THE ANNALS
OF
AMERICA

President-elect Jimmy Carter addresses congressmen while on a visit to Washington, D.C., November 22, 1976.

THE ANNALS OF AMERICA

Volume 20
1974-1976

The Challenge of Interdependence

ENCYCLOPÆDIA BRITANNICA, INC.

Chicago London Toronto Geneva Sydney Tokyo Manila Johannesburg Seoul

The editors wish to express their gratitude for permission to reprint
material from the following sources:

America Press Inc. for Selection 63. Reprinted by permission from *America*, June 26, 1976. Copyright '1976 by America Press, Inc.

The American Jewish Committee for Selection 25. Reprinted by permission from *Commentary* Magazine, December 1974. Copyright © 1974 by the American Jewish Committee.

The American Philosophical Society and Archibald MacLeish for Selection 74. Copyright © 1976 by the American Philosophical Society.

ARTnews for Selection 24. POP, Phyllis Tuchman, interviews with George Segal, James Rosenquist. Copyright © *ARTnews* 1974.

The Association of Trial Lawyers of America for Selection 59. Reprinted by permission from *Trial* Magazine, Vol. 12, No. 9, September 1976

Atlas World Press Review for Selection 75, parts 3, 4, 5, 6, 10, 11, 12, 13, 14, 15, 16, 17, 18, 19, 20. Reprinted by permission. Also for Selection 68, copyright © 1976 by Atlas World Press Review. Reprinted by permission.

Black Star for Selection 75, part 1 from *Stern* Magazine (West Germany). Copyright © 1976 by Black Star. Reprinted by permission.

Change Magazine for Selection 56. Reprinted with permission from Volume 8, Number 7, *Change* Magazine, New Rochelle, New York.

The Chicago Tribune for Selection 13. Copyright © 1974 *Chicago Today*. Used with permission, all rights reserved. Also for Selection 1, Copyright © 1974 *Chicago Tribune*. Used with permission, all rights reserved.

The Christian Century Foundation for Selection 23. Copyright © 1974 Christian Century Foundation. Reprinted by permission from the November 13, 1974, issue of *The Christian Century*.

Christianity and Crisis, Inc. for Selection 21, A & B. Reprinted from the September 16, 1974 issue of *Christianity and Crisis*, copyright © 1974 by Christianity and Crisis, Inc.

Commonweal Publishing Company, Inc. for Selection 26. Reprinted by permission from *Commonweal*. Also for Selection 54A. Reprinted by permission from *Commonweal*.

The Council of State Governments for Selection 34. Reprinted by permission from the Spring 1975 issue of *State Government*.

The Council on Foreign Relations, Inc. for Selection 18. Excerpted by permission from *Foreign Affairs*, October

Contents

1975

1975–1976

1976

THE CHALLENGE OF INTERDEPENDENCE

In Pictures

Transition 28–29

The Nixon presidency commenced as an attempt to "bring us together," but it took four years to wind down the war, and no sooner had that been accomplished than Watergate emerged to harass an already frustrated society. The inauguration of President Gerald R. Ford in August 1974 served at least to restore respectability and integrity to the nation's highest office.

Women's World 155–158

In the late 1960s, several movements arose to challenge the "Establishment" and to criticize the traditional assumptions and beliefs of many Americans. One of the most important and widespread movements was women's liberation. Patterning itself after the "black power" rebellion of the mid-1960s, it took to the streets in protest, using strident slogans and occasionally bizarre tactics to attract attention. By the 1970s push for women's rights was channeling itself into positive attempts to attain specific and realizable economic and social goals.

Freedom's Fading Light? 247–252

For a time, in the 1950s and early 1960s, it seemed that the areas of human freedom might expand as many more nations rejected colonialism and gained independence, but government "by the people" has come more and more to be superseded by dictatorial regimes. This should not surprise Americans, for most areas of the world have no centuries-long tradition of constitutional government as we have in the West.

Looking Backward, Looking Forward 317–320

The Bicentennial celebration of 1976 was overshadowed by a presidential campaign that saw a field of a dozen Democratic hopefuls narrowed down by the primaries to former Georgia governor Jimmy Carter, and a strong challenge to President Ford mounted by Ronald Reagan, former governor of California. The national celebration of the anniversary of the Declaration of Independence ended on July 4, 1976. 1976 was, in a real sense, Jimmy Carter's year. America was ripe for change and new directions. What the directions would be, no one could say. And the very narrowness of Carter's November victory did little to clarify the matter.

Introduction

The contents of this volume of *The Annals of America* are bracketed by the dissolution of the Nixon presidency and the beginning of the Carter presidency. To proceed from the beginning of 1974 to the end of 1976 is to go from a known but unhappy ending to an unknown but hopeful beginning. However, these three years themselves seem anticlimactic. Many of the problems that had emerged during President Nixon's years in the White House remained unsolved, but few new issues were raised. One is tempted to say the nation was caught in a period of inertia.

To let it go at that, however, would be a most ungenerous assessment of the presidency of Gerald Ford. For years the United States had been in turmoil. The civil rights movement and its backlash; the Vietnam War and the protests against it; the youth rebellion and the disruptions of the campuses; and finally Watergate itself had all left the nation emotionally drained and ready for a respite, a time of relative calm. When President Ford arrived at the White House, such a period of calm set in. The office of the presidency could once more be viewed with respect and approbation. The Vietnam War ended, not favorably to be sure; but it did end, and that, at the time, seemed the important thing. If the problems centering on the energy crisis, the decay of cities, swelling welfare roles, segregated education, high crime rates, inflation, and unemployment were not solved, that was not surprising. No one in the White House, the Congress, the universities, or the councils of big business had the answers.

The one thing that was certain was that times had changed. The post-World War II era was over. In the quarter-century after 1945 the United States dominated much of the world, both by its military might and by its burgeoning economic power. It seemed that the combination of "Pax Americana" and prosperity might go on forever. But between 1968 and 1973 the dream unravelled. The United States found itself in a war that it could not win, and the nation no longer stood alone as the economic leader of the world. Europe and Japan had rebuilt after the war and had become industrial giants in their own right. The Soviet Union, so utterly devastated by World War II, had recouped dramatically, particularly in the area of military might. And even some countries of the "Third World" had awakened to an awareness of their economic power: the Arab nations of the Middle East, along with Iran, had, through the seizure and control of their oil resources, gained a huge advantage against the industrial West and Japan. Paradoxically, as the Bicentennial of the Declaration of Independence approached, the United States was not so independent as it had once been. The nations of the world had become, as Secretary of State Kissinger asserted in a 1974 speech, "interdependent."

While many Americans probably did not bother to reflect much about the state of the world, what they did realize was that everything at home cost more. The economy was evidently in worse shape than it had been for a long time. Yet, although unemployment climbed to a high of more than 9 percent in 1975, prosperity did not

The Tall Ships arrive in New York Harbor for the observance of the Bicentennial, July 4, 1976.

suddenly vanish, as it had done during the Great Depression. Wages kept rising and the economy kept expanding, although at a slower rate than one had been accustomed to. Some industries, for example, housing and automobile manufacturing, went through severe recession doldrums; but there did not seem to be any reason to believe that the dislocations would be permanent.

The troubled economy not only disturbed individuals in their private lives; it also affected many public institutions. Spiralling costs and chronic money shortages forced cutbacks in public services, education, mass transit, and the postal service. The plight of New York City, as it verged on bankruptcy, epitomized on a grand scale what was happening in many sections of the country.

A shortage of funds was only one of many factors that disturbed U. S. institutions in this period. They also were plagued by a crisis of public confidence that, starting with politics and government, touched much else besides. The schools were continually criticized for failing to educate adequately. The major denominations were in turmoil over many issues, social and theological. The image of big business was tarnished by evidence of corruption, bribery, and profiteering. Public esteem for the legal and medical professions reached new lows. The constitutional guarantees of the Bill of Rights were eroded by the illegal activities carried on by several of the investigatory agencies of the federal government.

In foreign affairs, American policies continued much as they had under President Nixon, but without the dead weight of Vietnam. Détente with the Soviet Union persisted in spite of much criticism. The various trouble spots in the world remained troublesome, and to their number was added a new area of critical concern: Africa.

For the first time in American history it became necessary to take the problems of sub-Saharan Africa seriously. The new interest in that continent was occasioned by the civil war in Angola, a conflict in which the Soviet Union and China both saw fit to get involved. The possibility of Communist meddling in such potentially dangerous areas as Rhodesia and South Africa prompted the U. S. government to take a new look at racial conflicts, that, should they explode, could engulf most of Africa.

Socially, Americans were not quite the same as they had been in the 1960s. After the civil rights movement, brown power and red power movements, women's liberation, the campus rebellion, gay liberation, a new self-consciousness among the so-called "Ethnics," and a steady belaboring of every possible social problem, we may not have become more equal; but we were certainly much more aware of the many inequities that persist in American life. And as a result of the domestic conflicts of the past decade, the United States is probably a more open society than it has ever been.

What probably troubles most people is that they hear so much about problems and so little about solutions. It is the genius of the ever-present media—newspapers, magazines, radio, and especially television—to confront us daily with what is wrong almost everywhere in the world, so that our time seems to be an unrelieved tale of woe and misery. We are tempted to turn to the past, to nostalgia about the 1950s, or even the depressed 1930s, in search of a time it would have been emotionally satisfying to dwell in. This is not so much an escape as it is a kind of "pain reliever" for the 1970s.

Amidst all the distractions of our everyday existence, the Bicentennial of the Declaration of Independence and the Revolutionary War was observed with a measure of joy. To be sure, the jubilation was somewhat dampened by memories of Vietnam and Watergate and by the recession of 1974–76. But the Bicentennial *was* celebrated, and with great charm and ingenuity on the Fourth of July, 1976. From Mars Hill Mountain in Maine, where the dawn first appeared on that day, to American Samoa in the South Pacific, there were parades, pageants, bell ringing, picnics, sports events, church services. Perhaps most notable of the day's events was the "Tall Ships"—the arrival of more than 200 high-masted sailing ships in New York Harbor. In Philadelphia, President Ford, speaking at Independence Hall, asserted that "Liberty is a living flame to be fed, not dead ashes to be revered." His words may sound like traditional patriotic oratory. But it also seems probable that Americans in the 1970s are more conscious of rights, of liberty, of threats to freedom, of equality, and of the fragility of justice than they have been in many years.

Chronology: 1974-1976

1974

January. The major oil companies announce enormous profits for the last quarter of 1973.

January 1. The Census Bureau announces that the population of the U.S. stands at 211.7 million.

January 1. President Nixon impounds $3 billion of $7 billion that Congress has authorized for construction of sewage treatment plants.

January 2. The 55-mile-per-hour speed limit bill becomes law.

January 3. Professional football player O. J. Simpson is named offensive player of the year for the 1973 season, having set a record of 2,003 yards rushing.

January 7. Secretary of Defense James R. Schlesinger warns that a continuance of the Arab oil embargo may provoke the American public into demanding force be used to end the ban.

January 8. The trial of Russell Means and Dennis Banks, militant American Indian leaders of the Wounded Knee, South Dakota, hostilities in 1973, begins at St. Paul, Minnesota. **September 16.** Judge Fred Nichol dismisses all charges against the two.

January 8. The United States Supreme Court rules that grand juries can use evidence illegally obtained when questioning a witness.

January 11. U.S. District Court Judge Aubrey Robinson, Jr., rules that the Justice Department must tell the extent of illegal wiretaps and surveillance of anti-war protesters in 1968–69.

January 11. Newspapers disclose that a military spy ring had been operating within the National Security Council prior to 1971, passing diplomatic secrets to Pentagon officials. The Pentagon denies the allegation.

January 13. The Miami Dolphins win the football Superbowl with a 24–7 win over the Minnesota Vikings.

January 15. The Federal Energy Office publishes fuel allocation rules favoring industrial and public service users over private use.

January 16. Mickey Mantle and Whitey Ford are elected to the Baseball Hall of Fame.

January 17. The Commerce Department announces a general slowdown in economic growth, soaring inflation, increased personal income, and a severe slump in the housing industry.

January 18. The U. S. Export-Import Bank announces approval of nearly $38 million in credits to the Soviet Union to aid in the purchase of industrial equipment from American companies.

January 18. Israel and Egypt sign an agreement, negotiated through the efforts of Secretary of State Henry Kissinger, to disengage troops along the Suez Canal.

January 20. Johnny Miller becomes the first golfer to win three PGA tournaments in a row since 1962, with his victory at the Dean Martin–Tucson Open.

January 23. The Department of the Interior grants permission for construction of the Alaskan oil pipeline.

January 24. U. S. Court of Appeals rules that President Nixon's impounding of funds for sewage treatment is illegal.

January 28. The Commerce Department announces a 1973 trade surplus of $1.68 billion, the first such surplus since 1970.

January 28. President Nixon vows continued aid to Cambodia in its war against Communist insurgents.

January 30. President Nixon delivers his State of the Union address. He pledges that there will be no recession. On his political troubles he states that "One year of Watergate is enough," and he will not resign the presidency.

January 31. Veteran Hollywood producer Samuel Goldwyn dies at the age of 91 in Los Angeles.

February 4. President Nixon submits a budget of $304.4 billion to Congress for fiscal 1975. It is the first budget to exceed $300 billion.

February 5. Mariner 10 spacecraft flies to within 3,600 miles of the planet Venus, sending back photographs and measurements. It then continues in its trajectory toward Mercury.

February 5–6. The Senate defeats ratification of the United Nations treaty outlawing genocide.

February 6. Secretary of State Henry Kissinger asserts that continuation of the Arab oil embargo "must be construed as a form of blackmail."

February 7. Ohio becomes the 33rd state to ratify the Equal Rights Amendment.

February 8. The 84-day Skylab space station mission ends. It is the last manned spaceflight by the U.S. before the joint Soviet-U.S. mission of 1975. Astronauts are Gerald P. Carr, Edward G. Gibson, and William R. Pogue.

February 11–13. Representatives of 13 oil-consuming nations meet at Washington, D.C., to discuss the energy crisis. France disagrees with the U.S. plan for a comprehensive program to deal with it.

February 19. The Senate passes the emergency energy bill. It is approved by the House on **February 27**, but vetoed by President Nixon on **March 6**. The Senate sustains the veto.

February 21–23. Foreign ministers of Western Hemisphere countries meet at Mexico City to discuss mutual economic and political problems.

February 28. Egypt and the U.S. resume full diplomatic relations for the first time since 1967.

February 28. The House passes a pension reform bill setting standards for private pension plans and individual retirement accounts.

March 3. A joint commission of American Roman Catholic and Lutheran theologians states that the primacy of the Pope need not be an insurmountable barrier to reconciliation between the two denominations.

March 5. Sol Hurok, noted impresario, dies at the age of 85 in New York City.

March 7. The wreckage of the famed Civil War vessel, U. S. S. *Monitor*, is located on the ocean floor near Cape Hatteras, North Carolina. The ship went down in a storm on December 31, 1862.

March 13. The Senate passes a bill to restore the death penalty for crimes of treason, hijacking, espionage, kidnapmurder, and attacks on a President and other public officials.

March 15–17. The second National Black Political Convention meets at Little Rock, Arkansas. The convention is divided between those who favor separatism and those who would work within the present political system.

March 17. The Democratic Party approves a requirement to hold a mid-term party conference every four years between the national conventions.

March 18. Seven Arab nations lift their oil embargo against the U.S.

March 29. Mariner 10 spacecraft trans-

mits photographs and data on Mercury, showing that the planet has an atmosphere much less dense than Earth's.

March–April. The streaking fad, first reported in the news on March 7, gains popularity on college campuses and at public events.

April 2. At the annual Academy Awards presentation, *The Sting* receives the Oscar for best motion picture. Jack Lemmon and Glenda Jackson are best actor and actress.

April 6–7. President Nixon attends the funeral of French President Georges Pompidou in Paris. He also confers with other world leaders.

April 8. Hank Aaron breaks Babe Ruth's home run record by hitting his 715th home run. By the end of the baseball season in October, his total is 733 runs. His lifetime record reaches 752 runs by the time he decides to retire in 1975.

April 11. The Senate passes a comprehensive campaign reform law.

April 11. Former United Mine Workers president W. A. "Tony" Boyle is convicted of three counts of first-degree murder in the 1969 killing of Joseph Yablonski, his wife, and daughter.

April 13. Pioneer 10 spacecraft sends back radio signals from Jupiter to Earth, revealing that the temperature of the planet's upper atmosphere reaches 800°F.

April 15. Agreements are signed by nine steel companies, the United Steel Workers, and the federal government, providing for more job opportunities for women and minorities.

April 17. William Simon is named Secretary of the Treasury to replace George Shultz.

April 20. U. S. District Court Judge Miles W. Lord orders Reserve Mining Company of Silver Bay, Minnesota, to stop discharging industrial wastes into Lake Superior. The plant is temporarily closed on Lord's order, but resumes operations on April 22 when a three-judge panel orders a stay of the ruling.

April 28. Secretary of State Kissinger begins his fifth Middle East peace mission.

April 30. The Economic Stabilization Act of 1970 expires. The law had allowed the president to impose wage and price controls.

May 2. The Securities and Exchange Commission charges the Penn Central Company and 12 of its officers with a massive fraud scheme that led to the railroad's collapse in 1970.

May 4. Cannonade wins the Kentucky Derby.

May 5. The *Yearbook of American and Canadian Churches* reports that conservative and fundamentalist denominations are gaining members, while old-line denominations are losing them.

May 7. The Federal Energy Administration is established by President Nixon.

May 9. As Republican criticism of President Nixon mounts, the *Chicago Tribune*, in a lead editorial, calls upon him to resign.

May 12. The Boston Celtics win the National Basketball Association championship, their 12th in 18 years.

May 14. In Washington, D.C., the United States Court of Appeals blocks disbursement of federal funds to school districts in which racial discrimination exists in teacher assignment.

May 16. Four Black Muslims are indicted by a San Francisco grand jury for murdering three white persons in the "Zebra" killings that had terrorized the city.

May 19. The Philadelphia Flyers win the National Hockey League's Stanley Cup.

May 24. Edward "Duke" Ellington, jazz musician and composer, dies at age 75 in New York City.

May 26. Johnny Rutherford wins the Indianapolis "500."

May 28. Senator J. William Fulbright is defeated for renomination in the Arkansas Democratic primary, losing to Governor Dale Bumpers.

May 29. The House of Representatives passes a bill abolishing the Office of Economic Opportunity.

May 31. As a result of Secretary of State Kissinger's peace mission, Syria and Israel sign a cease-fire and troop disengagement agreement in Geneva.

June 4. The attorney general's list of "subversive organizations" is abolished by order of the president.

June 8. The U.S. and Saudi Arabia sign an agreement covering economic and military cooperation.

June 9. Katharine Cornell, one of the leading actresses of the American stage, dies at Vineyard Haven, Massachusetts, at age 81.

June 11. During a news conference in Salzburg, Austria, Secretary of State Kissinger threatens to resign because of charges against him concerning illegal wiretapping.

June 14. President Nixon, during a tour of the Middle East, signs an agreement with Egypt to provide the nation with nuclear technology.

June 20. The 3rd United Nations Conference on the Law of the Sea opens in Caracas, Venezuela. Goal of the conference is to draft a treaty on the use of the oceans.

June 27–July 3. President Nixon attends a summit meeting with Soviet leaders in Moscow.

June 27. The Defense Department announces cessation of naval practice shelling of the island of Culebra, near Puerto Rico.

June 28. Occidental Petroleum Company signs a 20-year agreement with the Soviet Union for two-way trade.

June 30. Mrs. Alberta Williams King, mother of the late Dr. Martin Luther King, Jr., is shot to death by a young black man during church services in Atlanta, Georgia.

July 1. Secretary of the Army Howard Callaway reports that the volunteer army is successful, with enlistments running higher than the minimum strength authorized by Congress.

July 1–August 27. Players of the National Football League are on strike, necessitating cancellation of the 41st College All-Star game.

July 9. Former Chief Justice of the U. S. Supreme Court Earl Warren dies in Washington, D. C., at age 83.

July 9. The Senate votes to create an Amateur Sports Board to oversee United States participation in the Olympic Games.

July 15. Following the overthrow of Cyprus president Makarios, the U.S. government issues a statement opposing war on the island and supporting independence. **July 20.** Turkey invades Cyprus. **July 22.** A cease-fire goes into effect as a result of combined British–U.S. efforts. **July 23.** In Greece the military dictatorship resigns in favor of a civilian government. **July 30.** Turkey, Greece, and Great Britain sign an agreement allowing Turkey to keep forces on the island.

July 17. Jay Hanna "Dizzy" Dean, former St. Louis Cardinals pitcher, dies at age 63 in Reno, Nevada.

July 22. Former Senator Wayne Lyman Morse of Oregon dies at age 73 in Portland, Oregon.

July 23. The Census Bureau reports that the Southern states show a continued increase in population, while Midwestern and Northeast states have a moderate out-migration.

July 25. The U.S. Supreme Court disallows school integration by means of cross-district busing.

July 29. Contravening the polity of the Episcopal Church, four bishops ordain eleven women to the priesthood in a ceremony in North Philadelphia. The ordination of women divides the denomination, but it becomes the policy of the church at its convention in the fall of 1976.

July 29–31. The Energy Coordination Group, a consortium of twelve nations, meets in Brussels, Belgium. It agrees on a plan for pooling oil in the event of another energy crisis.

August 9. President Nixon resigns. Gerald R. Ford is sworn in as 38th President of the United States.

August 14. The 40-year ban on private ownership of gold is ended by President Ford.

August 15. Senator Mike Mansfield, as of today, has held the post of Senate majority leader longer than any other individual. He assumed the post on January 3, 1961. In 1977 he retires from office, having declined to run for another Senate term.

August 19–23. Members of the United Mine Workers hold a memorial week for men killed or injured in the mines. This work stoppage idles 1,200 mines in twelve states.

August 19. Rodger P. Davies, U. S. ambassador to Cyprus, is slain in Nicosia by Greek Cypriot terrorists.

August 20. A report issued by the Atomic Energy Commission states that dangers from nuclear power plants are slight.

August 20. President Ford names former New York governor Nelson Aldrich Rockefeller to be the next vice president. He is confirmed by the Senate on December 10 and by the House on December 19.

August 26. Charles Augustus Lindbergh, America's most celebrated 20th-century hero, dies at age 72 on Maui, Hawaii.

September. A dispute over public school textbooks erupts in Kanawha County, West Virginia, with protest marches, school boycotts, and a coal miners' strike.

September 1. A U.S. Air Force SR-71 flies from New York to London in one hour and 55 minutes, setting a new record for the 3,490-mile Atlantic crossing.

September 4. Former Republican National Chairman George Bush is named envoy to China by President Ford.

September 4. Diplomatic relations are established between the U.S. and East Germany.

September 4. General Creighton Abrams, Army chief of staff, dies at age 59 in Washington, D.C.

September 8. President Ford grants former President Nixon a full pardon for all federal crimes "he committed or may have committed or taken part in while in office."

September 8. Covert activities by the Central Intelligence Agency in Chile from 1970–73 become the topic of a major controversy in Washington.

September 8. Motorcyclist Evel Knievel fails in his attempt to jump the Snake River Canyon at Twin Falls, Idaho, on a rocket-propelled motorcycle.

September 12. Protests and violence erupt in Boston over forced busing for integration. Busing is a political issue through the 1976 presidential campaign.

September 16. President Ford signs a proclamation offering amnesty to a limited number of Vietnam draft evaders and deserters.

September 18. President Ford addresses the U.N. General Assembly to urge a "global strategy for food and energy."

September 18. The second round of Strategic Arms Limitation Talks (SALT) resumes in Geneva, Switzerland.

September 22–23. The first national black economic conference is held in Washington, D.C. It urges public works programs to combat unemployment.

September 23. President Ford addresses the World Energy Conference in Detroit, warning the oil-producing countries against continued price increases. On the same day, Secretary of State Kissinger addresses the U.N. General Assembly, stressing the same theme.

September 27. An "economic summit" meeting takes place in Washington, D.C., to devise a plan for combating inflation and recession.

October. The price of sugar has increased 300% on the nation's commodity markets during the year, although there is no shortage. On October 23, Great Western United, largest of the beet sugar companies, announces third quarter profits 1200% higher than the previous year.

October. A major reform of federal election laws is approved by the Senate on October 8 and by the House two days later. President Ford signs the legislation on the 15th.

October. In Chicago three prominent members of the Democratic Party are convicted of felonies: Alderman Thomas Keane of mail fraud and conspiracy; Alderman Paul Wigoda of income tax fraud; and Earl Bush, Mayor Daley's press secretary, of mail fraud.

October 7. A car containing Rep. Wilbur Mills, chairman of the House Ways and Means Committee, and four other persons is stopped by U.S. Park Service police at 2 a.m. in Washington, D.C. All the occupants have been drinking, and one of them, Annabel Battistella (also known as Fanne Foxe), leaps into the Tidal Basin. In spite of this touch of scandal, Mills is re-elected in November, but he retires as chairman of the committee. He is replaced by Democrat Al Ullman of Oregon. On December 30, Mills reveals that he has been an alcoholic, but pledges total abstinence in the future.

October 8. Franklin National Bank of New York is declared insolvent. The FDIC, as receiver, takes over the bank's liabilities and assets.

October 9–15. Secretary of State Kissinger resumes his Middle East peace negotiations, visiting seven countries involved in the Arab–Israeli settlement.

October 13. Ed Sullivan, Broadway columnist and master of ceremonies of the popular TV variety show from 1948 to 1971, dies at age 73 in New York.

October 13–15. George Emil Palade of the Yale University School of Medicine and Paul J. Flory of Stanford University are named Nobel prizewinners in physiology and chemistry respectively.

October 14. The Palestine Liberation Organization is recognized by the United Nations as the representative of the Palestinian people.

October 17. Oakland wins the World Series by defeating the Los Angeles Dodgers four games out of five. The A's are the first team in 21 years to win the series three years in a row.

October 19. Secretary of the Treasury William Simon announces that the Soviet Union will be allowed to purchase a restricted amount of wheat and corn from the U. S. through June 1975.

October 29. Former President Nixon has surgery for phlebitis and remains in critical condition for some days afterward.

October 30. Muhammad Ali defeats George Foreman to regain the world heavyweight boxing championship, in a bout in Zaire, Africa.

October–November. The largest cash theft in the nation's history takes place on October 20, when the Purolator Company in Chicago is robbed of $3.4 million. On November 7 six men are indicted in the robbery. Only a portion of the money, $1.5 million, is thus far recovered.

November 5. The mid-term elections are a Democratic landslide, giving the party 291 seats in the House of Representatives and 61 in the Senate, as well as 36 governorships.

November 5. The United Nations World Food Conference opens in Rome for a ten-day session. Secretary of State Kissinger and Secretary of Agriculture Earl Butz address the gathering.

November 8. Eight former Ohio National Guardsmen are acquitted of charges relating to the deaths of four Kent State University students in May 1970.

November 18–26. President Ford visits Japan, Korea, and Vladivostok on a tour of the Far East. Meeting with Soviet Communist Party leader Leonid Brezhnev, he agrees to limits on strategic nuclear offensive weapons.

November 28. Twenty Latin American nations form a cartel, the Group of Latin American and Caribbean Sugar Exporting Countries, to sustain world sugar prices.

November–December. The American automobile industry, in a serious recession, cuts production schedules and orders numerous temporary plant shutdowns and massive layoffs.

December 1. The worst U.S. aviation disaster of the year occurs when a TWA 727 crashes in the Blue Ridge Mountains, killing all 92 persons aboard.

December 2. Pioneer II spacecraft passes within 26,000 miles of Jupiter on its way to Saturn, a destination it will not reach until 1979.

December 3. Secretary of the Treasury Simon announces that the U.S. will sell two million ounces of gold at public auction on January 6, 1975.

December 6–8. The Democrats hold a "mini-convention" in Kansas City. They adopt a formal charter and discuss the problems of economic recovery.

December 7. The Labor Department announces that unemployment has reached a thirteen-year high of 6.5% and is expected to rise during 1975.

December 14. Walter Lippmann, noted political journalist and author, dies at age 85 in New York.

December 15–16. President Ford and French President Valéry Giscard d'Estaing meet on the island of Martinique to confer on energy and economic problems.

December 21. The *New York Times* reports that the Central Intelligence Agency has conducted a "massive illegal domestic intelligence operation" against antiwar and other dissidents. These activities, increasing during the Nixon Administration, began in the 1950s. On December 26, CIA Director William Colby tells President Ford that the allegations are true.

December 23. The U.S. Supreme Court rules that the President's power to pardon criminals cannot be "modified, abridged, or diminished by Congress."

December 26. Jack Benny, one of America's most celebrated comedians, dies at the age of 80 in Los Angeles.

1974 - 1975

On January 22–23, 1974, the new World Football League holds its draft of college players in preparation for the first season of play. On March 31. Miami Dolphin players Larry Csonka, Paul Warfield, and Jim Kiick sign three-year contracts with the WFL Toronto team for the 1975 season. This leads other NFL players to sign lucrative contacts with the WFL. NFL teams obtain restraining orders to keep their players from signing out of the league. The first WFL season is far from successful, and financial troubles cause it to fold in the middle of its second season in 1975.

1974 - 1976

January–February 1974. Theological controversy dividing the Lutheran Church-Missouri Synod results in the firing of Concordia Seminary President John H. Tietjen on January 20. A student strike follows. On February 19 nearly 400 students, joined by some professors, leave to found a seminary in exile (Semi-

nex) to continue their studies. The rift in the church remains, after the 1975 convention fails to deal with the situation for fear of causing a split in the denomination. But in the fall of 1976, representatives of a number of congregations, meeting in Chicago, form the American Evangelical Lutheran Church, and sever ties with the synod.

February 4, 1974. Patricia Hearst, daughter of newspaper publisher Randolph A. Hearst, is kidnapped at Berkeley, California, by members of the "Symbionese Liberation Army." February 19. In response to demands by kidnappers Mr. Hearst sets up a $2-million food giveaway plan. April 3. A tape recording from Miss Hearst says she has chosen to join the SLA. April 15. She participates in a bank robbery in San Francisco with other members of the SLA. April 24. She claims, via another recording, that she was a willing participant in the robbery and has not been brainwashed by the SLA. May 17. In a gun battle with police in Los Angeles, six members of the SLA are killed. May 19. The FBI issues a warrant for the arrest of Miss Hearst on charges of violating the National Firearms Act. May 22. The Los Angeles County district attorney files 19 charges against Miss Hearst, covering such crimes as assault, murder, kidnapping, and intent to commit robbery. June 6. Patricia Hearst is indicted by a San Francisco grand jury on charges of bank robbery. September 18, 1975. Miss Hearst and her companions, Emily and William Harris, are captured by FBI agents in San Francisco. January 26, 1976. Miss Hearst's trial on armed robbery charges begins in San Francisco. March 20. She is found guilty. September 24. She is sentenced to seven years in prison. November 19. She is freed on one million dollars bail, with the provision she live with her parents.

1975

January 1. Militant Menominee Indians in central Wisconsin seize the Alexian Brothers novitiate at Gresham, demanding the property be turned over to them for use as a hospital. On February 4 the Indians leave voluntarily after the Alexian Brothers agree to turn the property over to Indian tribal government.

January 3. The Labor Department announces that unemployment has reached 7.1%. On January 7, the Chrysler Corporation announces a new policy of offering rebates to buyers of new cars. The other auto firms soon follow suit.

January 5. President Ford names an eight-member panel to study illegal domestic spying by the CIA. Chairman of the commission is Vice President Nelson Rockefeller.

January 12. The Pittsburgh Steelers defeat the Minnesota Vikings to win the National Football League Superbowl.

January 13. In an interview with *Business Week* magazine Secretary of State Kissinger suggests the possibility of using American military force in the Middle East "to prevent strangulation of the industrialized world."

January 14. A British publisher issues *Inside the Company; A CIA Diary,* written by former CIA agent Philip Agee, detailing operations of the agency, especially in Latin America. The book is also published in the U.S.

January 14. Edward Levi, president of the University of Chicago, is named Attorney General by President Ford.

January 14. About fifty persons are killed in a severe blizzard in the Central Plains States and the Midwest.

January 15. President Ford's State of the Union message focuses on the economy. He asks for a $16-billion tax cut, an increase in the tax on crude oil, and limits on federal spending. He predicts large budget deficits for the next two years.

January 19. Thomas Hart Benton, one of the country's most noted artists, dies at age 85 in Kansas City, Missouri.

January 23. President Ford raises tariffs on oil imports and denounces any Congressional plan to impose gas rationing.

January 27. The Commerce Department announces that the 1974 trade deficit of $3.07 billion is the second-worst in the nation's history after the 1972 deficit of $6.4 billion.

January 27. The Senate votes to create a committee to investigate illegal activities by the CIA, FBI, and other government investigative agencies. Frank Church of Idaho is chairman.

February 3. President Ford's proposed budget for fiscal 1976 is $349 billion, with a probable $51.9 billion deficit.

February 3–8. In Senegal, representatives of 110 Third World countries convene to discuss getting higher prices for raw materials on the world market.

February 7. The Labor Department announces that unemployment has reached 8.2%, the highest level since the Great Depression.

February 8. Former Boston Celtics basketball player Bill Russell is elected to the National Basketball Hall of Fame. In a public announcement the next day, Russell declines the honor.

February 9. The Census Bureau announces that in the 15 largest metropolitan areas, more people have moved out of the cities than into them since the 1970 census.

February 14. P. G. Wodehouse, playwright and novelist, dies at age 93 in Long Island, New York.

February 25. Elijah Muhammad, leader of the Black Muslims (Nation of Islam), dies at age 77 in Chicago. He is succeeded by his son, Wallace D. Muhammad.

February 26. The U.S. Railway Association proposes a plan to restructure the rail systems of the Northeast. The lines would be taken over by a federally supported corporation, Consolidated Rail Corporation (ConRail). The financing is not approved by Congress until December. The system goes into operation in 1976.

February 26. The Senate Subcommittee on Multinational Corporations releases a list of 1,500 American firms blacklisted by Saudi Arabia because of business dealings with Israel.

February 27. Attorney General Edward Levi reveals that the late J. Edgar Hoover, director of the FBI until May 1972, had kept secret files of information on prominent persons, including Presidents and Congressmen.

March 1. The American Revolution Bicentennial Commemoration begins. It will last until December 31, 1976.

March 17. The U.S. Supreme Court rules that the federal government, not the states, controls oil exploration rights in the off-shore area beyond the three-mile limit.

March 17–20. More than 2,000 physicians strike New York hospitals. It is the first such major doctors' strike in American history. The leading complaint is working schedules.

March 18. Newspaper reports allege that the CIA, in the summer of 1974, financed raising of a portion of a sunken Soviet submarine in the Pacific Ocean. The vessel used to raise the submarine is the *Glomar Explorer*.

March 18–25. Eighteen defendants in the Equity Funding Corporation fraud scheme are sentenced to jail terms and assessed fines.

March 21. The *Chicago Daily News* reports that the Chicago Police Department has kept files on prominent persons and organizations and has infiltrated community and civic organizations critical of the city administration.

March 29. President Ford signs a bill calling for a $22.8 billion tax cut.

March 31. UCLA wins the NCAA basketball championship for the 10th time in 12 years. The team's coach, John Wooden, announces his retirement.

March 31. President Ford's clemency program for Vietnam era draft evaders and deserters ends. Of the more than 124,000 men eligible for the program, only 25,500 have signed up to return.

April 1. Richard J. Daley is elected to an unprecedented sixth term as mayor of Chicago.

April 3. Bobby Fischer has his world

chess title taken away for refusing to accept World Chess Federation rules in a championship match.

April 4. The *Wall Street Journal* reports that New York City may be forced to default on its debts and file bankruptcy. This begins a controversy that receives nationwide attention. A solution, albeit temporary in nature, is achieved by the end of the year when Congress passes, and President Ford signs, a federal aid authorization bill for the city.

April 8. At the Academy Awards presentation, *The Godfather, Part II* receives the Oscar for best picture. Art Carney and Ellen Burstyn are best actor and actress.

April 12. Josephine Baker, American singer and dancer who became one of the most celebrated stage personalities of the century after moving to France in the 1920s, dies in Paris at age 68.

April 13. Jack Nicklaus wins the Masters Golf Tournament for the fifth time.

April 16. The Cambodian government falls to the Khmer Rouge rebels.

April 17. Former Texas governor and Secretary of the Treasury John Connally is acquitted of charges of accepting a $10,000 bribe from the Associated Milk Producers, Inc., in 1971 for helping gain increased federal milk price supports.

April 24. Congress authorizes emergency evacuation procedures and humanitarian aid for South Vietnam. On April 30 the government of South Vietnam surrenders to the Viet Cong and North Vietnam forces.

May. The medical malpractice crisis continues to spread across the nation. Several states contemplate measures to stem the epidemic of suits. The number of malpractice cases has risen 1000% since 1969, according to an announcement made by the American Medical Association on May 2. Physicians face huge increases in their insurance premiums.

May 2. The Securities and Exchange Commission reports that Gulf Oil Corporation has paid $4.2 million in bribes to foreign officials over the past several years. Gulf admits the truth of the allegation and adds that $5.4 million has been paid to American politicians. This is among the first of several admissions by large corporations that large overseas bribes have been paid to foreign officials for the privilege of doing business in various countries. Among the largest of such "donors" is Lockheed Aircraft, one of the Defense Department's largest contractors. These revelations cause scandal and political turmoil in several foreign countries, including Italy, Japan, and The Netherlands.

May 5. As the number of Vietnamese refugees reaching the U. S. approaches 150,000, President Ford asks Congress to appropriate $507 million to aid in their resettlement.

May 12–14. An American merchant vessel, the *Mayaguez,* is seized by Cambodians in the Gulf of Siam. The ship and its 39 crewmen are released after President Ford orders a military operation.

May 21. President Ford nominates Daniel P. Moynihan to be U.S. Ambassador to the United Nations.

May 25. The Golden State Warriors win the National Basketball Association championship by defeating Washington 4 games to 0.

May 25. Bobby Unser wins the Indianapolis "500" race.

May 27. The Alaska Supreme Court hands down a ruling that has the effect of legalizing the use of marijuana in one's own home.

May 27. The Philadelphia Flyers win the National Hockey League's Stanley Cup by defeating Buffalo 4 games to 2.

May 28–June 3. President Ford visits Europe and confers with NATO leaders in Brussels and government heads in Spain and Italy. He also meets with President Anwar Sadat of Egypt at Salzburg, Austria.

May 28. A month-long strike of California physicians protesting malpractice insurance rate increases ends when Governor Brown signs emergency legislation providing for underwriting of the policies. Similar actions by physicians have been under way or are threatened in other states.

June 8. The Labor Department reports that unemployment has reached 9.2%. This is the highest it would go during the 1974–76 recession. By the end of 1976 the rate is still about 8%.

June 10. The Rockefeller Panel report on the CIA is released to the public.

June 24. An Eastern Airlines 727 crashes near Kennedy International Airport in New York, killing 113 persons. It is the worst single aircraft disaster in American history.

June 26. Exiled Russian author and Nobel Prize winner Aleksandr Solzhenitsyn arrives in the U. S. for a visit. His attacks on détente with the Soviet Union hinder any meeting between him and President Ford.

July 5. Arthur Ashe beats Jimmy Connors at the Wimbledon tennis tournament in England.

July 8. President Ford announces that he will be a candidate for the Republican nomination for the presidency in 1976.

July 12. Exxon Corporation admits having paid bribes totaling more than $46 million to Italian politicians between 1963 and 1972.

July 15–24. The joint Soviet–United States space venture takes place. Apollo–Soyuz Test Project begins on July 15 with the launching of the two ships several hours apart. Link-up occurs on the 17th at 12:09 Eastern Daylight Time, 140 miles up over the Earth. The link-up ends on the 18th, and Soyuz returns to land on the 21st. Apollo remains aloft until the 24th.

July 16–17. Large Soviet purchases of wheat from the U. S. and Canada are announced. The total involves 3.2 million metric tons. A few days later additional sales of 4.5 million metric tons are reported.

July 30. James Hoffa, former president of the Teamsters Union, disappears from outside a restaurant in Bloomfield Township, Michigan. No trace of him has been found by the end of 1976, and it is presumed he is dead.

July 30. An international conference of leaders from 35 nations convenes at Helsinki, Finland. President Ford leads the U.S. delegation. All 35 heads of government sign the conference declaration on **August 1.** The document, entitled "Final

Act of the Conference on Security and Cooperation in Europe," contains principles for assuring permanent peace in Europe and for defining the boundaries between nations. This is the largest European conclave since the Congress of Vienna which met following the Napoleonic Wars.

August 20 and September 9. Two Viking space ships are launched on a flight to Mars. They will reach the planet in the summer of 1976.

August 31. News reports allege that the National Security Agency is monitoring nearly all overseas telephone and telegraphic communications from the U.S.

September. Violence erupts in Louisville, Kentucky, over court-ordered school busing for integration.

September 3. *Variety*, the show business journal, reports that the movie *Jaws* has become the number 1 moneymaker in film history.

September 4. Egypt and Israel sign a troop withdrawal agreement at Geneva, Switzerland. The agreement is in great part the result of negotiations conducted by Secretary of State Kissinger.

September 5. Lynette Fromme makes an assassination attempt on the life of President Ford while he is in Sacramento, California. On **November 26** she is convicted of the crime, and she is sentenced to life imprisonment on **December 17.**

September 6–8. Cuba is host to representatives from 79 countries who convene to promote Puerto Rican independence. The Ford Administration calls the conference an uncalled-for interference in American affairs.

September 14. Elizabeth Ann Bayley Seton is canonized by the Roman Catholic Church in a ceremony at St. Peter's basilica in Rome. She is the first native-born American to be made a saint.

September 22. President Ford escapes a second assassination attempt within one month while in California. A woman identified as Sara Jane Moore fires a handgun that is deflected by Oliver Sipple, a former marine. On **December 12,** in a court appearance, she pleads guilty to the attempt.

September 27. The Organization of Petroleum Exporting Countries raises the price of oil by ten per cent on the world market.

September 29. Charles D. "Casey" Stengel, baseball player, coach, and manager, dies at age 85 in Glendale, California.

October 2. W. T. Grant Company, a large national retail chain, files for bankruptcy in New York. **October 15.** It is reported that thus far in 1975 there have been 254,484 bankruptcy petitions filed in the U. S., most of them by individuals.

October 9–23. The following Americans win Nobel Prizes: Tjalling C. Koopmans, Yale economist; David Baltimore, medical researcher at Massachusetts Institute of Technology; Howard M. Temin, medical researcher at the University of Wisconsin; and L. James Rainwater, Columbia University physicist.

October 16. The Federal Reserve Board issues regulations banning discrimination against women in the issuing of credit.

October 17. The Social, Humanitarian, and Cultural Committee of the United Nations General Assembly passes a resolution declaring Zionism to be a form of racism. The resolution is severely denounced by U.S. Ambassador Daniel P. Moynihan.

October 20. A five-year agreement on grain purchases is reached between the Soviet Union and the U.S.

October 22. The Cincinnati Reds win the World Series, defeating the Boston Red Sox four out of seven games.

November 2. President Ford dismisses Secretary of Defense James Schlesinger and CIA Director William Colby. Donald Rumsfeld becomes Secretary of Defense and George Bush is named to the CIA post.

November 2. A National Hispanic Caucus is founded, comprised of Spanish-speaking citizens. It will affiliate with the Democratic Party.

November 3. Vice President Rockefeller, in a letter to President Ford, withdraws his name from consideration in the 1976 vice-presidential nomination.

November 10. A Great Lakes oreboat, the *Edmund Fitzgerald,* sinks in Lake Superior during a severe storm. All 29 crewmen are believed lost.

November 12. Associate Justice William O. Douglas announces his retirement from the U.S. Supreme Court, after serving for more than 36 years, longer than any other justice in American history.

November 15–17. The U. S., Japan, and four European nations hold an economic summit meeting in Paris, France. President Ford attends on behalf of the U.S. The main topics are high unemployment and recovery from the recession.

November 18. After a seven-year, self-imposed exile from the U.S., Eldridge Cleaver returns and surrenders to the FBI. He faces charges growing out of a 1968 shootout between Oakland police and the Black Panthers.

November 24. Secretary of State Kissinger, in a speech at Detroit, expresses concern over Cuban and Soviet intervention in the civil war in Angola.

November 24. Governor Marvin Mandel of Maryland and five associates are indicted by a federal grand jury in Baltimore on charges of mail fraud, bribery, racketeering, and income tax evasion.

December 1–5. President Ford visits China while on a tour of Asia. In Honolulu on December 7, he announces his "Pacific Doctrine" detailing the U.S. position with respect to Japan, China, Korea, and other Asian nations.

December 2. Archie Griffin, Ohio State football player, wins the Heisman trophy for the second year in a row. He is the only player who has won the award twice.

December 4. Hannah Arendt, political philosopher and teacher, dies at age 69 in New York City.

December 7. Thornton Wilder, novelist and dramatist who wrote the play "Our Town", dies at age 78.

December 17. The Senate confirms the nomination of John Paul Stevens of Illinois to the Supreme Court to replace retired William O. Douglas.

December 18. Governor Arch A. Moore of West Virginia is indicted by a federal grand jury at Charleston on extortion charges.

December 19. The U.S. Senate bans further aid to factions fighting in the Angolan civil war.

December 28. First-class postage goes from 10 cents to 13 cents per ounce.

December 29. A bomb explodes in the baggage area of La Guardia Airport in New York, killing 11 persons and injuring 70 others.

1976

January 1. Physicists report the discovery of indestructible subatomic particles known as "charmed quarks."

January 1. About 100,000 gallons of oil are spilled into the Hudson River when a barge hits a bridge abutment.

January 2. President Ford vetoes a construction site picketing bill that has been supported by his Secretary of Labor, John T. Dunlop. On January 14, Dunlop resigns his post. The labor members of the President's Collective Bargaining Committee in Construction have previously resigned their positions on January 8.

January 4. The 127-day National Airlines strike ends with an agreement with flight attendants. It has been the third-longest strike in the history of the airline industry.

January 7. David S. Fine is arrested by the FBI in connection with the 1970 bombing of a science building at the University of Wisconsin in Madison. Only one of the other four persons charged in this crime has previously been caught and convicted.

January 8. Delegates to the International Monetary Fund meeting in Kingston, Jamaica, agree on plans to reform the world's currency system. The new plan will abolish fixed parity rates and recognize the floating exchange rates.

January 9. In a collision of two Chicago Rapid Transit trains, one person is killed and more than 400 injured.

January 13. Sara Caldwell, first woman to conduct the Metropolitan Opera orchestra, leads a production of *La Traviata.*

January 13. In Paris, France, the newspaper *Libération* publishes the names of 32 persons it claims are CIA agents working in France. Other foreign newspapers publish similar lists from time to time, primarily in Greece, Germany, Italy, England, and the Netherlands.

January 15. Gulf Oil Company's board of directors fires its chairman and three other company officials because of bribery and slush fund scandals.

January 18. The Pittsburgh Steelers win the National Football League Superbowl game, beating the Dallas Cowboys 21–17.

January 19. President Ford delivers his State of the Union Address to Congress, calling for reduced taxes and cuts in the budget. On January 21 he submits his budget for fiscal 1977 to Congress. It totals $394.2 billion, with a projected deficit of $43 billion.

January 20. The Food and Drug Administration bans *Red No. 2,* the most widely used food dye in the U.S., because it is believed to be a cancer-causing agent.

January 21. A new X-ray device, the vascular image processor, is unveiled at the University of Southern California. It is able to picture the insides of arteries, enabling physicians to determine the likelihood of heart attacks.

January 23. Paul Robeson, actor, singer, and long-time black activist who was once denounced as a Communist, dies at age 77 in Philadelphia.

January 26. Busing for school integration begins peacefully in Detroit. This is the largest school system thus far to begin busing under federal court orders.

January 29. Congress overrides President Ford's veto of a $45 billion appropriation bill for health, welfare, and manpower plans.

January 29. Anne L. Armstrong is confirmed by the Senate as the first woman ambassador to England.

January 30. The U. S. Supreme Court voids part of the 1974 Federal Election Campaign Act setting limits on presidential campaign expenses. The court does uphold financial disclosure and the federal financing portions of the act.

February 2. Daniel P. Moynihan resigns as U.S. Ambassador to the United Nations. On February 25, President Ford appoints William Scranton, former governor of Pennsylvania, to the post. In the fall, Moynihan runs for the U.S. Senate from New York and wins the election, defeating one-term Conservative-Republican Senator James Buckley.

February 3. Three engineers at General Electric quit their jobs in a protest against the dangers of nuclear power plants.

February 4. Lockheed Aircraft Company admits paying a $7.1 million bribe to Japanese businessmen to promote the sale of its L-1011 jet in Japan. Payoffs have also been made to officials in Italy, Germany, the Netherlands, Turkey, Hong Kong, and several South American countries. The governments of some of these countries are severely shaken, and in Japan the government falls and the former premier is indicted for accepting a bribe.

February 4. Secretary of Transportation William T. Coleman announces his decision to allow the British-French supersonic aircraft, Concorde, to land at New York and Washington airports on a sixteen month trial basis. The flights are to begin May 24. Flight time from New York to London and Paris is just under four hours. Environmentalists' protests keep the New York landings from beginning, but regular service does begin at the Washington airport.

February 4–15. In the Winter Olympics at Innsbruck, Austria, American athletes win 3 gold, 3 silver, and 4 bronze medals. Gold medalists are Sheila Young and Peter Mueller for speed skating and Dorothy Hamill for figure skating. Silver medalists are Sheila Young and Leah Poulos in speed skating and Bill Koch in cross-country skiing. Bronze medalists are Cindy Nelson in downhill skiing, Dan Immerfall and Sheila Young in speed skating, and the team of Colleen O'Connor and Jim Millns in ice dancing.

February 5. The Department of Labor announces that unemployment has fallen from a 1975 high of 9.2% to 7.8% in January.

February 5. A 35-day slowdown by physicians in Southern California ends. They have been protesting astronomical increases in their malpractice insurance premiums.

February 6. Many of the nation's banks are reported in trouble. The Comptroller of the Currency lists 28 national banks in critical condition, and the FDIC says 35 banks have "problems." On February 15, the Hamilton National Bank of Chattanooga, Tennessee, is declared insolvent. Its parent firm, Hamilton Bancshares, files for bankruptcy on February 20. It is the third largest bank failure in U.S. history.

February 8. The Fermi National Accelerator Laboratory in Illinois reports the discovery of a new atomic particle, the upsilon.

February 13. Lily Pons, longtime Metropolitan Opera soprano, dies in Dallas at age 69.

February 16–24. Secretary of State Kissinger tours portions of Central and South America.

February 24. The northern Mariana Islands are granted commonwealth status by the U. S.

February 24. H. Allen Smith, journalist and humorous writer, dies at age 68.

February 24. President Ford defeats Ronald Reagan in the New Hampshire Republican primary by a narrow margin of 51% to 49%. Among the Democratic contenders, former Georgia governor Jimmy (James Earl) Carter wins over four competitors.

February 28. News correspondent Daniel Schorr, Columbia Broadcasting System, reveals that the CIA has been involved in plots to assassinate foreign leaders, including Fidel Castro of Cuba. Schorr's release of a secret House committee report on the CIA to the New York newspaper, *The Village Voice,* stirs up controversy in Congress and prompts an investigation of him by the House ethics committee. Testifying before the committee in September, Schorr refuses to divulge the source from whom he got the report.

March 4. Senate majority leader Mike Mansfield of Montana announces his retirement at the end of the session. He has served longer in the post than any previous majority leader.

March 24. The United States Supreme Court rules that minority employees are entitled to retroactive job pay as well as seniority.

March 24. President Ford urges a $135 million federally funded program to inoculate the whole U. S. population against a new influenza virus to stave off a possible epidemic. The program is passed by Congress on April 12 and is signed by the President three days later. The vaccinations begin in the fall. On December 16, owing to reports of 94 cases of a rare paralysis called Guillain-Barre syndrome, the immunization program is halted. It will not be revived unless an epidemic threatens.

March 28. The FBI reveals that during the years from 1960 to 1966 it burglarized the New York offices of the Socialist Workers Party at least 92 times. In response the SWP is suing the FBI for $27 million. The burglaries are only a small part of those committed by the FBI against several organizations between 1942 and 1968.

March 29. At the Academy Awards presentation in Los Angeles, *One Flew Over the Cuckoo's Nest* wins the Oscar as best film of the year. Jack Nicholson and Louise Fletcher are best actor and actress.

April 1. President Ford presents pianist Arthur Rubinstein with the Medal of Freedom, the nation's highest civilian award.

April 1. The Consolidated Rail Corporation, a quasi-governmental corporation, begins operation of bankrupt railroads in the Northeast section of the U. S.

April 9. The House of Representatives approves funds for the Air Force B-1 bomber. Eventual cost is expected to reach $21 billion for 244 planes. Production of the B-1 is delayed until a new president takes office in January 1977.

April 10. The Soviet Union and the U.S. agree on a treaty to limit underground nuclear tests for peaceful purposes.

April 14. The two dollar bill is reissued by the U.S. mint.

April 20. The U. S. Supreme Court rules that federal courts can order low-cost housing for white suburbs in order to relieve segregation in a city.

April 23. Volkswagen, the West German auto manufacturer, has decided to invest $250 million in an assembly plant to be located in Pennsylvania.

April 26. The Senate Select Committee on Intelligence issues its lengthy report on illegal activities committed by U.S. investigatory agencies. On May 6 the Senate votes to create a committee to monitor all intelligence-gathering agencies.

April 27. The U.S. Supreme Court broadens police powers by ruling that an individual can be convicted of selling contraband, even if it is supplied and purchased by law enforcement officers themselves. The degree of government participation in such crime is deemed to be of no significance.

April 27. Secretary of State Kissinger, on a tour of Africa, makes a major foreign policy speech at Lusaka, Zambia, declaring support for black rule in Rhodesia and urging an end to apartheid in South Africa.

April 27. An American Airlines 727 jet with 88 passengers aboard crashes at Charlotte Amalie's airport in the Virgin Islands, killing 37 persons.

May. The American auto industry has recovered from its slump. Sales are well above the same period a year ago.

May 1. Ronald Reagan wins four out of five Republican primaries, including Texas with its 96 convention delegates. This makes him a strong contender for the Republican nomination.

May 1. Bold Forbes wins the 102nd running of the Kentucky Derby.

May 2. A Pan American Airlines 747 completes the longest nonstop commercial flight, covering a distance of 8,088 miles from New York to New Delhi, India, in 13 hours and 31 minutes.

May 5. The Federal Election Commission begins to distribute matching campaign funds to nine presidential candidates.

May 7. A federal grand jury indicts Allied Chemical Corporation on 1,094 criminal charges involving the dumping of industrial waste into the James River. Among the chemicals was Kepone, a powerful insecticide. On October 5 the corporation is fined $13.3 million, the largest fine thus far assessed for violating federal environmental standards.

May 15. Samuel Eliot Morison, American historian, naval officer, and Harvard professor, dies at age 88 in Cambridge, Massachusetts.

May 15. New rules are issued by the Federal Trade Commission to protect consumers purchasing defective goods.

May 21. Twenty-eight high school choir members are killed in a bus crash at Yuba City, California.

May 25. The largest default in the history of the commodity trading industry takes place when speculators at the New York Mercantile Exchange default on 997 potato futures contracts for the delivery of about 50 million pounds of Maine potatoes.

May 25. Rep. Wayne L. Hays of Ohio, one of the most powerful members of the House of Representatives, admits having had an affair with Elizabeth Ray, one-time member of his staff. In spite of the news, he is renominated by the people of his district for another term. But he is gradually forced to resign his committee chairmanships. Eventually he decides against running for re-election, and on September 1 he resigns from the House.

May 25. An $800,000 theft at Kennedy Airport in New York is the largest in the history of the postal service.

May 25. The U. S. Supreme Court rules that pharmacies may advertise prices on prescription drugs.

May 29. A fiscal crisis at City University of New York forces a temporary closing. It will be necessary to charge tuition for the first time in 129 years.

May 30. Johnny Rutherford wins the Indianapolis "500" auto race.

June 1. Seven oil companies are indicted by a federal grand jury in Baltimore for fixing retail prices on gasoline in the Mid-Atlantic region.

June 5. The Teton River Dam in Idaho collapses, flooding 300 square miles, destroying 4,000 homes and businesses, and killing at least nine persons.

June 6. American billionaire J. Paul Getty dies at age 83 at his Surrey, England, estate.

June 6. The Boston Celtics win their 13th National Basketball Association championship, defeating the Phoenix Suns four games to two.

June 9. James A. Farley, an influential leader of the Democratic Party during the New Deal, and one-time postmaster general, dies at age 88 in New York City.

June 10. Adolph Zukor, founder of Paramount Pictures and producer of the first feature film in the U. S., dies at age 103 in Los Angeles.

June 13. Don Bolles, investigative reporter for the *Arizona Republic,* dies in Phoenix as the result of a bomb explosion in his car on June 7. He was looking into connections between local politicians and organized crime.

June 15. Proposition 15 on the California primary ballot is defeated. It would have limited construction of nuclear power plants in the state.

June 16. Francis E. Meloy, Jr., U. S. Ambassador to Lebanon, is assassinated in Beirut, along with an aide, Robert O. Waring, and their Lebanese driver.

June 17. A bus containing 26 school children and the driver disappears near Chowchilla in central California. They reappear the next day. Three men are captured as kidnappers.

June 22. The West Point honor system and a mass cheating scandal at the school come under the scrutiny of the Senate Armed Services Committee.

June 25. Composer Johnny Mercer dies at age 66 in Belair, California.

June 26. The United States Supreme Court rules that the Civil Rights Act of 1965 protects whites as well as blacks against racial discrimination.

June 28. Seven industrial nations hold a summit meeting in San Juan, Puerto Rico, to discuss problems of world economic recovery and control of inflation.

July. The American Bicentennial is celebrated all across the nation. On July 2, 200 "tall ships" begin arriving in New York Harbor. From July 6 to 12, Queen Elizabeth II pays a state visit to Washington, D.C., Newport, Philadelphia, and Boston. Nearly every city and town in the U. S. has some form of celebration over the Fourth of July weekend.

July 2. The U. S. Supreme Court upholds the death penalty for murder convictions.

July 8. Mrs. Patricia Nixon, wife of the former President, suffers a stroke at her San Clemente, California, home.

July 12–15. The Democratic Party Convention, meeting at New York's Madison Square Garden, nominates Jimmy Carter for the presidency and Walter Mondale for the vice presidency.

July 17–August 1. The Summer Olympic Games are held in Montreal. The U.S. wins a total of 94 medals: 34 gold, 35 silver, and 25 bronze.

July 20. Viking 1, the U.S. spacecraft launched to explore Mars, lands on the planet's surface at 7:53 a.m. Eastern Daylight Time. September 3. Viking 2 lands on Mars at 6:38 EDT, about 4000 miles away from Viking 1.

August. Twenty-seven persons die from a mysterious "legionnaire's disease" after attending an American Legion convention at the Bellevue Stratford Hotel in Philadelphia. The cause of the deaths has not been ascertained.

August 1. A heavy downpour sends floodwaters down Big Thompson Canyon in Colorado, near Loveland. The death toll reaches 138, with dozens of persons still missing.

August 1–8. The 41st International Eucharistic Congress of the Roman Catholic Church is held in Philadelphia.

August 9. Bob Lemon, Robin Roberts, Fred Lindstrom, and two deceased players, Oscar Charleston and Roger Connor, are elected to the Baseball Hall of Fame.

August 9. William and Emily Harris, members of the Symbionese Liberation

Army and former associates of Patricia Hearst, are convicted in Los Angeles of kidnapping, armed robbery, and car theft.

August 9–10. Hurricane Belle hits the East Coast from North Carolina to New York, killing at least 12 persons and causing an estimated 23.5 million dollars worth of damage.

August 15. About 100 black youths terrorize an audience at a rock music concert in Detroit's Cobo Hall.

August 16–19. The Republican Party Convention, meeting at Kansas City's Kemper Arena, nominates Gerald R. Ford for the presidency and Robert J. Dole for the vice presidency.

August 18. Two American army officers are killed by North Koreans in the Demilitarized Zone between North and South Korea.

August 29. A Senate committee investigation reveals that billions of dollars of Medicaid program funds are lost annually through fraud and waste in several cities.

September 8. Federal Judge William B. Bryant rules in Washington, D.C., that the annual football draft of college players is illegal, violating the anti-trust laws.

September 10. Croatian nationalists hijack a TWA jet en route from New York to Chicago. The passenger-hostages are later released in Paris and the hijackers surrender.

September 11–13. The Episcopal Church, at its general convention in Minneapolis, votes for ordination of women to the priesthood, intensifying what is becoming a major schism.

September 23. The first of three televised debates between presidential contenders Gerald Ford and Jimmy Carter takes place at Philadelphia. The second debate is held on October 6 and the last on October 22. The vice presidential candidates, Walter Mondale and Robert Dole, debate in Houston on October 15.

September 29. President Ford vetoes a $56 billion Health-Education-Welfare bill. Congress overrides the veto two days later.

October 4. Secretary of Agriculture Earl L. Butz resigns. His telling of a joke involving a racial slur, while on a flight to California from the Republican convention in Kansas City, has made him an issue in the campaign.

October 8. Two members of the American Bicentennial Everest Expedition, Chris Chandler and Bob Cormack, reach the top of Mt. Everest.

October 14. President Ford presents the Medal of Freedom to Martha Graham, dancer and choreographer.

October 14–21. All seven winners of this year's Nobel Prizes are Americans: Milton Friedman of the University of Chicago, for economics; Dr. Baruch S. Blumberg of the University of Pennsylvania and Dr. Daniel Carleton Gajdusek of the National Institutes of Health, for medicine; Saul Bellow of the University of Chicago, for literature; William Nunn Lipscomb, Jr., of Harvard University, for chemistry; and Burton Richter and Samuel Chao Chung Ting of Massachusetts Institute of Technology, for physics.

October 20. A ferryboat, the *George Prince,* collides with the Norwegian tanker, *Frosta,* in the Mississippi River about 20 miles upstream from New Orleans. The death toll is estimated at 100.

October 21. The Cincinnati Reds win the World Series, defeating the New York Yankees four games in a row.

October 21–23. A large, representative convention of Roman Catholics meets at Detroit. The 1,340 delegates discuss issues of social justice. On November 8–11, the National Conference of Catholic Bishops meets in Washington, D. C., amid controversy occasioned by the Detroit convention's resolutions.

October 24. Twenty-five persons die in an arson fire at a Puerto Rican social club in New York City.

November 2. In the general election, Jimmy Carter, former governor of Georgia, defeats President Ford. Carter will become the 39th President on January 20, 1977. The voter turnout of 80 million is numerically the highest in U.S. history but represents only about 54 percent of the electorate. Democrats will keep control of the House and Senate, and they have possession of 37 of the 50 governorships.

December. During the month five Liberian oil tankers experience difficulties in or near the United States. On the 17th, an 810-foot tanker explodes in Los Angeles Harbor. Four other tankers run aground. One off Nantucket Island breaks in half, spilling more than five million gallons into the Atlantic. On the Delaware River near Philadelphia the *Olympic Games* runs aground, spilling 34,000 gallons of oil. A third runs aground, on the Thames River in Connecticut, spilling some oil. Off the south coast of Puerto Rico, the *Daphne* runs aground on December 28, but is successfully floated again.

December 3–4. A new denomination, the Association of Evangelical Lutheran Churches, has its founding convention in Chicago. The group has broken away from the Lutheran Church-Missouri Synod.

December 7. The U. S. Supreme Court rules that federal civil rights laws do not require company disability programs to cover pregnancy or childbirth benefits.

December 20. Richard J. Daley, mayor of Chicago for nearly 22 years, dies at age 74.

December 21. The industrialized nations of the world sign an agreement in Paris, calling for the pooling of solar energy in order to lessen dependence on oil.

December 31. President Ford recommends that Puerto Rico become the 51st state of the Union.

The Watergate Chronology

(continued and concluded).

1974

January 2. The Internal Revenue Service announces that it is examining President Nixon's tax returns for 1969–1972.

January 4. President Nixon informs the Senate Watergate Committee that he will not comply with a subpoena for tape recordings and documents.

January 8. The President releases information on the milk price support decision of 1971 and on the ITT anti-trust suit dropped by the Justice Department.

January 12. Special Watergate Prosecutor Leon Jaworski resists turning over White House tapes and documents to the House Judiciary Committee.

January 15. A preliminary report by a panel of experts indicates that the 18½-minute gap in one tape was probably accomplished by manual manipulation.

January 18. Judge John Sirica orders Watergate grand jury number 3 to investigate the possibility of unlawful destruction of evidence and related offenses.

January 22. Senator Hugh Scott, Republican minority leader, states that the White House has information that will clear the President of any wrongdoing in the Watergate affair.

January 24. Egil Krogh, former White House aide and head of the "plumbers" unit, is sentenced to six months in prison.

January 28. Herbert L. Porter, former member of the Committee to Re-elect the President, pleads guilty to lying to the FBI during the original Watergate investigation.

January 29. The CIA admits destroying tape recordings dealing with the Watergate break-in.

February 6. John W. Dean III, former Nixon aide, is disbarred by a Virginia state court.

The House of Representatives votes to give the House Judiciary Committee powers to conduct an impeachment inquiry. Rep. Peter Rodino, Democrat of New Jersey, is committee chairman.

February 19. The Senate Watergate Committee, under chairman Sen. Sam Ervin, Jr., ends its public hearings.

The trial of John N. Mitchell and Maurice Stans for perjury and obstruction of justice opens in New York City. On April 28 they are acquitted of the charges.

February 21. In a report prepared for the House Judiciary Committee, special counsel John Doar and Republican counsel Albert E. Jenner state that violation of criminal law is not required for impeachment to be voted.

February 25. President Nixon announces that he will not appear to testify before the Watergate grand jury.

Herbert Kalmbach, formerly the President's lawyer and fund-raiser, pleads guilty to violations of campaign finance laws. On June 17 he is sentenced to a 6 to 18 month jail term and ordered to pay a fine of $10,000.

March 1. The federal government indicts John Mitchell, John Ehrlichman, H. R. Haldeman, Charles Colson, Robert Mardian, and Kenneth Parkinson.

March 7. A federal grand jury indicts John Ehrlichman, Charles Colson. Gordon Liddy, Bernard Barker, Felipe DeDiego, and Eugenio Martinez for conspiracy to violate the rights of Dr. Lewis Fielding, Daniel Ellsberg's psychiatrist, by breaking into his office in 1971.

March 15. President Nixon makes a series of public and televised appearances to rally public support for himself. He visits Chicago, Nashville, and Houston.

March 18. Judge Sirica rules that the House Judiciary Committee may have access to the federal grand jury's secret Watergate report and to other relevant materials concerning possible presidential involvement.

April 3. The White House announces that President Nixon will pay back taxes amounting to $432,787.

Lieutenant governor Edwin Reinecke of California is indicted by a Watergate grand jury on a charge of perjury before a Senate committee in connection with the investigation of the 1972 ITT antitrust case. He is found guilty on July 27, but his conviction is later overturned by a federal appeals court.

April 5. Dwight Chapin is found guilty of lying during the Watergate investigation. He is sentenced to from 10 to 30 months in prison.

April 11. The House committee votes to subpoena 42 Presidential tapes and sets April 25 as deadline for compliance.

April 16. Special Prosecutor Jaworski subpoenas 64 of the White House tapes.

April 29. On a nationally televised broadcast, President Nixon says he will give the committee 1200 pages of edited transcript and let two committee members listen to the tapes. Rep. Rodino states that transcripts will not be sufficient.

April 30. The edited transcripts are delivered to the Judiciary Committee.

May 1. The House committee votes to inform the President that he has not complied with its subpoena by sending transcripts of his tapes.

The President tells Judge Sirica that he will not turn over 64 tapes to Leon Jaworski.

May 2. Former Vice President Spiro Agnew is disbarred by the Maryland Court of Appeals.

May 9. The House Judiciary Committee opens hearings to determine on the impeachment of President Nixon.

May 20. Judge Sirica orders the President to turn over 64 tapes to Special Prosecutor Jaworski.

May 21. Jeb Stuart Magruder is sentenced to a prison term of from 10 months to four years for his part in the Watergate break-in.

May 24. The White House files a suit with the U. S. Court of Appeals in an effort to keep from turning tapes over to Jaworski. The Special Prosecutor asks the U. S. Supreme Court to intervene and settle the case directly.

May 31. The U. S. Supreme Court agrees to take up the case of the tapes.

June 3. Charles Colson pleads guilty in the case of Ellsberg's psychiatrist, Dr. Fielding. He is sentenced to from one to three years in prison and fined $5,000.

June 7. Former Attorney General Richard Kleindienst is given a suspended sentence for his "technical" law violation in testifying before a Senate committee.

June 15. Newspaper reports that President Nixon has been named an unindicted co-conspirator by the Watergate grand jury are confirmed.

July 9. The committee releases transcripts of eight recorded White House conversations showing significant differences from the edited transcripts released by the President.

July 10. President Nixon says he did not know in advance about the Watergate break-in.

July 12. John Ehrlichman, Gordon Liddy, Bernard Barker, and Eugenio Martinez are convicted of conspiracy in connection with the break-in at Dr. Lewis Fielding's office.

The Senate Watergate Committee releases its final report on illegalities committed during the 1972 Presidential campaign.

July 24. The U. S. Supreme Court, in an 8-0 decision, rules that the President must turn over tapes to Judge Sirica for possible use in the coverup trial because executive privilege does not apply to the case. The President's lawyer announces that Mr. Nixon will comply with the court's ruling.

July 24–27, 29–30. The House Judiciary Committee holds six days of televised debate on impeachment evidence.

July 27. The committee votes to recommend impeachment for obstruction of justice in the Watergate coverup.

July 29. The committee votes to recommend impeachment for general abuse of presidential powers.

July 30. The committee votes to recommend impeachment for President Nixon's refusal to comply with subpoenas for White House tapes.

August 2. John W. Dean III is sentenced to from 1 to 4 years for his part in the Watergate affair.

August 5. The President releases three transcripts of White House conversations with H. R. Haldeman that took place on June 23, 1972. These conversations are extremely damaging to the President's cause, for they show that as of that date he had planned to get the FBI to halt its inquiry into the break-in. Nixon admits a serious "act of omission" in his previous accounts of the coverup story. With the release of these tapes and this admission, his support in Congress virtually disappears.

August 7. In a meeting with his cabinet, the President vows not to resign.

Three Republican leaders of Congress, Sen. Barry Goldwater, Sen. Hugh Scott, and Rep. John Rhodes, meet with the President to confirm that he no longer has support in Congress.

August 8. In a nationally televised statement, President Nixon announces he will resign the next day.

August 9. President Nixon bids farewell to his administration and to members of the White House staff.

At 12:03 p.m. Gerald R. Ford takes the oath of office to become the 38th President of the United States.

August 16. The President orders all Nixon tapes and documents to be held at the White House until the Watergate matters are all resolved.

September 8. President Ford grants Nixon an unconditional pardon for all federal crimes "he committed or may have committed or taken part in" while President.

Over the next few days the national and Congressional reaction to the pardon is generally negative and hostile. President Ford denies that any bargain had been made with the former President before he left office which would result in the pardon.

October 1. The Watergate coverup trial begins in Washington.

October 12. Special Prosecutor Leon Jaworski announces his resignation, to be effective October 25.

December 4. After thirty months of service, the original Watergate grand jury is dismissed. Two other grand juries remain in session.

1975

January 1. The Watergate coverup trial ends with verdicts of guilty for the four defendants: H. R. Haldeman, John Ehrlichman, John Mitchell, and Robert C. Mardian.

January 8. John W. Dean III, Herbert Kalmbach, and Jeb Stuart Magruder are released from jail, having had their sentences reduced by Judge Sirica to the time already served.

March 12. Former Secretary of Commerce Maurice Stans pleads guilty to violations of federal campaign spending laws.

June 10. Former President Nixon, in a letter to the U. S. Supreme Court, resigns the practice of law.

July 3. Former Attorney General John Mitchell is disbarred by the New York State Supreme Court.

The third Watergate grand jury is dismissed by U. S. District Chief Judge George L. Hart.

1976

January 7. A panel of federal judges upholds a 1974 law giving control of former President Nixon's papers and tape recordings to the government.

*****

The foregoing chronology is but a skeletal outline of all the happenings that became entangled in and derived from the Watergate affair. What happened in the country during the administrations of President Nixon will doubtless continue to have repercussions for years to come. Associated with the Watergate affair, but not directly part of it, are also the scandals relating to illegal campaign contributions to public officials, the revelations about enormous bribes paid by American companies to officials in foreign nations, and the various illegalities committed by the Federal Bureau of Investigation and the Central Intelligence Agency, as well as other government agencies. The unraveling of these situations will stretch beyond the time span of this volume.

The Crisis of the Presidency
A Special Section

In his State of the Union message on January 30, 1974, President Nixon, affirming his determination to remain in office, asserted that: "One year of Watergate is enough." To which someone soon responded: "One year of Watergate is too much." But it was to be several months more before the presidential crisis wound to its inexorable conclusion. The word "inexorable" seems to have the benefit of hindsight, but actually the whole country sensed that the Nixon presidency was doomed after the famed "Saturday night massacre" of October 20, 1973, when Special Prosecutor Archibald Cox and assistant Attorney General William Ruckelshaus were fired, and Attorney General Elliot Richardson resigned. Within a few days several resolutions of impeachment were introduced into the House of Representatives.

The President's fate was bound up with the disposition of his own tape recordings, and it was the tapes, finally, that brought about his resignation. The new Special Prosecutor, Leon Jaworski, pressed for the release of more tapes and documents. President Nixon went on national television on April 29 to announce that he was releasing to the House Judiciary Committee the edited transcripts of 46 tapes of discussions between himself and his advisors. The committee accepted the transcripts, but continued to insist on the actual tapes. When the transcripts were made public the first week of May, the public reaction was highly unfavorable. The public outcry for impeachment or resignation increased dramatically when it was learned just what kind of conversations went on in the White House, among the most powerful men in the land.

Judge John Sirica ordered a subpoena issued on the White House for all the material that Jaworski demanded. (It must be remembered that there were two separate investigations under way by this time: that of the Special Prosecutor and that of the House Judiciary Committee. The one was concerned with criminal liability and the other with malfeasance in office. Both had subpoena power, but if the President gave tapes and documents to Jaworski, the House committee did not necessarily have access to them, and vice versa.) Nixon's failure to comply with the subpoena led Jaworski to petition the U. S. Supreme Court to hear the case. On July 24 the Court ruled that Nixon must give the Special Prosecutor the tapes and documents that he requested.

That same day, the House Judiciary Committee began nationally televised hearings on the impeachment issue. The committee, once its investigation was completed, voted three articles of impeachment on each of three days, July 27, 29, and 30.

The President still expressed confidence that he could weather both a House vote and the Senate trial. But on August 5 the most damaging evidence came to light, and from the President himself. At his lawyer's request, he released transcripts of tapes made on June 23, 1972. These conversations, with his chief advisor H. R. Haldeman, showed a clear intent to obstruct justice: the President had ordered Haldeman to stop the FBI investigation of the Watergate break-in because evidence was pointing to members of the President's re-election committee. When this news came out, virtually all of the President's remaining support in Congress evaporated.

Two days later, three Republican congressional leaders, Senators Barry Goldwater and Hugh Scott, and Rep. John Rhodes, went to the White House to tell the President he no longer had sufficient support in Congress to survive the Senate trial, much less an impeachment vote. The next evening, President Nixon went on national television to announce to the country that he would be resigning August 9. On the morning of August 9 the President bade farewell to the White House staff and then departed for his home at San Clemente, California.

Gerald R. Ford became the 38th President of the United States. One month later, on September 8, a Sunday, President Ford granted Nixon an unconditional pardon for any federal crimes "he committed or may have committed or taken part in" during his presidency. Public outrage over the pardon was vehement, but whether President Ford's standing with the American people was permanently damaged was impossible to discern. All euphoria that Congress and the public had felt over having a new President had vanished, however.

The selections in this special section comprise the key documents (apart from the voluminous transcripts) in the dissolution of the Nixon presidency. They are:

1. The *Chicago Tribune* editorial of May 9, urging the President to resign.
2. The Supreme Court ruling of July 24.
3. Portions of the final report of the House Judiciary Committee's inquiry.
4. President Nixon's August 5 statement on releasing the transcripts of June 23, 1972.
5. President Nixon's speeches of August 8 and 9, and his letter of resignation.
6. The swearing in of President Ford.
7. President Ford's first address to Congress.
8. President Ford's pardon of former President Nixon.

President Nixon with edited transcripts of the White House tapes.

1974

1.

Listen, Mr. Nixon . . .

In its May 9 edition, the Chicago Tribune *published a long editorial summing up the case against President Nixon and urging him to resign. To call this editorial a key document in the Watergate affair may presume too much. But it does mark a turning point. It was a signal that even the conservative Republican establishment had finally turned against the President. To be sure, there were holdouts — diehards who would believe in the President until it was impolitic to favor him any longer. The occasion of this editorial was the President's own release of the tape transcripts, making it possible for all Americans to view the inner workings of the Nixon White House.*

Source: *Chicago Tribune,* May 9, 1974.

LISTEN MR NIXON . . .

WE SAW the public man in his first administration, and we were impressed. Now in about 300,000 words we have seen the private man, and we are appalled.

What manner of man is the Richard Nixon who emerges from the transcripts of the White House tapes?

We see a man who, in the words of his old friend and defender, Sen. Hugh Scott, took a principal role in a "shabby, immoral and disgusting performance."

The key word here is immoral. It is a lack of concern for morality, a lack of concern for high principles, a lack of commitment to the high ideals of public office

that make the transcripts a sickening exposure of the man and his advisers. He is preoccupied with appearance rather than substance. His aim is to find a way to sell the idea that disreputable schemes are actually good or are defensible for some trumped-up cause.

He is humorless to the point of being inhumane. He is devious. He is vacillating. He is profane. He is willing to be led. He displays dismaying gaps in knowledge. He is suspicious of his staff. His loyalty is minimal. His greatest concern is to create a record that will save him and his administration. The high dedication to grand principles that Americans have a right to expect from a President is missing from the transcript record.

Mr. Nixon's strategy backfired when he released the transcripts. It was also a strategic error for him to release the record of his income taxes. Both stripped the man to his essential character, and that character could not stand that kind of scrutiny. Both miscalculations demonstrated an essential Nixon defect—an insensitivity to the standards of ethics and morality that Americans expect of their leaders.

He thought disclosure of the records would help him. He has had a demonstration that his countrymen are not that tolerant.

And it should be noted here that the transcripts and the income tax statement were not the fabrications of his enemies. These were self-created instruments of destruction.

His decision Tuesday to disclose no more information leaves the record as it now stands. And as it stands that record leaves no doubt that he lacks the qualities that could edify and inspire his countrymen with confidence in these difficult times.

The statement of his counsel, James St. Clair, that the President is ready for a confrontation with Congress and his own special prosecutor is ominous.

The balance among the coordinate branches of our government—Executive, Judicial, and Legislative—is fragile. It has been established on rather comfortably loose terms by nearly 200 years of experience in practicing the special virtues of American government.

The limits of executive privilege, of congressional power, of judicial authority are not rigidly fixed. We would not relish the prospect of forcing the Supreme Court to make hard decisions in the distorting heat of partisan controversy. This is one confrontation this country does not need and we pray Mr. Nixon will not insist on it. The President is right in urging a quick end to the Watergate affair. His country needs a swift and merciful termination of this agony.

Two roads are open. One is resignation. The other is impeachment. Both are legitimate and would satisfy the need to observe due process.

. . . The Two Choices . . .

Resignation of the President would be quick and simple and a qualified successor stands ready to assume office.

Impeachment is the judicial process prescribed by the Constitution for removing a President. The House can, and probably will, vote a bill of impeachment quickly. A trial in the Senate would be, and indeed should be, long and deliberate. No suggestion of haste or mob justice could be tolerated. The White House could be expected to seize every opportunity for challenge and delay, and the final outcome might be two years in coming.

The objection to resignation that has been raised—and we have raised it ourselves—is that it would not resolve the issues. It would not answer many of the questions about the President's behavior and degree of complicity. It would leave at least a suspicion that the President had been persecuted instead of properly prosecuted out of office. To some he might remain a martyr. To many it would seem a miscarriage of justice, an example of political exorcism.

The transcripts have changed all that. Tho they may clear Mr. Nixon of direct complicity in the Watergate burglary and the early stages of the coverup, nobody of sound mind can read them and continue to think that Mr. Nixon has upheld the standards and dignity of the Presidency which he proclaimed himself as a candidate in 1960. He hoped that, if elected, a mother or father would be able to "look at the man in the White House . . . and say, 'Well, there is a man who maintains the kind of standards personally that I would like my child to follow.'"

We do not share the White House belief that impeachment requires evidence of a specific crime. We believe a President may be removed simply for failing to do his job, or for so discrediting himself that he loses public respect and with it, his ability to govern effectively.

It is true that this vagueness may tempt opponents to seek to remove a President for political or otherwise inadequate reasons, as they did with Andrew Johnson. But that risk must be accepted. The ultimate arbiter in this matter must be the public, and the public reaction today is clearly one of revulsion. Republican politicians are defecting in droves. The evidence against Mr. Nixon is in his own words, made public at his own direction. There can no longer be a charge that he was railroaded out of office by vengeful Democrats or a hostile press. The fundamental questions have been answered. Filling in the gaps in the transcripts can only make the case against the President stronger.

And so the objections to resignation have largely vanished.

Since the President has rejected this course, we urge the House to act quickly on a bill of impeachment. As the impeachment process progresses, as public opinion becomes clear, and as Mr. Nixon sees support dwindling in the Senate, he will have to reconsider his stand and recognize that resignation will spare the country the ordeal of a trial.

. . . And the Cost of Inaction

There are three urgent reasons for turning the reins of government over to a new President who can concentrate on his job, and for doing so quickly.

First, without decisive leadership in either foreign or domestic matters, the country will drift along aimlessly during one of the most critical periods of history. In country after country, governments are being toppled and threatened because of popular frustration over inflation, hunger, the energy shortage, and the apparent inability of governments to deal with them. It would be a tragedy for the richest and most powerful country in the world to stagger along, immobile, during such a period.

Second, Mr. Nixon has become a liability to his political party as well as to the Republic. The longer he remains in office as a symbol of Watergate and all it stands for, the more likely it is that the Republican Party will be incapacitated for years to come. The health of our two-party system depends on separating the Republican Party from the evils of Watergate and the character of the President.

Third, it is equally important for the future of the Presidency itself that it be separated from the man who now holds it. We must return to the day when people can shiver with pride instead of shudder with embarrassment when they see the flag or hear "Hail to the Chief." Many of the prerogatives of the Presidency are essential to the country, including secrecy when properly justified for reasons of national security or executive privilege. These principles have been prostituted in order to preserve Mr. Nixon himself and those around him. The longer this goes on, the more likely these prerogatives are to be forfeited — in the public mind if not by act of Congress.

It is saddening and hard to believe that for the first time in our history, it is better that the President leave office than fight to keep it. But things have reached such a state that Mr. Nixon's departure, one way or another, is the best course for the Presidency, the country, and the free world. To perpetuate a state of confrontation between the Executive and Congress—in order to define the limits of power which are probably better undefined—will be tragically costly in the eyes of history and the world.

2.

WARREN E. BURGER: *United States* v. *Richard M. Nixon*

There are actually two cases at issue here: the one in the selection title and "Richard M. Nixon, President of the United States, Petitioner, v. United States." The substance of the cases was whether, by any claim of executive privilege, the President could keep from turning over tapes and documents as evidence to Special Prosecutor Leon Jaworski. A lower court ruling had gone against the President, so appeal was made to the Supreme Court. The major portion of Chief Justice Burger's lengthy ruling of July 24 is reprinted here.

Source: 418 US 683.

MR. CHIEF JUSTICE BURGER delivered the opinion of the Court.

These cases present for review the denial of a motion, filed on behalf of the President of the United States, in the case of *United States* v. *Mitchell et al.* (D. C. Crim. No. 74–110), to quash a third-party subpoena *duces tecum* issued by the United States District Court for the District of Columbia, pursuant to Fed. Rule Crim. Proc. 17 (c). The subpoena directed the President to produce certain tape recordings and documents relating to his conversations with aides and advisers. The court rejected the President's claims of absolute executive privilege, of lack of jurisdiction, and of failure to satisfy the requirements of Rule 17 (c). The President appealed to the Court of Appeals. We granted the United States' petition for certiorari before judgment, and also the President's responsive cross-petition for certiorari before judgment, because of the public importance of the issues presented and the need for their prompt resolution. . . .

On May 20, 1974, the District Court denied the motion to quash and the motions to expunge and for protective orders. It further ordered "the President or any subordinate officer, official or employee with custody or control of the documents or objects subpoenaed," to deliver to the District Court, on or before May 31, 1974, the originals of all subpoenaed items, as well as an index and analysis of those items, together with tape copies of those portions of the subpoenaed recordings for which transcripts had been released to the public by the President on April 30. The District Court rejected jurisdictional challenges based on a contention that the dispute was nonjusticiable because it was between the Special Prosecutor and the Chief Executive and hence "intra-executive" in character; it also rejected the contention that the judiciary was without authority to review an assertion of executive privilege by the President. The court's rejection of the first challenge was based on the authority and powers vested in the Special Prosecutor by the regulation promulgated by the Attorney General; the court concluded that a justiciable controversy was presented. The second challenge was held to be foreclosed by the decision in *Nixon* v. *Sirica*, 487 F. 2d 700 (1973).

The District Court held that the judiciary, not the President, was the final arbiter of a claim of executive privilege. The court concluded that, under the circumstances of this case, the presumptive privilege was overcome by the Special Prosecutor's prima facie "demonstration of need sufficiently compelling to warrant judicial examination in chambers. . . ." The court held, finally, that the Special Prosecutor had satisfied the requirements of Rule 17 (c). The District Court stayed its order pending appellate review on condition that review was sought before 4 p. m., May 24. The court further provided that matters filed under seal remain under seal when transmitted as part of the record.

On May 24, 1974, the President filed a timely notice of appeal from the District Court order, and the certified record from the District Court was docketed in the United States Court of Appeals for the District of Columbia Circuit. On the same day, the President also filed a petition for writ of mandamus in the Court of Appeals seeking review of the District Court order.

Later on May 24, the Special Prosecutor also filed, in this Court, a petition for a writ of certiorari before judgment. On May 31, the petition was granted with an expedited briefing schedule. On June 6, the President filed, under seal, a cross-petition for writ of certiorari before judgment. This cross-petition was granted June 15, 1974, and the case was set for argument on July 8, 1974.

I
Jurisdiction

The threshold question presented is whether the May 20, 1974, order of the District Court was an appealable order and whether this case was properly "in," 28 U. S. C § 1254, the United States Court of Appeals when the petition for certiorari was filed in this Court. Court of Appeals jurisdiction under 28 U. S. C. § 1291 encompasses only "final decisions of the district courts." Since the appeal was timely filed and all other procedural requirements were met, the petition is properly before this Court for consideration if the District Court order was final.

The finality requirement of 28 U. S. C. § 1291 embodies a strong congressional policy against piecemeal reviews, and against obstructing or impeding an ongoing judicial proceeding by interlocutory appeals, This requirement ordinarily promotes judicial efficiency and hastens the ultimate termination of litigation. In applying this principle to an order denying a motion to quash and requiring the production of evidence pursuant to a subpoena duces tecum, it has been repeatedly held that the order is not final and hence not appealable. This Court has consistently held that the necessity for expedition in the administration of the criminal law justifies putting one who seeks to resist the production of desired information to a choice between compliance with a trial court's order to produce prior to any review of that order, and resistance to that order with the concomitant possibility of an adjudication of contempt if his claims are rejected on appeal. *United*

States v. *Ryan*, 402 U. S. 530, 533 (1971).

The requirement of submitting to contempt, however, is not without exception and in some instances the purposes underlying the finality rule require a different result. For example, in *Perlman* v. *United States*, 247 U. S. 7 (1918), a subpoena had been directed to a third party requesting certain exhibits; the appellant, who owned the exhibits, sought to raise a claim of privilege. The Court held an order compelling production was appealable because it was unlikely that the third party would risk a contempt citation in order to allow immediate review of the appellant's claim of privilege. *Id.*, at 12–13. That case fell within the "limited class of cases where denial of immediate review would render impossible any review whatsoever of an individual's claims," *United States* v. *Ryan, supra,* at 533.

Here too the traditional contempt avenue to immediate appeal is peculiarly inappropriate due to the unique setting in which the question arises. To require a President of the United States to place himself in the posture of disobeying an order of a court merely to trigger the procedural mechanism for review of the ruling would be unseemly, and present an unnecessary occasion for constitutional confrontation between two branches of the Government. Similarly, a federal judge should not be placed in the posture of issuing a citation to a President simply in order to invoke review. The issue whether a President can be cited for contempt could itself engender protracted litigation, and would further delay both review on the merits of his claim of privilege and the ultimate termination of the underlying criminal action for which his evidence is sought. These considerations lead us to conclude that the order of the District Court was an appealable order.

The appeal from that order was therefore properly "in" the Court of Appeals, and the case is now properly before this Court on the writ of certiorari before judgment.

II
Justiciability

In the District Court, the President's counsel argued that the court lacked jurisdiction to issue the subpoena because the matter was an intra-branch dispute between a subordinate and superior officer of the Executive Branch and hence not subject to judicial resolution. That argument has been renewed in this Court with emphasis on the contention that the dispute does not present a "case" or "controversy" which can be adjudicated in the federal courts. The President's counsel argues that the federal courts should not intrude into areas committed to the other branches of Government. He views the present dispute as essentially a "jurisdictional" dispute within the Executive Branch which he analogizes to a dispute between two congressional committees. Since the Executive Branch has exclusive authority and absolute discretion to decide whether to prosecute a case, *Confiscation Cases*, 7 Wall. 454 (1869), *United States* v. *Cox*, 342 F. 2d 167, 171 (CA5), cert. denied, 381 U. S. 935 (1965), it is contended that a President's decision is final in determining what evidence is to be used in a given criminal case. Although his counsel concedes the President has delegated certain specific powers to the Special Prosecutor, he has not "waived nor delegated to the Special Prosecutor the President's duty to claim privilege as to all materials . . . which fall within the President's inherent authority to refuse to disclose to any executive officer." Brief for the President 47. The Special Prosecutor's demand for the items therefore presents, in the view of the President's counsel, a political question under *Baker* v. *Carr*, 369 U. S. 186 (1962), since it involves a "textually demonstrable" grant of power under Art. II.

The mere assertion of a claim of an "intra-branch dispute," without more, has never operated to defeat federal jurisdiction; justiciability does not depend on such a surface inquiry. In *United States* v. *ICC*, 337 U. S. 426 (1949), the Court observed, "courts must look behind names that symbolize the parties to determine whether a justiciable case or controversy is presented."

Our starting point is the nature of the proceeding for which the evidence is sought—here a pending criminal prosecution. It is a judicial proceeding in a federal court alleging violation of federal laws and is brought in the name of the United States as sovereign. *Berger* v. *United States*, 295 U. S. 78, 88 (1935). Under the authority of Art. II, § 2, Congress has vested in the Attorney General the power to conduct the criminal litigation of the United States Government. It has also vested in him the power to appoint subordinate officers to assist him in the discharge of his duties. Acting pursuant to those statutes, the Attorney General has delegated the authority to represent the United States in these particular matters to a Special Prosecutor with unique authority and tenure. The regulation gives the Special Prosecutor explicit power to contest the invocation of executive privilege in the process of seeking evidence deemed relevant to the performance of these specially delegated duties.

So long as this regulation is extant it has the force of law. In *Accardi* v. *Shaughnessy*, 347 U. S. 260 (1953), regulations of the Attorney General delegated certain of his discretionary powers to the Board of Immigration Appeals and required that Board to exercise its own discretion on appeals in deportation cases. The Court held that so long as the Attorney General's regulations remained operative, he denied himself the authority to exercise the discretion delegated to the Board even though the original authority was his and he could reassert it by amending the regulations. *Service* v. *Dulles*, 354 U. S. 363, 388 (1957), and *Vitarelli* v. *Seaton*, 359 U. S. 535 (1959), reaffirmed the basic holding of *Accardi*.

Here, as in *Accardi*, it is theoretically possible for the Attorney General to amend or revoke the regulation defining the Special Prosecutor's authority. But he has not done so. So long as this regulation remains in force the Executive Branch is bound by it, and indeed the United States as the sovereign composed of the three branches is bound to respect and to enforce it. Moreover, the delegation of authority to the Special Prosecutor in this case is not an ordinary delegation by the Attorney General to a subordinate officer: with the authorization of the President, the Acting Attorney General provided in the regulation that the Special Prosecutor was not to be removed without the "consensus" of eight designated leaders of Congress.

The demands of and the resistance to the subpoena present an obvious controversy in the ordinary sense, but that alone is not sufficient to meet constitutional standards. In the constitutional sense, controversy means more than disagreement and conflict; rather it means the kind of controversy courts traditionally resolve. Here at issue is the production or nonproduction of specified evidence deemed by the Special Prosecutor to be relevant and admissible in a pending criminal case. It is sought by one official of the Government within the scope of his express authority; it is resisted by the Chief Executive on the ground of his duty to preserve the confidentiality of the communications of the President. Whatever the correct answer on the merits, these issues are "of a type which are traditionally justiciable." *United States* v. *ICC*, 337 U. S., at 430. The independent Special Prosecutor with his asserted need for the subpoenaed material in the underlying criminal prosecution is opposed by the President with his steadfast assertion of privilege against disclosure of the material. This setting assures there is "that concrete adverseness which sharpens the presentation of issues upon which the court so largely depends for illumination of difficult constitutional questions." *Baker* v. *Carr,* 369 U. S., at 204. Moreover, since the matter is one arising in the regular course of a federal criminal prosecution, it is within the traditional scope of Art. III power. *Id.,* at 198.

In light of the uniqueness of the setting in which the conflict arises, the fact that both parties are officers of the Executive Branch cannot be viewed as a barrier to justiciability. It would be inconsistent with the applicable law and regulation, and the unique facts of this case to conclude other than that the Special Prosecutor has standing to bring this action and that a justiciable controversy is presented for decision.

III
Rule 17 (c)

The subpoena *duces tecum* is challenged on the ground that the Special Prosecutor failed to satisfy the requirements of Fed. Rule Crim. Proc. 17 (c), which governs the issuance of subpoenas *duces tecum* in federal criminal proceedings. If we sustained this challenge, there would be no occasion to reach the claim of privilege asserted with respect to the subpoenaed material. Thus we turn to the question whether the requirements of Rule 17 (c) have been satisfied. See *Arkansas-Louisiana Gas Co.* v. *Dept. of Public Utilities*, 304 U. S. 61, 64 (1938); *Ashwander* v. *Tennessee Valley Authority*, 297 U. S. 288, 346–347 (1936). (Brandeis, J., concurring.)

Rule 17 (c) provides:

A subpoena may also command the person to whom it is directed to produce the books, papers, documents or other objects designated therein. The court on motion made promptly may quash or modify the supoena if compliance would be unreasonable or oppressive. The court may direct that books, papers, documents or objects designated in the subpoena be produced before the court at a time prior to the trial or prior to the time when they are to be offered in evidence and may upon their production permit the books, papers, documents or objects or portions thereof to be inspected by the parties and their attorneys.

A subpoena for documents may be quashed if their production would be "unreasonable or oppressive," but not otherwise. The leading case in this Court interpreting this standard is *Bowman Dairy Co.* v. *United States*, 341 U. S. 214 (1950). This case recognized certain fundamental characteristics of the subpoena *duces tecum* in criminal cases: (1) it was not intended to provide a means of discovery for criminal cases. *Id.,* at 220; (2) its chief innovation was to expedite the trial by providing a time and place *before* trial for the inspection of subpoenaed materials. *Ibid.* As both parties agree, cases decided in the wake of *Bowman* have generally followed Judge Weinfeld's formulation in *United States* v. *Iozia*, 13 F. R. D. 335, 338 (SDNY 1952), as to the required showing. Under this test, in order to require production prior to trial, the moving party must show: (1) that the documents are evidentiary and relevant; (2) that they are not otherwise procurable reasonably in advance of trial by exercise of due diligence; (3) that the party cannot properly prepare for trial without such production and inspection in advance of trial and that the failure to obtain such inspection may tend unreasonably to delay the trial; (4) that the application is made in good faith and is not intended as a general "fishing expedition."

Against this background, the Special Prosecutor, in order to carry his burden, must clear three hurdles: (1) relevancy; (2) admissibility; (3) specificity. Our own review of the record necessarily affords a less comprehensive view of the total situation than was available to the trial judge and we are unwilling to conclude that the District Court erred in the evaluation of the Special Prosecutor's showing under Rule 17 (c). Our conclusion is based on the record before us, much of which is under seal. Of course, the contents of the subpoenaed tapes could not at that stage be described fully by the Special Prosecutor, but there was a sufficient likelihood that each of the tapes contains conversations relevant to the offenses charged in the indictment. *United States* v. *Gross*, 24 F. R. D. 138 (SDNY 1959). With respect to many of the tapes, the Special Prosecutor offered the sworn testimony or statements of one or more of the participants in the conversations as to what was said at the time. As for the remainder of the tapes, the identity of the participants and the time and place of the conversations, taken in their total context, permit a rational inference that at least part of the conversations relate to the offenses charged in the indictment.

We also conclude there was a sufficient preliminary showing that each of the subpoenaed tapes contains evidence admissible with respect to the offenses charged in the indictment. The most cogent objection to the admissibility of the taped conversations here at issue is that they are a collection of out-of-court statements by declarants who will not be subject to cross-examination and that the statements are therefore inadmissible hearsay. Here, however, most of the tapes apparently contain conversations to which one or more of the defendants named in the indictment were party. The hearsay rule does not automatically bar all out-of-court statements by a defendant in a criminal case. Declarations by one defendant may also be admissible against other defendants upon a sufficient showing, by independent evidence, of a conspiracy among one or more other defendants and the declarant and if the declarations at issue were in furtherance of that conspiracy. The same is true of declarations of coconspirators who are not defendants in the case on trial. *Dutton* v. *Evans*, 400 U. S. 74, 81 (1970). Recorded conversations may also be admissible for the limited purpose of impeaching the credibility of any defendant who testifies or any other coconspirator who testifies. Generally, the need for evidence to impeach witnesses is insufficient to require its production in advance of trial. See, *e. g., United States* v. *Carter*, 15 F. R. D. 367, 371 (D. D. C. 1954). Here, however, there are other valid potential evidentiary uses for the same material and the analysis and possible transcription of the tapes may take a significant period of time. Accordingly, we cannot say that the District Court erred in authorizing the issuance of the subpoena *duces tecum*.

Enforcement of a pretrial subpoena *duces tecum* must necessarily be committed to the sound discretion of the trial court since the necessity for the subpoena most often turns upon a determination of factual issues. Without a determination of arbitrariness or that the trial court finding was without record support, an appellate court will not ordinarily disturb a finding that the applicant for a subpoena complied with Rule 17 (c).

In a case such as this, however, where a subpoena is directed to a President of the United States, appellate review, in deference to a coordinate branch of government, should be particularly meticulous to ensure that the standards of Rule 17 (c) have been correctly applied. *United States* v. *Burr*, 25 Fed. Cas. 30, 34 (No. 14,692d) (1807). From our examination of the materials submitted by the Special Prosecutor to the District Court in support of his motion for the subpoena, we are persuaded that the District Court's denial of the President's motion to quash the subpoena was consistent with Rule 17 (c). We also conclude that the Special Prosecutor has made a sufficient showing to justify a subpoena for production *before* trial. The subpoenaed materials are not available from any other source, and their examination and processing should not await trial in the circumstances shown. . . .

IV
The Claim of Privilege
A

Having determined that the requirements of Rule 17 (c) were satisfied, we turn to the claim that the subpoena should be quashed because it demands "confidential conversations between a President and his close advisors that it would be inconsistent with the public interest to produce." App. 48a. The first contention is a broad claim that the sepa-

ration of powers doctrine precludes judicial review of a President's claim of privilege. The second contention is that if he does not prevail on the claim of absolute privilege, the court should hold as a matter of constitutional law that the privilege prevails over the subpoena *duces tecum*.

In the performance of assigned constitutional duties each branch of the Government must initially interpret the Constitution, and the interpretation of its powers by any branch is due great respect from the others. The President's counsel, as we have noted, reads the Constitution as providing an absolute privilege of confidentiality for all presidential communications. Many decisions of this Court, however, have unequivocally reaffirmed the holding of *Marbury* v. *Madison*, 1 Cranch 137 (1803), that "it is emphatically the province and duty of the judicial department to say what the law is." *Id.*, at 177.

No holding of the Court has defined the scope of judicial power specifically relating to the enforcement of a subpoena for confidential presidential communications for use in a criminal prosecution, but other exercises of powers by the Executive Branch and the Legislative Branch have been found invalid as in conflict with the Constitution. *Powell* v. *McCormack, supra: Youngstown, supra.* In a series of cases, the Court interpreted the explicit immunity conferred by express provisions of the Constitution on Members of the House and Senate by the Speech or Debate Clause, U. S. Const. Art. I, § 6. Since this Court has consistently exercised the power to construe and delineate claims arising under express powers, it must follow that the Court has authority to interpret claims with respect to powers alleged to derive from enumerated powers.

Our system of government "requires

that federal courts on occasion interpret the Constitution in a manner at variance with the construction given the document by another branch." *Powell* v. *McCormack, supra,* 549. And in *Baker* v. *Carr,* 369 U. S., at 211, the Court stated:

[d]eciding whether a matter has in any measure been committed by the Constitution to another branch of government, or whether the action of that branch exceeds whatever authority has been committed, is itself a delicate exercise in constitutional interpretation, and is a responsibility of this Court as ultimate interpreter of the Constitution.

Notwithstanding the deference each branch must accord the others, the "judicial power of the United States" vested in the federal courts by Art. III, § 1 of the Constitution can no more be shared with the Executive Branch than the Chief Executive, for example, can share with the Judiciary the veto power, or the Congress share with the Judiciary the power to override a presidential veto. Any other conclusion would be contrary to the basic concept of separation of powers and the checks and balances that flow from the scheme of a tripartite government. The Federalist, No. 47, p. 313 (C. F. Mittel ed. 1938). We therefore reaffirm that it is "emphatically the province and the duty" of this Court "to say what the law is" with respect to the claim of privilege presented in this case. *Marbury* v. *Madison, supra,* at 177.

B

In support of his claim of absolute privilege, the President's counsel urges two grounds one of which is common to all governments and one of which is peculiar to our system of separation of powers. The first ground is the valid need for protection of communications between high government officials and those who advise and assist them in the performance of their manifold duties; the importance of this confidentiality is too plain to require further discussion. Human experience teaches that those who expect public dissemination of their remarks may well temper candor with a concern for appearances and for their own interests to the detriment of the decisionmaking process. Whatever the nature of the privilege of confidentiality of presidential communications in the exercise of Art. II powers the privilege can be said to derive from the supremacy of each branch within its own assigned area of constitutional duties. Certain powers and privileges flow from the nature of enumerated powers; the protection of the confidentiality of presidential communications has similar constitutional underpinnings.

The second ground asserted by the President's counsel in support of the claim of absolute privilege rests on the doctrine of separation of powers. Here it is argued that the independence of the Executive Branch within its own sphere, *Humphrey's Executor* v. *United States,* 295 U. S. 602, 629–630; *Kilbourn* v. *Thompson,* 103 U. S. 168, 190–191 (1880), insulates a president from a judicial subpoena in an ongoing criminal prosecution, and thereby protects confidential presidential communications.

However, neither the doctrine of separation of powers, nor the need for confidentiality of high level communications, without more, can sustain an absolute, unqualified presidential privilege of immunity from judicial process under all circumstances. The President's need for complete candor and objectivity from advisers calls for great deference from the courts. However, when the privilege depends solely on the broad, undifferentiated claim of public interest in the confidentiality of such conversations, a confrontation with other values arises. Absent a claim of need to protect military, diplomatic or sensitive national security secrets, we find it difficult to accept the argument that even the very important interest in confidentiality of presidential communications is significantly diminished by production of such material . . . with all the protection that a district court will be obliged to provide.

The impediment that an absolute, unqualified privilege would place in the way of the primary constitutional duty of the Judicial Branch to do justice in criminal prosecutions would plainly conflict with the function of the courts under Art. III. In designing the structure of our Government and dividing and allocating the sovereign power among three coequal branches, the Framers of the Constitution sought to provide a comprehensive system, but the separate powers were not intended to operate with absolute independence.

While the Constitution diffuses power the better to secure liberty, it also contemplates that practice will integrate the dispersed powers into a workable government. It enjoins upon its branches separateness but interdependence, autonomy but reciprocity. *Youngstown Sheet & Tube Co. v. Sawyer,* 343 U. S. 579, 635 (1952) (Jackson, J., concurring).

To read the Art. II powers of the President as providing an absolute privilege as against a subpoena essential to enforcement of criminal statutes on no more than a generalized claim of the public interest in confidentiality of nonmilitary and nondiplomatic discussions would upset the constitutional balance of "a workable government" and gravely impair the role of the courts under Art. III.

C

Since we conclude that the legitimate needs of the judicial process may outweigh presidential privilege, it is necessary to resolve those competing interests in a manner that preserves the essential functions of each branch. The right and indeed the duty to resolve that question does not free the judiciary from according high respect to the representations made on behalf of the President. *United States* v. *Burr,* 25 Fed. Cas. 187, 190, 191–192 (No. 14,694) (1807).

The expectation of a President to the confidentiality of his conversations and correspondence, like the claim of confidentiality of judicial deliberations, for example, has all the values to which we accord deference for the privacy of all citizens and added to those values the necessity for protection of the public interest in candid, objective, and even blunt or harsh opinions in presidential decision-making. A President and those who assist him must be free to explore alternatives in the process of shaping policies and making decisions and to do so in a way many would be unwilling to express except privately. These are the considerations justifying a presumptive privilege for presidential communications. The privilege is fundamental to the operation of government and inextricably rooted in the separation of powers under the Constitution. In *Nixon* v. *Sirica,* 487 F. 2d 700 (1973), the Court of Appeals held that such presidential communications are "presumptively privileged," *id.,* at 717, and this position is accepted by both parties in the present litigation. We agree with Mr. Chief Justice Marshall's observation, therefore, that "in no case of this kind would a court be required to proceed against the President as against an ordinary individual." *United States* v. *Burr,*

25 Fed. Cas. 187, 191 (No. 14,694) (CCD Va. 1807).

But this presumptive privilege must be considered in light of our historic commitment to the rule of law. This is nowhere more profoundly manifest than in our view that "the twofold aim [of criminal justice] is that guilt shall not escape or innocence suffer." *Berger* v. *United States*, 295 U. S. 78, 88 (1935). We have elected to employ an adversary system of criminal justice in which the parties contest all issues before a court of law. The need to develop all relevant facts in the adversary system is both fundamental and comprehensive. The ends of criminal justice would be defeated if judgments were to be founded on a partial or speculative presentation of the facts. The very integrity of the judicial system and public confidence in the system depend on full disclosure of all the facts, within the framework of the rules of evidence. To ensure that justice is done, it is imperative to the function of courts that compulsory process be available for the production of evidence needed either by the prosecution or by the defense.

Only recently the Court restated the ancient proposition of law, albeit in the context of a grand jury inquiry rather than a trial,

> 'that the public . . . has a right to every man's evidence' except for those persons protected by a constitutional, common law, or statutory privilege, *United States* v. *Bryan*, 339 U. S., at 331 (1949); *Blackmer* v. *United States*, 284 U. S. 421, 438; *Branzburg* v. *United States*, 408 U. S. 665, 688 (1973).

The privileges referred to by the Court are designed to protect weighty and legitimate competing interests. Thus, the Fifth Amendment to the Constitution provides that no man "shall be compelled in any criminal case to be a witness against himself." And, generally, an attorney or a priest may not be required to disclose what has been revealed in professional confidence. These and other interests are recognized in law by privileges against forced disclosure, established in the Constitution, by statute, or at common law. Whatever their origins, these exceptions to the demand for every man's evidence are not lightly created nor expansively construed, for they are in derogation of the search for truth.

In this case the President challenges a subpoena served on him as a third party requiring the production of materials for use in a criminal prosecution on the claim that he has a privilege against disclosure of confidential communications. He does not place his claim of privilege on the ground they are military or diplomatic secrets. As to these areas of Art. II duties the courts have traditionally shown the utmost deference to presidential responsibilities. In *C. & S. Air Lines* v. *Waterman Steamship Corp.*, 333 U. S. 103, 111 (1948), dealing with presidential authority involving foreign policy considerations, the Court said:

> The President, both as Commander-in-Chief and as the Nation's organ for foreign affairs, has available intelligence services whose reports are not and ought not to be published to the world. It would be intolerable that courts, without the relevant information, should review and perhaps nullify actions of the Executive taken on information properly held secret. *Id.*, at 111.

In *United States* v. *Reynolds*, 345 U. S. 1 (1952), dealing with a claimant's demand for evidence in a damage case against the Government the Court said:

> It may be possible to satisfy the court, from all the circumstances of the case, that there is a reasonable danger that compulsion of the evidence will expose

military matters which, in the interest of national security, should not be divulged. When this is the case, the occasion for the privilege is appropriate, and the court should not jeopardize the security which the privilege is meant to protect by insisting upon an examination of the evidence, even by the judge alone, in chambers.

No case of the Court, however, has extended this high degree of deference to a President's generalized interest in confidentiality. Nowhere in the Constitution, as we have noted earlier, is there any explicit reference to a privilege of confidentiality, yet to the extent this interest relates to the effective discharge of a President's powers, it is constitutionally based.

The right to the production of all evidence at a criminal trial similarly has constitutional dimensions. The Sixth Amendment explicitly confers upon every defendant in a criminal trial the right "to be confronted with the witnesses against him" and "to have compulsory process for obtaining witnesses in his favor." Moreover, the Fifth Amendment also guarantees that no person shall be deprived of liberty without due process of law. It is the manifest duty of the courts to vindicate those guarantees and to accomplish that it is essential that all relevant and admissible evidence be produced.

In this case we must weigh the importance of the general privilege of confidentiality of presidential communications in performance of his responsibilities against the inroads of such a privilege on the fair administration of criminal justice. The interest in preserving confidentiality is weighty indeed and entitled to great respect. However we cannot conclude that advisers will be moved to temper the candor of their remarks by the infrequent occasions of disclosure because of the possibility that such conversations will be called for in the context of a criminal prosecution.

On the other hand, the allowance of the privilege to withhold evidence that is demonstrably relevant in a criminal trial would cut deeply into the guarantee of due process of law and gravely impair the basic function of the courts. A President's acknowledged need for confidentiality in the communications of his office is general in nature, whereas the constitutional need for production of relevant evidence in a criminal proceeding is specific and central to the fair adjudication of a particular criminal case in the administration of justice. Without access to specific facts a criminal prosecution may be totally frustrated. The President's broad interest in confidentiality of communications will not be vitiated by disclosure of a limited number of conversations preliminarily shown to have some bearing on the pending criminal cases.

We conclude that when the ground for asserting privilege as to subpoenaed materials sought for use in a criminal trial is based only on the generalized interest in confidentiality, it cannot prevail over the fundamental demands of due process of law in the fair administration of criminal justice. The generalized assertion of privilege must yield to the demonstrated, specific need for evidence in a pending criminal trial.

D

We have earlier determined that the District Court did not err in authorizing the issuance of the subpoena. If a president concludes that compliance with a subpoena would be injurious to the public interest he may properly, as was done here, invoke a claim of privilege on the return of the subpoena. Upon receiving a claim of privilege from the Chief Executive, it became the further duty of the District Court to treat the subpoenaed material as presumptively privileged and to require the Special Prosecutor to demonstrate that the presidential material was "essential to the justice of the [pending criminal] case." *United States* v. *Burr, supra*, at 192. Here the District Court treated the material as presumptively privileged, proceeded to find that the Special Prosecutor had made a sufficient showing to rebut the presumption and ordered an *in camera* examination of the subpoenaed material. On the basis of our examination of the record we are unable to conclude that the District Court erred in ordering the inspection. Accordingly we affirm the order of the District Court that subpoenaed materials be transmitted to that court. We now turn to the important question of the District Court's responsibilities in conducting the *in camera* examination of presidential materials or communications delivered under the compulsion of the subpoena *duces tecum*.

E

Enforcement of the subpoena *duces tecum* was stayed pending this Court's resolution of the issues raised by the petitions for certiorari. Those issues now having been disposed of, the matter of implementation will rest with the District Court. "[T]he guard, furnished to [President] to protect him from being harassed by vexatious and unnecessary subpoenas, is to be looked for in the conduct of the [district] court after the subpoenas have issued; not in any circumstances which is to precede their being issued." *United States* v. *Burr, supra*, at 34. Statements that meet the test of admissibility and relevance must be isolated; all other material must be excised. At this stage the

District Court is not limited to representations of the Special Prosecutor as to the evidence sought by the subpoena; the material will be available to the District Court. It is elementary that *in camera* inspection of evidence is always a procedure calling for scrupulous protection against any release or publication of material not found by the court, at that stage, probably admissible in evidence and relevant to the issues of the trial for which it is sought. That being true of an ordinary situation, it is obvious that the District Court has a very heavy responsibility to see to it that presidential conversations, which are either not relevant or not admissible, are accorded that high degree of respect due the President of the United States. Mr. Chief Justice Marshall sitting as a trial judge in the *Burr* case, *supra*, was extraordinarily careful to point out that:

[I]n no case of this kind would a Court be required to proceed against the President as against an ordinary individual. *United States* v. *Burr*, 25 Fed. Cases 187, 191 (No. 14,694).

Marshall's statement cannot be read to mean in any sense that a President is above the law, but relates to the singularly unique role under Art. II of a President's communications and activities, related to the performance of duties under that Article. Moreover, a President's communications and activities encompass a vastly wider range of sensitive material than would be true of any "ordinary individual." It is therefore necessary in the public interest to afford presidential confidentiality the greatest protection consistent with the fair administration of justice. The need for confidentiality even as to idle conversations with associates in which casual reference might be made concerning political leaders within the country or foreign statesmen is too obvious to call for further treatment. We have no doubt that the District Judge will at all times accord to presidential records that high degree of deference suggested in *United States* v. *Burr, supra*, and will discharge his responsibility to see to it that until released to the Special Prosecutor no *in camera* material is revealed to anyone. This burden applies with even greater force to excised material; once the

decision is made to excise, the material is restored to its privileged status and should be returned under seal to its lawful custodian.

Since this matter came before the Court during the pendency of a criminal prosecution, and on representations that time is of the essence, the mandate shall issue forthwith.

Affirmed.

3.

Articles of Impeachment

Beginning on July 24, 1974, the House Judiciary Committee, Peter W. Rodino, chairman, held six days of nationally televised hearings to debate the impeachment evidence. Out of five proposed articles, three were accepted by the committee. They charged President Nixon with obstruction of justice in the Watergate coverup, general abuse of presidential powers, and refusal to comply with subpoenas for evidence. The two articles voted down by the committee concerned the secret bombing of Cambodia, income tax fraud, and the unlawful use of public funds on the Nixon properties in Florida and California. The final 528-page report of the committee was released on August 20. By this time Mr. Nixon had already resigned his office. The impeachment articles are reprinted here.

Source: *Impeachment of Richard M. Nixon, President of the United States.* Report of the Committee on the Judiciary, House of Representatives. 93 Congress, 2 Session. Washington, D.C., 1974.

THE COMMITTEE on the Judiciary, to whom was referred the consideration of recommendations concerning the exercise of the constitutional power to impeach Richard M. Nixon, President of the United States, having considered the same, reports thereon pursuant to H. Res. 803 as follows and recommends that the House exercise its constitutional power to impeach Richard M. Nixon, President of the United States, and that articles of impeachment be exhibited to the Senate as follows:

RESOLUTION

Impeaching Richard M. Nixon, President of the United States, of high crimes and misdemeanors.

Resolved, That Richard M. Nixon, President of the United States, is impeached for high crimes and misdemeanors, and that the following articles of impeachment be exhibited to the Senate:

Articles of impeachment exhibited by the House of Representatives of the United States of America in the name of itself and of all of the people of the

United States of America, against Richard M. Nixon, President of the United States of America, in maintenance and support of its impeachment against him for high crimes and misdemeanors.

Article I. In his conduct of the office of President of the United States, Richard M. Nixon, in violation of his constitutional oath faithfully to execute the office of President of the United States and, to the best of his ability, preserve, protect, and defend the Constitution of the United States, and in violation of his constitutional duty to take care that the laws be faithfully executed, has prevented, obstructed, and impeded the administration of justice, in that:

On June 17, 1972, and prior thereto, agents of the Committee for the Re-election of the President committed unlawful entry of the headquarters of the Democratic National Committee in Washington, District of Columbia, for the purpose of securing political intelligence. Subsequent thereto, Richard M. Nixon, using the powers of his high office, engaged personally and through his subordinates and agents, in a course of conduct or plan designed to delay, impede, and obstruct the investigation of such unlawful entry; to cover up, conceal and protect those responsible; and to conceal the existence and scope of other . . . covert activities.

The means used to implement this course of conduct or plan included one or more of the following:

(1) making or causing to be made false or misleading statements to lawfully authorized investigative officers and employees of the United States;

(2) withholding relevant and material evidence or information from lawfully authorized investigative officers and employees of the United States;

(3) approving, condoning, acquiescing in, and counseling witnesses with respect to the giving of false or misleading statements to lawfully authorized investigative officers and employees of the United States and false or misleading testimony in duly instituted judicial and congressional proceedings;

(4) interfering or endeavoring to interfere with the conduct of investigations by the Department of Justice of the United States, the Federal Bureau of Investigation, the Office of Watergate Special Prosecution Force, and Congressional Committees;

(5) approving, condoning, and acquiescing in, the surreptitious payment of substantial sums of money for the purpose of obtaining the silence or influencing the testimony of witnesses, potential witnesses or individuals who participated in such unlawful entry and other illegal activities;

(6) endeavoring to misuse the Central Intelligence Agency, an agency of the United States;

(7) disseminating information received from officers of the Department of Justice of the United States to subjects of investigations conducted by lawfully authorized investigative officers and employees of the United States, for the purpose of aiding and assisting such subjects in their attempts to avoid criminal liability;

(8) making false or misleading public statements for the purpose of deceiving the people of the United States into believing that a thorough and complete investigation had been conducted with respect to allegations of misconduct on the part of personnel of the executive branch of the United States and personnel of the Committee for the Re-election of the President, and that there was no involvement of such personnel in such misconduct; or

(9) endeavoring to cause prospective defendants, and individuals duly tried and convicted. to expect favored treat-

ment and consideration in return for their silence or false testimony, or rewarding individuals for their silence or false testimony.

In all of this, Richard M. Nixon has acted in a manner contrary to his trust as President and subversive of constitutional government, to the great prejudice of the cause of law and justice and to the manifest injury of the people of the United States.

Wherefore Richard M. Nixon, by such conduct, warrants impeachment and trial, and removal from office.

Article II. Using the powers of the office of President of the United States, Richard M. Nixon, in violation of his constitutional oath faithfully to execute the office of President of the United States and, to the best of his ability, preserve, protect, and defend the Constitution of the United States, and in disregard of his constitutional duty to take care that the laws be faithfully executed, has repeatedly engaged in conduct violating the constitutional rights of citizens, impairing the due and proper administration of justice and the conduct of lawful inquiries, or contravening the laws governing agencies of the executive branch and the purposes of these agencies.

This conduct has included one or more of the following:

(1) He has, acting personally and through his subordinates and agents, endeavored to obtain from the Internal Revenue Service, in violation of the constitutional rights of citizens, confidential information contained in income tax returns for purposes not authorized by law, and to cause, in violation of the constitutional rights of citizens, income tax audits or other income tax investigations to be initiated or conducted in a discriminatory manner.

(2) He misused the Federal Bureau of Investigation, the Secret Service, and other executive personnel, in violation or disregard of the constitutional rights of citizens, by directing or authorizing such agencies or personnel to conduct or continue electronic surveillance or other investigations for purposes unrelated to national security, the enforcement of laws, or any other lawful function of his office; he did direct, authorize, or permit the use of information obtained thereby for purposes unrelated to national security, the enforcement of laws, or any other lawful function of his office; and he did direct the concealment of certain records made by the Federal Bureau of Investigation of electronic surveillance.

(3) He has, acting personally and through his subordinates and agents, in violation or disregard of the constitutional rights of citizens, authorized and permitted to be maintained a secret investigative unit within the office of the President, financed in part with money derived from campaign contributions, which unlawfully utilized the resources of the Central Intelligence Agency, engaged in covert and unlawful activities, and attempted to prejudice the constitutional right of an accused to a fair trial.

(4) He has failed to take care that the laws were faithfully executed by failing to act when he knew or had reason to know that his close subordinates endeavored to impede and frustrate lawful inquiries by duly constituted executive, judicial, and legislative entities concerning the unlawful entry into the headquarters of the Democratic National Committee, and the cover-up thereof, and concerning other unlawful activities, including those relating to the confirmation of Richard Kleindienst as Attorney General of the United States, the electronic surveillance of private citizens, the break-in into the offices of Dr. Lewis Fielding, and the campaign financing practices of

the Committee to Re-elect the President.

(5) In disregard of the rule of law, he knowingly misused the executive power by interfering with agencies of the executive branch, including the Federal Bureau of Investigation, the Criminal Division, and the Office of Watergate Special Prosecution Force, of the Department of Justice, and the Central Intelligence Agency, in violation of his duty to take care that the laws be faithfully executed.

In all of this, Richard M. Nixon has acted in a manner contrary to his trust as President and subversive of constitutional government, to the great prejudice of the cause of law and justice and to the manifest injury of the people of the United States.

Wherefore Richard M. Nixon, by such conduct, warrants impeachment and trial, and removal from office.

Article III. In his conduct of the office of President of the United States, Richard M. Nixon, contrary to his oath faithfully to execute the office of President of the United States and, to the best of his ability, preserve, protect, and defend the Constitution of the United States, and in violation of his constitutional duty to take care that the laws be faithfully executed, has failed without lawful cause or excuse to produce papers and things as directed by duly authorized subpoenas issued by the Committee on the Judiciary of the House of Representatives on April 11, 1974, May 15, 1974, May 30, 1974, and June 24, 1974, and willfully disobeyed such subpoenas. The subpoenaed papers and things were deemed necessary by the Committee in order to resolve by direct evidence fundamental, factual questions relating to Presidential direction, knowledge, or approval of actions demonstrated by other evidence to be substantial grounds for impeachment of the Presi-

The House Judiciary Committee's roll call vote on the impeachment of President Nixon, July 27, 1974.

dent. In refusing to produce these papers and things, Richard M. Nixon, substituting his judgment as to what materials were necessary for the inquiry, interposed the powers of the Presidency against the lawful subpoenas of the House of Representatives, thereby assuming to himself functions and judgments necessary to the exercise of the sole power of impeachment vested by the Constitution in the House of Representatives.

In all of this, Richard M. Nixon has acted in a manner contrary to his trust as President and subversive of constitutional government, to the great prejudice of the cause of law and justice, and to the manifest injury of the people of the United States.

Wherefore Richard M. Nixon, by such conduct, warrants impeachment and trial, and removal from office.

4.

RICHARD M. NIXON: Release of Additional Transcripts

By the time the Judiciary Committee recessed on July 30, having voted three articles of impeachment, support for the president had seriously eroded in Congress; but there was still some hope that he might get through the Senate trial and keep his office. After August 5, however, whatever remaining support he may have had quickly disappeared. On that day the President released transcripts of conversations he had had with H. R. Haldeman on June 23, 1972, six days after the original Watergate break-in. Nixon, learning that the FBI investigation was leading to members of his re-election committee, instructed Haldeman to order the FBI to stop its inquiries.

Source: *Weekly Compilation of Presidential Documents,* August 12, 1974.

I HAVE today instructed my attorneys to make available to the House Judiciary Committee, and I am making public, the transcripts of three conversations with H. R. Haldeman on June 23, 1972. I have also turned over the tapes of these conversations to Judge Sirica, as part of the process of my compliance with the Supreme Court ruling.

On April 29, in announcing my decision to make public the original set of White House transcripts, I stated that "as far as what the President personally knew and did with regard to Watergate and the coverup is concerned, these materials—together with those already made available—will tell it all."

Shortly after that, in May, I made a preliminary review of some of the 64 taped conversations subpoenaed by the Special Prosecutor.

Among the conversations I listened to at that time were two of those of June 23. Although I recognized that these presented potential problems, I did not inform my staff or my Counsel of it, or those arguing my case, nor did I amend my submission to the Judiciary Committee in order to include and reflect it. At the time, I did not realize the extent of the implications which these conversations might now appear to have. As a result, those arguing my case, as well as those passing judgment on the case, did so with information that was incomplete and in some respects erroneous. This was a serious act of omission for which I take full responsibility and which I deeply regret.

Since the Supreme Court's decision 12 days ago, I have ordered my Counsel to analyze the 64 tapes, and I have listened to a number of them myself. This process has made it clear that portions of the tapes of these June 23 conversations are at variance with certain of my previous statements. Therefore, I have ordered the transcripts made available immediately to the Judiciary Committee so that they can be reflected in the Committee's report and included in the record to be considered by the House and Senate.

In a formal written statement on May 22 of last year, I said that shortly after the Watergate break-in I became concerned about the possibility that the FBI investigation might lead to the exposure either of unrelated covert activities of the CIA or of sensitive national security matters that the so-called "plumbers" unit at the White House had been working on, because of the CIA and plumbers connections of some of those involved. I said that I therefore gave instructions that the FBI should be alerted to coordinate with the CIA and to ensure that the investigation not expose these sensitive national security matters.

That statement was based on my recollection at the time — some 11 months later — plus documentary materials and relevant public testimony of those involved.

The June 23 tapes clearly show, however, that at the time I gave those instructions I also discussed the political aspects of the situation, and that I was aware of the advantages this course of action would have with respect to limiting possible public exposure of involvement by persons connected with the re-election committee.

My review of the additional tapes has, so far, shown no other major inconsistencies with what I have previously submitted. While I have no way at this stage of being certain that there will not be others, I have no reason to believe that there will be. In any case, the tapes in their entirety are now in the process of being furnished to Judge Sirica. He has begun what may be a rather lengthy process of reviewing the tapes, passing on specific claims of executive privilege on portions of them, and forwarding to the Special Prosecutor those tapes or those portions that are relevant to the Watergate investigation.

It is highly unlikely that this review will be completed in time for the House debate. It appears at this stage, however, that a House vote of impeachment is, as a practical matter, virtually a foregone conclusion, and that the issue will therefore go to trial in the Senate. In order to ensure that no other significant relevant materials are withheld, I shall voluntarily furnish to the Senate everything from these tapes that Judge Sirica rules should go to the Special Prosecutor.

I recognize that this additional material I am now furnishing may further damage my case, especially because attention will be drawn separately to it rather than to the evidence in its entirety. In considering its implications, therefore, I urge that two points be borne in mind.

The first of these points is to remember what actually happened as a result of the instructions I gave on June 23. Acting Director Gray of the FBI did coordinate with Director Helms and Deputy Director Walters of the CIA. The CIA did undertake an extensive check to see whether any of its covert activities would be compromised by a full FBI investigation of Watergate. Deputy Director Walters then reported back to Mr. Gray that they would not be compromised. On July 6, when I called Mr. Gray, and when he expressed concern about improper attempts to limit his investigation, as the record shows, I told him to press ahead vigorously with his investigation — which he did.

The second point I would urge is that the evidence be looked at in its entirety and the events be looked at in perspective. Whatever mistakes I made in the handling of Watergate, the basic truth remains that when all the facts were brought to my attention I insisted on a full investigation and prosecution of those guilty. I am firmly convinced that the record, in its entirety, does not justify the extreme step of impeachment and removal of a President. I trust that as the constitutional process goes forward, this perspective will prevail.

5.

RICHARD M. NIXON: Resignation from the Presidency

Following the release of the tape transcripts on August 5, many members of Congress urged the President to resign to save the country the ordeal of a protracted debate on impeachment in the House and a trial in the Senate. On August 7, three leading congressional Republicans, Senators Barry Goldwater and Hugh Scott and Representative John Rhodes, went to the White House to tell the President he had virtually no support left in Congress, even among members of his own party. Therefore, on Thursday evening, August 8, President Nixon addressed the nation via television to announce that he would be resigning his office the next day. On the morning of the 9th, after bidding farewell to the White House staff, he and his family flew to their home in California. While he was airborne, his resignation became effective; and Gerald R. Ford was sworn in as the 38th President. This selection reprints both of President Nixon's final speeches and his letter of resignation.

Source: *Weekly Compilation of Presidential Documents*, August 12, 1974.

A. Television Address Announcing the Intention to Resign

Good evening.

This is the 37th time I have spoken to you from this office, where so many decisions have been made that shaped the history of this Nation. Each time I have done so to discuss with you some matter that I believe affected the national interest.

In all the decisions I have made in my public life, I have always tried to do what was best for the Nation. Throughout the long and difficult period of Watergate, I have felt it was my duty to persevere, to make every possible effort to complete the term of office to which you elected me.

In the past few days, however, it has become evident to me that I no longer have a strong enough political base in the Congress to justify continuing that effort. As long as there was such a base, I felt strongly that it was necessary to see the constitutional process through to its conclusion, that to do otherwise would be unfaithful to the spirit of that deliberately difficult process and a dangerously destabilizing precedent for the future.

But with the disappearance of that base, I now believe that the constitutional purpose has been served, and there is no longer a need for the process to be prolonged.

I would have preferred to carry through to the finish whatever the personal agony it would have involved, and my family unanimously urged me to do so. But the interest of the Nation must always come before any personal considerations.

From the discussions I have had with Congressional and other leaders, I have concluded that because of the Watergate matter I might not have the support of the Congress that I would consider necessary to back the very difficult decisions and carry out the duties of this office in the way the interests of the Nation would require.

I have never been a quitter. To leave office before my term is completed is abhorrent to every instinct in my body. But as President, I must put the interest of America first. America needs a full-time President and a full-time Congress, particularly at this time with problems we face at home and abroad.

To continue to fight through the months ahead for my personal vindication would almost totally absorb the time and attention of both the President and the Congress in a period when our entire focus should be on the great issues of peace abroad and prosperity without inflation at home.

Therefore, I shall resign the Presidency effective at noon tomorrow. Vice President Ford will be sworn in as President at that hour in this office.

As I recall the high hopes for America with which we began this second term, I feel a great sadness that I will not be here in this office working on your behalf to achieve those hopes in the next 2½ years. But in turning over direction of the Government to Vice President Ford, I know, as I told the Nation when I nominated him for that office 10 months ago, that the leadership of America will be in good hands.

In passing this office to the Vice President, I also do so with the profound sense of the weight of responsibility that will fall on his shoulders tomorrow and, therefore, of the understanding, the patience, the cooperation he will need from all Americans.

As he assumes that responsibility, he will deserve the help and the support of all of us. As we look to the future, the first essential is to begin healing the wounds of this Nation, to put the bitterness and divisions of the recent past behind us, and to rediscover those shared ideals that lie at the heart of our strength and unity as a great and as a free people.

By taking this action, I hope that I will have hastened the start of that process of healing which is so desperately needed in America.

I regret deeply any injuries that may have been done in the course of the events that led to this decision. I would say only that if some of my judgments were wrong, and some were wrong, they were made in what I believed at the time to be the best interest of the Nation.

To those who have stood with me during these past difficult months, to my family, my friends, to many others who joined in supporting my cause because they believed it was right, I will be eternally grateful for your support.

And to those who have not felt able to give me your support, let me say I leave with no bitterness toward those who have opposed me, because all of us, in the final analysis, have been concerned with the good of the country, however our judgments might differ.

So, let us all now join together in affirming that common commitment and in helping our new President succeed for the benefit of all Americans.

I shall leave this office with regret at not completing my term, but with gratitude for the privilege of serving as your President for the past 5½ years. These years have been a momentous time in the history of our Nation and the world. They have been a time of achievement in which we can all be proud, achievements that represent the shared efforts of the Administration, the Congress, and the people.

But the challenges ahead are equally great, and they, too, will require the support and the efforts of the Congress and the people working in cooperation with the new Administration.

We have ended America's longest war,

but in the work of securing a lasting peace in the world, the goals ahead are even more far-reaching and more difficult. We must complete a structure of peace so that it will be said of this generation, our generation of Americans, by the people of all nations, not only that we ended one war but that we prevented future wars.

We have unlocked the doors that for a quarter of a century stood between the United States and the People's Republic of China.

We must now ensure that the one quarter of the world's people who live in the People's Republic of China will be and remain not our enemies but our friends.

In the Middle East, 100 million people in the Arab countries, many of whom have considered us their enemy for nearly 20 years, now look on us as their friends. We must continue to build on that friendship so that peace can settle at last over the Middle East and so that the cradle of civilization will not become its grave.

Together with the Soviet Union we have made the crucial breakthroughs that have begun the process of limiting nuclear arms. But we must set as our goal not just limiting but reducing and finally destroying these terrible weapons so that they cannot destroy civilization and so that the threat of nuclear war will no longer hang over the world and the people.

We have opened the new relation with the Soviet Union. We must continue to develop and expand that new relationship so that the two strongest nations of the world will live together in cooperation rather than confrontation.

Around the world, in Asia, in Africa, in Latin America, in the Middle East, there are millions of people who live in terrible poverty, even starvation. We must keep as our goal turning away from production for war and expanding production for peace so that people everywhere on this earth can at last look forward in their children's time, if not in our own time, to having the necessities for a decent life.

Here in America, we are fortunate that most of our people have not only the blessings of liberty but also the means to live full and good and, by the world's standards, even abundant lives. We must press on, however, toward a goal of not only more and better jobs but of full opportunity for every American and of what we are striving so hard right now to achieve, prosperity without inflation.

For more than a quarter of a century in public life I have shared in the turbulent history of this era. I have fought for what I believed in. I have tried to the best of my ability to discharge those duties and meet those responsibilities that were entrusted to me.

Sometimes I have succeeded and sometimes I have failed, but always I have taken heart from what Theodore Roosevelt once said about the man in the arena, "whose face is marred by dust and sweat and blood, who strives valiantly, who errs and comes short again and again because there is not effort without error and shortcoming, but who does actually strive to do the deed, who knows the great enthusiasms, the great devotions, who spends himself in a worthy cause, who at the best knows in the end the triumphs of high achievements and who at the worst, if he fails, at least fails while daring greatly."

I pledge to you tonight that as long as I have a breath of life in my body, I shall continue in that spirit. I shall continue to work for the great causes to which I have been dedicated throughout my years as a Congressman, a Senator, a Vice President, and President, the cause of peace not just for America but among all nations, prosperity, justice, and opportunity for all of our people.

There is one cause above all to which I have been devoted and to which I shall always be devoted for as long as I live.

When I first took the oath of office as President 5½ years ago, I made this sacred commitment, to "consecrate my office, my energies, and all the wisdom I can summon to the cause of peace among nations."

I have done my very best in all the days since to be true to that pledge. As a result of these efforts, I am confident that the world is a safer place today, not only for the people of America but for the people of all nations, and that all of our children have a better chance than before of living in peace rather than dying in war.

This, more than anything, is what I hoped to achieve when I sought the Presidency. This, more than anything, is what I hope will be my legacy to you, to our country, as I leave the Presidency.

To have served in this office is to have felt a very personal sense of kinship with each and every American. In leaving it, I do so with this prayer: May God's grace be with you in all the days ahead.

B. Farewell to the White House Staff

Members of the Cabinet, Members of the White House Staff, all of our friends here:
I think the record should show that this is one of those spontaneous things that we always arrange whenever the President comes in to speak, and it will be so reported in the press, and we don't mind because they have to call it as they see it.

But on our part, believe me, it is spontaneous.

You are here to say goodby to us, and we don't have a good word for it in English. The best is *au revoir*. We will see you again.

I just met with the members of the White House staff, you know, those who serve here in the White House day in and day out, and I asked them to do what I ask all of you to do to the extent that you can and, of course, are requested to do so: to serve our next President as you have

served me and previous Presidents—because many of you have been here for many years—with devotion and dedication, because this office, great as it is, can only be as great as the men and women who work for and with the President.

This house, for example, I was thinking of it as we walked down this hall, and I was comparing it to some of the great houses of the world that I have been in. This isn't the biggest house. Many, and most, in even smaller countries are much bigger. This isn't the finest house. Many in Europe, particularly, and in China, Asia, have paintings of great, great value, things that we just don't have here, and probably will never have until we are 1,000 years old or older.

But this is the best house. It is the best house because it has something far more important than numbers of people who serve, far more important than numbers of rooms or how big it is, far more important than numbers of magnificent pieces of art.

This house has a great heart, and that heart comes from those who serve. I was rather sorry they didn't come down. We said goodby to them upstairs. But they are really great. And I recall after so many times I have made speeches, and some of them pretty tough, yet, I always come back, or after a hard day—and my days usually have run rather long—I would always get a lift from them because I might be a little down, but they always smiled.

And so it is with you. I look around here, and I see so many on this staff that, you know, I should have been by your offices and shaken hands, and I would love to have talked to you and found out how to run the world—everybody wants to tell the President what to do, and boy he needs to be told many times—but I just haven't had the time. But I want you to know that each and every one of you, I know, is indispensable to this Government. I am proud of this Cabinet. I am proud of all the members who have served in our Cabinet. I am proud of our sub-Cabinet. I am proud of our White House Staff. As I pointed out last night, sure we have done some things wrong in this Administration, and the top man always takes the responsibility, and I have never ducked it. But I want to say one thing: We can be proud of it—5½ years. No man or no woman came into this Administration and left it with more of this world's goods than when he came in. No man or no woman ever profited at the public expense or the public till. That tells something about you.

Mistakes, yes. But for personal gain, never. You did what you believed in. Sometimes right, sometimes wrong. And I only wish that I were a wealthy man— at the present time I have got to find a way to pay my taxes—[laughter]—and if I were, I would like to recompense you for the sacrifices that all of you have made to serve in Government.

But you are getting something in Government—and I want you to tell this to your children, and I hope the Nation's children will hear it, too—something in Government service that is far more important than money. It is a cause bigger than yourself. It is the cause of making this the greatest nation in the world, the leader of the world, because without our leadership the world will know nothing but war, possibly starvation, or worse, in the years ahead. With our leadership it will know peace, it will know plenty.

We have been generous, and we will be more generous in the future as we are able to. But most important, we must be strong here, strong in our hearts, strong in our souls, strong in our belief, and strong in our willingness to sacrifice, as you have been willing to sacrifice, in a pecuniary way, to serve in Government.

There is something else I would like for you to tell your young people. You know, people often come in and say, "What will I tell my kids?" They look at government and say it is sort of a rugged life, and they see the mistakes that are made. They get the impression that everybody is here for the purpose of feathering his nest. That is why I made this earlier point—not in this Administration, not one single man or woman.

And I say to them, "There are many fine careers. This country needs good farmers, good businessmen, good plumbers, good carpenters."

I remembered my old man. I think that they would have called him sort of a little man, common man. He didn't consider himself that way. You know what he was? He was a streetcar motorman first, and then he was a farmer, and then he had a lemon ranch. It was the poorest lemon ranch in California, I can assure you. He sold it before they found oil on it. [Laughter]

And then he was a grocer. But he was a great man because he did his job, and every job counts up to the hilt, regardless of what happens.

Nobody will ever write a book, probably, about my mother. Well, I guess all of you would say this about your mother— my mother was a saint. And I think of her, two boys dying of tuberculosis, nursing four others in order that she could take care of my older brother for 3 years in Arizona, and seeing each of them die, and when they died, it was like one of her own. Yes, she will have no books written about her. But she was a saint.

Now, however, we look to the future. I had a little quote in the speech last night from T.R. As you know, I kind of like to read books. I am not educated, but I do read books—[laughter]—and the T.R. quote was a pretty good one.

Here is another one I found as I was reading, my last night in the White House, and this quote is about a young man. He was a young lawyer in New York. He had married a beautiful girl, and they had a lovely daughter, and then suddenly she died, and this is what he wrote. This was in his diary.

He said: "She was beautiful in face and form and lovelier still in spirit. As a flower she grew and as a fair young flower she died. Her life had been always in the sunshine. There had never come to her a single great sorrow. None ever knew her who did not love and revere her for her bright and sunny temper and her saintly unselfishness. Fair, pure and joyous as a maiden, loving, tender and happy as a young wife. When she had just become a mother, when her life seemed to be just begun and when the years seemed so bright before her, then by a strange and terrible fate death came to her. And when my heart's dearest died, the light went from my life forever."

That was T.R. in his twenties. He thought the light had gone from his life forever—but he went on. And he not only became President but, as an ex-President, he served his country always in the arena, tempestuous, strong, sometimes wrong, sometimes right, but he was a man.

And as I leave, let me say, that is an example I think all of us should remember. We think sometimes when things happen that don't go the right way; we think that when you don't pass the bar exam the first time—I happened to, but I was just lucky; I mean my writing was so poor the bar examiner said, "We have just got to let the guy through." [Laughter] We think that when someone dear to us dies, we think that when we lose an election, we think that when we suffer a defeat, that all is ended. We think, as T.R. said, that the light had left his life forever.

Not true. It is only a beginning always. The young must know it; the old must know it. It must always sustain us because the greatness comes not when things go always good for you, but the greatness comes when you are really tested, when you take some knocks, some disappointments, when sadness comes, because only if you have been in the deepest valley can you ever know how magnificent it is to be on the highest mountain.

And so I say to you on this occasion, as we leave, we leave proud of the people who have stood by us and worked for us and served this country.

We want you to be proud of what you have done. We want you to continue to serve in Government, if that is your wish. Always give your best, never get discouraged, never be petty; always remember others may hate you, but those who hate you don't win unless you hate them, and then you destroy yourself.

And so, we leave with high hopes, in good spirit and with deep humility, and with very much gratefulness in our hearts. I can only say to each and every one of you, we come from many faiths, we pray perhaps to different gods, but really the same God in a sense, but I want to say for each and every one of you, not only will we always remember you, not only will we always be grateful to you but always you will be in our hearts and you will be in our prayers.

Thank you very much.

The President's Letter to the Secretary of State.
August 9, 1974

Dear Mr. Secretary;
I hereby resign the Office of President of the United States.
Sincerely,

RICHARD NIXON

A tearful moment as President and Mrs. Nixon bid farewell to the White House.

TRANSITION

Three times in American history has the office of the presidency been the focal point of major scandal. President Grant survived the corruption of his first administration to win re-election in 1872. President Harding died in office just as the sordid facts of his administration were coming to light. Richard Nixon has been the only president driven from office by the very real threat of impeachment and almost certain conviction in a Senate trial. The Watergate affair dominated the news for twenty months before it was finally resolved by Mr. Nixon's resignation and the swearing in of Gerald R. Ford. Watergate's most serious impact, however, was not on the presidency; a more enduring effect was the implanting in the American people of skeptical attitudes about their government and about politicians in general.

The White House helicopter lifts off, taking President and Mrs. Nixon to their airplane, August 9, 1974. Gerald R. Ford is sworn in as the 38th President of the United States by Chief Justice Warren E. Burger.

6.

A New President Is Sworn In

On Friday, August 9, at noon, Chief Justice Warren E. Burger administered the oath of office to President Gerald Ford. The new President then made a short speech to members of Congress and other friends assembled in the East Room of the White House.

Source: *Weekly Compilation of Presidential Documents,* August 12, 1974.

Oath of Office Taken by the President at a Ceremony in the East Room at the White House. August 9, 1974

I, Gerald R. Ford, do solemnly swear that I will faithfully execute the Office of President of the United States, and will to the best of my ability, preserve, protect and defend the Constitution of the United States, so help me God.

The President's Remarks Following His Swearing In as the 38th President of the United States. August 9, 1974

Mr. Chief Justice, my dear friends, my fellow Americans:

The oath that I have taken is the same oath that was taken by George Washington and by every President under the Constitution. But I assume the Presidency under extraordinary circumstances, never before experienced by Americans. This is an hour of history that troubles our minds and hurts our hearts.

Therefore, I feel it is my first duty to make an unprecedented compact with my countrymen. Not an inaugural address, not a fireside chat, not a campaign speech —just a little straight talk among friends.

And I intend it to be the first of many.

I am acutely aware that you have not elected me as your President by your ballots, and so I ask you to confirm me as your President with your prayers. And I hope that such prayers will also be the first of many.

If you have not chosen me by secret ballot, neither have I gained office by any secret promises. I have not campaigned either for the Presidency or the Vice Presidency. I have not subscribed to any partisan platform. I am indebted to no man, and only to one woman—my dear wife—as I begin this very difficult job.

I have not sought this enormous responsibility, but I will not shirk it. Those who nominated and confirmed me as Vice President were my friends and are my friends. They were of both parties, elected by all the people and acting under the Constitution in their name. It is only fitting then that I should pledge to them and to you that I will be the President of all the people.

Thomas Jefferson said the people are the only sure reliance for the preservation of our liberty. And down the years, Abraham Lincoln renewed this American article of faith asking, "Is there any better way or equal hope in the world?"

I intend, on Monday next, to request of

the Speaker of the House of Representatives and the President pro tempore of the Senate the privilege of appearing before the Congress to share with my former colleagues and with you, the American people, my views on the priority business of the Nation and to solicit your views and their views. And may I say to the Speaker and the others, if I could meet with you right after these remarks, I would appreciate it.

Even though this is late in an election year, there is no way we can go forward except together and no way anybody can win except by serving the people's urgent needs. We cannot stand still or slip backwards. We must go forward now together.

To the peoples and the governments of all friendly nations, and I hope that could encompass the whole world, I pledge an uninterrupted and sincere search for peace. America will remain strong and

united, but its strength will remain dedicated to the safety and sanity of the entire family of man, as well as to our own precious freedom.

I believe that truth is the glue that holds government together, not only our Government, but civilization itself. That bond, though strained, is unbroken at home and abroad.

In all my public and private acts as your President, I expect to follow my instincts of openness and candor with full confidence that honesty is always the best policy in the end.

My fellow Americans, our long national nightmare is over.

Our Constitution works; our great Republic is a Government of laws and not of men. Here the people rule. But there is a higher power, by whatever name we honor Him, who ordains not only righteousness but love, not only justice but mercy.

As we bind up the internal wounds of Watergate, more painful and more poisonous than those of foreign wars, let us restore the golden rule to our political process, and let brotherly love purge our hearts of suspicion and of hate.

In the beginning, I asked you to pray for me. Before closing, I ask again your prayers, for Richard Nixon and for his family. May our former President, who brought peace to millions, find it for himself. May God bless and comfort his wonderful wife and daughters, whose love and loyalty will forever be a shining legacy to all who bear the lonely burdens of the White House.

I can only guess at those burdens, although I have witnessed at close hand the tragedies that befell three Presidents and the lesser trials of others.

With all the strength and all the good sense I have gained from life, with all the confidence my family, my friends, and my

President Ford at a news conference in February 1976.

Dennis Brack—Black Star

dedicated staff impart to me, and with the good will of countless Americans I have encountered in recent visits to 40 States, I now solemnly reaffirm my promise I made to you last December 6: to uphold the Constitution, to do what is right as God gives me to see the right, and to do the very best I can for America.

God helping me, I will not let you down.

Thank you.

7.

GERALD R. FORD: First Address to Congress and the Nation

On Monday evening, August 12, President Ford addressed a joint session of Congress. Although his remarks contained few legislative proposals, they did set the tone of his administration by urging fiscal restraint to fight inflation and by suggesting the willingness to veto any measures he deemed too costly. The purpose of the message was primarily to acquaint the American people with their new President.

Source: *Weekly Compilation of Presidential Documents*, August 19, 1974.

Mr. Speaker, Mr. President, distinguished guests and my very dear friends:

My fellow Americans, we have a lot of work to do. My former colleagues, you and I have a lot of work to do. Let's get on with it.

Needless to say, I am deeply grateful for the wonderfully warm welcome. I can never express my gratitude adequately.

I am not here to make an inaugural address. The Nation needs action, not words. Nor will this be a formal report of the State of the Union. God willing, I will have at least three more chances to do that.

It is good to be back in the People's House. But this cannot be a real homecoming. Under the Constitution, I now belong to the executive branch. The Supreme Court has even ruled that I am the executive branch, head, heart, and hand.

With due respect to the learned Justices — and I greatly respect the judiciary — part of my heart will always be here on Capitol Hill. I know well the co-equal role of the Congress in our constitutional process. I love the House of Representatives.

I revere the traditions of the Senate despite my too-short internship in that great body. As President, within the limits of basic principles, my motto toward the Congress is communication, conciliation, compromise, and cooperation.

This Congress, unless it has changed, I am confident, will be my working partner as well as my most constructive critic. I am not asking for conformity. I am dedicated to the two-party system, and you know which party I belong to.

I do not want a honeymoon with you. I want a good marriage.

I want progress, and I want problem-solving which requires my best efforts and also your best efforts.

I have no need to learn how Congress speaks for the people. As President, I intend to listen.

But I also intend to listen to the people themselves—all the people—as I promised last Friday. I want to be sure that we are all tuned in to the real voice of America.

My Administration starts off by seeking unity in diversity. My office door has always been open, and that is how it is going to be at the White House. Yes, Congressmen will be welcomed—if you don't overdo it. [*Laughter*]

The first seven words of the Constitution and the most important are these: We, the people of the United States. We, the people, ordained and established the Constitution and reserved to themselves all powers not granted to Federal and State government. I respect and will always be conscious of that fundamental rule of freedom.

Only 8 months ago, when I last stood here, I told you I was a Ford, not a Lincoln. Tonight I say I am still a Ford, but I am not a Model T.

I do have some old-fashioned ideas, however. I believe in the very basic decency and fairness of America. I believe in the integrity and patriotism of the Congress. And while I am aware of the House rule that no one ever speaks to the galleries, I believe in the first amendment and the absolute necessity of a free press.

But I also believe that over two centuries since the First Continental Congress was convened, the direction of our Nation's movement has been forward. I am

here to confess that in my first campaign for President—of my senior class in South High School in Grand Rapids, Michigan—I headed the Progressive Party ticket, and lost. Maybe that is why I became a Republican. [*Laughter*]

Now I ask you to join with me in getting this country revved up and moving. . . .

The first specific request by the Ford Administration is not to Congress but to the voters in the upcoming November elections. It is this, very simply: Support your candidates, Congressmen and Senators, Democrats or Republicans, conservatives or liberals, who consistently vote for tough decisions to cut the cost of government, restrain Federal spending, and bring inflation under control.

I applaud the initiatives Congress has already taken. The only fault I find with the Joint Economic Committee's study on inflation, authorized last week, is that we need its expert findings in 6 weeks instead of 6 months.

A month ago, the distinguished majority leader of the United States Senate asked the White House to convene an economic conference of Members of Congress, the President's economic consultants, and some of the best economic brains from labor, industry, and agriculture.

Later, this was perfected by resolution to assemble a domestic summit meeting to devise a bipartisan action for stability and growth in the American economy. Neither I nor my staff have much time right now for letterwriting. So I will respond. I accept the suggestion, and I will personally preside.

Furthermore, I propose that this summit meeting be held at an early date, in full view of the American public. They are as anxious as we are to get the right answers.

My first priority is to work with you to bring inflation under control. Inflation is domestic enemy number one. To restore economic confidence, the Government in Washington must provide some leadership. It does no good to blame the public for spending too much when the Government is spending too much.

I began to put my Administration's own economic house in order starting last Friday.

I instructed my Cabinet officers and Counsellors and my White House Staff to make fiscal restraint their first order of business, and to save every taxpayer's dollar the safety and genuine welfare of our great Nation will permit. Some economic activities will be affected more by monetary and fiscal restraint than other activities. Good government clearly requires that we tend to the economic problems facing our country in a spirit of equity to all of our citizens in all segments of our society.

Tonight, obviously, is no time to threaten you with vetoes. But I do have the last recourse, and I am a veteran of many a veto fight right here in this great chamber. Can't we do a better job by reasonable compromise? I hope we can.

Minutes after I took the Presidential oath, the joint leadership of Congress told me at the White House they would go more than half way to meet me. This was confirmed in your unanimous concurrent resolution of cooperation, for which I am deeply grateful. If, for my part, I go more than half way to meet the Congress, maybe we can find a much larger area of national agreement.

I bring no legislative shopping list here this evening. I will deal with specifics in future messages and talks with you, but here are a few examples of how seriously I feel about what we must do together.

Last week, the Congress passed the elementary and secondary education bill, and I found it on my desk. Any reservations I might have about some of its provisions — and I do have — fade in comparison to the urgent needs of America for quality education. I will sign it in a few days.

I must be frank. In implementing its provisions, I will oppose excessive funding during this inflationary crisis.

As Vice President, I studied various proposals for better health care financing. I saw them coming closer together and urged my friends in the Congress and in the Administration to sit down and sweat out a sound compromise. The Comprehensive Health Insurance Plan goes a long ways toward providing early relief to people who are sick.

Why don't we write — and I ask this with the greatest spirit of cooperation — why don't we write a good health bill on the statute books in 1974, before this Congress adjourns?

The economy of our country is critically dependent on how we interact with the economies of other countries. It is little comfort that our inflation is only a part of a worldwide problem or that American families need less of their paychecks for groceries than most of our foreign friends.

As one of the building blocks of peace, we have taken the lead in working toward a more open and a more equitable world economic system. A new round of international trade negotiations started last September among 105 nations in Tokyo. The others are waiting for the United States Congress to grant the necessary authority to the executive branch to proceed.

With modifications, the trade reform bill passed by the House last year would do a good job. I understand good progress has been made in the Senate Committee on Finance. But I am optimistic, as always, that the Senate will pass an acceptable bill quickly as a key part of our joint prosperity campaign.

I am determined to expedite other international economic plans. We will be working together with other nations to find better ways to prevent shortages of food and fuel. We must not let last winter's energy crisis happen again. I will push Project Independence for our own good and the good of others. In that, too, I will need your help.

Successful foreign policy is an extension of the hopes of the whole American people for a world of peace and orderly reform and orderly freedom. So, I would say a few words to our distinguished guests from the governments of other nations where, as at home, it is my determination to deal openly with allies and adversaries. Over the past 5½ years in Congress and as Vice President, I have fully supported the outstanding foreign policy of President Nixon. This policy I intend to continue. . . .

Our job will not be easy. In promising continuity, I cannot promise simplicity. The problems and challenges of the world remain complex and difficult. But we have set out on a path of reason, of fairness, and we will continue on it.

As guideposts on that path, I offer the following:

—To our allies of a generation in the Atlantic community and Japan, I pledge continuity in the loyal collaboration on our many mutual endeavors.

—To our friends and allies in this hemisphere, I pledge continuity in the deepening dialog to define renewed relationships of equality and justice.

—To our allies and friends in Asia, I pledge a continuity in our support for their security, independence, and economic development. In Indochina, we are determined to see the observance of the Paris agreement on Vietnam and the cease-fire and negotiated settlement in Laos. We hope to see an early compromise settlement in Cambodia.

—To the Soviet Union, I pledge continuity in our commitment to the course of the past 3 years. To our two peoples, and to all mankind, we owe a continued effort to live and, where possible, to work together in peace; for in a thermonuclear age there can be no alternative to a positive and peaceful relationship between our nations.

—To the People's Republic of China, whose legendary hospitality I enjoyed, I pledge continuity in our commitment to the principles of the Shanghai communiqué. The new relationship built on those principles has demonstrated that it serves serious and objective mutual interests and has become an enduring feature of the world scene.

—To the nations in the Middle East, I pledge continuity in our vigorous efforts to advance the progress which has brought hopes of peace to that region after 25 years as a hotbed of war. We shall carry out our promise to promote continuing negotiations among all parties for a complete, just, and lasting settlement.

—To all nations, I pledge continuity in seeking a common global goal: a stable international structure of trade and finance which reflects the interdependence of all peoples.

—To the entire international community—to the United Nations, to the world's nonaligned nations, and to all others—I pledge continuity in our dedication to the humane goals which throughout our history have been so much of America's contribution to mankind.

So long as the peoples of the world have confidence in our purposes and faith in our word, the age-old vision of peace on earth will grow brighter.

8.

GERALD R. FORD: The Pardon of Richard Nixon

*On Sunday, September 8, in a surprise announcement, President Ford issued a
pardon to former President Nixon for "all offenses against the United States which
he . . . has committed or may have committed" while in office. The pardon surprised
and shocked the nation and seriously damaged the President's popularity. The full
pardon was contrasted unfavorably with the limited clemency offer made to Vietnam
draft evaders and deserters. Many people suspected that the pardon was the result
of a "deal" worked out before Nixon resigned. To quash such rumors President Ford
appeared before a congressional panel on October 17 to affirm that no prior
arrangement had led to the pardon.*

Source: *Weekly Compilation of Presidential Documents*, September 16, 1974.

*The President's Remarks Announcing His
Decision to Grant the Pardon.*

Ladies and gentlemen, I have come to a
decision which I felt I should tell you and
all of my fellow American citizens, as
soon as I was certain in my own mind and
in my own conscience that it is the right
thing to do.

I have learned already in this office that
the difficult decisions always come to this
desk. I must admit that many of them do
not look at all the same as the hypothetical questions that I have answered freely
and perhaps too fast on previous occasions.

My customary policy is to try and get
all the facts and to consider the opinions
of my countrymen and to take counsel
with my most valued friends. But these
seldom agree, and in the end, the decision
is mine. To procrastinate, to agonize, and
to wait for a more favorable turn of
events that may never come or more compelling external pressures that may as
well be wrong as right, is itself a decision
of sorts and a weak and potentially dan-

gerous course for a President to follow.

I have promised to uphold the Constitution, to do what is right as God gives me
to see the right, and to do the very best
that I can for America.

I have asked your help and your prayers, not only when I became President but
many times since. The Constitution is the
supreme law of our land and it governs
our actions as citizens. Only the laws of
God, which govern our consciences, are
superior to it.

As we are a Nation under God, so I am
sworn to uphold our laws with the help of
God. And I have sought such guidance
and searched my own conscience with
special diligence to determine the right
thing for me to do with respect to my
predecessor in this place, Richard Nixon,
and his loyal wife and family.

Theirs is an American tragedy in which
we all have played a part. It could go on
and on and on, or someone must write the
end to it. I have concluded that only I can
do that, and if I can, I must.

There are no historic or legal precedents to which I can turn in this matter,

none that precisely fit the circumstances of a private citizen who has resigned the Presidency of the United States. But it is common knowledge that serious allegations and accusations hang like a sword over our former President's head, threatening his health as he tries to reshape his life, a great part of which was spent in the service of this country and by the mandate of its people.

After years of bitter controversy and divisive national debate, I have been advised, and I am compelled to conclude that many months and perhaps more years will have to pass before Richard Nixon could obtain a fair trial by jury in any jurisdiction of the United States under governing decisions of the Supreme Court.

I deeply believe in equal justice for all Americans, whatever their station or former station. The law, whether human or divine, is no respecter of persons, but the law is a respecter of reality.

The facts, as I see them, are that a former President of the United States, instead of enjoying equal treatment with any other citizen accused of violating the law, would be cruelly and excessively penalized either in preserving the presumption of his innocence or in obtaining a speedy determination of his guilt in order to repay a legal debt to society.

During this long period of delay and potential litigation, ugly passions would again be aroused. And our people would again be polarized in their opinions. And the credibility of our free institutions of Government would again be challenged at home and abroad.

In the end, the courts might well hold that Richard Nixon had been denied due process, and the verdict of history would even more be inconclusive with respect to those charges arising out of the period of his Presidency, of which I am presently aware. But it is not the ultimate fate of Richard Nixon that most concerns me, though surely it deeply troubles every decent and every compassionate person. My concern is the immediate future of this great country.

In this, I dare not depend upon my personal sympathy as a long-time friend of the former President, nor my professional judgment as a lawyer, and I do not.

As President, my primary concern must always be the greatest good of all the people of the United States whose servant I am. As a man, my first consideration is to be true to my own convictions and my own conscience.

My conscience tells me clearly and certainly that I cannot prolong the bad dreams that continue to reopen a chapter that is closed. My conscience tells me that only I, as President, have the constitutional power to firmly shut and seal this book.

My conscience tells me it is my duty, not merely to proclaim domestic tranquillity but to use every means that I have to insure it.

I do believe that the buck stops here, that I cannot rely upon public opinion polls to tell me what is right.

I do believe that right makes might and that if I am wrong, 10 angels swearing I was right would make no difference.

I do believe, with all my heart and mind and spirit, that I, not as President, but as a humble servant of God, will receive justice without mercy if I fail to show mercy.

Finally, I feel that Richard Nixon and his loved ones have suffered enough and will continue to suffer, no matter what I do, no matter what we, as a great and good Nation, can do together to make his goal of peace come true.

Proclamation 4311. September 8, 1974

GRANTING PARDON TO RICHARD
NIXON

By the President of the United States of America a Proclamation

Richard Nixon became the thirty-seventh President of the United States on January 20, 1969 and was reelected in 1972 for a second term by the electors of forty-nine of the fifty states. His term in office continued until his resignation on August 9, 1974.

Pursuant to resolutions of the House of Representatives, its Committee on the Judiciary conducted an inquiry and investigation on the impeachment of the President extending over more than eight months. The hearings of the Committee and its deliberations, which received wide national publicity over television, radio, and in printed media, resulted in votes adverse to Richard Nixon on recommended Articles of Impeachment.

As a result of certain acts or omissions occurring before his resignation from the Office of President, Richard Nixon has become liable to possible indictment and trial for offenses against the United States. Whether or not he shall be so prosecuted depends on findings of the appropriate grand jury and on the discretion of the authorized prosecutor. Should an indictment ensue, the accused shall then be entitled to a fair trial by an impartial jury, as guaranteed to every individual by the Constitution.

It is believed that a trial of Richard Nixon, if it became necessary, could not fairly begin until a year or more has elapsed. In the meantime, the tranquility to which this nation has been restored by the events of recent weeks could be irreparably lost by the prospects of bringing to trial a former President of the United States. The prospects of such trial will cause prolonged and divisive debate over the propriety of exposing to further punishment and degradation a man who has already paid the unprecedented penalty of relinquishing the highest elective office of the United States.

NOW, THEREFORE, I, GERALD R. FORD, President of the United States, pursuant to the pardon power conferred upon me by Article II, Section 2, of the Constitution, have granted and by these presents do grant a full, free, and absolute pardon unto Richard Nixon for all offenses against the United States which he, Richard Nixon, has committed or may have committed or taken part in during the period from January 20, 1969 through August 9, 1974.

IN WITNESS WHEREOF, I have hereunto set my hand this eighth day of September, in the year of our Lord nineteen hundred and seventy-four, and of the Independence of the United States of America the one hundred and ninety-ninth.

Gerald R. Ford

◆

Politicians in all democracies are always obsessed with holding on to or regaining power, not using it while it remains in order to accomplish positive results for the national good.

C. L. SULZBERGER, *The New York Times,*
February 7, 1976

9.

World Energy Conference Communiqué

The Arab oil embargo of 1973-74, coming as it did at the onset of a severe inflationary recession, threatened severe damage to the economies of the industrialized nations. Some countries rationed gas, banned Sunday driving, lowered speed limits, and reduced the use of electricity. While the effect of the embargo and the greatly increased oil prices was not so severe in the United States, there was great concern about the nation's dependence on imported fuel. The Nixon administration announced "Project Independence," intended to free the U. S. of the need for overseas oil by 1980. But the project was an illusion. By 1976 we were importing a higher proportion of our oil than in 1973. While the embargo was still on, representatives of thirteen industrial nations met in Washington, D.C., for an international energy conference to seek both short- and long-range solutions to the fuel crisis. The selection below reprints the communiqué issued at the end of the conference.

Source: *Department of State Bulletin*, March 6, 1974.

1. FOREIGN MINISTERS of Belgium, Canada, Denmark, France, the Federal Republic of Germany, Ireland, Italy, Japan, Luxembourg, The Netherlands, Norway, the United Kingdom, the United States met in Washington from February 11 to 13, 1974. The European Community was represented as such by the President of the Council and the President of the Commission. Finance Ministers, Ministers with responsibility for Energy Affairs, Economic Affairs and Science and Technology Affairs also took part in the meeting. The Secretary General of the OECD also participated in the meeting. The Ministers examined the international energy situation and its implications and charted a course of actions to meet this challenge which requires constructive and comprehensive solutions. To this end they agreed on specific steps to provide for effective international cooperation. The Ministers affirmed that solutions . . . should be sought in consultation with producer countries and other consumers.

2. They noted that during the past three decades progress in improving productivity and standards of living was greatly facilitated by the ready availability of increasing supplies of energy at fairly stable prices. They recognized that the problem of meeting growing demand existed before the current situation and that the needs of the world economy for increased energy supplies require positive long-term solutions.

3. They concluded that the current energy situation results from an intensification of these underlying factors and from political developments.

4. They reviewed the problems created by the large rise in oil prices and agreed with the serious concern expressed by the International Monetary Fund's Committee of Twenty at its recent Rome meeting

over the abrupt and significant changes in prospect for the world balance of payments structure.

5. They agreed that present petroleum prices presented the structure of world trade and finance with an unprecedented situation. They recognized that none of the consuming countries could hope to insulate itself from these developments, or expect to deal with the payments impact of oil prices by the adoption of monetary or trade measures alone. In their view, the present situation, if continued, could lead to a serious deterioration in income and employment, intensify inflationary pressures, and endanger the welfare of nations. They believed that financial measures by themselves will not be able to deal with the strains of the current situation.

6. They expressed their particular concern about the consequences of the situation for the developing countries and recognized the need for efforts by the entire international community to resolve this problem. At current oil prices the additional energy costs for developing countries will cause a serious setback to the prospect for economic development of these countries.

7. *General Conclusions.* They affirmed, that, in the pursuit of national policies, whether in trade, monetary or energy fields, efforts should be made to harmonize the interests of each country on the one hand and the maintenance of the world economic system on the other. Concerted international cooperation between all the countries concerned including oil producing countries could help to accelerate an improvement in the supply and demand situation, ameliorate the adverse economic consequences of the existing situation and lay the groundwork for a more equitable and stable international energy relationship.

8. They felt that these considerations taken as a whole made it essential that there should be a substantial increase of international cooperation in all fields. Each participant in the Conference stated its firm intention to do its utmost to contribute to such an aim, in close cooperation both with the other consumer countries and with the producer countries.

9. They concurred in the need for a comprehensive action program to deal with all facets of the world energy situation by cooperative measures. In so doing they will build on the work of the OECD. They recognized that they may wish to invite, as appropriate, other countries to join with them in these efforts. Such an action program of international cooperation would include, as appropriate, the sharing of means and efforts, while concerting national policies, in such areas as:

— The conservation of energy and restraint of demand.

— A system of allocating oil supplies in times of emergency and severe shortages.

— The acceleration of development of additional energy sources so as to diversify energy supplies.

— The acceleration of energy research and development programs through international cooperative efforts.

10. With respect to monetary and economic questions, they decided to intensify their cooperation and to give impetus to the work being undertaken in the IMF, the World Bank and the OECD on the economic and monetary consequences of the current energy situation, in particular to deal with balance of payments disequilibria. They agreed that:

— In dealing with the balance of payments impact of oil prices they stressed the importance of avoiding competitive depreciation and the escalation of restrictions on trade and payments or disruptive actions in external borrowing.

—While financial cooperation can only partially alleviate the problems which have recently arisen for the international economic system, they will intensify work on short-term financial measures and possible longer-term mechanisms to reinforce existing official and market credit facilities.

—They will pursue domestic economic policies which will reduce as much as possible the difficulties resulting from the current energy cost levels.

—They will make strenuous efforts to maintain and enlarge the flow of development aid bilaterally and through multilateral institutions, on the basis of international solidarity embracing all countries with appropriate resources.

11. Further, they have agreed to accelerate wherever practicable their own national programs of new energy sources and technology which will help the overall world-wide supply and demand situation.

12. They agreed to examine in detail the role of international oil companies.

13. They stressed the continued importance of maintaining and improving the natural environment as part of developing energy sources and agreed to make this an important goal of their activity.

14. They further agreed that there was need to develop a cooperative multilateral relationship with producing countries, and other consuming countries that takes into account the long-term interests of all. They are ready to exchange technical information with these countries on the problem of stabilizing energy supplies with regard to quantity and prices.

15. They welcomed the initiatives in the UN to deal with the larger issues of energy and primary products at a world-wide level and in particular for a special session of the UN General Assembly.

16. They agreed to establish a coordinating group headed by senior officials to direct and to coordinate the development of the actions referred to above. The coordinating group shall decide how best to organize its work. It should:

—Monitor and give focus to the tasks that might be addressed in existing organizations;

—Establish such *ad hoc* working groups as may be necessary to undertake tasks for which there are presently no suitable bodies;

—Direct preparations of a conference of consumer and producer countries which will be held at the earliest possible opportunity and which, if necessary, will be preceded by a further meeting of consumer countries.

17. They agreed that the preparations for such meetings should involve consultations with developing countries and other consumer and producer countries.

A late afternoon traffic jam on the Harbor Freeway in Los Angeles suggests that gasoline use is as high as ever.

NYT Pictures

10.

HENRY KISSINGER: American Policy Toward Southeast Asia

Early in 1973, American and other allied troops had been withdrawn from South Vietnam, in accord with the truce agreement signed in Paris on January 27, 1973. A cease fire, enforced by an International Commission of Control and Supervision, had not worked out; and the war continued. The military and economic situation of South Vietnam continued to deteriorate, while Congress was much less willing to spend huge sums for aid to Indochina. By the middle of the year funds for direct military action in the region had been cut off even as infiltration from North Vietnam was stepped up. Yet the administration kept pressing for continued aid. On March 13, 1974, Senator Edward Kennedy wrote Secretary of State Kissinger asking precisely what the American objectives were in relation to Indochina. In a lengthy letter of March 25, reprinted here in part, Kissinger responded to the inquiry.

Source: *Department of State Bulletin*, April 22, 1974.

1) "The general character and objectives of American policy towards Indochina as a whole and towards each government or political authority in the area;"

There are two basic themes in our policy toward Indochina. The first is our belief that a secure peace in Indochina is an important element in our efforts to achieve a worldwide structure of peace. Conversely, we believe that an evolution toward peace in other troubled areas helps bring about the stability for which we strive in Indochina. Consequently, our Indochina policy has been geared to bring about the conditions which will enable the contending parties to find a peaceful resolution of their differences.

A resolution of differences can, of course, be achieved by other than peaceful means. For example, North Viet-Nam might seek to conquer South Viet-Nam by force of arms. Such a resolution, however, would almost certainly be a temporary one and would not produce the long-term and stable peace which is essential.

Therefore, a corollary to our search for peace, and the second theme of our policy, is to discourage the takeover of the various parts of Indochina by force. Forcible conquest is not only repugnant to American traditions but also has serious destabilizing effects which are not limited to the area under immediate threat.

We would stress the point that the United States has no desire to see any particular form of government or social system in the Indochina countries. What we do hope to see is a free choice by the people of Indochina as to the governments and systems under which they will live. To that end we have devoted immense human and material resources to assist them in protecting this right of choice.

Our objective with regard to the Government of Viet-Nam, the Government of the Khmer Republic and the Royal Lao Government is to provide them with the material assistance and political encouragement which they need in determining their own futures and in helping to create conditions which will permit free decisions. In Laos, happily, real progress has been made, partly because of our assistance. The Vientiane Agreement and Protocols give clear evidence of the possibility for the peaceful settlement our policies are designed to foster. We have supported the Royal Lao Government and, when it is formed, we will look with great sympathy on the Government of National Union. We welcome a peaceful and neutral Laos and, where appropriate, we will continue to encourage the parties to work out their remaining problems.

In Cambodia we are convinced that long-term prospects for stability would be enhanced by a cease-fire and a negotiated settlement among the Khmer elements to the conflict. Because such stability is in our interests we are providing diplomatic and material support to the legitimate government of the Khmer Republic, both in its self-defense efforts and in its search for a political solution to the war.

Our objective in Viet-Nam continues to be to help strengthen the conditions which made possible the Paris Agreement on Ending the War and Restoring Peace in Viet-Nam. With this in mind we have supported the Republic of Viet-Nam with both military and economic assistance. We believe that by providing the Vietnamese Government the necessary means to defend itself and to develop a viable economy, the government in Hanoi will conclude that political solutions are much preferable to renewed use of major military force. The presence of large numbers of North Vietnamese troops in the South demonstrates that the military threat from Hanoi is still very much in evidence. Because of that threat we must still ensure that the Republic of Viet-Nam has the means to protect its independence. We note, however, that the level of violence is markedly less than it was prior to the cease-fire and believe that our policy of support for South Viet-Nam has been instrumental in deterring major North Vietnamese offensives.

Our objective with regard to the Democratic Republic of Viet-Nam, and its southern arm, the Provisional Revolutionary Government, is to encourage full compliance with the Paris Agreement. We have been disappointed by North Viet-Nam's serious violations of important provisions of the Agreement. However, we still believe that the Agreement provides a workable framework for a peaceful and lasting settlement, and we will continue to use all means available to us to support the cease-fire and to encourage closer observance of it. Our future relations with Hanoi obviously depend in large part on how faithfully North Viet-Nam complies with the Agreement.

2) *"The general content and nature of existing obligations and commitments to the governments in Saigon, Phnom Penh and Vientiane:"*

The U.S. has no bilateral written commitment to the Government of the Republic of Viet-Nam. However, as a signator of the Paris Agreement on Ending the War and Restoring Peace in Viet-Nam, the United States committed itself to strengthening the conditions which made the cease-fire possible and to the goal of the South Vietnamese people's right to self-determination. With these commitments in mind, we continue to provide to the Republic of Viet-Nam the means necessary for its self-defense and for its economic viability.

We also recognize that we have derived a certain obligation from our long and deep involvement in Viet-Nam. Perceiving our own interest in a stable

Viet-Nam free to make its own political choices, we have encouraged the Vietnamese people in their struggle for independence. We have invested great human and material resources to support them in protecting their own as well as broader interests. We have thus committed ourselves very substantially, both politically and morally. While the South Vietnamese Government and people are demonstrating increasing self-reliance, we believe it is important that we continue our support . . .

6) *"The current status of negotiations between Washington and Hanoi on American reconstruction assistance to North Viet-Nam."*

Following the conclusion of the Peace Agreement last year, preliminary discussions of post-war reconstruction were held in Paris between U.S. and North Vietnamese members of the Joint Economic Commission. These talks have been suspended since last July. The Administration's position, which we believe is shared by the great majority of members of Congress, is that the U.S. cannot at this time move forward with an assistance program for North Viet-Nam. To date, North Viet-Nam has failed substantially to live up to a number of the essential terms of the Agreement, including those relating to the introduction of troops and war materiel into South Viet-Nam, the cessation of military activities in Cambodia and Laos, and the accounting for our missing-in-action. Should Hanoi turn away from a military solution and demonstrate a serious compliance with the Agreement, then we would be prepared, with the approval of Congress, to proceed with our undertaking regarding reconstruction assistance to North Viet-Nam.

7) *"The Department's assessment on the implementation of the ceasefire agreements for both Viet-Nam and Laos:"*

The cease-fire in Viet-Nam has resulted in a substantial decrease in the level of hostilities; for example, military casualties since the cease-fire have been about one-third the level of casualties suffered in the years preceding the Paris Agreement. Nonetheless, it is unfortunately evident that significant violence continues to occur and that the cease-fire is far from scrupulously observed. The fundamental problem is that the North Vietnamese are still determined to seize political power in the South, using military means if necessary. To this end they have maintained unrelenting military pressure against the South Vietnamese Government and have continued widespread terrorism against the population. In particularly flagrant violation of the Agreement North Viet-Nam has persisted in its infiltration of men and materiel into the South, bringing in more than one hundred thousand troops and large quantities of heavy equipment since the cease-fire began. South Vietnamese forces have reacted against these attacks by North Vietnamese forces and several sizable engagements have taken place.

Despite these serious violations, we continue to believe that the Paris Agreement has already brought substantial benefits and continues to provide a workable framework for peace. After more than a quarter century of fighting it would have been unrealistic to expect that the Agreement would bring an instant and complete end to the conflict. What it has done, however, is to reduce the level of violence significantly and provide mechanisms for discussion. The two Vietnamese parties are talking to each other and are achieving some results, even if these results are much less than we would like to see. The final exchange of prisoners which was completed on March 7 is illustrative.

We assess the cease-fire agreement in Laos as being so far largely successful. The level of combat was reduced substantially immediately following the cease-fire and has since fallen to a handful of incidents per week. There is hope that if developments continue as they have, the Laos cease-fire will work and the Lao, through their own efforts, will be able to establish a coalition government and a stable peace in their country.

8) *"The Department's assessment of the overall situation in Cambodia and the possibility for a ceasefire agreement."*

Despite continued pressure by the Khmer insurgents, now generally under the control of the Khmer Communist Party, the Khmer armed forces have successfully repulsed two major insurgent operations, one against Kompong Cham and, more recently, against Phnom Penh, with no U.S. combat support. Serious military problems remain, and continued hard fighting during the next few months is expected, both in the provinces and around the capital.

A broadened political base, a new Prime Minister and a more effective cabinet offer signs of improvements in the civil administration. The enormous dislocation of war, destroying production, producing over a million refugees and encouraging spiralling inflation, face the leaders of the Khmer Republic with serious problems.

Nonetheless, we are convinced that with U.S. material and diplomatic support the Khmer Republic's demonstration of military and economic viability will persuade their now intransigent opponents to move to a political solution of the Cambodian conflict. The Khmer Republic's Foreign Minister on March 21 reiterated his government's position that a solution for Cambodia should be peaceful and not forced by arms or capitula-tion. Instead, his government will continue to seek talks with the other side. His government hopes their efforts for peace will achieve some results after the current insurgent offensive.

9) *"Recent diplomatic initiatives, involving the United States, aimed at a reduction of violence in Indochina and a greater measure of normalization in the area."*

Since the signing of the Viet-Nam cease-fire agreement, the United States has been in constant liaison with the interested parties, including those outside of the Indochina area. While it would not be useful to provide details of all of these contacts, we can assure the Congress that we have used every means at our disposal to encourage a reduction in the level of violence and an orderly resolution of the conflict. We believe these measures have had some success. The level of fighting is down substantially from 1972 and the Vietnamese parties have taken at least beginning steps toward a satisfactory accommodation. Further, the interested outside parties remain basically committed to building on the framework of the cease-fire agreement.

When Hanoi established a pattern of serious violations of the Agreement shortly after its conclusion, Dr. Kissinger met with Special Adviser Le Duc Tho and negotiated the Paris communique of June 13, 1973, with a view to stabilizing the situation. Secretary Kissinger returned to Paris in December, 1973, to again discuss with Special Adviser Tho the status of the implementation of the Agreement. We will continue to maintain such contacts with Vietnamese and other parties in the hope that Hanoi will eventually be persuaded that its interests lie in peaceful development rather than in conflict.

In Laos, we have offered every encouragement to an evolution toward peace. At this time the Laotian parties are making great progress in the formation of a government of national union. We can help in this regard with our sympathy and encouragement while properly leaving the issue in the hands of those most interested, the Lao people.

The Government of the Khmer Republic, with our complete endorsement, has made notable efforts to terminate the hostilities in that country. Following the cease-fire in Viet-Nam, the Cambodian Government unilaterally ceased hostile activity by its forces in the hope that the other side would respond.

Unfortunately that striking gesture was rebuffed. On frequent occasions thereafter the Khmer Republic made proposals designed to move the conflict from the battlefield to political fora, with our strong support in each instance. Although all of those proposals have been ignored by the Khmer Communists, we continue to hope that the current relative military balance will make apparent to the other side what the Khmer Republic has already perceived, that peace is a far more hopeful prospect for Cambodia than incessant conflict.

11.

HENRY KISSINGER: The Challenge of Interdependence

The Arab oil embargo and the new highly inflated oil prices destabilized the economies of the industrialized nations and threatened them all with depression. The "Third World," or underdeveloped, countries, were in even worse shape. They lacked the economic resiliency of an industrialized society, while the necessities for their very livelihood were costing them far more. But oil was not the only issue in the energy crisis. There was increased worldwide concern over the price and allocation of all natural resources and food. The problems were not confined to any one nation, but were international in scope. On April 15, 1974, Secretary of State Henry Kissinger dealt with this issue in an address to the United Nations General Assembly.

Source: *Department of State Bulletin*, May 6, 1974.

WE ARE gathered here in a continuing venture to realize mankind's hopes for a more prosperous, humane, just, and cooperative world.

As members of this organization, we are pledged not only to free the world from the scourge of war but to free mankind from the fear of hunger, poverty, and disease. The quest for justice and dignity — which finds expression in the eco-

nomic and social articles of the United Nations Charter — has global meaning in an age of instantaneous communication. Improving the quality of human life has become a universal political demand, a technical possibility, and a moral imperative.

We meet here at a moment when the world economy is under severe stress. The energy crisis first dramatized its fragility. But the issues transcend that particular crisis. Each of the problems we face—of combating inflation and stimulating growth, of feeding the hungry and lifting the impoverished, of the scarcity of physical resources and the surplus of despair—is part of an interrelated global problem.

Let us begin by discarding outdated generalities and sterile slogans we have—all of us—lived with for so long. The great issues of development can no longer realistically be perceived in terms of confrontation between the "haves" and "have-nots" or as a struggle over the distribution of static wealth. Whatever our ideological belief or social structure, we are part of a single international economic system on which all of our national economic objectives depend. No nation or bloc of nations can unilaterally determine the shape of the future.

If the strong attempt to impose their views, they will do so at the cost of justice and thus provoke upheaval. If the weak resort to pressure, they will do so at the risk of world prosperity and thus provoke despair.

The organization of one group of countries as a bloc will, sooner or later, produce the organization of potential victims into a counterbloc. The transfer of resources from the developed to the developing nations—essential to all hopes for progress—can only take place with the support of the technologically advanced countries. Politics of pressure and threats will undermine the domestic base of this support. The danger of economic stagnation stimulates new barriers to trade and to the transfer of resources. We in this Assembly must come to grips with the fact of our interdependence.

The contemporary world can no longer be encompassed in traditional stereotypes. The notion of the northern rich and the southern poor has been shattered. The world is composed not of two sets of interests but many: developed nations which are energy suppliers and developing nations which are energy consumers, market economies and nonmarket economies, capital providers and capital recipients. The world economy is a sensitive set of relationships in which actions can easily set off a vicious spiral of counteractions deeply affecting all countries, developing as well as technologically advanced. Global inflation erodes the capacity to import. A reduction in the rate of world growth reduces export prospects. Exorbitantly high prices lower consumption, spur alternative production, and foster development of substitutes.

We are all engaged in a common enterprise. No nation or group of nations can gain by pushing its claims beyond the limits that sustain world economic growth. No one benefits from basing progress on tests of strength.

For the first time in history, mankind has the technical possibility to escape the scourges that used to be considered inevitable. Global communication insures that the thrust of human aspirations becomes universal. Mankind insistently identifies justice with the betterment of the human condition. Thus economics, technology, and the sweep of human values impose a recognition of our interdependence and of the necessity of our collaboration.

Let us therefore resolve to act with both realism and compassion to reach a new understanding of the human condition. On that understanding, let us base a new relationship which evokes the commitment of all nations because it serves the interests of all peoples. We can build a just world only if we work together. . . .

First, a global economy requires an expanding supply of energy at an equitable price.

No subject illustrates global interdependence more emphatically than the field of energy. No nation has an interest in prices that can set off an inflationary spiral which in time reduces income for all. For example, the price of fertilizer has risen in direct proportion to the price of oil, putting it beyond the reach of many of the poorest nations and thus contributing to worldwide food shortages. A comprehension by both producers and consumers of each other's needs is therefore essential:

—Consumers must understand the desires of the producers for higher levels of income over the long-term future.

—Producers must understand that the recent rise in energy prices has placed a great burden on all consumers, one virtually impossible for some to bear.

All nations share an interest in agreeing on a level of prices which contributes to an expanding world economy and which can be sustained over the long term.

The United States called the Washington Energy Conference for one central purpose—to move urgently to resolve the energy problem on the basis of cooperation among all nations. The tasks we defined there can become a global agenda:

—Nations, particularly developed nations, waste vast amounts of existing energy supplies. We need a new commitment to global conservation and to more efficient use of existing supplies.

—The oil producers themselves have noted that the demands of this decade cannot be met unless we expand available supplies. We need a massive and cooperative effort to develop alternative sources of fuels.

—The needs of future generations require that we develop new and renewable sources of supply. In this field, the developed nations can make a particularly valuable contribution to our common goal of abundant energy at reasonable cost.

Such a program cannot be achieved by any one group of countries. It must draw on the strength and meet the needs of all nations in a new dialogue among producers and consumers.

In such a dialogue, the United States will take account of—and take seriously—the concern of the producing countries that the future of their peoples not depend on oil alone. The United States is willing to help broaden the base of their economies and to develop secure and diversified sources of income. We are prepared to facilitate the transfer of technology and to assist industrialization. We will accept substantial investment of the capital of oil-producing countries in the United States. We will support a greater role for oil producers in international financial organizations as well as an increase in their voting power.

Second, a healthy global economy requires that both consumers and producers escape from the cycle of raw material surplus and shortage which threatens all our economies.

The principles which apply to energy apply as well to the general problem of raw materials. It is tempting to think of cartels of raw material producers to negotiate for higher prices. But such a course could have serious consequences for all countries. Large price increases coupled with production restrictions involve potential disaster: global inflation followed by global recession from which no nation could escape. . . .

Third, the global economy must achieve a balance between food production and population growth and must restore the capacity to meet food emergencies. A condition in which one billion people suffer from malnutrition is consistent with no concept of justice.

Since 1969, global production of cereals has not kept pace with world demand. As a result, current reserves are at their lowest level in 20 years. A significant crop failure today is likely to produce a major disaster. A protracted imbalance in food and population growth will guarantee massive starvation — a moral catastrophe the world community cannot tolerate. . . .

The United States is determined to take additional steps. Specifically:

— We are prepared to join with other governments in a major worldwide effort to rebuild food reserves. A central objective of the World Food Conference must be to restore the world's capacity to deal with famine.

— We shall assign priority in our aid program to help developing nations substantially raise their agricultural production. We hope to increase our assistance to such programs from $258 million to $675 million this year.

— We shall make a major effort to increase the quantity of food aid over the level we provided last year. . . .

Fourth, a global economy under stress cannot allow the poorest nations to be overwhelmed.

The debate between raw material producers and consumers must not overlook that substantial part of humanity which does not produce raw materials, grows insufficient food for its needs, and has not adequately industrialized. This group of nations, already at the margin of existence, has no recourse to pay the higher prices for the fuel, food, and fertilizer imports on which their survival depends.

Thus, the people least able to afford it — a third of mankind — are the most profoundly threatened by an inflationary world economy. They face the despair of abandoned hopes for development and the threat of starvation. Their needs require our most urgent attention. The nations assembled here in the name of justice cannot stand idly by in the face of tragic consequences for which many of them are partially responsible.

We welcome the steps the oil producers have already taken toward applying their new surplus revenues to these needs. The magnitude of the problem requires, and the magnitude of their resources permits, a truly massive effort.

The developed nations, too, have an obligation to help. Despite the prospect of unprecedented payment difficulties, they must maintain their traditional programs of assistance and expand them if possible. Failure to do so would penalize the lower income countries twice. The United States is committed to continue its program and pledges its support for an early replenishment of the International Development Association. In addition, we are prepared to consider with others what additional measures are required to mitigate the effects of commodity price rises on low-income countries least able to bear the burden.

Fifth, in a global economy of physical scarcity, science and technology are becoming our most precious resource.

No human activity is less national in character than the field of science. No development effort offers more hope than joint technical and scientific cooperation.

Man's technical genius has given us laborsaving technology, healthier populations, and the Green Revolution. But it has also produced a technology that consumes resources at an ever-expanding rate, a population explosion which presses against the earth's finite living space, and an agriculture increasingly dependent on the products of industry. Let us now apply science to the problems which science has helped to create:

— To meet the developing nations' two most fundamental problems, unemployment and hunger, there is an urgent need for farming technologies that are both productive and labor intensive. The United States is prepared to contribute to international programs to develop and apply this technology.

— The technology of birth control should be improved.

— At current rates of growth, the world's need for energy will more than triple by the end of this century. To meet this challenge, the U.S. Government is allocating $12 billion for energy research and development over the next five years, and American private industry will spend over $200 billion to increase energy supplies. We are prepared to apply the results of our massive effort to the massive needs of other nations.

— The poorest nations, already beset by manmade disasters, have been threatened by a natural one: the possibility of climatic changes in the monsoon belt and perhaps throughout the world. The implications for global food and population policies are ominous. The United States proposes that the International Council of Scientific Unions and the World Meteorological Organization urgently investigate this problem and offer guidelines for immediate international action.

Sixth, the global economy requires a trade, monetary, and investment system that sustains industrial civilization and stimulates growth.

Not since the 1930's has the economic system of the world faced such a test. The disruption of the oil price rises, the threat of global inflation, the cycle of contraction of exports and protectionist restrictions, the massive shift in the world's financial flows, and the likely concentration of invested surplus oil revenue in a few countries — all threaten to smother the dreams of universal progress with stagnation and despair.

A new commitment is required by both developed and developing countries to an open trading system, a flexible but stable monetary system, and a positive climate for the free flow of resources, both public and private. To this end the United States proposes that all nations here pledge themselves to avoid trade and payment restrictions in an effort to adjust to higher commodity prices.

The United States is prepared to keep open its capital markets so that capital can be recycled to developing countries hardest hit by the current crisis.

In the essential struggle to regain control over global inflation, the United States is willing to join in an international commitment to pursue responsible fiscal and monetary policies.

To foster an open trading world the United States, already the largest importer of the manufactures of developing nations, is prepared to open its markets further to these products. We shall work in the multilateral trade negotiations to reduce tariff and nontariff barriers on as wide a front as possible. In line with this approach we are urging our Congress to authorize the generalized tariff preferences which are of such significance to developing countries. . . .

Let us affirm today that we are faced with a common challenge and can only meet it jointly. Let us candidly acknowledge our different perspectives and then proceed to build on what unites us. Let us transform the concept of world community from a slogan into an attitude.

In this spirit let us be the masters of our common fate so that history will record that this was the year that mankind at last began to conquer its noblest and most humane challenge.

12.

Francis A. J. Ianni: The Ethnic Succession in Organized Crime

Organized crime in the United States has always been primarily a matter of economic opportunity. It has never been confined to one social or ethnic group. But since the early 19th century, it has happened that members of some ethnic groups were more visible than others in the perpetration of crime. They were usually newly arrived immigrants who found themselves in a disadvantageous position socially and economically. Many of them turned to crime in order to realize their version of the "American dream." The fact that there were at any given time so many Irish, Jews, or Italians involved in crime lent credence to the utterly erroneous notion that some groups were more prone to crime than others. There has been an apparent ethnic succession in organized crime, but it is really a succession of the economically disadvantaged. In the past few years, among the newer urban poor, blacks, Mexican Americans, and Puerto Ricans, some few have turned to crime. Professor Francis Ianni of Teachers College, Columbia University, has spent several years investigating the ethnic factors of organized crime. His 1974 book, Black Mafia, *presented his findings on the sociological changes taking place in urban crime. He summed up his work in an article, "New Mafia: Black, Hispanic and Italian Styles," for* Society *magazine. A portion of the article is reprinted here.*

Source: *Society*, March-April, 1974.

ORGANIZED CRIME is more than just a criminal way of life; it is an American way of life. It is a viable and persistent institution within American society with its own symbols, its own beliefs, its own logic and its own means of transmitting these systematically from one generation to the next. As an integral part of economic life in the United States it can be viewed as falling on a continuum which has the legitimate business world at one end and what we have come to call organized crime at the other. Viewed in this way, organized crime is a functional part of the American social system and, while successive waves of immigrants and migrants have found it an available means of economic and social mobility, it persists and transcends the involvement of any particular group and even changing definitions of legality and illegality in social behavior.

At present organized crime is in a period of transition. Italian domination has begun to give way to that of a new group: the blacks and Hispanics. During the next decade we will see the presently scattered and loosely organized pattern of their emerging control develop into a new Mafia. This black and Hispanic involvement can be examined as part of the process of ethnic succession. They, like other minorities before them, are inheriting a major instrument to social and economic mobility. . . .

A description of the future of organized crime must be speculative. It is instructive, however, to look at the present pattern of organization, which we found in our study, and the degree of control or power now possessed by the blacks and Hispanics. At present, their networks could not be characterized as big operations, like Italian-American crime families with many layers of authority and countless functionaries and associates, many of whom are not aware of the roles of the others. Black and Hispanic organized crime networks have not yet reached that level of development. We do, however, have enough data on hierarchical arrangements and placement within some of the networks to conclude that while they are growing in complexity, they are still dependent on external sources for supplies and protection. In the Paterson network (the most highly developed of the black networks we examined), the two lowest levels, the street operators who sell drugs, numbers or their bodies as well as their immediate supervisors, the numbers controllers, pimps and small-scale drug suppliers, are all black. It is the next highest, "boss" level which now seems in ethnic transition as Bro Squires, a black, struggles to replace Joe Hajar, a white, as the big man on the hill. Both Squires and Hajar, however, are still dependent on the Italians for police and political protection as well as for drug supplies.

In Harlem and in Bedford-Stuyvesant, black networks seem to be free of such dependence on the Italians for protection, but not as yet for drugs except in those cases where they are switching to the Cuban Connection. Internally, these networks do not seem to have developed any new forms of hierarchical arrangement as yet. In the numbers games, the traditional pattern of the carefully articulated runner-controller-banker hierarchy which is still in use by the Italians is also used by both blacks and Puerto Ricans. As we fol-

lowed the networks upward through the layers of individual black and Puerto Rican entrepreneurs, each with his own little entourage of employees and followers, however, it became obvious that while only in Paterson did we find a direct connection with an Italian syndicate, most of these individual entrepreneurs must relate to Italian families or alternately to the Cuban Connection for drug supplies and for other high-level services such as lay-off banking. Nowhere in our networks did we find blacks or Puerto Ricans who have risen to the point where they are providing major services to other criminals. Neither did we find any systematic pattern of exchange of such services among the various networks. Where we did find any contact among the networks, the individual entrepreneurs seem to be connected to one another either through occasional joint ventures or through straight, one shot deals for sales or services.

This lack of organizational development in black and Puerto Rican criminal structures coincides with both the newness of blacks and Puerto Ricans in control positions and with the nature of the types of criminal activities which we discovered in these networks. Just as the lack of a sufficient period of time in control positions has hindered any large-scale organizational development, it has also tended to keep the networks in specific types of criminal activities rather than allowing them to achieve hegemony in any one territory. Once again the only exception was in Paterson, where the Italians are still in control. Throughout the networks, however, there is evidence of some embryonic diversification of criminal activity involved in the networks as black control is consolidated. The combinations seem to be fairly stylized: prostitution and drugs, theft and petty gambling, numbers and narcotics are typical patterns. We also found evidence that black crime activists are starting to acquire some legitimate fronts: a boutique, for example, serves to shade some illegal activities, while a gypsy cab is sometimes used for drug transactions and prostitution.

Within this emergent system, mobility is based upon both efficiency needs and power through the accumulation of wealth and territorial control. There is a set of fairly strict rules and norms governing such movement. So it was among the Italians and the evidence suggests that it is becoming so among blacks and Hispanics in organized crime. Successful operations are gaining power increments over time through the scope, extent and intensity of their dealings. In crime organizations as in more legitimate business enterprises, small operations grow into larger ones and then join with others to maintain territorial control over rich market areas. The market for illegal goods and services is not restricted to the ghetto but at present, with the exception of prostitution, the black or Puerto Rican organized crime networks are excluded from the larger markets which are still dominated by Italians. This same condition prevailed among the Italians in the earlier part of the century until prohibition provided a source for extra-ghetto profit and power and allowed the Italian mobs to grow into control. But since the present networks among blacks and Hispanics are still relatively small operations, they continue to specialize and have yet to develop into large empires or even interconnected baronies. There are of course a number of indications of connections among networks in the same line of business and some of the activities we observed were on their way to becoming large, but the evidence from our study seems to indicate

that the present pattern of loosely structured, largely unrelated networks has now reached its highest stage of development and that what seems to be necessary for these networks to become elaborated into larger combines, like those now present among Italians are: (1) greater control over sectors of organized crime outside as well as inside the ghetto; (2) some organizing principle which will serve as kinship did among the Italians to bring the disparate networks together into larger criminally monopolistic organizations; and (3) better access to political power and the ability to corrupt it.

The first of these conditions, monopolistic control over some sector or sectors of organized crime, can only come about by wresting or inheriting such control from the Italians or, alternately, by developing new forms of illicit goods and services for sale to the public. The current sectors of organized crime — drugs, stolen goods, gambling, prostitution and loan sharking are presently in a state of transition and their availability to blacks and Hispanics as a source of illicit profit differs. At present, the numbers game is the major organized crime sector coming into obvious and immediate control of blacks and, to a lesser extent, Puerto Ricans. But the short period of control by blacks in this area seems certain to come to an early end. The reasons for its demise are precisely the same as was true in an earlier period when the game's popularity attracted the interest and attention of Jewish and Italian crime syndicates. Now it is the government which seems to be attracted to the immense profits which accrue in this form of gambling. Over the last decade a number of forms of gambling have been legalized, largely as a means of gaining additional revenue for near-bankrupt cities and for state governments as well. In New York, for example, the first step was the establishment of a lottery, ostensibly to defray the costs of education. The success of the lottery, and the lack of a public outcry against it, led to the legalizing of gambling on horse races through the establishment of the Off-Track Betting system. The latter was proposed simply as a means of diverting profits from gambling away from organized crime. . . .

There are now proposals in a number of cities to legalize the numbers as well. Here, however, the conflict between community sentiments and a revenue-hungry government is already beginning to emerge. When Off-Track Betting was established in New York, a number of spokesmen for the black community indicated that now the white middle class had managed to legalize its own preferred form of gambling and even added the convenience of placing the betting parlors throughout the city, doing away with the need to even go to the track. The numbers, however, was a black thing and it remained illegal. Thus, they said it was illegal for blacks to gamble but not for whites. The ghetto dweller's sense of white establishment hypocrisy in legalizing most other forms of gambling while continuing to condemn the numbers is not difficult to understand. On March 6, 1973, the New Jersey edition of the *New York Times* ran a full-column story reporting a police raid on a Puerto Rican numbers operation in East Harlem. The article described the raid by over 40 policemen and detectives, the arrest of 13 people and the confiscation of thousands of dollars worth of equipment. At the bottom of the column, there appeared the black-bordered box which is now present in every issue of the paper:

The winning New Jersey daily
lottery number yesterday was:
25113

The movement to legalize the numbers seems assured of success within the next few years. The proposals being advanced by a number of blacks are for a system of community control through licensing or franchising arrangements and even the granting of amnesty to present black numbers operators who can run the legal numbers games. The chances for such community control are minimal and even in the unlikely event that it does occur, the important point here is that the numbers, at present the most lucrative form of black organized crime, will certainly disappear through legalization in the near future.

Prostitution, while predominantly organized by black pimps and already operating outside the ghetto, does not actually offer a large enough financial base for further expansion so that among the present forms of organized crime, loan sharking, the theft and sale of goods, and drugs remain as possibilities. Loan sharking and the sale of stolen goods do not seem possible as means of expansion outside the ghetto for black crime activists. It is difficult to imagine that most white Americans would deal with a black salesman pushing stolen goods and even more difficult to envision whites borrowing money from black loan sharks. Thus, while these forms of illicit enterprise may well expand in the ghetto, it is not very probable that blacks can use them as a basis for extending their control over organized crime outside it.

The one sector of organized crime which does seem to present some possibility for black and Hispanic monopolization as a basis for expansion both within and outside the ghetto is drug traffic. First, narcotics and the drug traffic have the same pattern of relationships which surrounded alcohol and bootlegging during the prohibition era. Although there is not as wide a public acceptance of drugs and social opprobrium of hard drug use remains strong, all of the other conditions prevail. Drugs are illegal but in demand. In order for drugs to be produced and wholesaled, some safe haven is necessary for the crime operatives, a place in which they can be assured of at least tacit protection from police by their neighbors. The present movement toward tougher drug laws and stiffer penalties will reduce competition in the drug traffic so that blacks can begin to supply drugs outside the ghetto. Here, as in prostitution, the willingness of disenfranchized blacks to take risks that other groups need not take to escape poverty will combine with the color blindness of the needs of drug users to break down the racial barriers which impede loan sharking and the sale of stolen goods.

Finally, there is the possibility of corrupting police and other governmental officials without whose protection no form of organized crime could long endure. When the numbers are legalized, the major source of police graft will disappear leaving drugs one of the few remaining sources for the payment of substantial sums to police. All of the conditions for control of distribution within the ghetto are now operative and all that seems necessary is for the blacks and Hispanics to take over the sources of supply and then move into extra-ghetto distribution. In the East Harlem-Brooklyn Hispanic network, the Cuban Connection is already developing these sources. The importance of cocaine as a street drug has grown tremendously in the last two years and the Cuban Connection has grown apace. Both the police and the underworld, until recently preoccupied with the heroin trade, are now realizing the enormous profits which can be made in cocaine. Its growing popularity among the affluent drug public in penthouses and luxury apartments as well as on the street is equally obvious today. If blacks, either in concert or in competition with Hispanic groups, can take over control of this area then they can develop a national and even international base for operations. Then, as happened among the Italians, they can take their profits and reinvest them in other illicit enterprises. Whether they can also follow the pattern of Italians and use these same monies as a basis for movement into legitimate areas is, however, another question.

The second condition for the elaboration of black organized crime networks into larger combines is the development of some organizing principle which will serve to coalesce black and Hispanic organized crime networks as kinship did for the Italians. Hispanics in organized crime —particularly the Cubans—may well adopt and adapt the existing family model of organization used by the Italians. As we have noted, the bonds of kinship seem stronger in the Hispanic networks we observed than they did among blacks. In fact, there is growing evidence that Hispanics are working in concert with Italian families to a much greater extent than is true of blacks. In September of 1972, for example, Cubans operated the gambling concessions at the San Gennaro festival, New York's annual Italian street fair. Until 1972, of course, the gambling tables and wheels were always operated by Italians. Obviously some arrangement must have been made for the Italians to allow the Cubans to operate, even under franchise, in the heart of Little Italy. While there is a cultural base for a family-type organization among Hispanics, this is not true among blacks.

Instead of family or kinship, however, the blacks may be able to use black militancy as their organizing principle. Previous ethnic groups involved with organized crime—the Irish, the Jews and the Italians—were desperately trying to become white Americans. Now, however, the blacks are beginning to become important in organized crime at a time when being black, being a brother or a sister, serves to create a family-type structure based upon militancy. Even the terminology—brother, sister, mother—expresses a sense of rights and responsibilities to the "family of blacks." More important, blacks and Puerto Ricans involved in organized crime may rightfully feel themselves bound together by the oppressiveness of a system which rejects their attempts at social and political mobility and that during this period when much of black power is negative power—that is demanded and given out of fear—banding together to beat the system by any means may serve as a powerful incentive and organizer.

Patronage, acceptance and admiration define the attitudes of many of the blacks and Puerto Ricans we spoke with toward blacks and Puerto Ricans in organized crime. The reasons are not difficult to find; the crime activist is making it and he is making it in spite of and in conflict with an oppressive white establishment. Also, the activities he engages in—gambling, boosting and fencing, prostitution and loan sharking—are not considered socially harmful by many ghetto dwellers or indeed by many non-ghetto dwellers. Community attitudes toward crime activists change sharply when the drug problem is discussed, but solidarity is even apparent here. The narcotics trafficker is universally detested in the ghetto. Yet the local pusher, even though he is black or Puerto Rican (perhaps because he is black or Puerto Rican) is often not held responsible for the problem of drug addiction.

The community's attitude toward the drug pusher is ambiguous. On the one hand, he is a visible symbol of the narcotics traffic and as such becomes an easy target for verbal, sometimes physical abuse. People living in the community, overwhelmed by the magnitude of the drug problem and not knowing how to deal with it, identify the problem with the pusher. The pusher comes to represent the narcotics problem and the shame and fear community residents feel about drugs. At the same time, community residents assign the responsibility for widespread drug addiction to forces operating on the community from the outside. A conspiracy theory of drugs is widely held in the black and Puerto Rican communities. According to community residents, the widespread use of drugs in the ghetto is the result of a white establishment plot to kill off black and Puerto Rican youths by allowing or even encouraging drugs in these areas. The role of Italian-American criminal syndicates in narcotics importing and sale is also widely accepted in the ghetto. Community people believe it is Italian-Americans, not blacks and Puerto Ricans, who profit most from the drug trade. Again, this belief mitigates the community's attitude toward the local pusher.

Like most Americans living in our consumer society, ghetto dwellers are hungry for money and for the goods and services it can procure. Ghetto dwellers are cut off from many legitimate ways of obtaining financial security. At the same time they have fewer opportunities than middle-class Americans to achieve the psychological security that can reduce the incidence of crime. When a man is financially secure, happy in his work, has a stable family life and lives in a stable community, he has little reason to consider criminal activity as a vocational possibility. But blacks and Puerto Ricans, like other ethnics before them, see organized crime as one of the few available routes to success, to financial and thus psychological security. In every society, criminals tend to develop under those social conditions which seem to offer no other way of escaping bondage. Poverty and powerlessness are at the root of both community acceptance of organized crime and recruitment into its networks. Conditions of poverty also nurture community desires for the services organized criminal operations provide. Escapism accounts in part for both widespread drug use and numbers gambling; the resentment that poverty and powerlessness arouse in the subordinated population makes drugs and gambling attractive as mechanisms of rebellion. Organized crime is esteemed for the very reason that society outlaws it. . . .

The third condition for the elaboration of black and Hispanic crime networks is better access to political power and the ability to corrupt it. The evidence here is more difficult to deal with because it is to some extent contradictory. On the one hand, it is well established in the social history of the city that ethnic groups succeed to power in politics as they do in crime and that the two forms of mobility are often connected. There is evidence that blacks are moving ahead in politics in the large urban areas just as they are in organized crime. What is less evident is that the necessary connections between politics and its corruptability and black movement in organized crime will coincide. While it is a maxim in the underworld that graft and corruption are color-blind and that police and politicians will take graft regardless of the color of the hand that delivers it, it is difficult to imagine that blacks will be able to insinuate themselves into the kinds of social rela-

tionships with white politicians within which deals are made, bribes are offered or sought and protection developed. Again, the black movement in both politics and crime, like so many other processes of social advance among them, comes at a time when much of the power and profit has already been milked from the system by the groups which preceded them. The rampant corruption of our political system reaching up to and now obviously including the White House, could put the costs of corruption to a point where it is prohibitive. This already seems to be the case in New York City where the revelations of the Knapp Commission on bribe taking by the police seem to have doubled the costs of bribery in just one year's time.

While the growth of a new Mafia is fairly well known or at least perceived in black and Puerto Rican neighborhoods, it would not be unfair to say that, aside from the occasional newspaper headlines, there is little public knowledge that it is going on. To judge from its actions, the greater society seems to consider black and Puerto Rican organized crime as one of the small prices it must pay for the continuance of the many psychological and economic comforts that accrue from the existence of an ethnic underclass. Indeed, when measured against the cost of eliminating such crime, the costs are small. The most visible cost—of the thefts and muggings by narcotic addicts—touch only a few people in the large urban areas. In many respects there is also a continuation of that traditional attitude of the criminal justice system: so long as ghetto dwellers keep their crimes within the ghetto and do not spill outside, leave them to themselves. It is when the muggings and the robberies have reached the non-ghetto areas that there is a strong outcry. This attitude, which has traditionally been part of our law enforcement value system, allows organized crime to thrive within the ghetto. Once the organized crime networks find profitable sources of revenue outside the ghetto then the growing economic, political and social impact of organized crime becomes a matter of public interest and social policy. In the meantime, blacks and His-panics must continue to face the same basic dilemma which confounded earlier generations of Irish, Jews and Italians: How do you escape poverty through socially approved routes when such routes are closed off from the ghetto? Organized crime resolves the dilemma because it provides a quick if perilous route out.

13.

WARREN SHORE: Social Security — A Great Ripoff?

By 1973 the annual social security tax for a worker and his employer was more than 4 times what it had been in 1965. As of January 1974 the fixed annual rate was raised to 5.85% on a base salary of $13,200. In effect this meant each employer and employee would pay $722.20 in the social security fund. Despite this almost yearly increase in the tax, the amount being paid out in benefits continued to surpass income. Inflation was one reason for this. As the cost of living rose, social security benefits were raised according to an escalator clause in amendments to the Social Security Act. There was widespread concern that the social security system was headed for enormous deficits that would eventually bankrupt the plan. In a series of articles published in Chicago Today *from April 29 to May 3, 1974, reporter Warren Shore examined the problems facing the Social Security Fund and proposed some alternatives to the program. The first of his articles is reprinted here.*

Source: *Chicago Today,* April 29, 1974.

THE FEDERAL government prints a little blue booklet entitled "Your Social Security" which begins: "Nine out of 10 working people in the United States are now building protection for themselves and their families under the Social Security program."

If you believe the little blue booklet, the decision could cost you more than $200,000 and wipe out your chances for a secure future.

The huge loss is real, spendable income. It represents the difference between the protection value a wage earner gets for his Social Security payroll taxes and the value he could buy himself for the same money.

For the generation of American workers now under 45, Social Security no longer works. Tho today's over-45 worker may get a fair value for what he paid [since much of his tax was paid in the low-rate '40s and '50s], Social Security is actually tearing down the financial future of today's young wage earner.

Here are the startling facts:

• During the last 20 years the taxes we pay for Social Security have grown a staggering 800 per cent—more than 10 times the cost of living rise for the same years.

• During the same period, while the taxpayers' bill for Social Security grew from $5 billion to $40 billion annually, the average monthly benefit check went from $55 to $140—less than one-third the tax rise and always below the poverty level.

• It is now possible to pay as much as $14,602 in Social Security taxes and not be eligible for any retirement benefits at all, whether or not you work after 65.

• The household in which the husband earns $11,000 and his wife $9,000 annually must pay $32 per month MORE in Social Security taxes than the household of a $100,000-a-year executive.

• During the last 10 years Social Security payment checks have averaged HALF the maximum amount possible in any benefit category. The same amount of money, during the same years, paid to a private fund would have provided TWICE the government maximum in any benefit category.

• The Social Security restrictions against earning more than a poverty wage [$2,880 per year] while drawing benefits remain in full force until age 72, when more than 99 per cent of Americans are either fully retired or dead.

• More than half of all American taxpayers pay more to the Social Security Administration than they pay in income tax, and the percentage is growing.

How could the system, called "a ray of hope" in 1937 when it was enacted, have become what University of California economist Peter Somers recently termed "the biggest single roadblock to the security of the American wage earner"?

The answer is that Social Security has not done any of what it set out to do.

Designed to act as a "financial cushion which would encourage saving to supplement it," the opposite has resulted. The system now takes so much from the U. S. paycheck that saving is discouraged.

Intended to help the low-income worker, Social Security is instead paying maximum benefits to those who can afford not to work and a reduced benefit to those who must work.

Consider savings first. During the 1940s, when Social Security was in its early years, the amount collected in taxes represented only a small percentage of what Americans could afford to save out of their pay.

According to census and financial data, in 1942 the average American household, after all tax deductions and living expenses were paid, could afford to put $767 in the bank.

During that year, for every $100 an American could afford to save, $3.70 was being taken out of U. S. payrolls by the Social Security Administration for the retirement fund.

Then began the silent squeeze. By 1945 Americans were earning more but Social Security was taking more and taking it faster. Average household saving dropped to $740 a year. For every $100 we could afford to save, $4.30 was taken from payrolls.

In 1948 Social Security took $12.60 for every $100 we could save. By 1950 the payroll bite had grown to $20.40 for every $100, and by 1955 it was $36.20 for every $100 in household savings.

The tax that was supposed to encourage saving continued to grow faster than Americans could afford to save. In 1960 average yearly household saving in the richest country in the world had slumped to $320—a dismal 140 per cent drop in 18 years.

That year Social Security took $63.90

for every $100 we still had left. And still the tax was growing bigger.

Last year was the worst in history. Even tho the average American household was saving at slightly above 1945 levels, the Social Security Administration took $84 for every $100 we saved.

Professor Milton Friedman, a University of Chicago economist, has termed the last 20 years of Social Security "a crushing defeat for the average wage earner."

"Where is the incentive to save," Friedman asks, "when such a huge proportion of that saving is confiscated for a retirement plan a younger worker could buy for one-third of the price?"

All the examples cited include only the amount of Social Security tax earmarked for retirement and death benefit checks. Billions more are taken to finance other federal insurance plans.

What have we bought for an increase in "premiums" equal to six times private insurance increases?

"Pitifully little," says a spokesman for the Illinois Department of Insurance. "If a private insurance company attempted to sell a plan in Illinois which cost so much and paid so little, we would drum them out of the state as frauds."

Nor is Social Security going to stand still. Beginning this year, no more congressional votes are needed to raise Social Security taxes. The hikes will come automatically from now on, tied each year to cost of living increases.

Today's young worker can look forward to:

• Paying at least $1,000 a year to Social Security during the next five to six years.

• Seeing the insurance value of what he buys grow steadily lower.

• Paying the most during his middle years when his federal insurance is worth least to him.

• A retirement plan which will pay him less than half than a plan he could buy on his own, if he can afford to take the benefits.

He will become, in short, part of a generation of victims.

14.

The Foreign Grab for U.S. Land

Saudi Arabia is the wealthiest of the Middle East's oil producing states. In 1974 its income was $21 billion. By 1975 it was $30 billion. In another few years it is estimated that these oil countries will control most of the world's monetary reserves. They will, in other words, have enough money to buy majority ownership in all of American business enterprise. They are buying, and one of the commodities that interests them is land. And not only the Arab countries, but the other industrialized nations—Japan and Western Europe—also are buying into America. This article by the editorial staff of Dun's *magazine relates the extent of foreign investment in land in the U. S.*

Source: *Dun's*, May 1974.

BLINKING in the brilliant midday sunshine, a string of prosperous but pallid Bavarians marched off their Martin 404 jet one day this past winter and onto the warm sands of Marco Island, a select piece of palm-fringed real estate on Florida's west coast. Squired by the Deltona Corp., a large land developer in Miami, the visiting Bavarians wined, dined and gazed in delighted wonderment at the lush foliage, clear skies and soothing waters. And a week later when the suntanned Bavarians climbed back on board their jet, many carried away with them a little bit of Marco Island—contracts to buy thousands of dollars worth of its semitropical real estate.

Sometimes it seems that the entire U.S. is up for sale these days; the rate at which foreign investors have been buying a hunk of America is phenomenal. Germans and Italians, frightened of uncertainties in their home economies, have been plucking choice pieces of Florida real estate (except, of course, in Miami, which, as everyone knows, has already been sold to expatriate Cubans and other Latin Americans). The Japanese, squeezed into one of the most densely populated islands on earth, have been buying up expensive hotels, ranches and golf clubs in California.

The British have stepped up their purchases of top-grade real estate in such urban centers as New York, Boston and Baltimore. And now the Arabs have joined the land rush, as they seek out places to invest their swelling reserves of oil dollars, which, according to an estimate by the Chase Manhattan Bank, will reach $400 billion by 1980.

The deals seem endless. The Sebu department stores of Japan, for example, recently bought a large chunk of backwoods California from Boise Cascade Corp., broke the land up into one-acre lots and then sold the deeds across the counter. Land-hungry Japanese shoppers bought up the slices of California faster than tempura tidbits off a hot hibachi.

Meanwhile, Shah Mohammed Riza Pahlevi of Iran gave the imperial nod and bought the DePinna Building on Manhattan's Fifth Avenue for $8.6 million. The property is across the avenue from the prime location where Greek shipping tycoon Aristotle Onassis is constructing his 51-story Olympic Tower. And both addresses are within easy walking distance of numerous other high-cost properties that are owned by foreigners, including the General Motors Building, which although it sounds as all-American as the George Washington Bridge, is actually owned by British interests.

Not surprisingly, the influx of foreign investment has produced a backlash among some Americans who fear a foreign take-over of huge agricultural tracts and even crucial industries. Those fears are inflamed by reports that, for instance, German and Japanese interests are out shopping for a substantial number of U.S. cattle ranches this year. Currently, there are few restrictions on foreign investment in the U.S. (one exception: Iowa, where a non-citizen is forbidden to own more than 640 acres of farmland). But there are three bills before Congress that would seriously curtail foreign investment, and since early this year Senator Adlai Stevenson's Subcommittee on International Finance has been conducting hearings on the possible impact of foreign investment on national interests.

Precisely how much of the U.S. is now owned by foreign investors is difficult to measure. Some of the more spectacular transactions have been widely publicized, such as the British purchase of Gimbels department stores in New York and the purchase by the Kuwait Investment Co.

of Kiawah Island off Charleston, South Carolina for $17.4 million. But thousands of other transactions, most of them made quietly by American representatives acting on behalf of foreign customers, have been noted only in the ledgers of county land offices scattered across the country.

Stevenson estimates that foreign holdings in the U.S. now amount to close to $15 billion and could grow to more than $35 billion in the next ten years. But even the Stevenson estimate might be low. President Richard King of the Center for International Business in Los Angeles believes that the Japanese will invest $1 billion in U.S. real estate this year alone. President Benjamin V. Lambert of Eastdil Realty Inc., an affiliate of Blyth Eastman Dillon & Co., estimates that the Arabs will invest about $1 billion in U.S. property in the next two years, and others think his estimate is far too conservative and that the total might be as high as ten times that much.

Despite the exotic excitement that surrounds their purchases, however, the Arabs and the Japanese have not yet displaced such traditional investors as the Swiss, Dutch, Canadians and especially the English as the U.S.' biggest absentee landowners. Conceivably, foreign investment in the U.S. will soon be growing at the rate of $5 billion a year, which is roughly the equivalent of all the commercial and residential property in the city of Atlanta.

Each national group apparently has its own motives for investing in the U.S., its own style and its own objectives. British investment is being conducted almost exclusively by professionals who are counted among the shrewdest land shoppers in the world.

Following the lead of the royal family, which has long had extensive holdings in some of the highest rent districts in the U.S., British real-estate firms began to invest heavily in American real estate several years ago. They were motivated partly because land investment elsewhere had become increasingly unattractive. Canada and Australia, Britain's traditional overseas property markets, are curbing direct foreign investment and, at least according to Peter Kirvan-Taylor, a director of the English Property Corp., development in the U.K. itself has become unprofitable because interest charges are well above net rental returns, and values are falling. "But in the U.S.," he says "there is an immediate 2% income margin, and one can expect a 15%-to-20% annual increase in cash flow."

In three years, English Property has acquired over $150 million worth of U.S. urban real estate, including the Fisher and First National buildings in Detroit. Through cooperative ventures with local realtors, the firm is also building the $21-million Park Regis apartments in Manhattan as well as a $200-million hotel on Times Square. Within two years, the company plans to expand its holdings to about $500 million, much of it in the rapidly developing Southwest.

British Land Corp. has stopped all major property transactions in Britain and is now concentrating its efforts in the U.S. Within the past year and a half, British Land has spent $30 million buying up office buildings in Baltimore and Los Angeles and is aggressively scouting the country for more. "The U.S. market has not yet gone through the big rental upsurge we've had in Britain, and we believe this must come," explains Secretary John Weston-Smith. "Moreover, construction costs are rising so rapidly that it is unlikely good buildings will be replaced at anything like the current rates of rental."

London's Town & City Properties has

just acquired over $55 million worth of real estate in Boston. Trust House Forte, another major British investor, recently bought Travelodge International with 460 motels across the U.S., as well as Manhattan's elegant Pierre Hotel. And Hammerson Property in London, which already owned $75 million worth of U.S. real estate, boosted its total substantially by the recent purchase of a major block of office buildings in Houston.

While the British are generally regarded as skillful and prudent buyers who carefully invest in proven properties, even they get stung on occasion. "They are very sharp," says New York real-estate man Julien Studley. "But they did pick up one property that had been kicking around here for a year that none of us would touch. I don't think it would be fair to mention what it is."

The Japanese are widely reputed to be the most avid and free-spending of foreign investors, and sometimes the least discriminating. (Sebu is now being sued by customers who claim that the slices of California they were sold are all but inaccessible.) Because real-estate prices in land-poor Japan are so outrageous, Japanese investors in California seem grateful to be able to buy a piece of property at $7,500 an acre, even when the spread next door is selling for only $5,000 an acre. The Japanese are also reputed to buy such spacious properties as golf courses for prestige value. Hideshi Kubozono, a Japanese soft-drink manufacturer, paid $1.2 million for Dean Martin's estate in Hidden Valley, California.

Other observers point out that the Japanese often compete against one another for the most sensational purchase. "If someone from Mitsubishi buys John Wayne's ranch, someone from Mitsui has to buy William Holden's ranch," says Ronald F. Hagerthy, executive vice

president of Carlsberg Financial Corp., a Los Angeles real-estate firm. "It often makes no economic sense. They will sacrifice profits to get a larger piece of a market."

But other real-estate professionals contend that even though the Japanese may have overpaid for some of their acquisitions, the properties they have picked up are so desirable that the overcharge will be wiped out in no time by inflation and the natural increase in the value of the property. "They bought a piece of property on the ocean in Santa Monica," says real-estate man Studley. "They paid a high price—I think about $20 million for 150,000 square feet. But they have something truly unique. We always say in this business, it's location, location."

Until now, the Japanese have invested heavily in entertainment and leisure-time properties, partly at least to accommodate the swelling ranks of Japanese tourists. The Japanese reportedly own one-third of the hotel rooms in Honolulu and major hotels in San Francisco, Los Angeles and Pasadena. But when the Arabs quadrupled the price of oil and the Japanese were threatened with an $8 billion-$9 billion-a-year increase in their fuel bill, Tokyo placed severe restrictions on the outflow of Japanese cash. The Japanese these days are still eagerly buying up American real estate, but their interest has shifted towards industrial properties and real estate that includes natural resources. Mitsui has bought 3,500 acres of timberland not far from Seattle and has also invested $125 million in a joint venture with American Metal Climax Corp. to build an aluminum plant in Warrenton, Oregon.

The most intriguing, and in the eyes of some Americans, the most ominous investors are the Arabs. Certainly, the prospect of the Arabs buying up $400 billion

worth of the U.S. with their petrodollars is a sobering one. So far, however, the Arabs have been moving cautiously. And if they have also been moving secretly, the reason seems to be not that they have a sinister master plan for the take-over of the U.S. but because they want to avoid exposing themselves to hustlers. The Arabs feel that they have been flummoxed in past dealings with American promoters—most specifically, when they poured money into American stocks at the very height of the 1968 market. Still, the attraction of American property holdings seems irresistible. "Arabs have traditionally liked real estate—it's something they can understand," says Emerson Kailey, the Paris representative of Dallas' Henry S. Miller Realty company. "They like something they can see, of which they can say, 'That's my building.'"

So far, the Kuwaitis seem to be the most aggressive investors. They plan to spend more than $100 million to develop Kiawah Island as a residential resort over the next fifteen years. In addition, they want to put up $10 million for a project in Atlanta that will include a new Hilton hotel. The Kuwaitis have also bought a cattle feedlot in Idaho and land in California's San Remo Valley. They have also put up some of the capital for a $250-million real-estate project in Louisville, Kentucky.

Other Arab projects seem less definite at the moment. But a group of Arab banks is setting up First Arabian Bank and First Arabian Corp. as vehicles for buying interests in U.S. banks. And Abu Dhabi and Saudi Arabia have talked over the possibility of building a large oil refinery in Puerto Rico in cooperation with a New York-based firm. Raymond Jallow, chief economist of the United California Bank and an Iraqi himself, says he knows of several shopping centers and office buildings that Arabs have bought in California, ranging in price from $1 million to $10 million. Dr. Jallow was quoted by *Time* magazine as saying that he expects such investment to increase "twentyfold in the next two years."

A far different type of influx from abroad are the amateur investors of Continental Europe, many of them doctors, lawyers and prosperous farmers anxious to ship their savings out of what they believe to be the ailing economies of Western Europe into a healthier climate in the New World. Although a few Europeans are beginning to invest in commercial properties in the U.S., by far the largest amount of money has been poured into retirement and vacation property, particularly in Florida. Predictably, the eagerness of the Europeans has attracted the attention of some quick-stepping salesmen and promoters, who are sometimes thought to sell less than desirable property at more than reasonable prices.

Last year Europeans reportedly bought up to $30 million worth of lots and condominiums in Florida, and so far this year sales are running noticeably higher. "The limiting factor," says John Williamson, the Brussels-based representative of Florida's Lehigh Acres Inc., "is not the European willingness to buy. The market will absorb a great deal more. The only limitation is the capacity of the existing sales force."

Germans have been the most enthusiastic buyers for several reasons. They have more money than other Europeans, no restrictions on spending their deutschemarks overseas, and they have become increasingly edgy about the destiny of their savings under Socialist Chancellor Willy Brandt.

Most of the German buyers are small-time investors who purchase no more than two or three lots at $3,000 to $5,000 a lot. But one German client recently bought an entire promontory of Marco Island for $800,000, and others have invested as much as $1.5 million in Florida acres. "Wherever you turn there is business, and the surface has barely been scratched yet," says Richard Essex, Munich representative of AMREP Corp., which sells Florida real estate. "Investors are even walking into our office off the street asking about U.S. land."

Panicky Italians, trying to protect their capital from political and economic chaos, are smuggling suitcases of lire across the Alps. Although much of the money takes up residence in Swiss bank vaults, increasingly large amounts are finding their way into Florida lots. And even the steady Swiss may be getting a little nervous. One Swiss recently plunked down $500,000 in cash for his Florida retreat. "Switzerland is strong now," the Swiss buyer explains. "But anything could happen the next time there is a crisis."

The long-range implications of foreign investment are difficult to discern. Foreign competition for U.S. land, particularly by the Japanese and British, who are accustomed to paying soaring prices, seems certain to drive up the price of real estate, perhaps substantially. For Americans who are selling real estate, that is clearly good news; for those who are buying, it is just as clearly bad news. Many people may well find themselves paying higher rent.

Whether foreign investment, particularly by the Arabs, poses a security threat is another matter. One observer quickly pooh-poohs it. "Last year it was the Yellow Peril everybody was worried about," he observes. "This year it's the sinister sheik."

From the government point of view, one Nixon Administration aide explains, there are already sufficient safeguards to keep vital resources from being taken over by outsiders. The way he sees it, far from being dangerous or disruptive, a heavy Arab investment in the U.S. would have a stabilizing influence on world economics and politics.

If the U.S. did decide to restrict foreign investment in U.S. real estate, it seems almost inevitable that the rest of the world would quickly retaliate and that U.S. businesses, as the world's biggest overseas investors, would suffer most. And Americans who feel threatened by foreign competition for their real estate can take comfort in the fact that in the eyes of the rest of the world U.S. land as an investment is as good as gold or perhaps better. "Europeans see it this way," explains one real-estate salesman. "If America goes bust, then we're all going bust anyway."

15.

Egyptian-American Relations

In June 1974, President Nixon made a one-week tour of the Middle East, with a three-day stay in Egypt as his first stop. Diplomatic relations between the United States and Egypt, severed in 1956, were restored. Nixon and Egyptian President Anwar El-Sadat, on June 14, signed an agreement entitled "Principles of Relations and Cooperation," the most controversial provision of which declared that the U.S. would sell nuclear reactors and fuel to Egypt. The new feeling of good will between the two countries came about with the successful negotiation by Secretary of State Kissinger of an Israeli-Egyptian truce in January and an Israeli-Syrian settlement earlier in June.

Source: *Weekly Compilation of Presidential Documents*, June 24, 1974.

THE PRESIDENT of the Arab Republic of Egypt, Muhammed Anwar el-Sadat, and the President of the United States of America, Richard Nixon,

—Having held wide-ranging discussions on matters of mutual interest to their two countries,

—Being acutely aware of the continuing need to build a structure of peace in the world and to that end and to promote a just and durable peace in the Middle East, and,

—Being guided by a desire to seize the historic opportunity before them to strengthen relations between their countries on the broadest basis in ways that will contribute to the well-being of the area as a whole and will not be directed against any of its states or peoples or against any other state.

Have agreed that the following principles should govern relations between Egypt and the United States.

I. GENERAL PRINCIPLES OF BILATERAL RELATIONS

Relations between nations, whatever their economic or political systems, should be based on the purposes and principles of the United Nations Charter, including the right of each state to existence, independence and sovereignty; the right of each state freely to choose and develop its political, social economic and cultural systems; non-intervention in each other's internal affairs; and respect for territorial integrity and political independence.

Nations should approach each other in the spirit of equality respecting their national life and the pursuit of happiness.

The United States and Egypt consider that their relationship reflects these convictions.

Peace and progress in the Middle East are essential if global peace is to be assured. A just and durable peace based on full implementation of U.N. Security Council Resolution 242 of November 22, 1967, should take into due account the legitimate interest of all the peoples in the Mid East, including the Palestinian people, and the right to existence of all states in the area. Peace can be achieved only through a process of continuing negotiation as called for by United Nations Security Council Resolution 338 of October 22, 1973, within the framework of the Geneva Middle East Peace Conference.

In recognition of these principles, the Governments of the Arab Republic of Egypt and the United States of America set themselves to these tasks:

They will intensify consultations at all levels, including further consultations between their Presidents, and they will strengthen their bilateral cooperation whenever a common or parallel effort will enhance the cause of peace in the world.

They will continue their active cooperation and their energetic pursuit of peace in the Middle East.

They will encourage increased contacts between members of all branches of their two governments—executive, legislative and judicial—for the purpose of promoting better mutual understanding of each other's institutions, purposes and objectives.

They are determined to develop their bilateral relations in a spirit of esteem, respect and mutual advantage. In the past year, they have moved from estrangement to a constructive working relationship. This year, from that base, they are moving to a relationship of friendship and broad cooperation.

They view economic development and commercial relations as an essential element in the strengthening of their bilateral relations and will actively promote them. To this end, they will facilitate cooperative and joint ventures among appropriate governmental and private institutions and will encourage increased trade between the two countries.

They consider encouragement of exchanges and joint research in the scientific and technical field as an important mutual aim and will take appropriate concrete steps for this purpose.

They will deepen cultural ties through exchanges of scholars, students, and other representatives of the cultures of both countries.

They will make special efforts to increase tourism in both directions, and to amplify person-to-person contact among their citizens.

They will take measures to improve air and maritime communications between them.

They will seek to establish a broad range of working relationships and will look particularly to their respective Foreign Ministers and Ambassadors and to the Joint Commission on Cooperation, as well as to other officials and organizations, and private individuals and groups as appropriate, to implement the various aspects of the above principles.

II. JOINT COOPERATION COMMISSION

The two governments have agreed that the intensive review of the areas of economic cooperation held by President El-Sadat and President Nixon on June 12 constituted the first meeting of the Joint Cooperation Commission, announced May 31, 1974. This Commission will be headed by the Secretary of State of the United States and the Minister of Foreign Affairs of Egypt. To this end, they have decided to move ahead rapidly on consultations and coordination to identify and implement programs agreed to be mutually beneficial in the economic, scientific and cultural fields.

The United States has agreed to help strengthen the financial structure of Egypt. To initiate this process, United States Secretary of the Treasury William Simon will visit Egypt in the near future for high level discussions.

III. NUCLEAR ENERGY

Since the atomic age began, nuclear energy has been viewed by all nations as a double-edged sword—offering opportunities for peaceful applications, but raising the risk of nuclear destruction. In its international programs of cooperation, the United States Government has made its nuclear technology available to other nations under safeguard conditions. In this context, the two governments will begin negotiation of an Agreement for Cooperation in the field of nuclear energy under agreed safeguards. Upon conclusion of such an agreement, the United States is prepared to sell nuclear reactors and fuel to Egypt, which will make it possible for Egypt by the early 1980s to generate substantial additional quantities of electric power to support its rapidly growing development needs. Pending conclusion of this Agreement, the United States Atomic Energy Commission and the Egyptian Ministry of Electricity will this month conclude a provisional agreement for the sale of nuclear fuel to Egypt.

16.

ARTHUR A. HARTMAN: U. S.—Soviet Détente.

One of the major achievements of President Nixon's first term was improved relations with the Soviet Union. He had visited Moscow in May 1972 for a week of summit talks and concluded agreement on several matters, notably arms limitation. Events within the Soviet Union and in Eastern Europe made it evident that the Russians were as eager for détente as the Americans. But subsequent trade agreements, coupled with the steady Soviet arms buildup, soured many Americans on the whole concept of détente. On May 15, 1974, Assistant Secretary of State for European Affairs Arthur Hartman testified before the House Committee on Foreign Affairs to explain administration policy toward the Soviet Union and the advantages of this policy for the United States. Portions of his remarks are reprinted here.

Source: *Department of State Bulletin,* June 3, 1974.

EVEN A cursory review of what has been achieved in the last few years shows, I believe, that there has been a substantial and perhaps fundamental alteration in relations between the United States and the Soviet Union.

—In Berlin, the rights of the Western Powers have been recognized and affirmed, and the city is not now a point of recurrent tensions and East-West confrontation.

—In the Strategic Arms Limitation Talks, we have for the first time placed limitations on the most central armament and are now continuing the process of moving the negotiations toward a permanent and even more far-reaching limitation on nuclear armament.

— We have agreed on specific measures to prevent incidents at sea between our two navies in the first agreement since World War II between the military services of our two countries. Provocative actions at sea have diminished as a result, and technical experts meet periodically to review our experience with the agreement.

— We have concluded agreements providing for joint cooperative endeavors in a number of important fields. Building on the experience of previous cultural, scientific, and technical exchanges, these agreements now cover such diverse fields as space, peaceful uses of atomic energy, science and technology, environment, health and medicine, transportation, agriculture, and oceanography.

— The leaders of our two countries have pledged, in an agreement signed at the 1972 summit, to govern their conduct in foreign affairs by agreed basic principles. Under this agreement, they undertook an obligation to exercise restraint in their mutual relations, to do their utmost to prevent situations that could lead to military confrontation, and to refrain from efforts to obtain unilateral advantage at the expense of the other. Under a separate agreement, signed at the 1973 summit, we agreed to develop our relations with each other, and with other countries, so as to exclude the outbreak of nuclear war.

The development and expansion of economic ties between the two countries form an integral part of this framework of cooperation. The political momentum developed at the 1972 summit resulted in a formula to settle the stubborn problem of our lend-lease account, which led, in turn, to the extension of Export-Import Bank credits and guarantees needed for sustained trade expansion with the U.S.S.R. We have concluded a maritime agreement under which 40 ports in each country have been opened to prompt access by merchant and research vessels of the other. We have signed a carefully balanced trade agreement designed to take into account the structural asymmetries of trade between a market and a state-trading economy. In 1973 we concluded a tax treaty and signed protocols opening commercial offices in our respective countries and establishing a Joint Trade and Economic Council to foster the development of U.S.-Soviet trade.

A few concrete indicators demonstrate, I think, the progress that has been achieved over the last few years in diversifying our relations with the Soviet Union and in expanding contacts and communication between us.

Of the some 105 treaties and other international agreements that have been concluded between the United States and the Soviet Union since diplomatic relations were first established in 1933, 58 have been concluded since the end of January 1969. Forty-one of these agreements were signed in the last two years alone.

Collectively the bilateral cooperation agreements, although not of crucial significance in themselves, have resulted in a substantial two-way flow of ideas, information, and individuals between our two countries. Under the eight specialized agreements and the General Agreement on Exchanges, nearly 60 joint working groups, some with numerous subprojects, have been established to pursue the range of activities foreseen in the agreements. In 1973 the total number of persons traveling back and forth under these agreements rose to over 4,000, an increase of nearly 2,500 over 1971, the last year before the Moscow summit.

Let me review briefly some of the joint programs that are now underway in such fields as the peaceful uses of atomic energy, protection of the environment, and science and technology—fields that are relevant to all Americans, not simply to the technicians and specialists from both sides who actually plan and implement these projects.

In the field of atomic energy, the resources that the United States and the Soviet Union can commit to nuclear research hold out the promise that bilateral cooperative programs can bring greater results, and bring them sooner, than would be the case were each country to proceed on its own. This week, for example, a U.S. delegation is meeting with counterparts in Moscow to map out the search for a feasible thermonuclear technology that we hope will engage the leading nuclear scientists of both countries for much of the remainder of this century. In another program, a Soviet scientific team is midway through an experiment in high-energy physics at the National Accelerator Laboratory at Batavia, Illinois, employing that unique facility in conjunction with an apparatus developed in the Soviet Union and shipped to the United States for the purpose of the experiment.

The agreement on environmental protection signed at the 1972 summit is now in its second full year of implementation. Exchanges of information and experience are developing into genuinely cooperative joint projects in 36 areas, ranging from protection of the urban environment to arctic and subarctic ecosystems. Since both countries have large land, lake, and inland-sea areas, a variety of climates, and large urban-industrial concentrations, cooperative programs greatly extend the data base and theoretical

framework for environmental research in each country. Techniques acquired through exchanges can often be directly applied to ongoing theoretical studies. For example, in work now underway at the Lamont-Doherty Geological Observatory of Columbia University, an earthquake-prediction technique is being employed which was developed in the Soviet Union.

Under the agreement on science and technology, signed at the 1972 summit, we are seeking to move beyond the exchanges of delegations that have taken place during the past 15 years to the development of cooperative projects. Consultations on standards and on patent and licensing procedures and regulations, for example, are of direct interest to many U.S. corporations seeking to do business in the Soviet Union. In this area, government and private commercial interests are closely interwoven. Many of the participants on our side are representatives of U.S. firms and nongovernmental organizations such as the Industrial Research Institute.

Clearly a great deal has been accomplished in modifying our relationship with the Soviet Union. But the basic question remains: What are the dimensions of détente as perceived by both sides?

We have consistently sought to make clear that our pursuit of a relaxation of tensions in U.S.-Soviet relations is not based on any newly discovered compatibility in our domestic systems. It is based on the premise that the two nuclear superpowers must do everything in their power to spare mankind the dangers of a nuclear holocaust. In the world as it is today—not as it has been, and not as we might wish it to be—the United States and the Soviet Union share a responsibilty to minimize the danger of accident, miscalculation, or misunderstanding, to work out rules of mutual conduct, to recognize the interconnection of our interests, and to enhance communication between us.

At the same time, Secretary Kissinger has emphasized other aspects of our conception of détente. We will oppose the attempt by any nation to achieve a position of predominance, globally or regionally; we will resist any attempt to exploit a policy of détente to weaken our alliances; and we will react if a relaxation of tensions is used as a cover to exacerbate conflicts in international trouble spots. I think that the events in the Middle East last October demonstrated that the last of these principles cannot be disregarded without endangering the entire U.S.-Soviet relationship.

The Soviet Union, too, has made clear its perception of the limits to coexistence. Coexistence, for the Soviets, does not imply the right of others to seek to weaken what it calls the unity of the Socialist camp. It must not be used to erode the ideological base of socialism or to otherwise interfere in its internal affairs. Nor does coexistence suggest to the Soviets any incompatibility between cooperation with the West, on the one hand, and what the Soviets see as the evolution of the class struggle between socialism and capitalism, on the other — particularly in the ideological sphere.

However the dimensions of détente are perceived, both sides, it seems, agree that détente is necessary because of the danger posed by the accumulation of nuclear weapons; that détente is necessary not because we do not have opposing interests in many parts of the world or because our systems are not totally different — but precisely because these conditions do prevail; and that while occasional conflicts of interest will occur, détente makes possible a more rapid settlement and insures a certain restraint. And finally, both sides

seem to agree that détente is necessary because there simply is no other rational alternative.

Any appraisal of détente must frankly acknowledge from the outset that fundamental differences exist between us and that we and the Soviets remain adversaries in many ways and in many places. But at the same time, the present improvement in relations appears to be judged by each side to serve its own national interests, thus providing an incentive for both countries to try to minimize and contain the consequences of their differences, to persevere in the difficult process of negotiation, and to avoid any deliberate return to hostility and confrontation.

Our objective in the years ahead is to make the process of improving U.S.-Soviet relations irreversible. But habits formed on both sides during 20 years of confrontation are not easily set aside.

We recognize, moreover, that there is not a uniform perception in this country, or in any country for that matter, of the meaning of détente. Some argue that cooperation with a country whose domestic system is incompatible in many respects with American traditions and values can only be pursued at the expense of our ideals and moral principles. Others contend that we should take advantage of the Soviet interest in trade and technology to attach political conditions requiring basic changes in Soviet domestic practices.

The administration, as I have indicated, does not agree. We sympathize with the natural tendency of Americans to want others to share the rights and freedoms we value so highly. But if the United States attempts to make increased freedom within the Soviet Union a rigid precondition for improved relations, we will risk obtaining neither — neither improved relations nor an increased regard in the

Soviet Union for human rights. We will, of course, not abandon our ideals in pursuing improved relations with the Soviet Union. But we are convinced that our foreign policy must be aimed principally at influencing the foreign policies of other governments and not their domestic structures.

Secretary Kissinger addressed this issue in his testimony before the Senate Finance Committee on March 7 when he said:

Since détente is rooted in a recognition of differences and based on the prevention of disaster, there are sharp limits to what we can insist upon as part of this relationship. We have a right to demand responsible international behavior from the U.S.S.R.; we did not hesitate to make this clear during the Middle East crisis. We also have a right to demand that agreements we sign are observed in good faith.

But with respect to basic changes in the Soviet system, the issue is not whether we condone what the U.S.S.R. does internally; it is whether and to what extent we can risk other objectives—and especially the building of a structure of peace—for these domestic changes.

Trade is also an important component of our overall policy of détente with the Soviet Union. We have assumed that trade and commercial relations with the Soviet Union could not flourish if our political relations remained hostile. Thus, only after we had made progress in reducing sources of political tension with the U.S.S.R. did we undertake explorations in the economic sphere. At the same time, we have preserved controls to prohibit export of items that could directly enhance Soviet military capabilities. But for us to continue to insist on conducting our commercial relations with the U.S.S.R. on the same basis as during the worst years of the cold war would, in our opinion, de-prive the Soviets of an important incentive for improving relations with the United States.

Nor does détente bear any relationship to appeasement. We are not dealing with the Soviet Union from a position of weakness. On the contrary, the preservation of our military strength is a prerequisite for détente, and military strength inferior to none is the only national defense posture which can ever be acceptable to the United States. We cannot expect Soviet leaders to exercise restraint in their relations with us out of good will but only because they respect our strength, which is the underpinning of our diplomacy.

We are fully conscious of our responsibility to preserve an environment which enhances stability and encourages further efforts to limit nuclear arms. Our objective in the SALT negotiations is to obtain what we refer to as essential equivalence. In pursuit of this goal, we are prepared to reduce, stay level, or if need be, increase our level of strategic arms. That level will be influenced by the policies and decisions of the Soviet Union. We are not prepared to bargain away or compromise in any fashion the long-term strategic requirements of our security in seeking détente with the Soviet Union.

Nor can détente be pursued in isolation from our allies. To preserve an international military equilibrium, it is essential to maintain the strength, integrity, and steadfastness of our free-world alliances. Nowhere is this more important than in Europe. The Berlin agreement, which we negotiated in concert with our British and French allies, not only constituted an important stepping stone in our own relations with the U.S.S.R.; it also contributed to a general improvement of the climate in Europe, where we and our allies are now engaged in important multilateral East-West negotiations in the Conference on Security and Cooperation in Europe and on mutual and balanced force reductions (MBFR).

As you know, the Conference on Security and Cooperation in Europe, or CSCE as it is called, began in July 1973. We expect that it will conclude with a high-level meeting in the summer or early fall. Your subcommittee, Mr. Chairman, held extensive hearings on CSCE in April and again in September of 1972, when it heard the testimony of my predecessors Assistant Secretaries Hillenbrand and Stoessel. It remains our belief that nothing will emerge from the conference that could replace the security arrangements embodied in NATO. Rather, the conference should be seen as one element in a much broader and ongoing pattern of East-West negotiations that can reduce the risks of confrontation and open the way to more stable relationships in Europe. We hope, in particular, that CSCE can reach an understanding that will lower some of the barriers to the movement of people and information between East and West.

Five years after the allies proposed mutual and balanced East-West force reductions in Central Europe, preparatory talks opened in Vienna in January 1973. Formal negotiations began in October and are continuing. Both sides are proceeding from the premise that the talks should result in undiminished security for all parties. Specifically, the allies have proposed numerically larger Eastern than Western reductions in order to reach a common ceiling for overall ground-force manpower, in which the Warsaw Pact currently enjoys a 150,000-man advantage. The approach put forward by the Eastern side, in contrast, seeks to preserve the existing ratio between the force components of East and West.

At issue in MBFR is each side's perception of the crucial military balance in Central Europe. Thus, difficult negotiations lie ahead. The cohesion of the Western allies has been excellent. Both sides, moreover, are negotiating seriously, and the talks so far have clarified the basic issues at stake. We hope for further progress during the weeks ahead, leading ultimately to a more stable balance at lower force levels along the central front — an area vital to European and international peace.

Both of these important negotiations are concrete examples of our efforts to move from confrontation to negotiation. Both demonstrate that for détente to be meaningful, it must not lead to diminished security for either side.

In the long run, the stability of our relationship with Moscow will depend on the extent to which we both come to perceive the benefits of normalization as real and not illusory. This process is by no means an automatic one, given the deep differences in our ideological and political outlooks. These differences will limit the depth and quality of our mutual communication and will obviously not lead to the intimacy we would expect in relations with close friends and allies. But the changes that have occurred in U.S.-Soviet relations in recent years have encouraged us to believe that we will be able to continue to move away from the rigid hostilities of the past into a new relationship characterized by mutual restraint and a greater degree of stability — which is, after all, the goal of détente.

17.

RICHARD M. NIXON: Address to the People of the Soviet Union

At the end of June 1974, President Nixon flew to Moscow for a week of talks with Soviet leaders. This trip was not nearly so fruitful as his 1972 visit because no permanent arms limitation agreement was reached. Part of the failure to achieve lasting results must be credited to the President's greatly weakened domestic position owing to the Watergate scandal. Nevertheless, on the evening of July 2, the day before his departure for home, the President made a television address to the Soviet people on the potential offered by détente between the two nations.

Source: *Weekly Compilation of Presidential Documents,* July 8, 1974.

Dobryy vecher [Good evening]:

Two years ago, at the first of these summit meetings, your Government gave me the opportunity to speak directly with you, the people of the Soviet Union. Last year, at our second meeting, General Secretary Brezhnev spoke on radio and television to the people of the United States. And now, tonight, I appreciate this opportunity to continue what has become a tradition, a part of our annual meetings.

In these past 2 years, there has been a dramatic change in the nature of the relationship between our two countries. After a long period of confrontation, we moved to an era of negotiation, and now we are learning cooperation. We are learning to cooperate not only in lessening the danger of war, but in advancing the work of peace.

We are thereby helping to create not only a safer but also a better life for the people of both of our countries. By reflecting on how far we have advanced, we can better appreciate how strong a foundation we have laid for even greater progress in the future.

At our first summit meeting 2 years ago, we signed the first agreement ever negotiated for the limitation of strategic nuclear arms. This was an historic milestone on the road to a lasting peace — and to mankind's control over the forces of his own destruction.

We have many difficulties yet to be overcome in achieving full control over strategic nuclear arms. But each step carries us closer and builds confidence in the process of negotiation itself.

Our progress in the limitation of arms has been vitally important. But it has not been the only product of our work at the summit. We have also been steadily building a new relationship that over time will reduce the causes of conflict.

In the basic principles for our mutual relations, agreed to in Moscow in 1972, and in the agreement on prevention of nuclear war, signed last year in Washington, we have established standards to guide our actions toward each other in international affairs generally so that the danger of war will be reduced and the possibility of dangerous confrontations will be lessened.

What is particularly significant is that our negotiations have been far wider than the reduction of arms and the prevention of wars and crises. The pattern of agreements reached between us has opened new avenues of cooperation across the whole range of peaceful relations.

For example, we are working together in programs which will bring better health, better housing, a better environment, as well as in many other fields. Trade between our two countries totaled a record $1.4 billion in 1973. That is more than twice the level of the previous year. This means more goods and a greater choice available for the people of both of our countries.

It was exactly 15 years ago next month when I was here in Moscow as Vice President that I first spoke to the people of the Soviet Union on radio and television. In that speech I said, "Let our aim be not victory over other peoples, but the victory of all mankind over hunger, want, misery and disease, wherever it exists in the world."

The agreements we have reached at these summit meetings—on health, for example, including this year's agreement on artificial heart research—will help us toward that great victory. At the same time, they will give the people of both of our countries a positive stake in peace.

This is crucially important.

Traditionally, when peace has been maintained, it has been maintained primarily because of the fear of war. Negotiators have been spurred in their efforts either by the desire to end a war or by the fear that their failure would begin a war.

The peace we seek now to build is a permanent peace. And nothing permanent can be built on fear alone. By giving both of our nations a positive stake in peace—by giving both of our peoples hope, something to look forward to as the results of peace—we create a more solid framework on which a lasting structure of peace can be built and on which it then can stand strong through the years.

The peace we seek to build is one that is far more than simply the absence of war. We seek a peace in which each man, woman, and child can look forward to a richer and a fuller life. This is what the people of the Soviet Union want. This is what the people of America want. And this is what the people of all nations want.

Our two nations are great nations. They are strong nations, the two strongest nations in the world.

Too often in the past, the greatness of a nation has been measured primarily in terms of its success in war. The time has come to set a new standard for the measure of greatness of a nation. Let our measure of greatness be not by the way we use our strength for war and destruction, but how we work together for peace and for progress for ourselves and for all mankind.

Let us recognize that to be great, a strong nation need not impose its will on weaker nations. A great nation will establish its place in history by the example it sets, by the purposes for which its power is used, by the respect that it shows for the rights of others, by the contribution it makes toward building a new world in which the weak will be as safe as the strong.

In these meetings, we have been seeking to ensure that the power of both of our nations will be used not for war and destruction, but rather for peace and for progress.

Our two nations will continue to have differences. We have different systems. And, in many respects, we have different values. Inevitably our interests will not always be in accord.

But the important thing is that we are learning to negotiate where we have differences, to narrow them where possible, and to move ahead together in an expanding field of mutual interests.

One of the most important aspects of our developing new relationship might be stated this way: Just as a cloth is stronger than the threads from which it is made, so the network of agreements we have been weaving is greater than the sum of its parts. With these agreements, we have been creating a pattern of interrelationships, of habits of cooperation and arrangements for consultation—all of which interact with one another to strengthen the fabric of the new relationship. Thus each new agreement is important not only for itself but also for the added strength and stability it brings to our relations overall. . . .

When we first met at the summit two years ago, both sides were venturing into the untried waters of something new. And we were, perhaps, a bit uncertain, even apprehensive, about where it would lead.

But now, we and the leaders of the Soviet Union have come to know one another. Each of us has a much fuller understanding of the policies of the other country, even where those policies differ.

Thus, we have been able to meet this year, as we will meet again next year in the United States, not in an atmosphere of crisis, but rather in an atmosphere of confidence—confidence that the work we have embarked on is going forward.

In fact, it might be said that the most remarkable thing about this summit meeting is that it is taking place so routinely, so familiarly—as a part of a continuing pattern that would have seemed inconceivable just a few years ago.

Peace is not only a condition; if it is to last, it must also be a continuing process. And these meetings are an example of that process in action.

As allies in World War II, we fought side by side in the most terrible war in all human history. And together with our allies we won the victory. In winning that victory, the people of the Soviet Union and the people of the United States shared a common hope that we also had won a lasting peace. That hope was frustrated, but now we have a new opportunity.

Winning victory in war is difficult. It requires extraordinary courage, stamina, and dedication from every individual citizen in the nation. But in some ways, the building of a lasting peace is even more difficult than waging war because it is more complex. We must bring to the task of building that peace the same kind of courage, of stamina, of dedication that inspired us in our struggle for victory in war.

And the fact that our task of building peace is more complex does not mean that we cannot succeed.

Let me give a striking example which demonstrates that point. In the whole field of modern technology, no mission is more complex than the mission of sending men into space. The joint Soviet-American space mission planned for next year—the joint Soyuz-Apollo mission—is in many ways symbolic of the new relationship we are building between our two nations.

It is symbolic for several reasons—reasons which carry important lessons about that new relationship.

For one thing, the rocket technology developed for war is being used for peace.

And for another, Soviet and American spacemen, starting from their separate countries, will find their way toward one another and join with one another—just as we are doing and must continue to do across the whole range of our relationship.

By standardizing their docking techniques, they will make international rescue missions possible in case future space missions encounter trouble in space; thus they will make space safer for the astronauts and the cosmonauts of both of our countries—just as our new relationship can make life on earth safer for the people of both of our countries.

Finally, and perhaps more important, this joint mission—for which our astronauts are now here in the Soviet Union training alongside your cosmonauts—is being made possible by careful planning, by precise engineering, by a process of working and building together, step by step, to reach a goal that we share, and this is the way that together we can build a peace, a peace that will last.

One of the greatest of your writers, Leo Tolstoy, once told this story. A very old man was planting apple trees. He was asked: "What are you planting apple trees for? It will be a long time before they bear fruit, and you will not live to eat a single apple."

The old man replied, "I will never eat them, but others will, and they will thank me."

Our two nations bear a shared responsibility toward the entire world. And we, too, must plant now so that future generations will reap a harvest of peace—a peace in which our children can live together as brothers and sisters, joining hands across the ocean in friendship, and ushering in a new era in which war is behind us, and in which together, in peace, we can work toward a better life for our people and for all people.

Spasibo, y do svidaniye. [Thank you and goodby.]

18.

WALTER MONDALE: Beyond Détente

By late 1974 the discussion over Soviet-American détente had become three-sided. First, there were those who wished to pursue and improve on the policies established by President Nixon. Second, there were those who had serious second thoughts about the new attitudes toward the Soviets. They saw Russia getting all the benefits from détente, while continuing its adherence to domestic tyranny and foreign imperialism. Third, there was a growing number of persons who felt that détente was too limited a policy, given the new economic complexities of the international situation. They wanted a more comprehensive approach for foreign affairs. One proponent of such systematic international effort was Senator Walter F. Mondale of Minnesota. In 1976 Mondale was elected Vice President of the United States.

Source: *Foreign Affairs*, October 1974.

THE ECONOMIC and financial dislocations created by last year's fourfold increase in oil prices pose the most urgent set of issues with which we must deal. The size of the price increase and the abrupt manner in which it was imposed (not to mention the use of oil as a political weapon) smacked of economic aggression. The first task of a foreign policy aimed at enhancing economic security should be to try to get an oil price rollback. Because of overproduction and decreased consumption there is some prospect for lower oil prices. We should do all we can to encourage the trend (and ensure its being "passed through" to the consumer), but as a realistic matter we must also plan our economic strategy on the assumption that high oil prices will continue.

The oil price hike is like a huge tax levied on most of the world's economies. However, it is a form of taxation without representation, for the size and expenditure of this tax is beyond the control of those who pay it or of their governments. Most of the payments made to the oil producers are remaining in Geneva, London and New York, where they are recycled back into the world economy. Nonetheless important problems remain:

—the burden of recycling the oil receipts is threatening to undermine the stability of the international banking system;

—the recycling of oil "tax" receipts is not putting funds into the hands of those who need it most.

To these pressing issues must be added the longer-term problem of how to handle the continued acquisition of foreign exchange reserves by the oil-producing countries—an accumulation which could reach over a trillion dollars by 1980.

Today oil revenues are taking the form of short-term demand deposits in European, and increasingly American, banks, while the banks themselves must make longer-term loans for normal purposes such as capital investment, and now also to help governments meet the balance-of-payments cost of the oil price increases. The possibility of being caught in the squeeze (borrowing short and lending long) is real, particularly since no one knows how volatile the oil funds will prove to be.

Banks are also being pressed to hedge against potential exchange rate fluctuations stemming at least in part from the balance-of-payments drain of higher oil prices. This can involve extensive foreign exchange dealings of the kind that drove Franklin National and Herstatt to the wall.

The private international banking system must not be asked to take on alone this task of recycling oil receipts. Not only is it too great a burden on the system, but it also means that the recycling, the loans that are made, will be on the basis of commercial criteria when larger political and security objectives often should be controlling. Thus we find bankers understandably concerned about the creditworthiness of countries such as Italy, when unfortunately the overriding issue is whether democracy will survive or be replaced with a far Left or rightist revolutionary regime—with profound effects on NATO and stability in the Mediterranean.

To ensure that such political and strategic requirements are met, and to calm the anxieties of the international banking community, governments must now take on the task of reapportioning credit and financial resources. Acting together with the central banks and the IMF, governments must in some fashion assume the responsibility of lender of last resort. Clearly, certain safeguards must be built-in so that private banks do not have a blank check that they can cash to save themselves from the consequences of imprudence and mismanagement. But this risk is far less significant than the risk of collapse of major financial institutions and even of governments.

Such support for the international banking system, hopefully, will be sufficient to meet the reallocation problems of the industrialized countries without the need to resort to large-scale direct government aid, although such a possibility has been the object of lively debate among policy planners in Washington throughout the summer. For the have-not nations of the Fourth World, however, a substantial governmental aid effort is required.

The poorest countries—primarily on the Indian subcontinent, in Africa, and in parts of Latin America—are suffering severely from the oil price hike. It has been estimated that the increase in the oil bill for the developing countries this year more than cancels out the aid they are receiving. The skyrocketing costs of food and fertilizer are equally large. As a result, the developing countries face a total increase in import costs this year of $15 billion, which is twice the amount of all the aid they receive.

While some of the developing countries will get by, for others—notably India, Pakistan and Bangladesh—it is not an exaggeration to characterize the situation as desperate. Just to get through this year will require an estimated $3 to $4 billion in additional aid, if the lives of nearly one billion people are not to be threatened by economic collapse and ultimately starvation. The special $3 billion oil loan facility set up last June by the IMF will be of some help, but because of the IMF's formula for lending to its 126 members, the poorest countries cannot get sufficient assistance from this source.

Additional help is needed; it can take many forms, from financial assistance to concessional sales of food, fertilizer, and energy. The U.N. Secretary-General's effort to develop a special emergency fund or the IMF's Committee of 20 proposal for an IMF-World Bank joint Ministerial Committee on aid to the less-developed countries could become means to work out a package of emergency help. Moreover, the joint Ministerial Committee in particular, to be set up in October with its membership from both the developed and developing countries and strong representation by finance ministers, holds out the possibility of becoming a much needed vehicle for more long-term planning and greater support for international economic development.

Whatever the means of international cooperative action, the main need now is for the United States, the other industrialized countries, and the oil-producing countries to make a firm commitment. We have to stop waiting for the other fellow to act, and as a practical matter this means the United States must take the lead in proposing a specific commitment for itself. Once that decision is made, the logjam should break on other countries' contributions, and we can turn to the resolution of technical issues such as whether assistance will be in the form of debt rescheduling, food assistance, etc.

Even though American leadership is essential, the United States cannot, and should not, become the primary source of increased development assistance—which by 1980 should amount to an estimated $12 to $13 billion annually according to a World Bank study. Along with Western Europe and Japan, the oil-producing countries and the Soviet Union need to pick up their share of this responsibility. The oil-producing Arab countries in particular will soon have massive reserves and liquidity. By the end of this decade it is estimated that Saudi Arabia, Kuwait, Qatar, the United Arab Emirates and Libya may accumulate up to $966 billion in reserves. A significant part of this should somehow be brought to bear on the plight of the Fourth World.

The vast projected increase in Arab financial reserves underscores the fact that the oil price crisis is not a one-shot affair. Even if oil prices soften, the balance-of-payments drain will go on and on. Loans and interest will pile up. The burden will be great not only in the developing countries but also on the industrialized countries which are the oil producers' largest customers. There will be a continuing challenge to handle the stresses of recycling on the banking system and the industrialized economies.

Over time there is hope that the oil producers will put their excess funds into longer-term securities and equity investments. We should welcome such investment. However, there may be real limits, political and economic, to the amount of Arab equity investment that can be absorbed in the Western industrialized countries, including the United States.

The problem is not just economic nationalism, although there is already popular concern in the United States about Arab and Japanese purchases of American industry and real estate — and it is not hard to imagine the reactions to a Saudi Arabian purchase of 25 percent of U.S. Steel along the lines of the recent Iranian investment in Krupp. There are serious policy questions, too. For example, we regard equity investment as an essentially long-term proposition, but it is not clear the Arabs view it the same way. If Arab countries bought large holdings and then pulled out from companies like General Motors or General Electric, this could have a major impact not only on the companies, but on the stock market and the U.S. economy. We and others will want some measure of control to provide safeguards against these and other possible actions inimical to our overall national interest.

On the other hand, Arab governments will be concerned about the hospitality their investments are to receive. Although they are now in the process of taking over the holdings of the international oil companies in the Middle East, they clearly do not want the same thing to happen to their foreign investments. Given the benefits and potential risks for both sides, there appears to be a reasonable incentive to work out reciprocal assurances on how Arab equity investments will be handled in the industrialized world.

Thus the outline of a new pattern of cooperative effort can be envisioned. The oil-producing countries should be granted a larger role in the IMF and the World Bank, where today they have almost no executive positions. The developed countries could make commitments to protect the equity investments of the oil-producing states in their countries in return for appropriate assurances about the stability of such investments. In addition, the oil producers should put some of their reserves into the international lending institutions and engage in long-term aid to the less-developed countries (and possibly provide some short-term balance-of-payments assistance to troubled developed countries). Such a broader distribution of oil producers' revenues would also serve to reduce somewhat the volume of short-term bank deposits, ease the pressure on the banking system, and limit the size of equity investments in the developed countries.

The difficulty in arriving at such a new pattern of relationships and responsibilities cannot be overstated. There is an impressive lack of enthusiasm on the part of the oil producers toward helping their former brethren of the Third World, apart from Arab nations and a few others with whom they seek special ties. But there are a few encouraging signs, too. The World Bank is apparently finding it possible to borrow from Saudi Arabia, Kuwait and even Venezuela, and if the rate is not exactly concessional (reportedly eight percent), it is a step in the right direction.

If some such pattern of greater cooperation is to come about, American leadership is again essential. The United States has the largest single voice in the World Bank and the IMF. It is our overall support that reduces the risks to the oil producers who are channeling funds to the less-developed countries through loans to the World Bank. The United States is the greatest potential market for Arab equity investment, and the response of the American government in providing assurances and establishing rules for such investment is likely to set the standard for the rest of the world. . . .

The handling of trade policy will have a major impact on whether we are effective in fighting inflation and holding the line against recession. In the short run, the most urgent task is to head off increasing pressures for trade restrictions. In the long run, we need to find ways to assure fair access to commodities and raw materials at prices which are stable and reasonable.

The liberal international trading system that exists today, and which has been one of the key elements in the growth of the international economy over the last two decades, is now under serious political and economic pressure. Increasing unemployment and sluggish growth in sectors of national economies are tempting governments to control imports and to subsidize exports in selected cases. At the same time, inflation or shortages in still other economic sectors encourage export controls.

With interest rates as high as they are, the utility of monetary policy alone as a tool to manage economies is approaching its limit, and the use of fiscal policy is constrained in many countries by the dictates of internal social and political cohesion. There is therefore a real prospect of increasing reliance by governments on a patchwork of import and export controls to manage their national economies. The likelihood of turning to trade restrictions is, of course, increased in many countries by the balance-of-payments drain resulting from high oil prices.

An encouraging sign came from the OECD in July when the members pledged not to resort to such controls. However, without more concrete action on the underlying economic issues, the pledge may count for little. Italy slapped on import restrictions in the teeth of major Common Market obligations. While she faced a clear emergency and the import control measures are supposedly temporary, other countries may face similar emergencies. Moreover, there is doubt about how temporary these controls are, since the consequences of the oil price rise will continue indefinitely.

To contain such pressures, it is imperative to start up the long-immobilized trade negotiations. The Europeans and Japanese, once reluctant participants, are now eager to move ahead before protectionist pressures in their countries intensify to the point that negotiations become impossible. The Europeans want to begin serious bargaining this fall and fear that further delay, even to December, could entail serious risks.

This requires prompt action on the trade bill which is before the Senate. The reasons for the delay on the trade bill illustrate the pull between the issues of the past and those of the future on our response to the international economic crisis.

From the outset, the Nixon Administration pursued the strategy of linking most-favored-nation treatment for the Soviet Union, a matter more political than economic, to the broader economic purposes of the trade bill. Confronted with the issue of the right of Jews in the Soviet Union to emigrate free of harassment, President Nixon stalled, apparently hoping the problem would either go away or that the need for the other parts of the bill, combined with the threat of a veto if an emigration amendment were included, would be sufficient to get the bill he wanted. In other words, his Administration viewed the trade bill primarily as a vehicle to advance its détente objectives rather than as an essential means for dealing with the grave international economic issues that confront us. Understandably, a vast majority of U.S. Senators also found it appropriate to pursue what they considered valid political objectives vis-à-vis the Soviet Union by tying MFN to freer emigration.

At this writing there are encouraging signs of progress on the emigration issue, as the Executive has come to realize that the only approach is to work out a firm agreement on this subject with the Soviet Union. Such a solution would pave the way for prompt passage and an early start to the next round of trade negotiations.

A major long-term issue, which should be given priority attention at the trade negotiations, is the issue of access to commodities and raw materials. The rules of the General Agreement on Tariffs and Trade (GATT) focus on the problem of access to markets. What is also needed are rules and other arrangements providing for fair access to sources of supply at reasonable and stable prices.

The impulse to assure access to supplies is not a new form of colonialism. First, while the oil price increases are one obvious example of the kind of irresponsible price-fixing that should be brought under control, it is important to recognize that this is not solely, or even primarily, an issue between the less-developed and industrialized countries. The U.S. embargo on soybeans, the Japanese embargo on fertilizer, and widespread controls on scrap iron are all examples of steps by industrialized countries inimical to international economic stability.

Second, complicated equities are involved. Supplier countries which are also underdeveloped have an economic and moral case for an increased return on their products. Cartel pricing of oil and the efforts to build producer cartels in bauxite and copper are in part aimed at redressing what developing countries have always considered unfair terms of trade. Rightly or wrongly, they have felt that the industrialized countries set the price of their commodity exports as well as the price of their imports, and did so to the developing countries' disadvantage.

The problems the copper- and bauxite-producing countries have encountered in developing a cartel arrangement lend weight to the view that commodity cartels are difficult to achieve. However, efforts to construct such cartels have a destructive impact even if they fail; and continued inflation in the price of imported industrial goods will further stimulate efforts to raise commodity prices — if not by cartels then possibly by unilateral tax increases such as those imposed on bauxite by Jamaica.

The desire on the part of producers of raw materials to revalue their output is also based on concern over the exhaustibility of their resources. The developing countries now have a clearer appreciation of the enormity of the development task as well as little reason to believe that they can depend on anyone but themselves for the resources required. Those with finite resources are therefore particularly anxious to squeeze all they can out of them and are not likely to be very responsive to lectures on economic morality by the developed world.

Third, there may be justifiable reasons for individual countries to impose export controls in legitimate short-supply situations. However, the objective of such controls should be to allocate the short supplies equitably between the domestic economy and foreign purchasers and not solely to export inflation. Otherwise export controls can lead to retaliation, disruption in trade, and further disorder in the international economic system.

Stability in the price and supply of commodities is important if we are to deal with inflation over the long term. In comparison with other goods, most commodities were, until recently, low priced and there was thus a low rate of investment in producing them. With the surge in demand in 1972–73, production could not respond, causing shortages and large price increases. New investment in commodity production will bring the cycle down again, but this wide up-and-down swing in commodity supplies and prices is both wasteful and inflationary. It operates to the disadvantage of suppliers and consumers of commodities alike. To deal with this issue, as well as head off pressures for further cartels, means must be found for stabilizing individual commodity prices and supplies to the extent possible.

The United States bears a special responsibility and burden in this regard. We are now the major source of foodstuffs traded in world markets. Since 1971 U.S. farm exports have more than doubled and in 1973 amounted to $18 billion. The United States and Canada control a larger share of grain exports than the Middle East does of oil. The world has literally come to depend on U.S. agriculture for its well-being. At the same time, the surge in world food demand has also directly affected inflation in the United States. The temptation to resort to export controls, as we did briefly for soybeans last year, could well recur.

On the other hand, the United States also has a big stake in unfettered access to raw materials. For example, we import 100 percent of our chromium and tin and more than 90 percent of such important commodities as platinum and nickel. The United States thus has a particular interest in developing reasonable rules governing export controls, along with arrangements for assuring access to supplies at reasonable and stable prices. These rules must protect the domestic economy of countries from world inflation, and yet provide a responsible source of supply.

In addition to the clear need for new GATT rules on access to resources, and the urgent need to explore stabilization arrangements for specific commodities, there is the question of commodity reserves. At present the United States has large strategic reserves of several key raw materials, which might be used to help stabilize world prices more than has been the case to this point. However, if we move in this direction it should be in concert with others, and under arrangements through which other countries would share in the cost.

The creation of a world food reserve is urgent. This is a complex problem, made more difficult and pressing because American and Canadian reserves have been drawn down to perilously low levels in recent years. They should now be reconstituted, but if they are to form the bulk of a world food reserve (designed both for price stability and to meet famine situations) then others must act in parallel and the direct and indirect costs must be fairly apportioned.

Moreover, it is inconceivable that the United States could take on the task of world food supplier through a reserve system, while markets for American food exports are restricted and denied by trade barriers. The forthcoming World Food Conference can be a major forum for addressing proposals for world food reserves. At the same time the trade negotiations should give priority attention to reducing trade barriers to American foodstuffs. . . .

From this examination of the specific immediate and long-term actions now required, it is possible to envision the general outlines of a system of international economic security:

— A deeper measure of coordination of national and international economic policies among the industrialized nations in Europe, North America, and Japan.

— A new role for the oil-producing countries in the management of the international economy and new responsibilities for aiding stability, growth, and in the poorest countries, economic development.

— A new relationship between the industrialized and raw material producing countries assuring more stable prices and supplies.

— A more constructive involvement of the Communist countries, particularly the Soviet Union, in world trade and the task of economic development.

Not all of these broad objectives should be pursued at the same time or with equal vigor. Some of the specific issues in the present crisis are clearly more urgent than others, and for a few problems there

may not be ready answers. But the important thing is that U.S. policies be informed by a comprehensive vision of the kind of world economic system we hope to achieve.

And we must begin at once. With each passing week the economic problems we face become less susceptible to wise solutions. Progress on the urgent issues will facilitate tackling the longer range questions.

Initiatives and cooperation must come from many quarters if such a vision of worldwide economic relationships is to be realized. In particular, American leadership is indispensable. We are still the largest single economy and have the greatest impact on international trade and finance. Only if the United States plays its full part can the current trend toward economic fragmentation and disorder be turned around in the direction of a comprehensive and global effort of economic cooperation.

At present our government is poorly equipped in terms of talent and organization to handle such a role. Compared to the credentials of the Secretary of State and Secretary of Defense in the field of international security, those charged with international economic affairs are by no means the kind of strong group the United States put together in 1947 on a bipartisan basis and could surely assemble again.

Organizational remedies are no substitute for political commitment and capable people. But one clear need is to coordinate the diverse governmental organizations that affect international economic policy: State, Treasury, Commerce, Agriculture, the Council of Economic Advisers, the Federal Reserve, etc. The present Council on International Economic Policy has never been able to perform the task of developing coherent policies and strategies. Perhaps what is needed is something more akin to the National Security Council, with a statutory base and a strong substantive staff that can cut through the welter of conflicting interests and views to develop clear policy alternatives.

But there should be at least one major difference from the NSC system: the director of such a staff on international economic policy must be accessible to the Congress and to the public. The issues involved are too closely related to domestic policy to be shrouded from public view by the trappings of diplomatic or even presidential confidentiality. And the Congress must, as it did in 1947 and 1948, play a crucial affirmative role. For this it will need to exert greater efforts to coordinate the work of the many committees and subcommittees that have an impact on our economy. The new Budget Committee and the congressional Office of the Budget can make an important contribution in this regard by exerting more responsive and responsible control over fiscal policy.

Finally, an effective international economic policy must be grounded on a sound and equitable domestic economic program. Help for the international banking system or emergency aid for the have-not nations cannot possibly command the necessary support if the new Administration turns a blind eye to six percent unemployment. President Ford has an opportunity now to explain the facts of our current economic crisis to the American people and to take and propose decisive action. There may be strong differences over the right combination of policies and how the cost of meeting our present difficulties should be apportioned, but there is also a tremendous desire in Congress and the public for firm and bold leadership.

Because international economic issues bear so directly on our domestic concerns, moving toward a new system of international economic security and making it our first priority in world affairs could provide a basis for rebuilding the consensus among the American people in support of our foreign policy. The source of increasing isolationist sentiment in the United States is not some atavistic streak in the American character, but rather the fact that the ordinary American no longer sees his primary interests as being served by the current definition of American foreign policy.

If we can redefine our foreign policy and our national security to include not only the concern over strategic position and political influence but also the basic issues of inflation, economic stability, jobs and growth, and in fact make these a key concern, we will find that once again a broad consensus on our world role is possible. If such domestic needs gain a prominent place in our diplomacy, the American people will not only support efforts of international leadership, but will be willing as they have been in the past to accept short-term sacrifices in order to achieve long-range success. To meet the threat we now face to our economic security, foreign policy must truly become the extension of domestic policy by other means.

◆

This broad arrangement, in which the United States steers clear of hostilities in its direct relations with the Soviet Union but fights the Soviet Union to the death in Africa and Asia through the expedient of proxy war, was once called the Cold War and is now called détente.

Notes and Comment, *The New Yorker*, Jan. 5, 1976

19.

GERALD R. FORD: Amnesty Program for Military Deserters and Draft Evaders

On August 19, 1974, President Ford surprised the Veterans of Foreign Wars convention in Chicago by the announcement that he favored an amnesty program for Vietnam era draft evaders and military personnel who had deserted to avoid service in Southeast Asia. On September 16 he laid out the specifics of his program in a series of executive proclamations. They provided limited initiatives toward "earned re-entry" by means of alternative service, and the offer of clemency was likewise limited. A clemency review board composed of nine members, under the chairmanship of former Senator Charles E. Goodell, was to be set up. War resisters at home and abroad immediately denounced the program as both punitive and overcautious and compared it unfavorably with the unconditional pardon granted former President Nixon. They urged unconditional amnesty for those who had evaded the war. President Ford's remarks introducing the amnesty program are reprinted here.

Source: *Weekly Compilation of Presidential Documents,* September 23, 1974.

IN MY FIRST week as President, I asked the Attorney General and the Secretary of Defense to report to me, after consultation with other Governmental officials and private citizens concerned, on the status of those young Americans who have been convicted, charged, investigated, or are still being sought as draft evaders or military deserters.

On August 19, at the national convention of Veterans of Foreign Wars in the city of Chicago, I announced my intention to give these young people a chance to earn their return to the mainstream of American society so that they can, if they choose, contribute, even though belatedly, to the building and the betterment of our country and the world.

I did this for the simple reason that for American fighting men, the long and divisive war in Vietnam has been over for more than a year, and I was determined then, as now, to do everything in my power to bind up the Nation's wounds.

I promised to throw the weight of my Presidency into the scales of justice on the side of leniency and mercy, but I promised also to work within the existing system of military and civilian law and the precedents set by my predecessors who faced similar postwar situations, among them Presidents Abraham Lincoln and Harry S. Truman.

My objective of making future penalties fit the seriousness of each individual's offense and of mitigating punishment already meted out in a spirit of equity has proved an immensely hard and very complicated matter, even more difficult than I knew it would be.

But the agencies of Government concerned and my own staff have worked with me literally night and day in order to develop fair and orderly procedures and completed their work for my final approval over this last weekend.

I do not want to delay another day in resolving the dilemmas of the past, so that we may all get going on the pressing problems of the present. Therefore, I am today signing the necessary Presidential proclamation and Executive orders that will put this plan into effect.

The program provides for administrative disposition of cases involving draft evaders and military deserters not yet convicted or punished. In such cases, 24 months of alternate service will be required which may be reduced for mitigating circumstances.

The program also deals with cases of those already convicted by a civilian or military court. For the latter purpose, I am establishing a Clemency Review Board of nine distinguished Americans whose duty it will be to assist me in assuring that the Government's forgiveness is extended to applicable cases of prior conviction as equitably and as impartially as is humanly possible.

The primary purpose of this program is the reconciliation of all our people and the restoration of the essential unity of Americans within which honest differences of opinion do not descend to angry discord and mutual problems are not polarized by excessive passion.

My sincere hope is that this is a constructive step toward a calmer and cooler appreciation of our individual rights and responsibilities and our common purpose as a nation whose future is always more important than its past.

At this point, I will sign the proclamation that I mentioned in my statement, followed by an Executive order for the establishment of the Clemency Board, followed by the signing of an Executive order for the Director of Selective Service, who will have a prime responsibility in the handling of the matters involving alternate service.

Thank you very much.

20.

Allocation of the World's Resources

During September 1974, President Ford made two major addresses on the problems of the energy crisis and the use of the world's resources. He addressed the opening of the 29th session of the United Nations General Assembly on the 18th, and he spoke to the World Energy Conference in Detroit on the 23rd. His remarks brought forth immediate and somewhat vehement disagreements from many of the world's leaders, especially in the oil-producing countries and in the "Third World." They considered his statements about oil prices versus American food export policy to be little more than veiled threats. One of those who responded at length to the President's U.N. speech was Carlos Andres Pérez, the President of Venezuela. In an open letter published in many newspapers, Pérez stated the case of the Third World nations against the industrialized countries. Most of Ford's U.N. address and all of the Pérez letter are reprinted here.

Sources: A. *Weekly Compilation of Presidential Documents*, September 23, 1974.
B. *International Herald Tribune*, September 27, 1974.

A. President Ford's United Nations Speech

The nations in this hall are united by a deep concern for peace. We are united as well by our desire to ensure a better life for all people.

Today, the economy of the world is under unprecedented stress. We need new approaches to international cooperation to respond effectively to the problems that we face. Developing and developed countries, market and nonmarket countries—we are all a part of one interdependent economic system.

The food and oil crises demonstrate the extent of our interdependence. Many developing nations need the food surplus of a few developed nations. And many industrialized nations need the oil production of a few developing nations.

Energy is required to produce food and food to produce energy—and both to provide a decent life for everyone. The problems of food and energy can be resolved on the basis of cooperation, or can, I should say, be made unmanageable on the basis of confrontation. Runaway inflation, propelled by food and oil price increases, is an early warning signal to all of us.

Let us not delude ourselves. Failure to cooperate on oil and food and inflation could spell disaster for every nation represented in this room. The United Nations must not and need not allow this to occur. A global strategy for food and energy is urgently required.

The United States believes four principles should guide a global approach:

First, all nations must substantially increase production. Just to maintain the present standards of living the world must almost double its output of food and energy to match the expected increase in the world's population by the end of this century. To meet aspirations for a better life, production will have to expand at a significantly faster rate than population growth.

Second, all nations must seek to achieve a level of prices which not only provides an incentive to producers but which consumers can afford. It should now be clear that the developed nations are not the only countries which demand and receive an adequate return for their goods. But it should also be clear that by confronting consumers with production restrictions, artificial pricing, and the prospect of ultimate bankruptcy, producers will eventually become the victims of their own actions.

Third, all nations must avoid the abuse of man's fundamental needs for the sake of narrow national or bloc advantage. The attempt by any nation to use one commodity for political purposes will inevitably tempt other countries to use their commodities for their own purposes.

Fourth, the nations of the world must assure that the poorest among us are not overwhelmed by rising prices of the imports necessary for their survival. The traditional aid donors and the increasingly wealthy oil producers must join in this effort.

The United States recognizes the special responsibility we bear as the world's largest producer of food. That is why Secretary of State Kissinger proposed from this very podium last year a world food conference to define a global food policy. And that is one reason why we have removed domestic restrictions on food production in the United States.

It has not been our policy to use food as a political weapon, despite the oil embargo and recent oil prices and production decisions.

It would be tempting for the United

States — beset by inflation and soaring energy prices — to turn a deaf ear to external appeals for food assistance, or to respond with internal appeals for export controls. But however difficult our own economic situation, we recognize that the plight of others is worse.

Americans have always responded to human emergencies in the past, and we respond again here today. In response to Secretary General Waldheim's appeal and to help meet the long-term challenge in food, I reiterate: To help developing nations realize their aspirations to grow more of their own food, the United States will substantially increase its assistance to agricultural production programs in other countries.

Next, to ensure that the survival of millions of our fellow men does not depend upon the vagaries of weather, the United States is prepared to join in a worldwide effort to negotiate, establish, and maintain an international system of food reserves. This system will work best if each nation is made responsible for managing the reserves that it will have available.

Finally, to make certain that the more immediate needs for food are met this year, the United States will not only maintain the amount it spends for food shipments to nations in need but it will increase this amount this year.

Thus, the United States is striving to help define and help contribute to a cooperative global policy to meet man's immediate and long-term need for food. We will set forth our comprehensive proposals at the World Food Conference in November.

Now is the time for oil producers to define their conception of a global policy on energy to meet the growing need and to do this without imposing unacceptable burdens on the international monetary and trade system. A world of economic confrontation cannot be a world of political cooperation.

If we fail to satisfy man's fundamental needs for energy and food, we face a threat not just to our aspirations for a better life for all our peoples but to our hopes for a more stable and a more peaceful world. By working together to overcome our common problems, mankind can turn from fear towards hope.

From the time of the founding of the United Nations, America volunteered to help nations in need, frequently as the main benefactor. We were able to do it. We were glad to do it. But as new economic forces alter and reshape today's complex world, no nation can be expected to feed all the world's hungry peoples.

Fortunately, however, many nations are increasingly able to help. And I call on them to join with us as truly united nations in the struggle to produce, to provide more food at lower prices for the hungry and, in general, a better life for the needy of this world.

America will continue to do more than its share. But there are realistic limits to our capacities. There is no limit, however, to our determination to act in concert with other nations to fulfill the vision of the United Nations Charter, to save succeeding generations from the scourge of war, and to promote social progress and better standards, better standards of life in a larger freedom.

Thank you very, very much.

B. The Pérez Letter to President Ford

I have read with careful attention and particular interest the unofficial version of your speech to the United Nations

General Assembly. I hasten to inform you that your words hold a clear significance for Venezuela because our country has been an indefatigable and resolute defender of international petroleum prices over the last 15 years and has not failed to involve itself in the just controversy over the world raw materials situation in order to defend the position of our countries in respect of the so-called terms of trade. The great world forum in which you chose to present the views of the Government of the United States on the most important issues which today affect or preoccupy all the peoples of the world makes it possible and advisable for me to communicate with you publicly and directly, rather than through the customary diplomatic channel, in order to inform you of my Government's reaction to the views expressed by the United States Government.

For many decades, we in Latin America have persistently demanded just and equitable treatment by the developed countries and primarily, of course, by our neighbor and traditional friend, the United States of America. We have repeatedly pointed to the impoverishment of our countries as dependents of the North American economy. Before the energy crisis and before petroleum prices reached the levels at which they stand today, the raw materials produced by our countries were purchased year after year at prices which were never in proportion to or in equilibrium with the prices of the manufactured goods which our countries require for their development and which have been purchased largely in the United States, not only for geographical reasons but also because of the credits tied to the United States economy that have traditionally been made available to us.

Each year we, the countries which produce coffee, meat, tin, copper, iron or petroleum, have been handing over a larger amount of our products in order to obtain imports of machinery and other manufactured goods, and this has resulted in a constant and growing outflow of capital and impoverishment of our countries.

In Latin America, as in the other developing countries, we can assert that the developed countries have been taking advantage of the fundamental needs of the Latin American, Asian or African man. To cite the particular case of Venezuela, petroleum prices showed a steady decline for many years, while our country was obliged to purchase manufactured goods from the United States at ever-higher prices, which, day after day, restricted even further the possibilities of development and well-being for Venezuelans.

The establishment of the Organization of Petroleum Exporting Countries (OPEC) was a direct consequence of the developed countries' use of a policy of outrageously low prices for our raw materials as a weapon of economic oppression. In a sense, this fact demonstrates the truth of your statement to the United Nations that any attempt by a country to use a product for political purposes will inevitably tempt other countries to use their products for their own purposes. At this very time, we are seeing how the refusal of the developed countries, including the United States of America, to agree to just and fair prices for coffee has resulted in the inaction of the International Coffee Organization, which was established precisely to achieve a satisfactory and just equilibrium between producers and consumers. The coffee-producing countries of Latin America and Africa will lose roughly 30 per cent of their foreign-exchange earnings, while manufactured goods from the developed nations have doubled or tripled in price.

The world food crisis is a consequence, *inter alia*, of the high prices at which the developed nations sell us agricultural and industrial machinery and other inputs essential to agriculture and the growth of our economies.

My Government shares the view which you expressed before the United Nations General Assembly, that a world of economic confrontation cannot be a world of political co-operation. The economic confrontation has been created by the major Powers, which refuse to allow the developing countries equal participation in the search for an indispensable balance in the terms of trade. Within the Organization of Petroleum Exporting Countries (OPEC), Venezuela has not used and will not use its energy resources as a political weapon because that is not and never has been the purpose for which that organization was established; rather, its purpose was to protect the basic wealth extracted from our subsoil at prices that have never compensated for the costs of our imports and of the technology needed for our development.

Venturing to interpret the policy of OPEC, I would assure you that it is the hope of our petroleum-producing countries that an agreement between the countries producing raw materials and the industrialized countries which will be equitable and bring international justice can be reached, through a world body such as the United Nations, with a view to striking a proper and acceptable balance between the prices paid to us for the labor of the men and women of our poverty-stricken countries and those paid by our economies for the imports we require.

This policy of our country — which is supported by all parties and all segments of opinion and by our people — has been developed as part of our national education which conveys and disseminates the conviction that Venezuela is an oil country producing and selling an increasingly valuable, scarce and strategically vital commodity. We see no other way to confront the economic totalitarianism that has been coming to the fore in business and world trade and portends as much evil for the world as was threatened by political totalitarianism in the form of Nazi fascism, against which your great country fought, rendering the world a heroic and splendid service that earned the gratitude of all mankind.

The World Food Conference which FAO is preparing to hold in November will not be able to achieve its lofty objectives if we in the developing countries do not succeed in guaranteeing remunerative prices for the raw materials we produce, prices that are in the necessary and fitting balance with the prices of the manufactured goods we import.

I would remind Your Excellency that in the various international forums that have been set up to study the great inequalities and injustices prevailing in international trade, the developed countries have undertaken to contribute 1 per cent of their national product to the developing countries. This target has never been achieved. Our country is prepared, as it has consistently demonstrated, to make its economic contribution, but we demand and hope that the powerful countries will provide the co-operation to which they have committed themselves. It is our countries that have always borne the unacceptable burdens of international trade. Our complaints and demands have never been heeded, and our legitimate aspirations have been frustrated. It is a well-known fact, confirmed by figures provided by organizations of recognized and indisputable authority in the world, that oil prices account for only an insignificant percentage of production costs in the

United States and the other developed countries.

My Government has a sincere interest in maintaining the most cordial and fruitful relations with your Government, and to this end we engage in co-operative efforts in keeping with the interests of our country and the protection of our economy, particularly with regard to the management of our natural resources. On a previous occasion, on 15 July 1974, replying to a memorandum from the United States Embassy in Caracas, I gave instructions to the Venezuelan Ministry of Foreign Affairs to dispatch a memorandum of reply which is being made public today and in which my Government expressed the concerns that I have recapitulated in the present message, namely, the lack of understanding between the major developed countries, including your own, and our countries in regard to the need to arrive at satisfactory formulas for equal treatment and mutual respect in economic matters with a view to safeguarding the interests of each country in ensuring the well-being of its people.

In view of your important statement in the United Nations, I wish to place on public record this statement of Venezuela's position and the willingness of my Government to work in an international forum to establish a balanced relationship between the raw materials produced by our countries, on the one hand, and the manufactured goods and technology, on the other, which are possessed by the developed countries and are in essence the source of economic marginality and growing poverty in which over half of mankind continues to live.

Venezuela perforce takes a sympathetic view of any attempt at finding solutions to the great problems of our time in global terms, but only if a global perspective does not mean that the large countries will prevail over the small countries. It would be dangerous, ineffective and harmful for global and universal solutions to lose sight of the fact that the world includes us as well. It cannot be supposed, Mr. President, that consumers are limited to one part of the world. I share your hope and wish that petroleum-producing and petroleum-consuming countries will arrive at broad, sensible, sound, lasting and equitable agreements. It is my aim in this message, Mr. President, to convey my thoughts and feelings to you in all candor, which cannot and should not be interpreted, by any means, as a hostile reaction to what you said in your important message to the United Nations. However, it seems to me, as President of Venezuela, that I am contributing to good relations between our countries in sending you the clearest and most representative statement of our Latin American interests, which is not incompatible or in conflict with the national interest of your country or of any other nation that wishes to act within the true limits of international justice and not of unilateral domination.

You may count on the co-operation and support of Venezuela, a country with a history of long and continuing friendship for your own, in seeking to achieve the above-mentioned objectives.

◆

If there were no Israel and there were no Arabs there would still have been an oil crisis sooner or later. The era of cheap energy is over, and the adjustment will be painful.
I. F. Stone, *New York Review of Books*, February 6, 1975

21.

The Ordination of Women

For a number of years several Protestant denominations have accepted the ordination of women to full clergy status. Among the major branches of the Christian Church opposing this trend have been the Eastern Orthodox, the Roman Catholic, and the Anglican communions. In July 1974 serious controversy arose in the Episcopal (Anglican) Church in the United States when eleven women deacons were ordained to the priesthood by three retired bishops and one Costa Rican bishop at a public ceremony in North Philadelphia. At a meeting on August 16, the House of Bishops declared the ordinations invalid: but at a later meeting they endorsed the ordination of women in principle. In 1975 the bishops who conducted the service were censured, although the new priests continued to serve in their offices. The whole issue could not be resolved until the 1976 General Convention of the Church. This selection reprints three documents concerning the July 1974 ordination: 1. A letter from the ordaining bishops stating their intent; 2. A statement by Carter Heyward, one of the women involved, giving her impressions of the meeting of the House of Bishops; 3. A letter from Paul Moore, Jr., Episcopal Bishop of New York.

Sources: 1 & 2. *Christianity and Crisis*, September 16, 1974.
3. *New York Times*, November 23, 1974.

An Open Letter

On Monday, July 29, 1974, the Feasts of Sts. Mary and Martha, God willing, we intend to ordain to the sacred priesthood some several women deacons. We want to make known as clearly and as widely as we can the reflections on Christian obedience which have led us to this action.

We are painfully conscious of the diversity of thinking in our Church on this issue, and have been deeply sobered by that fact. We are acutely aware that this issue involves theological considerations, that it involves biblical considerations, that it involves considerations of Church tradition, and that it raises the vexing question of amicable consensus in our household of faith.

We are convinced that all these factors have been given due consideration by the Church at large, and by us. We note that the House of Bishops is on record as being in favor of the ordination of women. We note that a majority of the clergy and laity in the House of Deputies is also on record as being in favor, even though an inequitable rule of procedure in that House has frustrated the will of the majority.

All of the foregoing factors, by themselves, would not necessarily dictate the action we intend. Nor, even, would this intended action necessarily be required by the painful fact that we know pastorally the injustice, the hurt, the offense to women which is occasioned by the present position of our Church on this issue.

However, there is a ruling factor which does require this action on our part. It is our obedience to the Lordship of Christ, our response to the sovereignty of his Spirit for the Church.

One of the chief marks of the Church is its being the community of the Resurrection. Ours is a risen Lord. He was raised in the power of the Spirit so that we might participate, however inadequately, in his triumph against sin and separation, proclaim the good news of his victory, and occasionally ourselves walk in newness of life. His Spirit is the Lord of the Church. Hearing his command, we can heed no other. We gladly join ourselves with those who in other times and places, as well as here and now, have sought obedience to that same Spirit.

This action is therefore intended as an act of obedience to the Spirit. By the same token it is intended as an act of solidarity with those in whatever institution, in whatever part of the world, of whatever stratum of society, who in their search for freedom, for liberation, for dignity, are moved by that same Spirit to struggle against sin, to proclaim that victory,. . . to walk in newness of life.

We pray this action may be, as we intend it, a proclamation of the Gospel — that God has acted for us and expects us, in obedience, to respond with appropriate action.

THE RT. REV. DANIEL CORRIGAN
THE RT. REV. ROBERT DEWITT
THE RT. REV. EDWARD R. WELLES II

B. Remarks by Carter Heyward

As in all the churches of the saints, the women should keep silence in the churches. For they are not permitted to speak, but should be subordinate, as even the law says (I. Cor. 14-33b-34).

Now before faith came, we were confined under the law, kept under restraint until faith should be revealed. So that the law was our custodian until Christ came, that we might be justified by faith. But now that faith has come, we are no longer under a custodian: for in Christ Jesus you are all sons of God, through faith. For as many of you as were baptized into Christ have put on Christ. There is neither Jew nor Greek, there is neither slave nor free; there is neither male nor female; for you are all one in Christ Jesus (Gal. 3:23-28).

Solemnly and intently, eight of us newly ordained women priests watched and listened as the Episcopal House of Bishops voted us into "invalidity." We were not really surprised; and yet, as ever, we were appalled that men would sit in judgment on women's vocations without once even acknowledging our presence and without making any serious or persistent effort to discuss the possibility that the resolution being voted on related to "women" at all. The agenda at hand, we heard echoing through the bishops' chamber, was "order, not orders"; constitution and canons, not justice; collegiality among bishops, not women's ordination. Law of man, not law of God.

Accordingly, in the best mode of gentlemanly collegiality, resting solidly on canon law and order, the House of Bishops stated to us its opinion of our priesthood: "invalid." And so as to be sure that we do not feel that our personhood has been somehow invalidated, those who call themselves our "Fathers in God" were thoughtful enough to establish a pastoral commission to look after us in the wake of the travesty.

Dear bishops, to decry our priesthood is to decry our personhood. And we accept neither your judgment nor your pastoral commission. We are persons and we are priests, and our pastors are those who see us and accept us as we are.

The time at hand is a very human time.

The journey is experiential; the faith, Christian and existential and growing. Rather than write systematically either a "theological" or a "legal" brief today (though a number of these must be written soon), I share with you bits and pieces of my reflections over recent months and years, as they relate to this particular journey—into and through the impasse.

C. Open Letter from Bishop Moore

WOMEN PRIESTS—the phrase gives some people shivers. *Women priests!* Strange combination of words, conflict of images.

The word "priest" has a luminous quality, a mystique summoning up deep associations: The Great High Priest of some ancient pagan rite sitting splendid in an exotic temple, the medieval Grand Inquisitor sending Joan of Arc to the stake, Bing Crosby cuddling urchins in "Going My Way," the holy Curé d'Ars eating raw potatoes as he listens to the confessions of the poor.

The word "priestess" carries even more freight—temple prostitution, pagan fertility cults, vestal virgins.

These deep emotional associations and the unconscious linkages between sexuality and religion make it difficult for church people to be objective about women priests. But the time has come to face the issue squarely because behind it lurks sexism projected on the very image of God.

In the Judaeo-Christian tradition, arising as it does from a patriarchial society, the analogy of God as father has been the most natural and obvious way by which to interpret the mystery of Being: an ideal father is powerful and loving, just, yet compassionate, intimately related yet somehow set apart.

However, even the adequate image of Father is at best only an analogy. In the Bible, God is also called fire, spirit, rock, wind, and even compared, by analogy, to woman. But God as Father has overwhelmed these other images.

Christians acknowledge Jesus as divine. God's special presence in our human life was, as it happened, in a young Jewish male living 2,000 years ago in a small province in the Roman Empire. And so the Christ figure dominates Christian spirituality with masculinity.

However, all Jewish and Christian theology declares the godhead beyond sexuality, declares such masculine projections to be merely analogies.

Thus, for theological reasons, it is appropriate to begin to move God's image away from total maleness.

Thus, a woman standing before a holy altar dressed in the ancient vestments of Christian priesthood, a woman's voice proclaiming the word of God, a woman's hand feeding the people of God with the sacrament of Holy Communion will move the religious depths of the human psyche in this direction and will help us to comprehend more fully the rich variety of God's being.

Furthermore, the freeing of women in our society for the full potential of their development cannot occur until God is understood to be as feminine as masculine.

For this reason the seemingly unimportant struggle of women to attain priesthood in the Episcopal Church has extraordinary implications for liberation.

And by the same token, the depth and emotional power of resistance to this movement can only be understood by perceiving that it arises not only from theology but also from the psychic linkage of sexuality and religion.

The Episcopal Church has been wrestling with this issue in recent years. On July 29, eleven women were ordained priests illegally in Philadelphia. This ordination cannot be recognized, nor can more women be ordained regularly, until the Episcopal Church nationally (in its triennial General Convention) moves to do so.

Because of the great importance of this move it is essential that it come to pass in a regular fashion. A recent three-to-one vote by the Episcopal Church's House of Bishops makes such legislation likely in 1976.

In the meantime, the waiting candidates are under great pressure to be ordained. The women ordained uncanonically in July are under great pressure to exercise priesthood, and many people are impatient for the talents of these outstanding women to be used. Understandably, many church people are shaken by the prospect, objecting in good conscience and with much traditional logic in hurt and anguish.

Such revolutionary developments reaching to the furthest flights of human imaginings and into the deepest probings of human feeling causes great turmoil. I ask for understanding as we seek to resolve this issue with justice and compassion.

22.

HERBERT SCHLOSSER: Responsibility and Freedom in Television

During the administrations of President Nixon, the television industry was often under fire both from the public and from elected officials on a number of matters: program violence, biased news broadcasts, licensing practices, and the so-called "fairness doctrine." In June 1974 the Federal Communications Commission reported that it would be more restrained in its enforcement of the fairness doctrine in programs featuring controversial issues. In September commercial TV won a judicial victory when a U.S. Court of Appeals ruled that NBC had not violated fairness in broadcasting with a documentary entitled, "Pensions: The Broken Promise." Broadcasters felt that investigative journalism would be seriously hampered if the fairness doctrine were strictly enforced. The president of the National Broadcasting Company dealt with these and other matters in an address to the Association of National Advertisers in convention at Hot Springs, Virginia, on October 29, 1974.

Source: *Vital Speeches*, December 1, 1974.

COMMERCIAL TELEVISION has earned its way in a crowded, competitive marketplace. It has done this by recognizing—as a mass medium must—that the public has no single taste or preference. Television is many different things to different people. It comes before them variously as a source of fun and laughter; as the bearer of good news and bad; and as teacher and salesman. It is a theater for drama, and an arena for the greatest sports events. It is a political tool and a civics course. It is an art form. It is a profitable business.

This multiple personality presents a variety of responsibilities, but I want to focus on just four of them: our responsibility for the kind of entertainment we present; our responsibility to keep proper standards of taste in this programming; our responsibility for news and fairness in presenting the news; and our responsibility to preserve the free broadcasting system itself.

In entertainment, television has always faced a challenge no other medium confronts. It has to offer thousands of programs in the course of a year to engage the great majority of the public every day of the year.

In a society as diverse as ours, that means fashioning entertainment schedules that offer something to almost everyone. That is our first responsibility.

The public expects diversion. Comedy, fantasy and light entertainment will always be part of television programming. But the audience also lives in today's world, and it expects entertainment that reflects the concerns and realities of today. We have tried to respond to that expectation, and we will continue to do so.

We are not pursuing message theater. We do not seek through entertainment to create a new morality. But we must serve the millions of viewers who want at least part of their entertainment to relate to experiences of the real world with which they can identify. In keeping pace with the times, we do not intend to leap too far ahead of what viewers will accept, but we cannot lag so far behind that they leave us and turn elsewhere.

We have to strike the delicate balance between following public taste and leading it by offering new forms and styles of entertainment. Today the believability of television comedy has made instant hits out of such new shows as "Chico and the Man" and "Rhoda." And television's more serious dramatic programs, usually

motion picture features, made especially for television—we call them World Premieres—represent a new and exciting form. Many are topical. They deal with human problems and the issues of our time.

This kind of programming is increasing. It has ranged from "My Sweet Charlie" to "That Certain Summer." From "The Autobiography of Miss Jane Pitman" to "A Case of Rape." From "The Execution of Private Slovik" to "The Law." Programs like these—and I have mentioned only a few—come from creative people with something to say. They are reaching viewers who respond in large numbers, and with deep personal involvement—a real value for television and those with a stake in it.

This healthy trend has given television new problems in drawing that elusive line between mature and realistic treatments and those that may offend substantial numbers of viewers.

No matter what appears on the television screen, someone will be unhappy with it. What one viewer finds absorbing, perceptive and moving, another may find repugnant. This fact creates our second responsibility—to balance a respect for creative freedom with an equal respect for the sensitivities of an audience with a wide diversity of tastes and interests. Let me say it another way: to make sure that what we do is consistent with generally accepted standards of taste and propriety.

This is a task borne mainly by the networks' broadcast standards departments. It is an everyday, every-program job, carried out by experienced people who review every program through the production process—from outline to finished form. They make literally thousands of decisions a year on program content. They are human, so they sometimes make mistakes. But they do their jobs conscientiously, and with good will and with the interest of the audience uppermost in their minds.

Sex and violence are part of the real world and they cannot be ignored in television drama that deals with that world. The important point is *how* they are treated — with integrity or sensationalism? We insist on the former and reject the latter.

Television is the *only* medium that maintains such a comprehensive and ambitious surveillance of its content. It must do so because it is a medium that goes directly to peoples' homes.

We will never be complacent in this area. And we should not allow the occasional burst of controversy or strong complaint over a particular program to obscure the fact that the public generally finds we are meeting our obligations for standards of taste in the massive amount of entertainment programming television presents.

There is another vital dimension in television's overall service — its efforts in news and public affairs — and this area poses other important responsibilities.

The network news service reaches across the country to millions of people who might not otherwise be informed of differing views about the issues and events that concern their lives. . . .

There has been a dramatic increase over the years in the amount and quality of television news reporting and analysis and in the variety of news and information programs on the air. We have come a long way from the 15-minute evening network newscasts to the half-hour nightly news programs of Chancellor, Cronkite and Reasoner and Smith.

We have weekly news interview programs on all the networks and news magazines such as NBC's "Weekend," CBS's "60 Minutes" and ABC's "Rea-

soner Report." NBC pioneered in preempting the entire evening schedule for a comprehensive report on a single subject. We produced the first one in 1963, on civil rights. We have done others on foreign policy and organized crime. Last September, well before energy crisis became a household phrase we did a three-hour examination of the nation's energy problems.

In January we will take an entire evening to present a program dealing with the changing roles of women and men over the last 10 years.

News and information programs can evolve and grow in importance, and NBC's "Today" program is a case in point. It began as an entertainment show with newscasts inserted, and it has evolved into America's most important national forum, and its potential is still expanding.

Over the next two years, for example, as part of NBC's Bicentennial programming effort, "Today" will devote one program a week to a salute to each of our 50 states as well as our territories. These unusual presentations will include a mixture of live remotes, tape and film features, interviews, historical background and entertainment — an in-depth look at America. And a fitting one.

I have been talking about network news, but in total, the volume of local television news originated by hundreds of stations around the country far exceeds that of network news programs. And it is growing. The NBC Owned Stations in New York and Los Angeles, for example, are now programming two hours of local evening news, compared to the half-hour "Nightly News" on the network. Longer news programs have begun to appear in other major cities, and many local stations are building superb records in documentaries and investigative reporting.

Most encouraging in all of this is the fact that advertisers are aware of the growing importance of news programs, local and network, and are giving them increasing support.

News programming, in all its variety, has made the American public the best and most honestly informed people in history. And as it has done so, it has tried conscientiously to be accurate and fair.

Fairness is not a precise mathematical balance of all contrasting views on an issue. This is not possible. Fairness means treating an issue so that the audience recognizes what the issue is about and can arrive at an informed judgment. This calls for the professional skills of the journalist, who seeks to uncover facts and supply background and responsible analysis, without grinding a partisan ax.

Over the years, the FCC has developed a Fairness Doctrine designed to hold broadcasters to this responsibility. We do not quarrel with the concept of that doctrine. But we believe that fairness must be achieved through *news* judgments that are part of the daily work of the journalist.

Recently the Court of Appeals reached a decision in a landmark case. It overturned an FCC ruling that NBC had violated the Fairness Doctrine in a program about pensions. The essence of the Court's decision is simple and straightforward. It holds that the broadcaster—not a government agency—has—in the Court's words—"both initial responsibility and primary responsibility" for editorial judgments in news programs dealing with controversy. It also makes clear that the courts will not permit the broadcasters' news decisions to be disturbed unless they are plainly unsupportable. The decision emphasizes the values of television for increasing public awareness. And it affirms the special capability of broadcast journalism to inform the public.

We do not regard the Court's decision so much as a victory for NBC on one program; or for the news departments of the networks; or even for the freedom it affirms for all the local stations throughout America.

More than that, it is a victory for the people, who need—who must have—an independent and unafraid source of information about matters that affect their lives. . . .

The future for television's growth is a bright one. But we must all recognize the dangers that could come from the efforts of government and special interest groups who would shape television to fit their own design.

In many cases, these pressures come from well-intentioned people. But good intentions are not enough. As Justice Brandeis said so wisely, "Experience should teach us to be more on our guard to protect liberty when the government's purposes are beneficent . . . The greatest dangers to liberty lurk in insidious encroachment by men of zeal, well-meaning but without understanding."

It isn't necessary to dwell on the government threats to broadcasting and advertising. They include limitations on network program operations, proposals for countercommercials and the suggested prohibition of premium advertising. They should convince us that our services can be damaged, step by step, until it is too late for the public to retrieve what it has lost.

We stand with you in resisting these threats. We also recognize our obligations to eliminate flaws in our own operations and to adjust to the attitudes of a rapidly changing society. And I believe we can do these things better than the government can do them for us.

Too much of public value is at stake— for our free economy, for freedom to advertise and for a free broadcasting system — to ignore unjust threats from any quarter. We intend to fight hard against those threats. And we believe our greatest strength lies in meeting the responsibilities I've discussed here today.

In an age when our major institutions are under attack and many are declining in public esteem, the American system of television has managed to retain its popularity. That says something very positive about what we have built. And it should tell us we have something well worth preserving.

23.

JUNE K. EDWARDS: The Textbook Controversy

There was violence in Kanawha County, West Virginia, in the autumn of 1974, as angry parents vowed to keep their children out of school in protest against the use of certain new textbooks in the public schools. The protest, led by a group of Fundamentalist ministers, specifically attacked a new language arts series designed for grades 7 through 12. Many outsiders, including striking coalminers, joined the school boycott. Two schools were bombed in a rural area near Charleston. In this selection, June Kirkhuff Edwards, herself a West Virginia teacher, analyzes the meaning of the protest.

Source: *The Christian Century*, November 13, 1974.

THE STRONG PROTEST being mounted in Virginia and West Virginia against textbooks used in English classes in the public high schools of those states strikes those of us of liberal persuasion as outrageous. Never will we let ultra-rightists dominate our schools, telling students what they may and may not read. We want our children to be broadminded, to empathize with people of different backgrounds, and to experience vicariously some of the harsh realities of life that, we hope, they will never encounter themselves. As it happens, the textbooks in question (primarily the "Responding" series published by Ginn and Company) accord admirably with our views. They are relevant, ethnically inclusive and *interesting*. The students are "responding" to these books as never before, and they are lov-

ing what they read. And now come the die-hard "Christians" trying to squelch all that is at last good in a high school English class, trying to bring back the "good old days" of censored classics, traditional teaching and sheer boredom. Can we, should we, let them succeed?

I suggest that this liberal reaction is overhasty, for in fact the controversy in the Virginias raises far more fundamental questions of ethics, politics and educational theory. The protest of these angry parents against the literature books has a legitimate, perhaps even healthy, base. Their concern over "dirty" words is only a focus for a much deeper concern: who shall control the education of their children? But this, surely, should be a concern of all of us, whatever our political and theological leanings.

If the protest were merely a matter of choosing "safe" books over "suggestive" ones, the case could be quickly closed. For what books could possibly be chosen that do not contain at least some objectionable words, allusions to sex, slurs about race, religion or gender, or graphic depictions of lives lived in cruel circumstances? Think now. Can you name even one? Certainly not the Bible. Nor Shakespeare. Nor Chaucer. Nor Mark Twain with his use of "nigger" and his treatment of Injun Joe. Nor Louisa May Alcott with her goody girls behaving in traditional ways. No matter what book were chosen, someone somewhere would find it offensive. Clearly, choosing "safe" books is neither a realistic nor a possible solution.

Look more closely at the situation of our schools to see what the deeper problem really is. In the past 50 years our educational systems have grown from small one-room community centers to large and complex county or metropolitan bureaucracies. Time was when the teacher was a well-known local figure, directly accountable to the people he or she served. Today the walls of many schools are impregnably high. Often not even the teachers have a voice in determining curriculum or selecting textbooks. There is a semblance of "openness." PTA meetings sometimes *inform* parents about school decisions, but rarely are either parents or students allowed to share in policy-making, and rarely do parents insist that they be included. The textbook controversy in the Virginias is one of the few instances of open rebellion.

In an attempt to upgrade the quality of our schools, emphasis has shifted more and more toward professional expertise. Public school teachers and administrators have long envied the prestige enjoyed by physicians, lawyers and college professors, and have longed for the salaries that go with such recognition. It seems that the more esoteric the knowledge an individual possesses, the more the public is willing to pay him or her. The public schools' rebuttal to low salaries and low prestige has been to make the services they render more elusive, less easily observed. Just what do schools do these days? What books *are* the children reading? What ideas are they encountering daily in the classroom? Unless one is employed in a school or does volunteer work there, the answers are not easily come by. This is not to suggest that schools are any different—any better or any worse—than they have always been; it is simply to say that, bureaucratic as they are today, it is more difficult to find out what they are doing. The myth of "expertise" has all but taken over.

The Virginia fight against the English textbooks, then, is in reality a fight against the theory that professional educators have the right to control all decisions in a school system. It springs from the frustrated desire of parents to have some say about the education of their children—whether the parents' viewpoint be left, right or middle. In the case in question, people holding fundamentalist religious beliefs are rebelling against the more liberal-minded educators on the textbook selection committees. If these right-wingers have their way and force school boards to remove from classroom and library shelves all books they find objectionable, liberals and radicals will no doubt rebel in their turn, and for the same reason: to determine who has the right to control the schools.

The current controversy may die down, but it is not likely to die out, for the question it raises is fundamental to education in a democracy. If we are to find an answer, we shall have to consider making certain changes in public education.

First, the ethics of a compulsory school system in a supposedly free country must be dealt with. The law requires that every child attend school until age 16. Does that requirement endow educators with the right to control what each child reads and does every step of the way? Not, certainly, by standards of human decency. (Children *are* human, we tend to forget.)

It is true that a child who does not want to read a particular piece of poetry or fiction (or, usually, whose *parent* does not want him to read it) can normally be excused from doing so. But to a child, peer conformity is a force as compelling as is the law or the teacher. Hence being singled out embarrasses the child and can be psychologically detrimental to him. If compulsory school laws were repealed, or if the age were lowered as suggested by the Commission for the Reform of Secondary Education, parents who object to the books prescribed in the curriculum could at least have the choice of sending or not sending their children to school.

Yet if all citizens are to continue to be taxed for public education, perhaps this is not a fair solution. What parents are asking for is schooling *of their own choice.* This seems to me a legitimate request, and one that suggests another possibility. An educational system could provide within its jurisdiction alternative schools open to all students living in the area (within the limits set by overcrowding); in other words, a form of voucher system. For example, vocational-technical training could be emphasized in one or two schools, and traditional subjects and methods in one or two others. The open-concept school could be another. Parents and children would be free to choose the school which was most in line with their educational philosophy and career aspirations.

But this solution again has its unfair aspects, the primary problem being trans-portation. Busing children to the nearest school is headache enough; busing them to the school of their choice will be more troublesome. To make parents responsible for getting their children to schools not in their immediate area will not answer. It would penalize the poor and favor the well-to-do, since only the latter could afford the transportation costs that allowed their children to be mobile.

So I suggest a third solution, one that seems to me the most immediately practicable; namely, offering alternative courses within existing schools. This arrangement would necessitate a completely elective program, particularly for the areas most subject to controversy: English and social studies. It would perhaps mean an imbalance in teacher-pupil ratios. But just as in special education and compensatory programs, the needs of students do not fall neatly into 30-pupils-per-class divisions.

With regard to the controversy in the Virginias, I see ethical merit in setting up a class with a willing teacher for students of fundamentalist background who desire a particular type of textbook and method of teaching, even though they may be in the minority. As taxpaying citizens, as human beings in a democratic society, fundamentalist parents are entitled to the same consideration for their wishes as anyone else. And conversely, students who want to read books like the "Responding" series should have an equal right to enjoy a stimulating class without interference from people who personally object to these books. The majority should not rule in either case, nor the minority. All children and all parents have the right to demand that their interests, needs and desires be respected in the schools—especially since they have no choice about being there.

Our churches and our schools have al-

ways been political arenas, despite the
pretense of religious leaders and educators that they are not. Today's controversy over "filthy" English books is simply another move in the age-old power
struggle for the control of children's
minds. The struggle will go on as long as

each side insists on the triumph of its own
views. The only ethical and politically
practical answer to one group's manipula-
tive domination of another is the establishment of alternatives in education and
of freedom for students to choose their
own direction.

24.

Pop Art

*Pop art first drew a great deal of attention in the United States in the early 1960s.
Artists such as Andy Warhol, George Segal, Roy Lichtenstein, and Robert Indiana
used many motifs derived from outside the art world to create innovative forms and
images. By the mid-1970s pop art had flourished and become widely accepted. In
1974 Phyllis Tuchman, of the School of Visual Arts in New York, interviewed
several of the artists to learn how they regarded their achievements. The interviews
with two of the artists, George Segal and James Rosenquist, are reprinted here.*

Source: *Art News*, May 1974.

A. Interview with George Segal

PT: *What does the term, Pop art mean to
you?*

GS: I feel detached from the phrase Pop
art and yet I have a fondness for it. It's
been ten years since the Pop art movement; it's pronounced dead every season.
I look back at it with more warmth and
regard than when I lived through it. In
retrospect, it was a time of wide-open invention—a new life style—rock music,
costuming; a burst of optimism, joyous-
ness. A lot of that innocent frivolity got
displaced by violence and cynicism and
soberness and political action, assassination, disillusionment. Now we have this
law-and-order reaction. What seemed to
be heedless, mindless and frivolous in the
early '60s will, I think, in retrospect ap-

pear as some of the best work ever produced in America. Pop art is a great label
for a serious movement that produced a
lot of excellent work. Writers responded
to the strength, vitality and shock of the
new work; they didn't quite understand it.
You turn on your TV set to be amused or
shocked or entertained. Pop art did a lot
of that with its color, its size, its outra-
geousness. I never believed the magazine
definitions of Pop art. When eight, ten or
twelve talents emerge, they're called a
school. But each one is incredibly different the way Rothko is different from de
Kooning. What's called Pop art is a clus-
tering of very different individuals. And,
after the public excitement dies down,
each man is always thrust on his own resources. I never mistook that public excitement for the fullness of a private stu-
dio experience.

When you moved to sculpture, were you rejecting Abstract Expressionism?

It wasn't that simple. I accepted attitudes and ambitions from Abstract Expressionism, but I rejected the means. I'm schizophrenic in my love and hate of Abstract Expressionism. I love the ambition. I love the seeking to grasp ineffable experience. I liked the idea art could be more than decoration. I objected to the aspect of it which said. "Do it in this particular way." That meant handling the paint in a specific fashion and obeying certain restrictions—like rejecting imagery. I furiously objected to those limitations. My objection ultimately became theological. I thought that Abstract Expressionists,- in placing spirit on a high plane, accepted a dictum of the Catholic church: that the higher the plane of spirit, the more divorced it was from material, from real stuff. That was my own point of departure. I absolutely couldn't accept that. I've always tried to achieve a close connection between spirit and material. I had to include what was inside my head with actions and material from the outside world.

Why did you introduce words into some of your pieces?

The words were incorporated from the physical environments I saw: real signs. I dealt with them as words, as visual phenomena, esthetic shape, as something to silhouette a form against. It's the encounter of a person in a street at night. The fluorescent light, the dots of street lights, moving traffic, I'm forever seeing people against that imagery. So it's visual; that's the way I see things. On the other hand, restraint is necessary to intensify my vision. When I made the *Bus Driver,* my friends razzed me. I had come back from the scrapyard in Newark and said I could

have bought a whole old abandoned bus for 25 dollars. What a piece of art material! Early on, I could have used whole buses, whole streets, mountains, deserts. It's all implicit. Many of the Happening ideas have made that leap, say, to Nevada or the Sahara with Heizer and de Maria. And I think that's an absolutely valid jump. There is still so much to do. It just depends on what means the most to you.

Have Hollywood or European movies influenced you?

When I was a kid I went to the movies a lot and I suppose unconsciously learned about different characters and different places. Even now when they show a movie on television from the 1930s, I get excited. Old movies tend to get black and white and lose all the middle grays—especially when you see a nighttime scene or a train with all its smoke pulling into the station. Those were the years when Hollywood cameramen were knocked out by Eisenstein's films and there was an awful lot of art. When you see a good movie one night and a bad movie the next night, you begin to realize how high it can go as art. It was possible to tell a story sharply, probe very deeply into character, you could compose every frame, edit fast with no fat. Sure. I think we were all brought up—consciously or not—on film as art work.

Where are you now?

I still feel primitive in my work. That feeling comes from two contradictory impulses. My original impulse was to make total environments that incorporated everything, movement, smells, audience participation, the old Happening ideas. They were formless ideas at that point. As I worked, I had to reject more and more.

There's my contradiction. I had to reject the movement, the smells, the audience participation in order to intensify the quality of my own experience. I'm always tempted to use words, to introduce movement. I've combined that with film and with still objects. Then I decided to use my own body and the bodies of my friends and put them in places that I had been. That meant reconstructing them. Those sculptures depend on the quality of the empty space and the specific relationship of gestures to every physical object. The final piece accumulates on many levels answering twelve questions simultaneously. How does it hit me esthetically? How true is it psychologically? How many levels and conflicts are revealed by space and encounter?

B. Interview with James Rosenquist

PT: *What do you associate with Pop art?*

JR: Pop art is a term invented to describe a lot of energetic people working at the same time. It was a turn away from non-objective painting. The reasons for my work are not like other artists' reasons. My ideas of 1960-61 came from painting billboards in Times Square, doing window displays for Bonwit Teller and studying art with Cameron Booth and at the Art Students League. After several years of painting large signs ten and 20 stories up and mixing gallons of flesh and gallons of orange whiskey colors, I began to realize that the rate of identification of objects could be controlled by scale. Some fragments painted true to scale wouldn't be noticed until last. I had little interest in images, I was interested in the color. But it is because the images were recognizable that I was called a Pop artist. Actually, I was first considered a "New Realist." The

critics thought my work was like the New French Cinema: stark, stark realism. But I didn't know what anybody meant by New Realism. Then I was called a Pop artist because my work had things people recognized. It had popular images and it seemed to be a soft, easy term. There are vast differences between Pop artists, and our being lumped together is silly. Like Abstract Expressionism could hardly cover Rothko, Newman, de Kooning . . .

Why do you think artists developed similar images?

The imagery of the '60s may have had to do with the beat generation and the rejection of material things. Remember the abundance of material things in the 1950s? The look of the front ends of new automobiles was a vacant vision, like direct emptiness. Painting the front of an automobile was neither nostalgic nor passionate for me. I wasn't concerned with nostalgia. I had an abstract attitude toward my painting, I thought by using images that were a little out-of-date and style, you would have a little harder time being excited about them.

How did the painting of billboards affect your art?

At Artkraft/Strauss, there was a desk where I'd pick up sketches to paint. Everything was about 30 by 40 feet, and sometimes even 60 by 70 feet. I'd pick up a fragment. Once I picked up something and didn't know what it was. The boss said, "I think it's a prison picture: it must be stones on a prison wall." So I painted it to look like a stack of bricks. I forgot about it, and then about a month later, I was walking home through Times Square and I looked up at this billboard and two people were embracing with bilious clouds in back of them. Right in the middle of the clouds were those bricks! That was my part—bricks stuck on a cloud. And I thought, well, you can't mistake a brick for a cloud! Someone can't mistake a banal object. That's one reason I use them. It began that simply. I made a painting of a front of a car, a fragment of spaghetti and two people lying down, one whispering in the other's ear. People said, "Oh, that's a car crash with people's guts spilled out." I wasn't involved in that. It was really an attitude of making a picture of seeing something there and something there. It was the idea of seeing a flash, flash, flash. It has to do with the speed of identification. You're walking along the street and you're looking at someone's legs and then you're almost hit by a taxi. That's dangerous. You never see the whole taxi, but you do see someone eating a sandwich while they're holding the steering wheel. You see a sandwich, a steering wheel and somebody's legs. You go, "Whoops, I'm in trouble," and you move. It's automatic reflexes. People think they see an abstract relation. but they really don't.

Why do you use blurred edges?

I'll give you an example. Once I was asked to paint Juliette Greco's name on a billboard. The letters were 40 feet high— black letters on a yellow ground. I started to draw this O. My helper, Marty Parillo, painted the yellow and I cut in with black. The edges of the letter sort of took off down the side of the building. When I went down to the sidewalk, it looked terrible. The O looked like it was doing the rumba, wiggling like a melted eggplant. It was wrong. So I went back up and started trimming the edges to make a nice O out of it. I went down and looked at it again. It was better but it was still wrong. So I took a four-inch brush and blended the black line into the yellow so it went

from black to green to yellow. When I got down to the sidewalk again, it snapped right out as an O. You couldn't see the soft edges. The hard-edge shape had looked tough and every wiggle and discrepancy showed. But blended, the letter O just zonked. It came out very strong as a letter. I blended the rest of the letters in Greco and they really looked hard edge. You couldn't tell they were soft edge from 100 feet away—and it's the same with colors.

How did you use color?

As a billboard painter, I painted things magnified and close up. While I was painting them, I couldn't see them. I would be painting a big strawberry shortcake, but tactilely, it was just a lot of red, yellow and pink creamy oil paint. If I felt like painting a certain color, I'd take a picture of a strawberry shortcake to paint. I was really painting color using magnified imagery (I took objects and painted them in different scales: you could recognize them because they were known objects). I was always sick or afraid something would tend to be pretty. Why use light green? For what emotional reason? So I thought why not use light rose pink and make it look like terrible Franco-American spaghetti. When I was painting billboards, I painted huge bottles of Schenley Whiskey. Salesmen would come in and say, "No, we're sorry, but that whiskey looks more like orange soda. That's the wrong color. You've got to have a little more malt in that whiskey." I'd paint a 50-foot-wide glass of beer, and I'd use yellows, tans, browns and whites. The salesman would say. "That beer hasn't got enough hops in it. We can't accept it." So to put hops in the beer, I'd set the whole thing up so it was one half shade lighter or darker. It became very peculiar.

25.

Culture in America

In September 1974, Commentary *magazine and the Rockefeller Foundation's Humanities Program cooperated in an all-day round table discussion on the topic "Culture and the Present Moment." The occasion of the seminar was the 35th anniversary of the publication in the* Partisan Review *of Clement Greenberg's famous article, "Avant-Garde and Kitsch" on the relations between high culture and modern society. Participants in the seminar were Norman Podhoretz, editor of* Commentary; *writer Edward Grossman; Hilton Kramer,* New York Times *art critic; author Michael Novak; novelist and critic Cynthia Ozick; playwright Jack Richardson; and Lionel Trilling, noted literary critic and professor at Columbia University. Selections from the discussion are reprinted here.*

Source: *Commentary*, December 1974

Hilton Kramer: For me, rereading "Avant-garde and Kitsch" for I suppose the twentieth time, and also rereading Ortega y Gasset's *The Revolt of the Masses,* which I regard as a classic text on this question, what is especially striking is not so much the reasoned defense of high culture as the fact that the concept of kitsch, or lowbrow culture, remains thoroughly unexamined by these authors. It is simply assumed by Ortega and by Greenberg that kitsch or lowbrow culture is both monolithic and easily identifiable. What is more, lowbrow culture is assumed to be something a healthy culture might do without and *should* do without, for its own good.

This does not conform to my sense of the cultural realities. First of all, a vast cultural terrain exists below the mountain peaks of high culture, and in that terrain there are many levels and many kinds of accomplishment, many contending values; for me, indeed, these constitute the most interesting part of the entire problem. Secondly, the relationship be-

tween avant-garde and kitsch is no longer one of civil war, if it ever was. Ortega speaks in one place of the way in which "the mass crushes beneath it everything that is different, everything that is excellent, individual, qualified, and serious." Now, I ask myself in what sense "the mass" could be said to have "crushed" *Ulysses,* or *Les Demoiselles d'Avignon,* in 1930—the year Ortega's book was published—or in what sense "the mass" in previous centuries could be said to have crushed Rembrandt, or Shakespeare. The answer is, in no sense that I can identify or isolate.

A year before Ortega published his analysis, the Museum of Modern Art was founded in New York. In my view of modern cultural history, the founders of the Museum of Modern Art had a much shrewder understanding of where "the mass" stood in relation to culture than Ortega did. They understood, for instance, that there was a public, a society, out there that was multi-leveled in its education, in its taste, in its appetites, and that the products of high artistic culture could be made accessible to a variety of levels through institutionalization. The values of high culture, in the view of the founders of the Museum of Modern Art, did not necessarily have to be *fully* experienced in order to be experienced at some level of value. That is to say, the values of high culture were transmissible at many different levels of appreciation and attachment. This, for me, goes to the heart of the issue of high culture in a democratic society. Unlike the situation in earlier societies, the fate of high culture in a democratic society is intimately related to the democratization of power. Culture is no longer the monopoly of a particular class, but is shared and debated, and is constantly being renewed through that sharing and that debate.

Lionel Trilling: I'm in accord with you about that. I think one of the things that fails in Greenberg's essay is the sense of history. You spoke of the founding of the Museum of Modern Art in 1929. I happened just yesterday to be looking at the life of John Quinn, and in particular at the facts of the sale of Quinn's collection here in 1927. This superb collection, which could in itself have constituted the basis of the Museum of Modern Art, was let go at insanely low prices. Nobody wanted it. It was said that there was no "public" for it. And yet within a very few years the Museum of Modern Art was founded and people were crowding into its galleries. It turned out there was a public after all, and a very large one.

I agree with you too about the inadequate representation in Greenberg's essay of the notion of "low" culture. I had an interesting experience this summer at the Aspen Institute. At a party given to mark the end of a conference one of the guests sat down at a piano and out of an enormous memory began playing popular songs, untold numbers of them. Some young people began to sing to his playing. They too seemed to know every song that had been written and after a while I was drawn to join them and I discovered that I knew dozens, scores, hundreds of songs from the time of my childhood, from the time of my mother's childhood—that I knew and adored them. It suddenly came to me that I was filled with the most enchanting music from popular culture, and I thought what a splendid thing it was to be in possession of these songs, which certainly do not in any way make against my notion of what high culture is. Indeed, in an important and striking way they are continuous with it.

Podhoretz: Could I ask you to elaborate on that? The assumption reflected in Greenberg's essay is that, far from continuity, there is a radical disjunction between popular art and high art. Popular songs are especially tainted because they are written purely for money, purely for the market, and are therefore somehow not genuine, whereas real art, even if bad, at least is created out of the effort of an individual to say something to someone else, irrespective of financial reward. Would you deny any validity at all to that distinction? It is a very widely held notion, even today, that if something is done for money it is by definition disreputable.

Trilling: The relation between money and art is an enormously complicated one, of course. I am reminded of Schumpeter's terrible observation that there is a clandestine alliance between the avant-garde and the bourgeoisie. Greenberg fails to take account of this connection. He sees the avant-garde as single-minded and innocent.

As for the avant-garde's own view of

itself, and especially what you refer to as the effort of an individual to say something to someone else, it seems to me that one of the characteristics of the avant-garde, as we experienced it in the 30's, was its continuation of the artistic effort of the 19th century. The avant-garde had a profound will to impose itself morally. It wanted to change people's sensibility, to change people's view of life. I think this can no longer be said. At the present time there is implicit in the conception of the avant-garde a certain tendency to say that we are not finally serious in the old way. Irony has come in, a devaluation of clear moralizing intention, and with it that diminution of distinction between high art and low art which we are so conscious of at the moment.

Cynthia Ozick: Is it irony or parody, parody without irony? Parody seems to be the loophole, the solution, for all these difficulties with high and low art. If as an artist you don't know what to do with the remnants of high culture, you parody them; if you don't know what to do with kitsch, you simply invite it in, adding further to the parody. Take, for instance, a work like Thomas Pynchon's *Gravity's Rainbow*, or the stories of Donald Barthelme. Twenty years hence, every such fiction is going to require an addendum— complete citations of the work and tone and attitude it parodies. What seems implicit now, because of its currency as memory or tradition, will have to be made explicit later, for the sake of comprehension, when tradition is forgotten and memory is dead. And meanwhile, the trouble with parody is that it is endlessly reflective, one parody building on a previous parody, and so on, until eventually the point becomes ingenuity in the permutations of derivativeness, and you lose sight of any original objective notion

of what literature can be about, of the real sources of literature.

Trilling: Yes. I think that what is implicit in this parody, or irony, is really a rejection of the vestigial religious intention of art. It would be interesting to consider the relation of the great artists of the avant-garde to their religious backgrounds. Joyce, Lawrence, Eliot, Gide—all are somehow involved either with Catholicism or Protestantism; most of them rejected religion but also they affirmed it.

This situation no longer prevails. A hiatus has occurred in religious instruction, and it is no longer a significant act for a young man to say, I'm giving up the religion of my fathers. This is largely what is being mocked or parodied today, all those notions that consort with religion—the notions of salvation, of the shaping of a life which can be approved, and so on. At any rate this is true in literature, and I believe a similar case could be made for its being true in the visual arts.

Edward Grossman: Cynthia Ozick uses the words "remnants of avant-garde culture." That is depressing, but also instructive—it explains something. One would have thought it was the identifiable, somehow coherent, *materials* of past art, rather than the shards or leftovers, that an artist has to begin by working through if he can. This is a theme in Hilton Kramer's "The Age of the Avant-Garde," that process by which a Picasso, to permit myself the obvious example, first of all familiarized himself with what had gone before him in Western, and also in his case later in non-Western, art. His own contribution then took the form partly of a parody, but it was parody intended, and executed, with lusty seriousness. Much of parody in books today, by contrast, is sickly under its lively mask, and it is disrespectful among other things to the artist's own intention and sense of himself. The past, what he knows of it, is a mess; but so is he a mess, and his work too. It is almost as if an announcement were being made that the enterprise is no longer really worth the trouble.

Kramer: One way of putting it might be that the element of parody today has something facetious about it. The parodic impulse was certainly at work in *Ulysses* and in other great works of high culture in the 20's, but it was as you say serious in its intentions. The facetiousness we see today with regard to the artistic enterprise itself has as its unacknowledged function the warding off of any kind of moral commitment.

Podhoretz: Does that kind of facetiousness derive from Dada?

Kramer: Dada was the phenomenon that released its most explicit energies. This new facetiousness is a kind of institutionalization of Dada.

Podhoretz: I would suggest myself that the religious element still exits today but in a highly debased form. It is hard to think of a single serious novel or film of the past few years that does not in some sense invite the reader to join with the author in a celebration of their mutual superiority to everyone else in the world. This affirmation of virtue, of membership in an elect, by means of invidious comparison with everyone else, is a vulgarization and debasement of the original priestly element in the avant-garde enterprise, and is a development that has its parallels in the history of organized religion itself.

Trilling: Everybody wants to get into that particular act — I mean, is impelled to demonstrate his superiority to everyone else. But one way the sense of superiority gets expressed is through the idea that we really are not worth very much. We know we're better than others but sometimes our betterness consists in our awareness that we aren't very good. This too involves the repudiation of those notions I spoke of as consorting with religion, the Victorian ideals of "nobility," of "making a good life," of "fulfilling an ideal." These used to control literature, both what was expressed in literature and the literary enterprise itself, and they no longer do so.

Podhoretz: Still, the serious culture — again, it's hard to locate it precisely — does frequently assert its sense of superiority in a simple way as well. It is true our superiority consists in knowing we are no good, but in another sense we are superior — so this culture says over and over again — because we are living on the frontiers of human experience, and all our failures and unhappinesses — our divorces, the fact that our children are coming out badly, our alcoholism, our drug addiction, our nihilism — are all really a tribute to us, the necessary wounds we incur in living out there on the frontier, exploring new human possibilities.

Kramer: That is a very exact parody of the old avant-garde ideal — Everyman doing his Rimbaud bit and deranging his senses. I suppose it was inevitable that the old avant-garde scenario of achieving some ideal state of mind would be democratized in this way.

Ozick: I once drew up a list of the burdens every new young fiction writer has to bear, a kind of credo which seems to me

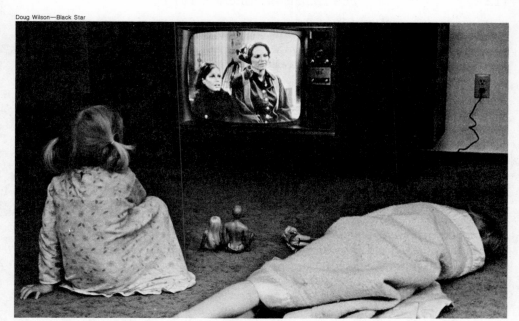

The influence of TV on children continues to be a debated issue.

horrifically idealistic in that sense. It has nine assertions:

1) That each new crop of mass births must reinvent culture.

2) That models are unthinkable.

3) That each succeeding generation is inherently brighter and more courageous than the one before.

4) That "establishments" are closed.

5) That whatever has won success is by definition stale.

6) That "structurelessness," that is, incoherence, must be understood as a paradox, since incoherence is really coherence.

7) That "innovation" is endlessly possible and endlessly positive, and that the more unprecedented a thing is, the better.

8) That "alternative forms" are salvational.

9) That irrational or "psychedelic" states represent artistic newness.

Kramer: That seems to me a perfect list. It represents the established ideal, the avant-garde inheritance. Hearing it read off that way is profoundly depressing, because it embodies such a clear historical *cul de sac.* But on the other hand I don't think we can reject the possibility that it might represent one of those necessary fictions that enable artists to accomplish something.

Ozick: It means you always dump your progenitor, though, and it seems to me that experiment in art is not the same as innovation in the human psyche; just the opposite. Experiment in art has as its motivation the extension of humanity, not a flow of spite against it. Culture is the continuation of expectations. The difference between barbarian and civilized expectations is the difference between the will to dominate and the will toward regeneration. To dominate, you must throw the rascals out; to regenerate, you have to take them with you. The point of the risk of art, especially the risk of innovative art, is the continuation of a recognizably human enterprise. I don't know how dumping one's progenitors, or finding the past useless, can be a leavening for creation.

Grossman: It can't. The list sounds like an alphabet of errors, and I don't see how anyone who strictly adheres to it from the beginning can produce art worth anything. On the other hand, a certain strong, outwardly unruly, conscious sense of rebellion, and informed discontent with what has gone before, what has been tried before and achieved or failed at, is a necessary element for new achievement in the arts of any sort, especially for productions that are not merely talented but actually masterful.

Kramer: Well, historically it can't be denied that certain writers, functioning—consciously functioning—on the basis of the principles defined in that list created masterpieces. Whether these masterpieces were also based on an unacknowledged commitment to their inherited culture is another matter. That was one of the things I was concerned to explore in my essay, that avant-garde culture has for the most part operated on two levels, an avowed repudiation of inherited traditions and an unavowed building on them. . . .

Is it possible to maintain high culture for an indefinite historical term without the recognition that there are certain classics, certain masterworks, that must be transmitted as the central body of culture from one generation to another? I don't think we are acquainted with any high cultures in which such a transmission has not occurred. To some extent, the universities, the museums, the serious journals, such as they are, still operate on the assumption that there exists a cultural class in possession of this central body of

works, but we all know that in reality that class becomes smaller and smaller each year.

Richardson: We should make a distinction when we speak of high culture between a certain attitude of mind on the one hand and, on the other, the cultural data that are used by the universities in their courses of study. There is something unchanging about the former; whereas the latter is very much subject to historical fashion. A seminar on Doris Lessing—that does take me aback somewhat; but I imagine that when Dickens was taught in the universities for the first time and Latin and Greek were dropped as prerequisites, people felt that as a bad omen too.

Kramer: And they were right.

Richardson: That is another case that could be argued.

Kramer: No, I agree, modifications can occur, and should occur, in our notion of what the central body of masterworks consists of, but the point is it shouldn't be absolutely fluid.

Now, I myself am much more disturbed about seminars on John Ford than I am about seminars on Doris Lessing.

Podhoretz: That's your visual parochialism.

Kramer: But Doris Lessing is still what you might call a "reading experience." Her books deal with serious and often difficult experience.

Richardson: The point I'm trying to make is that high culture is not a series of works that must be read, listened to, or looked at.

Ozick: Why isn't it?

Kramer: Whether it is or not, can it exist without that body of works?

Richardson: I should have said that it's not a coextensive definition: you don't say high culture and then list every great work you approve of and rest on that. Culture then becomes nothing but a question of individual biography.

If there is anything like a definition of high culture, then it must be found in a quality of mind, a spiritual need for investigation that need not be linked to any particular work of art, or any particular style, or any particular mode of expression. It is this desire to study life intensely that needs defending from vulgarization. This is the attitude that I think is threatened in a democratic society, is in danger of becoming — what shall I say? — overcome by the notion of polls, publicity, of referenda, things like that.

Culture is being catered to in our democracy, but what is being produced except some satisfaction over the expense involved? So far as drama is concerned, public support of culture has put up about twenty-five terrible repertory companies throughout the country. But what else?

Ozick: If the repertory companies are awful, and the high cultural spirit is absent, might that not be related in some way to the loss of that attitude in the universities which required Chaucer, Milton, and Shakespeare? It is true that Dickens was once regarded as a popular frivolity, and it took a few generations for his work to achieve classic stature, but that was simply a matter of waiting for posterity to seize its perspective, it did not signify that the canon of masterpieces was closed. The

canon is always open; it's a question of accretion and time. But there has to be a link, doesn't there, between an education that stresses the spiritual attitude of investigation and the consequences of that attitude in the world of artistic creation? If there are undistinguished repertory companies and subliterate poets, it means somebody isn't getting educated. . . .

Trilling: I would like to ask a question which I think a few of us have already adumbrated. What is the basis of our society's belief that art is so important? What do we expect of it? Only good, it seems. I am quite open to the idea that art can produce bad effects as well as good ones, even that what might be called good art can produce bad effects.

I am not altogether comfortable seeing the great number of students who are committed to literature and who read the kinds of things they do read — my sense is that something may be happening to their personal fiber which I am not sure I like, and I often feel that I would much rather see them doing history, or philosophy, or anthropology, or politics — almost any humane subject rather than literature.

To the question I referred to, why art is thought to be important and beneficent, the answer commonly given is that art makes one more conscious, more aware, more sensitive, and that the more conscious, aware, and sensitive one is, the more sympathetic and responsive one is to other people. I am not sure that art actually does have this effect, and I would like to hear why, apart from its usefulness as entertainment, art should be supported.

Podhoretz: I'm delighted to see you turning from Dostoevsky to Tolstoy — this is a new development in the intellectual growth of Lionel Trilling.

Trilling: Oh, this is old with me.

Podhoretz: But it *is* very Tolstoyan, this question. Can anyone answer it?

Richardson: What can one say? It is an open point. Art certainly can have bad effects, depending upon the person judging those effects, of course. You can say that certain books have not made life easier for a lot of people. I think you can say that the whole artistic experience doesn't make life easier for anybody.

Kramer: The assumption has been that the great value that is placed on art, apart from its value as a pastime, as an entertainment, is that it puts one in a more profound possession of reality. As far as I'm concerned, that is sufficient defense.

Trilling: That's what it does ideally. That is what we, when we deal with it as part of education, say we believe. But I wonder whether it is not in fact *blinding* people to reality, making them concerned only with themselves, creating such self-pity, such self-regard, that they can't respond to reality. . . .

Novak: High culture is terribly important, but we also need to find ways of strengthening popular cultures, which are presently being wiped out in large part by television and cinema. I am thinking now of that still great majority that does not go to college—that shares, now, in weaker and weaker cultural networks of any sort. Young children growing up are already learning a form of rebellion and discontent from the television set right in the living room. Parental authority, the authority of the mind, of the community, no longer exist—there is a nihilism in working-class neighborhoods that is frightening. The children in one community I know tied a child to a tree and left him there; another time they threw rocks at a child they had tied to a tree. Few parents can compete with the power of the images of the media, and if the media version of reality wins out on the level of the working class and the non-university class, we will have very deep trouble no matter how strong a high culture we have. Culture is ultimately of a piece.

Trilling: Why do you assume that it's nihilism that television is offering? It seems to me that one of the things we have to be aware of is the "virtue" that is promulgated by the media and the popular culture. You get a degree of cultural sophistication among masses of people today which, if I recall correctly, is exactly what we were trying to achieve in Columbia College thirty years ago, that readiness to criticize people in authority, that sense of the contradictions in culture. All this is being made available to everybody and is very quickly picked up.

Archibald Cox, in the opening sentence of his report on the Columbia disturbance in 1968, stated that today's younger generation, in the opinion of everyone, is the most gifted, the most intelligent, the most responsible generation the world has ever known. Where did that "intelligence" and "responsibility" come from? It came at a very early age, from the media. It is, to be sure, a false intelligence, it is a false responsibility, but it certainly has all the appearance of the real thing.

If you watch Dr. Welby, or Kojak, or Cannon, you will be filled with the highest ideals. You will learn tolerance and understanding, you will learn that the conventional way of doing things is not right. Nothing, it seems, is easier than to hold those ideals we fought so hard for in the 30's. Nothing is more self-justifying.

We needn't now take time to consider that nothing stops one's further development more effectually than this ready-made self-justification. But with the appearance of intelligence and responsibility so facilely supplied by television, who needs literature?

Podhoretz: That's an argument against education.

Trilling: In a certain sense I am arguing against education.

Kramer: No, no, quite the contrary—it goes again to prove that literature is a more profound mode of moral instruction than television.

Trilling: It depends. Literature can be a more profound mode of instruction than television can probably ever be. But not necessarily.

Kramer: Not necessarily? Well, I think I would even say necessarily.

Novak: What I want to plead for, in any case, is a greater concentration of intellectual resources in the criticism of these media. They carry cultural functions that other agencies are losing.

Kramer: That is an interesting point. There really never has existed a sustained criticism of television with any intellectual force to it. The New Yorker, for example, has tried over and over again to induce gifted writers of one kind or another to address themselves to television and the results have been abortive. One of the reasons for this has to do with something that is endemic to the higher criticism of mass culture, which is that it tends to become simply another mode of the consumption of mass culture. A great

many of the intellectuals who wrote in the old days about mass culture in Commentary or Partisan Review were really disguising their appetite for it.

Podhoretz: Some of us were bragging about our appetite for it.

Kramer: That was a later development. I think, though, there is something about the serious analysis of mass culture that is extremely difficult to sustain inherently, because in a sense mass culture doesn't offer an object for criticism. It offers a Zeitgeist, not the kind of object that the critical intelligence is formed to analyze.

Novak: I don't think it is the fault of the mass culture in the case of television. I have come to believe that there are limitations in the medium. That is, there are certain things you cannot do in film, or video, that are terribly important to human relations. These media deal poorly with complicated human involvements and emotions. A novel can disentangle these; they can't be grasped by looking in from the outside, no matter how skillfully. What the camera tends to do is make up with intensity for what it lacks in subtlety and nuance and irony. We spoke about discontinuity. One such discontinuity, in sensibility and in intellectual habit, I have noticed in my university students, whose experience has been formed by television and by movies. There is no way to break through and open them up to the world of literature —or, in my case, the world of philosophy —unless one can locate and define the limitations in their own modes of perception.

If you ignore the problem, or are overawed by it—a few years ago this rather new power burst upon us and critics were overawed by its new idiom, and inflated its significance—you cripple yourself from the outset.

Ozick: In other words, you want to use criticism of the visual media as a bridge, as a stepping stone, into literature?

Novak: You have to grasp the limitations of the media if you are going to teach philosophy or literature.

Kramer: So you want a certain kind of intelligence-gathering about the effect of the popular media on the minds of the young.

Novak: No. I simply want sensitive and subtle critics to reflect on the impact of the popular media on *them.*

Kramer: But their criticisms are not going to reach this audience that is being damaged.

Novak: Not in the first place, but we have to begin somewhere and there is not now in existence a protracted criticism of television—I mean, longer than what you get in the daily paper.

Grossman: Isn't *Sesame Street* the most important example of the thing you are talking about? Perhaps it is the most important television show in America. If we are discussing the future of high culture and literacy, we have to take *Sesame Street* and its spin-offs into account. Even in public schools that are not considered advanced or forward-looking, the techniques, not to say mystique, of *Sesame Street* become ubiquitous. Maybe that is not worth crying about. Anyway, nothing could be more elementary, basic, than this fact: letters are supposed to come easy, now. I wonder if the next generations will be able or will even wish to or feel a need to read books that are as tough and hard as the ones we are talking about.

Podhoretz: I have to reverse ground here. The facts of the case, once again, are that far from resulting in a decline in reading, television is highly correlated with an increase in reading. You can say nobody is appreciating or understanding what he reads, but the predictions that people would read less as a result of being brought up on television are proving to be false. More books are bought, and presumably read, than before television came on the scene—all kinds of books. Moreover, books are now available in places in America that used to be innocent of their presence. If there were any conclusion to be drawn from the effect of television on literacy, it would be that television has increased literacy and increased the appetite for books, not the other way around. I can testify to this personally as a parent who has raised several children in the age of television.

In general, the apocalyptic views of the effects of television seem to me highly exaggerated. What television has done, however, has been to make us one culture, one country, for the first time. Neither radio nor the movies could effectively unite the country, but now everybody is more or less aware of the same things at the same time. This has had profound political consequences, in setting the agenda of important problems. It has undoubtedly also had profound cultural consequences, in the transmission of attitudes, ways of life, and values. It is no accident that the media have become such a major issue. Spiro Agnew did not invent that issue, it arose because in fact something new has happened: there are no quarantined communities or protected enclaves any longer. Everybody now lives in the same country.

1975

26.

EDWARD S. HERMAN: The United States and the Third World
Economies

*The inflationary recession of 1974-75 resulted in an industrial slowdown in the
United States, Western Europe, and Japan; but the blow it dealt the underdeveloped
countries was far more severe. The one billion poorest people of Asia and Africa
found the economies of their areas reduced to zero growth at best, while some places
actually lost ground. They were victims of an unfavorable trade balance as prices for
their natural resources (apart from oil) dropped, while the cost of imported
manufactured goods rose sharply. This pattern of rich versus poor nations divided
the world into two blocs, with the great majority of the planet's population in the
poorer societies. And the Communist bloc nations, whether industrialized or not,
tended to side with the less-developed countries in international disputes. The
following selection, part of a longer article on income redistribution, was written by
Edward S. Herman of the Wharton School of Economics at the University of
Pennsylvania.*

Source: *Commonweal*, January 3, 1975. "The Income Counter-Revolution."

THE "ONE WORLD" of Second World War
euphoria has obviously not materialized.
Among the many ways of looking at the
fractured world of our day, one that has
become commonplace is the division between the "rich," "developed" nations
and the "poor," "under" or "less developed" countries (LDCs) of the "Third
World." Contrary to the expectations of
many, this division has sharpened since
1945 as the rich countries have, on average, grown faster in per capita incomes
than the poor lands. (The expectation of
a shrinking differential was based in part
on the belief that Western technology
could work productivity miracles in the
now "aware" Third World, a belief which
reflected a failure to grasp the nature and
intractability of the institutional obstacles
to development widely prevalent in the
LDCs.)

Gunnar Myrdal wrote in 1968 that "it
is abundantly clear that the discrepancy
between the economic well-being of the
haves and the have-nots, so far as South
Asia is concerned, is rapidly widening."

Data extending beyound Asia on rates of growth of real per capita income for the period 1950-1971 indicate that the rich countries of the "free world" continue to grow somewhat faster than the poor. Given the enormous initial income discrepancies between rich and poor, this means that the absolute income gains in the rich countries are huge, and steadily widening, relative to those in the poor countries: the 3.6 percent rate of per capita real gain for the developed countries, 1960-1971, applied to the 1959 per capita U.S. figure of $2,830, represents a per person increment of $102 a year; the 3.1 percent rate for LDCs, applied to India's base of about $80, represents an increment of $2.48. It will be noted that the U.S. per person *increment* exceeds the original *total* per capita income figure for India.

There is little basis for optimism that increasing world inequality will be reversed in the near future. It is true that oil profits have bolstered the position of some relatively underdeveloped countries, such as Iran, Saudi Arabia and Indonesia, but others have suffered in the same process. Among them oil importers like India and Pakistan have been unable even to sustain their unsatisfactory growth rates of earlier years and show signs of stagnation and even retrogression. The worldwide rise in the price of food and other raw materials has had a mixed impact on poor countries, depending on their structure of imports and exports, but on balance it has been unfavorable. And its damaging effects have been greatest on the poorest (India, Pakistan, Sub-Saharan Africa), often suffering from elemental hunger and dependent on a shrinking external largesse.

A few of the totalitarian free enterprise LDCs such as Brazil, Iran, Indonesia and South Korea have grown rapidly in recent years, but by a process combining the turning over of a large part of development to external interests and ignoring or deliberately depressing the condition of the underlying population. (The income distribution effects of this phenomenon are discussed in the next section.) The military plays a large role in these societies and absorbs a large fraction of aid plus increments to social output. The recent huge arms sale arranged by the Pentagon with Iran, a country with a 70 percent illiteracy rate, involving $2.5 billion in advanced planes, helicopters and missiles, is a reminder of the sobering fact that arms purchases in the Third World are growing twice as rapidly as its overall economic growth. This not only involves huge direct waste that these countries cannot afford, it also has an obvious sociopolitical component, helping to keep the lid on any internal challenges to the rule of traditional elites. As U.S. direct intervention recedes, in response to the impact of Vietnam, the capacity of neo-colonial elites to protect themselves from their own people must be enlarged accordingly.

In sum, as a recent study by Irving Kravis notes, there is a "growing polarization of income levels in the world," with three-fifths of the human race having per capita incomes of $310 or less a year and the gap between rich and poor nations increasing. "The inescapable conclusion," says Kravis, "is that the benefits of economic progress have been confined to a minority of the world's population." And by and large the trade-investment-aid package offered by the West has provided neither adequate growth nor minimally humane social orders among Free World LDCs.

Not only has growth been slow on the average among the poor countries, income distribution within them has tended to become more unequal. In their recent invaluable study of this subject, *Economic Growth and Social Equity in Developing Countries*, Irma Adelman and Cynthia Taft Morris state in their preface that

> The results of our analyses came as a shock to us ... we had shared the prevailing view that economic growth was economically beneficial to most nations. We had also not greatly questioned the relevance today of the historical association of successful economic growth with the spread of parliamentary democracy. Our results proved to be at variance with our preconceptions.

On the basis of an elaborate analysis of data for 43 LDCs, they found that,

> The position of the poorest 60 percent typically worsens, both relatively and absolutely, when an initial spurt of narrowly based dualistic growth is imposed on an agrarian subsistence economy ... The gains of the top 5 percent are particularly great in very low income countries where a sharply dualistic structure is associated with political and economic domination by traditional or expatriate elites.

The idea of temporary regression in mass welfare at some stage in the growth process had been suggested earlier by Kuznets and others on the basis of Western historical evidence. But recent developments have been based on special factors of the modern era and may not be a passing abnormality or transitional phase of the growth process. A number of these special factors arise from the extreme division of today's world into rich and poor countries and the ready communication and unequal power relations among them. One factor is the extent to which the aggressive development and marketing of new consumer goods by rich countries to local poor country elites results in a perverse "international demonstration effect," which absorbs in autos, gasoline, roads, gadgets, and luxury housing resources that might otherwise contribute to basic development. These elites "need" any growth dividend to meet a rising international consumption standard, so that with sufficient force at their command they may capture all surpluses and even depress further the real incomes of the masses (frequently via inflation in a context of downward pressures on money wages).

As just implied, a second factor is the ability and willingness of these elites to use force to assure their privileged command over income. Where they are actually threatened with income redistribution downward via democratic processes, the termination of democracy in favor of "order" and "austerity" is a foregone conclusion (*vide* Brazil, Uruguay, and even more conspicuously, Chile). And the threats to domination by privileged elites tend to be greater today than in the early years of Western capitalist development, again partly because of the duality between rich and poor countries and the spread of ideas and knowledge of the possibilities of a better life for both rich and poor alike (although by radically different processes).

Another special factor in the modern era has been the efforts of the rich countries to shape the post-colonial developments in the Third World, not according to their own image, as in the common cliché, but according to their interest. This has meant interventionist efforts to create and sustain a neo-colonial elite. As the greatest world power after 1945, the U.S. has been the leader in this process. Despite a mass of rhetoric claiming devotion to democracy and self-determination, the clear essence of U.S. policy has been the unremitting support of counter-revolution in this age of Third World upheaval. A community of interest has united Third World elites and the leaders of the U.S., resulting in a huge influx of military and intelligence "aid" into the LDCs, occasional violent intrusions (Vietnam, the Dominican Republic), and a steady general support for conservative, increasingly military-dominated regimes.

The building up of a large neo-colonial military force, linked to the U.S. by training and material aid, has had as its main purpose the provision of an "insurance policy" against internal social revolution. The community of interest rests on the need of Third World elites for external support, given their lack of any mass domestic constituency; and, on the U.S. side, the interest of the leadership both in the "open door" for its expanding economy and dependable political allies. Bankers Trust, as well as the Pentagon, is "bullish on Brazil" under junta auspices (quoting a recent widely placed ad by the bank)—its open door is wide, its support of U.S. leadership is reliable, and its use of torture and stifling of a democratic order does not bother either Bankers Trust or the military. Nor are they unduly troubled by the fact that the Brazilian income distribution has worsened markedly under the junta, the relative share of the richest 5 percent increasing from 29 percent in 1960 to 38 percent in 1970, the real income of the poorest 40 percent falling absolutely.

The Dominican Republic provides an even clearer case study of the regressive impact of U.S. policy on the distribution of income and wealth in poor countries subject to dominant U.S. influence. In that client state hunger is rampant, with much of the potentially rich agricultural land unused or misused, and with fewer than 1 percent of the farmers owning 47.5 percent of the land, many of the rest operating under semi-feudal tenure conditions. A *Wall Street Journal* report (Sept. 9,

1971) cites one foreign economic expert as saying that "Per capita income is about the same as before 1965, but it's less equitably distributed." The invasion of 1965, however, preserved a large U.S. investment stake, and tax subsidies and low wages have encouraged a considerable further influx. Low wages are assured by stagnation plus U.S.-supported terror. Even the *Wall Street Journal* noted that "the [U.S.] embassy has done nothing publicly to dissociate itself from the terror. The U.S. continues to provide substantial aid, including training, equipment and arms to the Dominican police and army." And the *Journal* also described the more specific ways in which repression affects the class distribution of income:

> When a union attempted to organize construction workers at a foreign-owned ferronickel mill project last year, Mr. Balaguer sent in the army to help straighten things out. While the soldiers kept order, the contractor fired 32 allegedly leftist leaders . . . The strike was broken in eight days.

The *Wall Street Journal* also reported the use of army troops in the Dominican Republic to evict peasants from land needed for the construction of a plush foreign-owned vacation resort in which George Meany, among others, had an interest; which may have added something personal to Meany's well-known acquiescence in the crushing of free unionism in America's client states.

Adelman and Morris found sociopolitical factors to be of great importance in explaining cross-country differences in income distribution; in case after case, "the more firmly entrenched the expatriate financial, commercial and technical elite, the greater the concentration of income in the hands of the top 5 percent. . . . ;" and "broad-based economic growth provides a way to achieve redistribution only where accompanied by social and educational development as well as substantial broadening of political participation."

In brief, then, income distribution has tended to worsen in the poor countries of the Free World because rapid growth has generated wealth that has been used not to improve the condition of the masses but to serve the growing consumption needs of a neo-colonial elite. The preservation of their position has required a costly diversion of resources into the military (the "insurance policy") and a subordination of development and welfare needs to the consumption-oriented demands of U.S. open-door entrants and affluent domestic consumers. Lon Nol, Thieu, Park, Balaguer, Suharto, Marcos, etc., all have in common institutionalized venality, terrorization of the masses, and service to the needs of "the expatriate financial, commercial, and technical elites" specified by Adelman and Morris as tied in closely with a worsening income distribution. The Nixon Doctrine formalized a support of such regimes, which was, however, in practical effect well before Nixon and is being continued under the Ford Administration.

27.

WILLIAM I. SPENCER: Policies of the Multinational Corporations

Multinational corporations have the ability to locate and extract worldwide resources, develop new technology, and provide the impetus for economic growth in the lesser developed countries. But they are also able, in conjunction with industrial nations, to hold the underdeveloped societies in a state of economic peonage. Frequently, too, because of the poverty of the Third World, these corporations choose to invest their money and talent in other already prosperous countries where the immediate return will be greater. In the past few years the multinationals have come under severe criticism for the ways they use their money and power both at home and abroad. Especially condemned has been their involvement in the domestic politics of foreign countries. In an interview with Harvard Business Review, *William I. Spencer, president of Citicorp, answered much of the criticism and explained the relation of the multinationals to the countries in which they operate. Citicorp itself has installations in 103 overseas countries. Portions of the interview are reprinted here.*

Source: *Harvard Business Review*, November-December 1975. "Who Controls MNCs?"

HBR: Before we discuss the many issues that operating Citicorp and Citibank raises, could we touch on the media's recent hard questioning of the ethics of U.S. businessmen? Should we expect higher ethical standards of our business people when they negotiate with officials of foreign countries?

Spencer: Of course we should expect, and demand, higher standards, but we've got to be careful how we draw the line. Consider the case of a corporation operating in a country where it's the accepted custom for people like import agents to take 1% off the top. Now, this can be bribery–but it can also be a sales commission. It's properly regarded as a sales commission, I think, if it's the accepted custom in the country and if the figure goes into the books. Now, the fact that some countries have such a custom doesn't mean we shouldn't deal with them. We may not like that kind of situation, but in our enthusiasm for our own moral codes I don't think we should try to write ethical standards for the rest of the world. We can, however, insist on proper accounting procedures consistent with our own standards of business conduct.

The criterion, then, is whether the sales commission is accounted for openly and aboveboard?

For U.S. marketers, yes. Let me use a hypothetical example. Suppose I'm selling helicopters to some foreign country. Let's say its president has an ambitious program for building up the country. He's a one–man band surrounded by many ministers. He says to me, "Okay, Spencer, here's what we want, and this is our price, and I want you to supply the best fleet of helicopters you can." Then his defense minister tells me, "I happen to own the helicopter sales agency that sells all helicopters to the government, and so you must work through me. For sales from your country, we get a 5% commission."

Now, this is part of the quotation price, and if I don't pay it, I don't get the business. The French or the English or some other developed country will—because they will pay the commission. To me, this outcome doesn't make sense.

How important is it to know where the commission money finally goes?

I don't want to appear to be too much of a devil's advocate, nor do I want to put my imprimatur on bribery as a way of doing business, but I don't think that's the question. Somebody in the country is get-

ting 5%. It may end up in the minister's pocket, or go to a Swiss bank account, or wind up in the national treasury—we don't know. If the commission is paid aboveboard, if it's on the books, that satisfies the criterion.

Is this the guideline, then, that you ask Citibank people to follow if they encounter problems of this nature?

No. While I don't condemn the practice for other marketers, I won't have it as far as Citibank is concerned. We simply will not do business if we have to pay some "squeeze" to a minister or other official, even if that is consistent with the mores in that country and it's recorded on the books for the transaction. The business we're in, the financial services industry, can't operate successfully with that sort of thing going on. To the best of my knowledge, this hasn't been a problem for us.

Many critics, including Senator Church, chairman of the Senate subcommittee on multinational corporations of the Committee on Foreign Relations, have demanded that MNCs subscribe to a mandatory code of conduct that would align their activities with the national interests of countries in which they operate.

I prefer a voluntary code to a mandatory one because of problems relating to enforcement. I would be extremely wary of a code that could be unilaterally and subjectively interpreted by each country on its own authority or by a less than impartial international body.

What could such a code be expected to accomplish?

If an attempt is going to be made to develop a common code of conduct, it will have to spell out the obligations of governments as well as the obligations of companies. A crucial step is recognition by the host countries that they need to spell out clearly to MNCs the role they can expect to play in achieving national objectives. The critics of MNCs talk about the misconduct of MNCs, but they use a double standard. They apply different regulatory and procurement standards to local companies than they do to companies with foreign parents. In other words, if there is sin, it is to be found on both sides—and the preachers ought to take that into account in their sermonizing on the subject. I'm not condoning the errors of MNCs. I'm just saying that in the real world their behavior looks a little different than it does to the critics.

Observers like Raymond Vernon of the Harvard Business School believe that a code of conduct would be trivial in comparison with the difficult problems confronting MNCs.

Yes, I also believe that an international code of conduct would be of limited use. It seems to me that the vast majority of MNCs already try to be good citizens of the countries where they do business, and so I tend to agree with Professor Vernon that such questions as taxes and capital formation are far more important. Actually, if you came up with a code that was general enough to be accepted by all countries, it would probably be too general to be meaningful to any. . . .

Some business leaders feel there's a growing tendency in developing nations for the host government to bargain harder and tougher. And I wonder if that's a tendency your people have noted too.

Well, I think it is established without any real debate among serious economists that a relatively untrammeled flow of goods and services provides more things at lower prices by virtue of competition than anything else. Now, to a certain extent, a country wishes to control its own destiny. For instance, some country may conclude that it wants to reduce imports severely. That would qualify as a country coming head on with a multinational

company's aspirations, I suppose. Let's hope that we and our host governments learn something as we go along—that to the degree we keep the flow of goods and services across the whole spectrum at its greatest depth, our own people have a better standard of living; they can buy more things more cheaply. But to the degree that a government tries to build walls around its borders and do its own thing, whether you're a manufacturer, an exporter, or a financial institution, the atmosphere is not conducive to doing business.

Has this environment been more hostile recently than in the past? Is negative reaction to companies like yours what you find in host countries?

It pops up here and there. With 103 countries, you're always going to have something unfavorable somewhere. There's an irregularity of economic health in these countries, and sure, I guess there are head-on collisions. Cuba nationalized our 20 branches there when Castro took over and assumed all our assets and liabilities. Egypt nationalized our branches in 1957 but paid us full compensation. Chile nationalized our branches in 1970 and gave us negotiated compensation. The People's Republic of China placed our branches in liquidation in 1950. The Soviet Union closed our branches in 1917. Other banks have had foreign branches nationalized in these countries too.

What exactly happens when you're expropriated?

Whenever we're asked to leave a country, we try to do so as gracefully as possible. Our conduct has been such that Egypt, Chile, and the USSR have invited us back, and now we're operating in these countries again. I wouldn't be surprised if we returned to the People's Republic of China one of these days, back to our old quarters in Shanghai. As for reimbursement, it varies, as I've indicated.

Putting the shoe on the other foot, multinational corporations have come under a lot of criticism from writers, members of Congress and others who say that MNCs are not subject to enough effective control in developing countries and that the powerful companies manipulate the governments there.

That's nonsense. MNCs come under government control in every country where they do business. *Any* company operating abroad is dependent on the sufferance of the host government, not the other way around. After all, governments in developing countries do expropriate foreign companies. In addition, they set requirements on the kinds of loans we can make, the amount of loans, our debt/asset and other capital ratios—many things. They do all this at will, regardless of how their gross national products compare with the total world sales of the MNC— all of us have seen comparisons showing that some MNCs are "bigger" than their host countries. But I see no evidence that governments abroad, including the smallest ones, have lost the capacity to influence their economic and political destinies.

Suppose MNCs keep growing in size and number. Might they become a threat to national sovereignty then? Some have said that MNCs may be on the way to succeeding in creating a global mechanism for administering the affairs of our planet.

No way. The idea that MNCs could become capable of exercising sovereign powers is fantasy. Sovereignty embraces the power to levy taxes, to raise and support armies, to license business activities, and to nationalize property with or without compensation, among other things. These are not powers MNCs possess. Basically, MNCs try to rationalize their economic activities on an international scale, and national sovereignty is a fact and force they have to reckon with and adjust to in order to accomplish their objectives.

Some critics argue that Washington should be doing more policing of U.S.-based corporations operating abroad.

I've said I'm in favor of prohibiting the undercover payment of bribes. But we should be under no illusion that U.S. legislation will end the practice of foreign nationals soliciting bribes—only the governments abroad can do that. Moreover, in some cases U.S. legislation can have an adverse effect on the fortunes of U.S. companies operating overseas. This might happen if, say, we tried to apply some of our domestic collective bargaining requirements to all other countries. In addition, I wonder if there isn't a philosophical contradiction in criticizing MNCs for ignoring the sovereignty of host governments at the same time that we argue for Washington to do more policing of the activities of our MNCs in foreign countries. . . .

To make doing business in a foreign country worthwhile, you can probably stand only a limited amount of regulation and control. How much would you say an international bank like yours can tolerate?

Let me turn your question around from "How much control can you accept?" to "How much freedom do you require?"

We require free movement of people, plants, equipment, and money—the tools we need to do our job. This means a commitment on the local government's part to participate in the needs of a global economy. Also, we have to be free to make our own management decisions; we can work under guidelines and regulations, but we really can't be partners with local governments in making day-to-day business decisions.

We find, by the way, that the countries

that impose the fewest controls generally turn out to be the most prosperous. West Germany is a good example in Europe. In South America, Brazil is progressing swiftly . . . Singapore, which is essentially a free port, is one of the fastest growing countries in Asia.

We've mentioned a number of obstacles to economic development. What do you consider to be the most important threat to the future of the world economy?

Nationalism, provincialism. There's bound to be unevenness in wealth and trade. How does a country cope with it? The way of nationalism is to put a circle around its business and try to protect it by tariff barriers. "All we need to do is keep imports down" is the attitude. It's very easy, then, for the attitude to spread to other countries. "Well, if they're going to do that to us," they say, "we're going to do the same to them." So artificial price levels are created, and production and distribution become uneconomic. Imagine what would happen to the United States if Michigan started to put tariffs on goods made in New York!

If there's one decisive influence on the future world economy, I'd have to say it's success or failure in keeping international barriers down. For the positive side, look at the achievement of the groups of countries that have gradually lowered tariff barriers since World War II.

Is there any chance that MNCs will control themselves enough to make each nation feel that there's no need to raise barriers?

I'd say there's a good chance. Multinational banks, for instance, are only financial institutions, not political ones, so their very nature limits their power.

Lending money doesn't confer control. Banks bid competitively to lend to many corporations, and the corporations can pick and choose which banks will get their borrowing business.

How can one small country protect itself from the power of a large corporation to balance its sales, capital expenditures, and profits over the entire globe?

A country can make its own economic policy. Some less developed countries, for example, have adopted national development plans that enable them to judge the value of individual investments in terms of their overall benefit to the country. Some countries have chosen to reserve key sectors of their economies for local entrepreneurs and to restrict the amount of foreign direct investment. Other countries — notably West Germany and Brazil — have left more operating room for the private sector than for the public and have done very well with that approach. I believe that reliance on the private profit motive is an extremely effective way of directing resources to their best use.

Aren't some of these policies barriers?

Not really. A barrier restricts production and distribution in an industry in such a way as to make it unprofitable. These national policies assign certain industries to local businessmen and allow free enterprise to take its course, with the help of MNCs, in other industries.

What curative effect can a big bank like Citibank have on the ups and downs of international trade?

I think that in that matter we are essentially captive. What happens in ups and downs is governmental policies, and they have to do with closing off imports, fostering exports, tripling the speed of the printing press to flood a country with currency, and all the resulting inflationary problems. We are captive to those, and what we try to do is deal with them in our mix of assets and liabilities. So, we are performing our function within the confines of financing trade and manufacturing — this sort of thing. But as far as having any real strength goes, that's deeply rooted in the economic policy of a government, and there's very little we can do about that.

Barnet and Müller assert that nine large banks, Citibank among them, control the most important MNCs. "In the vaults of these Wall Street giants," they state, "are $1 trillion worth of corporate securities." How much control in reality do the leading banks exert over the MNCs?

This alleged fact is so sweepingly misleading that it's difficult to respond briefly. Citibank owns no stock for its own account. However, it does serve as trustee or investment advisor or executor on behalf of our trust customers and, as such, invests in the stock of major corporations, many of them multinationals. In 1974, assets held and managed amounted to $15.6 billion, of which $7 billion was common stock. In addition, we also serve as asset custodian for many other customers.

The $7 billion of equity assets held in our investment management group represents the combination of assets of thousands of individuals, institutions, and corporate clients with a variety of investment objectives. These assets are clearly held for the benefit of the client, and our objective is to provide clients with investment performance consistent with their individual requirements and not to assist in any effort by Citibank to exercise any sort of "control."

Among the 100 largest common stock holdings held by our investment management group for its clients at year-end 1974, in only two cases did this group vote over 5% of the outstanding shares. And among these 100 largest holdings, the average percent of outstanding shares voted by Citibank in its trustee capacity was 1.8%.

Voting decisions are made by the senior management of our investment management group—no commercial bankers are involved—on the basis of protecting the long-term economic interests of our clients. From a perfectly practical viewpoint, if our investment people do not like the way a company is operating, they sell the stock. Therefore, I don't know in what possible sense we could've exercised the "control" attributed to us. . . .

I'd like to switch the subject for a moment to the question of all the money flowing from the OPEC countries. Is it a big problem to handle these flows of cash?

No, I think this has been one of the most highly overrated problems of our time. You recall all of the doomsday cries following the oil embargo in 1973 and the worry that hundreds of billions of dollars would be washing around the world and upsetting the financial equilibrium of nations. The facts are that, to a degree, there's been a safety net provided to handle some of the exchange, and it's been very comfortably handled by the private sector. There are growing demands in all those countries, and our view is that in the next 10 to 15 years the OPEC countries' surplus of funds will diminish quite sharply as their appetites for new goods, services, and imports continue to grow.

A year ago, we were saying, "Let's not panic; the normal system of flows and demands have a way of compensating for these things." But we were crying alone in the wilderness at that time. Nothing's happened. Remember the horror stories that all the banks were going to have all their deposits from OPEC countries and that the oil producers could move them at a whim and that this would render banks impotent? It just isn't so. . . .

Can a bank like Citibank help prevent international recession and financial collapse? Or is it true, as some critics assert, that the growth of multinational banking stretches world credit to its limit and makes widespread failure more probable?

A bank's power to cause or cure inflation or recession is seriously exaggerated. Banks don't print money; nor do they control the world's supply. Governments do. Only the controllers of the money supply can really cause or prevent major dislocations. Banks just move money, and to the extent that they do this job efficiently, they can ameliorate the severity of these dislocations. By efficiently channeling petro-dollars from the producers back to the consumers, banks have in fact lately relieved the pressure tremendously.

Far from stretching world credit to its limit and making failure probable, international banks have actually monitored credit in such a way as to make world business more stable. A bank's most important job is to assess credit and ensure that each credit decision is sound and prudent. A bank's function is to protect both the bank and the borrower. Fear of stretching world credit "to the limit" assigns an artificial ceiling to credit. Credit is essentially an advance against work to be done or goods to be produced tomorrow. As long as the credit advanced remains realistically within the range of tomorrow's production, it may be expanded without risk.

28.

The Sports Boom Is Going Bust

The collapse of the World Football League in 1975 and the dissolution of the American Basketball Association and its merger with the NBA in 1976 were sure signs that all was not well with the multi-billion dollar sports establishment in the United States. This article explains why the franchise over-expansion program backfired on the team owners and players.

Source: *Forbes*, February 15, 1975.

LITTLE 5-foot 2-inch Fran Monaco sat shaking his head in his cramped office surrounded by football gear and explained in a halting voice how his Jacksonville Sharks football team—his first love—had eaten him alive. In one season, the 48-year-old Florida businessman seems to have lost every cent he made in the last 22 years on his medical laboratory business and running a supper club. "Before, I had a good reputation," said Monaco, wincing. "I paid my debts."

But no more. Thanks to his beloved Sharks, for which he paid the new World Football League $650,000 last year, Monaco now has total liabilities of around $1.8 million.

Monaco said sadly: "This is like a nightmare."

Little Fran Monaco has company. A growing number of owners and promoters are learning that the easy days are over for the sports boom, which created scores of new teams, fostered more than a score of new arenas and stadiums costing over $1 billion and saturated television with "spectaculars" like the wrist wrestling championship.

Teams are folding in football, basketball and tennis—to name a few—and some sports insiders now insist that the recession will eat up entire leagues. Two candidates: the World Football and World Hockey outfits. Beyond question, the in word in sports today is shrinkage.

The sports boom is ending with a bang and a lot of whimpers:

Veteran builder and sports mogul Robert Schmertz lost around $1 million operating the World Football League's New York Stars' franchise last year. Besides, he recently gave away 50% of his Boston Celtics basketball team to settle a $3.7-million suit. That must really hurt, since the stock of his Leisure Technology retirement home company has collapsed, and he has just been indicted for bribery in connection with a realty deal. But he's hoping the public will help him out by buying the WFL team, now known as the Charlotte, N.C. Hornets, for $100 a share.

Sambo's Restaurants' Sam Battistone Jr. and friends are likely to lose about $1 million operating the National Basketball Association's New Orleans Jazz this season. Last year he and his friends paid $6.2 million for the privilege (and franchise). Battistone and other partners stand to lose another $1 million on the WFL Hawaiians. Poor Sam! He jumped from his frying pans into a fire.

Some even think that sports troubles may have been one factor that led investment counselor Charles W. Call Jr. to shoot and kill his wife, a son and then himself last month in New Jersey. According to one organizer, Sean Downey, Call was committed to investing $600,000 in the World Baseball Association, a new league that is supposed to challenge the two entrenched leagues.

There are even rumors that Jack Kent Cooke, chairman of TelePrompTer and the biggest sports mogul of all, wants to sell out. That's doubly significant, because Cooke's timing is usually as impeccable as his wardrobe. He entered sports in the Fifties, later going to Los Angeles from Canada, where he owned a string of radio stations. For around $20 million invested over the years, he got a slew of sports franchises, including basketball's Los Angeles Lakers, and built the 18,000-seat Forum. His rumored asking price: $90 million. But as the boys on Seventh Avenue say, "Wait; he'll take less."

What happened to pro sports isn't very surprising. All boom businesses are started by the truly shrewd, then inevitably become saturated by the misguided souls who can't resist getting in on a good thing. And, of course, sports is especially attractive to investors. It makes instant celebrities out of unknowns—like the son of a rich man or perhaps the anonymous executive referred to as "what's-his-name, the toilet-seat king."

Sports isn't dying; it is merely shrinking to a more healthy size. America's love of sports assures ever more sports revenues. But those bigger dollars will continue to be stretched to the breaking point by too many teams in too many leagues, sharply higher ticket prices and the escalating cost of living. Sports' inevitable shrinkage is just being hastened these days by inflation, recession and by a rash of serious lawsuits that could kick the financial pinnings out from under the owners.

To see why the sports explosion is backfiring, look back a little. Until the Sixties, professional sports was more an avocation than a business. Most teams were owned by sportsmen—rather than businessmen—and ownership changed about as often as the height of the pitcher's mound. Connie Mack, "the grand old man of baseball" (as the saying goes), served as owner-manager of the Philadelphia (now Oakland) Athletics for 49 years, from 1901 to 1950.

Nobody made much money; nobody lost much. In the old days, the founder of the New York football Giants, Tim Mara, covered his team's modest annual losses with profits from his bookmaking operation. Art Rooney, whose Pittsburgh Steelers finally won the football championship in January, used to come out ahead by betting horses.

As late as 1961, the National Football League's 14 teams were filling half their seats and clearing, at most, $100,000 each a year.

But then pro sports boomed. Since 1961, revenues have *tripled*—to more than $1 billion. Add to that another $16 billion bet illegally each year on all sports. Looking back, insurance magnate and Oakland Athletics outspoken owner Charles O. Finley says: "Oh, it's been happy days, golden days."

Since 1961, the overall number of big-league football teams has expanded from 14 to 38; the number of basketball teams from nine to 28; hockey from six to 32 and baseball from 16 to 24. In addition, promoters have created team competition where none existed before—in tennis, track, volleyball, boxing, lacrosse and other sports. About the only game that hasn't been organized and peddled to franchise investors is tiddledywinks.

Texas oilman Lamar Hunt, H.L.'s son, ushered in the new era in 1960 by creating the American Football League to challenge the old, arrogant National Football League. Despite its early losses, the AFL landed a league-saving TV contract with the National Broadcasting Co., successfully bid for star players and eventually forced the old NFL into a money-saving merger. The value of the original AFL franchises jumped from $25,000 to today's valuation of $16 to $20 million.

Sports was big business. Out went the nickel-and-dime owners and in came expansion-minded businessmen. They, in turn, sold new franchises in every big city in sight for at least two reasons. First, as the fried chicken people had shown, selling franchises was an easy way to make money; the up to $19.5 million that new buyers paid was split among each team's existing owners. Second, by blanketing the major TV markets, the owners hoped to discourage the creation of competition through new rival leagues.

The expansion policy, however, didn't stop the competition. New leagues popped up as often as Dizzy Dean. Suddenly, instead of professional basketball adding, say, two teams every couple of years or so, the sport got 11 ABA and two new NBA teams overnight in 1967—a 130% increase. The World Hockey Association did the same thing to hockey in 1972; then the WFL did it to football last year and now promoters are threatening baseball, too.

It was too much, too soon. Up went player salaries, as the leagues began bidding for anyone who could run and chew gum at the same time. Also up went ticket prices, as the owners scrambled to pay for their high-priced talent. And finally, up went the number of TV hours devoted to the so-called sports boom.

The elements were in place; the bust, as always, was brewing in the midst of the boom.

Interestingly, one group of Newport Beach, Calif. cronies seems to be behind most of the new leagues. The group is led by a blond, boyish 40-year-old tax lawyer named Gary Davidson. He and his friends became rich by introducing the franchise game to one sport after another, beginning with basketball in 1967 (the ABA), hockey in 1972 (the WHA) and football last year (the WFL). A disgusted Lamar

Hunt says: "It is now basically the franchise hucksters who are in sports."

To establish themselves as "big league," the new owners threw money around like confetti. As player salaries and operating expenses soared, so did the potential for losses. An owner could now lose $1 million a year—easily. Some of Davidson's early basketball investors lost more. Construction man James J. Kirst bought the Los Angeles Stars from an original franchise owner for $250,000, and then dropped about $1.7 million before he sold out to a Salt Lake buyer for about $345,000.

Ticket prices climbed. But the owners knew that gate receipts could never bail them out. There was only one salvation— a nationwide TV contract. Besides the money (the NFL's 26 teams split $55 million a year from the networks), the TV broadcasts popularized sports and helped lure fans to the stadium despite higher ticket prices.

Michael Burke, who ran the New York Yankees for CBS and now heads the New York Knickerbockers, acknowledges that TV is sports' golden crutch. He says: "If sports lost those [TV] revenues, we'd all go out of business."

At first, TV couldn't get enough sports with its high ratings and big male audiences. But the inevitable happened: Sports saturated TV. Today roughly 1,000 hours of TV time a year are devoted to big-time sports, double the number in 1969. And that doesn't include all the games, even high school games, that creep across the screen at such odd hours as Saturdays at midnight and Sundays at 9 a.m. Says *The New York Times* columnist, Red Smith: "I like football, but holy smoke! I like ice cream, too, but I don't want anyone to rub it in my hair."

Now many viewers—not just wives— are asking: "Isn't the game over yet?"

Regular season football ratings on CBS, to cite one example, are down 4.2% from last year. CBS recouped a bit with "Rhoda"; the situation comedy often outpointed ABC's Monday Night Football. Now NBC may drop hockey, and perhaps replace it with ABA basketball.

It may come to that. To get one sport on TV, an old one must go.

The viewer disinterest that is hurting the ratings is also reflected at the box office. While Broadway and movies staged comebacks, overall NFL football attendance dropped 4.6% last season. NFL Commissioner Pete Rozelle, a former press agent, blames the "no-shows" on a two-season-old federal law that permits local broadcast of games sold out 72 hours in advance. But there is more to it than that. A recent Harris Poll notes that only tennis and horse racing gained popularity last year.

Mixing metaphors the way a broken-field runner zigzags, football's Hunt says: "When the tide shifts, things can go downhill awful fast." Two years ago, his Kansas City Chiefs had a 5,000-seat waiting list for season tickets. No more. This season there were a lot of no-shows at Chiefs' games in the fancy new Arrowhead Stadium. Says Hunt: "We have big salary budgets, more administrative overhead and stadium leases to pay. There's plenty of pressure on the downside."

So there you have a formula for sports shrinkage: too many teams fighting for roughly the same sports dollars, too little new TV money, a decline at the gate. And all this while player salaries and other operating expenses are soaring.

Fans forget that athletes used to be underpaid. Remember Sam Huff, the football Giants' sensational middle linebacker? In 1959 when he was Defensive Lineman of the Year, Huff made only $9,000.

Times have changed. Football salaries went up 35% last year. In hockey, seven of the 20 New York Rangers' players are said to be making between $100,000 and $200,000 a year. In baseball, the New York Yankees (which CBS sold at a $3.2-million loss in 1973) outbid 21 other teams for free-agent superstar Jim (Catfish) Hunter. The bid: $3 million for five years, or around $15,000 for each game Hunter pitches. And basketball salaries are even higher. The median NBA salary is $95,000 a year, up from $65,000 three years ago. The superstars make much more—up to roughly $500,000 a year for the Milwaukee Bucks' star center, Kareem Abdul-Jabbar.

The biggest sports disaster so far is Davidson's WFL. Last year, during its first season, the World Football League's 12 teams lost an estimated $11 million to $22 million. Some say the league is now headed toward well-deserved oblivion....

As if sports didn't have enough troubles, there is also more than a whiff of scandal in the air. The stories have been splashed all over page one. Just to list a few, the New York Giants' former orthopedic surgeon consorted with bookmakers; the Justice Department suspects football players of betting for and against their teams; organized baseball suspended Cleveland shipbuilder George Steinbrenner, principal owner of the New York Yankees, after he pleaded guilty to making illegal political contributions; and a young woman under arrest said that she delivered drugs to football players all around the country. In addition, the owner of the National Hockey League's Toronto franchise, Harold Ballard, was sent to jail for one year for manipulating the funds of his Toronto arena. He was in line to get a new NBA franchise.

Fans can only read those stories with disgust. Their inevitable conclusion must be that big businessmen and pampered athletes are corrupting the children's games that are called organized sports.

Commissioner of Baseball Bowie Kuhn tries to put a good face on the situation: "I think that sports' piece of the entertainment dollar will continue to grow." But even he adds: "I think you will see teams disappearing in the near future. There has been a too great overexpansion of sports."

There is a bright side to this bleak picture for the fan. For years now, fans have complained that expansion has deflated the quality of play while it inflated the ticket prices. Today, with ticket prices up 50% in five years at Madison Square Garden, a family of four that drives in for a modest dinner and an equally modest Knickerbocker basketball game will spend around $100 for one night out.

However, if there is shrinkage, marginal players will be cut and the best will be lumped together on the remaining squads. The result: Fans might start getting close to their money's worth of entertainment again. The NBA Players Association General Counsel Larry Fleisher, who at 44 still talks about basketball with a teen-ager's enthusiasm, says: "Can you imagine a team with the New York Nets' Julius Erving *and* the Knicks' Earl Monroe *and* the Detroit Pistons' Bob Lanier? Man, what basketball that would be."

That, at least, may come to pass in the shrinking world of pro sports.

29.

RON FIMRITE: Baseball Is Bigger Than Ever

While professional football and basketball teams were experiencing financial difficulties, baseball had one of its best years in 1975. How the teams managed to lure fans to the ballparks in spite of television coverage of the games is described by reporter Ron Fimrite in this article from Sports Illustrated.

Source: *Sports Illustrated*, August 11, 1975. "It's A Grand New Game."

IT IS CONSIDERED bad form among baseball people to dash about issuing clamorous pronouncements on how the national pastime is booming, how it is enjoying a new and unprecedented popularity and making a heartwarming comeback from a time when its critics declared it too slow, too dull, too pastoral for the bloodthirsty modern sports fan. Such tasteless crowing, they say, is a mark of insecurity, behavior more characteristic of the professional football, basketball and hockey Philistines. It is baseball's party line that during all those years when its competitors were dismissing the game as little more than an occasionally charming anachronism, it was quietly setting attendance records. Baseball men claim their game is not coming back but that it never went away.

"Baseball was a media straw man during the so-called pro football boom," says Chub Feeney, president of the National League. "The pendulum never swung away from baseball."

"While Evel Knievel was crashing," adds Phillies Vice-President Bill Giles, "baseball survived."

"Baseball has been the victim of a lot of generalities," says Fred Claire, vice-president for public relations and promotions of the enormously successful Dodgers. "A lot of people on the fringe of sports got the impression the game was losing popularity. That impression persisted when it was obviously not substantiated by attendance figures and television and radio ratings."

But if the game was in good health before, it is positively radiant today. And no matter how modest baseball officials may be, it is booming. Attendance at major league games is up about 550,000 from last year when the two leagues drew 30,025,608, only 83,318 shy of the record attendance of 1973. Thirteen of the 24 teams have increased attendance this year, and even in those cities where crowds are down radio and television ratings are up. Some of the increases are astonishing. The Dodgers, whose paid attendance of 2,632,474 last year was easily the highest in baseball, are more than 200,000 ahead of that pace. They passed one million on June 9 (after only 27 home dates), the earliest any team ever reached that figure, and they will probably pass two million this week, which would be the earliest any team has done that. Los Angeles seems assured of breaking the one-season attendance record of 2,755,184 it set in 1962. San Diego, which drew more than a million fans for the first time last year, is also more than 200,000 ahead of 1974 and conceivably could draw 1.5 million with a mediocre team. The Reds again should join Los Angeles in the two million class, and so might the Phillies. Eight of the 12 American League teams are ahead of last year's attendance rates, and six of them are up more than 100,000. Two clubs, the Brewers and Yankees, show increases in excess of 200,000. Overall the league is running more than 600,000 ahead of 1974 and will probably break its season high of 13,433,604 set in 1973. The Reds have even drawn 28,000 for an 11 a.m. baseball clinic, and 20,600 Red Sox faithful sat patiently through a five-hour rain-delayed game late last month.

Some trouble spots remain, most notably in California's Bay Area, where the Oakland A's and San Francisco Giants compete to their mutual detriment, and in Atlanta and Minnesota. Still, both the Twins and the A's are drawing better this year than last. Attendance is significantly down in Detroit, Kansas City and Chicago in the American League and in Houston and Montreal in the National, but it is likely that the lackluster performances of the teams in those communities are making them poor draws, not any general decline of interest.

The attendance increases are even more noteworthy considering there is only one moderately close divisional race in the two major leagues. And they are still more impressive in view of the economic climate, which, as we are relentlessly reminded, is not exactly healthy. But with ticket prices significantly lower than in other major professional sports, baseball is better able to cope with hard times than its rivals. The Dodgers, for example, have not raised their ticket prices in the 18 years they have been in Los Angeles. It is still possible for a 12-year-old to buy a seat in Dodger Stadium for 75¢. In the past 20 years, baseball prices

have increased 54%, while movies have gone up 227%, bread 135%, hamburgers 110% and gasoline 96%. The average cost of a major league ticket is $1.94, compared to $6.75 for pro football, $5.88 for basketball and $6.26 for hockey. While these sports' high prices are threatening to make them available only to upper-middle-class male adults, baseball remains . . . cheap enough to qualify as family entertainment.

And the times do seem to be changing. Social trends can be ridiculously over-intellectualized, but Feeney's pendulum may well be swinging away from the violence, restlessness and dead seriousness of the '60s, a time when professional football was appropriately on the rise.

"Baseball has benefited from the nostalgia craze," says Peter Bavasi, the young and, yes, progressive general manager of the Padres. "The values in American society seem to be returning to another time. There is less dwelling now on the sensational. In the past, baseball has been criticized for its conservative approach. We've never changed our rules that much. Now that's proving to be an advantage. We're helping draw people back to the good old days."

Mention of the "good old days" or anything else that smacks of stodginess sends shudders through the game's modernists, but there is a ring of truth to such talk. A game that remains essentially the same — even the designated hitter, the most radical change of this decade, has not altered baseball's basic framework — has certain advantages in a time when changes in other aspects of life occur too rapidly to be assimilated. What is more significant is that while baseball remains a grand old game on the field, its front offices are no longer content to sit back and wait for fans to pound on the gates. Alarmed by the growth of its competitors, the club-owners have done a selling job.

The young people jamming parks from Boston to Los Angeles are just one indication of their salesmanship. During the time when baseball was purportedly in decline, the standard analysis of the game's following was that it consisted largely of Little Leaguers, whose interest would last only until they moved on to more adult diversions, and aged fans, who would take the game with them when they died. That profile was never correct, and even excluding pre-teens (whose increased enthusiasm is attested to by players who report being badgered more than ever for autographs), baseball now attracts the youngest fans in pro sports. Tube-topped adolescent girls, many of them such rabid rooters that fan clubs are enjoying a revival, have become as much a part of the scene in the stands as beer vendors. And so have teen-aged boys, college students and all sorts of people in their 20s.

"At our park you find a tremendous number of spectators in the 18 to 30 category," says Oriole General Manager Frank Cashen. "There are more of them than ever before. Baseball has even become a popular form of dating, and a lot of young fans are arriving in couples."

"We have a very young audience," says Reds Vice-President Dick Wagner. "Our attendance profile is an absolute duplicate of the federal census, except our percentages aren't as high in the 50-and-over and the 5-and-under groups. That belies a lot of what's been said about baseball."

The availability of tickets, their inexpensiveness, a turning-away from more violent games and even the fact that beer is often cheaper at the park than it is in many bars have all contributed to baseball's youth movement. But probably nothing has done more to attract young fans—and their elders, for that matter—

than the enlightened approach of the game's owners, who not too long ago feared that promotions would tarnish baseball's image.

"Our boom is the result of five years' hard work," says Dick Hackett, vice-president of marketing for the Brewers. "A couple of years ago, I took some of our players on a winter goodwill tour. In one city not one kid knew who our catcher was, not one knew our second baseman and not one could name a starting pitcher. Then Phil Roof, our catcher, asked the people, 'Who's the Packer quarterback?'' and they yelled in unison, 'Bart Starr.' Right there, I said, we've got a job to do."

"The big difference now is that we're marketing our game," says Angel President Red Patterson, who proudly describes himself as "the dean of baseball's promotin' guys." "When I went with the Yankees in 1946 as a combination road secretary, public-relations man and promotin' guy, I think I was the only one in the league with a job specifically involving promotions. Now everyone has a promotions department. In those days, the Yankees didn't even have souvenir stands. They didn't want to sell baseball caps in the Stadium because they thought it would lower the dignity of the cap. I'm not talking about giving the caps away the way we do now. I'm talking about *selling* them. When I first suggested we do this, George Weiss [then the Yankee general manager] looked shocked. 'Red,' he said, 'we don't want every kid in town running around with a Yankee cap on.' Then I looked shocked. 'Why in the heck not?' I said."

Caps are for sale in every park now, but there is seldom any need to buy them. Along with helmets, bats, balls, batting gloves, jackets, sweatbands, T shirts, halter tops and Lord knows what else, caps are given away on the myriad promotion days and nights. Sixty-three of the Padres' 77 home dates are promotions. The Dodgers have had 10 crowds of more than 50,000 this season; five have come on giveaway nights. . . .

Still, with all the huckstering, the game remains the essential ingredient. As Giles says, "Baseball survives while Evel Knievel and outside linebackers recklessly come and go. Played well, it is a study in grace; played poorly it can be an excruciating bore. But then there is always tomorrow, for baseball is not so much an event as it is a fact of life. Sometimes we forget how much pleasure it can give."

"To the youngsters," says the Dodgers' Claire, "it is a magic game. As we get older we tend to say the game is not what it used to be. We forget that there are 10-year-olds who come out to the park with stars in their eyes. To them, the game is everything. We older people say the game has lost something. We are wrong. The game hasn't lost anything. It is we who have lost something. We have lost our youth."

30.

CLAUDE E. WELCH: Medical Malpractice

As the number of medical malpractice suits increased dramatically from 1973 to 1975, the malpractice insurance premiums for physicians and hospitals went up at alarming rates. Many doctors gave up the practice of medicine rather than pay the huge fees. In some areas of the country physicians went on strike to enforce demands for revision of state malpractice laws. Boston physician Dr. Claude Welch explains the malpractice crisis and its effect on the public in this selection.

Source: *New England Journal of Medicine,* June 26, 1975.

SUDDENLY THE TERM "medical malpractice" has become familiar to the public. Journals and newspapers proclaim that a true crisis has developed. Staggering rises in medical costs are predicted if adequate protection for the public is to be maintained.

This crisis had been foreseen by the medical and legal professions for many years. In 1971, the President directed the Secretary of Health, Education, and Welfare to appoint a Commission on Medical Malpractice; the report appeared on January 16, 1973, before it had received a full discussion by all the members. The report engendered many critical statements, even from members of the Commission, and essentially none of their suggestions have been activated. However, a body of important information was collected. It was not until the recent precipitate withdrawal of insurance companies from the field of professional liability insurance or the imposition of fantastic increases in premiums that the public finally became alert to what is now a public-health problem that almost certainly will require either state or even national legislation to correct.

The purpose of this brief article is to

summarize some of the known facts and to consider methods of solution that have been suggested.

The medical profession has always preferred to use the term "professional liability" to indicate responsibility for unhappy results; the term is applicable to other professionals such as dentists, lawyers, and architects. "Medical malpractice" is specific; it has been defined by the Commission as an injury to a patient caused by a health-care provider's negligence. A malpractice claim is an allegation with or without foundation that an injury was caused by negligence. "Injury" implies either physical or mental harm that occurs in the course of medical care whether or not it is caused by negligence.

Compensation to patients for malpractice therefore requires proof both of an injury and of professional negligence. On the other hand, it may be argued that it is reasonable to compensate patients for injuries, particularly of a major type, even if no negligence has been involved. The Commission's report implies that there are many medical injuries that have never been discovered but should be placed in a compensable category. Needless to say, if a patient is to be compensated for such minor problems as subjective statements of pain, the inflationary effects on medical costs could be serious.

Nevertheless, it is in the public interest that severe injuries should be atoned for by a just settlement. Such items, for example, as the loss of an extremity, paraplegia, or brain death are easily identified. However, knotty problems remain. Who, for example, is responsible for a death if a patient with a disease that is known to be incurable dies somewhat before his expected time?

If medical malpractice and other injuries not due to negligence are to receive compensation, it is necessary to determine who will pay for such reimbursement. At present insurance companies maintain that greatly increased premiums are necessary to balance costs, or have withdrawn from such insurance business. Many reasons have been advanced for this action. Obviously, the enormous awards given by some juries in the past few years, even though not numerous, have made it apparent that the financial reserves of insurance companies could be exhausted by a few such calamities. Furthermore, such reserves have decreased considerably during the recession. The prospect that all injuries, as well as negligent actions, might eventually have to be compensated makes the private insurance field much less attractive. Spiraling inflation makes any accurate prognosis of future costs very difficult and has led companies to suggest abandonment of the present system of insurance coverage for the "claims-made" type. At present, for example, if a doctor should be sued in 1980 for an action committed in 1975, he would be covered by the insurance company that covered him in 1975; in the "claims-made" policy he would be covered by the company that is insuring him in 1980. By this method doctors would be required to maintain continuous insurance even long after they had retired, and even after they had died, their estates might be subject to judgments.

Some data suggest that insurance companies either charge unduly high rates or fail to return proper amounts to injured patients. For example, in 1970 it was estimated that 39 per cent of the incidents reported to the companies did not reach the claims stage. About 65 per cent of the claims were disposed of before trial, and less than 10 per cent went to trial. Eighty million dollars was paid out in this year for the 12,000 incidents in which claims files were settled; the median claim settlement was $2,000, and only 3 per cent of plaintiffs received awards of $100,000 or more. It was considered that at that time there were 279,000 practicing doctors, so that a charge of less than $300 per doctor would have sufficed to have paid all malpractice actions (exclusive of business costs for the insurance companies) in that year. These estimates are not exact since it was impossible for the Commission to obtain complete data from insurance companies.

Recent figures indicate that in 1973 in New York State, where approximately 20,000 practitioners were insured by a single company, 769 claims were settled for an average payment of $22,694; the average cost per doctor of the total $17,-452,000 would be slightly less than $900; yet the average premium of 1974 was $3,218. A recent statement indicated that in 1974 in California malpractice costs were about $30 million, or an average of $750 per doctor; meanwhile, the average annual premium per doctor was $3,500. In effect, insurance companies are making doctors set up their own insurance pool.

If a curve is drawn of the rising dollar value of awards it is apparent that company reserves could quickly become exhausted by a few unusually large awards that could be made several years later, because of the applicability of present statutes, which allow the institution of suits many years after the injury. Insurance companies can in turn reinsure themselves against large losses, but this method is also expensive. This development prompts the question why such huge awards are made. Perhaps because of sympathy for the defendant, perhaps because of the huge figures that are tossed around glibly these days, or swayed by the salaries of professional athletes that may be in the millions of dollars, a

jury or a judge is apt to award a large amount to a poor patient in the thought that the sum can easily be handled by a wealthy insurance company or by a doctor. The fact that this money ultimately will be withdrawn from society itself is not apparent in individual cases.

The physician places blame on a combination of litigation-conscious public, aggressive trial lawyers, and a liberal court, as well as on the breakdown of the insurance system and inflation. The legal profession stresses faults of the physician. The public expects too much. All critics agree that poor communication between physician and patient is of prime importance.

It is pertinent to point out some of the most common differences between the points of view of the medical and legal professions. Lawyers state that physicians may neglect the necessity of obtaining informed consent, may have inadequate training, and in some cases abandon a patient or clearly be guilty of negligence. It has been suggested that if doctors were better educated, many of these problems would disappear. There is considerable doubt, however, that they would. For example, 91 per cent of the claims cited in the Secretary's report were from hospitals certified by the Joint Commission for Accreditation of Hospitals, and 43 per cent of them had residency training programs. Furthermore, there has been no time in history when medical knowledge has been as advanced as it is today, but claims, instead of diminishing, have risen exorbitantly. Indeed, more sophisticated machines used in diagnosis and treatment lead to increased chances of injury.

There has been much recent criticism of the medical profession such as the statement "it does not clean its own house." Many more lawyers, for example, have been disbarred from practice than doctors. It could be commented that this criticism is true but also that for many years only boards of registration have had the power to carry out revocation of license. The greatest penalty that a state medical society or a professional organization may impose is the expulsion from such a society. Many hospitals have been unable because of legal appeals to restrict the activities of doctors whose professional performance is substandard. A great deal more power must be given the medical profession if it is to accomplish more. Conceivably, the establishment of the Professional Standards Review Organizations will have an important influence, though it is too early to know whether or not these organizations in themselves can effect important changes.

I believe that recertification by boards and relicensure on the basis of continuing education or peer review could have beneficial effects, but licensure procedures require an entirely new approach. Until the turn of the present century the power of licensure in Massachusetts rested in the hands of the Massachusetts Medical Society, and there is no question that its peer review has been much more effective than that of the State Board of Registration in recent years. National licensure and relicensure would establish identical qualifications throughout the country, and undoubtedly will be pushed strongly in future years.

The medical profession believes that many legal doctrines that vitiate what doctors believe are honest decisions. Obviously, however, many of these legal doctrines work to the benefit of the physician as well, though unfortunately the interpretation of some of them may be different when they are applied to the medical profession from the interpretation when they are applied to other groups, The relative influence of these factors in determining the outcome of an original claim is not known. However, in a study by the Commission of the important legal doctrines arranged in order of frequency as applied to malpractice appeals, the following are listed:

1. Burden of proof. This rests upon the plaintiff.

2. Expert testimony. In general terms, such testimony is required to establish negligence.

3. Standards of care. The usual standards of care must be maintained. Formely, the locality rule was employed in which doctors were judged on the basis of standards of care maintained in similar communities. This rule had been abolished in Massachusetts and is rapidly disappearing in other parts of the country because it is assumed that all doctors now have access to medical information wherever it may originate.

4. Proximate cause. It must be determined whether the injury was due to the underlying disease or due to the physician.

5. Res ipsa loquitur—"the thing speaks for itself." As an example of this doctrine, a patient who had lost a leg after treatment for a fractured knee could be shown to the jury. The surgeon will have the burden of proof, and unless he could in some way establish his innocence, would be judged guilty. This doctrine is not recognized in Canada.

6. Procedural issues. For example, instructions to juries by judges may include statements to which one of the lawyers had raised objections; this lapse could be considered a cause to initiate an appeal.

7. Statute of limitations. They may be influenced by the date of injury, the discovery rule, and fraudulent concealment. Suits may be brought, depending upon state laws, either during a specified period after commission of the in-

jury or after discovery of the injury. ("Discovery" usually relates to retained foreign bodies after surgery.) Statutes of limitations regularly specify longer periods for infants or children than for adults. Statutes of limitations vary in different states. In New York, for example, it is three years except for injuries to infants, in which it is three years after the age of 18. Owing to liberal interpretations of such rules by the courts, New York physicians believe that the statute of limitations is virtually inactive in that state.

8. Erroneous instructions to juries by judges.

9. Respondeat superior. By this doctrine an employer is held responsible for the acts of his employees. Hospitals are affected by this consideration.

10. Informed consent. "Informed consent" requires more than the blanket approval for anything that might transpire during a hospital admission. Without belaboring the point, it is obvious that this consent could be made so detailed that it might become an actual danger for a patient. Any unauthorized procedure, even for a patient's good, could legally be construed as a battery. Furthermore, oral assurance of good results by doctors has been made the basis for suits; Dr. C. A. Hoffman has emphasized that this is true in no other field of law.

11. Charitable and governmental immunity. Charitable immunity is not applicable in Massachusetts since by statute charitable institutions can be held liable for injuries. The federal government may be sued for injuries caused by individuals; if negligence is proved, as in the case of a medical office, the government pays the award.

12. Breach of contract. If a physician has guaranteed a complete cure, which is not attained, suit may be brought for this purpose.

Many states have eliminated or modified some of these doctrines. It would seem that a concerted attack, however, would be necessary to gain important changes. For example, the most galling of these doctrines is that of res ipsa loquitur. It is doubtful if abolition of this doctrine in itself would be very effective. For example, in the state of Alaska, where the doctrine has been abolished by law, insurance companies are now withdrawing their protection. Statutes of limitations, on the other hand, are of great importance and would become even more important if "claims-made" policies were established. "Claims made" become more palatable as the period is shortened.

The medical profession would approve several changes in the present tort system. Besides elimination of res ipsa loquitur and revisions of the statutes of limitations, elimination of the ad damnum clause and changes in the contingency fee are the most common criticisms. The ad damnum clause refers to the specification of an amount asked as damages from a defendant; absurd amounts can be placed on claims that have little or no merit. For example, a defendant could be sued for a thousand or a million dollars for the same misadventure; it is obvious that if the latter amount were claimed, the suit would appear to have gained corresponding importance. A recent suit in California is said to have specified five billion dollars for damages.

Contingency fees have been regarded as important culprits by the medical profession. They are often blamed for the high cost of insurance in this country as compared with that in Great Britain or Canada. Thus, a general surgeon in New York State will now pay about $5,000 a year, or 10 times the fee of his Canadian neighbor. Meanwhile, malpractice insurance for a physician in Great Britain was raised to $65 in 1973. Attitudes about such fees are entirely different in many countries. For example, contingency fees are "expressly forbidden to lawyers in Great Britain and it would be a serious disciplinary offense if it were proved that any lawyer in Great Britain had undertaken a case on that basis." Bernstein stated, on the basis of interviews with leading solicitors and barristers in New Zealand, that all of them believed that contingent fees were unacceptable, and even barbaric.

In Canada the use of the contingency fee is permitted in many of the provinces, but the lawyer's share is usually 15 to 20 per cent rather than the average third that is taken by an attorney in the United States.

There are obviously arguments for and against contingency fees. In the United States the legal profession clings firmly to this process in the belief that it is the only way in which an impecunious patient can obtain legal services. At present it seems very unlikely that contingency fees can be abolished. However, it is gratifying to note that the Commission, which contained many lawyers in its group, recommended that the fee rate should decrease as the recovery amount increases.

The public, for the first time, has begun to appreciate the dangers of the present situation. For example, the projected annual insurance premium for a New York City orthopedic surgeon is about $40,000; under these circumstances it is certain that many older surgeons would close their offices, and young men would find it impossible to start practice. Anesthesiologists are particularly vulnerable; if they cannot receive adequate coverage, elective surgical procedures could be eliminated, as they are at this moment in sections of California.

As the situation worsens, many states are making important changes in their statutes. However, the possibility of action by the national Congress becomes more probable if prompt changes are not made. The methods that can be used fall essentially in five categories. They are (1) continuation of the present tort system, but with important modifications of legal doctrines and continued solution by litigation, (2) expansion of present grievance procedures, (3) the use of screening panels, (4) the formation of arbitration panels, and (5) the introduction of no-fault insurance, Various combinations of these methods are also possible. The medical profession would, in particular, seek important reductions in statutes of limitations, and the imposition of a dollar limit on awards.

1. Maintenance of the present system of litigation, unless drastic changes are made, would continue all the faults that are so apparent today. They include the long delay to trial. A relatively small return goes to the patient; this amount may average 18 to 20 per cent of the total settlement. The great burden of unhappiness on the affected members of the medical profession should not be forgotten.

The expenses of defensive medicine, approached only tentatively by the Commission, have become exceedingly high and promise to continue to escalate. Altemeier has estimated the cost of medical malpractice at nearly $6 billion a year, at least half of which is due to defensive medicine. For example, if it were decided to make all injuries compensable and if postoperative infection were considered to be such an injury, the use of antibiotics and consequent expenses would escalate enormously. The public eventually would have to pay for all these charges. The withdrawal of insurance companies from this field or the imposition of premiums that are almost insupportable are further evidence that the present policy must be changed.

2. Grievance procedures are highly developed in many institutions and in most medical societies and are capable of expansion. Patient complaints can often be resolved by the doctor or hospital staff; compromises on fees may solve some problems. However, it is very doubtful if this mechanism can provide any important solution for the major problems of professional liability.

3. Screening panels may be made up of a few physicians who decide whether or not a claim is worthy of further investigation. It is apparent that panels composed only of physicians do become somewhat suspect because they are likely to be influenced in favor of the profession. Consequently, screening panels that include representatives of the legal profession and the public are more desirable. Screening panels have been established under court systems in New Jersey and New York and by statute in New Hampshire. A total of 34 panels of various types is decribed in the Commission's report. These panels can dispose of many nuisance claims and small claims, but the major ones are still left to the court.

4. The possibility that arbitration panels can be the answer to the whole problem of malpractice claims is gaining momentum every day. Such arbitration panels could be set up on a model of the industrial-accident panels, including, for example, doctors, lawyers, and members of the public. Decisions of the arbitration panels could be compulsory, or the right to appeal could be retained by either plaintiff or defendant.

Arbitration panels conceivably could be inconsistent with the Seventh Amendment, which guarantees the right of trial by jury. This constitutional question was considered in detail in the Commission's report by Adams and Bell, with the conclusion that "a medical malpractice arbitration plan would survive the test of constitutionality under any theory so far devised and that a judicial establishment would be increasingly inhospitable to suits alleging constitutional deficiencies in arbitration. Compulsory arbitration has been established on a national model for Health Maintenance Organizations and has been specified in other prepayment plans such as the Ross-Loos Clinic.

It is of interest that except for actions of libel or slander, civil actions in England and Scotland are now tried by a judge alone and not by a jury. Trial by jury is much less common in Canada than in the United States and is usually refused on the basis of complicated medical evidence. If a right to appeal from an arbitration panel is retained, it would seem that a much more just settlement could be obtained in a trial before a judge; on the other hand, it could be argued that the individual patient might receive a more sympathetic treatment from a jury.

5. No-fault insurance. This insurance would require a payment by every person who enters the hospital or who becomes a patient in an office to establish a fund that could then be used to pay for medical injuries. This suggestion was fostered by the success of the no-fault insurance in the automobile liability industry; however, application to the medical field is much more difficult. If all injuries were compensable, the number of claims would undoubtedly proliferate; many nuisance claims would have to be processed, and the system would become unduly expensive. It is conceivable, on the other hand, that some type of insurance of this nature could have its benefits restricted to injuries of a permanent nature that are of major importance. Specified amounts could be set for each one of these injuries. For example, brain death, paraplegia or quadriplegia, or blindness

would receive specific awards. Such minor injuries as postoperative pain, a broken tooth, or infection could be handled by simple grievance procedures.

It is apparent that any correction of the present situation requires a long-range solution following the models or combinations thereof mentioned above. Short-range prospects, however, are grim. Insurance pools set up by professional organizations such as the American Medical Association, state medical or national specialty societies will continue the evils of the present system and postpone effective action. There is the very real possibility that many medical facilities will close or have to raise their rates high enough to establish an insurance pool for their staffs if state or national action is not taken soon. However, as a stop-gap measure joint underwriting associations set up by insurance companies appear to be the only solution.

31.

No Alternative to Nuclear Power

In 1973 the Atomic Energy Commission published a report stating that the possibility of a major accident in a nuclear power plant was negligible. This finding was immediately challenged by opponents of nuclear power plants, including scientists, consumer groups, and environmentalists. But in the face of possible oil shortages and higher fuel prices, there seemed no alternative to the continued construction of these plants. In 1975, thirty-two scientists under the chairmanship of Dr. Hans Bethe of Cornell University issued this statement on the urgency for nuclear energy as a chief source of electric power.

Source: *Bulletin of the Atomic Scientists,* March 1975.

WE, AS SCIENTISTS and citizens of the United States, believe that the Republic is in the most serious situation since World War II. Today's energy crisis is not a matter of just a few years but of decades. It is the new and predominant fact of life in industrialized societies.

The high price of oil which we must now import in order to keep Americans at their jobs threatens our economic structure — indeed, that of the Western World. Energy is the lifeblood of all modern societies and they are currently held hostage by a price structure that they are powerless to influence.

In the next three to five years conservation is essentially the only energy option. We can and we must use energy and existing energy sources more intelligently. But there must also be long-range realistic plans and we deplore the fact that they are developing so slowly. We also deplore the fact that the public is given unrealistic assurances that there are easy solutions. There are many interesting proposals for alternative energy sources which deserve vigorous research effort, but none of them is likely to contribute significantly to our energy supply in this century. Conservation, while urgently necessary and highly desirable, also has its price. One man's conservation may be another man's loss of job. Conservation, the first time around, can trim off fat, but the second time will cut deeply.

When we search for domestic energy sources to substitute for imported oil, we must look at the whole picture. If we look at each possible energy source separately, we can easily find fault with each of them, and rule out each one. Clearly, this would mean the end of our civilization as we know it.

Our domestic oil reserves are running down and the deficit can only partially be replaced by the new sources in Alaska; we must, in addition, permit off-shore exploration. Natural gas is in a similar critical condition; in the last seven years new discoveries have run far below our level of gas consumption. Only with strong measures could we hope to reverse this trend.

We shall have to make much greater use of solid fuels. Here coal and uranium are the most important options. This represents a profound change in the character of the American fuel economy. The nation has truly great reserves of these solid fuels in the earth. Our economically recoverable coal reserves are estimated to be 250 billion tons and exceed the energy of the world's total oil reserves. Our known uranium ores potentially equal the energy of 6,000 billion tons of coal; lower grade ore promises even more abundance.

The U.S. choice is not coal *or* uranium; we need both. Coal is irreplaceable as the basis of new synthetic fuels to replace oil and natural gas.

However, we see the primary use of solid fuels, especially of uranium, as a source of electricity. Uranium power, the culmination of basic discoveries in physics, is an engineered reality generating electricity today. Nuclear power has its critics, but we believe they lack perspective as to the feasibility of non-nuclear power sources and the gravity of the fuel crisis.

All energy release involves risks and nuclear power is certainly no exception. The safety of civilian nuclear power has been under public surveillance without parallel in the history of technology. As in any new technology there is a learning period. Contrary to the scare publicity given to some mistakes that have occurred, no appreciable amount of radioactive material has escaped from any commercial U.S. power reactor. We have confidence that technical ingenuity and care in operation can continue to improve the safety in all phases of the nuclear power program, including the difficult areas of transportation and nuclear waste disposal. The separation of the Atomic Energy Commission into the Energy Research and Development Administration and the Nuclear Regulatory Commission provides added reassurance for realistic management of potential risks and benefits. On any scale the benefits of a clean, inexpensive, and inexhaustible domestic fuel far outweigh the possible risks.

We can see no reasonable alternative to an increased use of nuclear power to satisfy our energy needs.

Many of us have worked for a long time on energy problems and therefore we feel the responsibility to speak out. The energy famine that threatens will require many sacrifices on the part of the American people, but these will be reduced if we marshal the huge scientific and technical resources of our country to improve the use of known energy sources.

32.

ROBERT H. BOYLE: The PCB Menace

Polychlorinated biphenyls are highly stable mixtures of organic compounds with several industrial uses. They serve as lubricants, heat-resistant fluids, and protective coatings on wood, metal, and concrete. When dumped as industrial waste the PCBs are highly toxic to fish and pose a real threat to wildlife and humans. In this selection, reporter Robert H. Boyle details the extent of the PCB threat to humans as it has been recognized in the past few years.

Source: *Sports Illustrated*, December 1, 1975.

THERE WAS IRONIC LAUGHTER in the coffee shop of Chicago's Pick-Congress Hotel last Friday when Nathaniel P. Reed, Assistant Secretary of the Interior for Fish and Wildlife and Parks, glanced at the menu and said, "Ah, fresh salmon sandwich!" Only an hour before, at the concluding session of the National Conference on Polychlorinated Biphenyls (PCBs), Reed had delivered a blistering speech on PCB contamination of fish, including Great Lakes salmon.

"The problem is a national problem," Reed had emphasized to some 400 scientists, bureaucrats and conservationists. "I am deeply shocked by the pervasiveness of PCBs; they are literally everywhere. I am very troubled by the exceedingly high levels found in fish in all our drainage systems, and I do not mean just the Hudson and the entire Great Lakes system, but the Merrimac and Connecticut rivers of the Atlantic Coast, the Mississippi and Ohio rivers of the Midwest, the Columbia River system in the northwest, the Sacramento in the West, the Rio Grande and other Gulf Coast streams . . . even the Yukon in Alaska."

Reed called for the elimination of all sources of PCBs in the U.S. environment within three years. With a candor unusual for a federal official, he criticized the sponsor of the conference, the U.S. Environmental Protection Agency, which has done little protecting, and the U.S. Food and Drug Administration, which has established a "tolerance" level of five parts per million of PCBs in fish for human consumption.

"Quite frankly," Reed ended his speech, "I am thoroughly disgusted by the gnashing of teeth, wailing and rubbing of hands. To the agencies which have the enforcement responsibilities, a word on behalf of the bewildered but concerned American people—*get on with it!*"

PCBs are chlorinated hydrocarbon compounds used by industries throughout the world because of their resistance to heat. More durable than DDT, PCBs are a proved menace to animal organisms, ranging from invertebrates to man. In 1968 an estimated 1,200 Japanese came down with *Yusho* disease after using rice oil heavily contaminated with PCBs. The clinical effects included stillbirths, undersized infants, bone and joint deformities and various neurological disorders including loss of libido.

In this country, in a recent experiment

on laboratory rats, PCBs caused liver cancer. Last week in Chicago the scientist in charge of that experiment, Dr. Renate D. Kimbrough of the U.S. Public Health Service, delivered a paper in which she warned, "Because of these findings in experimental animals, ingestion of PCBs in humans must be curtailed." The EPA estimates that about half the public now carries around with it from one to three parts per million of PCBs in its fatty tissues.

Another speaker at the Chicago meeting was Dr. James R. Allen of the University of Wisconsin Medical School, who fed eight female rhesus monkeys a diet that included 2.5 ppm of Aroclor 1248 (one of the nine trademarked PCB compounds made by the sole domestic manufacturer, Monsanto Industrial Chemicals Company) for six months. They were then bred to normally fed male rhesus monkeys. Two females resorbed their fetuses, one suffered a stillbirth, and the five infants born were all undersized. Two of the infants died while nursing. The three survivors are now eight months old, and although they have been on a PCB-free diet for four months, preliminary observations by Dr. Diane H. Norback, a colleague of Dr. Allen, indicate that the youngsters are hyperactive.

The PCB problem, which has been growing for years, began to receive nationwide attention last summer when Ogden R. Reid, commissioner of the New York State Department of Environmental Conservation, warned the public against eating striped bass from the Hudson River or salmon from Lake Ontario. Reid issued his warning after receiving a report from EPA scientists who noted that two General Electric plants at Hudson Falls and Fort Edward were discharging at least 30 pounds of PCBs per day into the river. In September, Reid brought action against G.E. to force the

company to reduce its discharge to two pounds a day by Dec. 31 and to zero by Sept. 30 of next year. The action is now before a state hearing officer, and G.E. is contesting it all the way. It is worth noting, however, that in response to a state interrogatory before the hearing began, G.E. admitted, "During the past 15 years, 49 employees have reported to the dispensaries complaining of allergic dermatitis, diagnosed as having been caused by contact with PCBs."

No one really knew that PCBs were present in the world environment until 1966 when Sweden's Dr. Sören Jensen isolated and identified the compounds that had been baffling researchers working on DDT residues. PCBs were then commonly used in a wide variety of everyday products, such as paints, sealants and caulking compounds. In 1971 Monsanto announced it would restrict sales of PCBs to use in so-called "closed cycle" systems, such as capacitors and transformers. U.S. industry turns out more than 100 million capacitors a year, including those for home air conditioners. When junked, such an item is commonly taken to a dump, where the chance exists that PCBs can leach through the soil to bodies of water. In western New York state several companies have been draining PCBs from old transformers, mixing them with crankcase oil and selling the gunk to municipalities to put on roads as a dust suppressor. There is also a report the PCBs have been spread on airport runways in Maryland to prevent skidding in wet weather.

Beyond such practices, there is the danger that transformers can rupture or leak. According to EPA records available in Chicago, a transformer leak occurred on April 16, 1974 on a railroad train running between Philadelphia and Paoli, Pa. From 10 to 100 pounds of PCBs were spilled. The same type of spillage occurred on July 5 of last year from a transformer leak in Stamford, Conn.

On March 8, 1973, a truck developed a leak in Kingston, Tenn., and 630 gallons of PCBs were spilled. The contaminated soils were recovered in 11,500 drums and sealed in concrete at a cost of $1.7 million. It was paid by G.E., which was shipping the chemical. Local residents also brought damage suits against G.E. and last October a judge awarded them a total of $120,000.

The U.S. Department of Defense was involved in a Catch-22 PCB episode with other government agencies in Seattle. On Friday, March 13, 1974 an electrical transformer destined for an Air Force radar station in Shemya, Alaska fell on a pier in Seattle and 265 gallons of PCBs bled into the Duwamish River. Defense refused responsibility; so did the U.S. Coast Guard, which has the primary obligation to clean up oil and other harbor spills. The Coast Guard said PCBs were not among the chemicals it was required to recover. The EPA had to hire divers who brought up 70 to 90 gallons of the compound, and in February of this year the Defense Department finally agreed to pay the cost, $148,000.

But recovery from the Duwamish spill is far from ended. EPA officials estimate 60 to 80 gallons remain in the riverbed, and Defense has assigned the job to the U.S. Army Corps of Engineers. The Corps is scheduled to begin dredging 30,-000 cubic yards of river bottom sometime around the first of the year. Estimated cost of the project is between a quarter and half a million dollars.

Although the U.S. Food and Drug Administration allows up to five parts per million of PCBs in fish, the U.S. Fish and Wildlife Service regards the presence of a *half* part per million (.5 ppm) in a fish egg as a sure sign of trouble in a waterway. According to Charles R. Walker, Senior Environmental Scientist with the Service, who delivered two papers in Chicago, trouble spots on the Atlantic Coast range from the Merrimac River in Massachusetts to the St. Johns in Florida. On the Gulf Coast afflicted rivers extend from the Rio Grande east to the Apalachicola in the Florida panhandle. The Mississippi-Missouri system has its hot spots. On the West Coast, the Sacramento, Rogue, Columbia and Snake rivers have problems and they abound in the Great Lakes region and in the St. Lawrence. Last week, Canadian officials announced they were dropping edible fish tolerance levels from 5 ppm to two ppm and might well close the eel fishery in the St. Lawrence.

Obviously, some rivers are in worse shape than others. Here are some PCB values for fish sampled by the U.S. Fish and Wildlife Service: carp, Cincinnati, Ohio River, 133 ppm; two channel catfish, Marietta, Ohio, Ohio River, 38-77 ppm; walleye pike, Natrona Heights, Pa., Allegheny River, 35 ppm; white perch, Camden, N.J., Delaware River, 19 ppm; gizzard shad, Elizabethtown, N.C., Cape Fear River, 23 ppm; small-mouth buffalo, Redwood, Miss., Yazoo River, 73 ppm; yellow perch, Lowell, Mass., Merrimac River, 98 ppm; goldfish, Poughkeepsie, N.Y., Hudson River, 213 ppm.

The Fish and Wildlife Service does not sample every stream in the country—it extends itself to maintain even the 100 monitoring stations in existence—but research reveals other trouble spots. Half the lake trout analyzed from Lake George, N.Y. have more than 5 ppm. And eggs of striped bass taken in 1972 from the Nanticoke and Choptank rivers on the supposedly unspoiled eastern shore of Maryland had PCB levels that ranged from 2.8 to 20 ppm.

33.

Kenneth D. Kaunda: America's African Policy

Africa has always been the stepchild of American foreign policy. But events in 1975 and 1976 occasioned a drastic reassessment of policy in Washington. Soviet and Cuban interference in the Angolan civil war, an armed struggle against white rule in Rhodesia, riots in South Africa, and the civil war in Ethiopia were some of the issues that forced the Ford Administration to pay serious attention to what was happening in Africa. In April 1975, Dr. Kenneth Kaunda, president of Zambia, paid a state visit to Washington. In remarks at a White House dinner he surprised his audience by chiding the administration for its lack of policy in Africa, especially in the light of America's professed ideals.

Source: *New York Times*, April 28, 1975.

I FIRST WANT to express my deep appreciation and gratitude for inviting me to visit Washington D.C. I also thank you, the Government and the people of the United States for their warm welcome and kind hospitality given to my wife and I and the entire Zambian delegation.

We are happy to be in Washington D.C. It is a very brief visit, but since we come for specific objectives, it is not the duration that matters, but the results. So far, we have done a lot. We find we have a lot in common on vital issues affecting mankind. Our discussions have been characterized by a spirit of frankness and cordiality. This spirit coupled by the definition of areas of urgent action should move the U.S. and Africa closer towards the attainment of our common objectives.

We come to America with a clear purpose. We simply want to be understood. We seek American understanding of Africa's objectives and America's fullest support in the attainment of these objectives.

The relations between Zambia and the U.S. cause me no concern because they are cordial although there is room for improvement through more sound co-operation.

What gives Zambia and Africa great cause for concern is America's policy towards Africa or is it the lack of it—which, of course, can mean the same thing. For I have been told of U.N. tricks in which an abstention in a vote can be a vote for or against. A no-policy position may not be a neutral position, indicative of passive posture, but a deliberate act of policy to support the status quo or to influence events in one direction or the other at a particular time. We have in recent years been most anxious about the nature and degree of the United States participation in building conditions for genuine peace based on human equality, human dignity, freedom and justice for all particularly in southern Africa.

You will forgive us, Mr. President for our candour if we reaffirmed, on this occasion, our dismay at the fact that America has not fulfilled our expectations.

Our dismay arises from a number of

factors. We are agreed that peace is central to all human endeavours. Our struggle for independence was designed to build peace, and, thank God, our people have enjoyed internal peace. We are agreed that we must help strengthen peace wherever it is threatened.

There has been no peace in southern Africa for a very long time even if there was no war as such. The absence of war does not necessarily mean peace. Peace is something much deeper than that. The threat of escalation of violence is now real. It is our duty to avoid such an escalation. We want to build peace in place of violence, racial harmony in place of disharmony, prosperity in place of economic stagnation, security in place of insecurity now digging every family everyday. . . .

To build genuine peace in southern Africa, we must recognise with honesty the root causes of the existing conflict. First: Colonialism in Rhodesia and Namibia. The existence of a rebel regime in Rhodesia has since compounded that problem. Second: Apartheid and racial domination in South Africa. Over the last few years, a number of catalytic factors have given strength to these forces of evil. External economic and strategic interests have nourished colonial and apartheid regimes.

Realism and moral conscience dictate that those who believe in peace must join hands in promoting conditions for peace. We cannot declare our commitment to peace and yet strengthen forces which stand in the way to the attainment of that peace.

The era of colonialism has ended. Apartheid cannot endure the test of time. Our obligation is that these evil systems end peacefully. To achieve our aim, we need America's total commitment to action consistent with that aim.

So far, American policy let alone action has been low keyed. This has given psychological comfort to the forces of evil.

We become even more dismayed when the current posture of America towards Africa is set against the background of her historic performance in late 50's and early 60's. We cannot but recall:

America that did not wait for and march in step with colonial powers, but rather boldly marched ahead with the colonial peoples in their struggle to fulfill their aspirations. An America undaunted by the strong forces of reaction against the wind of change, whose nationals helped teach the colonial settlers about the evils of racial discrimination. An America whose Assistant Secretary for Africa Affairs "Soapy" Williams, could be slapped in the face by a white reactionary on our soil and yet, undaunted still smile, still stand by American principles of freedom, justice and national independence based on majority rule. Yes, the reactionaries hated Americans for "spoiling the natives," for helping to dismantle colonialism.

What has happened to that America? Have the principles changed? The aspirations of the oppressed have not changed. In desperation their anger has exploded their patience. Their resolve to fight if peaceful negotiations are impossible is borne out by history. So their struggle has now received the baptism of fire, victories in Mozambique and Angola have given them added inspiration. Africa has no reason not to support the liberation movements.

Can America still end only with declaration of support for the principles of freedom and racial justice? This will not be enough. Southern Africa is poised for a dangerous armed conflict. Peace is at stake. The conflict with disastrous consequences can be averted but there is not much time. Urgent action is required.

At this time, America cannot realistically wait and see what administering powers will do or to pledge to support their efforts when none are in plan. America must heed the call of the oppressed. America, once an apostle in decolonisation, must not be a mere discipline of those which promise but never perform and thus give strength to evils of colonialism and apartheid.

If we want peace we must end the era of inertia — in Rhodesia and Namibia and vigorously work for ending apartheid. America must now be in the vanguard of democratic revolution in southern Africa. This is not the first time we make this appeal. It is Africa's constant plea.

Now Africa has taken an unequivocal stand on decolonisation. We do not want to fight a war to win freedom and full national independence in southern Africa. Africa wants to achieve these objectives by peaceful means, i.e. through negotiations. Our declaration to give high priority to peaceful methods to resolve the current crisis is a conscious decision. We feel it to be our moral duty to avoid bloodshed where we can. We are determined to fulfill this obligation but not at any price, not at the price of freedom and justice. No.

Africa has made it clear that if the road to peaceful change is closed by the stone walls of racial bigotry and force of arms by minority regimes then we are equally duty-bound to take the inescapable alternative. The oppressed people have a right to answer force with force and Africa and all her friends in the world will support them. Liberation movements fought fascist Portugal. We supported them. They won. Now we must turn to Rhodesia and Namibia.

Can America stand and be counted in implementing the Dar-es-Salaam strategy adopted by Africa? In Dar-es-Salaam early this month Africa reaffirmed its commitment to a peaceful solution to the crisis in southern Africa as a first priority. Our strategy opens even new doors to peaceful change if those caught up in the crisis seek honourable exit. Here is a chance in a century to achieve peace based on human equality and human dignity without further violence.

We call upon America to support our efforts in achieving majority rule in Rhodesia and Namibia immediately, and the ending of apartheid in South Africa. If we are committed to peace, then let us join hands in building peace by removing factors underlying the current crisis. . . .

If the oppressed peoples fail to achieve these noble ends by peaceful means we call upon America, not to give any support to the oppressors. Even now we call upon America to desist from direct and indirect support to minority regimes. For this puts America in direct conflict with the interests of Africa i.e. peace, deeply rooted in human dignity and equality and freedom without discrimination.

We have recently demonstrated our readiness to make peaceful change possible in Mozambique and Angola. We are equally committed to assist the oppressed if they should convince us that the road to peaceful change is closed and armed struggle is the only alternative.

The rebels in Rhodesia, assisted by South African troops have committed some of the worst atrocities on the continent. Africa cannot allow them to continue and we urge America not to allow them to continue. Victory for the majority is a matter of time. Let us, therefore, make it as painless as possible to those who have dominated their fellowmen for years.

Mr. President, we wish America to understand our aims and objectives. We are not fighting whites, we are fighting an evil and brutal system. On this there must be no compromise. America should also understand our strategy. We want to achieve our objectives by peaceful methods first and foremost. Africa is ready to try this approach with patience and exhaust all possible tactics. For peace is too precious for all of us, but our patience and the patience of the oppressed has its limits.

Mr. President, we are here only for a short time. We have no other mission except to take the opportunity of the visit to put Africa's stand. We want to avoid confrontation, but let us not be pushed into it.

Once again on behalf of my wife and my compatriots and indeed on my own behalf I thank you for this warm welcome and hospitality. This is indeed a memorable visit, memorable because it has been fruitful and it coincides with the launching, only yesterday, of your bicentenary celebrations. We congratulate the people of the United States for their anti-colonialist struggle of their founding fathers.

34.

Pros and Cons of the Equal Rights Amendment

The Equal Rights Amendment to the Constitution was passed by Congress in 1972, at the height of the "women's lib" movement. But the drive to get the amendment ratified became a protracted one as opposition began to gather steam. By the end of 1975 thirty-four of the requisite thirty-eight states had voted in favor of ERA. Nonetheless, prospects for approval by the March 1979 deadline seemed to be growing more remote. Ratification was defeated in Florida, Illinois, Missouri, South Carolina, and North Carolina. Some states in fact retracted their previous ratification. The following selection reprints arguments for and against the ERA by two women state legislators. Writing in favor of the amendment is Elaine Gordon of the Florida House of Representatives. She is opposed by former Arizona state senator Trudy Camping.

Source: *State Government*, Spring 1975.

Elaine Gordon: For the ERA

Historically, the United States has defended people's rights to liberty, freedom, and equality around the world at great personal sacrifice and enormous cost in money and lives. It appears inconsistent that we refuse to insure the same lofty ideals for over 51 percent of our own citizens—women.

Women, as a class, enjoy only one guaranteed right under the Constitution—the right to vote. In all other respects they are governed by state statutes, codes, and rules and regulations. In a report to the U.S. Supreme Court, the Solicitor General revealed that 876 sections in the U.S. Code contained sex-based references. States have turned up hundreds of state statutes in need of revision.

Discrimination on the basis of sex affects property and inheritance rights, guardianship rights, management of earnings, access to education and employment, and even the right to retain one's own name. Denial of a woman's right to establish a domicile affects a broad spectrum of legal rights and duties, i.e., eligibility to register to vote, to run for office, pay taxes, serve on a jury, or be employed by a municipality.

Since there are more discrimination cases filed against the federal government than all of the cases against state statutes combined (most of which are challenges to federal codes and administrative rules and policies rather than statutes), the immediate impact of the addition of the Equal Rights Amendment to the Constitution would be on the federal government. It becomes evident, therefore, that merely changing state statutes will not be a solution to discrimination against women.

Opponents of the ERA choose to ignore the legislative history embodied in the majority report of a congressional committee which serves the purpose of "legislative intent," a term well recognized in the State Legislatures. It is this legislative intent, not the oft quoted and distorted Minority Report, that will guide the Supreme Court in its decisions. The argument that the courts could interpret present laws to include women is specious since they have historically refused to take such a position. The Supreme Court has been slow to move and has consistently chosen not to apply the Fourteenth Amendment to discrimination based on sex with the same vigor it applies the amendment to distinctions based on race.

Perhaps if the Court had held that discrimination based on sex is inherently "suspect," its rulings on sex discrimination cases would have been sweeping and could have applied nationwide to similar laws in other States. However, the Court has never held that sex, unlike discrimination based on race, is inherently suspect, and therefore subject to close judicial scrutiny.

Furthermore, the present Court, in its decision in the *Fronterio* case, stated "it is unnecessary for the Court in this case to characterize sex as a suspect classification, with all of the far reaching implications of such holding. By acting prematurely, the Court [will assume] decisional responsibility at the very time when state legislatures, functioning within the traditional democratic process, are debating the proposed amendment." It is apparent, therefore, that the Court will not render decisions of sweeping implications that would strike down discriminatory statutes and regulations because it is anticipating the ratification of the ERA.

The argument that men would no longer be required to support their families is one that proponents reject because one would have to believe that, upon ratification of ERA, all husbands would suddenly decide to withhold support from their families, thus forcing wives to go to work. More than 40 percent of the labor force is women and most of them have to work to supplement shrinking family purchasing power. It is not law, or lack of law, that forces women—or men —into the job market, but rather sheer economic necessity.

The draft is a moot question inasmuch as Pentagon officials continue to support a volunteer army. If the draft were reinstituted, women would have the same deferments available to them as men. Present policy of the armed forces is for no more than 2 percent of the military to be women. While the legality of that might be questioned, as long as the armed forces have powers to regulate troop makeup, those policies could remain the same.

Laws relating to homosexuality would

UPI Compix

Betty Ford expresses support for ERA.

not be construed to deny or abridge equality of rights on account of sex since the classification of persons as "homosexuals" is not a sex-based classification. Homosexuality is not a characteristic unique to one sex; thus statutes relating to homosexuality would apply to males and females equally. The ERA would prohibit discrimination between males and females on the basis of sex, and not among males and females on the basis of sexuality.

"Equality" does not mean "sameness." Thus, the ERA would not prohibit reasonable classifications based on characteristics unique to one sex. For example, a law providing for payment of the medical costs of child bearing could only apply to women. In contrast, if a particular characteristic is found among members of both sexes, then under the ERA it is not the sex factor but the individual factor which would be determinative. Since the childbearing characteristic is unique to one sex, regulations concerning that characteristic are not based on sex and are not reached by the ERA.

The question of "unisex" toilet facilities was clearly resolved when the *Griswald* v. *Connecticut* case, relating to rights of privacy, became part of the legislative intent of the Congress.

Rather than ERA "undermining" the family unit, ratification of the amendment would serve to reaffirm the contribution made by the woman working at home who chooses to invest her time in the creation of family life. The additional sharing of responsibility might free men to spend more time with their children.

The amendment itself will deal only with laws which discriminate between the sexes. Its effect will be a reexamination of the attitudes and lifestyles of both men and women which have made many marriages in 20th century America less than rewarding.

Section 2 of the resolution—"the Congress shall have the power to enforce, by appropriate legislation, the provisions of this article"—raises the question of States' rights. Articles 13, 14, 15, 19, 23, and 24 of the Constitution all contain similar wording and do not change the power of States. This wording grants Congress authority to act in the area of sex discrimination. Article 10 of the Bill of Rights empowers the States to legislate, and the ERA will not supersede that right just as the other articles did not deny the States their power to legislate appropriately.

Only if we fail to do our job as legislators will all jurisdiction over women's rights, domestic relations, property laws, family support, and privacy be transferred to the federal government. States, rather than the federal government, should control the fate of these laws. The legislative process then will not be weakened, the judicial system will not be undermined, and the citizens of each State will be able to retain "home rule."

Proponents cite several reasons for the

necessity of a constitutional amendment. First is the guarantee that the issue of equality will not be subject to the whim of the Legislatures from year to year and that full equality before the law—first-class citizenship—will be assured across state boundaries.

Second, state statutes cannot provide legal authority to correct inequities in federal laws, i.e., the 40-year-old Social Security Act which is dooming a disproportionate number of women to poverty in their old age. Third, once the Equal Rights Amendment is ratified, the burden of proving the reasonableness of disparate treatment on the basis of sex would shift to the United States or the State. Presently the burden is on the aggrieved individuals to show unreasonableness.

It is true that litigation will be required to resolve many of the knotty issues that will arise. But it was litigation that developed much of the discrimination at which the amendment is aimed.

The inherent right of all citizens to receive equal protection and equal treatment under the law should not be subject to the will or whim of even the majority. In almost all cases, civil liberties of minorities are protected by the law. Virtually all of the civil liberties now held by racial and religious minorities and others cannot be modified or abridged by the caprice or desire of even an overwhelming majority. Certainly, considerations of conscience and right compel and demand that these liberties be extended to all men and women.

Trudy Camping: Against the ERA

Only four more States remain before the necessary 38 will have ratified the Equal Rights Amendment, possibly making it the 27th addition to the United States Constitution. Before the remaining Legislatures undertake ratification, perhaps it would be best to determine if the Nation presently would not be better off with just 26 constitutional amendments, and supportive state and federal legislation. Is the Equal Rights Amendment needed, or will it bring even more problems to be solved?

The most important point to remember is that when the State Legislatures ratify the ERA, they are not merely agreeing with the symbolic and philosophical issues of women's rights, they are establishing legal language which must be strictly adhered to. If the U.S. Constitution contained the sentence, "Equality of rights under the law shall not be denied or abridged by the United States or by a State on account of sex," the language itself would admit to no exceptions. It would be an indiscriminate amendment, forcing completely equal treatment of the sexes when that is not particularly advantageous or desired. Such a rigid requirement of equality would be unworkable and would lead to greater injustices for women and men.

To examine the consequences of ratification, Virginia established a task force to study the effects of the ERA on that State's laws. The final report concluded that women's position would be extensively damaged by the ERA because it would all but destroy the protective legislation that has been enacted to help them. Statutory rights or exemptions now given women concerning employment, marital and child support, alimony, rape, seduction, and military draft would be completely invalidated rather than being extended to men. Separate sleeping and toilet facilities would not be legally justified if the ERA were ratified. Women cannot afford to lose these laws which have given protection in special areas of need. The far-reaching effects on family life and the status of women must not be passed over lightly.

However, I think the argument has been not so much over the desired equal status for women but rather the method for achieving this goal. The U.S. Constitution has a special purpose in that it must apply to all successive generations and it would be foolish to tinker with its provisions just to satisfy a philosophical desire for equality. Proponents of the ERA apparently think it would be easier to insert a small sentence in the Constitution than to identify specific wrongs and enact legislation to correct them. This has been of extreme concern to legislators because of the vagueness inherent in the ERA and also because of Section 2 of the proposed amendment.

Section 2 says that "Congress shall have the power to enforce, by appropriate legislation, the provisions of this article." If the ERA was ratified, it would preempt the present right of individual States to legislate in this area and that should not be allowed. It is essential that the States retain their right to enact laws for women. A federal, congressionally influenced set of equal rights for the sexes is not in the best interests of the States or the women and men living in them. In some instances, a national law has been useful, such as in civil rights, employment, or other legislative areas, but women's rights should be kept to the States. The ERA is a misdirected effort in the important work toward women's equality.

State legislation has many advantages, the most significant being that it could relieve a known problem without producing any undesirable side effects. It is difficult to predict all the repercussions of a constitutional amendment, but it is much easier to do so for legislation because it is necessarily more specific. The Nation should not gamble with the effects that could be produced by the Equal Rights Amendment. Specific legislation appears much more desirable.

The private sector would also come under the jurisdiction of legislation, thus granting additional benefits to working women in every area of private employment. Working-hour limitations, rest periods, disability leave, and weight-lifting regulations could all be handled by state legislation, but in this manner the laws would be tempered with rationality, not included in a one-sentence cure-all.

Some progress has been made with state action and court decisions. Litigation has expanded and will continue to expand definitions for women's occupational and marital rights and several States have enacted equal rights legislation. For example, the Arizona Legislature in 1973 enacted two bills dealing with employment, providing equal pay for equal work and allowing an employee to collect triple damages for wages wrongfully withheld. Another measure was an extensive piece of legislation providing equality under the law for both sexes. In 1975, several bills were introduced to amend the state constitution to conform with the antidiscrimination laws previously passed.

Other States should follow this example and enact positive equal rights legislation. The danger in the ERA is its potential to radically change established, time-proven family and sexual relationships. Something as basic as the American family cannot be altered without some expectation of profound disturbances of the Nation's foundation. No one can deny the need for equality between men and women, but the ERA is not the way to achieve it.

WOMEN'S WORLD

The upsurge of interest in women's rights was not confined to the United States. In most countries of the world, even in Communist societies and underdeveloped nations, women evinced some determination to attain social equality and better economic opportunities for themselves. The United Nations proclaimed International Women's Year for 1975, and an international conference was held in Mexico City to debate a "World Plan of Action," a ten-year-long project aimed at improving literacy, work rights, and educational opportunities. There was little unanimity at the conference, however, because Communist and "third world" countries were intent upon making a "new international economic order" and liberation from "capitalist imperialism" the leading priorities. The condition and needs of women thus took second place to these issues.

Veiled women leaving a mosque in Teheran (right). (Below) Delegates vote during a session of the World Conference of the International Women's Year held at Mexico City in July 1975.

Mrs. Ella Grasso, governor of Connecticut, above, attends the Democratic National Convention of 1976. Patricia Hearst photographed by a hidden bank camera during a robbery in San Francisco in April 1974.

In the United States it was impossible to judge whether, by the end of 1976, the women's liberation movement had lost momentum. Certainly the Equal Rights Amendment had become stalled, although only a very few states were needed to complete the ratification process. What had probably happened was a cooling down from the early furor of the movement: tactics of protest march and demonstration had given way to the slower but equally determined attempts to bring about change by means of legislation, government regulation, court cases, and economic policy changes. Yet the overall gains made by women since the late 1960s were hard to assess. There were some obvious improvements: more women were elected to public office; more were given responsible positions in government and industry; some Protestant denominations began to ordain women to the ministry (but this remained a very divisive issue in some churches); and women's sports events were given better national media coverage. In other words, women became more "visible" to the public. But it certainly was an open question whether the life of the average woman in America was much different. Many more women were working outside the home than ever before, either to support themselves or to help support their families. Did this represent greater equality of economic opportunity, or was it the result of sheer economic necessity, owing to spiraling prices and a severe recession? Given the traditional male-oriented biases of our society (even among millions of women), real social equality was a goal still to be attained.

Shelly Katz—Black Star

In ceremonies at Rome in 1975, Mother Elizabeth Seton, left, was proclaimed the first native-born American saint. This portrait in the Vatican Museum was painted by Joseph Dawley. Elizabeth Ray revealed that she had been mistress to an Ohio congressman while on his staff payroll. Dr. Mary Johnston, below, in training to be the first American spacewoman.

UPI COMPIX

Courtesy, NASA

Wide World

Recently ordained women priests celebrate their first holy communion at Riverside Church in New York. Left to right are the Reverends Carter Heyward, Alison Cheek, and Jeannette Piccard. Trans-sexual Renee Richards in a professional tennis tournament, 1976.

Leo Chaplin—Black Star

35.

PATRICIA HUTAR: International Women's Year

International Women's Year 1975 was proclaimed by the United Nations General Assembly in 1972. It was planned as an endeavor to promote the equality of women in all societies. The high point of the year was the international conference at Mexico City June 19 to July 2. The conference adopted a ten-year program entitled "World Plan of Action" and a declaration on women's rights. Unfortunately the proceedings of the conference were not harmonious. The Communist bloc and Third World nations attempted to politicize IWY by insisting that the issue of women's rights be subsumed under demands for a new international economic order. Because of numerous disagreements the United States delegation voted against the conference declaration. One of the members of the U. S. delegation was Patricia Hutar of the Commission on the Status of Women of the U.N. Economic and Social Council. She spoke to the conference on June 20.

Source: *Department of State Bulletin,* August 18, 1975.

Ladies and gentlemen:

I would like to begin by bringing you the personal greetings from the First Lady of the United States, Betty Ford:

As I am unable to be with you in Mexico City, I send my cordial greetings to President Echeverría and Mrs. Echeverría, to President of the Conference Ojeda Paullada, to Secretary General Waldheim, Secretary General of the Conference Mrs. Sipila, and to all who are attending this historic conference.

I wish you to know that the people and Government of the United States are firmly committed to the goals of the conference and to the work that must follow it if these goals are to be reached.

The high purpose of International Women's Year—to promote the equality of women—truly enhances the equality of us all. As my husband said on the occasion of announcing our own National Commission for the Observance of International Women's Year,

the search to secure rights for women frees both sexes from restrictive stereotypes. Liberation of the spirit opens new possibilities for the future of all individuals and of all nations. I am awed by the task you face. I am inspired by the opportunity you have for progress.

I know that the leaders of the U.S. delegation will work unceasingly with you in a spirit of cooperation to make the Conference on International Women's Year a landmark in the history of women's affairs and of humanity's search for peace and understanding. We are deeply grateful to President Echeverría for gracing our deliberation this afternoon and to the Government of Mexico for its generosity in volunteering to host this international conference. We thank the Government of Mexico for all the work it has done in making arrangements for us. The vibrance and beauty of this capital city are a stimulus to achievement. The hospitality of the Mexican people enhances our enjoyment of our brief time among them. We also wish to praise the extraordinary competence of those members of the U.N. Secretariat at all levels who completed the enormous task of preparing for a world conference of this magnitude in an unprecedentedly short period of time.

The representatives of the United States of America come to this conference with a deep sense of empathy and solidarity with women in all parts of the world. We desire to work together on the many concerns that are common to us all.

Discrimination based on sex is the most widely known kind of discrimination. It is found in all developed and developing societies, either openly or covertly, and it is manifested in diverse forms. The time is long overdue for women to eliminate discrimination based on sex. No rhetoric, however attractive it may be, should postpone the achievement of equal rights and responsibilities for women.

We in the United States had long felt the need for all countries of the world to come together to discuss the most important problems that affect over half the world's population, the women of the world. Therefore, with the cosponsorship of nine developing nations, we introduced a U.N. resolution to establish a World Conference for International Women's Year. We all are aware that declarations and statements of principle enunciated by the United Nations, though of great value, were not enough. There was a need to focus worldwide attention to dramatize the problems faced by women.

We will work with the other delegations to produce a plan of action that will impact on national governments for the implementation of the principles of International Women's Year — equality, development, and peace. But plans are not enough. Mechanisms need to be established to insure that real progress is made.

We in the United States expect to learn much from the accomplishments of our sisters around the world. In exchange, we offer to share with you the substantial progress made in the United States to further women's rights and responsibilities.

Much has been done, but there is much more that needs to be done to overcome the limitations and discriminatory practices of the past, reinforced by centuries of laws, traditions, and customs. We are proud in the United States of the legislation and government action that has been taken in the past several years to prohibit employment discrimination based on sex. Such legislation provides for equal pay for work of equal value, nondiscrimination in hiring, in discharging, and in compensation. Another piece of important legislation prohibits discrimination on the basis of sex in educational programs or activities.

These antidiscrimination laws and other social change have come about in our country through the joint efforts of voluntary organizations and the government. Traditionally the Government of the United States does not plan social change in the sense that some other governments do — it responds to the demands for reform made by citizens and/or voluntary associations and works with them in charting the mechanisms of social change.

We are also proud of the fact that we have established various national machinery to continue to monitor and implement nondiscrimination on the basis of sex. Some of these include a Special Assistant to the President of the United States for Women and an Office of Women's Programs in the White House; the Women's Bureau in our Department of Labor, established in 1920; a Women's Action Program in the Department of Health, Education, and Welfare; and a

Federal Women's Program Coordinator to monitor employment practices in every governmental body. We also have citizens actively involved in this machinery, including a President's Advisory Council on the Status of Women, Advisory Councils to the Secretaries of Labor, Defense, and Health, Education, and Welfare.

Though many general economic, political, and social changes are modifying the basic situation of women throughout the world—both in those countries now undergoing arduous processes of development and those which have already experienced the impact of industrialization—these changes will not automatically redress the balance. It requires positive efforts to identify and cope with the many factors which limit women and stand in the way of their full integration in development. I need mention only the lack of access to employment, education, and political integration to make the point that women are prevented from making their full and responsible contribution to the life of their societies and their full contribution to their families, their communities, and their nations.

International Women's Year has chosen as two of its basic goals equality for women and their integration in development. These goals are inextricably interrelated. Each is indispensable to the other.

Equality without development means shared misery and frustration. Development without equality may mean a worsened situation for many women, both those who are homemakers and those who are in the labor force. Similarly, achieving one of the goals helps achieve the other. Development creates new situations and changes which make it possible for women to win a new and more equal status. And the full, equal participation of women in the development process can make the difference between success and failure of development itself.

The U.S. Government is prepared to introduce at this conference a draft declaration on equality and development that embraces these two basic goals of the Year, which I have stated are intertwined.

But women cannot wait, with arms folded, for men to achieve a new order before women can achieve equality. On the contrary, women must continue their work, already begun, to achieve a truly equal partnership. Women must be in decisionmaking positions in the power structure along with men to build a more just world order.

Women have a strong sense of social responsibility and are searching for opportunities to share their vision of a new society free of hunger and poverty. We must have, though, the understanding and commitment of men to reach the goal of equality. We have heard pledges of such commitment already in this conference in our opening session. We welcome this pledge of partnership.

The third goal of International Women's Year is to strengthen the role of women in establishing world peace. To achieve it, women must mobilize their potential political power to assure that governments actively pursue the goal of disarmament.

The United States believes that disarmament negotiations should be directed toward general and complete disarmament under strict international control. It is our profound hope that women will not only use their influence to keep governments working toward this end but we believe also that women must equip themselves for and assert their right to serve in agencies of government and on international delegations that are responsible for arms control and disarmament.

Basically, the issue and challenge which we face is to develop and utilize the untapped potential of over half the world's population. There is a great scarcity of women in policymaking positions in the world. Women remain significantly absent from high-level posts in governments, in international affairs, in the professions, and in business.

Women want to share with men the responsibilities and the duties involved in decisions affecting peace and development as well as in decisions that affect their lives. But unless they are able to move into the top positions in their fields, their impact in national and world affairs will be negligible and the possibilities of helping other women to move ahead in their roles will be nil.

Women's presence must be felt if we want the policies of the public and the private sector to be altered so as to be more equitable for women and men. This is one of the major areas of concern and focus of our U.S. National Commission on the Observance of International Women's Year.

At this conference we must insist that the United Nations and its specialized agencies provide opportunities for women to rise to the highest levels.

During the last General Assembly the U.S. delegation introduced a resolution, inspired by Senator Charles Percy, designed to assure that priority is given to projects within the U.N. Development Program that integrate women into the development process. This is a step in the right direction; our responsibility now, though, is to assure that this resolution is carried out.

At the initiative of the U.S. delegation, too, the U.N. Secretariat has set up a personnel committee to make sure that there shall be no discrimination against women in hiring or promotion within the U.N. Secretariat. The next step is to secure the establishment of other personnel committees throughout the entire U.N. system.

Action by national governments will have a still broader effect upon the status of women than the international actions proposed above. A majority of governments have committed themselves to the principles of equality and of integrating women in development through their adherence to U.N. conventions and resolutions on these subjects.

This conference must build a plan of action that includes specific national measures for translating principles into action. Upon leaving this conference, participants must assume the responsibility for assuring that each of their governments puts into action the policy recommendations and provides the necessary resources to adopt the measures called for by the plan of action.

The U.S. delegation and the National Commission on the Observance of International Women's Year have held several meetings with our nongovernmental leaders to discuss the implementation of the World Plan of Action. We have a commitment to work together to insure the full implementation of the plan of action in our country upon our return from Mexico City.

I am pleased that so many nongovernmental leaders from around the world have assembled here in Mexico City to attend this conference and also the International Women's Year Tribune. I think that one of the strongest assets of the world conference is the interest of the nongovernmental organizations and the input they will provide the delegations to this U.N. conference.

In order to escalate the process of equality for women and for integration in development, we must devise strategies to change attitudes and behavior that have resulted from cultural conditioning. We cannot accomplish this by institutional change alone. Escalating strategies directed at attitudinal change involves not only the way men see women but also how women see themselves.

Women are learning that to compete is all right, for they are looking at themselves in a new light. They are learning that women must build support systems within existing structures — whether business, government, political, academic, or agriculture. Women must develop support systems to change the degrading sex-role stereotype and images of women in the mass media which perpetuate false depictions of women.

A myth prevails that women are not competitive — that they seem to lack motivation to progress and to participate in all phases of society.

However, we must keep in mind why this is perceived to be the case. We must remember the impact that conditioning has had on women. From the moment they are born, women's role in society has been dictated by culture and tradition. This affects the way their role is perceived by men, by the society, and by themselves.

We must examine and reassess old myths that society holds about the capacities, potential, and lifestyles of girls and women. Self-images for women are beginning to change, but the inaccurate and destructive sexist image projected must be rooted out.

We must make changes in the portrayal of women in program content and commercials in mass media — radio, television, newspapers. Educational materials in the schools — textbooks, visual aids, curricula — all need to be reexamined and changed to reflect the changing role of women and men in the society and to eliminate sex-role stereotyping.

To effect change in any area of life, women must seek and achieve leadership roles in management and public administration. Change will be accelerated when women serve in program planning, policymaking and decisionmaking roles in society.

Under the office of the Assistant Secretary for Education, the highest ranking official of education in the United States — currently a woman and a member of our delegation, I am proud to say — has developed programs based on special women's research being conducted at the National Institute of Education on changing sex roles in American culture, female role ideology, and educational aspiration, to mention a few.

Finally, this conference should serve as a stimulus to men as well as to women throughout the world. We hope that from this conference men will gain a vision of a more just society in which an equality for women and participation by them will mean a more varied and equitable sharing, to the benefit of men as well as women. It is the conviction of women globally that the goals of International Women's Year — of equality, development, and peace — are not goals for *women* but serious goals for a world society and that men no less than women stand to gain. It should be the objective of the conference to make this conviction take root and grow.

36.

HENRY KISSINGER: The Evacuation of Vietnam

On April 30, 1975, the South Vietnamese government collapsed and surrendered to North Vietnam. The long war had finally ended. Cambodia had already fallen thirteen days earlier, and Laos was soon to follow. In the days before Saigon's collapse, the United States conducted a massive evacuation project to bring out most of the Americans who were still there, as well as thousands of South Vietnamese who felt they would be endangered by the Communist takeover. On April 29 Secretary of State Kissinger held a news conference explaining the evacuation and answering reporters' questions on the future of American foreign policy. Portions of the news conference are reprinted here.

Source: *Weekly Compilation of Presidential Documents,* May 5, 1975.

Secretary Kissinger. Ladies and gentlemen, when the President spoke before the Congress, he stated as our objective the stabilization of the situation in Vietnam.

We made clear at that time, as well as before many Congressional hearings, that our purpose was to bring about the most controlled and the most humane solution that was possible and that these objectives required the course which the President had set.

Our priorities were as follows: We sought to save the American lives still in Vietnam; we tried to rescue as many South Vietnamese that had worked with the United States for 15 years, in reliance on our commitments, as we possibly could; and, we sought to bring about as humane an outcome as was achievable under the conditions that existed.

Over the past 2 weeks, the American personnel in Vietnam have been progressively reduced. Our objective was to reduce at a rate that was significant enough so that we would finally be able to evacuate rapidly, but which would not produce a panic which might prevent anybody from getting out.

Our objective was also to fulfill the human obligation which we felt to the tens of thousands of South Vietnamese who had worked with us for over a decade.

Finally, we sought through various intermediaries to bring about as humane a political evolution as we could.

By Sunday evening, the personnel in our mission had been reduced to 950, and there were 8,000 South Vietnamese to be considered in a particularly high-risk category—between five and eight thousand. We do not know the exact number.

On Monday evening Washington time, around 5 o'clock, which was Tuesday morning in Saigon, the airport in Tan Son Nhut was rocketed and received artillery fire.

The President called an NSC meeting. He decided that if the shelling stopped by dawn Saigon time, we would attempt to operate with fixed-wing aircraft from Tan Son Nhut airport for one more day to remove the high-risk South Vietnamese, together with all the Defense Attaché's Office [DAO], which was located near the Tan Son Nhut airport. He also ordered a substantial reduction of the remaining American personnel in South Vietnam.

I may point out that the American personnel in Saigon was divided into two groups; one with the Defense Attaché's Office, which was located near the Tan Son Nhut airport; the second one, which was related to the Embassy and was with the United States mission in downtown Saigon.

The shelling did stop early in the morning on Tuesday, Saigon time, or about 9 p.m. last night, Washington time. We then attempted to land C-130s, but found that the population at the airport had got out of control and had flooded the runways. It proved impossible to land any more fixed-wing aircraft.

The President thereupon ordered that the DAO personnel, together with those civilians that had been made ready to be evacuated, be moved to the DAO compound which is near Tan Son Nhut airport. And at about 11 o'clock last night, he ordered the evacuation of all Americans from Tan Son Nhut and from the Embassy as well.

This operation has been going on all day which, of course, is night in Saigon, under difficult circumstances. And the total number of those evacuated numbers about 6,500 — we will have the exact figures for you tomorrow — of which about a thousand are Americans.

Our Ambassador has left, and the evacuation can be said to be completed.

In the period since the President spoke to the Congress, we have therefore succeeded in evacuating all of the Americans who were in South Vietnam, losing the two Marines last night to rocket fire and two pilots today on a helicopter.

We succeeded in evacuating something on the order of 55,000 South Viet-

Vietnamese refugees are hauled aboard ship near the South Vietnamese city of Hue in March 1975, shortly before Saigon fell to the Communists.

namese, and we hope that we have contributed to a political evolution that may spare the South Vietnamese some of the more drastic consequences of a political change. But this remains to be seen; this last point remains to be seen.

As far as the Administration is concerned, I can only underline the point made by the President. We do not believe that this is a time for recrimination. It is a time to heal wounds, to look at our international obligations, and to remember that peace and progress in the world has depended importantly on American commitment and American convictions and that the peace and progress of our own people is closely tied to that of the rest of the world.

I will be glad to answer your questions. . . .

Q. Mr. Secretary, do you consider the United States now owes any allegiance at all to the Paris pact? Are we now bound in any way by the Paris agreements?

Secretary Kissinger. Well. as far as the

United States is concerned, there aren't many provisions of the Paris agreement that are still relevant. As far as the North Vietnamese are concerned, they have stated that they wish to carry out the Paris accords, though by what definition is not fully clear to me. We would certainly support this if it has any meaning.

Q. May I ask one followup? Do you now favor American aid in rebuilding North Vietnam?

Secretary Kissinger. North Vietnam?

Q. North Vietnam.

Secretary Kissinger. No, I do not favor American aid for rebuilding North Vietnam.

Q. How about South Vietnam?

Secretary Kissinger. With respect to South Vietnam, we will have to see what kind of government emerges and, indeed, whether there is going to be a South Vietnam. We would certainly look at particular specific humanitarian requests that can be carried out by humanitarian agencies, but we do believe that the primary responsibility should fall on those who supplied the weapons for this political change. . . .

Q. Mr. Secretary, what caused the breakdown of the intent which was spoken of earlier on the Hill to try to achieve a measure of self-determination for the people of South Vietnam, and what is your total assessment now of the effectiveness or the noneffectiveness of the whole Paris accord operation, which you said at the outset was intended to achieve peace with honor for the United States?

Secretary Kissinger. Until Sunday night, we thought there was some considerable hope that the North Vietnamese would not seek a solution by purely military means. And when the transfer of power to General Minh took place, a person who had been designated by the other side as a counterpart worth talking to—they would be prepared to talk with—we thought that a negotiated solution in the next few days was highly probable.

Sometime Sunday night, the North Vietnamese obviously changed signals. Why that is, we do not yet know, nor do I exclude that now that the American presence is totally removed and very little military structure is left in South Vietnam, that there may not be a sort of a negotiation. But what produced this sudden shift to a military option or what would seem to us to be a sudden shift to a military option, I have not had a sufficient opportunity to analyze.

Now, as to the effectiveness of the Paris accords, I think it is important to remember the mood in this country at the time that the Paris accords were being negotiated. I think it is worth remembering that the principal criticism that was then made was that the terms we insisted on were too tough, not that the terms were too generous.

We wanted what was considered peace with honor—was that the United States would not end a war by overthrowing a government with which it had been associated. That still seems like an objective that was correct.

Now, there were several other assumptions that were made at that time that were later falsified by events that were beyond the control of, and that were indeed unforeseeable by anybody who negotiated these agreements, including the disintegration of, or the weakening of executive authority in the United States, for reasons unconnected with foreign policy considerations.

So, the premises of the Paris accord in terms of aid, of the possibility of aid, and in terms of other factors, tended to disintegrate. I see no purpose now in reviewing that particular history. Within the context of the time, it seemed the right thing to do.

Q. Mr. Secretary, a followup question on that. What is the current relationship of the United States to the South Vietnamese political grouping, or whatever you would call it?

Secretary Kissinger. We will have to see what grouping emerges out of whatever negotiations should now take place between the two South Vietnamese sides. After we have seen what grouping emerges and what degree of independence it has, then we can make a decision about what our political relationship to it is. We have not made a decision on that.

Q. Would you say diplomatic relations are in abeyance with the government in South Vietnam?

Secretary Kissinger. I think that is a fair statement.

Q. Mr. Secretary, looking back on the war now, would you say that the war was in vain and, what do you feel it accomplished?

Secretary Kissinger. I think it will be a long time before Americans will be able to talk or write about the war with some dispassion. It is clear that the war did not achieve the objectives of those who started the original involvement, nor the objectives of those who sought to end that involvement, which they found on terms which seemed to them compatible with the sacrifices that had been made.

What lessons we should draw from it, I think we should reserve for another occasion. But I don't think that we can solve the problem of having entered the conflict too lightly by leaving it too lightly, either.

Q. Mr. Secretary, looking toward the future, has America been so stunned by the experience of Vietnam that it will never again come to the military or economic aid of an ally? I am talking specifically in the case of Israel.

Secretary Kissinger. As I pointed out in a speech a few weeks ago, one lesson we must learn from this experience is that we must be very careful in the commitments we make, but that we should scrupulously honor those commitments we do make.

I believe that the experience in the war, that the war has had, can make us more mature in the commitments we undertake and more determined to maintain those we have. I would therefore think that with relation to other countries, including Israel, that no lessons should be drawn by the enemies of our friends from the experiences in Vietnam. . . .

Q. Mr. Secretary, there is a new Asia developing after the Indochina situation. What will the priorities of the United States be in recognizing its existing commitments and in making new ones?

Secretary Kissinger. We will have to assess the impact of Indochina on our allies and on other countries in that area and on their perceptions of the United States. And we will have to assess, also, what role the United States can responsibly play over an indefinite period of time, because surely another lesson we should draw from the Indochina experience is that a foreign policy must be sustained over decades if it is to be effective and, if it cannot be, then it has to be tailored to what is sustainable.

The President has already reaffirmed our alliance with Japan, our defense treaty with Korea, and we, of course, also have treaty obligations and important bases in the Philippines. We will soon be in consultation with many other countries in that area, including Indonesia and Singapore and Australia and New Zealand, and we hope to crystallize an Asian policy that is suited to present circumstances with close consultation with our friends.

37.

GERALD R. FORD: The Mayaguez Incident

Although this May 15, 1975, letter from President Ford to the Congress contains the gist of the **Mayaguez** *affair, there was a great deal of confusion about it at the time; and the letter leaves many questions unanswered. As stated, the President ordered the Marines to rescue the ship and crew. On May 14, 250 Marines and eleven helicopters struck at Koh Tang island, but in spite of casualties exceeding the number of crew members on the ship, neither the ship nor its crew was there. On the same day, U. S. planes bombed a Cambodian air base some 200 miles away from Koh Tang island. The Cambodian government insisted that the ship and crew members had been released before the air strike. For several weeks afterward there were conflicting reports about exactly what had happened and how many American casualties were involved. If the incident had any lasting effect, it was in the worsening of relations between the U. S. and Thailand. The strike had used Thailand as a base against the wishes of the Thai government.*

Source: *Department of State Bulletin,* June 2, 1975.

Dear Mr. Speaker: (*Dear Mr. President Pro Tem:*)

On 12 May 1975, I was advised that the S. S. *Mayaguez,* a merchant vessel of United States registry en route from Hong Kong to Thailand with a U.S. citizen crew, was fired upon, stopped, boarded, and seized by Cambodian naval patrol boats of the Armed Forces of Cambodia in international waters in the vicinity of Poulo Wai Island. The seized vessel was then forced to proceed to Koh Tang Island where it was required to anchor. This hostile act was in clear violation of international law.

In view of this illegal and dangerous act, I ordered, as you have been previously advised, United States military forces to conduct the necessary reconnaissance and to be ready to respond if diplomatic efforts to secure the return of the vessel and its personnel were not successful. Two United States reconnaissance aircraft in the course of locating the *Mayaguez* sustained minimal damage from small firearms. Appropriate demands for the return of the *Mayaguez* and its crew were made, both publicly and privately, without success.

In accordance with my desire that the Congress be informed on this matter and taking note of Section 4(a) (1) of the War Powers Resolution, I wish to report to you that at about 6:20 a.m., 13 May, pursuant to my instructions to prevent the movement of the *Mayaguez* into a mainland port, U.S. aircraft fired warning shots across the bow of the ship and gave visual signals to small craft approaching the ship. Subsequently, in order to stabilize the situation and in an attempt to preclude removal of the American crew of the *Mayaguez* to the mainland, where their rescue would be more difficult, I directed the United States Armed Forces to isolate the island and interdict any movement between the ship or the island and the mainland, and to prevent movement of the ship itself, while still taking all possible care to prevent loss of life or injury to the U.S. captives. During the evening of 13 May, a Cambodian patrol boat attempting to leave the island disregarded aircraft warnings and was sunk. Thereafter, two other Cambodian patrol craft were destroyed and four others were damaged and immobilized. One boat, suspected of having some U.S. captives aboard, succeeded in reaching Kompong Som after efforts to turn it around without injury to the passengers failed.

Our continued objective in this operation was the rescue of the captured American crew along with the retaking of the ship *Mayaguez*. For that purpose, I ordered late this afternoon [May 14] an assault by United States Marines on the island of Koh Tang to search out and rescue such Americans as might still be held there, and I ordered retaking of the

Mayaguez by other marines boarding from the destroyer escort *Holt*. In addition to continued fighter and gunship coverage of the Koh Tang area, these marine activities were supported by tactical aircraft from the *Coral Sea*, striking the military airfield at Ream and other military targets in the area of Kompong Som in order to prevent reinforcement or support from the mainland of the Cambodian forces detaining the American vessel and crew.

At approximately 9:00 P.M. EDT on 14 May, the *Mayaguez* was retaken by United States forces. At approximately 11:30 P.M., the entire crew of the *Mayaguez* was taken aboard the *Wilson*. U.S. forces have begun the process of disengagement and withdrawal.

This operation was ordered and conducted pursuant to the President's constitutional Executive power and his authority as Commander-in-Chief of the United States Armed Forces.

38.

ELLSWORTH BUNKER: Panama and the United States

Control of the Panama Canal Zone has been a sorely controversial point between the two nations for many years. Pressing economic problems constitute one reason for Panama's desire to control the zone. On the other hand, apart from economic gains, American officials have long viewed the canal as vital to the U. S. defense system. The Nixon Administration, in 1973 and 1974, sent ambassador-at-large Ellsworth Bunker to confer with Panamanian Foreign Minister Juan Antonio Tack on a new treaty regulating the canal zone. Guidelines for the projected treaty provide for the abrogation of the 1903 treaty which had consigned the zone to the U. S. in perpetuity. In 1976 no new treaty had yet been signed, and the negotiations had become embroiled in the partisan politics of an election year. On May 22, 1975, Ambassador Bunker explained the developing relationship with Panama to the Rainier Club in Seattle, Washington. Portions of his remarks are reprinted here.

Source: *Vital Speeches*, July 1, 1975.

I AM HAPPY to be with you this afternoon and to have this opportunity to speak on the efforts now underway to create a new relationship between Panama and the United States.

I know that the arrangements for the future operation of the Panama Canal are of great interest to a major maritime city such as Seattle.

But there are broader reasons why negotiations over the future of the Canal should concern Americans. For the successful conclusion of a new agreement on the Canal:

— would demonstrate the possibility, in the conduct of our foreign relations, of resolving problems when they are susceptible to accommodation and compromise, rather than waiting until they raise the danger of confrontation and possible use of military force.

— would provide concrete evidence of our country's willingness to move toward a more mature partnership with Latin America, where we have often in the past been accused of paternalism or neglect. And,

— It would serve as an example of practical cooperation between a large and a small country, a developed and a less developed country. Such cooperation is indispensable if we are to achieve what the Secretary of State recently described as the aim of U.S. foreign policy: "to help shape a new structure of international relations which promotes cooperation rather than force; negotiation rather than confrontation, and the positive aspirations of people rather than the accumulation of arms by nations."

In the past, when serving as a U.S. negotiator, I have made it a habit to keep my mouth shut publicly while negotiations were in progress. The fact that I have decided to discuss today some of the key issues in the current Canal negotiations reflects another basic element of this Administration's conduct of foreign policy—the awareness that no foreign policy decision, and particularly no significant change in foreign policy, can take place without the advice and consent of Congress and the informed support of the American people, on the basis of candid and reasonable public discussion.

The story begins 72 years ago.

In 1903 the newly-independent Republic of Panama granted to the United States —in the Hay-Bunau-Varilla Treaty—a strip of its territory 10 miles wide and 50 miles long for the construction, maintenance, operation and protection of a Canal between the Atlantic and Pacific.

Panama also granted to the United States—in perpetuity—all of the rights, power and authority to act within that strip of territory as "if it were the sovereign." . . .

Panama has grown increasingly conscious of the fact that the Treaty is heavily weighted in our favor.

Consequently, the level of its consent to our presence there has—over the years —persistently declined.

And by Panama, I mean the Panamanian people of all strata—not simply their governments.

Among the aspects of the 1903 Treaty which have caused this decline in consent, Panama cites the following:

— The United States occupies a strip across the heartland of its territory— cutting the nation in two and curbing the natural growth of its urban areas.

— The United States rules as sovereign over this strip of Panama's territory—the Canal Zone.

— It maintains a police force, courts, and jails to enforce the laws of the United States—not only upon Americans, but upon Panamanians as well.

— It operates, on Panama's territory, a full-fledged government—a government which has no reference to the Government of Panama, its host.

— It operates virtually all commercial enterprises within the Canal Zone — and denies to Panama the jurisdictional rights which would permit private Panamanian enterprise to compete.

— It controls virtually all the deep-water port facilities which serve Panama.

— It holds idle large areas of land and water within the Canal Zone.

— The United States pays Panama but $2 million annually for the immensely valuable rights it enjoys on Panamanian territory.

— Finally — and perhaps most importantly — the United States can do all these things, the Treaty says, forever.

To these conditions Panama objects, saying that they deprive their country of dignity, of the ability to develop naturally, and indeed, of full independence.

The United States attempted to respond to some of the Panamanian objections in the past.

Treaty revisions were made in 1936 and 1955.

But the most objectionable feature from Panama's viewpoint — United States exercise of rights as if sovereign in the Canal Zone in perpetuity — has remained unchanged.

Panamanian frustrations over this state of affairs, and over the apparent disinclination of the United States to alter it has intensified over the years.

These frustrations culminated in demonstrations and riots in January 1964 when 21 Panamanians and 3 Americans were killed.

Diplomatic relations were broken.

Following a major reassessment of our policy toward Panama, President Johnson after consultations with President Truman and President Eisenhower committed us — publicly and with bipartisan support — to negotiate a wholly new treaty to replace the old one.

President Nixon and President Ford

subsequently renewed that commitment.

Our purpose was, and continues to be this — to lay the foundations for a new — a more modern — relationship between the two countries.

Without such a changed relationship I believe it safe to say that Panama's already low level of consent to our presence will become lower still.

It will approach zero.

While it is true — of course — that we could attempt to maintain our present position with regard to the Panama Canal, we would have to do so in an increasingly hostile atmosphere.

In these circumstances we would likely find ourselves engaged in hostilities with an otherwise friendly country — a conflict that, in my view, the American people would not long accept.

At the same time, we should bear in mind that the Canal is vulnerable to sabotage and terrorist acts.

We would find it difficult, if not impossible, to keep the Canal running against all-out Panamanian opposition.

The problem — in my opinion — simply will not go away.

Attitudes — not only in Panama but in the Hemisphere at large — have changed.

The Latin American nations have made our handling of the Panama negotiation a test of our intentions in the Hemisphere. We no longer can be — nor would we want to be — the only country in the world exercising extra-territoriality on the soil of another country.

The evidence — it seems to me — strongly favors some form of partnership with Panama.

Partnership with Panama would help the United States preserve what it needs most respecting the Canal.

Partnership would provide an environment conducive to effective operation and defense of the Canal by the United States.

It would provide Panama with a meaningful stake in the operation and defense of the Canal.

It would help stimulate the cooperation and friendship both of the Panamanian people and of whatever government exists in Panama at any given time.

In short, partnership would mean that the United States would not have to divert any of its energies in Panama from the functions required for the efficient operation of the Canal.

Putting it simply, I believe our interest in keeping the Canal open and operating for our own strategic and economic purposes is best served by a partnership agreement for a reasonably additional period of time. . . .

Such a new relationship involves giving up something of what we now possess.

We want to keep the power but discard what is nonessential to our purpose in Panama.

Three examples should serve to explain my meaning:

—First, we will retain control over Canal operations for the duration of the Treaty, *but* Panama will participate progressively in these operations in preparation for its future role.

—Second, we will keep the lands and facilities we need to control and defend the Canal, *but* return what we can do without.

—Third, we will have defense rights, *but* perform our defense tasks with Panamanian participation.

Simply stated, we will work together, *but*—for the Treaty's life—we will operate the Canal.

We will secure the lands we need by releasing what we do not need.

By having Panamanian participation in operation and defense we will have a more secure Canal.

In sum, we see a new Treaty as the most practical means for protecting our interest.

Whereas continuance of the *status quo* will lead surely to prolonged problems—possible loss of what we are trying to preserve—partnership promises a greater assurance of success in achieving our essential interest—a Canal that is open, efficient and neutral.

In reality we have never claimed sovereignty over the Canal Zone.

Under the 1903 Treaty we have extensive rights.

The new Treaty would grant us continued rights to operate and defend the Canal, but we would relinquish some rights which we don't need to accomplish these missions.

Our essential requirement is not abstract sovereignty but the specific rights —accepted by Panama—that give the control we need.

Second, we need to overcome the idea that perpetuity is essential to defense and operation of the Canal.

On the contrary United States insistence on perpetual control is likely to create the kind of hostile environment which will jeopardize our ability to operate and defend the Canal for an extended period of time.

What is required is a relationship based on mutual respect and dignity.

Third, we must overcome the belief that the Canal Zone is part of the United States or a United States territory.

In the 1903 Treaty Panama granted us "rights, powers and authority within the Zone . . . which the United States would possess . . . if it were the sovereign of the territory."

We were not granted "sovereignty" as such.

The United States for many years has considered the Canal Zone as Panamanian territory, albeit under the United States jurisdiction.

Fourth,—and last—we must overcome the notion that a new Treaty will somehow lead inevitably to the Canal's closure and loss. This concern appears based upon an erroneous view of the Panamanians as well as a lack of knowledge about our negotiating objectives.

There are still people who believe that Panamanians lack the technical aptitude and the inclination to manage the operation of the Canal.

These people ignore the fact that Panamanians already comprise over ¾ of the employees of the Canal enterprise.

While it is true that many of these employees have not held supervisory positions, no one who has been to Panama and seen its thriving economy can persuasively argue that Panamanians—given the proper training—would not be able to keep the Canal operating effectively and efficiently.

Whereas Panama's participation in the Canal's operation and defense would increase its stake in the Canal and provide it with a greater incentive to help us keep the Canal open and operating efficiently, adherence to the *status quo* would more likely lead to the Canal's closure and loss.

I firmly believe that our most critical problem at home is not fundamental antipathy to a new relationship with Panama.

It is ignorance of why the new relationship is needed to protect our interests.

We need a straightforward and productive dialogue.

Considerable public education is needed if a new Treaty is not to be regarded as bad politics domestically.

Debate on an issue of such national import is not only inevitable but desirable.

After education, dialogue and debate I believe that we will emerge with a reasonable and mutually satisfactory Treaty which will be examined and which will stand, on its merits.

39.

ALEKSANDR SOLZHENITSYN: America, You Must Think About the World

Universally regarded as one of the 20th century's great writers, Solzhenitsyn was awarded the Nobel Prize for Literature in 1970. But, as a strong critic of Soviet rule, he was not allowed to leave Russia to accept his prize until the Soviet government expelled him on February 13, 1974, and deprived him of his citizenship. The immediate occasion for this action was publication in the West of Solzhenitsyn's Gulag Archipeligo, *volume I, a description of the Soviet prison camp system. Having left Russia, the author settled in Zurich, Switzerland, with his family. As his fame spread throughout Western Europe and America, he did a great deal of traveling and lecturing. His trip to the United States in the summer of 1975 proved to be a controversial one because of the embarrassment it caused the Ford Administration. Although he was pointedly not invited to the White House, he did speak in Washington, D.C., on June 30. The Administration's reluctance to meet with Solzhenitsyn stemmed from the President's impending trip to the Helsinki summit conference. Portions of Solzhenitsyn's June 30 address are reprinted here.*

Source: *Society*, November-December 1975.

THROUGH THE DECADES of the 1920s, the 1930s, the 1940s, the 1950s, the whole Soviet press wrote: Western capitalism, your end is near.

But it was as if the capitalists had not heard, could not understand, could not believe this.

Nikita Khrushchev came here and said, "We will bury you!" They didn't believe that, either. They took it as a joke.

Now, of course, they have become more clever in our country. Now they don't say "we are going to bury you" anymore, now they say "detente."

Nothing has changed in Communist ideology. The goals are the same as they were, but instead of the artless Khrushchev, who couldn't hold his tongue, now they say "detente."

In order to understand this, I will take the liberty of making a short historic survey—the history of such relations, which in different periods have been called "trade," "stabilization of the situation," "recognition of realities," and now "detente." These relations now are at least 40 years old.

Let me remind you with what sort of system they started.

The system was installed by armed uprising.

It dispersed the Constituent Assembly.

It capitulated to Germany—the common enemy.

It introduced execution without trial.

It crushed workers' strikes.

It plundered the villagers to such an unbelievable extent that the peasants revolted, and when this happened it crushed the peasants in the bloodiest possible way.

It shattered the Church.

It reduced 20 provinces of our country to a condition of famine.

This was in 1921, the famous Volga famine. A very typical Communist technique: To seize power without thinking of the fact that the productive forces will collapse, that the fields will not be sown, the factories will stop, that the country will decline into poverty and famine—but when poverty and hunger come, then they request the humanitarian world to help them. We see this in North Vietnam today, perhaps Portugal is approaching this also. And the same thing happened in Russia in 1921. When the three-year civil war, started by the Communists—and "civil war" was a slogan of the Communists, civil war was Lenin's purpose; read Lenin, this was his aim and his slogan—when they had ruined Russia by this civil war, then they asked America, "America, feed our hungry." And indeed, generous and magnanimous America did feed our hungry.

The so-called American Relief Administration was set up, headed by your future President Hoover, and indeed many millions of Russian lives were saved by this organization of yours.

But what sort of gratitude did you receive for this? In the USSR not only did they try to erase this whole event from the popular memory—it's almost impossible today in the Soviet press to find any reference to the American Relief Administration—but they even denounce it as a clever spy organization, a clever scheme of American imperialism to set up a spy network in Russia. I repeat, it was a system that introduced concentration camps for the first time in the history of the world. . . .

The scope and the direction of my speech today do not permit me to say more about pre-revolutionary Russia. I will just say that information about pre-revolutionary Russia was obtained by the West from persons who were either not sufficiently competent or not sufficiently conscientious. I will just cite for the sake of comparison a number of figures which you can read for yourself in Gulag Archipelago, volume 1, which has been published in the United States, and perhaps many of you may have read it. These are the figures:

According to calculations by specialists, based on the most precise objective statistics, in pre-revolutionary Russia, during the 80 years before the revolution—years of the revolutionary movement when there were attempts on the Tsar's life, assassination of a Tsar, revolution—during these years about 17 persons a year were executed. The famous Spanish Inquisition, during the decades when it was at the height of its persecution, destroyed perhaps 10 persons a month. In the Archipelago—I cite a book which was published by the Cheka in 1920, proudly reporting on its revolutionary work in 1918 and 1919 and apologizing that its data were not quite complete—in 1918 and 1919 the Cheka executed, without trial, more than a thousand persons a month! This was written by the Cheka itself, before it understood how this would look to history.

At the height of Stalin's terror in 1937–38, if we divide the number of persons executed by the number of months, we get more than 40,000 persons shot per month! Here are the figures: 17 a year, 10 a month, more than 1,000 a month, more than 40,000 a month! Thus, that which had made it difficult for the democratic West to form an alliance with pre-revolutionary Russia had, by 1941, grown to such an extent and still did not prevent the entire united democracy of the world —England, France, the United States, Canada, Australia and small countries— from entering into a military alliance with the Soviet Union. How is this to be explained? How can we understand it? Here we can offer a few explanations. The first, I think, is that the entire united

democracy of the world was too weak to fight against Hitler's Germany alone. If this is the case, then it is a terrible sign. It is a terrible portent for the present day. If all these countries together could not defeat Hitler's little Germany, what are they going to do today, when more than half the globe is flooded with totalitarianism? I don't want to accept this explanation.

The second explanation is perhaps that there was simply an attack of panic—of fear—among the statesmen of the day. They simply didn't have sufficient confidence in themselves, they simply had no strength of spirit, and in this confused state decided to enter into an alliance with Soviet totalitarianism. This is also not flattering to the West.

Finally, the third explanation is that it was a deliberate device. Democracy did not want to defend itself. For defense it wanted to use another totalitarian system, the Soviet totalitarian system.

I'm not talking now about the moral evaluation of this, I'm going to talk about that later. But in terms of simple calculation, how shortsighted, what profound self-deception!

We have a Russian proverb: "Do not call a wolf to help you against the dogs." If dogs are attacking and tearing at you, fight against the dogs, but do not call a wolf for help. Because when the wolves come, they will destroy the dogs, but they will also tear you apart.

World democracy could have defeated one totalitarian regime after another, the German, then the Soviet. Instead, it strengthened Soviet totalitarianism, helped bring into existence a third totalitarianism, that of China, and all this finally precipitated the present world situation.

Roosevelt, in Teheran, during one of his last toasts, said the following: "I do not doubt that the three of us"—meaning Roosevelt, Churchill and Stalin—"lead our peoples in accordance with their desires, in accordance with their aims." How are we to explain this? Let the historians worry about that. At the time, we listened and were astonished. We thought, "when we reach Europe, we will meet the Americans, and we will tell them." I was among the troops that were marching towards the Elbe. A little bit more and I would have reached the Elbe and would have shaken the hands of your American soldiers. But just before that happened. I was taken off to prison and my meeting did not take place.

But now, after all this great delay, the same hand has thrown me out of the country and here I am, instead of the meeting at the Elbe. After a delay of 30 years, my Elbe is here today. I am here to tell you. as a friend of the United States, what, as friends, we wanted to tell you then, but which our soldiers were prevented from telling you on the Elbe.

There is another Russian proverb: "The yes-man is your enemy, but your friend will argue with you." It is precisely because I am the friend of the United States, precisely because my speech is prompted by friendship, that I have come to tell you: "My friends, I'm not going to tell you sweet words. The situation in the world is not just dangerous, it isn't just threatening, it is catastrophic."

Something that is incomprehensible to the ordinary human mind has taken place. We over there, the powerless, average Soviet people, couldn't understand, year after year and decade after decade, what was happening. How were we to explain this? England, France, the United States, were victorious in World War II. Victorious states always dictate peace; they receive firm conditions; they create the sort of situation which accords with their philosophy, their concept of liberty, their concept of national interest.

Instead of this, beginning in Yalta, your statesmen of the West, for some inexplicable reason, have signed one capitulation after another. Never did the West or your President Roosevelt impose any conditions on the Soviet Union for obtaining aid. He gave unlimited aid, and then unlimited concessions. Already in Yalta, without any necessity, the occupation of Mongolia, Moldavia, Estonia, Latvia, Lithuania was silently recognized. Immediately after that, almost nothing was done to protect eastern Europe, and seven or eight more countries were surrendered.

Stalin demanded that the Soviet citizens who did not want to return home be handed over to him, and the western countries handed over 1.5 million human beings. How was this done? They took them by force. English soldiers killed Russians who did not want to become prisoners of Stalin, and drove them by force to Stalin to be exterminated. This has recently come to light—just a few years ago—a million and a half human beings. How could the Western democracies have done this?

And after that, for another 30 years, the constant retreat, the surrender of one country after another, to such a point that there are Soviet satellites even in Africa; almost all of Asia is taken over by them: Portugal is rolling down the precipice.

During those 30 years, more was surrendered to totalitarianism than any defeated country has ever surrendered after any war in history. There was no war, but there might as well have been.

For a long time we in the East couldn't understand this. We couldn't understand the flabbiness of the truce concluded in Vietnam. Any average Soviet citizen understood that this was a sly device which made it possible for North Vietnam to take over South Vietnam when it so chose. And suddenly, this was rewarded by the Nobel Prize for Peace—a tragic and ironic prize.

A very dangerous state of mind can arise as a result of this 30 years of retreat: give in as quickly as possible, give up as quickly as possible, peace and quiet at any cost.

This is what many western papers wrote: "Let's hurry up and end the bloodshed in Vietnam and have national unity there." But at the Berlin Wall no one talked of national unity. One of your leading newspapers, after the end of Vietnam, had a full headline: "The Blessed Silence." I would not wish that kind of "blessed silence" on my worst enemy. I would not wish that kind of national unity on my worst enemy.

I spent 11 years in the Archipelago, and for half of my lifetime I have studied this question. Looking at this terrible tragedy in Vietnam from a distance, I can tell you, a million persons will be simply exterminated, while 4 to 5 million (in accordance with the scale of Vietnam) will find themselves in concentration camps and will be rebuilding Vietnam. And what is happening in Cambodia you already know. It is genocide. It is full and complete destruction but in a new form. Once again their technology is not up to building gas chambers. So, in a few hours, the entire capital city—the guilty capital city—is emptied out: old people, women, children are driven out without belongings, without food. "Go and die!"

This is very dangerous for one's view of the world when this feeling comes on: "Go ahead, give it up." We already hear voices in your country and in the West—"Give up Korea and we will live quietly. Give up Portugal, of course; give up Japan, give up Israel, give up Taiwan, the

Philippines, Malaysia, Thailand, give up 10 more African countries. Just let us live in peace and quiet. Just let us drive our big cars on our splendid highways; just let us play tennis and golf, in peace and quiet; just let us mix our cocktails in peace and quiet as we are accustomed to doing; just let us see the beautiful toothy smile with a glass in hand on every advertisement page of our magazines."

But look how things have turned out: Now in the West this has all turned into an accusation against the United States. Now, in the West, we hear very many voices saying, "It's your fault, America." And, here, I must decisively defend the United States against these accusations.

I have to say that the United States, of all the countries of the West, is the least guilty in all this and has done the most in order to prevent it. The United States has helped Europe to win the First and the Second World Wars. It twice raised Europe from post-war destruction— twice—for 10, 20, 30 years it has stood as a shield protecting Europe while European countries were counting their nickels, to avoid paying for their armies (better yet to have none at all) to avoid paying for armaments, thinking about how to leave NATO, knowing that in any case America will protect them anyway. These countries started it all, despite their thousands of years of civilization and culture, even though they are closer and should have known better.

I came to your continent—for two months I have been travelling in its wide open spaces and I agree: here you do not feel the nearness of it all, the immediacy of it all. And here it is possible to miscalculate. Here you must make a spiritual effort to understand the acuteness of the world situation. The United States of America has long shown itself to be the most magnanimous, the most generous country in the world. Wherever there is a flood, an earthquake, a fire, a natural disaster, disease, who is the first to help? The United States. Who helps the most and unselfishly? The United States.

And what do we hear in reply? Reproaches, curses, "Yankee Go Home." American cultural centers are burned, and the representatives of the Third World jump on tables to vote against the United States.

But this does not take the load off America's shoulders. The course of history—whether you like it or not—has made you the leaders of the world. Your country can no longer think provincially. Your political leaders can no longer think only of their own states, of their parties, of petty arrangements which may or may not lead to promotion. You must think about the whole world, and when the new political crisis in the world will arise (I think we have just come to the end of a very acute crisis and the next one will come any moment) the main decisions will fall anyway on the shoulders of the United States of America. . . .

The Soviet system is so closed that it is almost impossible for you to understand from here. Your theoreticians and scholars write works trying to understand and explain how things occur there. Here are some naive explanations which are simply funny to Soviet citizens. Some say that the Soviet leaders have now given up their inhumane ideology. Not at all. They haven't given it up one bit.

Some say that in the Kremlin there are some on the left, some on the right. And they are fighting with each other, and we've got to behave in such a way as not to interfere with those on the left side. This is all fantasy: left . . . right. There is some sort of a struggle for power, but they all agree on the essentials.

There also exists the following theory, that now, thanks to the growth of technology, there is a technocracy in the Soviet Union, a growing number of engineers and the engineers are now running the economy and will soon determine the fate of the country, rather than the party. I will tell you, though, that the engineers determine the fate of the economy just as much as our generals determine the fate of the Army. That means zero. Everything is done the way the party demands. That's our system. Judge it for yourself. . . .

So what are we to conclude from that? Is detente needed or not? Not only is it needed, it's as necessary as air. It's the only way of saving the earth—instead of a world war to have detente, but a true detente, and if it has already been ruined by the bad word which we use for it—"detente"—then we should find another word for it.

I would say that there are very few, only three, main characteristics of such a true detente.

In the first place, there would be disarmament—not only disarmament from the use of war but also from the use of violence. We must stop using not only the sort of arms which are used to destroy one's neighbors, but the sort of arms which are used to oppress one's fellow countrymen. It is not detente if we here with you today can spend our time agreeably while over there people are groaning and dying and in psychiatric hospitals. Doctors are making their evening rounds, for the third time injecting people with drugs which destroy their brain cells.

The second sign of detente, I would say, is the following: that it be not one based on smiles, not on verbal concessions, but it has to be based on a firm foundation. You know the words from the Bible: "Build not on sand, but on rock." There has to be a guarantee that this will not be broken overnight and for this the other side—the other party to the agreement—must have its acts subject to public opinion, to the press, and to a freely elected parliament. And until such control exists there is absolutely no guarantee.

The third simple condition—what sort of detente is it when they employ the sort of inhumane propaganda which is proudly called in the Soviet Union "ideological warfare"? Let us not have that. If we're going to be friends, let's be friends, if we're going to have detente, then let's have detente, and an end to ideological warfare.

The Soviet Union and the Communist countries can conduct negotiations. They know how to do this. For a long time they don't make any concessions and then they give in a little bit. Then everyone says triumphantly, "Look, they've made a concession; it's time to sign." The European negotiators of the 35 countries for two years now have painfully been negotiating and their nerves were stretched to the breaking point and they finally gave in. A few women from the Communist countries can now marry foreigners. And a few newspapermen are now going to be permitted to travel a little more than before. They give 1/1,000th of what natural law should provide. Matters which people should be able to do even before such negotiations are undertaken. And already there is joy. And here in the West we hear many voices, saying: "Look, they're making concessions; it's time to sign."

During these two years of negotiations, in all the countries of eastern Europe, the pressure has increased, the oppression intensified, even in Yugoslavia and Romania, leaving aside the other countries. And it is precisely now that the Austrian chancellor says, "We've got to sign this agreement as rapidly as possible."

What sort of an agreement would this be? The proposed agreement is the funeral of eastern Europe. It means that western Europe would finally, once and for all, sign away eastern Europe, stating that it is perfectly willing to see eastern Europe be crushed and overwhelmed once and for all, but please don't bother us. And the Austrian chancellor thinks that if all these countries are pushed into a mass grave, Austria at the very edge of this grave will survive and not fall into it also.

And we, from our lives there, have concluded that violence can only be withstood by firmness.

You have to understand the nature of communism. The very ideology of communism, all of Lenin's teachings, are that anyone is considered to be a fool who doesn't take what's lying in front of him. If you can take it, take it. If you can attack, attack. But if there's a wall, then go back. And the Communist leaders respect only firmness and have contempt and laugh at persons who continually give in to them. Your people are now saying—and this is the last quotation I am going to give you from the statements of your leaders—"Power, without any attempt at conciliation, will lead to a world conflict." But I would say that power with continual subservience is no power at all.

But from our experience I can tell you that only firmness will make it possible to withstand the assaults of Communist totalitarianism. We see many historic examples, and let me give you some of them. Look at little Finland in 1939, which by its own forces withstood the attack. You, in 1948, defended Berlin only by your firmness of spirit, and there was no world conflict. In Korea in 1950 you stood up against the Communists, only by your firmness, and there was no world conflict. In 1962 you compelled the rockets to be removed from Cuba. Again it was only firmness, and there was no world conflict. And the late Konrad Adenauer conducted firm negotiations with Khrushchev and thus started a genuine detente with Khrushchev. Khrushchev started to make concessions and if he hadn't been removed, that winter he was planning to go to Germany and to continue the genuine detente.

Let me remind you of the weakness of a man whose name is rarely associated with weakness — the weakness of Lenin. Lenin, when he came to power, in panic gave up to Germany everything Germany wanted. Just what it wanted. Germany took as much as it wanted and said, "Give Armenia to Turkey." And Lenin said, "Fine." It's almost an unknown fact but Lenin petitioned the Kaiser to act as intermediary to persuade the Ukraine and, thus, to make possible a boundary between the Communist part of Russia and the Ukraine. It wasn't a question of seizing the Ukraine but rather of making a boundary with the Ukraine.

We, we the dissidents of the USSR, don't have any tanks, we don't have any weapons, we have no organization. We don't have anything. Our hands are empty. We have only a heart and what we have lived through in the half century of this system. And when we have found the firmness within ourselves to stand up for our rights, we have done so. I's only by firmness of spirit that we have withstood. And if I am standing here before you, it's not because of the kindness or the good will of communism, not thanks to detente, but thanks to my own firmness and your firm support. They knew that I would not yield one inch, not one hair. And when they couldn't do more they themselves fell back.

This is not easy. In our conditions this was taught to me by the difficulties of my own life. And if you yourselves — any one of you — were in the same difficult situation, you would have learned the same thing. Take Vladimir Bukovsky, whose name is now almost forgotten. Now, I don't want to mention a lot of names because however many I might mention there are more still. And when we resolve the question with two or three names it is as if we forget and betray the others. We should rather remember figures. There are tens of thousands of political prisoners in our country and — by the calculation of English specialists — 7,000 persons are now under compulsory psychiatric treatment. Let's take Vladimir Bukovsky as an example. It was proposed to him, "All right, we'll free you. Go to the West and shut up." And this young man, a youth today on the verge of death said: "No, I won't go this way. I have written about the persons whom you have put in insane asylums. You release them and then I'll go West." This is what I mean by that firmness of spirit to stand up against granite and tanks. . . .

Today there are two major processes occurring in the world. One is the one which I have just described to you which has been in progress more than 30 years. It is a process of shortsighted concessions; a process of giving up, and giving up and giving up and hoping that perhaps at some point the wolf will have eaten enough.

The second process is one which I consider the key to everything and which, I will say now, will bring all of us our future; under the cast-iron shell of communism — for 20 years in the Soviet Union and a shorter time in other Communist countries — there is occurring a liberation of the human spirit. New generations are growing up which are steadfast in their struggle with evil; which are not willing to accept unprincipled compromises; which prefer to lose everything—salary, conditions of existence and life itself—but are not willing to sacrifice conscience; not willing to make deals with evil.

This process has now gone so far that in the Soviet Union today, Marxism has fallen so low that it has become an anecdote, it's simply an object of contempt. No serious person in our country today, not even university and high school students, can talk about Marxism without smiling, without laughing. But this whole process of our liberation, which obviously will entail social transformations, is slower than the first one—the process of concessions. Over there, when we see these concessions, we are frightened. Why so quickly? Why so precipitously? Why yield several countries a year?

I started by saying that you are the allies of our liberation movement in the Communist countries. And I call upon you: let us think together and try to see how we can adjust the relationship between these two processes. Whenever you help the persons persecuted in the Soviet Union, you not only display magnanimity and nobility, you're defending not only them but yourselves as well. You're defending your own future.

So let us try and see how far we can go to stop this senseless and immoral process of endless concessions to the aggressor—these clever legal arguments for why we should give up one country after another. Why must we hand over to Communist totalitarianism more and more technology—complex, delicate, developed technology which it needs for armaments and for crushing its own citizens? If we can at least slow down that process of concessions, if not stop it all together—and make it possible for the process of liberation to continue in the Communist countries—ultimately these two processes will yield us our future.

On our crowded planet there are no longer any internal affairs. The Communist leaders say, "Don't interfere in our internal affairs. Let us strangle our citizens in peace and quiet." But I tell you: Interfere more and more. Interfere as much as you can. We beg you to come and interfere.

Understanding my own task in the same way, I have perhaps interfered today in your internal affairs, or at least touched upon them, and I apologize for it. I have traveled a lot around the United States and this has been added to my earlier understanding of it; what I have heard from listening to the radio, from talking to experienced persons.

America—in me and among my friends and among people who think the way I do over there, among all ordinary Soviet citizens—evokes a sort of mixture of feelings of admiration and of compassion. Admiration at the fact of your own tremendous forces which you perhaps don't even recognize yourselves. You're a country of the future; a young country; a country of still untapped possibilities; a country of tremendous geographical distances; a country of tremendous breadth of spirit; a country of generosity; a country of magnanimity. But these qualities—strength, generosity and magnanimity—usually make a man and even a whole country trusting, and this already several times has done you a disservice.

I would like to call upon America to be more careful with its trust and prevent those wise persons who are attempting to establish even finer degrees of justice and even finer legal shades of equality—some because of their distorted outlook, others because of short-sightedness and still others out of self-interest—from falsely using the struggle for peace and for social justice to lead you down a false road. Because they are trying to weaken you; they are trying to disarm your strong and magnificent country in the face of this fearful threat—one which has never been seen before in the history of the world. Not only in the history of your country, but in the history of the world.

And I call upon you: ordinary working men of America—as represented here by your trade union movement—do not let yourselves become weak. Do not let yourselves be taken in the wrong direction. Let us try to slow down the process of concessions and help the process of liberation!

40.

GERALD R. FORD: Address to the Helsinki Conference

The 35-nation summit conference at Helsinki, Finland, in July-August of 1975, was the largest such gathering since the Congress of Vienna in 1815. Purpose of the summit was the signing of the Final Act of the Conference on Security and Cooperation in Europe. The document was not a treaty and thus not legally binding on the signatories, but it did spell out principles for assuring a permanent peace in Europe, for inviolable national boundaries, and for international cooperation. President Ford addressed the conference on August 1. Portions of his speech are reprinted here.

Source: *Weekly Compilation of Presidential Documents,* August 11, 1975.

NOWHERE ARE THE CHALLENGES and the opportunities greater and more evident than in Europe. That is why this Conference brings us all together. Conflict in Europe shakes the world. Twice in this century we have paid dearly for this lesson; at other times, we have come perilously close to calamity. We dare not forget the tragedy and the terror of those times.

Peace is not a piece of paper.

But lasting peace is at least possible today because we have learned from the experiences of the last 30 years that peace is a process requiring mutual restraint and practical arrangements.

This Conference is a part of that process—a challenge, not a conclusion. We face unresolved problems of military security in Europe; we face them with very real differences in values and in aims. But if we deal with them with careful preparation, if we focus on concrete issues, if we maintain forward movement, we have the right to expect real progress.

The era of confrontation that has divided Europe since the end of the Second World War may now be ending. There is a new perception and a shared perception of a change for the better, away from confrontation and toward new possibilities for secure and mutually beneficial cooperation. That is what we all have been saying here. I welcome and I share these hopes for the future.

The postwar policy of the United States has been consistently directed toward the rebuilding of Europe and the rebirth of Europe's historic identity. The nations of the West have worked together for peace and progress throughout Europe. From the very start, we have taken the initiative by stating clear goals and areas for negotiation.

We have sought a structure of European relations, tempering rivalry with restraint, power with moderation, building upon the traditional bonds that link us with old friends and reaching out to forge new ties with former and potential adversaries.

In recent years, there have been some substantial achievements.

We see the Four-Power Agreement on Berlin of 1971 as the end of a perennial crisis that on at least three occasions brought the world to the brink of doom.

The agreements between the Federal Republic of Germany and the states of Eastern Europe and the related intra-German accords enable Central Europe and the world to breathe easier.

The start of East-West talks on mutual and balanced force reductions demonstrate a determination to deal with military security problems of the continent.

The 1972 treaty between the United States and the Soviet Union to limit anti-ballistic missiles and the interim agreement limiting strategic offensive arms were the first solid breakthroughs in what must be a continuing, long-term process of limiting strategic nuclear arsenals.

I profoundly hope that this Conference will spur further practical and concrete results. It affords a welcome opportunity to widen the circle of those countries involved in easing tensions between East and West.

Participation in the work of détente and participation in the benefits of détente must be everybody's business—in Europe and elsewhere. But détente can succeed only if everybody understands what détente actually is.

First, détente is an evolutionary process, not a static condition. Many formidable challenges yet remain.

Second, the success of détente, of the process of détente, depends on new behavior patterns that give life to all our solemn declarations. The goals we are stating today are the yardstick by which our performance will be measured.

The people of all Europe, and, I assure you, the people of North America are thoroughly tired of having their hopes raised and then shattered by empty words and unfulfilled pledges. We had better say what we mean and mean what we say, or we will have the anger of our citizens to answer.

While we must not expect miracles, we can and we do expect steady progress that comes in steps—steps that are related to each other that link our actions with words in various areas of our relations.

Finally, there must be an acceptance of mutual obligation. Détente, as I have often said, must be a two-way street. Tensions cannot be eased by one side alone. Both sides must want détente and work to achieve it. Both sides must benefit from it.

Mr. Chairman, my colleagues, this extraordinary gathering in Helsinki proves that all our peoples share a concern for Europe's future and for a better and more peaceful world. But what else does it prove? How shall we assess the results?

Our delegations have worked long and hard to produce documents which restate noble and praiseworthy political principles. They spell out guidelines for national behavior and international cooperation.

But every signatory should know that if these are to be more than the latest chapter in a long and sorry volume of unfulfilled declarations, every party must be dedicated to making them come true.

These documents which we will sign represent another step—how long or short a step only time will tell — in the process of détente and reconciliation in Europe. Our peoples will be watching and measuring our progress. They will ask how these noble sentiments are being translated into actions that bring about a more secure and just order in the daily lives of each of our nations and its citizens.

The documents produced here represent compromises, like all international negotiations, but these principles we have agreed upon are more than the lowest common denominator of governmental positions:

— They affirm the most fundamental human rights: liberty of thought, conscience, and faith; the exercise of civil and political rights; the rights of minorities.

— They call for a freer flow of information, ideas, and people; greater scope for the press, cultural and educational exchange, family reunification, the right to travel and to marriage between nationals of different states; and for the protection of the priceless heritage of our diverse cultures.

— They offer wide areas for greater cooperation: trade, industrial production, science and technology, the environment, transportation, health, space, and the oceans.

— They reaffirm the basic principles of relations between states: nonintervention, sovereign equality, self-determination, territorial integrity, inviolability of frontiers, and the possibility of change by peaceful means.

The United States gladly subscribes to this document because we subscribe to every one of these principles.

Almost 200 years ago, the United States of America was born as a free and independent nation. The descendants of Europeans who proclaimed their independence in America expressed in that declaration "a decent respect for the opinions of mankind" and asserted not only that all men are created equal but they are endowed with inalienable rights to life, liberty, and the pursuit of happiness.

The founders of my country did not merely say that all Americans should have these rights, but all men everywhere should have these rights. And these principles have guided the United States of America throughout its two centuries of nationhood. They have given hopes to millions in Europe and on every continent.

I have been asked why I am here today.

I am here because I believe, and my countrymen believe, in the interdependence of Europe and North America — indeed in the interdependence of the entire family of man.

I am here because the leaders of 34 other governments are here — the states of Europe and of our good neighbor, Canada, with whom we share an open border of 5,526 miles, along which there stands not a single armed soldier and across which our two peoples have moved in friendship and mutual respect for 160 years.

I can say without fear of contradiction that there is not a single people represented here whose blood does not flow in the veins of Americans and whose culture and traditions have not enriched the heritage which we Americans prize so highly.

When two centuries ago the United States of America issued a declaration of high principles, the cynics and doubters of that day jeered and scoffed. Yet, 11 long years later our independence was won and the stability of our Republic was really achieved through the incorporation of the same principles in our Constitution. But those principles, though they are still being perfected, remain the guiding lights of an American policy. And the American people are still dedicated, as they were then, to a decent respect for the opinions of mankind and to life, liberty, and the pursuit of happiness for all peoples everywhere.

To our fellow participants in this Conference: My presence here symbolizes my country's vital interest in Europe's future. Our future is bound with yours. Our economic well-being, as well as our security, is linked increasingly with yours. The distance of geography is bridged by our common heritage and our common destiny. The United States, therefore, intends to participate fully in the affairs of Europe and in turning the results of this Conference into a living reality.

To America's Allies: We in the West vigorously pursue the course upon which we have embarked together, reenforced by one another's strength and mutual confidence. Stability in Europe requires equilibrium in Europe. Therefore, I assure you that my country will continue to be a concerned and reliable partner. Our partnership is far more than a matter of formal agreements. It is a reflection of beliefs, traditions, and ties that are of deep significance to the American people. We are proud that these values are expressed in this document.

To the countries of the East: The United States considers that the principles on which this Conference has agreed are a part of the great heritage of European civilization, which we all hold in trust for all mankind. To my country, they are not cliches or empty phrases. We take this work and these words very seriously. We will spare no effort to ease tensions and to solve problems between us. But it is important that you recognize the deep devotion of the American people and their Government to human rights and fundamental freedoms and thus to the pledges that this Conference has made regarding the freer movement of people, ideas, information.

In building a political relationship between East and West, we face many challenges.

Berlin has a special significance. It has been a flashpoint of confrontation in the past; it can provide an example of peaceful settlement in the future. The United States regards it as a test of détente and of the principles of this Conference. We welcome the fact that, subject to Four-Power rights and responsibilities, the results of CSCE apply to Berlin as they do throughout Europe.

Military stability in Europe has kept the peace. While maintaining that stability, it is now time to reduce substantially the high levels of military forces on both sides. Negotiations now underway in Vienna on mutual and balanced force reductions so far have not produced the results for which I had hoped. The United States stands ready to demonstrate flexibility in moving these negotiations forward, if others will do the same. An agreement that enhances mutual security is feasible—and essential.

The United States also intends to pursue vigorously a further agreement on strategic arms limitations with the Soviet Union. This remains a priority of American policy. General Secretary Brezhnev and I agreed last November in Vladivostok on the essentials of a new accord limiting strategic offensive weapons for the next 10 years. We are moving forward in our bilateral discussions here in Helsinki.

The world faces an unprecedented danger in the spread of nuclear weapons technology. The nations of Europe share a great responsibility for an international solution to this problem. The benefits of peaceful nuclear energy are becoming more and more important. We must find ways to spread these benefits while safeguarding the world against the menace of weapons proliferation.

To the other nations of Europe represented at this Conference: We value the work you have done here to help bring all of Europe together. Your right to live in peace and independence is one of the major goals of our effort. Your continuing contribution will be indispensable.

To those nations not participating and to all the peoples of the world: The solemn obligation undertaken in these documents to promote fundamental rights, economic and social progress, and well-being, applies ultimately to all peoples.

Can we truly speak of peace and security without addressing the spread of nuclear weapons in the world or the creation of more sophisticated forms of warfare?

Can peace be divisible between areas of tranquillity and regions of conflict?

Can Europe truly flourish if we do not all address ourselves to the evil of hunger in countries less fortunate than we?

— To the new dimensions of economic and energy issues that underline our own progress?

— To the dialog between producers and consumers, between exporters and importers, between industrial countries and less developed ones?

— And can there be stability and progress in the absence of justice and fundamental freedoms?

Our people want a better future. Their expectations have been raised by the very real steps that have already been taken — in arms control, political negotiations, and expansion of contacts and economic relations. Our presence here offers them further hope. We must not let them down.

If the Soviet Union and the United States can reach agreement so that our astronauts can fit together the most intricate scientific equipment, work together and shake hands 137 miles out in space, we as statesmen have an obligation to do as well on Earth.

History will judge this Conference not by what we say here today, but by what we do tomorrow — not by the promises we make, but by the promises we keep.

Thank you very much, Mr. Chairman.

41.

NORMAN MACRAE: Agenda for a World Leader

Concerning the amount of the world's natural resources and the problems of food supply, there have been a great many gloomy prophecies and warnings since the 1973–74 oil embargo. This selection by British journalist Norman Macrae takes a much more optimistic outlook. The article is part of a much longer piece entitled "America's Third Century," an assessment of the United States on the eve of the Bicentennial.

Source: *The Economist*, October 25, 1975.

ON THE FIRST DAY of our Lord, when the order had gone out from Caesar Augustus that all the world should be counted, there were probably around 250m human beings, with an average annual income per head of $100 in terms of today's money. On the first day of the United States, on July 4th of 1776, there were probably around 700m human beings, with the same average annual income per head. The world then stood at one minute to dawn after 10,000 years of technological stagnation.

The average Roman citizen in AD 1 seems to have had a slightly higher annual income (guessed at today's equivalent of just under $300 a head) than his successor citizen 1775 years later in the next great republic (just under $200 a head for the United States in 1776). The man of 1776 used much the same energy sources as the man of AD 1 (animal muscle, wind and water); he could travel much the same tiny maximum distance per day; he used much the same materials for tools (wood and iron) and had much the same average expectation of life (to his late 30s or early 40s), although Rome's standards of big-city-sanitation were better. Rome reached a population of a million, which no subsequent city dared to do until London after 1800, because the million-people-megalopolis did not seem safe under post-Roman but pre-1800 standards of cleanliness, plague control, law and order protection, and unmechanised transport of peasant or feudal agriculture's products into the towns. The two really big technological advances between AD 1 and 1776 were in killing power (gunpowder by 1776 had several times the killing area of arrows) and information technology (Gutenberg's printing press after 1441 increased the circulation potential of each written word several hundredfold).

Then, shortly after 1776, all the charts scattered through this survey took off with a whoosh.

Between 1776–1975 world population has increased sixfold, real gwp eightyfold, the distance a man can travel a day between a hundredfold and a thousandfold, the killing area of the most effective megadeath weapon over a millionfold, the amount of energy that can be released from a pound of matter over 50 millionfold (with much more to come) and the range and volume of information technology several billionfold (although how do you compare the range of an orator's voice in 1776 with Neil Armstrong's telecast from the moon to everybody's drawing room, or an abacus with a computer?).

Note that the things which cause gwp to increase (potential energy, information technology, etc) have already increased by thousands or even millions of times more than gwp itself, so that there is a lot of existing technology still to work through to living standards as well as even more new technology to come. In 1975, when it is fashionable to forecast that world growth is about to stop, technological realism suggests that growth is more probably at an early stage of an extraordinary acceleration.

The eightyfold increase in real gwp since 1776 has been based on man's increase in control over matter and energy, at a pace that has risen in each of the last 20 decades after having stood still in the previous 10,000 years. To this matter-cum-energy-revolution there has been added in the past two decades a breakthrough in the processing of information (computers, etc) and a nascent breakthrough in the distribution of information (telecommunications by satellite, the beginnings of packaged and computerised "learning programmes," maybe even at last a start towards understanding of the learning process itself).

During 1950–73 real gwp was increasing at an annual average 5%, which meant that it doubled about every 14 years. It will be surprising if during most of America's third century 1976–2076 the world does not have the potential to grow considerably more quickly than that, But note, first, that even if only 5% annual growth were continued, then by 2045 today's $5½ trillion gwp would be over $175 trillion and by 2059 it would be over $350 trillion. My guess is that by 2059 world population might be around 15 billion, and people probably would not want a gwp much higher than that trebling for every human of America's present gnp per head. Note, second, . . . the distribution of income with which the world starts. Two-thirds of mankind are still living at pre-1776 levels of under $300 a head. The other third of us have average incomes between five and 25 times as high. Trillion in this survey means, in the American language, one million million; and billion means a thousand million.

There is a temptation to preach to any world leader . . . on the way in which he should determine to help distribute these many chickens for every pot. But what may stop them from being hatched?

American ecologists—who for some reason think that all the post-1776 charts which have risen with a whoosh will now drop with a whoosh—say growth is going to be stopped by a shortage of energy, food and raw materials (especially metals) plus high pollution and high birth rates. These seem, in fact, the five least likely forecasts for the next 20 years. Instead, the three biggest worries over the next three decades may be: a fall in the old people's death rate, a growth in mass-killing-power, and the danger that new knowledge will expand out of control. But consider the five red herrings first.

There are many thousand possible ways of releasing energy from storage in matter. They range from petty ways, like 25 BTUs per pound of matter by letting a pound of elastic bands untwist; through fairly petty ways, like 20,000 BTUs by burning a pound of petrol; through more sophisticated ways like 250m BTUs from the fission of the U-235 isotope in one pound of natural uranium; up to 260 thousand billion BTUs from the fusion to helium of a pound of hydrogen. Note that this last system, in which the waters of the oceans could serve as a limitless reservoir of fuel, would be over 10,000,000,000 times more effective per pound of matter than burning a pound of the Arabs' oil.

The trend since 1776 has been for new technology to drive on in sudden bursts towards the cleaner power sources nearer the top of the range. The present "energy crisis"—ie, the raising to 100 times its marginal cost of the asking-price for the inconvenient mineral slime that is temporarily considered the most transportable energy source—must make the next burst a bit faster. The likely speed of the coming glut in oil might best be gauged by the speed with which other sources were displaced when oil became cost-effective (oh, those poor interwar coal-miners and horses), by the range of known future alternatives (unprecedented, including fusion, solar, geothermal, ocean-gradient, renewable-cellulose-into-clean-alcohol, a lot of others) and by the inefficiency with which all industrial countries have used fossil fuels (generation, storage and transmission mechanisms have long been archaic).

A big advantage is that each new energy source tends to be much less pollutant than the last one. A horse dragging a cart through an urban mile emits 600 grams of solid pollutant and 300 grams of liquid pollutant; a motor car emits only 6 grams of pollutant of any sort; a battery-driven car will emit . . .? Pittsburgh and London peasoup fogs have largely disappeared with soft King Coal.

The present world political system is that nearly all poor countries (under an annual $500 a head) rig their economic policies against their farmers—and then find that the universally-high elasticity of supply in agriculture means that their countries are very short of food; while nearly all rich countries (over $1,000 a head) rig their economic policies in favour of their farmers—and then find that the universally-high elasticity of supply in agriculture saddles them with butter mountains. Over the next three decades most countries will move above the $1,000 a head mark, and we will suddenly find ourselves swimming in food gluts.

Shortages in food supply per head of local population are not nowadays well correlated with soil conditions. India-Pakistan-Bangladesh, the most tragic area, has more arable land than the United States, great ability for multiple cropping, a more bountiful water supply. More interestingly, the elasticity of food supply (ie, the usual % rise in supply in response to a % rise in real price) is not nowadays well correlated with social conditions.

In the five years after 1965 there were huge increases in wheat and rice yields in India-Pakistan (aided by the politicians' temporary emphasis on agriculture, by favourable terms of trade for petroleum-based fertilisers, by the green revolution, maybe by good weather), so that India temporarily became self-sufficient in agriculture. If these increases in yields had been continued for a century, the world would have been destroyed because its entire surface would have been covered by rice to a depth of three feet. But then Indian and Pakistani politicians turned to concentrate their budgets on more bellicose things, and higher energy prices moved the terms of trade against the farmers.

Agriculture in the rich countries is now uneconomically energy-intensive, so it is easy for those who count in megajoules to say there is wild exaggeration in the argument that if all the land now cultivated were brought up to Dutch standards of efficiency, then the world could feed 60 billion people, 15 times today's population. Instead, there is understatement. This estimate refers only to the tiny 3% of the globe's surface that is now farmed. It ignores the fact that in most poor countries there has not been a serious "green revolution" study of the best methods and crops. It underestimates the fact that 70% of crops in some poor parts of the world are eaten by easily-destroyable pests. It takes no account of the way plant growths can already be increased between tenfold and a hundredfold in plastic greenhouses or other scientifically-controlled chambers free of diseases and pests. And the chemical equivalent of outdoor protection by plastic greenhouses is bound to come.

Above all, it ignores the waste in the present extraordinary agricultural system of turning grain into meat through very inefficient livestock converters.

The world's pigs today eat seven times more primary protein than the world's North Americans. The world's horses (now often a recreational animal) eat more than its Chinese. The world's cows (a third of them Afro-Asian nonproducers) eat more grain than all the world's people. With apologies to cows, our children will move to rearing food by conversion of cellulose by enzymes and of petroleum wastes by single-cell high-protein organisms. Listen to America's J. Leon Potter:

A pound of bacteria, feeding on crude oil so worthless that it is burned as waste, can grow fast enough to produce 10 pounds of protein in a day. If a yearling calf were able to manufacture protein at the same rate, it would end the day roughly the size of a three-car garage and it would have consumed several tons of expensive grain in the process. The cost of protein produced from waste effluents is approaching 3 cents/-pound, compared with agriculture and animal protein at 10 cents/pound. Algae produces protein at a rate of 30 to 50 tons/acre/year, compared with the conventional agriculture of 3 to 5-tons/acre/year.

Will this food from bugs be made palatable? Unfortunately, yes. It is already possible to make sewage taste like stew.

The real food problem for the future is rich men's habit of eating more food than is good for health, partly because of the accident that "entertaining," both social and business, has morbifically become attached to this natural function, rather than to the two that are assumed to be more disgusting than a drunken guzzle (defecation and sex), or than to the civilised Roman one. It will be wise in this next century to go back to holding social gatherings and informal business negotiations in what could now be various exciting sorts of baths.

Five of the world's 16 main metals are in virtually limitless supply (iron, aluminium, magnesium, titanium, silicon). Four others are subject to continuing improvements in the mining process, and the next will be the big step of just picking up nodules from the ocean floor (copper, cobalt, manganese, nickel). That leaves seven whose long-term prices might rise sharply if today's "known reserves" were the most economic way of mining them (chromium, lead, zinc, tin, gold, silver, mercury). But the whole anti-intellectual concept of talking about "known reserves" of anything, including oil, is often the last refuge of the scoundrelly oil company's public relations officer. Listen instead to Professor Wilfred Beckerman:

Given the natural concentrations of the key metals in the earth's crust, as indicated by a large number of random samples, the total natural occurrence of most metals in the top mile of the earth's crust has been estimated to be about a million times as great as present known reserves. Since the latter amount to about a hundred years' supplies this means we have enough to last about one hundred million years. Even though it may be impossible at present to mine to a depth of one mile at every point in the earth's crust, by the time we reach the year AD 100,000,000 I am sure we will think up something.

Other rather obvious points: the world does not actually consume metals at all, but employs them in ways that make them available for re-use after anything between 3 and 25 years (ie "known reserves" should include all the already-used metals eventually available for recycling); most of the industrial materials used today were not even conceptually recognised a short time ago, and most of the materials that will be used in the coming century are not conceptually recognised today; substitutions through plastics, etc, will hugely increase; and microminiaturisation with integrated circuits means that it is going to be increasingly economic to put on to a chip the size of a postage stamp properly connected electrical circuits which would previously have required assemblies of machinery that fill a room.

One mineral probably is going to be short for a while, because countries have foolishly made it a free good: water.

At last year's World Population Conference in Bucharest, the United Nations Secretariat presented a World Plan for Action (on which it had been working for years), calling for a reduction of world population growth to 1.7% a year by 1985. Nobody liked to point out that world population growth had probably fallen to 1.7% a year already.

The anti baby hysteria of the 1960s was a classic of trendy innumeracy. It came after a fall in fertility rates had been made certain by the breakthrough in both birth control technology (the pill, etc) and in birth control attitudes (acceptance of abortion and of papal fallibility). By 1972 the World Bank was already reporting a decline in fertility in 56 of the 66 countries for which meaningful data on births are available; but those whose jobs depended on the continued organisation of the anti-baby World Population Year pressed on regardless. The result will now be a risk of emotion the other way. It is already fashionable to say that the present 4 billion world population will still be under 6 billion by the year 2000. This is probably wrong, because the next problem has not been foreseen.

Awkwardly, medicine is bound eventually to make a breakthrough in curing the main degenerative diseases, so that old people will start to exist longer. This will set the real population problem. As the death rate drops, mankind will probably have to move towards acceptance of euthanasia and even planned death (with a hell of a going-away party on your 85th birthday?).

My guess is that mankind will accept this smoothly. Witness how abortion was a word you could not mention to auntie 15 years ago, but today any woman could get an abortion in most cities by next weekend. It will not be at all surprising if there is in some quite near decade-and-a-half a similarly swift and equally civilised dash to acceptance of killing off old codgers (by then, like me) as there has been, in so short a twinkling, towards the more emotive act of killing unborn babies. Acceptance of planned death means that mankind must then surely alter all the lifestyles for all the ages of present individual existence as well.

42.

The U. S. Postal Service Crisis

Since 1970 when the Postal Service became a semi-independent, corporation-like, government agency, there have been numerous complaints abount continued deficits, deteriorating service, and rate increases. In the light of the postal "crisis," the issue was again raised whether the mail system should continue as a federally subsidized monopoly or whether it should be a completely private corporation. The Los Angeles Times *looked at the problems of the post office in a pair of articles on August 3, 1975. Writing in favor of federal subsidy is Robert J. Myers, publisher of the* New Republic. *Favoring an independent corporation is Tom Winter, editor of* Human Events *magazine*

Source: *Los Angeles Times*, August 3, 1975. "The Mail Mess."

THE CASE FOR FEDERAL
SUBSIDY

Why is it that at this particular time the U.S. Postal Service is coming apart at the seams? Why is it that service is worse, costs are higher and labor relations more touchy than at any other time in the postal system's history? Why, in a word, is the mail a mess?

These questions become truly intriguing when you consider that just five years ago—in July, 1970—Congress passed the Postal Reorganization Act, which was designed to prevent all this from ever happening. In fact, the answers to these pressing questions are to be found in that legislation itself. From the beginning, it was a classic case of a faulty perception of the problem leading to well-intentioned, but wrong-headed analysis, and the befuddlement of Congress when it attempted to confront a complex problem.

It should now be clear that, despite the Reorganization Act's good intentions, the postal system is not a business but a public service and as such requires and deserves the federal revenues necessary to maintain it. Indeed, the attempt to turn the post office into a profit making—or at least self-supporting—enterprise is at the root of many of the system's current problems.

For almost 200 years, the Post Office was considered solely as a public service. The system moved west with the frontier and provided a visible link with the federal government in Washington. Most of its fiscal support was raised through the sale of first-class stamps, and the proliferation of periodicals was encouraged by low rates on the assumption that public interest was served through low-cost dissemination of the written word.

Usually, the postal system lost money. "Lost money"—what a phrase! What other branch of the American government—defense, agriculture, commerce—earns money? Indeed, the Post Office's "losses" over the years were hardly staggering. (It even turned a profit during the Civil War, when it did not have to service so many rural Southern routes.)

Yet despite the essential nature of the postal system's public service function, Congress grumbled about the deficit. It was loath to provide money for modern buildings and mechanization, and the whole system began to deteriorate. By 1966 there was a "mail crunch" in Chicago and Lawrence O'Brien, the postmaster general, announced that the Post Office was in a "race with catastrophe." So, a presidential commission was appointed.

Ordinarily in Washington that would have been the end of the matter—but for the postal system that's when trouble really began. The commission, headed by the distinguished former chairman of AT&T, Frederick R. Kappel, produced dramatic recommendations. Kappel argued that the costs of the postal system could be reduced by at least 20 percent by abandoning the public service concept in favor of "proper management."

Proper management included investment in mechanization (then standing at only $1,145 per worker compared to $35,630 at AT&T), elimination of political appointments at the top levels, as well as at the local postmaster level, and the creation of a government corporation, free of congressional restraints on rates and labor negotiations. The post office, in short, was to become a business, designed to break even by 1984, and not a public service.

This swift and ill-considered departure from a long-established tradition has had lamentable effects—less service, higher costs. There was a rush into fancy, but untried, sorting equipment, bulk mail centers, and sectional centers which required multibillion dollar investments. The new management also agreed to a demand by the postal unions, which control 80 percent of the workers, that there be a "no layoff" clause in their contracts.

By 1975 there were more permanent postal employees than in 1970. Naturally, the capital investment program pushed costs higher, but productivity actually declined. The labor contract, meanwhile, provided pay raises with unlimited cost of living escalators, making Postal Service workers the envy of the federal bureaucracy. Indeed, this vast bureaucracy is now demanding wages and fringe benefits comparable to those of postal workers — an unhappy competition for taxpayers.

But the biggest headaches have resulted from two of the Reorganization Act's other innovations. The board of governors, which guides the system, is selected by senators and approved by the President — with the essential qualification that they have not previously been involved with postal matters. One can, of course, support the concept that parties with a vested interest should not sit on the board, but while most of the governors are competent in other areas, are they really suited to supervise postal specialists?

If any single innovation could be said to be wrecking the system, however, it is the creation of an independent Postal Rate Commission. Postal rates have traditionally been a highly political matter, subject to lobbying by special interest groups such as the magazine, book and record industries, and religious and labor groups.

But out of that traditional process, which included congressional hearings and interplay between a skilled congressional staff and post office specialists,

came an approximation of justice in rates. Strict cost accounting, which disregards the system's public service role, results in recommendations such as the one recently made by the Government Accounting Office to shut down more than 12,000 rural post offices.

It is not unusual nowadays to look back to the good old days. But users of the mail, who feel so inclined, need look back no further than five years. It is obvious that the Postal Service, which touches the lives of all Americans, should not remain in the hands of an independent board of governors and be run as a government corporation. The postal system should be responsible to the people through their Congress and should be supported by the Treasury, when necessary, as a beneficial and enlightened use of tax dollars.

THE CASE FOR COMPETITION

"The post office is both a monopoly and a government bureau — so it should occasion no surprise that it is costly, inefficient and backward."

As is so often the case, economist Milton Friedman is again correct in his analysis of a pressing national problem: As long as first-class mail (so-called "letter" mail) is a monopoly of the federal government there is no real chance that service will improve or that costs will be held in check.

When the old Post Office Department became the Postal Service, some commentators and members of Congress actually believed that near miracles would occur by "taking the Post Office out of politics." Sound business practices, it was thought, would produce better service and eliminate sky rocketing postal deficits.

But just as Prof. Friedman had predicted in 1967 when such a switch was proposed by Postmaster General Lawrence O'Brien, nothing of the kind has occurred. "That (the Postal Reorganization Act) would change only form, not substance," wrote Friedman. "As a monopoly it would still be costly; as a government organization, it would still be backward."

And so it is today. As John Haldi and Joseph F. Johnston, Jr., pointed out in an excellent, comprehensive study for the American Enterprise Institute: "The statutory (first-class) postal monopoly has no economic justification. The monopoly is no longer an important source of governmental revenue and in no way promotes better and cheaper mail service. In fact, it probably impedes the development of better systems for delivering written communications."

Because the law permits it, there is currently some competition with the Postal Service in the delivery of other classes of mail, particularly third (bulk advertising circulars) and fourth (parcel post). More than a dozen companies around the country now deliver third-class mail more cheaply and efficiently than the Postal Service—and make a profit doing it. The biggest competitor in the fourth-class field is United Parcel Service, which now handles close to 50 percent of the national package volume. UPS makes a profit and pays taxes, while the Postal Service just about breaks even on parcel post, although its rates are higher and it pays no taxes.

The Postal Service has responded to competitive pressures, however, and has started to mechanize its package sorting and distributing procedures and is supposedly even setting up separate handling treatment for packages marked "fragile." This is the kind of change that comes about through competition. In fact, studies show that most improvements in mail service over the last 200 years have been developed by private companies attempting to compete with a government monopoly. The typical pattern has been for government to adopt the new idea and then strengthen its monopoly to crush the competitor.

This pattern need not continue. Every year since 1970, Rep. Philip M. Crane (R-Ill.) has introduced a bill to end the Postal Service monopoly over first-class mail. Despite the growing appeal of such a change—to liberals and conservatives alike—no committee hearings have ever been held on this bill and this year's measure (H.2651) is receiving equal neglect.

Why? There are two standard replies: The Postal Service is a "natural monopoly," and if competitors were permitted to exist they would just engage in "cream skimming"—i.e., take the most profitable business and leave the remainder to the Postal Service.

The answer to the first objection is simple enough. Judging from the performance so far there is no "economy of steel" that makes postal delivery a natural monopoly. If it were, no law would be needed to protect it.

The second objection is somewhat harder to handle because of the emotionalism and politics involved. People who live in less populated areas now receive subsidized mail and do not want to pay more for a first-class letter than city dwellers and suburbanites. And they have let their congressmen know this in clear terms.

There is no available evidence, however, on which to predict what first-class rates—or any other rates—would be in a competitive situation. With government alone involved, there is no real yardstick against which to make projections. There are some rough indications nonetheless, of what might happen. The president of the Independent Postal System of America, for example, says his system can deliver mail for about four cents a letter. While the cost in rural areas would undoubtedly be higher than that, it still might be lower than the 13 cents the Postal Service may soon charge for first-class.

In fact, it is the mechanism of competition that makes abolishing the postal monopoly a good risk for everyone—the isolated rural resident as well as the city dweller, who now pays *too much* for his first-class mail. As editor of a publication sent out at supposedly subsidized second-class rates (although in dollar value we do approximately as much first-class mailing), I am willing to take the chance. In my view, new techniques in mail handling will ultimately result in savings, even for second-class users, over what the present Postal Service has in store for us.

What do we have to lose by trying? Very little. Since mail delivery is so labor intensive, there would be no need for large capital investments which might damage the economy if they went sour. As the American Enterprise Institute study points out: "If by any chance repeal (of the monopoly provision) should turn out to be a mistake, unprofitable private posts would disband and the resources (mostly labor and delivery vehicles) could be quickly and readily transferred to other productive uses in the economy. The costs of any specialized equipment which might have to be written off would be small."

As John Ryan, former chairman of the Postal Rate Commission, recently told the House subcommittee on postal service: "Open competition has always been the condition which best serves the customer, short of compelling theoretical or practical evidence to the contrary. Such evidence has not been produced concerning mail service. In any case, it is not properly up to the proponents of competition to prove their case. It is up to the monopolists to prove the case for monopoly, and I don't believe that they can do so."

43.

FLOYD HARRINGTON: CB Radios

The citizens band radio fad was a by-product of the Arab oil embargo. After the speed limit on the nation's highways was reduced to 55 miles per hour in 1973, many truck drivers installed the radios to be able to warn each other of highway police and radar traps. Publicity about this usage led many automobile owners to buy CB radios for their cars for the same reason and as an entertainment while driving. By mid-1976 there were more than 20 million CB radios in use, an increase of 19 million since 1967; and a whole CB cult had grown up with its own peculiar slang and its own magazines. Because of the sudden congestion of the airwaves, the Federal Communications Commission ruled in 1976 that effective in January 1977 the number of channels would be increased from 23 to 40. This article describes the CB fad as it developed from 1973 to 1975.

Source: *Soldiers*, October 1975.

SOME PEOPLE THINK [CB's are] the greatest thing since sliced bread; others get downright violent over them. Some people have never heard of them, let alone know what their purpose is.

What CB is supposed to be is a short-range communication service for a person's business or personal needs. The service began in 1958 with the use of the 23 CB channels strictly governed by Federal Communications Commission's (FCC) Rules and Regulations, Volume VI, Part 95. CB isn't intended to compete with amateur radio as a hobby.

Joining the CB radio craze is easy. Buy a radio (there are more than 40 types of units on the market ranging in price from $50 to $600), read FCC's Part 95, fill out an application (FCC Form 505) and send it, along with $4, to: FCC, 334 York Street, Gettysburg, Pa. 17325. You can operate your set *after* you get your license and call letters.

How long you have to wait for your license depends on the workload of the FCC's Amateur and Citizens Division. By mid-1975, more than 1.4 million licenses were issued. According to Harvey Speck, senior attorney of FCC's Amateur and Citizens Division, new applications are pouring in at a rate of 200,000 a month, probably because the license fee was lowered from $20 to $4. "We're 16 days behind in opening up the mail, and there's a 6- to 8-week processing time."

Once you have your license you're ready to start operating. Since you've spent about 2 months reading and memorizing Part 95 (Rules and Regulations), you know the correct radio procedures. You turn on your radio and—unless you live out in the middle of nowhere—you hear something like this:

"Weeowwookhow 'bout that Dapper Dan, you got your ears ozztweedleDee, Tweedle Dee, do you read this ol' Twee-

dle Dum? Comzzztadio check. Break! Break! for a radio chezztreak! Break! How 'bout a 10-37 fzzt report on the Smokey situation south bounzzt Break! Break! Break! Breakity, Broke . . . "

What's all that gobbledygook, you say? It's the biggest problem with CB today. The 23 channels are overcrowded and there are both old and new CBers who couldn't care less about correct radio procedure.

"Handles," such as C. C. Rider, Trashman, Ridgerunner, Honey Bee, and thousands more are used for identification rather than call signs. If you listen to CB for any time at all you may think that the channels are being used just for the sake of chatter. For the most part you'd be right.

According to a newspaper interview with an FCC official, " . . . the abuses have grown so great that the actual use of Citizens Band radio has been threatened."

Abuses are considered to be: not using a call sign when transmitting, using offensive language over the air, using the radio as a hobby and talking "skip." For example, when conditions are right it's possible for a CBer in Ohio to talk to a CBer in Texas. Operating a CB with "boosts," some CBers hook up an amplifier that can boost their radio's power output from the legal 4 watts up to 1000 watts.

To curb CB abuses the FCC has five 8-member enforcement teams located throughout the country. These teams use directional finding equipment and tips from disgruntled informers to track down CBers who use the radio illegally. Informers could be just about anyone from a CBer who's a stickler for procedure to an irate housewife who's tired of her favorite TV program being interrupted with, "Break Tomcat, you got your ears on?"

"Between 25 to 30 percent of the abusers are unlicensed," says Speck. "They're the most difficult to detect because they don't operate with call signs."

While you're sitting there listening to the mumbo jumbo coming out of your speaker you have to decide how *you're* going to operate.

Without a doubt the easiest way is to think up a "handle" for yourself, key your mike (begin broadcasting) and start hollering. "Break, Break!" Someone may be kind to you and answer with a "Go break!" You can ask him, or her, for a 10-36 (time check) or radio check (you're asking for someone to tell you if your radio is working). You could even find out how heavy the traffic is on Main Street. This is all neat stuff you really need to know. If you're in luck you may even get an answer to your questions before another CBer breaks in on you — but don't bet on it.

Then again, you can do like a big percentage of responsible CBers do and wait until you have a real reason for keying your mike.

Mobility. Many families have both a base station in their home and a mobile unit in their car. If Mom wants Dad to stop at the store on his way home, she can call him on the base station and tell him. If they want to set up a get-together with another family by using CB radios, that's all right, too. On vacation they can use their mobile unit to ask for directions or find a good place to eat.

One Army family traveling from Alaska to the "lower 48" put their CB to good use in Canada. Just outside of Dawson Creek, British Columbia, they found the steel tongue on their travel trailer had started to shear off. They called a Canadian CBer who directed them to a welder in Dawson Creek.

While the tongue was being welded the Canadian radio operator came down to the shop, picked up the entire family and took them to his house for dinner. A few hours later they were on their way again, the trailer tongue fixed, and, thanks to their CB, they had found a new friend.

Specialist 5 Bill Riley, 365th Transportation Company, Fort McClellan, Ala., and his wife Ann are CB buffs (KBA 6779). His handle is "Wrestler" while she goes by "Lady Marion."

The couple has both a base station and mobile unit. Ann monitors the base station during the day and around 4:30 p.m., keeps an ear cocked for a call from her husband. "Bill will let me know when he's coming home so I'll have supper on the table when he gets here. Then too, if I need something from the store I can let him know." She also relays messages when her husband isn't at home.

SP5 Riley's big interest in CB is his membership in a local organization called the Alabama Emergency Local Patrol (AELP). The 50-member group works closely with the Alabama State Troopers. They spend their free time assisting stranded motorists and can provide a communications network in the event of an emergency or natural disaster. While on the road they also keep their eyes peeled for any kind of criminal activity.

AELP has a base station set up to monitor channel 10 and scan channel 9, the emergency channel, at the State Troopers Anniston, Ala., sub-station. AELP members take turns operating the set on weekends and holidays. They plan to have base stations set up eventually in all Alabama counties to relay weather warnings and other emergency information.

Corporal Lewis Mewborne, Alabama State Troopers, has a personal CB radio installed in his patrol car. He's all for AELP. "We're short-handed as it is, and when those CBers are on the road that 30 or 40 more sets of eyes really help out.

"Many times they're at the scene of an

accident long before we are. By using their radios to call for help they save lives. Over in Gaston they've also been responsible for helping stop a couple of robberies."

Trucker Lingo. Another thing you'll find when listening to channel 10 is the trucker's channel. It's called that because channel 10 is used by the big 18-wheelers to keep tabs on "Smokey" (state police), find out whether or not "chicken coops" (weigh stations) are open and to pass on other nice-to-know information, such as, "Hey Big Blue, check out the seat covers (the girl) on that red four-wheeler coming up alongside you."

There's probably not a CBer in the country who can honestly say he doesn't monitor the trucker's channel while on the road, particularly "greenstamps" like the Pennsylvania and Ohio Turnpikes. Turnpikes are called "greenstamps" because greenstamp is CB jargon for money and speeding tickets cost money.

The truckers warn each other as to the location of each Smokey, what kind of car he's in—a Tijuana Taxi (marked), plain black or brown wrapper (unmarked), where the picture-taking machines (radar) are and which direction they're headed. The theory is that you can speed until you hear there's a Smokey in the area and then you slow down until he's gone.

Unlike some state police, Mewborne doesn't mind if the truckers keep tab on him. He says his job is to slow down traffic and save lives. If the truckers know he's on the road they slow down for 15 miles in either direction.

"I like it when they know where I am. Before there were CB radios, they wouldn't slow down until they actually saw me," says Mewborne.

"Another good point is that those 18-wheelers report accidents, drunk drivers and cars in trouble just like AELP members do."

On the other hand there are state policemen who get upset by such things as this little ditty:

Smokies, smokies, in the trees,
You've got radar,
But we've got CBs!

A CBer in Beaver Falls, Wis., was arrested for using his radio to warn a trucker about Smokey. He was found guilty of "obstructing an officer in the performance of his duty," and fined $20.

The arresting officer was quoted as saying, "Our basic goal is to prevent accidents. If someone does something to deprive us of that ability, we are unable to properly serve the public . . . There are valid uses for Citizen's Band radios, but where they are used to obstruct justice, those individuals must be stopped." Both Alabama and Wisconsin are in the process of officially installing CB radios in their patrol cars.

It doesn't matter what state you live in, practically all of them have some kind of local organization like AELP that CBers can join. If they don't, you can join a national organization like REACT (Radio Emergency Action Team). They all do pretty much the same things—monitor channel 9, give assistance to motorists and set up a communication network in other emergencies.

Military Madmen. If you're interested in the social aspects of CB radio there are numerous clubs scattered around the country like the Military Madmen in Northern Virginia.

Staff Sergeant Paul McCreight, Headquarters, Installation Support Activity, Military District of Washington (KHZ 2306), says, "The Madmen is a social club where anyone interested in CB can get together and talk about CB. We take our families to a restaurant or maybe on a picnic and just have fun."

The 50-member club also assists anyone they can from stalled motorists to Park Rangers searching for a lost child.

Prospective Madmen members don't have to be licensed to join but the club makes every effort to help them get a license. "We stress legal operation of radios," says McCreight. "We're trying to get away from all these illegal operators who give us a bad name."

Without a doubt operating a CB can be fun and it can be a hobby *without* using the radio as a hobby. How you use it is up to you.

"... 73s your way and 88s if they apply. Have a good day today, a better day tomorrow and may the good Lord take a likin' to you. This is the Silver Dollar, KGR 1119, Clear!"

44.

ELDRIDGE CLEAVER: Why I Am Returning to the United States

Eldridge Cleaver first gained national prominence as a founder of the Black Panther Party in Oakland, California, and as author of the popular book, Soul on Ice. *Having little formal schooling, he had succeeded in educating himself while serving a prison sentence for a 1958 assault. After nine years he was paroled, but then got into a shootout with Oakland police. Rather than return to jail, he fled the country and lived abroad, mainly in Algeria and France. In 1975 he decided to return, even at the risk of facing the charges he had run away from. In an open letter published in November he told why he was returning home.*

Source: *New York Times*, November 18, 1975.

I AM OFTEN ASKED why I want to return to the United States. This question never fails to bowl me over, and I find it impossible to answer. I also feel that it is an improper question. In fact, most people who ask are not really interested in that question. What they actually want to know is what will I do if they allow me to return.

I always take the opportunity to explain why I left in the first place. Lots of people believe I left because I preferred to go live in a Communist country, and that now, several years and many Communist countries later, I find the grass not greener on the Communist side of the fence. So now, here I stand, locked outside the gates of the paradise I once scorned, begging to be let back in. Let me clarify.

On April 6, 1968, two days after Dr. Martin Luther King Jr. was assassinated, there was a gun battle between members of the Black Panther Party and the Oakland Police Department. Bobby Hutton was killed. Warren Wells and I received gunshot wounds. Two policemen were wounded. Eight party members, myself included, were arrested in the area of the gunfight.

After I received emergency treatment, guards from the California Department of Corrections transported me directly to San Quentin State Prison, in the spirit of

"Oh, boy, we got you now!" It seemed obvious to them that I had violated my parole. I, along with the others, was indicted by an Alameda County Grand Jury. And although bail was set on all of us, the Corrections Department refused to allow me to go free on bail, claiming jurisdiction over me as a parole violator.

I pleaded not guilty. Without a trial or hearing of any sort, the prison authorities were prejudging my case, declaring me guilty, and, in effect, sentencing me to prison. My attorneys filed a petition for a writ of habeas corpus. A hearing was held before Chief Judge Raymond J. Sherwin of the Solano County Superior Court.

Judge Sherwin ordered me free on bail. I quote two passages from his decision:

"The record here is that though the petitioner was arrested and his parole cancelled more than two months ago, hearings before the Adult Authority [the state parole board for male felons] have not even been scheduled.

"There is nothing to indicate why it was deemed necessary to cancel his parole before his trial on the pending criminal charges of which he is presumed innocent.

"It has to be stressed that the uncontradicted evidence presented to this Court indicated that the petitioner had been a model parolee. The peril to his parole status stemmed from no failure of personal rehabilitation, but from his undue eloquence in pursuing political goals, goals which were offensive to many of his contemporaries.

"Not only was there absence of cause for the cancellation of parole, it was the product of a type of pressure unbecoming, to say the least, to the law enforcement paraphernalia of this state."

Judge Sherwin's decision exploded like a bomb inside California legal, political and police circles, because it missed the whole point: From Gov. Ronald Reagan down, the politicians wanted me silenced, and here Judge Sherwin was talking about due process of law!

People who supported my fight for my rights posted $50,000 bail, and I was free.

The law-enforcement paraphernalia was not stopped by Judge Sherwin's condemnation, and the Adult Authority moved swiftly to have his ruling reversed in the Appellate Court. The court refused to examine the facts at issue in the case and instead simply affirmed the arbitrary power of the Adult Authority to revoke parole. Because of a technicality in court procedure, the ruling ordering me returned to prison could not become effective for sixty days. I was due to surrender on Nov. 27. That day, I was in Montreal. That was seven years ago.

History shows that when the American political system is blocked and significant segments of the population are unable to have their will brought to bear on the decision-making process, you can count upon the American people to revolt, to take it out into the streets, in the spirit of the Boston Tea Party.

During the 1960's, the chips were down in a fateful way, uniting the upsurge of black Americans against the oppressive features of the system, and the gargantuan popular opposition to the Indochina wars. It was left to the Nixon Administration to bring the issues to a head. In the end, the system rejected President Nixon and reaffirmed its own basic principles.

A fabulous new era of progress is opening up to the world, and coping with all of the problems unleashed by Watergate has opened up a creative era for American democracy. I believe that every American, regardless of his politics, has a duty to re-examine some of his beliefs.

This is particularly true of those active at both extremes of the political spectrum. Those of us who developed a psychology of opposition must take a pause and sum up our experiences. We must recognize that in a sense we are playing in a brand new ball game. The slogans of yesterday will not get us through the tasks at hand. I believe that for America to deal with problems posed on the world level, a fundamental reorientation in the relationship between the American people is absolutely necessary.

We can not afford to refight battles that have already been either won or lost. If Richard Nixon and his friends had accepted the verdict of the people in 1960, rejecting him at the polls, the nation would have been spared the debacle of Watergate. But the truth is that nations do get the leaders they deserve.

With all of its faults, the American political system is the freest and most democratic in the world. The system needs to be improved, with democracy spread to all areas of life, particularly the economic. All of these changes must be conducted through our established institutions, and people with grievances must find political methods for obtaining redress.

Each generation subjects the world it inherits to severe criticism. I think that my generation has been more critical than most, and for good reason. At the same time, at the end of the critical process, we should arrive at some conclusions. We should have discovered which values are worth conserving. It is the beginning of another fight, the fight to defend those values from the blind excesses of our fellows who are still caught up in the critical process. It is my hope to make a positive contribution in this regard.

45.

DANIEL P. MOYNIHAN: The United Nations Resolution on Zionism

On November 10, 1975, the United Nations General Assembly adopted a resolution equating Zionism with racism. Passage of the resolution by a vote of 72 to 35, with 32 abstentions, depended on Communist bloc and Third World countries. The United States vehemently opposed the resolution, as did the nations of Western Europe. On the day passage occurred, Daniel P. Moynihan, U. S. Ambassador to the U.N., enunciated the American position in the statement reprinted here. The text of the resolution is printed before the Moynihan address.

Source: *Department of State Bulletin,* December 1, 1975.

Text of Resolution

Elimination of all forms of racial discrimination

The General Assembly.

Recalling its resolution 1904 (XVIII) of 20 November 1963, proclaiming the United Nations Declaration on the Elimi-nation of All Forms of Racial Discrimination, and in particular its affirmation that "any doctrine of racial differentiation or superiority is scientifically false, morally condemnable [and] socially unjust and dangerous" and its expression of alarm at "the manifestations of racial discrimination still in evidence in some areas in the world, some of which are imposed by certain Governments by means of legislative, administrative or other measures",

Recalling also that, in its resolution 3151 G (XXVIII) of 14 December 1973, the General Assembly condemned, *inter alia,* the unholy alliance between South African racism and zionism,

Taking note of the Declaration of Mexico on the Equality of Women and their Contribution to Development and Peace, 1975 proclaimed by the World Conference of the International Women's Year, held at Mexico City from 19 June to 2 July 1975, which promulgated the principle that "international cooperation and peace require the achievement of national liberation and independence, the elimination of colonialism and neocolonialism, foreign occupation, zionism, *apartheid,* and racial discrimination in all its forms as well as the recognition of the dignity of peoples and their right to self-determination",

Taking note also of resolution 77 (XII) adopted by the Assembly of Heads of State and Government of the Organization of African Unity at its twelfth ordinary session, held in Kampala from 28 July to 1 August 1975, which considered "that the racist régime in occupied Palestine and racist régimes in Zimbabwe and South Africa have a common imperialist origin, forming a whole and having the same racist structure and being organically linked in their policy aimed at repression of the dignity and integrity of the human being",

Taking note also of the Political Declaration and Strategy to Strengthen International Peace and Security and to Intensify Solidarity and Mutual Assistance among Non-Aligned Countries, adopted at the Conference of Ministers for Foreign Affairs of Non-Aligned Countries, held in Lima from 25 to 30 August 1975, which most severely condemned zionism as a threat to world peace and security and called upon all countries to oppose this racist and imperialist ideology,

Determines that zionism is a form of racism and racial discrimination.

Statement by Ambassador Moynihan

The United States rises to declare before the General Assembly of the United Nations, and before the world, that it does not acknowledge, it will not abide by, it will never acquiesce in, this infamous act.

Not three weeks ago, the U.S. Representative in the Social, Humanitarian and Cultural Committee pleaded in measured and fully considered terms for the United Nations not to do this thing. It was, he said, "obscene." It is something more today, for the furtiveness with which this obscenity first appeared among us has been replaced by a shameless openness.

There will be time enough to contemplate the harm this act will have done the United Nations. Historians will do that for us, and it is sufficient for the moment only to note one foreboding fact. A great evil has been loosed upon the world. The abomination of anti-Semitism—as this year's Nobel peace laureate, Andrei Sakharov, observed in Moscow just a few days ago—the abomination of anti-Semitism has been given the appearance of international sanction. The General Assembly today grants symbolic amnesty—and more—to the murderers of the 6 million European Jews. Evil enough in itself, but more ominous by far is the realization that now presses upon us—the realization that if there were no General Assembly, this could never have happened.

As this day will live in infamy, it behooves those who sought to avert it to declare their thoughts so that historians will know that we fought here, that we were not small in number—not this time—and that while we lost, we fought with full knowledge of what indeed would *be* lost.

Nor should any historian of the event, nor yet any who have participated in it, suppose that we have fought only as governments, as chancelleries, and on an issue well removed from the concerns of our respective peoples. Others will speak for their nations; I will speak for mine.

In all our postwar history there has not been another issue which has brought forth such unanimity of American opinion.

The President of the United States has from the first been explicit: This must not happen. The Congress of the United States, in a measure unanimously adopted in the Senate and sponsored by 436 of 437 Representatives in the House, declared its utter opposition.

Following only American Jews themselves, the American trade union movement was first to the fore in denouncing this infamous undertaking. Next, one after another, the great private institutions of American life pronounced anathema on this evil thing—and most particularly, the Christian churches have done so. Reminded that the United Nations was born in the struggle against just such abominations as we are committing today—the wartime alliance of the United Nations dates from 1942—the United Nations Association of the United States has for the first time in its history appealed directly to each of the 141 other delegations in New York not to do this unspeakable thing.

The proposition to be sanctioned by a resolution of the General Assembly of the United Nations is that "zionism is a form of racism and racial discrimination." Now, this is a lie. But as it is a lie which the United Nations has now declared to be a truth, the actual truth must be restated.

The very first point to be made is that the United Nations has declared Zionism to be racism—without ever having defined racism. "Sentence first—verdict afterwards," as the Queen of Hearts said. But this is not Wonderland, but a real world, where there are real consequences to folly and to venality.

Just on Friday, the President of the General Assembly, speaking on behalf of Luxembourg, warned not only of the trouble which would follow from the adoption of this resolution but of its essential irresponsibility—for, he noted, members have wholly different ideas as to what they are condemning. "It seems to me," he said, and to his lasting honor he said it when there was still time, "It seems to me that before a body like this takes a decision they should agree very clearly on what they are approving or condemning, and it takes more time."

Lest I be unclear, the United Nations has in fact on several occasions defined "racial discrimination." The definitions have been loose, but recognizable. It is "racism," incomparably the more serious charge—racial discrimination is a practice; racism is a doctrine—which has never been defined. Indeed, the term has only recently appeared in U.N. General Assembly documents.

The one occasion on which we know its meaning to have been discussed was the 1644th meeting of the Third Committee on December 16, 1968, in connection with the report of the Secretary General on the status of the International Convention on the Elimination of All Forms of Racial Discrimination.

On that occasion—to give some feeling

for the intellectual precision with which the matter was being treated—the question arose as to what should be the relative positioning of the terms "racism" and "nazism" in a number of the preambular paragraphs. The distinguished delegate from Tunisia argued that "racism" should go first because nazism was merely a form of racism. Not so, said the no less distinguished delegate from the Union of Soviet Socialist Republics. For, he explained, nazism contained the main elements of racism within its ambit and should be mentioned first. This is to say that racism was merely a form of nazism.

The discussion wound to its weary and inconclusive end, and we are left with nothing to guide us, for even this one discussion of "racism" confined itself to word orders in preambular paragraphs and did not at all touch on the meaning of the words as such.

Still, one cannot but ponder the situation we have made for ourselves in the context of the Soviet statement on that not so distant occasion. If, as the distinguished delegate declared, racism is a form of nazism, and if, as this resolution declares, Zionism is a form of racism, then we have step by step taken ourselves to the point of proclaiming—the United Nations is solemnly proclaiming—that Zionism is a form of nazism.

What we have here is a lie—a political lie of a variety well known to the 20th century and scarcely exceeded in all that annal of untruth and outrage. The lie is that Zionism is a form of racism. The overwhelmingly clear truth is that it is not.

The word "racism" is a creation of the English language, and relatively new to it. It is not, for instance, to be found in the Oxford English Dictionary. The term derives from relatively new doctrines—all of them discredited—concerning the human population of the world, to the effect that there are significant biological differences among clearly identifiable groups and that these differences establish, in effect, different levels of humanity. Racism, as defined by Webster's Third New International Dictionary, is "the assumption that . . . traits and capacities are determined by biological race and that races differ decisively from one another." It further involves "a belief in the inherent superiority of a particular race and its right to domination over others."

This meaning is clear. It is equally clear that this assumption, this belief, has always been altogether alien to the political and religious movement known as Zionism. As a strictly political movement, Zionism was established only in 1897, although there is a clearly legitimate sense in which its origins are indeed ancient. For example, many branches of Christianity have always held that, from the standpoint of the biblical prophets, Israel would be reborn one day. But the modern Zionist movement arose in Europe in the context of a general upsurge of national consciousness and aspiration that overtook most other people of Central and Eastern Europe after 1848 and that in time spread to all of Africa and Asia.

It was, to those persons of the Jewish religion, a Jewish form of what today is called a national liberation movement. Probably a majority of those persons who became active Zionists and sought to emigrate to Palestine were born within the confines of Czarist Russia, and it was only natural for Soviet Foreign Minister Andrei Gromyko to deplore, as he did in 1948, in the 299th meeting of the Security Council, the act by Israel's neighbors of "sending their troops into Palestine and carrying out military operations aimed"—in Mr. Gromyko's words—"at the suppression of the national liberation movement in Palestine."

Now, it was the singular nature—if I am not mistaken, it was the unique nature—of this national liberation movement that, in contrast with the movements that preceded it, those of that time, and those that have come since, it defined its members in terms not of birth, but of belief.

That is to say, it was not a movement of the Irish to free Ireland or of the Polish to free Poland, not a movement of Algerians to free Algeria nor of Indians to free India. It was not a movement of persons connected by historic membership in a genetic pool of the kind that enables us to speak loosely but not meaninglessly, say, of the Chinese people, nor yet of diverse groups occupying the same territory which enables us to speak of the American people with no greater indignity to truth.

To the contrary, Zionists defined themselves merely as Jews and declared to be Jewish anyone born of a Jewish mother or—and this is the absolutely crucial fact—anyone who converted to Judaism. Which is to say, in the terms of the International Convention on the Elimination of All Forms of Racial Discrimination, adopted by the 20th General Assembly, *anyone*—regardless of "race, colour, descent, or national or ethnic origin."

The State of Israel, which in time was the creation of the Zionist movement, has been extraordinary in nothing so much as the range of "racial stocks" from which it has drawn its citizenry. There are black Jews, brown Jews, white Jews, Jews from the Orient, and Jews from the West. Most such persons could be said to have been "born" Jews, just as most Presbyterians and most Hindus are "born" to their faith; but there are many Jews who are converts. With a consistency in the matter which surely attests to the importance of this issue to that religious and political culture, Israeli courts have held that a Jew who converts to another religion is no longer a Jew.

In the meantime the population of Israel also includes large numbers of non-Jews, among them Arabs of both the Moslem and Christian religions and Christians of other national origins. Many of these persons are citizens of Israel, and those who are not can become citizens by legal procedures very much like those which obtain in a typical nation of Western Europe.

Now, I should wish to be understood that I am here making one point, and one point only, which is that whatever else Zionism may be, it is not and cannot be "a form of racism." In logic, the State of Israel could be, or could become, many things—theoretically including many things undesirable—but it could not be and could not become racist unless it ceased to be Zionist.

Dangers to Cause of Human Rights

Indeed, the idea that Jews *are* a "race" was invented not by Jews, but by those who hated Jews. The idea of Jews as a race was invented by 19th-century anti-Semites such as Houston Stewart Chamberlain and Edouard Drumont, who saw that in an increasingly secular age, which is to say an age which made for fewer distinctions between people, the old religious grounds for anti-Semitism were losing force. New justifications were needed for excluding and persecuting Jews, and so the new idea of Jews as a race, rather than as a religion, was born. It was a contemptible idea at the beginning, and no civilized person would be associated with it. To think that it is an idea now endorsed by the United Nations is to reflect on what civilization has come to.

It is precisely a concern for civilization, for civilized values that are or should be precious to all mankind, that arouses us at this moment to such special passion. What we have at stake here is not merely the honor and the legitimacy of the State of Israel—although a challenge to the legitimacy of any member nation ought always to arouse the vigilance of all members of the United Nations. For a yet more important matter is at issue, which is the integrity of that whole body of moral and legal precepts which we know as human rights.

The terrible lie that has been told here today will have terrible consequences. Not only will people begin to say—indeed they have already begun to say—that the United Nations is a place where lies are told; but far more serious, grave, and perhaps irreparable harm will be done to the cause of human rights itself.

The harm will arise first because it will strip from racism the precise and abhorrent meaning that it still precariously holds today. How will the peoples of the world feel about racism, and about the need to struggle against it, when they are told that it is an idea so broad as to include the Jewish national liberation movement?

As this lie spreads, it will do harm in a second way. Many of the members of the United Nations owe their independence in no small part to the notion of human rights, as it has spread from the domestic sphere to the international sphere and exercised its influence over the old colonial powers. We are now coming into a time when that independence is likely to be threatened again. There will be new forces, some of them arising now, new prophets and new despots, who will justify their actions with the help of just such distortions of words as we have sanctioned here today.

Today we have drained the word "racism" of its meaning. Tomorrow, terms like "national self-determination" and "national honor" will be perverted in the same way to serve the purposes of conquest and exploitation. And when these claims begin to be made—as they already have begun to be made—it is the small nations of the world whose integrity will suffer. And how will the small nations of the world defend themselves, on what grounds will others be moved to defend and protect them, when the language of human rights, the only language by which the small can be defended, is no longer believed and no longer has a power of its own?

There is this danger, and then a final danger that is the most serious of all—which is that the damage we now do to the idea of human rights and the language of human rights could well be irreversible.

The idea of human rights as we know it today is not an idea which has always existed in human affairs. It is an idea which appeared at a specific time in the world and under very special circumstances. It appeared when European philosophers of the 17th century began to argue that man was a being whose existence was independent from that of the state, that he need join a political community only if he did not lose by that association more than he gained. From this very specific political philosophy stemmed the idea of political rights, of claims that the individual could justly make against the state; it was because the individual was seen as so separate from the state that he could make legitimate demands upon it.

That was the philosophy from which the idea of domestic and international rights sprang. But most of the world does not hold with that philosophy now. Most of the world believes in newer modes of political thought, in philosophies that do not accept the individual as distinct from and prior to the state, in philosophies that therefore do not provide any justification for the idea of human rights, and philosophies that have no words by which to explain their value. If we destroy the words that were given to us by past centuries, we will not have words to replace them, for philosophy today has no such words. But there are those of us who have not forsaken these older words, still so new to much of the world. Not forsaken them now, not here, not anywhere, not ever.

The United States of America declares that it does not acknowledge, it will not abide by, it will never acquiesce in, this infamous act.

46.

KONSTANTIN BUSHUYEV: A Soviet View of the Soyuz-Apollo Project

The United States and the Soviet Union conducted a joint space venture, the first such cooperative effort, in the summer of 1975. The American astronauts were Thomas P. Stafford, Vance D. Brand, and Donald K. Slayton. The Soviet crew consisted of Aleksey A. Leonov and Valery N. Kubasov. The Soyuz craft was launched on July 15, and Apollo was sent aloft some seven and one-half hours later. The two ships docked in space on July 17. During the flight a number of important space experiments were conducted. On July 19 the ships separated and docked once more in order to check out the mechanism and the maneuver. Final separation occurred the same day. Soyuz landed on July 21, and Apollo came down in the Pacific Ocean on the 24th. The selection below reprints an early assessment of the project by a member of the Soviet Academy of Sciences, K. Bushuyev, a technical director for the flight.

Source: *Space World*, November 1975.

THE SOVIET-AMERICAN joint test mission of the Soyuz and Apollo spacecraft came off successfully. For the first time in the history of space flight a space system consisting of spaceships of two countries with an international crew on board was set up and functioned in near-Earth orbit for two days. Soyuz and Apollo met in outer space but the true significance of their meeting can be seen best of all here on Earth.

The public and political leaders in different countries with ample reason see this flight as a historic event in the exploration of outer space and a signal contribution to the improvement of Soviet-American relations and the international situation in general.

With great excitement and deep gratitude the participants in the Soyuz-Apollo project have received greetings of the leaders of the Communist Party and the Soviet state to those who prepared and carried out the Soyuz-19 flight.

One needs time to fully appreciate the results of the Soyuz-Apollo test flight. However, even today it is safe to say that the program of the joint mission and its basic aims have been carried out in full. This experiment gave practical embodiment to the Soviet-American agreement on cooperation in the exploration and use of outer space for peaceful purposes signed three years ago.

During this time Soviet and American spacemen, scientists, engineers, technicians and other personnel worked tirelessly here on Earth, sharing their knowledge, experience and ideas in an effort to establish all conditions necessary to carry out the Soyuz-Apollo project, which is another step on the way to international space programs. Complex technical as well as human problems were solved in the process, and it was proved that sincere desire to cooperate can overcome any barriers.

During a comparatively short time after the signing of the agreement Soviet and American specialists held numerous meetings, various joint tests and training sessions, in the course of which they settled on a wide range of organizational and technical questions.

The last stage of joint preparations for the experiment came to an end on May 22, when the USSR Academy of Sciences and the American NASA signed a final document on readiness for the flight. Then came the day when the Soyuz and the Apollo lifted off from the cosmodromes in Baikonur and on Cape Canaveral.

From the first minute of the flight, the press, radio and television gave extensive and detailed coverage of each stage of the flight, so that the whole world could closely follow its progress.

Paying tribute to the work of those who were responsible for the development and flight of Soyuz-19, I would like to point out the following. Despite intolerably hot weather, the technical personnel at the cosmodrome and the launching team did a good job getting the space-rocket complex ready for launch and ensuring the smooth orbiting of Soyuz-19. We were satisfied with the accurate measurements made by ballistics experts and the smooth operation of the attitude and motion control system of the launch vehicle and the spacecraft. Soyuz-19 missed the docking orbit by 250 meters with the tolerance being 1,500 meters; the spacecraft reached the target area with the time deviation of 7.5 sec. with the tolerance standing at 90 sec.

The joint operations were carried out strictly on schedule, "to a minute or even to a second," as Alexei Leonov invariably reported from Soyuz-19. There were moments, however, when we and our American colleagues ran into some trouble. For several hours after the launch we could not obtain television transmission from Soyuz-19, while the Americans took too long to open the hatch and clear the passage from the Apollo command module to the docking module. Thanks to the recommendation of the Soviet Control Center experts and the skillfulness of Alexei Leonov and Valery Kubasov, the television system on board the Soyuz-19 spacecraft was repaired. Following recommendation from the ground control center, the American astronauts also managed to rectify the faults.

The first international docking was carried out on schedule. The whole world could watch the first international crew on board Soyuz-19.

The Soyuz and Apollo crews displayed courage and worked in close cooperation and mutual understanding during the flight.

The second, so-called "test" docking was an impressive experiment. This time, the Soyuz docking module was configured in active mode. The test docking was carried out successfully, although oscillations of Apollo which were very close to maximum put the docking module to a hard test. The Soyuz module bore the strain well and proved the dependability and accuracy of the design.

The staffs of the flight control centers maintained efficient cooperation through 13 channels of constant, direct television, telephone and telegraph communications. Soviet and US tracking stations were used for communication sessions with the Soyuz and Apollo crews and for measuring the orbit parameters. The flight went off smoothly and, according to Alexei Yeliseev, the flight director for the Soviet Union, it was easier to manage than during the training sessions because there were virtually no deviations in the work of the onboard and ground systems.

The planned joint and unilateral scientific experiments, radio and television reports from orbit and motion-picture filming and photographing from aboard the spaceships were successfully carried out.

The first joint experimental flight of the Soviet Soyuz and the American Apollo spacecraft was completed successfully. In its course the correctness of technical solutions to ensure the compatibility of rendezvous and docking means for future manned spacecraft and stations, as well as the validity of the chosen principles of cooperation between Soviet and US ground services in flight control from two centers located on different continents were checked and confirmed. There were tested out the elements of a compatible system of rendezvous in orbit, the docking of spacecraft with the aid of new androgynous units developed in the USSR and the USA was successfully carried out, and the technique of mutual transfer from spaceship to spaceship with different atmospheres was checked. Thereby the possibility of rescue operations in space was tested in practice.

The astrophysical, biological and technological experiments carried out during the flight permitted obtaining new information about the space surrounding us, checking an original method of studying of the solar corona—an artificial solar eclipse—and amassing some experience in carrying out the technological processes of obtaining materials in space. Of course, the five joint and a number of autonomous experiments do not exhaust the potential offered by the cooperation of the two countries and the use of two spacecraft.

The successful realization of the Soyuz-Apollo program became possible as a result of the big work done by engineers and workers in the thorough optimization of all the systems and equipment of the spaceships on the ground and in flight conditions. Of great importance was the experimental flight of the Soyuz spacecraft piloted by cosmonauts A. Filipchenko and N. Rukavishnikov.

The pooling of efforts has enriched Soviet and American specialists with an experience of realizing the complex technical and organizational tasks involved in carrying out a joint flight. The specialists of the two countries made a synthesis of advanced engineering ideas and technical solutions. The most diversed forms were used.

From May 1972 to this day there took place over 20 joint meetings, 11 joint tests of all types, 6 joint trainings of crews and 6—of the personnel of the flight control centers. The sides released over 1,500 documents ranging in size from several dozen to several thousand pages. During this time we, with Dr. Lunney, had 50 telephone conversations, and exchanged many letters and telegrams.

A coherent, overall approach to solving organizational and technical tasks, the efficient planning of joint activity and strict control over the fulfilment of plans, a convenient system of documentation and high standards of handling it, a strict division of powers and responsibility at all levels of the organizational structure and in examining any questions—all this to no small extent determined the success.

The amassed experience of cooperation and the organizational forms found lay a good basis for the further development of business contacts between Soviet and American specialists in the explora-tion and use of outer space for peaceful purposes in the interests of the development of world science.

The historical Soyuz-Apollo flight became possible only in the conditions of political detente, the successful realization in practice of the Peace Program proclaimed by the 24th Congress of the CPSU. It marks a stage in the development of cosmonautics and opens up new possibilities for cooperation between nations.

47.

Rockefeller Panel Report on Illegal CIA Activities

In the wake of the Watergate scandal much information and rumor was forthcoming about abuses of authority by the various investigative agencies of the Executive Branch; The Central Intelligence Agency, the Federal Bureau of Investigation, the Internal Revenue Service, the Defense Intelligence Agency, and the State Department's Bureau of Intelligence. The number of allegations about CIA activities prompted President Ford to create a commission, headed by Vice President Nelson Rockefeller, to investigate the agency. The President's directive was issued on January 4, 1975, and the panel finished its work and reported its findings in June. This selection reprints the commission's legal analysis of CIA authority.

Source: *Report to the President by the Commission on CIA Activities Within the United States.* Washington, 1975. Chapter 6.

THE CIA, like every other agency of the federal government, possesses only that authority which the Constitution or duly enacted statutes confer on it. And, like every other agency, it is subject to any prohibitions or restraints which the Constitution and applicable statutes impose on it. Congress vested broad powers in the CIA. Its purpose was to create an effective centralized foreign intelligence agency with sufficient authority and flexibility to meet new conditions as they arose.

But the Agency's authority under the Act is not unlimited. All its functions must relate in some way to foreign intelligence. The Agency is further restricted by the Act's prohibition on law enforcement powers and internal security functions, as well as by other Constitutional and statutory provisions.

Determining the lawfulness of particular Agency conduct requires analysis of its authority as well as any applicable restrictions. The process does not always produce clear and precise answers. Difficult questions of statutory and Constitutional interpretation are involved. There are few, if any, authoritative judicial decisions. The legislative history and the experience under the Act are an uncertain guide.

In many instances, the only appropriate test is one of reasonableness. Different persons are likely to hold different opinions as to what the statutes and Constitution authorize or prohibit in particular circumstances.

Legal questions are only the beginning of a complete analysis of the issues. A distinction must be drawn between what the law authorizes or prohibits and what may be desirable or undesirable as a matter of public policy. Activities which the law authorizes may, nonetheless, be undesirable as a matter of policy. Conversely, policy may create a compelling need for activities which have not been authorized; to the extent that no Constitutional restrictions pose an absolute barrier, authority for such activities may be sought if it does not now exist.

In the Commission's recommendations, both law and policy are considered. This chapter, however, is intended to deal only with the applicable law.

A. The Extent of the CIA's Authority

1. The Authority of the CIA as to Foreign Intelligence. Although the National Security Act does not expressly limit the CIA's intelligence activities to foreign intelligence, it appears from the legislative history as a whole and the consistent practice under the statute that the Agency's responsibility is so limited.

In deciding what constitutes "foreign intelligence," the subject matter of the information and not the location of its source is the principal factor that determines whether it is within the purview of

the CIA. This conclusion is supported by that portion of the legislative history which indicates the CIA may collect foreign intelligence in this country by overt means.

"Foreign intelligence" is a term with no settled meaning. It is used but not defined in National Security Council Intelligence Directives. Its scope is unclear where information has both foreign and domestic aspects.

The legislative history indicates general congressional concern that the Agency should not direct activities against United States citizens or accumulate information on them. However, Congress did not expressly prohibit any activities by the CIA except the exercise of law enforcement and internal security functions.

We believe the congressional concern is properly accommodated by construing "foreign intelligence" as information concerning the capabilities, intentions, and activities of foreign nations, individuals or entities, wherever that information can be found. It does not include information on domestic activities of United States citizens unless there is reason to suspect they are engaged in espionage or similar illegal activities on behalf of foreign powers.

The authority of the CIA to collect foreign intelligence in this country by clandestine means is also unclear. The Act neither expressly authorizes such collection nor expressly prohibits it. The National Security Council has never formally assigned this responsibility to the CIA. The Commission concludes that the CIA's authority in this area needs clarification.

2. Support Activities. In order to carry on its authorized intelligence functions within and without the United States, the CIA must necessarily engage in a variety of support activities. Such activities include the operation of its headquarters, the recruitment and training of employees, the procurement of supplies, communication with overseas stations, and the like.

The Commission finds that the authority to conduct foreign intelligence operations includes the authority to conduct such otherwise lawful domestic activities as are reasonably necessary and appropriate by way of support. This includes the authority to use those unusual cover and support devices required by the clandestine nature of the CIA.

3. Protection of Sources and Methods. The National Security Act requires the Director of Central Intelligence to protect intelligence sources and methods from unauthorized disclosure. The Commission believes that this provision and the inherent authority of the Director authorize the Agency to take reasonable measures not otherwise prohibited to protect the facilities and personnel of the Agency from outside threats and to ensure good security practices by persons affiliated with the Agency.

What measures are reasonable in a particular case depends on all the facts and circumstances. No general rule can be laid down, but some relevant factors can be suggested. Among them are:

— The degree of danger to the security of the Agency;

— The sensitivity of the activities involved;

— The extent and nature of the Agency's intrusions on individual privacy; and,

— The alternative means of protection available.

Because of the uncertainty inherent in a test of reasonableness, the Commission in the chapters which follow has recommended both statutory changes and a number of restrictions on the means which the Agency may employ to protect its sources and methods.

On rare occasions, the Agency has asserted that the Director's authority permits him to investigate any unauthorized disclosure that jeopardizes intelligence sources and methods. This claim has been made in cases where there was no reason to believe the disclosure came from a person in any way related to the Agency. Although the statutory language and legislative history are not precise, the Commission finds that such an interpretation is unwarranted, especially in light of the applicable NSCID that makes the CIA responsible only for unauthorized disclosures from the Agency.

In our judgment:

(a) The investigative authority of the Director is limited to persons affiliated with the Agency—that is, employees (including former employees and applicants for employment), contractors and their employees, knowing sources of intelligence, agents and similar persons used by the Agency in operations, and others who require clearance by the CIA for access to classified information. Such investigations must be conducted in a lawful manner consistent with the requirements of the Constitution and applicable statutes.

(b) Investigation of breaches of security by employees of other government agencies is the responsibility of the heads of those agencies or of the FBI.

(c) The CIA has no authority to investigate newsmen.

The Commission proposes statutory changes as well as an Executive Order to clarify these matters.

4. Other Authority. The CIA derives some authority from federal statutes of general application. The Economy Act of 1932 authorizes government agencies to provide services and equipment to each other where that course would be in the best interest of the government. Public

Law 90-331 requires all federal agencies to assist the Secret Service in the performance of its protective duties. The authority granted in these acts is often exercised by the CIA, but our investigation has disclosed no improprieties arising from that exercise.

The CIA may from time to time be delegated some of the President's inherent authority under the Constitution in matters affecting foreign relations. The scope of the President's inherent authority and the power of the Congress to control the manner of its exercise are difficult Constitutional issues not raised by the facts found by the Commission in carrying out its assignment.

B. The Restrictions on CIA's Authority

1. The Prohibition on Law Enforcement Powers or Internal Security Functions. The statutory proviso that "the Agency shall have no police, subpena, law-enforcement powers, or internal security functions" was initially designed to prevent the CIA from becoming a national secret police force. It was also intended to protect the domestic jurisdiction of the FBI. The statute does not define the terms.

Many matters related to foreign intelligence or the security of the Agency also relate to law enforcement or internal security. For example, an unauthorized disclosure of classified information by an Agency employee may also violate the espionage acts or other criminal statutes. Additionally, the Agency in the ordinary course of its business has relationships of various types with law enforcement agencies. Some of these relationships may raise questions of compliance with the proviso.

The Commission finds that whether Agency activity is prohibited depends principally on the purpose for which it is conducted. If the principal purpose of the activity is the prosecution of crimes or protection against civil disorders or domestic insurrection, then the activity is prohibited. On the other hand, if the principal purpose relates to foreign intelligence or to protection of the security of the Agency, the activity is permissible, within limits, even though it might also be performed by a law enforcement agency.

For instance, the mere fact that the Agency has files on or containing the names of American citizens is not in itself a violation of the statutory prohibition on law enforcement or internal security functions. The test is always the purpose for which the files were accumulated and the use made of them thereafter.

The Commission does not construe the proviso to prohibit the CIA from evaluating and disseminating foreign intelligence which may be relevant and useful to law enforcement. Such a function is simply an exercise of the Agency's statutory responsibility "to correlate and evaluate intelligence relating to the national security." Nor do we believe that the CIA is barred from passing domestic information to interested agencies, including law enforcement agencies, where that information was incidentally acquired in the course of authorized foreign intelligence activities. Indeed, where the Agency has information directly relevant to an ongoing criminal investigation, as it did in connection with the Watergate investigation, the Agency is under a duty to bring its evidence to the attention of the appropriate authorities.

So long as the Agency does not actively participate in the activities of law enforcement agencies, we find that it is proper for it to furnish such agencies with the benefits of technical developments and expertise which may improve their effectiveness.

In the past, the Agency has conducted some technical training of members of state and local police forces through the Law Enforcement Assistance Administration. A 1973 statute prohibited this practice. The Agency has interpreted the statute to evidence congressional intent that it terminate furnishing such training directly to local law enforcement agencies as well. The Commission approves the Agency's decision to leave to the FBI such training of state and local police officers.

2. *Constitutional Prohibitions.* The Central Intelligence Agency, like all organs of government, is required to obey the Constitution. The protections of the Constitution extend generally to all persons within the borders of the United States, even aliens who have entered the country illegally.

a. *The First Amendment.* — The First Amendment to the Constitution protects among other things freedom of speech, of the press, and of political association from abridgement by the government. These freedoms are not absolute. The Amendment, as Mr. Justice Holmes noted, does not "protect a man in falsely shouting fire in a theatre and causing a panic." Nevertheless, government conduct which inhibits the exercise of these Constitutional rights raises a substantial Constitutional question.

The interception of private communications and the undue accumulation of information on political views or activities of American citizens could have some inhibiting effect. Because the Commission has found these activities were improper for other reasons, it is unnecessary to explore the First Amendment questions in detail.

b. *The Fourth Amendment.* — The Fourth Amendment prohibits unreasonable searches and seizures. In ordinary criminal cases, law enforcement officers must obtain a judicial warrant before searching a person's residence, hotel room, or office,

except in "exigent circumstances." When the Supreme Court held in 1967 that private conversations were protected by the Fourth Amendment, it made it clear that all wiretaps and other forms of surreptitious electronic surveillance were within the field of investigative activities that ordinarily require prior judicial approval.

It is unclear whether the President can act without such approval in some cases where the national security is involved. The Supreme Court recently held that a warrant is required in national security cases having "no significant connection with a foreign power, its agents or agencies." However, the Court expressly reserved decision on whether a significant foreign connection would justify a different result. Some lower courts have held that no warrant is required in such cases.

Neither the Fourth Amendment nor any other Constitutional or statutory provision prohibits physical surveillance — the observation of the public comings and goings of an individual — unless such surveillance reaches the point of harassment. The use of undercover agents or informers is also largely uncontrolled by legal standards.

c. *Waiver and Consent* — Constitutional rights may be waived in certain circumstances. The Supreme Court has held that a valid waiver must be knowing and voluntary, and the evidence of such a waiver must be clear and unequivocal. The government cannot make waiver of Constitutional rights a condition of public employment, unless the demand for such a waiver is reasonably related to a proper governmental objective and the waiver is the least restrictive means available to achieve that objective. Whether a particular waiver is valid depends on all the facts of the case.

3. *Statutory Prohibitions.* a. *The Omnibus Crime Control and Safe Streets Act.* — Title

III of the Omnibus Crime Control and Safe Streets Act prohibits the interception of private conversations through wiretaps or other forms of electronic eavesdropping unless one party to the conversation consents or a judicial warrant is obtained. The statute expressly does not affect whatever power the President has to order warrantless wiretaps or eavesdropping in national security cases. An Executive Order, dated June 30, 1965, permits warrantless wiretaps so long as the written approval of the President or the Attorney General is obtained.

The statute defines "interception" to mean "the acquisition of the contents of any wire or oral communication through the use of any electronic, mechanical, or other device." A number of judicial decisions have held that the Act does not prohibit the collection of long-distance telephone billing records. These records show the telephone number called, the date and time of the call, and, in some cases, the names of the parties. They do not indicate the content of the call.

A different question is posed by the acquisition of communications incidental to the testing of interception equipment to be used abroad. On the face of the statute, such activities appear to be prohibited.

b. *Statutes Protecting the United States Mails.*—Opening first-class mail to examine its contents without a lawfully issued warrant is illegal. The statutes set forth no exception for national security matters.

The examination of the exterior of first-class mail without opening it presents a different problem. Lower federal courts have held that these so-called "mail covers" are valid if they are conducted within the framework of the postal regulations and there is no unreasonable delay of the mail. The Supreme Court has not passed on this issue.

c. *Disclosure of Income Tax Information.*—Federal statutes, Executive Orders, and Internal Revenue Service regulations prohibit disclosure of information from federal income tax returns except under carefully defined procedures. There is no exception to these requirements for the CIA. Indeed, CIA inspection of tax returns was one form of improper activity specifically mentioned in the 1947 Act's legislative history.

d. *Other Statutes.*—The Commission has not attempted to identify or analyze all statutes which might conceivably apply to activities by the CIA or on its behalf. Whether in any particular case a criminal or other prohibitory statute restricts the authority of the CIA within the United States is a question of interpretation of that statute in light of the National Security Act. The statute may contain an express or implied exception for activities required in the interest of national security; on the other hand, it may be an unqualified prohibition on certain conduct. Only an analysis of the language, any relevant legislative history, and the underlying policies can answer the question in a particular case.

Conclusions

The evidence within the scope of this inquiry does not indicate that fundamental rewriting of the National Security Act is either necessary or appropriate.

The evidence does demonstrate the need for some statutory and administrative clarification of the role and function of the Agency.

Ambiguities have been partially responsible for some, though not all, of the Agency's deviations within the United States from its assigned mission. In some cases, reasonable persons will differ as to the lawfulness of the activity; in others, the absence of clear guidelines as to its authority deprived the Agency of a means of resisting pressures to engage in activities which now appear to us improper.

Greater public awareness of the limits of the CIA's domestic authority would do much to reassure the American people.

The requisite clarification can best be accomplished (a) through a specific amendment clarifying the National Security Act provision which delineates the permissible scope of CIA activities, as set forth in Recommendation 1, and (b) through issuance of an Executive Order further limiting domestic activities of the CIA, as set forth in Recommendation 2.

Recommendation (1). Section 403 of the National Security Act of 1947 should be amended in the form set forth in Appendix VI to this Report. These amendments, in summary, would:

a. Make explicit that the CIA's activities must be related to *foreign* intelligence.

b. Clarify the responsibility of the CIA to protect intelligence sources and methods from unauthorized disclosure. (The Agency would be responsible for protecting against unauthorized disclosures within the CIA, and it would be responsible for providing guidance and technical assistance to other agency and department heads in protecting against unauthorized disclosures within their own agencies and departments.)

c. Confirm publicly the CIA's existing authority to collect foreign intelligence from willing sources within the United States, and, except as specified by the President in a published Executive Order, prohibit the CIA from collection efforts within the United States directed at securing foreign intelligence from unknowing American citizens.

Recommendation (2). The President should by Executive Order prohibit the CIA from the collection of information about the domestic activities of U.S. citizens (whether by overt or covert means), the evaluation, correlation, and dissemination of analyses or reports about such activities, and the storage of such information, with exceptions for the following categories of persons or activities:

a. Persons presently or formerly affiliated, or being considered for affiliation, with the CIA, directly or indirectly, or others who require clearance by the CIA to receive classified information;

b. Persons or activities that pose a clear threat to CIA facilities or personnel, provided that proper coordination with the FBI is accomplished;

c. Persons suspected of espionage or other illegal activities relating to foreign intelligence, provided that proper coordination with the FBI is accomplished.

d. Information which is received incidental to appropriate CIA activities may be transmitted to an agency with appropriate jurisdiction, including law enforcement agencies.

Collection of information from normal library sources such as newspapers, books, magazines, and other such documents is not to be affected by this order.

Information currently being maintained which is inconsistent with the order should be destroyed at the conclusion of the current congressional investigations, or as soon thereafter as permitted by law. The CIA should periodically screen its files and eliminate all material inconsistent with the order.

The order should be issued after consultation with the National Security Council, the Attorney General, and the Director of Central Intelligence. Any modification of the order would be permitted only through published amendments.

48.

CIA Assassination Plots

Along with allegations of illegal domestic spying, the Central Intelligence Agency was also said to have been involved in attempts to assassinate a number of foreign leaders whose policies were disliked by various Washington administrations from Eisenhower to Nixon. These and other allegations were investigated by the Senate Select Committee on Intelligence, with Senator Frank Church of Idaho as chairman. The report of the committee, published on November 20, 1975, was released over the strong objections of the Ford Administration. Portions of the introduction and summary of the report are reprinted here.

Source: *Alleged Assassination Plots Involving Foreign Leaders.* An Interim Report of the Select Committee to Study Government Operations with respect to Intelligence Activities. Washington, 1975.

THIS INTERIM REPORT covers allegations of United States involvement in assassination plots against foreign political leaders. The report also examines certain other instances in which foreign political leaders in fact were killed and the United States was in some manner involved in activity leading up to the killing, but in which it would be incorrect to say that the purpose of United States involvement had been to encourage assassination.

The evidence establishes that the United States was implicated in several assassination plots. The Committee believes that, short of war, assassination is incompatible with American principles, international order, and morality. It should be rejected as a tool of foreign policy.

Our inquiry also reveals serious problems with respect to United States involvement in coups directed against foreign governments. Some of these problems are addressed here on the basis of our investigation to date; others we raise as questions to be answered after our

investigation into covert action has been completed.

We stress the interim nature of this report. In the course of the Committee's continuing work, other alleged assassination plots may surface, and new evidence concerning the cases covered herein may come to light. However, it is the Committee's view that these cases have been developed in sufficient detail to clarify the issues which are at the heart of the Committee's mandate to recommend legislative and other reforms.

Thorough treatment of the assassination question has lengthened the Committee's schedule, but has greatly increased the Committee's awareness of the hard issues it must face in the months ahead. These issues include problems of domestic and foreign intelligence collection, counterintelligence, foreign covert operations, mechanisms of command and control, and assessment of the effectiveness of the total United States intelligence effort. The Committee intends, nevertheless, to complete, by February 1976, its main job of undertaking the first comprehensive review of the intelligence community. . . .

SUMMARY OF FINDINGS AND CONCLUSIONS

1. The Questions Presented. The Committee sought to answer four broad questions:

Assassination plots.—Did United States officials instigate, attempt, aid and abet, or acquiesce in plots to assassinate foreign leaders?

Involvement in other killings.—Did United States officials assist foreign dissidents in a way which significantly contributed to the killing of foreign leaders?

Authorization.—Where there was involvement by United States officials in assassination plots or other killings, were such activities authorized and if so, at what levels of our Government?

Communication and control.—Even if not authorized in fact, were the assassination activities perceived by those involved to be within the scope of their lawful authority? If they were so perceived, was there inadequate control exercised by higher authorities over the agencies to prevent such misinterpretation?

2. Summary of Findings and Conclusions on the Plots. The Committee investigated alleged United States involvement in assassination plots in five foreign countries:

Country	Individual involved
Cuba	Fidel Castro.
Congo (Zaire)	Patrice Lumumba.
Dominican Republic	Rafael Trujillo.
Chile	General Rene Schneider.
South Vietnam	Ngo Dinh Diem.

The evidence concerning each alleged assassination can be summarized as follows:

Patrice Lumumba (Congo/Zaire).—In the Fall of 1960, two CIA officials were asked by superiors to assassinate Lumumba. Poisons were sent to the Congo and some exploratory steps were taken toward gaining access to Lumumba. Subsequently, in early 1961, Lumumba was killed by Congolese rivals. It does not appear from the evidence that the United States was in any way involved in the killing.

Fidel Castro (Cuba).—United States Government personnel plotted to kill Castro from 1960 to 1965. American underworld figures and Cubans hostile to Castro were used in these plots, and were provided encouragement and material support by the United States.

Rafael Trujillo (Dominican Republic).—Trujillo was shot by Dominican dissidents on May 31, 1961. From early in 1960 and continuing to the time of the assassination, the United States Government generally supported these dissidents. Some Government personnel were aware that the dissidents intended to kill Trujillo. Three pistols and three carbines were furnished by American officials, although a request for machine guns was later refused. There is conflicting evidence concerning whether the weapons were knowingly supplied for use in the assassination and whether any of them were present at the scene.

Ngo Dinh Diem (South Vietnam).—Diem and his brother, Nhu, were killed on November 2, 1963, in the course of a South Vietnamese Generals' coup. Although the United States Government supported the coup, there is no evidence that American officials favored the assassination. Indeed, it appears that the assassination of Diem was not part of the Generals' pre-coup planning but was instead a spontaneous act which occurred during the coup and was carried out without United States involvement or support.

General Rene Schneider (Chile).—On October 25, 1970, General Schneider died of gunshot wounds inflicted three days earlier while resisting a kidnap attempt. Schneider, as Commander-in-Chief of the Army and a constitutionalist opposed to military coups, was considered an obstacle in efforts to prevent Salvador Allende from assuming the office of President of Chile. The United States Government supported, and sought to instigate a military coup to block Allende. U.S. officials supplied financial aid, machine guns and other equipment to various military figures who opposed Allende. Although the CIA continued to support coup plotters up to Schneider's shooting, the record indicates that the CIA had withdrawn active support of the group which carried out the actual kidnap attempt on October 22, which resulted in Schneider's death. Further, it does not appear that any of the equipment supplied by the CIA to coup plotters in Chile was used in the kidnapping. There is no evidence of a plan to kill Schneider or that United States officials specifically anticipated that Schneider would be shot during the abduction.

Assassination capability (Executive action). — In addition to these five cases, the Committee has received evidence that ranking Government officials discussed, and may have authorized, the establishment within the CIA of a generalized assassination capability. During these discussions, the concept of assassination was not affirmatively disavowed.

Similarities and differences among the plots. — The assassination plots all involved Third World countries, most of which were relatively small and none of which possessed great political or military strength. Apart from that similarity, there were significant differences among the plots:

(1) Whether United States officials initiated the plot, or were responding to requests of local dissidents for aid.

(2) Whether the plot was specifically intended to kill a foreign leader, or whether the leader's death was a reasonably foreseeable consequence of an attempt to overthrow the government.

The Castro and Lumumba cases are examples of plots conceived by United States officials to kill foreign leaders.

In the Trujillo case, although the United States Government certainly opposed his regime, it did not initiate the plot. Rather, United States officials responded to requests for aid from local dissidents whose aim clearly was to assassinate Trujillo. By aiding them, this country was implicated in the assassination, regardless of whether the weapons actually supplied were meant to kill Trujillo or were only intended as symbols of support for the dissidents.

The Schneider case differs from the Castro and Trujillo cases. The United States Government, with full knowledge that Chilean dissidents considered General Schneider an obstacle to their plans, sought a coup and provided support to the dissidents. However, even though the support included weapons, it appears that the intention of both the dissidents and the United States officials was to abduct General Schneider, not to kill him. Similarly, in the Diem case, some United States officials wanted Diem removed and supported a coup to accomplish his removal, but there is no evidence that any of those officials sought the death of Diem himself.

3. Summary of Findings and Conclusions on the Issues of Authority and Control. To put the inquiry into assassination allegations in context, two points must be made clear. First, there is no doubt that the United States Government opposed the various leaders in question. Officials at the highest levels objected to the Castro and Trujillo regimes, believed the accession of Allende to power in Chile would be harmful to American interests, and thought of Lumumba as a dangerous force in the heart of Africa. Second, the evidence on assassinations has to be viewed in the context of other, more massive activities against the regimes in question. For example, the plots against Fidel Castro personally cannot be understood without considering the fully authorized, comprehensive assaults upon his regime, such as the Bay of Pigs invasion in 1961 and Operation Mongoose in 1962.

Once methods of coercion and violence are chosen, the probability of loss of life is always present. There is, however, a significant difference between a cold-blooded, targeted, intentional killing of an individual foreign leader and other forms of intervening in the affairs of foreign nations. Therefore, the Committee has endeavored to explore as fully as possible the questions of how and why the plots happened, whether they were authorized, and if so, at what level.

The picture that emerges from the evidence is not a clear one. This may be due to the system of deniability and the consequent state of the evidence which, even after our long investigation, remains conflicting and inconclusive. Or it may be that there were in fact serious shortcomings in the system of authorization so that an activity such as assassination could have been undertaken by an agency of the United States Government without express authority.

The Committee finds that the system of executive command and control was so ambiguous that it is difficult to be certain at what levels assassination activity was known and authorized. This situation creates the disturbing prospect that Government officials might have undertaken the assassination plots without it having been uncontrovertibly clear that there was ex-plicit authorization from the Presidents. It is also possible that there might have been a successful "plausible denial" in which Presidential authorization was issued but is now obscured. Whether or not the respective Presidents knew of or authorized the plots, as chief executive officer of the United States, each must bear the ultimate responsibility for the activities of his subordinates.

The Committee makes four other major findings. The first relates to the Committee's inability to make a finding that the assassination plots were authorized by the Presidents or other persons above the governmental agency or agencies involved. The second explains why certain officials may have perceived that, according to their judgment and experience, assassination was an acceptable course of action. The third criticizes agency officials for failing on several occasions to disclose their plans and activities to superior authorities, or for failing to do so with sufficient detail and clarity. The fourth criticizes Administration officials for not ruling out assassination, particularly after certain Administration officials had become aware of prior assassination plans and the establishment of a general assassination capability.

There is admittedly a tension among the findings. This tension reflects a basic conflict in the evidence. While there are some conflicts over facts, it may be more important that there appeared to have been two differing perceptions of the same facts. This distinction may be the result of the differing backgrounds of those persons experienced in covert operations as distinguished from those who were not. Words of urgency which may have meant killing to the former, may have meant nothing of the sort to the latter.

While we are critical of certain individual actions, the Committee is also mindful of the inherent problems in a system which relies on secrecy, compartmentation, circumlocution, and the avoidance of clear responsibility. This system creates the risk of confusion and rashness in the very areas where clarity and sober judgment are most necessary. Hence, before reviewing the evidence relating to the cases, we briefly deal with the general subject of covert action.

49.

New York City's Fiscal Crisis

In 1975 New York City was on the verge of defaulting on its debt obligations and sinking into bankruptcy. It was a crisis that had been building for more than ten years because, while city expenses had increased by about 12% yearly, tax revenues only went up 4 or 5% a year. The resort to short-term borrowing to make ends meet was finally catching up with the city administration. By 1975 the total city debt had reached $12.3 billion, an increase of more than $7 billion since 1965. With an impending default of $792 million in June, the state created a Municipal Assistance Corporation to oversee long-term borrowing and to raise money through bond sales. The failure of this effort led Mayor Abraham Beame to order drastic cuts in city expenses. Appeals for federal aid met at first with little favorable response. President Ford, in an address to the National Press Club, spurned any federal support for the city. He later changed his mind, and legislation for short-term aid and the means to tide the city over cash shortages for three years quickly passed Congress. This selection reprints Mayor Beame's call for fiscal restraint on July 31, 1975, and Ford's October 29 speech.

Sources: 1. *New York Times*, August 1, 1975.
2. *Weekly Compilation of Presidential Documents*, November 3, 1975.

Abraham Beame: The Need for Financial Restraint

We are struggling to overcome a crisis of confidence in our fiscal integrity. Its roots trace back more than a decade. The role of our cities has changed dramatically in response to national trends, heightened aspirations and shifting policy.

We've seen the demand for city services soar, outstripping our ability to pay for them with local dollars. The very national and state programs which help defray some of the costs of providing these services also add to their cost because they require matching local contributions.

For example, welfare and medical assistance this year will cost New York City taxpayers approximately $1-billion, a legal obligation no other municipality in the nation remotely shares.

During the past decade the number of New York City employes in social services, health, education and related programs, many mandated by Federal and state requirements, increased by more than one-third.

In contrast, municipal workers assigned to such local services as police, fire, sanitation and water supply, remained fairly constant.

To make up the difference between its modestly growing revenues and rapidly escalating demands, the city during this current period of need had resorted increasingly to borrowing for the cash required to stretch the budget.

This kind of financing is questionable at best, even when the economy is strong. But the economy didn't remain solid. The city in effect gambled against a future which didn't come. Instead of economic expansion, we have deep recession; instead of stability, we have runaway inflation; instead of an enlightened political will to share national obligations more equitably, we've been told to go it alone.

That is why we must act today and act decisively. We have exhausted the possibilities for negotiation and discussion. Now our options in time are running out.

There must be financial restraint and service cutbacks.

There must be fiscal reform and management resolve. Our program of austerity must be accelerated. There must be immediate steps to restore our credit. These steps are necessary, painful and not easily taken.

But there is no choice. We must restore the city's fiscal integrity. We must demonstrate that despite unrelenting economic pressures and punitive isolation the city can and will meet its greatest challenge. I know this will impose an added burden upon us. I know it means great sacrifices. But I also know that we have the inherent strength and unflagging determination to do what must be done.

The city will hold the line on expenditures. We will concentrate our limited resources on the best possible delivery of essential services. We will also hold that line because I am determined not to make any unnecessary inroads into the already strained tax base of our city. Therefore I am implementing a program for recovery.

I am taking the following actions, and before I detail my plan I am happy to announce, as some of you may know, that I have recently heard from Deputy Mayor James Cavanagh at the Americana Hotel that the majority of the municipal unions have agreed to a voluntary wage freeze. And I am extremely pleased at this turn of events.

I'd like to express my personal thanks to the union leaders involved for their responsible, courageous and tough-minded action. The police, fire and education unions are not party to this agreement.

With this latest development in mind, let me return to my plan.

First, there will be a wage freeze, if not voluntary, then imposed. I'm submitting to the City Council legislation and a message of necessity to provide me with the emergency powers to declare a freeze on all wages subject to collective bargaining at the level paid on June 30, 1975.

I am requesting the Governor to be prepared to back up this action with state legislation, if necessary, to insure that the freeze remains in effect with the full force of law behind it. I am also freezing wages of all management and executive personnel to levels fixed on July 1, 1973, the last effective date of increases for such personnel.

The wages of other city personnel not falling within these categories are also frozen. There can be no wage increases now. These are hard, unyielding and unvarnished facts of the present economic reality.

David Burnett—Contact

Mayor Abraham Beame of New York City.

Demands cannot be met by funds that don't exist.

Second, in all future collective bargaining, we will concentrate on what comes out of the contract as well as what goes in it.

We can no longer tolerate contractual giveaways or frills. These, too, must be brought into line with reality.

Excesses should be eliminated from future contracts.

The obligation to work a full day is not seasonal. There should be no summer hours for any workers. No one needs two days to recover from the simple and decent act of donating blood. Overtime must be ordered only when needed to serve the public interest, not inflate individual pensions.

Third, acting on information gathered by the Office of Management and Budget, I am eliminating agencies or activities which can be consolidated, combined or absorbed by other agencies within or outside of city government.

I am also eliminating those functions which can no longer be justified under the present economic climate. Our priorities, of course, will be to preserve those programs which are essential to the city's health, safety and economic future.

Based on initial analysis I am issuing an executive order and submitting legislation to the City Council taking the following action:

The Department of Commerce is eliminated and its functions absorbed by the Office of Economic Development.

The Emergency Control Board Office of Civil Defense is eliminated and replaced by a designated mayoral liaison officer.

The Departments of Relocation and Development are consolidated to eliminate duplication and redundancy.

The Mayor's Office of Staten Island Planning and Development is eliminated, and its function shifted to the City Planning Department.

Now, in addition, studies are under way now to facilitate such further actions as: combining the Department of Ports and Terminals with the Department of Marine and Aviation; eliminating the Office of Veterans' Action and replacing it with a mayoral aide who will work with Federal and state offices of veterans affairs; reorganizing youth services programs which are currently spread through various units; combining the Board of Water Supply and the Department of Water Resources, which will require state legislation; merging the Mayor's Offices of Midtown and Lower Manhattan Planning and Development into a single business district office.

We will continue this approach. It will mean staff cuts and reductions in personal service costs. Initial savings will be relatively modest, but they will increase as we streamline government operations and make them more efficient.

Fourth, I am taking immediate steps to reduce and reform the capital budget. I am ordering the transfer of $30-million in operating personnel items from the capital to the expense budget. This, added to the $25-million reduction in the '75-'76 budget for this purpose, represents a $55-million first-phase cleaning out of non-capital costs from the capital budget.

Changes in the state equalization rate compel us and economic necessity dictates that we reduce the capital budget by $375-million.

This will mean rescindment of all but the highest priority, the most advanced projects. Our action will reduce the need to sell bonds, decrease our projected debt service and maintain our capital reserve.

Fifth, I have consulted with the chairman of the Metropolitan Transportation Authority and he is prepared to recommend to his board that subway and bus fares be increased by 15 cents on Sept. 1, 1975. To alleviate the impact of this increase on those who normally pay a double fare, I have also recommended a 25-cent transfer from bus to bus and bus to subway. The double fare would be 75 cents, not $1.

I also propose that the double fare currently paid by riders of the Rockaway line be eliminated. Even so steep a rise cannot eliminate a growing transit deficit.

Escalating operating costs and ridership losses associated with growing unemployment underscore the plain fact that mass transit cannot and should not depend solely on funds generated by the fare box.

I'll be meeting with Governor Carey to prepare a more realistic formula for state and national mass transit funding.

I've also called the M.T.A. to cut its costs as the city has to achieve the economies required of all in this time of crisis. Unnecessary overtime must be sharply curtailed. Similarly, everyone who uses mass transit facilities should pay a fare.

Now all uniformed personnel and transit authority employes are granted privileged status. No one is entitled to a free ride for personal transportation under today's conditions.

Sixth, I am instituting a $32-million cut in City University funds. The Board of Higher Education has voted to maintain free tuition, yet we must achieve drastic economies.

Seventh, I'm instituting a series of management and accounting reforms. I'm determined to make our government operate most efficiently and within its means. I'm directing agency heads to submit to me no later than 30 days from today plans to increase agency efficiency and productivity.

I'm establishing a Mayor's management council. I will ask top corporations to assign executive talent to work for the city for six months while paid by their respective firms to help review and implement these and other management and productivity reforms and to advise me on other fruitful areas for management study and action.

I hope to have as a chairman of this council one of the most outstanding people in our city in the business world.

I am also issuing executive orders holding managers strictly accountable for enforcement of work rules. Workers under their jurisdiction must come to work on time, put in a full day's work and leave only at the end of their working day.

A recording system is being developed to monitor excessive lateness and absences so that effective and appropriate disciplinary action can be taken expeditiously. And as part of our commitment to fiscal reform, we're changing our accounting system to conform to the State Controller's manual of accounts, which the Controller and I have discussed before.

Eighth, and final, I'm calling on the state to assume financial responsibility for state functions. In fairness, the state should absorb the cost of the courts, corrections and probation systems in New York City as it does for other local jurisdictions.

It goes beyond simple equity. The economies I have made in this city budget, the current '75-'76 budget, will save the state approximately $125-million. These savings could be used by the state to pay for these state services they should assume. And legislation is pending to achieve this transfer.

This program for economy follows hard upon the steps I have already taken. I have already instituted heavy cutbacks, a rigorous job freeze and massive layoffs. These actions and the program I present today will result in a near-zero growth budget as compared with the past fiscal years.

By comparison, consider the experience of other cities, like Pittsburgh and New Orleans, which show a 3 or 4 per cent increase; Detroit and Chicago, with a 4 to 5 per cent increase; San Francisco with a 7 per cent increase, and Boston with a 13 per cent increase. The New York State budget is up more than 9 per cent, and the Federal budget more than 11 per cent.

My program for recovery is addressed to the people of the city who must bear the further burden it imposes. There's nothing I've done in public life that has been more bitter than recommending these slashing economies that affect each and every one of us. I recognize the problem and difficulties a wage freeze brings to the families of our workers.

Yet it must be done and I will take all the required steps in the light of con-

flicting legal views to carry it out.

I have fought for a reasonable mass transit fare in the halls of Congress and in the White House and in Albany. I counted holding down the fare as an important achievement in my administration. I know the hardship a fare rise can cause.

I'm a product of the City University system, and not only received my training but a deep and abiding appreciation of the value of free education at City College. And I must demand slashing economies from the university which gave me and so many others the opportunity for a full and more rewarding life.

My program for recovery may not make good politics, but there can be no politics as usual when the survival of the city as we know it is at stake.

My fellow New Yorkers, we're a diverse people who speak many languages and respect different traditions. But we're capable of pulling together.

In times of crisis, this city has shown its great strength and great heart. The demands upon us are real. We must respond with boldness, understanding and determination. I know we will not be found wanting.

I believe that my program for recovery can succeed with your cooperation. The combination of fiscal probity and sound management I propose will place this city in a far better shape than it has been in decades.

To those who have demanded sharp evidence of reform I say we've cut to the bone, but we cannot and will not cut into the bone. We will sacrifice and change our life style, but we will not cripple or hobble our great city.

Now to the financial community, to the state and to the Federal Government I say, your readiness to invest now in the future of the city will determine how well and how fast New York recovers its momentum.

The commitment is ours, the decision now is yours.

President Ford: No Federal Bail-out of New York City

Mr. President, fellow members of the Press Club, ladies and gentlemen, guests:

I am deeply grateful for the opportunity to join you today and talk to you about a matter of very deep concern to all Americans. New York City, where one out of every 25 Americans lives, through whose "Golden Door" untold millions have entered this land of liberty, faces a financial showdown.

The time has come for straight talk — to these eight million Americans and to the other 206 million Americans to whom I owe the duty of stating my convictions and my conclusions, and to you, whose job it is to carry them throughout the world as well as the United States.

The time has come to sort facts and figures from fiction and fear-mongering in this terribly complex situation. The time has come to say what solutions will work and which should be cast aside.

And the time has come for all Americans to consider how the problems of New York and the hard decisions they demand foreshadow and focus upon potential problems for all governments — Federal, State, and local — problems which demand equally hard decisions for them.

One week ago, New York City tottered on the brink of financial default which was deferred only at the eleventh hour. The next day, Mayor Beame testified here in Washington that the financial resources of the city and the State of New York were exhausted. Governor Carey agreed.

They said it is now up to Washington, and unless the Federal Government intervenes, New York City within a short time will no longer be able to pay its bills.

The message was clear: Responsibility for New York City's financial problems is being left on the front doorstep of the Federal Government — unwanted and abandoned by its real parents.

Many explanations have been offered about what led New York City deeper and deeper into this quagmire. Some contend it was long-range economic factors such as the flight to the suburbs of the city's more affluent citizens, the migration to the city of poorer people, and the departure of industry.

Others argued that the big metropolitan city has become obsolescent, that decay and pollution have brought a deterioration in the quality of urban life and New York's downfall could not be prevented.

Let's face one simple fact: Most other cities in America have faced these very same challenges, and they are still financially healthy today. They have not been luckier than New York; they simply have been better managed. There is an old saying: "The harder you try, the luckier you get." And I kind of like that definition of luck.

During the last decade, the officials of New York City have allowed its budget to triple. No city can expect to remain solvent if it allows its expenses to increase by an average of 12 percent every year, while its tax revenues are increasing by only 4 to 5 percent per year.

As Al Smith, a great Governor of New York who came from the sidewalks of New York City, used to say: "Let's look at the record."

The record shows that New York City's wages and salaries are the highest in the United States. A sanitation worker with 3 years experience now receives a base salary of nearly $15,000 a year. Fringe benefits and retirement costs average more than 50 percent of base pay. There are 4-week paid vacations and unlimited sick leave after only one year on the job.

The record shows that in most cities, municipal employees have to pay 50 percent or more of the cost of their pensions. New York City is the only major city in the country that picks up the entire burden.

The record shows that when New York's municipal employees retire, they often retire much earlier than in most cities and at pensions considerably higher than sound retirement plans permit.

The record shows New York City has 18 municipal hospitals; yet, on an average day, 25 percent of the hospital beds are empty. Meanwhile, the city spends millions more to pay the hospital expenses of those who use private hospitals.

The record shows New York City operates one of the largest universities in the world, free of tuition for any high school graduate, rich or poor, who wants to attend.

As for New York's much-discussed welfare burden, the record shows more than one current welfare recipient in ten may be legally ineligible for welfare assistance.

Certainly, I do not blame all the good people of New York City for their generous instincts or for their present plight. I do blame those who have misled the people of New York about the inevitable consequences of what they were doing over the last 10 years.

The consequences have been a steady stream of unbalanced budgets, massive growth in the city's debt, extraordinary increases in public employee contracts, and total disregard of independent experts who warned again and again that the city was courting disaster.

There can be no doubt where the real responsibility lies. And when New York City now asks the rest of the country to guarantee its bills, it can be no surprise that many other Americans ask why.

Why, they ask, should they support advantages in New York that they have not been able to afford for their own communities?

Why, they ask, should all the working people of this country be forced to rescue those who bankrolled New York City's policies for so long—the large investors and big banks?

In my judgment, no one has yet given these questions a satisfactory answer. Instead, Americans are being told that unless the rest of the country bails out New York City, there will be catastrophe for the United States and perhaps for the world.

Is this scare story true? Of course, there are risks that default could cause temporary fluctuations in the financial markets. But these markets have already made a substantial adjustment in anticipation of a possible default by New York City.

Claims are made that because of New York City's troubles, other municipalities will have grave difficulty selling their bonds. I know that this troubles many thoughtful citizens.

But the New York City record of bad financial management is unique among municipalities throughout the United States. Other communities have a solid reputation for living within their means. In recent days and weeks, other local governments have gone to investors with clean records of fiscal responsibility and have had no difficulty raising funds.

The greater risk is that any attempt to provide a Federal blank check for the leaders of New York City would ensure that no long-run solution to the city's problems will ever occur.

I can understand the concern of many citizens in New York and elsewhere. I understand because I am also concerned. What I cannot understand—and what nobody should condone—is the blatant attempt in some quarters to frighten the American people and their representatives in Congress into panicky support of patently bad policy.

The people of this country will not be stampeded; they will not panic when a few desperate New York City officials and bankers try to scare New York's mortgage payments out of them.

We have heard enough scare talk. What we need now is a calm, rational decision as to what is the right solution—the solution that is best for the people of New York and best for all Americans.

To be effective, the right solution must meet three basic tests:

—It must maintain essential public services for the people of New York City. It must protect the innocent victims of this tragedy. There must be policemen on the beat, firemen in the station, nurses in the emergency wards.

—Second, the solution must assure that New York City can and will achieve and maintain a balanced budget in the years ahead.

—And third, the right solution must guarantee that neither New York City nor any other American city ever becomes a ward of the Federal Government.

Let me digress a minute to remind you that under our constitutional system, both the cities and the Federal Government were the creatures of the States. The States delegated certain of their sovereign powers—the power to tax, police powers, and the like—to local units of self-government. And they can take these powers back if they are abused.

The States also relinquished certain sovereign powers to the Federal Government—some altogether and some to be shared. In return, the Federal Government has certain obligations to the States.

I see a serious threat to the legal relationships among our Federal, State, and local governments in any Congressional action which could lead to disruption of this traditional balance. Our largest city is no different in this respect than our smallest town. If Mayor Beame doesn't want Governor Carey to run his city, does he want the President of the United States to be acting mayor of New York City?

What is the solution to New York's dilemma? There are at least eight different proposals under consideration by the Congress, intended to prevent default. They are all variations of one basic theme: that the Federal Government should or would guarantee the availability of funds to New York City.

I can tell you, and tell you now, that I am prepared to veto any bill that has as its purpose a Federal bail-out of New York City to prevent a default.

I am fundamentally opposed to this so-called solution, and I will tell you why. Basically, it is a mirage. By giving a Federal guarantee, we would be reducing rather than increasing the prospect that the city's budget will ever be balanced. New York City's officials have proved in the past that they will not face up to the city's massive network of pressure groups as long as any other alternative is available. If they can scare the whole country into providing that alternative now, why shouldn't they be confident they can scare us again into providing it 3 years from now? In short, it encourages the continuation of "politics as usual" in New York, which is precisely not the way to solve the problem.

Such a step would be a terrible precedent for the rest of the Nation. It would promise immediate rewards and eventual rescue to every other city that follows the tragic example of our largest city. What restraint would be left on the spending of other local and State governments once it becomes clear that there is a Federal rescue squad that will always arrive in the nick of time?

Finally, we must all recognize who the primary beneficiaries of a Federal guarantee program would be. The beneficiaries would not be those who live and work in New York City because the really essential public services must and will continue.

The primary beneficiaries would be the New York officials who would [thus] escape responsibility for their past follies and be further excused from making the hard decisions required now to restore the city's fiscal integrity.

The secondary beneficiaries would be the large investors and financial institutions who purchased these securities anticipating a high rate of tax-free return.

Does this mean there is no solution? Not at all. There is a fair and sensible way to resolve this issue, and this is the way to do it.

If the city is unable to act to provide a means of meeting its obligations, a new law is required to assure an orderly and fair means of handling the situation.

As you know, the Constitution empowers the Congress to enact uniform bankruptcy laws. Therefore, I will submit to the Congress special legislation providing the Federal courts with sufficient authority to preside over an orderly reorganization of New York City's financial affairs—should that become necessary.

How would this work? The city, with State approval, would file a petition with the Federal District Court in New York under a proposed new chapter XVI of the Bankruptcy Act. The petition would state that New York City is unable to pay its debts as they mature and would be accompanied by a proposed way to work out an adjustment of its debts with its creditors.

The Federal court would then be authorized to accept jurisdiction of the case. There would be an automatic stay of suits by creditors so that the essential functions of the city would not be disrupted.

This would enable an orderly plan to be developed so that the city could work out arrangements with its creditors. While New York City works out a compromise with its creditors, the essential governmental functions of the city would continue. In the event of default, the Federal Government will work with the court to assure that police and fire and other essential services for the protection of life and property in New York are maintained.

The proposed legislation will include a provision that as a condition of New York City petitioning the court, the city must not only file a good faith plan for payment to its creditors but must also present a program for placing the fiscal affairs of the city on a sound basis.

In order to meet the short-term needs of New York City, the court would be empowered to authorize debt certificates covering new loans to the city, which would be paid out of future revenues ahead of other creditors.

Thus, the legislation I am proposing will do three essential things:

— First, it will prevent, in the event of default, all New York City funds from being tied up in lawsuits.

— Second, it will provide the conditions for an orderly plan to be developed for payments to New York City's creditors over a long term.

—Third, it will provide a way for new borrowing to be secured by pledging future revenues.

I don't want anybody misled. This proposed legislation will not, by itself, put the affairs of New York City in order. Some hard measures must be taken by the officials of New York City and New York State. They must either increase revenues or cut expenditures or devise some combination that will bring them to a sound financial position.

Careful examination has convinced me that those measures are neither beyond the realm of possibility nor beyond the demands of reason. If they are taken, New York City will, with the assistance of the legislation I am proposing, be able to restore itself as a fully solvent operation.

To summarize, the approach I am recommending is this: If New York fails to act in its own behalf, orderly proceedings would then be supervised by a Federal court.

The ones who would be most affected by this course of action would be those who are now fighting tooth and nail to protect their authority and to protect their investments—New York City's officials and the city's creditors. The creditors will not be wiped out; how much they will be hurt will depend upon the future conduct of the city's leaders.

For the people of New York, this plan will mean that essential services will continue. There may be some temporary inconveniences, but that will be true of any solution that is adopted.

For the financial community, the default may bring some temporary difficulties, but the repercussions should not be large or longstanding.

Finally, for the people of the United States, this means that they will not be asked to assume a burden that is not of their own making and should not become their responsibility. This is a fair and sensible way to proceed.

There is a profound lesson for all Americans in the financial experience of our biggest and our richest city. Though we are the richest Nation, the richest Nation in the world, there is a practical limit to our public bounty, just as there is to New York City's.

Other cities, other States, as well as the Federal Government are not immune to the insidious disease from which New York City is suffering. This sickness is brought on by years and years of higher spending, higher deficits, more inflation, and more borrowing to pay for higher spending, higher deficits, and so on, and so on, and so on. It is a progressive disease, and there is no painless cure.

Those who have been treating New York's financial sickness have been prescribing larger and larger doses of the same political stimulant that has proved so popular and so successful in Washington for so many years.

None of us can point a completely guiltless finger at New York City. None of us should now derive comfort or pleasure from New York's anguish. But neither can we let that contagion spread.

As we work with the wonderful people of New York to overcome their difficulties—and they will—we must never forget what brought this great center of human civilization to the brink.

If we go on spending more than we have, providing more benefits and more services than we can pay for, then a day of reckoning will come to Washington and the whole country just as it has to New York City.

And so, let me conclude with one question of my own: When that day of reckoning comes, who will bail out the United States of America?

50.

Black Americans and the National Economy

In December 1975 the Third National Institute for Black Elected Public Officials convened in Washington to discuss the precarious situation of many black Americans during the inflationary recession that was then only beginning to subside. Unemployment in the urban black communities was much higher than the national average, and the development of new black-owned businesses was much slowed down. The 500 officials attending the meeting issued a seven-point statement of principles intended to serve as a basis for supporting presidential and other candidates in the 1976 elections.

Source: *Congressional Record*, 94 Congress, 1 Session. December 19, 1975.

BLACK ELECTED OFFICIALS of all levels and from all parts of the country have come together to deal with the conditions of blacks in America with particular emphasis on the disproportionate burden which blacks, the poor and other disadvantaged groups bear as a consequence of our economic policies.

It is recognized that the sorry state of the economy is a major concern of all Americans. However, the bold fact is that black Americans have less and suffer more than any other segment of the society.

It is also understood that many of the solutions to our problems must rest with local action and initiatives but are only possible if national policies and programs provide direction and funding.

The needs of black Americans today are not too different than they have been for the last decade and, therefore, the specific concerns and demands of this document are not new. They are a reaffirmation of what the country has been told over the years.

Yet, it was important for black elected officials to get together and discuss common problems and possible solutions. In an era of a declining economy and a clear withdrawal by the country from its constitutional commitment for justice, it is essential for black elected officials to become more vigilant and forceful in meeting the needs of their constituents. The general moral decline shall not deter us from the drive for economic justice for all Americans. Deprived as we are, we are not alone—millions of Americans suffer with us due to the lack of moral and programatic leadership. We all need jobs, housing, education and other essentials of a decent and humane life.

Notice is now served on all candidates of all parties and persuasions for high public office—the presidency in particular—that we have no permanent friends, no permanent enemies—just permanent interests, who seek high offices merit the support of black and other afflicted segments of the society. Old alliances, past party ties are to be reexamined—the sole criteria of what is to be done to alleviate the horrendous plight of blacks trapped at the bottom of the economic system.

Black Elected Officials representing

localities throughout the nation believe that the following principles and mandates must guide and serve as the basis for candidate support by our people in 1976 and beyond:

1. Full employment.—

The American economy belongs to all of the people. The burden of the economic recovery, of halting inflation, should not be placed with those least able to shoulder the costs. Jobs are our first priority in any economic recovery plan.

What is viewed as a recession by the Nation, is a virtual Depression in Black and poor communities. We cannot accept Alice-in-Wonderland definitions of full employment. In our view, there is no tolerable level of unemployment. At present, some eight to 10 million workers are unemployed. National unemployment in November, 1975 was 8.3%—with black jobless, "officially" estimated at nearly 14%.

The unemployment that has plagued the black community has had a particularly devastating impact on the increasing number of black women who are heads of household. These women earn wages that are generally below that of white men, white women, and black men.

Full Employment, a program which guarantees the right to useful and meaningful jobs for all those willing and able to work, now demands broad public understanding and support. The majority of American people are beginning to realize what the black community has always known—that there is no reasonable trade-off between high unemployment and the high cost of living; that a job is the only buffer most people have against high prices.

The Congress must, in the coming year, pass strong and effective full employment legislation. The Equal Opportunity and Full Employment Act (H.R. 50/-

S. 50) would do the job. H.R. 50 provides that the President must prepare a national purposes budget which will result in an unemployment rate of less than 3 percent in 18 months. This rate is to be reduced in 3 years to the point that every person willing and able to work is guaranteed a job. Government policies would encourage the private sector to hire the unemployed. The Federal government would serve as employer of last resort, maintaining a Job Guarantee Office and establishing a U.S. Full Employment Service.

We must focus at the same time on the new congressional budget process to implement full employment. The House Budget Resolution passed in November 1975 projected unemployment at 7.5 percent in one year, clearly an unacceptable figure.

2. Welfare reform—

For a number of years, there has been a great deal of discussion about welfare abuse, welfare reform and welfare replacement. Welfare, or income security, must be discussed now in human terms.

The Federal Government must assume a larger share of the welfare burden. There must be a guaranteed annual income. However, any measure for income security cannot be laden down with punitive, counterproductive requirements such as has happened in the past. As one simple example, it is ludicrous to talk about forced work requirements at a time of spiraling unemployment. Moreover, it is necessary to remove procedures and activities which result in invasions of privacy. It is also crucial to recognize that the majority of welfare recipients are heads of single family households, frequently with young children.

Any welfare replacement or income supplement program is doomed to failure unless it is tied to job development, job training, a vastly expanded child program and a thorough and far-reaching program to eradicate sex and racial discrimination in education, job training and employment.

3. National Health care—

The Congress must pass and the President must sign legislation to provide for a system of comprehensive health care. The legislation must provide full coverage with a high level of benefits. Legislation which provides coverage only in cases of catastrophic illness is not acceptable. There are six essentials which must be included in any legislation passed:

a. It must set forth a positive health concept, which includes preventive services, health maintenance and community education for personal and community health.

b. Health care must be recognized as a right, not merely as a privilege.

c. Health coverage must be comprehensive and include a full range of health care, preventive, diagnosis, treatment and rehabilitation regardless of one's ability to pay.

d. There must be progressive trust fund financing so that health care is insured of continuation as a permanent program.

e. Consumers, that is, the community residents, must be permitted and encouraged to participate in health care program operations.

f. The health care program must be reinforced with adequate financing for research, planning and administration.

4. Africa policy—

The United States has virtually ignored an entire continent rich in mineral and economic potential, but whose countries are in great need of financial and technical assistance. The lack of a responsive U.S. policy toward Africa is reflected in a number of international policy decisions in the United Nations and other forums at which many African nations vote contrary to the United States position.

Two key steps for a more positive African policy are: (1) for the administration to stop supporting minority rule in Southern Africa and (2) to take concrete steps to implement the final resolution at the Seventh United Nations Special Session providing for a new International Economic Order, specifically those relating to assuring just and stable prices for primary commodities. In addition, the U.S. should make a significant contribution to the African Development Fund.

Finally, the Congress must reverse itself and pass the legislation to prohibit importation of Rhodesian chrome in violation of United Nations sanctions. These are initial, but necessary steps in turning around the policy and the image of the United States with respect to Africa and to other developing nations.

5. Education—

Equal educational opportunity has increased significantly for blacks in this country over the past several years. Yet, while many gains have been made, much remains to be done. The black school child continues to be the victim of misguided efforts to retreat from the goal of school desegregation. The largest number of blacks are affected by policies in elementary and secondary education, but the increasing numbers of black college students face a parallel struggle, the struggle to find the financial assistance essential to higher education opportunity.

In the first part of 1976, the Congress will continue its work on major pieces of higher education legislation—extending the Higher Education Act and renewing the Vocational Education Act. We support the renewal of this legislation and state our particular concern about several aspects of these measures.

In extending the Higher Education Act, three goals must be met: (1) Eligibility for student financial aid must remain concentrated on those with the greatest need. We must resist efforts to open these programs to middle class students who have alternatives for financing their college education; (2) the Developing Institutions program must be continued with increased funding; and (3) the affirmative action obligations of institutions to hire and promote minorities and women must be vigorously enforced.

A renewed Vocational Education Act must contain provisions to ensure that handicapped and disadvantaged students receive substantial benefits from the programs. Moreover, legislative provisions must be added to substantially diminish administrative costs at the State level.

During the past few years, important educational policy questions have taken second place to a misleading and emotional debate over busing. This misdirected debate has obscured the essential thrust and purpose of school desegregation. That purpose was in 1954 and still is in 1975 to improve access for all children to quality education. Until and unless communities have alternative viable means of insuring high quality education for their children in integrated settings, busing remains a technique which must be supported wherever it has been judicially ordered, in order to reach that goal. The few communities in which the busing of school children has resulted in violent and vicious confrontation should be our shame, not our example.

6. Tax reform—The efforts of the House to bring about substantial tax reform were stymied by heavy lobbying of those who benefit most from the current inequitable tax laws.

Special interests have been able to write into the law additional benefits aimed at protecting their wealth.

Tax reform is crucial to any effort at redistribution of wealth. Tax shelters and loopholes permit wealthy individuals and corporations to pay no tax at all, or to pay at a rate considerably below that of the average American. For every dollar of income which escapes federal taxation through loopholes, the government is, in effect, providing a direct subsidy or appropriations. This forgone revenue has been labeled a "tax expenditure." The Congress must scrutinize these tax expenditures as closely as budget items.

7. Economic development and aid to minority businesses—Presently, many minority businesses are being liquidated because of the inability to repay federal loans. We recommend a one-year moratorium on federal loan repayments. There should be a significant increase in set-asides and subsidies to minority businessmen.

A system of tax concessions for financial institutions and other investors should be developed immediately. Such loans and investments should be made available for business development and mortgage financing in black and other poverty communities.

There are several federal programs that have begun to work effectively in minority communities to aid in the economic and business development of rural and urban low-income communities. Minority Enterprise Small Business Investment Corporations (MESBICs) and Community Development Corporations (CDCs) have been primary mechanisms for providing an economic base for these areas. A commitment must be given to these enterprises in order that they may play a greater role in resolving the dual problems of inflation and unemployment.

51.

David M. Alpern: Big Government

Some of the most popular officeholders during the 1970s were those who derided the notion that government could solve all the nation's problems. Governors Jerry Brown of California, Ella Grasso of Connecticut, and David Boren of Oklahoma and Mayor Michael Dukakis of Boston were among the most outspoken practitioners of "lowered expectations" and critics of "big government." In 1976 the three main presidential contenders, Gerald Ford, James Carter, and Ronald Reagan all pursued the nominations of their respective parties on a platform of pledges to cut back the huge Washington bureaucracy. That government at all levels had burgeoned greatly since the early New Deal days was true, but the extent to which most Americans felt intimidated by this growth was hard to gauge. It was perhaps not so much the size of government as it was the facts of corruption and inefficiency that bothered most citizens. Journalist David Alpern did a special report on government in 1975, spelling out some of the problems connected with over-regulation and red tape entailed by the huge federal establishment.

Source: *Newsweek*, December 15, 1975. Copyright © 1975 by Newsweek, Inc. All rights reserved. Reprinted by permission.

NOT QUITE A YEAR shy of its 200th birthday, the American system of government seems to be under siege again — this time by Americans themselves and some of their most powerful political leaders. "Any government big enough to give you anything you want is big enough to take everything you have," warns President Ford. Ronald Reagan pictures Washington, D.C., as an oppressive "foreign power" much as imperial England was two centuries ago. The cry echoes in the Democratic camp as well, and not just in the voice of George Wallace. "The pat answers of big government — the grants, the programs, the projects . . . often are not answers at all," says Presidential hopeful Lloyd Bentsen, a Texas millionaire. Populist candidate Fred Harris agrees. "Bigness in government is like bigness in business," he says. "It crushes competition, stifles the individual and just doesn't work." And the dean of the nation's new school of do-less public officials, California Gov. Jerry Brown, sounds an even more dour note. "All government," he says, "bothers my conscience."

Around the nation and across the political spectrum, big government has emerged as the hot new ideological issue in the politics of '76. To be sure, the problems that worry Americans most are two old favorites: inflation and unemployment. But not far behind in the opinion-poll rankings is a bitter dissatisfaction with a government that is perceived as inefficient, overindulgent, intrusive and just too damned expensive in an era of economic belt-tightening and post-Watergate cynicism. Big Government has consistently turned up second or third in recent Gallup Poll surveys of the nation's "most important problems." And in a recent CBS News poll, fully 39 per cent of those questioned cited dissatisfaction with government as a matter of serious concern.

Despite those statistics and the campaign-year rhetoric of the say-nay politicians, many political scientists contend that most Americans want better—not smaller—government. A recent survey conducted for the U.S. Commerce Department by the business-oriented Advertising Council showed that a surprising 56 per cent of the population believes still more government regulation of some economic activities is required in American life. "We will not cure all the problems that beset us merely by resorting to less government," argues Democratic Presidential contender Birch Bayh. "What we need is a better government [and] . . . a willingness to ask tough questions about our real priorities."

Beyond that, though most Americans may be against Big Government in the abstract, they raise howls of protest whenever a government service that benefits them is abolished. Just last week in Connecticut, for instance, demonstrating military veterans helped defeat Gov. Ella Grasso's emergency austerity program because, among other things, it would shift the state's veterans benefit fund into the general-fund coffers—and thus make it more difficult for the vets to collect benefits. And in agricultural communities across the nation, farmers are railing against a consolidation of 12,000 county offices set up by different branches of the U.S. Agricultural Department out of a fear that some Federal offices would be farther from their farms. "It's a funny thing," says one Agriculture official. "Rural people are against big government more than anybody. But try to change a

county office and they scream the loudest."

What's behind the bad rap on government today? Sheer size, for one thing. With a combined Federal, state and local work force of 14.6 million people and a total expenditure of $523.2 billion, government on all levels now accounts for 37 per cent of the gross national product—as against 12 per cent in 1929. For all the shouting, however, total government spending has remained fairly constant as a fraction of the nation's GNP in the last twenty years, and the Federal bureaucracy has increased only slightly: from 2.4 million civilian employees in 1946 to 2.9 million last year. What *has* grown astronomically is the size of Federally funded social programs and the state and local governments that must administer them. But the size of government would not draw the fire it does were it not for three key aspects of the way it works—or fails to:

● *Proliferating Programs*—what many Americans see as government's fundamentally goodhearted but wasteful tendency to mount endless and expensive programs against apparently intractable social problems. Despite a wealth of state and Federal school-enrichment programs, for example, a new study by Harvard University's Christopher Jencks suggests that there is still no clear-cut evidence that they improve students' test scores, educational attainment or eventual occupational status.

● *Over-Regulation*—which, to hear the contradictory complaints, is either hamstringing or coddling big business, thus destroying healthy competition and raising prices to the consumer for such intangible benefits as a cleaner environment or greater safety protection. To make matters worse, competing agencies of the Federal government often cannot even decide which rules to enforce. Recently, the Occupational Safety and Health Administration (OSHA) ordered vehicles at work sites to use back-up beepers; the Environmental Protection Agency then challenged the order because the beepers exceeded the EPA's allowable noise levels.

• *Burdensome Reporting Requirements* — the dark underside of even the most beneficial government program, wrapping tentacles of red tape and forms-in-triplicate around everyone from the executives of giant oil companies to the heads of local school boards. "If a foreign power really wanted to destroy this country, it could develop a chemical to destroy paper," says Dr. Richard Brautigan, superintendent of the eleven district schools in El Centro, Calif. "That would bring us to our knees."

Such problems raise the broadest questions of social philosophy and public administration. Has the nation, as some critics contend, gone beyond the essential limits set by the Founding Fathers and built a government that tries to do too much for (and to) its citizens? Is it simply a question of bureaucratic inefficiency? Or have the critics themselves seized on the issue of big government to mask an attack on the sweeping Federal social programs that began with the New Deal and evolved into the Great Society? What is needed, clearly, is a new definition of what government should do and what it can do given current economic limits — what Americans, in the end, are persuaded is worth paying for.

The answers will have to come from the political process, the traditional forum for tying up opposing threads of American national interest. The danger is that the debate will deteriorate into demagoguery. "It's the easiest speech in the world to blame everything on the bu-

reaucracy — to say that programs don't work," warns Sen. Hubert Humphrey. "But I challenge anybody that gets up and says that to tell me which ones they are going to take off."

Some officials — particularly in governors' mansions around the U.S. — are trying to do just that. "We are beginning to recognize that there are limits to what government can and should do," says Wisconsin's Gov. Pat Lucey, whose efforts to skin back are matched by fellow Democrats such as Brown in California and Michael Dukakis in Massachusetts — and Republicans Christopher Bond of Missouri and Iowa's Robert Ray, who has somehow managed to pile up a $200 million budget surplus while cutting state taxes. Yet in many cases, this hard-nosed approach by the governors has come as a shock to the people who elected them — and to whom they must eventually go for re-election. "The jury is still out on this tactic electorally," says Prof. Laurence E. Lynn Jr. of Harvard's John F. Kennedy School of Government. "Who repealed the New Deal? Not the American people," challenges Democratic theoretician Ben Wattenberg, a member of Scoop Jackson's brain trust. "Democrats will not win elections by renouncing the national policies we created, policies which helped America and elected Democrats."

The point is arguable, but pertinent nonetheless. For what is clear from history is that American government did not grow big only by accident. At almost every step of the way, it was inflated by the demands of an ever-increasing number of interest groups and by the visionary programs of the nation's most popular leaders. . . .

With the Depression of the 1930s, Franklin D. Roosevelt's New Deal gave a new stamp of acceptability to massive efforts at social engineering. And even during the tamped-down days of the Eisenhower Administration, there were indications of the new, activist spirit—from Ike's deployment of Federal troops to Little Rock (in line with the Supreme Court's historic school-desegregation ruling) to Congressional passage of the National Defense Education Act (putting U.S. schools into the space race with Russia) and the Kerr-Mills bill that added to Federal underwriting of health care for the elderly poor. Then came Kennedy's Camelot—manpower training, civil rights, interventionist economics—and Lyndon Johnson's Great Society, an even greater burst of Federal programs to help that minority of Americans still trapped in Depression-style poverty.

Oversold in the Johnsonian manner, the Great Society created unwieldy new mechanisms like the Office of Economic Opportunity and began "throwing dollars at problems"—in the words of urbanologist Daniel Patrick Moynihan, now U.S. ambassador to the United Nations. Spawned in the process were vast new constituencies of government bureaucrats and beneficiaries whose political clout later made it difficult to kill programs off.

Experience has shown that some of these programs were expensive exercises in futility. Others have done much good: only 12 per cent of the population now falls beneath the so-called poverty level, compared with 17 in 1965. And some of the Great Society's supporters argue that its failures were the result of too little money being spent, not too much. "To the degree that Federal programs did generate new problems while failing to cope with old ones," says socialist theorist Michael Harrington, "these failures occurred not because Washington acted too radically or too prodigiously, but because it acted too timidly, following corporate priorities even as it spoke in populist rhet-

oric." Sociologist Daniel Bell, on the other hand, blames the effort for touching off "a revolution of rising entitlements"—a shift in national focus from the traditional pursuit of equal opportunity to a new pursuit of equal outcomes and advantages as practically absolute rights of citizenship. The ceaseless demands thus made on government by competing interest groups, says Bell, now "threaten the stability of American society."

The costs are already mounting precipitously. Federal, state and local programs for direct-aid payments to individuals have grown more than 8 per cent a year for the past two decades—while the nation's economy has had a 3.5 per cent annual growth. The rates may well level off naturally. If not, some critics contend, these programs could boost the cost of government to 58 per cent of the gross national product, and most Americans would find themselves working more than half the time just to pay their taxes. . . .

Some experts suggest that Congress should write expiration dates into all legislation, so that programs would be regularly rethought before repassage. Congressmen now tend to let a law ride along unchecked, without an eye toward its unintended effects. Others suggest the inclusion of a well-defined performance standard in any new program, thus enabling the public to tell whether it is effective.

That might well produce even more paper work, but Congress could help ease the bureaucratic burden by consolidating many of the programs to which it has given birth. The agencies themselves might stress more efficiency and productivity among their workers, and make it a point to send young lawyers who write regulations into the field periodically to confront the practical problems they have created for businessmen and local officials.

At the grass roots, predictably, mayors and governors call for more revenue-sharing funds with as few strings as possible—although there are some signs in Washington that the $30.2 billion revenue-sharing program might conceivably be scuttled after 1976. The idea of decentralizing government even further is also increasingly fashionable, with advocates noting how ward captains in Richard Daley's Chicago and "little city halls" in Boston, Atlanta and elsewhere often help cut through bureaucratic red tape.

All the calls for tactical trimming, however laudable, skirt what some critics argue is the real issue: that government has simply tried to do too much. Americans have always prided themselves on being a can-do people; it has not been comfortable to the American spirit to suggest that there are national problems that cannot be solved. The outcry against Big Government is in large measure a call for a more modest approach, and the creation of a new public consensus that the government should do more of what it does well and less of what it has been shown to do poorly. The watchword, perhaps, should be neither Big Is Better nor Small Is Best, but Best Is the Best We Can Do.

52.

Objections to Astrology

The dozen or so years prior to 1975 witnessed a popular revival of interest in the occult: astrology, fortune telling, spiritualism, supernatural beings such as angels and demons, and life after death. Of these, astrology has by far the largest following, owing in great measure to the daily printing of horoscopes in the newspapers. Regarded as either a science or a pseudoscience, astrology has a history dating from at least the second millennium B.C., and it is concerned with the forecasting of events by observing the fixed stars and the movements of Sun, Moon, and planets. Alarmed at the current revival of astrology, the Humanist *magazine in 1975 published a statement of objections to it signed by 186 of the world's leading scientists, including 18 Nobel laureates. The statement, reprinted here, was drafted by Professor Bart J. Bok of the University of Arizona, Professor Paul Kurtz of the State University of New York at Buffalo, and Lawrence E. Jerome, science writer from Santa Clara, California.*

Source: *The Humanist,* November-December 1975.

SCIENTISTS in a variety of fields have become concerned about the increased acceptance of astrology in many parts of the world. We, the undersigned—astronomers, astrophysicists, and scientists in other fields—wish to caution the public against the unquestioning acceptance of the predictions and advice given privately and publicly by astrologers. Those who wish to believe in astrology should realize that there is no scientific foundation for its tenets.

"I'm Taurus, You're Taurus. We're all Taurus."

In ancient times people believed in the predictions and advice of astrologers because astrology was part and parcel of their magical world view. They looked upon celestial objects as abodes or omens of the Gods and, thus, intimately connected with events here on earth; they had no concept of the vast distances from the earth to the planets and stars. Now that these distances can and have been calculated, we can see how infinitesimally small are the gravitational and other effects produced by the distant planets and the far more distant stars. It is simply a mistake to imagine that the forces exerted by stars and planets at the moment of birth can in any way shape our futures. Neither is it true that the positions of distant heavenly bodies make certain days or periods more favorable to particular kinds of action, or that the sign under which one was born determines one's compatibility or incompatibility with other people. Why do people believe in astrology? In these uncertain times many long for the comfort of having guidance in making decisions. They would like to believe in a destiny predetermined by astral forces beyond their control. However, we must all face the world, and we must realize that our futures lie in ourselves, and not in the stars.

One would imagine, in this day of widespread enlightenment and education, that it would be unnecessary to debunk beliefs based on magic and superstition. Yet, acceptance of astrology pervades modern society. We are especially disturbed by the continued uncritical dissemination of astrological charts, forecasts, and horoscopes by the media and by otherwise reputable newspapers, magazines, and book publishers. This can only contribute to the growth of irrationalism and obscurantism. We believe that the time has come to challenge directly, and forcefully, the pretentious claims of astrological charlatans.

It should be apparent that those individuals who continue to have faith in astrology do so in spite of the fact that there is no verified scientific basis for their beliefs, and indeed that there is strong evidence to the contrary.

1975–76

53.

The Task of the Churches — Two Views

On January 18, 1975, a group of Protestant, Catholic, and Orthodox theologians met at Hartford Seminary to examine and denounce thirteen themes that they had found to be pervasive in American churches. They published their views in what has become known as "The Hartford Appeal," essentially a conservative reaffirmation of Christian thought. Nearly a year later, on January 6, 1976, another interfaith group met in Boston under the auspices of the Boston Industrial Mission to discuss current trends in the churches. The statement they issued, "The Boston Affirmations," was set in the context of the social implications of faith and posed a marked contrast to the Hartford document. Both statements underscored the conservative-liberal tension that has long existed in American Christianity. In the 1970s it appeared that most church members were shifting to conservative and fundamentalist points of view.

Sources: 1. *Christianity and Crisis,* July 21, 1975.
2. *Christianity and Crisis,* February 16, 1976

The Hartford Appeal

The renewal of Christian witness and mission requires constant examination of the assumptions shaping the church's life. Today an apparent loss of a sense of the transcendent is undermining the church's ability to address with clarity and courage the urgent tasks to which God calls it in the world. This loss is manifest in a number of pervasive themes. Many are superficially attractive, but upon closer examination we find these themes false and debilitating to the church's life and work.

Among such themes are:

Theme 1: Modern thought is superior to all past forms of understanding reality, and is therefore normative for Christian faith and life. In repudiating this theme we are protesting the captivity to the prevailing thought structures not only of the 20th century but of any historical period. We favor using any helpful means of understanding, ancient or modern, and insist that the Christian proclamation must be related to the idiom of the culture. At the same time we affirm the need for Christian thought to confront and be confronted by other world views, all of which are necessarily provisional.

Theme 2: Religious statements are totally independent of reasonable discourse. The capitulation to the alleged primacy of modern thought takes two forms: One is the subordination of religious statements to the canons of scientific rationality; the other, equating reason with scientific rationality, would remove religious statements from the realm of reasonable discourse altogether. A religion of pure subjectivity and nonrationality results in treating faith statements as being, at best, statements about the believer. We repudiate both forms of capitulation.

Theme 3: Religious language refers to human experience and nothing else, God being humanity's noblest creation. Religion is also a set of symbols and even of human projections. We repudiate the assumption that it is nothing but that. What is here at stake is nothing less than the reality of God: *We did not invent God: God invented us.*

Theme 4: Jesus can only be understood in terms of contemporary models of humanity. This theme suggests a reversal of "the imitation of Christ"; that is, the image of Jesus is made to reflect cultural and countercultural notions of human excellence. We do not deny that all aspects of humanity are illumined by Jesus. Indeed it is necessary to the universality of the Christ that he be perceived in relation to the particularities of the believers' world. We do repudiate the captivity to such metaphors, which are necessarily inadequate, relative, transitory and frequently idolatrous. Jesus together with the Scriptures and the whole of the Christian tradition cannot be arbitrarily interpreted without reference to the history of which they are part. The danger is in the attempt to exploit the tradition without taking the tradition seriously.

Theme 5: All religions are equally valid: the choice among them is not a matter of conviction about truth but only of personal preference or life style. We affirm our common humanity. We affirm the importance of exploring and confronting all manifestations of the religious quest and of learning from the riches of other religions. But we repudiate this theme because it flattens diversities and ignores contradictions. In doing so it not only obscures the meaning of Christian faith, but also fails to respect the integrity of other faiths. Truth matters; therefore differences among religions are deeply significant.

Theme 6: To realize one's potential and to be true to oneself is the whole meaning of salvation. Salvation contains a promise of human fulfillment, but to identify salvation with human fulfillment can trivialize the promise. We affirm that salvation cannot be found apart from God.

Theme 7: Since what is human is good, evil can adequately be understood as failure to realize human potential. This theme invites false understanding of the ambivalence of human existence and underestimates the pervasiveness of sin. Paradoxically, by minimizing the enormity of evil, it undermines serious and sustained attacks on particular social or individual evils.

Theme 8: The sole purpose of worship is to promote individual self-realization and human community. Worship promotes individual and communal values, but it is above all a response to the reality of God and arises out of the fundamental need and desire to know, love and adore God. We worship God because God is to be worshiped.

Theme 9: Institutions and historical traditions are oppressive and inimical to our being truly human; liberation from them is required for authentic existence and au-

thentic religion. Institutions and traditions are often oppressive. For this reason they must be subjected to relentless criticism. But human community inescapably requires institutions and traditions. Without them life would degenerate into chaos and new forms of bondage. The modern pursuit of liberation from all social and historical restraints is finally dehumanizing.

Theme 10: The world must set the agenda for the church. Social, political and economic programs to improve the quality of life are ultimately normative for the church's mission in the world. This theme cuts across the political and ideological spectrum. Its form remains the same, no matter whether the content is defined as upholding the values of the American way of life, promoting socialism or raising human consciousness. The church must denounce oppressors, help liberate the oppressed and seek to heal human misery. Sometimes the church's mission coincides with the world's programs. But the norms for the church's activity derive from its own perception of God's will for the world.

Theme 11: An emphasis on God's transcendence is at least a hindrance to, and perhaps incompatible with, Christian social concern and action. This supposition leads some to denigrate God's transcendence. Others, holding to a false transcendence, withdraw into religious privatism or individualism and neglect the personal and communal responsibility of Christians for the earthly city. From a biblical perspective, it is precisely because of confidence in God's reign over all aspects of life that Christians must participate fully in the struggle against oppressive and dehumanizing structures and their manifestations in racism, war and economic exploitation.

Theme 12: The struggle for a better humanity will bring about the Kingdom of God. The struggle for a better humanity is essential to Christian faith and can be informed and inspired by the biblical promise of the Kingdom of God. But imperfect human beings cannot create a perfect society. The Kingdom of God surpasses any conceivable utopia. God has his own designs which confront ours, surprising us with judgment and redemption.

Theme 13: The question of hope beyond death is irrelevant or at best marginal to the Christian understanding of human fulfillment. This is the final capitulation to modern thought. If death is the last word, then Christianity has nothing to say to the final questions of life. We believe that God raised Jesus from the dead and are " . . . convinced that there is nothing in death or life, in the realm of spirits or superhuman powers, in the world as it is or in the world as it shall be, in the forces of the universe, in heights or depths — nothing in all creation that can separate us from the love of God in Christ Jesus our Lord" (Romans 8:38 f.).

SIGNED BY: Peter L. Berger, Elizabeth Ann Bettenhausen, William Sloane Coffin Jr., Avery Dulles S.J., Neal Fisher, George W. Forell, James N. Gettemy, Stanley Hauerwas, Thomas Hopko, George A. Lindbeck, Ileana Marculescu, Ralph McInerny, E. Kilmer Myers, Richard J. Mouw, Richard John Neuhaus, Randolph W. Nugent Jr., Carl J. Peter, Alexander Schmemann, Nathan A. Scott Jr., Gerard Sloyan, Lewis B. Smedes, George H. Tavard, Bruce Vawter C.M., John D. Weaver, Robert Wilken.

The Boston Affirmations

The living God is active in current struggles to bring a Reign of Justice, Righteousness, Love and Peace. The Judeo-Christian traditions are pertinent to the dilemmas of our world. All believers are called to preach the good news to the poor, to proclaim release to the captives and recovery of sight to the blind, to set at liberty those who are oppressed and to proclaim the acceptable year of the Lord. Yet we are concerned about what we discern to be present trends in our churches, in religious thought and in our society. We see struggles in every arena of human life, but in too many parts of the church and theology we find retreat from these struggles. Still, we are not without hope nor warrants for our hope. Hopeful participation in these struggles is at once action in faith, the primary occasion for personal spiritual growth, the development of viable structures for the common life, and the vocation of the people of God. To sustain such participation we have searched the past and the present to find the signs of God's future and of ours. Thus, we make the following Affirmations:

Creation: God brings into being all resources, all life, all genuine meanings. Humanity is of one source and is not ultimately governed by nature or history, by the fabric of societies or the depths of the self, by knowledge or belief. God's triune activity sustains creative order, evokes personal identity, and is embodied in the dynamic movements of human history in an ever more inclusive community of persons responsibly engaged in all aspects of the ecosphere, history and thought.

Fall: Humanity is estranged from the source of life. We try to ignore or transcend the source and end of life. Or we try to place God in a transcendent realm divorced from life. Thereby we give license to domination, indulgence, pretense, triviality and evasion. We endanger creative order, we destroy personal identity, and we corrupt inspired communities. We allow tyranny, anarchy and death to dominate the gift of life.

Exodus and Covenant: God delivers from oppression and chaos. God chooses strangers, servants, and outcasts to be witnesses and to become a community of righteousness and mercy. Beyond domination and conflict God hears the cry of the oppressed and works vindication for all. God forms "nobodies" into a people of "somebodies," and makes known the laws of life. The liberation experience calls forth celebrative response, demands responsibility in community, and opens people and nations for a common global history.

Prophecy: In compassion God speaks to the human community through prophets. Those who authentically represent God have interpreted—and will interpret—the activity of God in social history. They announce the presence of God in the midst of political and economic life; they foretell the judgment and hope that are implicit in the loyalties and practices of the common life; and they set forth the vision of covenantal renewal.

Wisdom: The cultural insights and memories of many people and ages illuminate the human condition. The experience and lore of all cultures and groups bear within them values that are of wider meaning. Racism, genocide, imperialism, sexism are thus contrary to God's purposes and impoverish us all. Yet all wisdom must also be tested for its capacity to reveal the human dependence on the source of life, to grasp the depths of sin, to liberate, to evoke prophecy and to form genuine covenant.

The New Covenant: God is known to us in Jesus Christ. The source and end of life is disclosed in that suffering love which breaks the power of sin and death, which renders hope in the action of God to reconcile and transform the world, which shatters the barriers of ethnic, class, familial, national and caste restrictions. Meaning and divine activity are incarnate

The new St. Joseph's Ukrainian Catholic Church, Chicago, designed by architect Zenon Mazurkevich. The old house, serving as a rectory, is to be torn down.

in history and human particularity.

Church Traditions: God calls those who trust the power of suffering love to form into communities of celebration, care and involvement. Those called together enact renewing forms of association and movement to the ends of the earth, responding by word and deed to the implications of faith for each age and for us today:

— The early Eastern church celebrated the dependence of humanity upon the cosmos, and of the cosmos upon God, demanding a sacramental attitude toward the whole of creation.

— The Formers of doctrine set forth the meanings of faith in the face of cultured despisers, exposed the frail foundations of various secularisms, and gave new directions to both the faithful and civilization.

— The Monastics assumed vows to ex-emplify life styles beyond preoccupation with gain, freedom from familial and sexual stereotyping, and disciplined lives of service.

— The Scholastics engaged secular culture, demanding of each generation critical and synthetic reappropriation of tradition.

— The Reformers preached the word of protest against religious pretense and demanded reliance upon the gifts of divine empowerment.

— The Sectarians nurtured the spirit that cannot be contained by priesthood, dogma, hierarchy, authoritative word or any established power, and demanded democracy, freedom, toleration and the redistribution of authority, power and wealth.

— And today many reach out for wider fellowships, demanding ecumenical engagements and a witness which frees and unites.

Wherever the heirs of these movements are authentic, they confess their sins, worship the power that sustains them, form a company of the committed, and struggle for justice and love against the powers and principalities of evil.

Present Witnesses: The question today is whether the heritage of this past can be sustained, preserved and extended into the future. Society as presently structured, piety as presently practiced, and the churches as presently preoccupied evoke profound doubts about the prospects. Yet we are surrounded by a cloud of witnesses who prophetically exemplify or discern the activity of God. The transforming reality of God's reign is found today:

— In the struggles of the poor to gain a share of the world's wealth, to become creative participants in the common economic life, and to move our world toward an economic democracy of equity and accountability.

—In the transforming drive for ethnic dignity against the persistent racism of human hearts and social institutions.

—In the endeavor by women to overcome sexist subordination in the church's ministry, in society at large, and in the images that bind our minds and bodies.

—In the attempts within families to overcome prideful domination and degrading passivity, and to establish genuine covenants of mutuality and joyous fidelity.

—In the efforts by many groups to develop for modern humanity a love for its cities as centers of civility, culture and human interdependence.

—In the demands of the sick and the elderly for inexpensive, accessible health care administered with concern, advised consent and sensitivity.

—In the voices of citizens and political leaders who demand honesty and openness, who challenge the misplaced trust of the nation in might, and who resist the temptations to make a nation and its institutions objects of religious loyalty.

—In the research of science when it warns of dangers to humanity and quests for those forms of technology which can sustain human well-being and preserve ecological resources.

—In the humanities and social sciences when the depths of human meanings are opened to inquiry and are allowed to open our horizons, especially whenever there is protest against the subordination of religion to scientistic rationality or against [its] removal from realms of rational discourse.

—In the arts where beauty and meaning are explored, lifted up and represented in ways that call us to deeper sensibilities.

—In the halls of justice when righteousness is touched with mercy, when the prisoner and the wrongdoer are treated with dignity and fairness.

—And especially in those branches and divisions of the church where the truth is spoken in love, where transforming social commitments are nurtured and persons are brought to informed conviction, where piety is renewed and recast in concert with the heritage, and where such struggles as those here identified are seen as the action of the living God who alone is worshiped.

On these grounds, we cannot stand with those secular cynics and religious spiritualizers who see in such witnesses no theology, no eschatological urgency, and no Godly promise or judgment. In such spiritual blindness, secular or religious, the world as God's creation is abandoned, sin rules, liberation is frustrated, covenant is broken, prophecy is stilled, wisdom is betrayed, suffering love is transformed into triviality, and the church is transmuted into a club for self- or transcendental awareness. The struggle is now joined for the future of faith and the common life. We call all who believe in the living God to affirm, to sustain and to extend these witnesses.

The following members of the Boston Industrial Mission Task Force participated, with some variation of regularity, in the process of drafting this statement; Norman Faramelli, Harvey Cox, Mary Roodkowsky, Dave Dodson Gray, Jeanne Gallo, Robert Starbuck, Preston Williams, Max Stackhouse, Scott Paradise, George Rupp, Liz Dodson Gray, Ignacio Castuera, John Snow, Mary Hennessey, Constance Parvey, Joseph Williamson, Paul Santmire, Richard Snyder, Moises Mendez, Eleanor McLaughlin, Jerry Handspicker. In addition more than 200 church leaders—local, regional, theological and national—of several denominations were involved in the process of developing this statement at various stages.

FREEDOM'S FADING LIGHT?

In July 1975, delegates from 35 nations met in Helsinki, Finland, for a European Security Conference. The Final Act of the conference, signed by all the nations present, provided, among other things, for freer movement of peoples across national borders and for greater recognition of human rights. But, this agreement has done little to enlarge the area of freedom in the world. In fact, human liberty seems to be threatened more now than at any time since World War II. The "third world" revolution against colonialism has demonstrated that independence does not necessarily mean freedom. Many newly independent nations of Africa have become dictatorships. Tyrannical governments exist in all Communist societies, while rightwing dictatorships are the rule in Latin America. In 1975, India, the world's most populous democracy, had its freedoms subverted, albeit temporarily, by Prime Minister Indira Gandhi's "state of emergency." The Philippines, too, came under rule by decree when President Marcos set aside the constitution. And perhaps worst of all for us, America's commitment to human rights was ambiguous. While opposing the tyranny of Communism, our government yet supported numerous military dictatorships around the world, all in the name of national security and international stability.

The European Security Conference, with delegates from 35 countries, met at Helsinki, Finland, in July 1975. Exiled Russian author Aleksandr Solzhenitsyn addresses the AFL-CIO at Washington, D.C., on June 30, 1975.

Ledru/Nogues—Sygma

Dennis Brack—Black Star

Israeli commandos return from their successful raid to rescue hostages at Entebbe, in Uganda, July 1976. President Idi Amin of Uganda addresses the United Nations General Assembly, 1975. Secretary of State Henry Kissinger in Salzburg, Austria.

Alain Nogues—Sygma

Evidence of severe drought in the Sahel country of Africa. Such conditions threaten the most elemental of human rights—the right to live. Indira Gandhi addresses constituents during state of national emergency, Punjab, India.

J.P. Laffont—Sygma

Joseph and Julia, parents of Karen Quinlan, with a book of clippings about their daughter's right-to-die case. Gary Gilmore, seated in this chair, was executed for murder by a firing squad in Salt Lake City, Utah. The Supreme Court building is in Washington, D.C.

In the United States in the 1970s new areas of human rights made news. The issues of the "right to die" and the "right to live" both promised to be controversial for years to come. And the federal and state courts were in the center of both issues, as petitioners brought cases for and against execution and for and against the rights of the unborn. While the U.S. Supreme Court had previously decided in favor of abortion, by the end of 1976 it had not made definitive rulings on the death penalty or on the right to let terminally ill patients die by taking away mechanical life-support systems. The busing-for-integration controversy also persisted, most notably in South Boston where white citizens continued to denounce and combat integration of their schools.

Donlau—Sygma

Eldridge Cleaver, back from self-imposed exile abroad, makes a court appearance in San Francisco, January 1976. White students from South Boston High School attack a black man with a flag outside city hall. The students had been protesting busing for integration.

Stanley Forman—Boston Herald American

Congressional investigations revealed that, in the United States, the invasion of the constitutional rights of citizens by investigative agencies of the federal government had been going on since at least the 1930s, and presumably with the knowledge of presidents from Roosevelt to Ford. There had been opening of mail, tapping of telephones, breaking and entering, spying, use of informers, impeding the right to assembly, subversion of legally constituted organizations, and incitement to crime by those whose ostensible responsibility it was to uphold and enforce the laws. What limits, if any, would be imposed on the Federal Bureau of Investigation, the Central Intelligence Agency, and other branches of the Executive Department was still uncertain by the end of 1976.

Computerized fingerprint identification system at FBI headquarters in Washington, D.C.
Central Intelligence Agency headquarters in Virginia, near Washington, D.C.

54.

The Right to Die

The right to die and the right to live both were prominent issues in 1975–76. The anti-abortion forces played a vocal, if not unduly influential, role in the 1976 presidential campaign. In the last few months of 1976 the right, or virtually the demand, to die gained national notoriety through the efforts of convicted Utah murderer Gary Gilmore to promote his own execution by firing squad. Probably the most notable instance of the right to die issue was raised in 1975 in what has become known as the Quinlan case. Early in 1975 Karen Ann Quinlan of Dover, New Jersey, fell into a coma after taking a combination of pills and alcohol. Since it was virtually certain that recovery was impossible, her parents asked that life-support systems be removed so the girl could die "with grace and dignity." A county court ruling went against this petition, but in March 1976 the New Jersey Supreme Court ruled that if physicians in consultation with a hospital ethics committee decided Karen would be unlikely to recover from her comatose condition, the life-support systems could be withdrawn "without any civil or criminal liability." The court concluded that such difficult decisions ought to be made by the family, not by the state. Several other such cases cropped up during 1976. In some of them patients have been allowed to die, in others not. Because there have been no established procedures on caring for the incurably ill, hospitals have begun to formulate policies to define the circumstances under which patients should be allowed to die. Below are reprinted two selections relating to the right-to-die issue. The first is an article, "Death On Demand," by Patrick F. and Carol Altekruse Berger, discussing the social and religious implications of the Quinlan case. The Bergers teach medical ethics at the Metropolitan College of St. Louis University. Second is a report of the Clinical Care Committee of the Massachusetts General Hospital entitled "Optimum Care for Hopelessly Ill Patients." The policy described by the report was in effect at the hospital during most of 1976.

Sources: A. *Commonweal*, December 5, 1975.
     B. *New England Journal of Medicine*, August 1976.

A. Death on Demand

There is a theory, current in pro-life circles, that there is a "domino" relationship between abortion and euthanasia, that if we acquiesce to legalized abortion, euthanasia is sure to follow. Actually, there is a bit of surface truth to the theory. Legalized abortion is with us now,

and the inertia of law and custom present a formidable obstacle to those who would have it repealed. At the same time, we are witnessing increasing sentiment in favor of legalizing some forms of euthanasia. Nevertheless, the domino theory is basically inaccurate and misleading.

First of all, it seems to rest upon the presumption that abortion is the product

254 The Annals of America: 1975-76

of minds which are infected by a callous disregard for human life, and that anyone who would be so cruel as to kill a helpless infant, surely must be setting his sights on Grandma. Yet contact with pro-abortion activists often reveals them to be a rather high-minded, humanistic lot with an unfortunate tendency to short-sightedness — for the most part, they find it very difficult to see beyond the plight of the reluctant mother to the quite a bit more perilous plight of her unwanted offspring. Often their vision has been clouded by related issues such as population control and notions about a woman's right over her body. They are frequently very sympathetic persons; it is just that their sympathies have not, for one reason or another, been engaged on behalf of fetal life. Many pro-abortionists are, in fact, shocked by what they interpret as the "malice" of anti-abortionists whom they perceive as wanting to "punish" the unwilling mother.

The second defect of the "domino" theory is the ease with which it obscures the unique character and attitudes which have brought abortion to legal status, and seemingly eliminates the need to seek out and examine those distinct societal conditions which are presently germinating legalized euthanasia. While there are certain valid analogies to be drawn between the abortion and euthanasia debates, we believe that if death-on-demand becomes an institution in our culture, it will be for reasons quite different from those that brought abortion into our midst.

It seems rather certain, for instance, that the progress of medical science is one of the chief factors forcing the issues of death-by-choice, now that there is, in principle, no deadly, no incurable disease. As a result, the problem of euthanasia is leaving the sector of isolated, private cases of individuals who might opt for it,

either as agent or patient, and it is entering the arena of public legislation. Whether advocated by a person like Dr. Walter Sackett, a Miami practitioner who is also a member of the Florida Legislature and one who has introduced a death with dignity bill in Florida, or whether placed for discussion before the British Parliament for adoption as is currently the case in England, it seems almost inevitable that euthanasia will become legalized in some form, just as abortion-on-demand has been legalized.

If pro-life Christians should have learned anything from the abortion episode, it is that the core issues should be discussed now, in their entirety, not after euthanasia has passed into law as a *fait accompli*. For after all the discussion and controversy on the abortion issue, too many people are either for it or against it, without knowing the issues and the complicated reasoning behind the different stands. If one is to have a grasp on the situation, it is necessary to understand the most compelling and most agonizing of the euthanasia arguments; for it is the extreme case that will constantly be paraded before the public in the attempt to legalize the process.

Generally speaking, euthanasia falls into two categories: active (involving overt action such as a lethal injection) and passive (requiring nothing more than the refusal to use "extraordinary means" to prolong life). Passive euthanasia, both voluntary and involuntary, has been, in principle and in fact, acceptable to Catholic moral theologians for some time. It even received the endorsement of Pope Pius XII in a 1957 address to the International Congress of Anesthesiologists. The point of difficulty, however, is the ambiguity of the term "extraordinary." In a medical climate which has come to regard respirators and intravenous feeding tubes as basic hospital equipment, the line between ordinary and extraordinary is extremely difficult to draw. The unfortunate and well-publicized case of Karen Quinlan is an obvious example of this difficulty.

The extreme complexity of the Quinlan case simply overwhelms traditional thinking on the matter. It is not only a question of euthanasia, but a question about the meaning of death, as well. For amidst the current debate on the definition of death, there is a developing consensus that death can be said to occur when there is no measurable brain wave activity over a twenty-four-hour period and there is an absence of spontaneous heartbeat and respiration. Using these criteria, we must agree with the opinion of Miss Quinlan's doctors that she is not yet dead. But in what sense can she be said to be alive? Comatose since April, she does not even resemble her former self physically. Her body has gradually assumed a fetal position and her weight has been cut by half. She is said to be in a chronic vegetative state, with no hope of rehabilitation or recovery. Nothing remains of Karen Quinlan but a minimal degree of brain activity and occasional spontaneous breathing.

To many persons in the medical field the choice seems obvious: disconnect the respirator. But there is a deceptive simplicity in that decision, for one is actually making a decision regarding the *quality* of the life that Karen Quinlan may be expected to live should the respirator remain in use. And the decision is that it is a *life not worth living*. For in what way does the Quinlan situation differ from that of another who through catastrophic illness such as polio requires lifetime assistance to respirate? It differs only in that Karen Quinlan is severely brain damaged and we can presume that the polio victim is cerebrally unimpaired and is capable of fully human interaction with others.

In the Quinlan case it would seem that to force continued use of the respirator is to make a mockery of the sacredness of life. The art of medicine has long been dedicated to the frustration of natural forces—the appendix that wants to rupture and kill is removed before it can follow its natural course—but there must also be a time to submit when the struggle has lost its human meaning. To maintain a grotesque remnant of human life by artificial means is as clear a violation of natural law as any test-tube baby could be. But one must not lose sight of the awesomeness of declaring a life—even the artificially sustained life of Karen Quinlan—to be a life that is not worth living. In her case the course of action seems fairly clear, but what about cases that are less well-defined?

Some of the most difficult situations involving euthanasia concern the defective new-born. These complicated instances have been amply chronicled by Catholic philosophers and theologians, notably Daniel Maguire (*Death By Choice*) and Richard McCormick, S.J. ("To Save or Let Die," *America*, 7/13/74). The problems arise mainly because modern technology can keep alive seriously ill and defective infants who would have otherwise died merciful and natural deaths. Both Maguire and McCormick bring up the difficult cases of babies who are practically incapable of attaining any meaningful experience or human relationships. In these instances, both men tentatively argue that perhaps it is precisely to the infant's benefit to allow him to die. They mention the Johns Hopkins case in which a baby was born with Down syndrome (mongoloid) and in which minor surgery was required to open up a blocked duodenal tract. The parents opted against the surgery, and thus the baby died by starvation in fifteen days. Some of the agonizing questions to arise out of this were whether after the decision not to operate was made, should the child's death have been hastened by a merciful injection of pain-killer? What was to be gained by the fifteen-day period of starvation?

Maguire cites another case, that of Missy who was born with spina bifida with meningomyelocele of the lumbar spine. She had no reflex activity in either leg and could not control her anal or urinary sphincters; and she had club feet. Water on the brain develops in 90 percent of these cases, and even with complicated surgery and the insertion of a shunt drain, the child had a 50-50 chance of being mentally retarded. Maguire notes that ten years ago 80 percent of these babies died and today 75 percent survive. At the time that this case was discussed by a distinguished panel, two questions were raised, "Should the baby have been allowed to die from the meningitis that would normally ensue in such cases? Or should the medics have begun at once what would be for the child a lifetime of extraordinary care?" Maguire poses a third alternative for possible consideration—direct termination of life. Or more subtly stated so as to be protected under the murky state of the law, "The moral question then is whether the death should be entrusted to the imminent disease or whether it could be brought on by the administration of drugs or whether a compromise could be found whereby the drugs are used to comfort and to weaken in co-ordination with the meningitis."

Maguire is not championing any mad rush to eliminate by painless means all such infants who do not meet current demands for perfection. But he is suggesting the possibility of active involuntary euthanasia for infants in certain cases in which the life possibilities of the baby may function at a biological or physical level but not in any kind of spiritual, psychological, or relational manner. McCormick makes the same point by emphasizing that some babies might be let die, because if they survived in a state which demanded such extraordinary care and excessive hardship, then the "very possibility of growth in love of God and neighbor, and the like would be impossible." What these two theologians are saying is that problems of this type simply did not exist in the past when the death of some infants was determined by forces beyond our control. Now that science has brought us to a point where we can keep such infants biologically alive, these theologians are asking: does such survival constitute the fullest expression of respect for the natural law and the sanctity of life?

At the other end of the spectrum, what response does the Christian make to the hopelessly incurable who beg their doctor for some medication that will put them out of their physical and psychological misery? The active voluntary euthanasia of the rational aged, and/or ill, presents a serious moral problem. Walter Alvarez, a noted medical doctor and lecturer in this field, has recorded cases of elderly patients who have led productive lives, made peace with the world, and wanted only to die quickly with as little pain as possible. There is rather one poignant case in which he obtained a lethal dose of morphine for a dying man under such circumstances. A sixty-year-old man was suffering from inoperable cancer which was eating into a number of sensitive spots in his chest and spine. The man was suffering so terribly that Dr. Alvarez could not relieve him with the amount of morphine that he could safely give. The man told him that he had just talked with his son and was satisfied and that his unbearable wife was only adding to his misery. He could see no reason why the horrible process of his dying should be prolonged for another two or three months. He asked the doctor for enough morphine tablets so that he could take a fatal dose if he should so decide. Alvarez obtained the tablets for the man, but the suicide-euthanasia was unsuccessful because the man fainted when he tried to walk across the room to get them from his bureau, and the tablets were then discovered by his wife. Alvarez said that he barely escaped a lawsuit, but that he felt that he had done the correct thing and that doctors should let patients like this commit suicide if they so desire. But, he adds, the law certainly does not permit this.

Still, these very difficult and trying cases are not enough in themselves to create sufficient pressure to have pro-euthanasia laws formally placed on the books. There are other forces at work. In the case of abortion, the combination of overpopulation and the rise of the feminist movement helped to change attitudes towards abortion more quickly and more deeply than anyone realized and the central problem has been set aside—namely, is the fetus human and does he or she have any rights to be protected under the 14th Amendment? In much the same way the general beliefs are changing about euthanasia and suicide: namely, the belief in the right to die with dignity and the diminished effectiveness of the religious and cultural strictures against taking one's life. . . .

In fact there are even respected Christian moralists like Joseph Fletcher who are aware of the redemptive potential of suffering but who have lobbied for euthanasia in cases where a long painful death does more to dehumanize a person than to elevate him. In effect, what many

moralists are coming to the awareness of is that we have most certainly altered the natural law to live longer; why not alter it to live shorter since both are to our convenience? Likewise, to make the Commandment "Thou shalt not kill" apply in cases of suicide, even though we permit the involuntary homicide of criminals in capital punishment or even innocents in war is simply not coherent, St. Augustine's reasons to the contrary. For if we can make exemptions for criminals and war victims, we can just at least as easily exempt the suicide because there are things we can do to ourselves that we cannot do to others. Thus if Christians and other people concerned about the value of life are going to raise voices of protest against euthanasia, they are going to have to resort to other sources than authority or slogans like "Euthanasia is murder"—if, that is, they have learned anything from the abortion issue and its ready acceptance into the law books by society.

The debate will have to shift to other grounds. For one aspect often overlooked in the abortion debate is that far from giving women a choice in the matter, a subtle burden has been placed on a woman to have an abortion whether she desires one or not. We are reminded of a recent case in the news in which a young man, the father of a fetus being brought to term by an unmarried girl, saw his responsibility in the pregnancy absolved because, after all, he had urged her to obtain an abortion, and "She was too stupid to do it." The girl was placed in a bind and obviously looked like an irresponsible person if she did not abort.

The same sort of pressure would be placed on a large number of the elderly. Any number of old people would be coerced or feel coerced by their own sense of futility and the burdens that they are placing on their kin by their very troublesome and potentially expensive existence. On the other hand, would the relatives feel responsible for that fact that Grandfather does not want to live? What kind of guilt would be produced in them?

Another problem would be that of proper and valid consent. What may look like an unbearable day today could be much more hopeful tomorrow. How many dying and old people would opt for euthanasia if it became legal merely because they were in a deep, real, painful, but nonetheless curable or passing depression?

But if Christians are to have any credible input into the euthanasia debate, they are going to have to bear more witness to the care of the old, the dying and the unsuccessful. Both in a personal manner and in a structured institutional way. Christians must share the burdens of the despair experienced by the incurably pain-wracked people who are approaching death. Modern man has taken the task of dying out of the home, away from the sphere of familiar places, friends and routines, and placed this process in the professional yet antiseptic and cold confines of the hospital and old age home. Gone are the days when death was accepted as part of the natural processes of the family. . . .

For our part, we would be opposed to the legalization of euthanasia. It is our fear that for every Senecan sage who would be blessed by the cool and rational shortening of his days, there would be thousands of elderly persons who would be hastened to their deaths by the subtle coercion of a society which ranks the care of the aged and ill as one of its most onerous burdens. The legal option of euthanasia would perhaps, in time, erode the now and again begrudged privilege of the elderly and infirm to linger on for as long as the Lord lets them.

B. Optimum Care for Hopelessly Ill Patients

When advance life support and maximum therapeutic efforts are continued in a patient who is judged to be hopelessly ill and the anticipated outcome is death, serious medical, emotional, legal and economic questions concerning the justification for continued efforts arise. The responsible physician and the medical and nursing staff in the intensive-care unit (ICU) as well as the patient's relatives face the dilemma of deciding whether continued maximal efforts constitute a reasonable attempt at prolonging life or whether the patient's illness has reached a stage where further intensive care is, in fact, merely postponing death. Although relatively few such patients are encountered in most intensive-care units, their presence generates medical, moral and emotional problems out of proportion to their number. Lack of precise knowledge concerning the specifics of outcome often precludes a satisfactory solution under these circumstances, and the tendency is to persist in heroic measures until death by conventional criteria, whether cessation of circulation or cerebral function.

To study the growing issue of how best to manage the hopelessly ill patients, the Critical Care Committee created an ad hoc subcommittee composed of a psychiatrist as chairman, legal counsel, an assistant nursing director in charge of intensive-care nursing, an internist specializing in oncology, a general surgeon and a lay person who herself had been stricken with, and recovered from, serious neoplastic disease.

The subcommittee was charged with a study and recommendation concerning treatment of the hopelessly ill patient and utilization of critical-care facilities.

On the basis of the recommendations of

the ad hoc subcommittee, the Critical Care Committee submitted a report to the General Executive Committee recommending the formation of a patient-care classification system, ... and the establishment of a permanent committee on optimum treatment of the hopelessly ill patient. The classification system and other recommendations from the Critical Care Committee follow:

1. Whenever appropriate, critically ill patients should be classified according to the following system. Class A *Maximal therapeutic effort* without reservation. Class B *Maximal therapeutic effort* without reservation, but with daily evaluation because probability of survival is questionable. Class C *Selective limitation of therapeutic measures.*

The criterion which determines every aspect of the therapeutic regimen continues to be the overall welfare of the patient. At this time certain procedures may cease to be justifiable and become contraindicated. Particular attention must be given to resuscitation measures of all kinds. The therapeutic plan must be clearly detailed to the other members of the care team so that all understand and are united about their caring efforts and responsibilities. As an integral part of caring for the patient, appropriate notes specifically describing the therapeutic plan should be made in the patient's record. The patient's resuscitation status should be similarly recorded in conformance with the policy governing orders limiting full cardio-pulmonary resuscitation.

A Class C patient is not an appropriate candidate for admission to an Intensive Care Unit. A decision to transfer the patient out of the Intensive Care Unit is based upon the needs of the patient, and transfer is appropriate only after required comfort measures become manageable in a nonintensive care setting. Whatever the patient's location, however, and irrespective of the specific therapeutic measures that have been selectively limited, a Class C patient and his family require and must be given full general support.

Class D *All therapy can be discontinued.* Any measures which are indicated to insure maximum comfort of the patient may be continued or instituted.

2. (a) The Critical Care Committee recommends the establishment of an advisory committee to be referred to as the Optimum Care Committee. This group should be available to serve *in an advisory capacity* in situations where difficulties arise in deciding the appropriateness of continuing intensive therapy for critically ill patients. Although the ICU Director may *suggest* a review by the committee, *the ultimate request must come from the responsible physician.* When requested by the responsible physician, the Optimum Care Committee will act as expeditiously as possible to review all available information regarding the patient, calling on whatever resources it deems necessary. The committee will then recommend to the responsible physician what it considers to be an appropriate course of action. It should be emphasized that the committee's role is *advisory* and the responsible physician may accept or reject its decision.

(b) The Optimum Care Committee can most effectively deal with the highly sensitive issues by convening all members of the care team involved, i.e., responsible physician, ICU Director, consultants, nursing staff and committee members, to discuss the care of the patient and mutually explore what the best interests of the patient and his relatives require in the situation. The major aim will be the clarification of the treatment rationale for all concerned.

(c) The ICU Director may have recourse to the chief of service when the responsible physician does not wish to discuss the treatment rationale and the ICU Director feels such discussion is warranted. In the case of a disagreement between an ICU Director and responsible physician, the ICU Director may ask the permission of the chief of service to call the committee. In the event permission is granted and the committee offers a recommendation, the responsible physician nevertheless makes the final decision about treatment.

(d) The services of the Optimum Care Committee should be available to all Intensive Care Units and to individual physicians requesting advice in the management of critically ill patients confined outside the intensive care units.

On admission to the intensive-care unit, patients will be assumed to be Class A or B. Any patient who is not in Class A must be reassessed daily. It is stressed that the ultimate decision concerning treatment classification rests with the responsible physician. Whenever a question arises about the appropriateness of treatment of a patient with an irreversible illness the situation should be reviewed at unit rounds. Such questions may arise from the patient himself, the family, the responsible physician, the staff of the unit or its director, or consultants called by the responsible physician. If there is a consensus about treatment, no change in classification occurs. If patients or family or someone not at rounds has raised the question, the responsible physician, the director of the unit or an appropriate designee should explain the treatment rationale to the person who raised the question. If treatment rationale remains unclear at unit rounds, the patient should be assigned to Class B by the responsible physician. The purpose of assignment to Class B is twofold: to provide opportunity for the responsible physician to obtain

further consultation and support in the management of a difficult case; and to ensure dialogue between the primary physician and director and staff of the intensive-care unit through the forum of unit rounds. If the unit nurses and physicians do not understand the reasons for a specific treatment of a patient, or fail to see how a specific treatment may reverse the course of a patient's illness, they are encouraged to request clarification from the responsible physician or unit director, who may relay the request to the primary physician. Since communication failures can cause serious misunderstanding, use of unit rounds to clarify specific treatment considerations is strongly recommended.

When the responsible physician designates a patient for treatment in Class C, it is essential that he receive the support of the unit director, physicians, nursing staff and his own consultants. Concurrence is probably most conveniently given through discussion at unit rounds, although prior discussion may indicate that such supportive consensus is already clear. If the responsible physician is uncertain whether his clinical reasoning has been properly understood by the unit staff, he is encouraged to review the situation with the director.

Once a patient has been classified in the C category, the guidance of the responsible physician is even more heavily relied upon to specify indications for treatment of hypotension, ventilatory or cardiac failure, acute pulmonary edema, arrhythmias, metabolic intoxication and other crises heralded by failing organ systems. Nursing and resident staff skilled in use of defibrillators, vasopressors, pacemakers, endotracheal tubes or other lifesaving treatments feel especially threatened when the responsibility for initiating these efforts is left to their judgment.

These decisions must be made by the responsible physician. Efforts to ease the burdens of nurses and house staff in this regard will reduce most if not all of the potential for conflict. Nurses and house staff are also encouraged to voice their concerns at rounds so that clarification and guidance can be ensured.

At the transition from Class B to Class C the responsible physician, who must make this difficult decision, should avail himself of any consultation he wishes. Designation of Class C requires judgment entirely independent of the question of whether or not the patient should remain in the intensive-care unit. Because of the high cost of unit beds, considerable pressure may arise to make economic considerations primary in deciding where a particular patient should reside. This committee stresses that economic considerations must never serve as the sole criterion for disposition and treatment of patients.

Although Class C designation implies that death is the probable outcome, it may not necessarily be the case. With improvement, the patient's category may be changed to a more optimistic one. Similarly, with deterioration, therapy may be selectively limited, while the patient remains in Class C without necessarily being assigned to Class D.

Designation of a patient for Class D is to follow the same recommendations as those given for Class C. The definite act of commission, such as turning off a mechanical ventilator, is to be performed only by an appropriate physician after consultation with and concurrence of the family and appropriate hospital committee (or committees) where indicated. Assignment to Class D is generally reserved for patients with brain death, or when there is no reasonable possibility that the patient will return to a cognitive and sapient life.

Unless otherwise stated full resuscitation will be initiated for all patients. Any limitation on full resuscitative efforts must be stated precisely in the patient's record.

The classification system has been in use as a pilot study for six months involving 209 admissions to the Respiratory Intensive and Acute Care Unit, an 11-bed multidisciplinary critical-care unit. All patients were classified independently by the charge nurse and the Respiratory Unit staff physician on call upon admission and daily thereafter until discharge. Once all concerned personnel had gained a thorough understanding of the classification there was a remarkable degree of correlation of classification among nurses and physicians.

Requests for Optimum Care Committee consultation have been rare; 15 patients have been reviewed to date. The main benefits of the consultation have been clarification of misunderstanding about the patient's prognosis, reopening of communication, re-establishment of unified treatment objectives and rationale, restoration of the sense of shared responsibility for patient and family, and, above all, maximizing support for the responsible physician who makes the medical decision to intensify, maintain or limit effort at reversing the illness.

◆

What I'd like to see is the evolution of a more flexible attitude, an admission that wishing to die is not always unreasonable.
Charles Fried, *New England Journal of Medicine*, August 12, 1976

1976

55.

The Flow of Wealth and Population to the Sunbelt

On May 17, 1976, Business Week *published a special report entitled "The Second War Between the States." The point of the article was a striking change that has been taking place in the United States since the last decade: the steady shift of population and money to what is variously called the "Sunbelt" or the "Southern rim." The population in the South and the Southwest has grown six times as fast as in the Great Lakes region and ten times as fast as in the combined New England and Midwest regions. Industry and jobs are a part of this migration, and more federal money flows into the region than into the Northeast and Midwest. Consequently some sections of the United States are declining economically, while others are coming into a new prosperity. The economic portent of this shift was the subject of a survey by the* National Journal, *published in part here. The report was prepared by Joel Havemann and Rochelle L. Stanfield, staff correspondents, and Neal R. Peirce, contributing editor, with the assistance of Lawrence P. Malone and Jerry Hagstrom.*

Source: *National Journal,* June 26, 1976. "Federal Spending: The North's Loss is the Sunbelt's Gain."

FEDERAL TAX AND SPENDING policies are causing a massive flow of wealth from the Northeast and Midwest to the fast-growing Southern and Western regions of the nation, according to a *National Journal* survey of financial relationships between the states and the federal government.

The five Great Lakes states are hurt the most. They paid $62.2 billion in federal taxes in fiscal 1975, according to *National Journal* computations, while they received only $43.6 billion in federal outlays. Their "balance of payments" deficit

was $18.6 billion.

The Mid-Atlantic states lost $10 billion through their money exchange with Washington.

The misfortune of the old industrial states is the blessing of the Sunbelt. The 16 states of the South showed a balance of payments surplus of $11.5 billion, while the Pacific and Mountain states came out a total of $10.6 billion ahead.

The inequities are almost entirely accidental. Florida gets more than its share of social security outlays because many elderly persons live there. Defense spending is heavy in California because it is the home of the aerospace industry. Mississippi and New York, which both have high proportions of poor residents, receive substantial federal welfare payments.

Even when the federal government dictates where its money goes, the reasons often have little to do with the needs of the states that benefit. More often than not, defense bases are located in the states of powerful Members of Congress, not necessarily in regions that need economic help. Formulas for distributing federal grants to states and localities can be manipulated according to the needs of the recipients, but the number of local residents usually is the most important factor.

Political leaders of the Northeast are only beginning to protest the role that the federal government is playing in the shift of wealth away from their part of the country. Hugh L. Carey, the Democratic governor of New York, for example, has called for a "modern federalist" policy to correct the economic malaise of "the vast and aging industrial belt that stretches from Massachusetts to Illinois and beyond."

Rich get richer: Although there were notable exceptions, the study indicated a heavy flow of federal dollars away from —rather than toward—the states and regions of the nation in the most severe economic straits.

In general, those states in the most favorable balance of payments position with Washington were the ones in the South and the West that have been experiencing the heaviest population gains, the least unemployment and the strongest gains in per capita income.

The states at the receiving end of high federal outlays also tend to be those that tax their own citizens least for state and local government services.

On the other hand, the balance of payments situation generally is adverse in the Northeast and Midwest, where population is stagnant or declining, where unemployment is the most severe, where relative personal income is falling and where the heaviest state and local tax burdens are imposed.

Some regions are remarkably homogenous in their financial relations with Washington. Every Mid-Atlantic and Great Lakes state was a big loser, and all South Central and Mountain states except Nevada were winners.

Other parts of the country were not so uniform. The South Atlantic showed a balance of payments surplus largely due to the federal salaries paid by government agencies located in Maryland and Virginia; Delaware and North Carolina had deficits and Florida's surplus was tiny.

Previous studies have shown similar patterns of financial relationships between the states and the federal government. The Congressional Research Service, the Tax Foundation Inc. and the Dreyfus Corp. have found that federal dollars have been flowing for years from the Northeast and Midwest to the South and West.

While the flow of money has been consistent over the years, the economic characteristics of the winning and losing regions have not. With the recent economic development of the South, federal money now is moving away from economically stagnant regions—the Northeast and Midwest.

Spending and taxes: National Journal tallied total federal outlays—spending for salaries, defense contracts, public works, grants in aid and the like—for each state in fiscal 1975. It measured them against federal tax revenues sent to Washington that year by the states.

From spending, it subtracted interest payments on the national debt, for which state-by-state allocations are unreliable. To make total tax burden equal to total spending in a year in which there was a substantial deficit, a share of the deficit proportional to each state's population was added to the actual tax burden.

With these adjustments, the states as a whole sent as much money to Washington in taxes as they received in spending. But individual states showed enormous surpluses or deficits in their balance of payments with Washington.

The 10 Midwestern and Mid-Atlantic states that were the worst off suffered a total deficit of $30.8 billion. Three Midwestern states—Illinois, Michigan and Ohio—were at the bottom of the list, followed by New Jersey, New York and Pennsylvania.

After the District of Columbia, the 10 big winners, with a combined surplus of $15.6 billion, were in the South, West and D.C. orbit. California led the list, followed by Virginia, Washington, Mississippi and Maryland.

Another way to measure the federal balance of payments for each state—one that is independent of state population—is to look at how much it receives in the form of federal spending for each dollar it sends to Washington in taxes.

By this measure, the District of Columbia, where the federal government spends $7.67 for every tax dollar it collects, and Alaska ($2.60) are the leaders. Among the contiguous 48 states, New Mexico leads with $1.93 in spending for every $1 in taxes.

At the other end of the list is Michigan, which received only 65 cents in spending for every $1 in tax payments. New Jersey and Delaware, at 66 cents, were only a penny out of last place.

Significance: Throughout much of U.S.

history, economic investment, jobs and population have been shifting from the Northeast to the West and South. Virtually every indicator now shows, however, that the shift began to accelerate with unprecedented speed sometime around 1970. Spurred on by federal funds transfers—though other economic factors are equally if not more important—the movement has now reached such momentum in the eyes of a number of Northeastern spokesmen, that the economic underpinnings of the Northeast quadrant are threatened.

The shift has major intergovernmental implications, since the southerly and westerly flow of money and jobs has eroded the tax bases of many state and local governments in the East and Midwest and may force them to raise taxes to prohibitive levels or cut services so drastically that the quality of life would be severely diminished.

One major concern is that high unemployment is likely to persist in the Northeast quadrant, even as the rest of the nation returns to "full employment."

Another factor, according to Ralph R. Widner, former executive director of the Appalachian Regional Commission and now president of the Academy for Contemporary Problems, is that the large cities of the Northeast and Midwest have become "the nation's new cottonfields. . . . The rural poor of the South and elsewhere now reside in the cities of the Northeast."

New York's Gov. Carey said the national economy is intimately interrelated and national economic and spending policies have profound regional implications. "We can no longer allow economic illness to fester in any section of our nation, for, as it festers, it shall spread and in time consume every state and locality."

The Midwestern farm belt gets more

federal dollars for agriculture than the industrialized states of the Northeast—that's no surprise. Neither is it startling that the government spends more for welfare in New York than it does anywhere in the South. And why shouldn't the government spend more for construction of weapons systems in California than anywhere else, since California is the headquarters of the weapons industry?

In each category of spending, the disparities among the states are hardly surprising. But when they are added together and placed alongside the federal tax burden in each state, the results are astonishing indeed.

Kinds of spending: There are four basic ways in which the federal government spends money. Three of them do not lend themselves easily to manipulation aimed at changing the state-by-state distribution of federal dollars.

The government pays salaries to federal workers where the work takes place. The only way to change state-by-state spending for salaries is to move the workers around, not an efficient way to correct regional spending disparities.

Under such programs as social security and welfare, the government makes benefit payments to individuals. These payments occur where the beneficiaries are: the government hardly can move them around.

The government builds things—submarines and sewers, dams and highways—through contracts with private industry, and the choice of a contractor can depend on several different factors.

The decision on where to build a dam or bridge, for example, can rest on geographic and physical considerations alone or be related as well to the political influence exerted by Members of Congress from the area.

For the construction of weapons systems, which absorb most federal contract dollars, a contractor may be selected not only on the basis of whether he can do the job but also on whether the contractor's state or region needs the economic stimulus and on whether the local Member of Congress has sufficient political clout.

But the easiest kind of spending to manipulate is the federal grant. In fiscal 1975, there were 1,030 programs of grants to state and local governments, and the aid was distributed according to a variety of formulas, many of which rely heavily on population. Other factors can include poverty (general revenue sharing), jobless rates (job training) and the number of college students (higher education grants).

Federal grants reached a total of nearly $50 billion in fiscal 1975, or about 15 per cent of the federal budget. It is this 15 per cent that can be used most easily to influence spending among the states. "We are preparing to suggest changes in the formulas governing the 21 biggest grant programs," said James M. Howell, senior vice president of the First National Bank of Boston, which is pressing for more federal dollars for New England.

To the extent that they influence regional spending totals, grant outlays already are helping the Northeast, where they were $260 per capita in fiscal 1975. The West was second at $246, followed by the South at $220 and the Midwest at $197. Grant outlays for individual states ranged from $152 in Illinois to $354 in Wyoming.

Defense: Spending for defense accounts for nearly all the federal spending disparities among the Northeast, Midwest, South and West. The federal government spent $620 per capita for defense in the West, nearly triple the $210 rate of defense spending in the Midwest. Further, there are enormous disparities among the states in both major categories of defense spending: contracts and salaries.

When it contracts with private industry for the weapons systems it needs, the Defense Department makes no effort to distribute its money equitably among the states. "We work with the contractors who will do the best job for the least money," a department spokesman said.

Although the Northeast as a whole is a distant second to the West in spending for defense contracts, the leading state in the nation is Connecticut, where the government spent $763 per capita in fiscal 1975. The General Dynamics Corp. constructs nuclear submarines in Connecticut, and the Pratt & Whitney Aircraft Division of United Technologies Corp. builds engines for fighter planes there.

Next among the 48 continental states is Washington, where the Boeing Co. is a prime supplier for the Air Force. Then comes Mississippi, home of the Ingalls Shipbuilding Division of Litton Industries Inc., which builds destroyers and amphibious assault ships.

The Defense Department spent more money on contracts in California—$8.4 billion—than it did in the entire 12 states of the Midwest. Among the giant defense contractors in California are Aerojet-General Corp., Hughes Aircraft Co., Lockheed Aircraft Corp., Northrop Corp. and Rockwell International Corp.

Spending for defense salaries is high in states with large military bases. As a whole, the South and the West receive more than triple the outlays for defense salaries that go to the Northeast and the Midwest.

Alaska and Hawaii, where there are large military outposts in states with small populations, lead in spending for defense salaries per capita. They are followed by Virginia, which has not only the Pentagon but also the nation's largest naval installation at Norfolk.

Public works: Contracts for various kinds of public works projects also vary widely from region to region, with the Mountain states holding a clear lead. But public works spending is on a much smaller scale than defense spending, and so these variations are less significant than those that result from military contracts and salaries.

National Journal examined spending for the two biggest public works programs—highway and sewer construction—in each state. The Mountain states, where Interstate highway construction still is going on, consistently ranked ahead of the rest of the country in per capita spending for roads and sewers. The government spent $237 per capita in Wyoming, for example, and only $27 per capita in New York.

Many experts regard public works spending as more valuable for the regional economy than most other kinds of domestic spending. Thomas Muller, director of evaluation studies for the Urban Institute, said public works spending helps the development of local business, which may continue after federal spending runs out. He said spending for such income maintenance programs as welfare and social security, which are used largely for necessities, has a lesser impact.

Retirement programs: The federal government spends considerably more money for programs aiding persons who are no longer working because of age or disability. But spending for these kinds of programs is quite even from state to state.

National Journal looked at the money spent by the government in fiscal 1975 for eight retirement programs, including social security, the biggest of all. Spending in almost every state was between $350 and $450 per capita. The only major exception was Florida, the retirement capital of the nation—and even there, spending was only $570 per person.

Welfare: Spending for welfare was high both in states with urban poverty—New York leads the list at $181 per capita in fiscal 1975—and with rural poverty—Mississippi is second at $158 per person.

But a look at the component welfare programs shows a very different mix in the Northern industrialized states as opposed to the Southern states. There are two kinds of programs—those for which poor individuals qualify for federal benefits regardless of action by the states in which they live, and those in which the federal government matches state spending. The food stamp program is an example of the former, while medicaid requires state matching.

In the Northern states as a whole, spending was about equal for the two kinds of programs. In the Northeast, slightly more money was spent for the state matching programs than for those that benefit all poor residents regardless of state spending. But in the South, spending for the programs that require no state action was nearly double what was spent for programs in which federal payments matched state spending.

Other programs: There are many other programs that exhibit large state-by-state spending disparities, but they are considerably smaller than defense and income maintenance programs such as welfare and social security.

Agriculture and rural development programs, amounting to $5 billion in fiscal 1975, nationally, would figure to benefit the farm states of the Northern Plains, and they do, to the tune of $1.7 billion. Spending in the seven Northern Plains states amounted to $108 per person, triple the rate in any other region. At the bottom of the scale were the New England and Mid-Atlantic states, at $7 per

capita, and the Great Lakes states, at $14.

California was the recipient of nearly half the $3.2 billion spent in fiscal 1975 for space, science and technology. That meant $65 per person in California: outlays in this category in 19 other states were zero.

Taxes: If federal spending is distributed unequally among the states, federal taxes tend to make the inequalities even greater. New Mexico is the most startling example: federal spending there is 40 per cent greater than the national average, but New Mexico's share of the federal tax burden is 27 per cent below the national average.

By contrast, even though they get less than their share of federal spending, both the Northeast and the Midwest are under a federal tax burden that is greater than the national average. In the Northeast, federal taxes were 12 per cent greater than the national average in fiscal 1975, while spending was 4 per cent below; in the Midwest, taxes were 5 per cent greater and spending 20 per cent less.

The tax burden on the South, where spending was only 2 per cent below the national average, was 14 per cent less than the nation as a whole. In the West, where spending was 21 per cent ahead of the national average, the tax burden was only 1 per cent higher.

Federal taxes reflect income, and despite the relative deterioration of per capita income in recent years in the Northeast, Midwest and Pacific states, these areas still register higher income levels than the South. The cost of living in most parts of the South is still so much lower than in most Northern states, however, that the income differential may be largely illusory.

Cost of living figures make no difference when federal spending and tax burden are compared for the same state or region. A dollar of spending in Mississippi equals a dollar of taxes in Mississippi, even if it doesn't equal a dollar of spending in New York.

Thus, for every dollar sent to Washington in the form of taxes, New Mexico, for example, received the benefit of $1.93 in federal spending—no matter how much a dollar was worth in New Mexico.

The flow of federal dollars out of the Northeast and Midwest, into the South and West, has potentially explosive political ramifications. Many Northeastern and Midwestern states already have seriously declining economies marked by high unemployment, loss of population and flight of tax-paying and job-providing industries. The resulting financial squeeze on state and local governments in the two regions is producing increased tax burdens and major reductions in government services.

As the seriousness of the situation becomes apparent to the Northeast and Midwest, *Business Week* suggested in its May 17, 1976 edition, a "second war between the states" may emerge.

No one suggests that federal policy is solely responsible for the decline of the older, industrialized states and the attendant economic boom in the newly fabled American "Sunbelt" stretching from Virginia to Southern California. But a number of Northeastern spokesmen, alarmed by the economic hemorrhaging of their region, are beginning to suggest that federal spending patterns are one important reason—an area they might be able to affect by concerted political action.

The southerly and westerly movement of people and wealth caused little concern as long as the older, industrialized states themselves continued to grow economically, the traditional conditions of deep poverty in the South were being corrected, and both the South and West were being opened to investment opportunities welcomed by financial circles in the Northeast and Midwest and were purchasing the major portion of their industrial and consumer supplies from Northeast and Midwest industries.

But within the past five years, the shift appears to have achieved a critical mass, with grave implications for "older" America. The reasons are diverse, ranging from population shifts to the impact of recent recessions, from the cheaper labor available in the South and Southwest to the rise in the cost of energy.

Independence: The economic "coming of age" of the South and Southwest, resulting in growth that is self-sustaining rather than dependent on discretionary investment from outside the region, is a major factor in the national shift.

With increases in its population, the Sunbelt region has seen its markets grow and has attracted new industries and supporting services, thus reducing its dependency on the factories and the services of the Northeast and the Midwest.

Labor: Cheaper labor, weaker unions and less expensive land costs and factory and home construction costs in the Sunbelt states than in the older "frostbelt" region have helped to accelerate the shift.

Between 1969 and 1974, total nonfarm employment rose approximately 20 per cent in the South, 33 per cent in the Mountain states and 13 per cent in the Pacific states. But it increased only 7.1 per cent in New England, 1.8 per cent in the Mid-Atlantic states, 6.1 per cent in the Great Lakes region and 12.7 per cent in the Plains states. Without the Mid-Atlantic's 16 per cent increase in state and local government employment, that region actually would have suffered a total job loss in the 1969–74 period.

Among individual states, New York dropped 1.8 per cent in total nonfarm employment in 1969–74. Illinois gained only 1.4 per cent, Pennsylvania 3.5 per cent. But Arizona gained 44.2 per cent, Colorado 35.1 per cent, Florida 36.5 per cent.

Cumulative figures for manufacturing alone in the 15 years between 1960 and 1975 show a decline of 9.0 per cent in New England and 13.7 per cent in the Mid-Atlantic states, increases of 3.2 per cent in the Great Lakes states and 19.8 per cent in the Pacific states, compared with growth rates of 43.3 per cent and 67.3 per cent in the Southeast and Southwest respectively.

Recent recessions have tended to intensify the manufacturing losses of the Northeast and Midwest. As the Joint Economic Committee notes, these regions "contain the oldest, least efficient manufacturing facilities, which are the first to be closed as production is reduced."

According to Ralph L. Schlossten of the committee staff, each recession since the late 1960s has shown that unemployment figures for the Northeast and Great Lakes regions have risen more precipitously "and come back slower than the other regions of the country or the economy as a whole."

Energy: The nation's 13 major energy-producing states (oil, gas or coal) are all, with the exception of Indiana and Ohio, located in the South or West—Oklahoma, Texas, Louisiana, West Virginia, Utah, New Mexico, Alabama, Arkansas, Montana, Wyoming and Tennessee.

Schlossten observed: "For the foreseeable future—at least 10 or 15 years—the energy states will have a great economic advantage." The reason, he suggested, rests not only on the boost to local economies provided by energy-producing minerals with far higher prices than in the past, but also on the fact that the energy-producing states, through severance taxes

Harry Reol—Black Star

Housing developments sprawl across Arizona, one of the fastest growing states in the southwest.

on mineral extraction, are able to "export" their tax burdens to less fortunate states and regions.

Population: The shift of people among the regions has occurred at an accelerated rate in recent years. Between 1960 and 1970, the population of the South and West grew by 14.2 and 24.1 per cent respectively. But the Northeast, with a 9.7 per cent growth figure, and the Midwest, at 9.6 per cent, felt no immediate cause for concern.

Between 1970 and 1975, however, the population growth differentials from region to region became far more dramatic: an 8.4 per cent increase in the South and 8.7 per cent in the West, but only 0.8 per cent in the Northeast and 1.9 per cent in the Midwest. Population growth in the Pacific states was a relatively moderate 6.4 per cent, but stood at 16.3 per cent in the Mountain states. By comparison, the population of the nation as a whole grew by 4.8 per cent over that period.

Total population in the five-year period rose 23.0 per cent in Florida, 9.3 per cent in Texas, 25.3 per cent in Arizona and 14.7 per cent in Colorado—

but it actually declined 0.7 per cent in New York and 2.4 per cent in Rhode Island, and grew by only 2.4 per cent in Massachusetts, 0.2 per cent in Pennsylvania, 0.3 per cent in Illinois, 3.1 per cent in Michigan, and 1.0 per cent in Ohio.

According to figures compiled by Muller of the Urban Institute, based on Census data and his own estimates, all states in the Northeast and Midwest, with the exception of Maine and New Hampshire, either had no net migration movement or experienced out-migration between 1973 and 1975. Net out-migration from these regions totaled more than 2.5 million persons in 1970-75 — twice the rate of the previous five years. For example, New York, which had a net migration loss of 212,000 during the 1960s, lost 554,000 people in 1970-75 alone. New Jersey, which had a net in-migration of 454,000 in 1960-70, lost 44,000 in 1970-75.

By contrast, all states in the South and West except Delaware, Louisiana and Maryland gained population from immigration as well as from natural increases in 1970-75.

The dramatic falloff in black migration from the South to the North since 1970 has thrown into bold relief a long-term out-migration of the white population in the Northeast and Midwest. During the 1960s, for instance, the Census showed a net out-migration among whites of 1.3 per cent in the Northeast and 2.6 per cent in the Midwest. But those regions experienced a net black in-migration of 20.2 per cent and 11.1 per cent respectively — thus averting an over-all population loss.

Since 1970, it appears that the white out-migration from the Northeast and Midwest has continued and accelerated, while black in-migration has fallen off to a trickle.

But the black northward migration that does continue, together with Puerto Rican and other Latin American immigration, burdens the older regions of the nation with a less-educated, frequently dependent population — even while the southerly and southwesterly flow of an educated, managerial-scientific-technical and taxpaying white middle class continues or gathers momentum.

Thus the Northeast and Midwest gain dependent, low tax-paying populations and lose significant numbers of middle-class taxpayers; the South and West gain taxpaying residents. Taxes, as a result, go up in the Northeast and Midwest, but can be held more stable, because of the broadening tax base, in the growing regions.

For the nation's older regions and particularly their large cities, Schlosstein notes, "you have a situation of an almost self-feeding decline. Jobs, income and retail sales decline somewhat. So taxes go up, and people and jobs flee. It's a very difficult cycle to interrupt. New York's situation is not the worst of the older cities at all. If you look at the socio-economic base of places like Newark or Cleveland, Hartford or Baltimore, they are economically in worse shape than New York."

Northern and Midwestern policy makers — seeing the fortunes of their regions in decline — are beginning to seek a change in the federal policies that favor the South and Southwest at the expense of the Northeast and Midwest.

Change will require concerted regional action, they realize. But except in New England, regional cooperation generally remains an elusive goal for these strongly independent states.

Politicians and regional economists alike agree that the Northeast and Midwest will have to act soon because their relative population declines are ending their political power base.

56.

Martin Kaplan: The Ideologies of Tough Times

"In the sixties we were radicals; in the seventies we tended our own gardens . . ."
remarks the author of this selection, himself a recent PhD whose student days
spanned portions of two remarkably different decades, as different in their own way
as the Jazz Age 1920s differed from the Depression Thirties. The 1960s, the
"country of the young," were years of turbulent change, moral revolution, protest,
and nonconforming conformism. The Seventies pose a striking contrast in the mood of
the country and in the attitudes of the student generations of the respective decades.
In the article from which this selection is taken, Kaplan describes the rapid change
that has taken place in the values of American youth. He did his undergraduate
work at Harvard and received his doctorate from Stanford University.

Source: *Change*, August 1976.

TRASHING THE SIXTIES has become the initiation fee of the new right-center chic sweeping "serious" American culture. Any revisionist account of history, whether from the right or the left, is a kind of "Just So" story. It proceeds from what apparently happened to what "really" happened, from the official version to the underlying causes, from the symptoms to the origins. Rather than "How the Tiger Got Its Stripes," Midge Decter in *Liberal Parents, Radical Children* gives us "How the Radical Got His Ideology." She explains the sixties — dope, sex, communes, dropping out of school, and the critique of middle-class values — as the product of a child-rearing system gone haywire. Where my grandparents' generation fearlessly enforced the ethic of work, competition, individualism, trial, endurance, and accommodation, my parents' generation, according to Decter, fell under the sway of ersatz progressive values. Their Dr. Spock, their cult of self-realization, their indulgence, their fear of punishing, their liberal culture — all these

promoted in us, the children, a paralysis that renders us intellectual and moral cripples. And so what appear to be our assertions of social criticism, our ways of resisting and revising the society we will inherit, are actually the symptoms of our neurosis. . . .

I'd be delighted to admit that much of the rhetoric of America's young in the sixties was shockingly undistinguished — though no more so than, say, the speeches of its last three Presidents. I'd be happy to concede that some radicals were opportunistic — though no more so than, say, the corporate and military captains of the same period. I'd be more than willing to grant that the apologists for the nation's "greening" were an intellectual embarrassment — though no more so than, say, the elegant rationales delivered by the best and the brightest. I'd be perfectly content to deplore the decadence and irresponsibility of the hippie withdrawal to drugs and the post-hippie withdrawal to the California crafts farm — though no more so than, say, the middle class's addictions to valium and material consumption. But I refuse to accept Decter's tacit premise: that, in a conflict between self and society, it is accommodation of self to society that is the hallmark of adulthood. Is it too much to expect of our educations that they equip us with the skill to distinguish between disappointed whim and systematic frustration? Is it too much to hope of our parents that they enable us to move from a fairy-tale childhood where Mother and Father Know Best to a young adulthood in which a reasonable dialectic of critique and response takes the place of unimpeachable authority? Is it too much to want from our society that it allow us to distinguish work from drudgery, meaning from habit, commitment from cocktail banter, and whining from justified rage? . . .

Not too long ago, "absolutism," as a description of an ethical paradigm, carried little pejorative freight. There has always been a way of looking at the world in which, whenever questions of judgment arise, whenever one is called upon to sort, discriminate, choose, and assess worth, the ability to perform these essentially ethical maneuvers ineluctably depends on some higher, transcendent principles. Whether the sanctions for choices derive from God, parents, the Wisdom of Tradition, Reason, or the State, what characterizes all absolutist positions is the ability to separate right from wrong, good from bad. That ability might be imperfectly exercised, and the perceptions of its transcendent sources might be dishearteningly partial, but there was to be no mistaking that the choices made were suprapersonal, unfettered by local accidents of time, place, or idiosyncrasy. As it was seemly that generally unimpeachable authority accompany the exercise of values such as these, it was inevitable that the overwhelming rejection of transcendent wisdom that occurred in the sixties—the time of puberty and adolescence for today's college students—should have occasioned so much horror. . . .

Unfortunately, there was also available a far easier response to the decline of the old hegemonies than the assumption of critical responsibility. Relativism came into its own. Its message is conveyed by Andrew Greeley's too broad generalization: "The older generation didn't believe in anything." What he should have said was, "Many people, young and old, believed in no principles broader than local self-interest." The cult of the self was chosen over the rigors of collective insight. For relativists, if nothing can be eternally and objectively the case, then nothing at all—not even standards critically examined, historically bound, and consensually attained—can be the case. In such a relativized world any ideals are reduced to the mere personal ideological claims that they are seen to represent. Everyone is out for his own good, his own thing. At its bleakest, relativism brings torpor, nihilism, meaninglessness: humanity as a mass of impotent cockroaches. When not pressed to this dark extreme, relativism is opportunism and expedience, the core of the decadent hippie ideology whose "liberation" has so often been mistaken for the liberating responsibilities of radical criticism. This decadence springs in part from solipsistic origins. [John Lennon's song "God"], after sweeping out the old gods in a flurry of moral housekeeping, finally retreats from the burden of critical work and hibernates: He believes, finally, only in himself. . . .

By nearly all accounts, what seems to be occurring now in the schools and colleges is a competitiveness, a precocious careerism, an academic utilitarianism that surpasses even Decter's wildest hopes.

Young people today seem to want nothing more than to be told what to do, think, believe, and cherish by their teachers, so that they may dutifully regurgitate those approved facts and values, so that, in turn, the society in which they want so desperately to succeed will duly reward them. When they are not absorbed with making it, they are busily lending credence to the iconographic montage of society's seventies child: streaking, boozing, and—in a moment of sheer terminological inspiration—dancing "the hustle."

Preprofessional and prevocational courses are burgeoning everywhere. Authoritarian teaching methods and curricula once again seem seductive, gratifying, and plausible. Where they have not perished entirely, the liberal arts have become a service industry providing moral software for their more practically minded disciplinary brethren. In an almost dim past, the humanities were a repressive regimen, an unquestionably beneficent drum roll of great texts to measure up to. Just a while ago, there were many who hoped that the study of art and literature could be an occasion to learn critical responsibility, to confront society's characteristic ways of defining meaning and worth. Now, later still, the attempt to keep alive the humanities in the midst of the hustle ethic's renaissance is a barely disguised, institutionally condoned dilettantism: Rather than physics for poets and rocks for jocks, today the catalog lists poetry for physicists and lit for lawyers. Soon, perhaps, we may educate a fleet of advertising executives whose ads for vaginal deodorants will be festooned with faultlessly chosen Dickensian caricatures. Soon, perhaps, the boardrooms of our multinational corporations will be merrily alive with allusions to Marcuse; already, after all, they are hung with Mondrians.

When reasons are sought for the new careerism, we obediently trot out our recently acquired and already threadbare Marxist savoir faire in order to provide—ah!—an economic analysis. Inflation, recession, unemployment, the unmarketable liberal arts BA, Bureau of Labor Statistics figures, allocation of scarce resources, OPEC: Laying bare the fiscal roots of this new lust for serving authority and making it pay off is part of our intellectual cocktail party repertoire. Intoning what have become common-sense notions of economic cause and effect, we explain that a wise student today realizes that he —or, God forbid, she—will have a tough time of it when the privilege of the university's fiscal shelter has ended. Most good jobs—interesting, professional, well paid despite inflation, secure despite recession—today require some special post-collegiate training. Faced with the prospect of being screened by yet another admissions committee and, later, by the prospective employer, these students know that their dossiers are being stacked up against an ever growing number of other dossiers. To excel amid this competition, they psych out the achievements most likely to be rewarded; that is, they intuit the values of those committees and do their best to match them, legitimize and confirm them, and, occasionally, surpass them. They rack up A's to show hard work and drive. The pattern of their hardware-oriented courses is an arrowhead leading toward a specific vocational path. And they toss in a literature survey or a bout with music appreciation in answer to some faint Ivy League inner echo about the virtues of being well-rounded. These students are doing what makes sense: Academic five-year planning and student consumerism pay off. And hell, aren't all those radicals doing corporate law somewhere anyway?

In the seventies the new conformists, perhaps soon to be our new professional class, have chosen relativism as the best game in town. Instead of doubt, irony, inquiry, and foolish dreams, the dreams that made their older brothers and sisters cry, they have chosen the rewards of privatism, self-fulfillment, personal gratification, individualistic autonomy, and the burgherly hearthside virtues of coping, acquiescence, and accommodation. They are the real flower children of the seventies; their ontology is clear and crisp: "Yoko and me, that's reality." They haven't acceded dumbly to this world vision; it's the key moral tactic for the decade. They've chosen cynical relativism as the shrewdest strategy for operating within our premised economy; in so many ways, their choice is a wise one. With some persistence and some luck, they'll be financially rewarded. They'll acquire, perhaps, all the comforts of home: children to replace them, friends they like, tasteful possessions, healthy bodies, a yen for foreign food and old movies.

What they will lack is the dimension of outrage, the capacity to thunder "No" when some injustice has been wrought on something other than their own self-interests. What they will lack is the noisome drive to meddle, to risk their stability, to jeopardize their cherished assumptions, to doubt the worth of their ethos, to reassess their goals. Criticism, for them, will not be a burdensome responsibility. They will rarely sense that anything amiss beyond the perimeters of their lives exerts moral demands upon them. Few things larger than the achievement of their personally set goals will obtrude on their purposefulness. They will view conscience as an utterly private matter, and consensus as the *politesse* of the ballot box.

Their experiences of culture will be self-selected; by and large, they will enjoy those works whose tacit values and perceptions tend to confirm and legitimize the choices they have already made. Little will be at stake in their encounters with art; no requirement other than entertainment — albeit somewhat exclusive, witty, "better" entertainment — will be exacted from their diversions. From their government they will ask laissez-faire; from their God they will want succor when their ends are thwarted; from their school systems, they will expect a service industry, providing the socialization that brings order, the skill-training that brings profit, and the moral education that ensures replication. Chances are, they will have their way. . . .

Sad to say, one is hard pressed to point to more than a handful of disciplines in which it is considered proper to make value judgments, advocate moral and political positions, use words like "good" and "bad" or "conscience" and "dignity," explore the realm of personal choices, raise existential questions, be self-critical, or jeopardize the premises of one's discipline, pedagogy, institution, or career. The victories of the scientific point of view and the guild structure are very nearly total. Value-freedom has become a kind of postulate throughout the university. Genteel liberal pluralism, academic freedom, and the right to self-determination are the rationales most regularly offered for avoiding advocacy stances. Most teachers, if pressed to identify the moral suppositions that underpin their work, would mumble something about Cardinal Newman or Matthew Arnold and hope you would please leave them alone.

To succumb to this, goaded on by the stick of tough times, is an unconscionable abnegation. But for those to whom critical responsibility matters, and for whom "the sixties" and even "teacher" are really only convenient metaphoric shorthands — for those moral nudnicks, three questions urge to be asked: What are the value assumptions of my profession and my discipline? What ought those assumptions to be? How can I work to get to that "ought"?

Nothing is sadder to admit about American universities today than that these three questions would be generally regarded as hostile, irrelevant, and pointless by most faculty members, junior and senior. Nothing deepens the gloom of that admission more than the recognition that most undergraduates, too, would find these questions rhetorical, tedious, and off the wall. We strange survivors in a reactionary time determined to trash the decade that validated our queer ethical intensities — these three questions are where we live our professional lives.

What structures of personal relationships and hard funds could best serve our asking these questions is itself a topic for debate. Perhaps we need more socially legitimized occasions on which we might ask our tenured and value-free colleagues, Why does your discipline have the boundary lines it does? What constitutes a good argument in your field? A scored point? A breakthrough? What are the criteria for professional advancement, for assessing greatness? Why are you a teacher, anyway? What does the creden-tial you award mean to you, your student, your society? Who are your students, what is the nature of your authority in the university, and who has a say in determining your responsibilities toward those whom you teach?

Perhaps we need more techniques for worrying our students. We could use more ways to interrupt the unimpeded flow of fact from us to them, more ways to intervene and meddle in their moral lives, more ways to focus their attention on some questions that education seems recently to have forgotten — questions like, Who am I? and, Where do I want to go? and, What do I believe?

We scarcely need reminding that those questions ought properly to be addressed to ourselves as well. It is not enough to reject the pop sociology media montage that threatens to shape our historical self-image, though that rejection is an important one. It is not enough to combat the new revisionist stereotypes of social determinism, though that effort calls for keen energies. It is not enough to qualify the icy ahistoric universals of life cycles, though the resistance to latent ideologies of resignation requires a certain good-humored vigilance. What we also need to do is explore the terrain of inquiry suggested by the critically acknowledged limitations of our own vision.

◆

I had believed in intellectuals, whether they were my teachers or my friends or strangers whose books I had read. This is inexplicable to a younger generation, who look upon the 1930s radical and the 1930s Red-baiter with equal amusement. I don't much enjoy their amusement, but they have some right to it. As I now have some right to disappointment in what the good children of the Sixties have come to.

Lillian Hellman, *Scoundrel Time,* 1976

57.

Senate Committee Findings on Illegal Intelligence Activities

In December 1974, the New York Times *published a series of articles by Seymour M. Hersh about spying on American citizens by the Central Intelligence Agency. Subsequent to these revelations, the U. S. Senate, on January 17, 1975, established a select committee under chairman Frank Church to study illegal intelligence activities by agencies of the Federal Government. On April 26, 1976, the committee published the report of its fifteen-month investigation and urged Congress to adopt a law that would create charters for the majority of such agencies to limit the use of covert action as a tool of foreign policy. The multi-volume final report covered the work of all the major investigative agencies and made specific recommendations regarding each. This selection reprints a portion of the report concerning domestic spying on American citizens. Such surveillance, as many news stories have reported, was also undertaken by police forces of several cities and states.*

Source: *Intelligence Activities and the Rights of Americans.* Book II. Final Report of the Select Committee to Study Governmental Operations with respect to Intelligence Activities. April 26, 1976. Washington D. C. "Introduction and Summary."

THE RESOLUTION creating this Committee placed greatest emphasis on whether intelligence activities threaten the "rights of American citizens."

The critical question before the Committee was to determine how the fundamental liberties of the people can be maintained in the course of the Government's effort to protect their security. The delicate balance between these basic goals of our system of government is often difficult to strike, but it can, and must, be achieved. We reject the view that the traditional American principles of justice and fair play have no place in our struggle against the enemies of freedom. Moreover, our investigation has established that the targets of intelligence activity have ranged far beyond persons who could properly be characterized as enemies of freedom and have extended to a wide array of citizens engaging in lawful activity.

Americans have rightfully been concerned since before World War II about the dangers of hostile foreign agents likely to commit acts of espionage. Similarly, the violent acts of political terrorists can seriously endanger the rights of Americans. Carefully focused intelligence investigations can help prevent such acts.

But too often intelligence has lost this focus and domestic intelligence activities have invaded individual privacy and violated the rights of lawful assembly and political expression. Unless new and tighter controls are established by legislation, domestic intelligence activities threaten to undermine our democratic society and fundamentally alter its nature.

We have examined three types of "intelligence" activities affecting the rights of American citizens. The first is intelligence collection—such as infiltrating groups with informants, wiretapping, or opening letters. The second is dissemination of material which has been collected. The third is covert action designed to disrupt and discredit the activities of groups and individuals deemed a threat to the social order.

These three types of "intelligence" activity are closely related in the practical world. Information which is disseminated by the intelligence community or used in disruptive programs has usually been obtained through surveillance. Nevertheless, a division between collection, dissemination and covert action is analytically useful both in understanding why excesses have occurred in the past and in devising remedies to prevent those excesses from recurring. . . .

The Questions

We have directed our investigation toward answering the following questions:

Which governmental agencies have engaged in domestic spying?

How many citizens have been targets of Governmental intelligence activity?

What standards have governed the opening of intelligence investigations and when have intelligence investigations been terminated?

Where have the targets fit on the spectrum between those who commit violent criminal acts and those who seek only to dissent peacefully from Government policy?

To what extent has the information collected included intimate details of the targets' personal lives or their political views, and has such information been disseminated and used to injure individuals?

What actions beyond surveillance have intelligence agencies taken, such as attempting to disrupt, discredit, or destroy persons or groups who have been the targets of surveillance?

Have intelligence agencies been used to serve the political aims of Presidents, other high officials, or the agencies themselves?

How have the agencies responded either to proper orders or to excessive pressures from their superiors? To what extent have intelligence agencies disclosed, or concealed them from, outside bodies charged with overseeing them?

Have intelligence agencies acted outside the law? What has been the attitude of the intelligence community toward the rule of law?

To what extent has the Executive branch and the Congress controlled intelligence agencies and held them accountable? Generally, how well has the Federal system of checks and balances between the branches worked to control intelligence activity?

Summary of the Main Problems

The answer to each of these questions is disturbing. Too many people have been spied upon by too many Government agencies and too much information has been collected. The Government has often undertaken the secret surveillance of citizens on the basis of their political beliefs, even when those beliefs posed no threat of violence or illegal acts on behalf of a hostile foreign power. The Government, operating primarily through secret informants, but also using other intrusive techniques such as wiretaps, microphone "bugs," surreptitious mail opening, and break-ins, has swept in vast amounts of information about the personal lives, views, and associations of American citizens. Investigations of groups deemed potentially dangerous—and even of groups suspected of associating with potentially dangerous organizations—have continued for decades, despite the fact that those groups did not engage in unlawful activity. Groups and individuals have been harassed and disrupted because of their political views and their lifestyles.

Investigations have been based upon vague standards whose breadth made excessive collection inevitable. Unsavory and vicious tactics have been employed—including anonymous attempts to break up marriages, disrupt meetings, ostracize persons from their professions, and provoke target groups into rivalries that might result in deaths. Intelligence agencies have served the political and personal objectives of presidents and other high officials. While the agencies often committed excesses in response to pressure from high officials in the Executive branch and Congress, they also occasionally initiated improper activities and then concealed them from officials whom they had a duty to inform

Governmental officials—including those whose principal duty is to enforce the law—have violated or ignored the law over long periods of time and have advocated and defended their right to break the law.

The Constitutional system of checks and balances has not adequately controlled intelligence activities. Until recently the Executive branch has neither delineated the scope of permissible activities nor established procedures for supervising intelligence agencies. Congress has failed to exercise sufficient oversight, seldom questioning the use to which its appropriations were being put. Most domestic intelligence issues have not reached the courts, and in those cases when they have reached the courts, the judiciary has been reluctant to grapple with them.

Each of these points is briefly illustrated below. . . .

1. *The Number of People Affected by Domestic Intelligence Activity*

United States intelligence agencies have investigated a vast number of American citizens and domestic organizations. FBI headquarters alone has developed over 500,000 domestic intelligence files, and these have been augmented by additional files at FBI Field Offices. The FBI opened 65,000 of these domestic intelligence files in 1972 alone. In fact, substantially more individuals and groups are subject to intelligence scrutiny than the number of files would appear to indicate, since typically, each domestic intelligence file contains information on more than one individual or group, and this information is readily retrievable through the FBI General Name Index.

The number of Americans and domestic groups caught in the domestic intelligence net is further illustrated by the following statistics:

—Nearly a quarter of a million first class letters were opened and photographed in the United States by the CIA between 1953–1973, producing a CIA computerized index of nearly one and one-half million names.

—At least 130,000 first class letters were opened and photographed by the FBI between 1940–1966 in eight U.S. cities.

—Some 300,000 individuals were indexed in a CIA computer system and separate files were created on approximately 7,200 Americans and over 100 domestic groups during the course of CIA's Operation CHAOS (1967–1973).

—Millions of private telegrams sent from, to, or through the United States were obtained by the National Security Agency from 1947 to 1975 under a secret arrangement with three United States telegraph companies.

—An estimated 100,000 Americans were the subjects of United States Army intelligence files created between the mid-1960's and 1971.

—Intelligence files on more than 11,-000 individuals and groups were created by the Internal Revenue Service between 1969 and 1973 and tax investigations were started on the basis of political rather than tax criteria.

— At least 26,000 individuals were at one point catalogued on an FBI list of persons to be rounded up in the event of a "national emergency."

2. Too Much Information Is Collected For Too Long

Intelligence agencies have collected vast amounts of information about the intimate details of citizens' lives and about their participation in legal and peaceful political activities. The targets of intelligence activity have included political adherents of the right and the left, ranging from activist to casual supporters. Investigations have been directed against proponents of racial causes and women's rights, outspoken apostles of nonviolence and racial harmony; establishment politicians; religious groups; and advocates of new lifestyles. The widespread targeting of citizens and domestic groups, and the excessive scope of the collection of information, is illustrated by the following examples:

(a) The "Women's Liberation Movement" was infiltrated by informants who collected material about the movement's policies, leaders, and individual members. One report included the name of every woman who attended meetings, and another stated that each woman at a meeting had described "how she felt oppressed, sexually or otherwise." Another report concluded that the movement's purpose was to "free women from the humdrum existence of being only a wife and mother," but still recommended that the intelligence investigation should be continued.

(b) A prominent civil rights leader and advisor to Dr. Martin Luther King, Jr., was investigated on the suspicion that he might be a Communist "sympathizer." The FBI field office concluded he was not. Bureau headquarters directed that the investigation continue — using a theory of "guilty until proven innocent:"

The Bureau does not agree with the expressed belief of the field office that ---------------- is not sympathetic to the Party cause. While there may not be any evidence that ---------- is a Communist neither is there any substantial evidence that he is anti-Communist.

(c) FBI sources reported on the formation of the Conservative American Christian Action Council in 1971. In the 1950's, the Bureau collected information about the John Birch Society and passed it to the White House because of the Society's "scurrilous attack" on President Eisenhower and other high Government officials.

(d) Some investigations of the lawful activities of peaceful groups have continued for decades. For example, the NAACP was investigated to determine whether it "had connections with" the Communist Party. The investigation lasted for over twenty-five years, although nothing was found to rebut a report during the first year of the investigation that the NAACP had a "strong tendency" to "steer clear of Communist activities." Similarly, the FBI has admitted that the Socialist Workers Party has committed no criminal acts. Yet the Bureau has investigated the Socialist Workers Party for more than three decades on the basis of its revolutionary rhetoric — which the FBI concedes falls short of incitement to violence — and its claimed international links. The Bureau is currently using its informants to collect information about SWP members' political views, including those on "U.S. involvement in Angola," "food prices," "racial matters," the "Vietnam War," and about any of their efforts to support non-SWP candidates for political office.

(e) National political leaders fell within the broad reach of intelligence investigations. For example, Army Intelligence maintained files on Senator Adlai Stevenson and Congressman Abner Mikva because of their participation in peaceful political meetings under surveillance by Army agents. A letter to Richard Nixon, while he was a candidate for President in 1968, was intercepted under CIA's mail opening program. In the 1960's President Johnson asked the FBI to compare various Senators' statements on Vietnam with the Communist Party line and to conduct name checks on leading antiwar Senators.

(f) As part of their effort to collect information which "related even remotely" to people or groups "active" in communities which had "the potential" for civil disorder, Army intelligence agencies took such steps as: sending agents to a Halloween party for elementary school children in Washington, D.C., because they suspected a local "dissident" might be present; monitoring protests of welfare mothers' organizations in Milwaukee; infiltrating a coalition of church youth groups in Colorado; and sending agents to a priests' conference in Washington, D.C., held to discuss birth control measures.

(g) In the late 1960's and early 1970's, student groups were subjected to intense scrutiny. In 1970 the FBI ordered investigations of every member of the Students for a Democratic Society and of "every Black Student Union and similar group regardless of their past or present involvement in disorders." Files were opened on thousands of young men and women so that, as the former head of FBI intelligence explained, the information could be used if they ever applied for a government job.

In the 1960's Bureau agents were instructed to increase their efforts to discredit "New Left" student demonstrators by tactics including publishing photographs ("naturally the most obnoxious picture should be used"), using "misinformation" to falsely notify members events had been cancelled, and writing "telltale" letters to students' parents.

(h) The FBI Intelligence Division commonly investigated any indication that "subversive" groups already under investigation were seeking to influence or control other groups. One example of the extreme breadth of this "infiltration" theory was an FBI instruction in the mid-1960's to all Field Offices to investigate every "free university" because some of them had come under "subversive influence."

(i) Each administration from Franklin D. Roosevelt's to Richard Nixon's permitted, and sometimes encouraged, government agencies to handle essentially political intelligence. For example:

—President Roosevelt asked the FBI to put in its files the names of citizens sending telegrams to the White House opposing his "national defense" policy and supporting Col. Charles Lindbergh.

—President Truman received inside information on a former Roosevelt aide's efforts to influence his appointments, labor union negotiating plans, and the publishing plans of journalists.

—President Eisenhower received reports on purely political and social contacts with foreign officials by Bernard Baruch, Mrs. Eleanor Roosevelt, and Supreme Court Justice William O. Douglas.

—The Kennedy Administration had the FBI wiretap a Congressional staff member, three executive officials, a lobbyist, and a Washington law firm. Attorney General Robert F. Kennedy received the fruits of an FBI "tap" on Martin Luther King, Jr., and a "bug" on a Congressman both of which yielded information of a political nature.

— President Johnson asked the FBI to conduct "name checks" of his critics and of members of the staff of his 1964 opponent, Senator Barry Goldwater. He also requested purely political intelligence on his critics in the Senate, and received extensive intelligence reports on political activity at the 1964 Democratic Convention from FBI electronic surveillance.

— President Nixon authorized a program of wiretaps which produced for the White House purely political or personal information unrelated to national security, including information about a Supreme Court justice.

3. *Covert Action and the Use of Illegal or Improper Means*

(a) *Covert Action* — Apart from uncovering excesses in the collection of intelligence, our investigation has disclosed covert actions directed against Americans, and the use of illegal and improper surveillance techniques to gather information. For example:

(i) The FBI's COINTELPRO — counterintelligence program — was designed to "disrupt" groups and "neutralize" individuals deemed to be threats to domestic security. The FBI resorted to counterintelligence tactics in part because its chief officials believed that the existing law could not control the activities of certain dissident groups, and that court decisions had tied the hands of the intelligence community. Whatever opinion one holds about the policies of the targeted groups, many of the tactics employed by the FBI were indisputably degrading to a free society. COINTELPRO tactics included:

— Anonymously attacking the political beliefs of targets in order to induce their employers to fire them;

— Anonymously mailing letters to the spouses of intelligence targets for the purpose of destroying their marriages;

— Obtaining from IRS the tax returns of a target and then attempting to provoke an IRS investigation for the express purpose of deterring a protest leader from attending the Democratic National Convention;

— Falsely and anonymously labeling as Government informants members of groups known to be violent, thereby exposing the falsely labelled member to expulsion or physical attack;

— Pursuant to instructions to use "misinformation" to disrupt demonstrations, employing such means as broadcasting fake orders on the same citizens band radio frequency used by demonstration marshals to attempt to control demonstrations, and duplicating and falsely filling out forms soliciting housing for persons coming to a demonstration, thereby causing "long and useless journeys to locate these addresses";

— Sending an anonymous letter to the leader of a Chicago street gang (described as "violence-prone") stating that the Black Panthers were supposed to have "a hit out for you." The letter was suggested because it "may intensify . . . animosity" and cause the street gang leader to "take retaliatory action."

(ii) From "late 1963" until his death in 1968, Martin Luther King, Jr., was the target of an intensive campaign by the Federal Bureau of Investigation to "neutralize" him as an effective civil rights leader. In the words of the man in charge of the FBI's "war" against Dr. King, "No holds were barred."

The FBI gathered information about Dr. King's plans and activities through an extensive surveillance program, employing nearly every intelligence-gathering technique at the Bureau's disposal in order to obtain information about the "private activities of Dr. King and his advisors" to use to "completely discredit" them.

The program to destroy Dr. King as the leader of the civil rights movement included efforts to discredit him with Executive branch officials, Congressional leaders, foreign heads of state, American ambassadors, churches, universities, and the press.

The FBI mailed Dr. King a tape recording made from microphones hidden in his hotel rooms which one agent testified was an attempt to destroy Dr. King's marriage. The tape recording was accompanied by a note which Dr. King and his advisors interpreted as threatening to release the tape recording unless Dr. King committed suicide.

The extraordinary nature of the campaign to discredit Dr. King is evident from two documents:

— At the August 1963 March on Washington, Dr. King told the country of his "dream" that:

all of God's children, black men and white men, Jews and Gentiles, Protestants and Catholics, will be able to join hands and sing in the words of the old Negro spiritual, "Free at last, free at last, thank God Almighty, I'm free at last."

The Bureau's Domestic Intelligence Division concluded that this "demagogic speech" established Dr. King as the "most dangerous and effective Negro leader in the country." Shortly afterwards, and within days after Dr. King was named "Man of the Year" by *Time* magazine, the FBI decided to "take him off his pedestal," reduce him completely in influence, and select and promote its own candidate to "assume the role of the leadership of the Negro people."

— In early 1968, Bureau headquarters

explained to the field that Dr. King must be destroyed because he was seen as a potential "messiah" who could "unify and electrify" the "black nationalist movement." Indeed, to the FBI he was a potential threat because he might "abandon his supposed 'obedience' to white liberal doctrines (non-violence)." In short, a non-violent man was to be secretly attacked and destroyed as insurance against his abandoning non-violence.

(b) *Illegal or Improper Means.* — The surveillance which we investigated was not only vastly excessive in breadth and a basis for degrading counterintelligence actions, but was also often conducted by illegal or improper means. For example:

(1) For approximately 20 years the CIA carried out a program of indiscriminately opening citizens' first class mail. The Bureau also had a mail opening program, but cancelled it in 1966. The Bureau continued, however, to receive the illegal fruits of CIA's program. In 1970, the heads of both agencies signed a document for President Nixon, which correctly stated that mail opening was illegal, falsely stated that it had been discontinued, and proposed that the illegal opening of mail should be resumed because it would provide useful results. The President approved the program, but withdrew his approval five days later. The illegal opening continued nonetheless. Throughout this period CIA officials knew that mail opening was illegal, but expressed concern about the "flap potential" of exposure, not about the illegality of their activity.

(2) From 1947 until May 1975, NSA received from international cable companies millions of cables which had been sent by American citizens in the reasonable expectation that they would be kept private.

(3) Since the early 1930's, intelligence

agencies have frequently wiretapped and bugged American citizens without the benefit of judicial warrant. Recent court decisions have curtailed the use of these techniques against domestic targets. But past subjects of these surveillances have included a United State Congressman, a Congressional staff member, journalists and newsmen, and numerous individuals and groups who engaged in no criminal activity and who posed no genuine threat to the national security, such as two White House domestic affairs advisers and an anti-Vietnam War protest group. While the prior written approval of the Attorney General has been required for all warrantless wiretaps since 1940, the record is replete with instances where this requirement was ignored and the Attorney General gave only after-the-fact authorization.

Until 1965, microphone surveillance by intelligence agencies was wholly unregulated in certain classes of cases. Within weeks after a 1954 Supreme Court decision denouncing the FBI's installation of a microphone in a defendant's bedroom, the Attorney General informed the Bureau that he did not believe the decision applied to national security cases and permitted the FBI to continue to install microphones subject only to its own "intelligent restraint."

(4) In several cases, purely political information (such as the reaction of Congress to an Administration's legislative proposal) and purely personal information (such as coverage of the extra-marital social activities of a high-level Executive official under surveillance) was obtained from electronic surveillance and disseminated to the highest levels of the federal government.

(5) Warrantless break-ins have been conducted by intelligence agencies since World War II. During the 1960's alone,

the FBI and CIA conducted hundreds of break-ins, many against American citizens and domestic organizations. In some cases, these break-ins were to install microphones; in other cases, they were to steal such items as membership lists from organizations considered "subversive" by the Bureau.

(6) The most pervasive surveillance technique has been the informant. In a random sample of domestic intelligence cases, 83% involved informants and 5% involved electronic surveillance. Informants have been used against peaceful, law-abiding groups; they have collected information about personal and political views and activities. To maintain their credentials in violence-prone groups, informants have involved themselves in violent activity. This phenomenon is well illustrated by an informant in the Klan. He was present at the murder of a civil rights worker in Mississippi and subsequently helped to solve the crime and convict the perpetrators. Earlier, however, while performing duties paid for by the Government, he had previously "beaten people severely, had boarded buses and kicked people, had [gone] into restaurants and beaten them [blacks] with blackjacks, chains, pistols." Although the FBI requires agents to instruct informants that they cannot be involved in violence, it was understood that in the Klan, "he couldn't be an angel and be a good informant."

4. Ignoring the Law

Officials of the intelligence agencies occasionally recognized that certain activities were illegal, but expressed concern only for "flap potential." Even more disturbing was the frequent testimony that the law and the Constitution were simply ignored. For example, the author of the so-called Huston plan testified:

Question. Was there any person who

stated that the activity recommended, which you have previously identified as being illegal opening of the mail and breaking and entry or burglary—was there any single person who stated that such activity should not be done because it was unconstitutional?

Answer. No.

Question. Was there any single person who said such activity should not be done because it was illegal?

Answer. No.

Similarly, the man who for ten years headed FBI's Intelligence Division testified that:

> . . . never once did I hear anybody, including myself, raise the question: "Is this course of action which we have agreed upon lawful, is it legal, is it ethical or moral." We never gave any thought to this line of reasoning, because we were just naturally pragmatic.

Although the statutory law and the Constitution were often not "[given] a thought," there was a general attitude that intelligence needs were responsive to a higher law. Thus, as one witness testified in justifying the FBI's mail opening program:

> It was my assumption that what we were doing was justified by what we had to do . . . the greater good, the national security.

5. *Deficiencies in Accountability and Control*

The overwhelming number of excesses continuing over a prolonged period of time were due in large measure to the fact that the system of checks and balances—created in our Constitution to limit abuse of Governmental power—was seldom applied to the intelligence community. Guidance and regulation from outside the intelligence agencies—where it has been imposed at all—has been vague. Presidents and other senior Executive officials, particularly the Attorneys General, have virtually abdicated their Constitutional responsibility to oversee and set standards for intelligence activity. Senior government officials generally gave the agencies broad, general mandates or pressed for immediate results on pressing problems. In neither case did they provide guidance to prevent excesses and their broad mandates and pressures themselves often resulted in excessive or improper intelligence activity.

Congress has often declined to exercise meaningful oversight, and on occasion has passed laws or made statements which were taken by intelligence agencies as supporting overly-broad investigations.

On the other hand, the record reveals instances when intelligence agencies have concealed improper activities from their superiors in the Executive branch and from the Congress, or have elected to disclose only the less questionable aspects of their activities.

There has been, in short, a clear and sustained failure by those responsible to control the intelligence community and to ensure its accountability. There has been an equally clear and sustained failure by intelligence agencies to fully inform the proper authorities of their activities and to comply with directives from those authorities.

◆

The CIA, after all, is nothing more than the secret police of American capitalism, plugging up leaks in the political dam, night and day, so that shareholders of United States companies operating in poor countries can continue enjoying the rip-off.

Philip Agee, *Inside the Company; CIA Diary,* 1975

58.

DANIEL SCHORR: Congress and Freedom of the Press

During 1975–76, committees in both houses of Congress investigated allegations of illegal procedures on the part of the Federal Bureau of Investigation, the Central Intelligence Agency, and other information-gathering bureaus of the Federal Government. The House Select Committee on Intelligence, headed by Rep. Otis G. Pike, compiled an extensive study of activities of the CIA and other agencies. The committee voted to make the report public, but it was overridden by a vote of the full House in accordance with the wishes of President Ford. Nevertheless, CBS correspondent Daniel Schorr obtained a copy of the report and leaked it to the New York newspaper, The Village Voice, *in February 1976. Consequently, the House committee on ethics was assigned to investigate the circumstances of the report's release, namely, how did Mr. Schorr get a copy in the first place? On September 15, 1976, Schorr testified before the committee, refusing to divulge his sources. This selection reprints his opening statement.*

Source: *Investigation of Publication of Select Committee on Intelligence Report:* Hearings Before the Committee on Standards of Official Conduct, House of Representatives, 94th Congress, 2nd Session, Washington, D.C., 1976.

I APPEAR before this committee today under protest, in response to a subpena whose issuance I deeply deplore.

I had hoped that this committee, which has already learned a great deal about congressional procedures for handling intelligence information, could have completed its hearings without crossing that constitutional Great Divide which separates the roles of the Congress and the press.

Whatever happens hereafter at this hearing, it is my belief that your subpena, commanding the appearance of a reporter to discuss his journalistic activities, its effect can only be to establish an atmosphere of intimidation for the press.

Now, this subpena requires me to produce all records, papers, documents, correspondence, et cetera, and this is not inclusive, "which relate in any way" to the subject of your inquiry. It's a broad statement and I have tried to interpret it, and I will divide the material in my possession into four general categories.

First, many of the records in my possession are material in the public domain, such as speeches that I have made, newspaper articles and I guess copies of *Village Voice* containing the report of the house Intelligence Committee.

To the extent that these public materials are not already available to the committee and are desired by the committee, I am willing to provide them.

Second, since the publication of the report in the *Village Voice* I have received several thousand letters and telegrams. If the committee feels a need for such correspondence. I should like first to seek the permission of the persons involved out of respect for their privacy.

Third, I have notes taken during the coverage of the House Intelligence Investigation and I have draft scripts that were written in preparation for broadcasts.

Now, because of the internal news decisionmaking and the editing process, some of those scripts vary from what I actually did broadcast, and in fact, others were not broadcast at all.

All of this work product I must respectfully decline to submit. I believe that it falls under the category of reporters' notes, protected by the first amendment. I take now the same position that Dr. Frank Stanton, who was then President of CBS, Incorporated, took in 1971.

He refused to comply with the House Commerce Committee subpena demanding the scripts and the so-called out-takes of interviews filmed in preparation for the CBS television documentary, "The Selling of the Pentagon."

His position and mine today is that the internal process of preparing news for publication or for broadcast cannot be subjected to the compulsory process of subpena without subverting the purposes of the first amendment.

Now fourth, the subpena specifically demands "all drafts and copies of the report of the Select Committee on Intelligence which were in existence prior to January 29, 1976."

I cannot comply with that demand. The examination of the document could conceivably help to lead to discovery of the source, and as must now be manifest, if it has not been manifest before, I consider it a matter of professional conscience as well as a constitutional right not to assist you in discovering that source.

Now, this also means, obviously, and we may as well say it now, that I shall not respond to direct questioning about confidential sources, for in some 40 years of practicing journalism I have never yielded to a demand for a disclosure of a source that I had promised to protect, and I cannot do so now.

At the appropriate time, Mr. Chairman, Mr. Califano is ready to explain why, given the circumstances of this case, my role in the publication of the report, and my right to withhold the source, are indeed, protected by the Constitution.

But let me add that even if our legal position were not as strong as I believe it is, I could still not tell you my source, because for me this is a personal matter, and almost a visceral matter.

Mr. Chairman and members of the committee, we all build our lives around certain principles, and without those principles our careers simply lose their meaning.

For some of us, doctors, lawyers, clergymen, and yes, journalists it is an article of faith that we must keep confidential those matters entrusted to us only because of the assurance that they would remain confidential.

Now, for a journalist, the most crucial kind of confidence is the identity of a source of information. To betray a confidential source would mean to dry up many future sources for many future reporters.

The reporter and the news organization would be the immediate losers, but I would submit to you that the ultimate losers would be the American people and their free institutions.

And if you will permit me one last personal word, without all of this constitutional argument, I would like to go beyond all of this. To betray a source would be for me to betray myself, my career, and my life, and to say that I refuse to do it isn't quite saying it right.

I cannot do it.

That concludes my statement.

59.

STEPHEN A. BENNETT: Fair Trial *v.* Free Press

One of the most widely reported conflicts over the right of the press to report a trial centered on a 1975–76 Nebraska murder case. It was one of several such contests between the courts and the press in recent years, perhaps the most famous of which was the Pentagon Papers trial. Not all the decisions have favored the press, however. In some cases, reporters have been jailed for refusing to divulge their sources of information. In a 1971 Baton Rouge, Louisiana, murder-conspiracy trial, a U. S. district court judge forbade publication of testimony. Reporters ignored this order and were cited for contempt of court. An appellate court upheld the gag order, and the U. S. Supreme Court declined to rule on the case. Subsequently similar gag orders were issued by judges in several parts of the country. Then came the Nebraska case out of which came a ruling by the Supreme Court. Both the case and the Court's decision are discussed here by Stephen A. Bennett, an editor of Trial *magazine.*

Source: *Trial*, September 1976.

"Free speech and fair trial are two of the most cherished policies of our civilization, and it would be a trying task to choose between them."

— *Justice Hugo Black*
Bridges v. California, *1941*

ON THE NIGHT of October 18, 1975, Edwin Charles Simants borrowed his brother-in-law's .22 caliber rifle, walked to the house next door and proceeded to slaughter the James Henry Kellie family. He raped 10-year-old Florence, then shot her in the forehead, and as the other family members responded to her screams, he shot each one of them. There was evidence of necrophilia. The horrors took place in Sutherland, Neb., population 840. At 9:37 P.M. the community got word of the killings from WNOP-TV which broadcast a bulletin warning that "everyone should lock their doors and windows and admit no one." At 6:37 the next morning, an Associated Press bulle-

tin reported that Sheriff Hop Gilster said that Simants apparently told his father "that he was responsible for the killings." The scene was being set for a historical conflict between the right to an unbiased jury and the guarantee of freedom of the press.

A sad-looking character, an unemployed handyman with an IQ of 75, Simants turned himself in the next day. He was read his *Miranda* rights three times, and he confessed. At the preliminary hearing, Lincoln County Judge Ronald Ruff, 34, disallowed reporting of any testimony. Nebraska news organizations appealed the gag order to District Court Judge Hugh Stuart, who ended Judge Ruff's order and initiated his own.

Judge Stuart's gag order prohibited the press from publishing the confession, the results of the pathologist's report, the identity of the victims, and the description of the crimes. He agreed with Judge Ruff that the Nebraska bar-press guidelines, voluntary standards on reporting crimes and criminal trials, should become mandatory. Also, the press was not to be allowed to publish what was contained in the gag order.

The Nebraska Press Association, urged on by the national Reporters' Committee for Freedom of the Press, applied to the Nebraska Supreme Court on a writ of mandamus, but in the interim appealed the ruling to Justice Harry Blackmun, sitting as the Supreme Court's circuit justice. While modifying some of the gag order, including the mandatory directive on the bar-press guidelines, Justice Blackmun left standing the prohibition on confessions or admissions of guilt or other material "strongly implicative of the accused."

Then the Nebraska Supreme Court, balancing the "heavy presumption against . . . constitutional validity" that an order restraining publication bears, *New York Times v. United States,* 403 US 713, 714 (1971), against the importance of the defendant's right to trial by an impartial jury, declared that because of the publicity in this case the latter right was in jeopardy. An appeal was then taken to the full U.S. Supreme Court.

Gag orders were nothing new; in fact at the time this case went to court they were being issued all over the country by leaps and bounds. According to Fred W. Friendly, in an article on this case in the *New York Times Magazine* of March 21, the first gag order was issued in 1893 by a California judge who told a newspaper not to report on a divorce case he said was of "a filthy nature." That ruling was struck down by the California Supreme Court.

The first case of prior restraint—prepublication gags—was in 1931, wrote Friendly, not followed again until the famous Pentagon Papers case in 1971, when the Nixon Administration tried to prevent publication of those papers; but the Nebraska case was of the more recent vintage—a prior restraint in a criminal trial proceeding.

"We had no intention of publishing confessions or violating the spirit of the guidelines, which I helped write," Joe R. Seacrest, whose family owns the *Lincoln Journal* and the *North Platte Telegraph,* told Friendly. "But we wanted to do it voluntarily, not have some judge order us what not to print," Seacrest said.

Sutherland, Neb., is cattle country, a land not inhabited by a lot of people. Friendly described it as a "bleak prairie village." The people in the region are mainly ranchers and railroad workers on the Union Pacific. According to Nebraska law, a change of venue can only be made to an adjacent county, and the counties around Lincoln are just as bare of people. One has 650 residents. And the same newspapers cover the entire area.

So it was that Simants' right to a fair trial and the right of the press to publish came into conflict. The U.S. Supreme Court under Chief Justice Burger stepped in where Justice Black said he would fear to tread. But their opinions showed they largely agreed with the former Justice.

In a concurring opinion, Justice Brennan wrote:

"I unreservedly agree with Mr. Justice Black that 'free speech and fair trials are two of the most cherished policies of our civilization, and it would be a trying task to choose between them.' But I would reject the notion that a choice is necessary, that there is an inherent conflict that cannot be resolved without essentially abrogating one right or the other."

What did the Court decide?

The Court essentially said that judges

generally cannot issue gag orders in criminal cases, even if they believe such orders would help assure a fair trial. The unanimous opinion said the constitutional free press guarantee had been violated in the Nebraska case. But it did not rule out a gag order in some exceptional criminal cases. In the Court opinion written by Chief Justice Burger, prior restraint cases, including the Pentagon Papers case, were cited, and the Chief Justice wrote:

"The thread running through all these cases is that prior restraints on speech and publication are the most serious and the least tolerable infringements on First Amendment rights.

"A prior restraint, by contrast and by definition, has an immediate and irreversible sanction. If it can be said that a threat of criminal or civil sanctions after publication 'chills' speech, prior restraint 'freezes' it at least for the time."

The Court cited earlier sensational trials and said that "pretrial publicity — even pervasive, adverse publicity — does not inevitably lead to an unfair trial. . . . The trial judge has a major responsibility. What the judge says about a case, in or out of the courtroom, is likely to appear in newspapers and broadcasts. More important, the measures a judge takes or fails to take to mitigate the effects of pretrial publicity — the measures described in *Sheppard* [*Sheppard v. Maxwell*, 384 US 33 (1966)] — may well determine whether the defendant receives a trial consistent with the requirements of due process."

The Burger opinion went on to say:

"The authors of the Bill of Rights did not undertake to assign priorities as between First Amendment and Sixth Amendment rights, ranking one as superior to the other. In this case, the petitioners would have us declare the right of an accused subordinate to their right to publish in all circumstances. But if the authors of these guarantees, fully aware of the potential conflicts between them, were unwilling or unable to resolve the issue by assigning one priority over the other, it is not for us to rewrite the Constitution by undertaking what they declined.

"It is unnecessary, after nearly two centuries, to establish a priority applicable in all circumstances. Yet it is nonetheless clear that the barriers to prior restraint remain high unless we are to abandon what the court has said for nearly a quarter of our national existence and implied throughout all of it. . . ."

The Court concluded, "Our analysis ends as it began, with a confrontation between prior restraint imposed to protect one vital constitutional guarantee and the explicit command of another that the freedom to speak and publish shall not be abridged. We reaffirm that the guarantees of freedom of expression are not an absolute prohibition *under all circumstances* [editor's emphasis added], but the barriers to prior restraint remain high and *the presumption against its use continues intact* [editor's emphasis added]. . . ."

Shades of Hugo Black. But the press generally viewed it as a solid victory for freedom of expression. In this issue of *Trial,* the Supreme Court reporter for Newhouse Newspapers, Jack Landau, representing the Reporter's Committee for Freedom of the Press, argues the free press side . . . in light of the *Nebraska* decision. Taking the fair trial side in this issue is Professor Martin Shapiro, an author of several books on the Supreme Court. . . .

What happened to Simants? He was convicted of murder and sentenced to death in the electric chair. He told Friendly, who asked him if he had any resentments about members of his family who testified against him: "All they done was tell the truth."

60.

NEAL R. PEIRCE: The "Sunset" Challenge to Bureaucratic Growth

Since the mid-sixties there has developed among the American people a mood of unrest, even hostility, with regard to governmental bodies at every level. This mood has in part been engendered by the size of government, by constantly rising expenditures, and by the seemingly endless proliferation of agencies that do not appear responsive to the needs of the people. The multiplication of laws and bureaus is not matched by any increase in effectiveness. In 1975–76, Colorado legislators came up with an interesting and possibly workable solution to the growth of bureaucracy; a built-in self-destruct mechanism for all state regulatory agencies. Author and political scientist Neal R. Peirce described the Colorado experiment in an article for the Washington Post.

Source: *Washington Post,* March 16, 1976.

CAN THE mindless growth of bureaucracy, characterized by the layering of self-serving regulatory agencies that virtually defy public oversight and control, be stemmed? Perhaps not. But here in Colorado's state capital, the freshest and possibly most significant law of the '70s to do just that is moving toward passage.

The proposal has a catchy name—the "sunset" law. It would force automatic termination—the "sunset"—of state regulatory agencies every seven years, unless the legislature gives them a specific new lease on life.

No other state, and certainly not the federal government, has ever set up a comprehensive plan to review the operations of agencies and commissions on a systematic basis, with a triggering mechanism as effective as the threat of extinction.

It's not just the uniqueness of the Colorado law, however, that may make it one of the most important legislative initiatives of our times.

First, there is the law's sponsorship. It was conceived, and named, by the Colorado chapter of Common Cause. After some initial skepticism, national Common Cause has now made "sunset" one of its legislative priorities. That means a formidable lobbying force, both in Washington and state capitals, is in place to push the concept.

Second, the sunset idea has broad political appeal. The bill passed the Colorado House 55-11, with representatives of every ideological stripe in favor. The chief House sponsor was a consumer-oriented liberal Democrat, Gerald Kopel; the chief Senate sponsor, where passage seems imminent, is that body's conservative Republican president, Fred Anderson.

Third, Colorado is establishing a model that may be copied soon by Congress. Sen. Edmund S. Muskie, D-Maine, with co-sponsors including Sens. Henry S. Bellmon, R-Okla., John H. Glenn, D-Ohio, and the two Senate party leaders—Mike Mansfield, D-Mont., and Hugh Scott, R-Pa.—has even proposed putting all federal programs on a four-year authorization cycle. Senate hearings on the

Muskie bill start this Wednesday, with the Colorado Legislature sponsors and state Common Cause board chairman, Sidney Brooks, scheduled to testify Thursday.

Colorado has opted for a more modest pilot effort, striking first at that soft underbelly of state government—the multitude of regulatory boards and commissions that often turn out to be little beds of monopoly, restricting competition and driving up prices under the cloak of state power.

After a study of state licensing boards across the nation, the U.S. Labor Department concluded they are "fraught with chaotic and inequitable rules, regulations and requirements and prone to restrictive and exclusionary practices as a result of pressures exerted by special interest groups."

No one questions the need for state commissions to regulate utilities, or regulations to protect citizens against fraud or health-endangering products in such areas as drugs, dentistry or medicine. But why does New Jersey, for instance, need to license such occupational groups as goats' milk dealers, tree experts and well drillers? Why must Illinois regulate egg dealers and wholesale minnow dealers?

Colorado's Board of Cosmetology considers such problems as acne scars and split hair ends so grievous that a prospective hairdresser must undergo 1,650 hours of instruction, including 100 hours of supervised practice at shampooing.

Most frequently, state licensing boards are comprised of members of the regulated profession—a practice reminiscent of the exclusionary medieval guild system. Plumbers watch over plumbers, doctors police doctors, cemetery keepers and nursing home administrators take care of their own. The added costs for consumers probably number in the billions of dollars annually.

According to Brooks, the sunset bill will fight "regulatory obesity" through 1) the automatic termination provision; 2) shifting the burden of proof to an agency to show it is performing a valuable public service; 3) forcing the legislature to perform its often-neglected oversight responsibility; and 4) requiring public hearings on extending agencies, so that citizens and consumer groups can have a voice.

Several refinements have been added to the Colorado sunset bill. One requires that all agencies in a related field come up for review simultaneously, so they can be considered as a group and, in some cases, consolidated.

Another change provides a year's grace if the legislature fails to act on extending an agency. In that extra year, popular support for an important agency could be built up, even if a committee chairman had tried to bottle up an extension bill. The extra year would also minimize danger of arbitrary termination of a politically vulnerable agency, such as a civil rights commission.

Finally, Common Cause has agreed to an amendment by Sen. Anderson to require preparation, by an auditing arm of the legislature, of a full-scale performance audit report on each agency as it comes up for renewal. The report, Anderson claims, will provide "a solid case for judgment" on whether to extend a board or not, and reduce the influence of special interest lobbying.

On the surface, the sunset law looks quite different from the ethics issues—campaign spending, lobbying disclosure and "sunshine" laws to open up government meetings—on which Common Cause cut its teeth.

But ethics, sunshine and sunset laws have one thing in common: making government more accountable. Sunset has the virtue of appealing to conservatives as well as liberals. It has caused some conservative Colorado legislators to note, quite increduously, that they are making "common cause" with Common Cause for the first time.

Thus Colorado Common Cause may have developed a thrust that could keep the citizen's lobby, with so many successes in the ethics area already to its credit, alive and influential on the state and national scene for years to come.

The sunset law also places Common Cause at the cutting edge of an overriding issue of our times — controlling the growth of bureaucracies, lest government, by its very complexity and distance from average citizens, becomes paralyzed and incapable of performing its essential tasks.

61.

What Future for the American Family?

In 1975 there were about two million marriages and nearly one million divorces. This does not mean that half of the families in the United States are breaking up, but it is an indication that the institution of the family has undergone a great deal of stress in the 1970s. Prophets of gloom have suggested that the family is done for. Others are not so pessimistic, however. They realize that the moral-cultural revolution of the 1960s, the greater number of working mothers, the laxity of divorce laws, the increased independence of children, and the growing acceptance of single status have worked together to weaken traditional family relationships. But this is regarded as an extreme situation that will inevitably right itself eventually. This selection takes the more optimistic view, while readily acknowledging the seriousness of the present problems.

Source: *Changing Times*, December 1976.

FORGED IN THE cooler fires of simpler times, the framework of the American family is sagging noticeably in the heat of modern social and economic frictions. Evidence of the strain isn't hard to find.

Husbands and wives, once secure in the understanding of their separate roles and duties, now grope through confusion and emotional pain for a satisfactory way of accommodating current concepts of men's and women's places in the world.

Children, who look to the family for love, security and a sense of direction, too often don't seem to find it. Many are aimless and alienated, and alarming numbers of them have turned to drugs, alcohol, vandalism and violence.

The institution of marriage itself seems to be withering. Marriages end in divorce more often in the United States than anywhere else in the world, and the record has been getting worse each year.

What does it all mean? Is the family as we know it really headed for extinction, as some people have suggested? If it survives, will it be in a recognizable form? On the answers to these very difficult questions may ride the character and attitudes of future generations of Americans.

The history of the family, in which lie some useful clues to its present stress, is tied closely to the history of the nation itself. When Americans made their living largely from the soil and travel across great distances was difficult, families tended to stay put. Parents, children, grandparents, aunts, uncles and cousins often worked together. Together they constituted an "extended family," which each generation relied on for its economic security, social activity and emotional nourishment. The men and boys labored in the fields while the women and girls labored in the home.

Then, as the nation turned to industry as its principal means of livelihood, family patterns began to change, too. Men who might have tilled their own land in earlier times were drawn to the cities where the jobs were, leaving their extended families behind. Working long hours outside the home cut down on the time they could spend with their family, so the role of mother as the anchor around which home and family life were built became more important.

As time went on, economic pressures and upwardly mobile ambitions, plus social changes outside the family — chiefly the liberation of women from age-old constraints — encouraged increasing numbers of wives and mothers to take jobs outside the home. Women who might have been totally dependent on their husbands for support began to feel they were capable of supporting themselves.

In the meantime, there were other forces at work changing the complexion of the American family. Religious and social taboos that served to govern family behavior declined greatly in importance. Women who perceived the boundaries of homemaking and child rearing as too confining began to have access to more education that equipped them to compete for a variety of jobs outside the home.

It is the convergence of three major trends — the demand on parents' time outside the home, the demise of the extended family due to the frequent uprooting of its parts and the liberation of women — that has put the challenge to our traditional family structure. According to some authorities, the only need many families now supply for their members is emotional, leaving one fragile thread to hold together what once was bound by many. The inevitable result: more divorce. . . .

Many family experts are disturbed by what they see — trends, attitudes and situations that are not easily measured but which, they fear, are undermining the family's status and frustrating attempts to shore it up. Urie Bronfenbrenner, professor of family studies at Cornell University, finds today's family isolated and its members, especially the children, frustrated and alienated. Kenneth Keniston, chairman of the Carnegie Council on Children, feels the structure of society no longer supports the family. Anthropologist Margaret Mead feels the same. Philosopher-theologian Michael Novak observes that the notion of the family is so unpopular these days that a decision to have children, formerly a routine event in a young married couple's life, now requires an act of courage.

Look at what today's family is up against.

Frumpy images. The single, no-strings-attached life is often glamorized, with scant attention paid to its problems. "Work" is recognized as valuable only if it is paid employment. This feeds the image of the child-rearing role as servile and unappreciated. Television commercials frequently portray husbands as uninvolved in household tasks and wives as obsessed with them.

Diminishing influence of parents on children. Economic necessity used to be a major cause of family cohesion; now it is splitting families apart. When both mom and dad work, the kids must spend their days in the care of someone else. With the extended family a rarity, the task of raising children is shared with a host of family interlopers. Schools, day-care centers and baby-sitters spend more time with some children than their parents do. This is often "passive" care because the care givers aren't actively involved in the lives of the children. As their parents' roles diminish, children turn increasingly to peer groups and fall more heavily under their influence. Some social scientists find this a disturbing development, since research has shown that strong attachments to peer groups may be influenced by feelings of neglect at home.

Television is another major influence on children, and research suggests a link between the kinds of behavior certain children display and the behavior they see on television. With violence and aggression the staples of TV fare, such a link is troubling. To Professor Bronfenbrenner, however, what television prevents is just as important. It gets in the way of family conversations, games, even arguments, all of which play a large part in character development.

Age segregation. Family experts also lament the general pattern of age segregation developing in society. Many children are rarely exposed to elderly people, except perhaps during visits to grandparents who themselves may be neatly segregated in a retirement community. The fact that such separations are voluntary doesn't alter the effect: The young are increasingly isolated from the old, and vice versa, and different generations of the same family grow apart. Young people wishing to establish families of their own have adopted a variety of responses to the problems of doing so. Some have established or joined communes where several families share housekeeping and child-rearing tasks. A number have packed up and moved to remote areas of the country where they can carve out a living on farms or in small towns where traditional family life is still considered important.

The most common response, however, is simply to postpone marriage for a while in favor of other pursuits. The median age of men and women at the time of marriage is nearly a year older than it was 25 years ago. Nevertheless, though the proportion of people who do get married has declined a bit in recent years, it is still higher than it was 20 years ago.

The fact is, the family as we know it seems in little danger of destruction at the hands of the young. More than half of the nearly 200,000 college freshmen surveyed last year at 366 schools listed "raising a family" as one of the most important objectives of their lives, ahead of financial success and other goals. The survey, directed by Alexander Astin of UCLA, also revealed that these same young people don't find recent upheavals in social values incompatible with future family happiness. Nearly half said couples should live together before marrying, more than half felt large families should be discouraged, and better than 90% endorsed job equality for women.

There are other signs around for those concerned about the future of the family. Surveys find that people in general put "family" near the top when asked to name the most important sources of personal satisfaction, indicating that family discord may not be as damaging as some believe. And the characteristics that show up more and more in today's new families— later marriages, fewer children, shared decision-making—are the very characteristics, research shows, that successful families usually tend to have in common. Even most divorced people eventually remarry, which says something about their faith in traditional family life.

Far from the verge of collapse, then, the American family appears to be in a period of adjustment. When the smoke clears, most authorities expect that the family will still occupy the central position in most people's lives. Its contours may be changed, but the institution will be readily recognizable.

Even so, the family could use some nurturing. Following are some of the things that have been recommended to help it.

Better education and training for future parents. This means "parenting" courses in the schools, preferably with opportunities for adolescent students to work and play with small children. Along these lines, the National PTA and the March of Dimes are sponsoring a series of regional parenting conferences designed to get better curriculum materials.

Day-care facilities that encourage the participation of parents and other family members. This would allow the family, rather than child-care specialists, to retain primary responsibility for bringing up children. Other recommendations for easing the child-care problems of more working parents include tax breaks and child-care allowances.

Improved status for women. With this, it is hoped, will come wider recognition of child rearing as an important function, thus enhancing the status of mothers who choose to stay home.

More flexible working arrangements. Flexible hours for full-time workers, plus more opportunities for part-time work, could make it easier to be a mother or father while holding a job.

Revamped family income and health-care programs to replace the current system of welfare payments. The stability of poor families is shakiest of all, sometimes because welfare laws actually penalize them for getting back together. A common suggestion for reform is a guaranteed income policy and health-care arrangements that would encourage families to stay together in the face of economic pressures that tend to push them apart.

None of these ideas will come to pass overnight, of course, and some may never be realized. But with or without them, it's a pretty safe bet that the American family will find a way to survive.

62.

The Plight of American Education

Over the years, the schools have probably come in for more persistent criticism than any other American institution. In the 1970s public education has come under heavy fire because of the alarming decline in basic skills among students from grade school through college age. A report published in Newsweek *(December 8, 1975) asserted that: "Willy-nilly, the U.S. educational system is spawning a generation of semiliterates." The most dismal indication of the generally low level of educational achievement is the poor performance in basic literary and mathematical skills by the best-educated. Many post-graduate students have been found unable to express themselves in clear, accurate English. This selection reprints a portion of a Los Angeles* Times *study of American education by Jack McCurdy and Don Speich, tracing trends in the schools since the early 1960s.*

Source: *Chicago Sun-Times*, September 5, 1976. "U. S. Education on the Skids."

AFTER EDGING UPWARD for more than a century, the reading, writing and computational skills of American students from elementary school through college are now in a prolonged and broad-scale decline unequalled in U.S. history.

The downward spiral, which affects many other subject areas as well, began abruptly in the mid-1960s and shows no signs of bottoming out. By most measures, student achievement is now below the national average of a decade ago.

There are, in fact, some indications that the decline—reflected in a wide range of test results and other evidence of academic performance—is growing worse.

The decline, a Los Angeles Times investigation shows, encompasses all ethnic groups, all economic classes, and both private and public school students, at most achievement levels in all regions of the nation.

Furthermore, there is evidence that over a nine-year span, college students have been doing progressively worse on examinations required prior to entering graduate schools. This would indicate a drop in achievement in higher education as well as in elementary and secondary schools.

The only exception to this pattern has been in the reading level of pupils in the first three grades, and in science knowledge among college-bound students and college graduates. Test scores in these areas generally either have risen modestly or have held steady over a long period.

Evidence from a Los Angeles Times investigation shows that the drop in standards is the result of a shift in social and educational values during the 1960s—a shift to which schools and colleges both succumbed and contributed by reducing the number of basic academic classes, weakening graduation requirements and emphasizing electives that are academically less demanding.

Basic course requirements in English, history and foreign language, for example, were cut back or eliminated outright (in college alone by 22 per cent since 1967) and replaced by a host of electives or, in the case of high schools, by vocational education classes, where enrollment rose fourfold and funding tenfold between 1964 and 1974.

Grades are threatening to become almost meaningless as instructors drop traditional standards of academic quality and instead dispense A and B marks offhandedly to a growing number of students. Consequently, students now are able to get through school and college not only more easily and with less preparation, but also with higher grades than ever.

At the same time, more high school students have been working part time, absenteeism rates have climbed and students generally have spent less and less time in school over the last 10 years—particularly in basic academic subjects.

The drop in attendance is probably one reason for the achievement decline, but more to the point is the fact that, because of curriculum changes, students have been spending less time in basic academic classes. Moreover, in college the total number of hours required to obtain a baccalaureate degree has been cut back.

All of these things—curriculum shifts, drops in requirements, grade inflation, rising absenteeism—began in the mid-1960s and then swept through the educational system. Not until the 1970s, however, did they have their sharpest impact.

Much of this can be seen as the result of an educational system that became fragmented and confused about its mission as it faced repeated demands in the 1960s to justify the wisdom of its educational practices. Instead of justification, many educators offered almost instantaneous change.

Substituted for academic rigor — which, curiously, many found difficult to defend — was the notion that learning somehow should be less painful or, preferably, fun. It was an attitude of "I don't care how bright you are as long as you feel good," said Stanford University admissions dean Fred Hargadon in an interview.

If the pain could not be taken out of learning entirely, maybe a high grade would ease the transitory discomfort of (or, at least, quiet protest about) having to deal with something that was not easily identifiable as immediately relevant.

In some instances, the rationale behind curriculum changes was based on the concern of educators that, without flexibility in curriculum, disinterested students would remain untouched by an educational experience based on the time-worn — but not necessarily time-proven — methods of teaching.

Meanwhile, an enormous and highly successful push began to make education in the nation's high schools more than ever before a practical means toward a generally low-level occupational end.

A lower keyed but similar attitude crept into much of higher education. If an academic major ultimately led to an available slot in the labor market, it was blessed. If not, it was held suspect — if not threatened with extinction.

It is the fundamental and massive shift from basic academic requirements to a vast array of electives that seems to be the most direct contributor to the achievement decline in both schools and colleges.

The shift was fast, and it was pervasive. In colleges and universities across the country, for example, general education requirements dropped by 22 per cent between 1967 and 1974, according to a recent study by the Carnegie Council on Policy Studies in Higher Education.

Falling into this category are such things as history and literature survey courses, which, like others, traditionally have been required to assure that all students become acquainted with more than the subject area of their academic majors.

Additionally, the study noted, requirements in English, foreign language and mathematics "declined appreciably."

Nathaniel Teich, director of English composition at the University of Oregon, said in an interview: "There was just a staggering percentage of universities and colleges that cut their writing requirements and in some cases just dropped them."

Drops in requirements, moreover, occurred in each of the disciplinary areas of higher education, including humanities and social sciences — but in natural sciences to a much lesser degree. Such drops, the study said, were greatest in the humanities.

Results of the Times' investigation strongly indicate that in areas where electives have blossomed, such as the social sciences, the scores have dropped sharply. Conversely, in the natural sciences, where there are more requirements and fewer electives, scores have risen.

Between 1965-66 and 1973-74, for instance, scores on the Graduate Record Examination's history subtest dropped 41 points, while in biology they increased by 14 points.

Electives themselves are not bad, of course; but when they are used in a wholesale manner to replace basic courses, as they increasingly are in college, and are innovative in name but marginal in content, as many are in high school, then their worth is questionable.

"The elective curriculum has put hard subjects like composition in competition with things like playground supervision (and) rap sessions," said Paul White, special consultant on new program development and evaluation at the California state university system, in an interview. "Kids are kids, after all. Why should they sweat over writing, which is so damn hard to do, when they could act in a play?"

These are the conclusions of a four-month investigation. And although the reasons for the achievement decline and the relative importance of each are not as clear as the decline itself, all indications point to what occurred — or did not occur — within schools and colleges as the critical factors.

Other possibilities show up in a study by David Wiley of the University of Chicago, which assumes that it was basically external forces that impinged on education and brought about the achievement decline.

One such factor is television and its apparent subversive influence on youngsters' study habits and time once spent on an activity that is generally thought to bolster all other academic achievement: reading.

Another hypothesis involves changes in the family structure, particularly the sharp rise in the number of working mothers since World War II. The number of single-parent families also has jumped. The implication here is that the presence of adults in the family household has diminished, and that attention to school-work and academic discipline has suffered as a result.

A related factor concerns what many teachers see as reduced student motivation to do well in school, which may be a product of the "permissiveness" growing out of the changes in parental control.

Possibly linked to that is the growth of violence and disruptions in school and drug and alcohol use among youngsters, which many school people blame for destroying the atmosphere requisite for learning.

In light of the national controversy over school desegregation, many have cited busing as a possible reason, implying that learning has been undercut either by mixing children of different ethnic groups or by the dislocations caused by integration. This argument is easily disposed of: The achievement decline has affected all regions of the country, including school districts with desegregation as well as those without, and public as well as private schools.

There is another set of "in-school" factors that some have tried to blame. They have to do with budgets, personnel and the like. The financial squeeze that some school districts have experienced in recent years is cited. However, the material condition of public education in the United States has improved markedly in virtually every way over the last 10 years.

All of which does not mean that the nation's schools and colleges have entered a dark age, or that American students have suddenly stopped learning and know less than their counterparts of some golden era many decades ago.

The over-all decline on standardized tests represents roughly an average of 5 to 10 fewer correct answers per student on tests of around 75 questions.

What it does mean is that American education clearly appears to be on a dangerous course.

The trend seems to indicate that students are losing their ability to handle more complex matters, more sophisticated language, disciplined and articulate written discourse on any given subject, higher mathematical concepts and ideas that demand some critical thought.

63.

JOHN A. COLEMAN: The Crisis of American Catholicism

With 49 million members, the Roman Catholic Church is the largest denomination in the United States. In the 1970s it was also a troubled and divided church. The Second Vatican Council of 1962–65, convened by Pope John XXIII, opened windows through which the winds of change—and strife—blew. The accession of Pope Paul VI brought to the papacy a man who wanted to moderate change, while still imposing the traditional authoritarian rule. But once the church had been brought face to face with the realities of the 20th century and the old restraints were relaxed, it was impossible to impose them again. Catholics became restive under the church's attempt to govern their private lives. Modernists in the church pulled one way, and traditionalists another. For one reason or another, mass attendance declined markedly. Thousands of priests and nuns left their vocation. Several thousand parochial schools have been forced to close. In 1976 the divisions within the church were symbolized by two different gatherings of Catholics. In October a national assembly of Catholics convened in Detroit. It was made up of 1,300 delegates representing the whole spectrum of church membership. This broadly based assembly drafted a five year agenda for social justice urging such issues as allowing priests to marry, the ordination of women, abolition of nuclear weapons, the Equal Rights Amendment, and the ending of arms sales abroad by the U. S. In November, the American bishops met in conference at Washington, D.C., where they reiterated support for the traditional positions of the church and declared the Detroit convention to be unrepresentative of American Catholicism. The author of this selection, John A. Coleman, S.J., is a sociologist and a member of the faculty of the Jesuit School of Theology in Berkeley, California.

Source: *America*, June 26, 1976. "American Bicentennial, Catholic Crisis."

I AM GOING to add my voice to those who have spoken of a crisis state in American Catholicism.

I am using "crisis" in the classical sense to mean a decisive turning point in the life history of a people or an institution. One stage of development comes to a termination, history hangs in the balance, and it does not yet appear what shall be. David O'Brien captured this sense of the term when he stated: "The conflict and confusion within the Catholic Church in the United States . . . offers a promise of vital-ity and dedication that could have tremendous impact both on the church and on American society, but it offers as well the possibility of failure, dissipation of energies and gradual erosion of institutional relevance and personal commitment."

The relative quietus in the American church in the latter 1970's, compared to the "conflict and confusion" Mr. O'Brien cited, seems to me a possibly ominous sign of the darker potentialities latent in crisis. For the vitality and dedication that persisted as a residue of the collective élan in the last years of the church of the immigrants was historically specific. If the ready commitment of the generation that rode the crest of the victory years of the pre-Vatican II immigrant church with a highly salient Catholic self-identity is not tapped and channeled, there is no guarantee that succeeding generations will have the same energies and dedication. Much of it went untapped at the opportune moment. Thus, already there are those who refer to the church most of us over 30 grew up in as "The *Last* Amen."

Nevertheless, nostalgic evocations of that collective élan will not serve us in diagnosing the crisis. We do not have to denigrate the genuine faith achievements of Catholics during the years 1930–1960 to recognize also the shadow side to that rich Roman Catholic life. The catalog of its sins is numerous: clericalism; triumphalism; sexual prudery; ahistorical orthodoxy with its fear of open inquiry; a shallow interiority; a lack of serious commitment to civil liberties; the absence of symbolic foci to national Catholicism; institutional segmentation into uncoordinated and inefficient parochial units; the failure to generate critical alternative models either to the cold war or the smug American consumer and status-oriented society. Even much that was lovely in that era of Catholicism — group solidarity; a texture of personal loyalties; a vision of high idealism coupled with a healthy dose of realism; a rich feeling for sacramental signs to accompany every season and stage of life; a solid sense of joy and good humor in the face of life's limits; a toughness in facing the tragic dimensions of existence; an absence of moralism; a high commitment to rationality and an unmistakable taste for continuity and tradition — can never again be retrieved in the forms and vessels in which it was then embodied. We neither want to nor could

go home again.

I do not think it will do to lump the American Catholic crisis in one bin with crisis elements in worldwide Catholicism. American Catholicism is both culturally and structurally different from other national churches. Its history has been extraordinary and unique. Nor is the Vatican Council to blame for the crisis because it came "too late" or "too soon and unprepared." While it is obvious that the council precipitated the crisis because of the abruptness with which American Catholics have been called to face modernity, it is clear that American Catholicism by the time of the council was ready for a crisis on its own terms.

For, with the accession of John F. Kennedy to the American Presidency, the historic goals of American Catholicism had been achieved. Catholics had entered American history largely as a beleaguered minority of immigrants suffering cultural, religious and social-status deprivation. For 175 years, the primary goals of American Catholics were survival and personal and collective achievement. Since the time of Bishop John Hughes, Catholics had vigorously battled against a self-definition of America as a Protestant land, preferring, even forcing, a secularization of the public school system rather than accept its Protestant character. . . .

The strong and vigorous Catholic subculture, particularly as embodied in the parochial school, the urban neighborhood and the big-city political machine, served as an escalator of economic and social advancement for Catholics so that, by the 1960's, they were even more likely than Protestants to be achievement-oriented, in tune with the Puritan work ethic and firmly lodged in middle-class respectability. Even before the council, then, the days of the ghetto church, battling for equal justice in a hostile environment, were over. Victory, however, brought with it the taste of ashes as it laid bare just how shallow much of the classic program of the American church had been.

Upward mobility and acceptance by American culture constituted the core objectives of immigrant Catholics and their leaders. And yet, for all their achievements, American Catholics, as Richard Hofstader has noted, "have been influenced by the American environment to a far greater degree than they have influenced it." Recent historical work on American Catholicism, in forcing us to nuance Prof. Hofstader's judgment, recognizes the extent to which it mirrors a one-sided, Anglo-ethnic, assimilationist perspective. Thus, Michael Novak has referred to the ways in which Catholic ward politics softened the inhumane economic and political realities of a harsh urban life by a kind of participatory democracy — not participation in making the rules, but participation in a network of people who exchange services. Jay Dolan has documented the extent to which Catholic urban neighborhoods were the most diverse concentrations in terms of class and ethnicity within the American landscape. In its day-to-day living and institutions, Catholicism may well have been the best single embodiment of the often-flawed national ideal of unity amid pluralistic cultural diversity.

By the time of the accession of Kennedy, Catholics had acquired their full share of that upward mobility, status and respectability they had so long and earnestly pursued. The immediate aftermath of their moment of success in the questioning climate of Vatican II was a Catholic explosion upon the national political life as Catholic names such as Eugene McCarthy, James Groppi, the brothers Berrigan and Sargent Shriver burst upon the public scene. At Selma, and in anti-Vietnam activities and the war on poverty, Catholics played a prominent role and set a tone to an era. Soon, however, this ever so brief Catholic renaissance exhausted its shallow roots as disillusionment, institutional setbacks measured in terms of a falling rate of Mass attendance, declining numbers of pupils in parochial schools, a drastic drop in vocations to the priesthood and religious life and a sapping of communal identity became the indices of the impact of *aggiornamento* on Americanization.

Whatever the need from a historical perspective to nuance Prof. Hofstader's comments about Catholicism, it seems fair to conclude that, in the post-Vatican II period of drift, Catholics, with few exceptions, have, indeed, been more shaped by their American environment than they have reciprocally influenced it. For, in what can only be seen as delicious irony, many of those who argued vigorously for the substitution of a community/people paradigm to replace the institutional model for the church have largely forgotten the primitive sociological truism that a people prospers only when it lives out of richly textured communal symbols and achieves its own unique sense of history, heroes and collective story — what we can call in code words, its tradition and peculiar language. Today, however, Catholic America, like the larger nation, is a land without adequate symbols.

I have argued, thus far, that American Catholics achieved middle-class respectability at a time when their own distinctive identity was called into question and without having any clear program that might either challenge or at least complement the ethos and institutions of the wider American society. Most of their leaders and intellectuals, thereupon, proceeded to disregard or jettison much of historic Catholic tradition and sensibilities upon which such a program might have been based. The responses to the Catholic identity-crisis have been varied.

Very few in the American church have opted for what seems to me to be the only sensible and hopeful strategy for successfully weathering the crisis with some identity intact, namely, a profound and genuinely open-ended *resourcement*, which envisions creative engagement with the received Catholic symbols in a dialectical effort both to break them open to new purposes, experiences and questions and to allow these latter, in turn, to challenge the tradition.

Dialogue must have two partners if it is to exist at all. It cannot be entirely receptivity or entirely the imposing of one's own agenda. It implies for each partner a conversion to the process of growth and change. This is not the same, however, as the loss of family resemblances: a people's earlier story, myths and symbols. Openness is not the same as characterlessness. And yet, most American Catholics are near illiterates in their own history. American Catholic history is conspicuously absent from parochial schools, church colleges and even seminaries.

It is helpful to consider some of the cultural paradoxes in contemporary American Catholicism. In a nation noted for its one-sided, if not pathological, emphasis on activism, instrumental rationality and optimistic pragmatism, Catholic intellectuals seem to have suffered a bout of amnesia about their classic wisdom concerning contemplation, mysticism, passivity and receptive acceptance of inevitable and unavoidable limits. The church, which for Jung represented the strongest carrier of the feminine in Western Christianity, in its American incarnation has become almost exclusively masculine, with dominant concerns for action, success, building the new earth and results.

Some of its theologians seem to have reduced theology to ethics, thereby weakening both. Instead of creatively reformulating Marian devotion, which was, among other less noble things, freighted with a strong sense of one's passivity before God, it consigns it to benign neglect, without finding another substitute symbolic carrier for one's receptivity before God. In an age when environmental conditions are forcing a halt to endless industrial expansion and the compensatory cultivation of both sobriety and the limitation of superfluous learned needs, American Catholics seem curiously out of touch with an earlier Catholic rationale for ascesis, which could claim that "the cultivation and expansion of needs is the antithesis of wisdom; it is also the antithesis of freedom and peace." Finally and most importantly, the church seems to have suffered pastoral bankruptcy in dealing with a specifically *religious* agenda at a time when a kind of religious revival of interiority is occurring outside the church.

American Catholics have been bequeathed a centuries-old tradition of social Catholicism. Indeed, the American church, in particular, had given renewed vigor to that tradition in the 1930's in the thought of Msgr. John A. Ryan and his associates, and in the 1950's through the work of John Courtney Murray. With all its defects, social Catholicism offers rich resources for finding a middle way between the excessive individualism, greed and disproportionate competition fostered by capitalism, on the one hand, and the unmediated collectivism of statism, on the other. Against the former, social Catholicism argues for the priority of the common good and the necessity to find criteria of ethical judgment beyond pragmatic purposes in the more ultimate this-worldly goals of human society. It refused to legitimate excessive economic concentration of power on the premise that every argument in favor of private property which is acceptable to the Christian conscience is also an argument for its greatest possible distribution.

Against unmediated state control of the economic order, social Catholicism proposed a doctrine of the state which stressed equally the duties and limits of state competence and the state's subservience to a more profound order of inherent and inalienable human rights and liberties. With a shrewd sociological wisdom, its principle of subsidiarity favored, by a presumptive rule, smaller, more manageable and natural units such as the family, primary networks of friends and work associates, the neighborhood and the region over larger, impersonal bureaucratic units.

Recalling Lord Acton's byword concerning the corruptive dangers of unchecked power, social Catholicism showed a decided bias toward decentralization and a balance of power in the economic and political orders. In this century, a new sense of evolving history detached social Catholicism from scholastic cosmological premises concerning a static order to the universe or society. At least since the ground-breaking corpus of Emmanuel Mounier, who worked within the tradition, social Catholicism has included a much-needed commitment to personalism and human growth.

Referring to this tradition, the Protestant social ethicist John C. Bennett has remarked: "Roman Catholicism, unlike Protestantism, has always kept some distance from capitalism." The British economist, E.F. Schumacher has written a contemporary underground classic, *Small Is Beautiful,* whose extraordinary ethical

wisdom in great part relies upon Catholic notions of the common good, moral virtue and the principle of subsidiarity. And yet, for most of the post-Vatican II American church, it is as if that tradition never existed or were totally corrupt. Among Catholic social ethicists today perhaps only Ivan Illich continues to work within that tradition in new and exciting ways to give us some inkling of what a humane socialism or, as he perhaps more aptly terms it, a "convivial society" might look like.

In recent years the focus of concern of American Catholics, as of international Catholicism generally, has properly shifted to a global context. Imperialism, the armaments race, pollution, the inordinate and untamed power of the transnational corporations, the sad and steady decline of the Third World nations, the exploitation of women, international racism, the population explosion—these topics appropriately loom large in contemporary Catholic ethical discussions.

On the other hand, there has been an almost total obliviousness to the fate of the soft and fragile institutions such as the family, the community and parochial school, and the neighborhood. And yet, the church has had close intimate contact with and knowledge of these institutions. It has a doctrine of society that is biased toward them. Moreover, every sociological sensibility informs us that the neighborhood, the family, intimate networks of kin, friends and work colleagues and the ethnic and religious group are the primary loci for socialization to a sense of personhood, communal values, bonds of loyalty and—in hostile environments—resistance. It seems hardly worth arguing the fact that these soft institutions—or some functional substitute for them—must be vigorous as an indispensable prerequisite for a convivial society. Participation in them has been the source of what an earlier generation referred to as "common grace." They serve as workshops for apprenticeship in virtue, humane sensibility and practical wisdom.

These so-called institutions can also serve as key social turf to do battle against that unchecked economic and political bureaucratic centralization which makes life in contemporary America, with its exultant triumph of technical rationality, so often feel for some like Max Weber's image of the modern world as an "iron cage." . . .

I would argue, then, that special-priority status should be given to pastoral strategies aimed at both nurturing present strength and enabling new directions of growth for the family unit, the functional work unit, the neighborhood and the region. Where territorial units have totally lost functional meaning, priority should be given to creating "base-communities" consisting of networks of families and work associates. Even within traditional and unwieldy American parishes, this strategic concentration on creating real grass-roots communities seems preferable to a neo-Christendom paradigm directed to the impossible task of total territorial inclusion.

Where viable neighborhoods still exist, programs of community organizing may promise to do for the new, changed urban situations what the traditional neighborhood parish did for the old. There seems to be an elective affinity between the classic function of the Catholic parish as a neighborhood center and the goals of the community organization. Moreover, in black neighborhoods, the parochial school often serves a special neighborhood function. The American church, never conspicuous for its concern for black Americans, should commit itself as a pastoral priority to maintaining, even at

serious financial sacrifice, such parochial schools in the inner city.

I am prepared to argue further that American society at large has never adequately implemented the national ideal of cultural diversity. It has stubbornly resisted language pluralism, only reluctantly achieved its genuine religious pluralism and looked askance at deviations from the dominant symbol for politics, morality and the family. But neither has American Catholicism, which was spun out of a web of extraordinary ethnic diversity, sufficiently allowed its internal cultural pluralism to surface. In revising the historical record, recent historians of American Catholicism have seen that, to some extent, the German immigrant Catholics of the 19th century, who lost their historic battle with the Irish Americanizers over the question of cultural diversity within the church, represented a clearer ideal than that of the Irish — of Catholic unity amidst cultural pluralism. The Germans were also more likely than the Irish to be critical of the prevailing American ethos.

A tendency toward factionalism among the Germans, Irish superiority in language, political organization, urban concentration and numbers, as well as the organizational imperatives of the American church of that period, dictated that the Irish program should prevail. In the process, an enormous opportunity for a richer internal pluralism within American Catholicism was lost. Persisting resentments of Italians and, especially, Polish and Eastern European Catholics against the Irish style of dominance within the clergy and hierarchy is a witness to the Irish failure to do full justice to cultural diversity. And, yet, providentially, the opportunity has not been entirely lost.

There are still strong residues of ethnic

separateness among Italians, Poles and Eastern European Catholics and the more recent Hispanic immigrants from Puerto Rico, Cuba, Mexico and Central and South America, as well as the recently arrived Catholic refugees from Vietnam. Current statistics indicate that Hispanic Catholics in some dioceses constitute from a third to a half of the Catholic population. These ethnic groups are in touch with alternative cultural symbols which view authority, politics, morality, interpersonal loyalties, the structures of work and leisure, the rhythms of life and death, youth and old age and the dynamism of the human body in ways profoundly different from that of the dominant American symbolism.

The Catholic ethnic groups are mainly composed of the lower middle class and poor. I am enough of an economic determinist to think that the special American Catholic concern in the past for the cause of the working classes and poor, although perhaps prompted and given direction by the high intellectual tradition of social Catholicism, was largely rooted in the pastoral exigencies of working with a lower-class constituency. Because of its unique history and social-class basis, American Catholicism had much more impetus to become a champion of the encyclical tradition of international Catholicism than did many of the bourgeois-centered European churches. Hence, in America the Catholic working classes were not lost to the church.

The persistence of a significant base of lower-middle- and lower-class Catholics in its pastoral constituency may well be an indispensable link to keep the American church alert to calls from the Roman international center for a more just economic order and the strategic choice by the church to side with the cause of the least advantaged. America's Catholic eth-

nic groups could be a necessary bridge to narrow the gap between the overly Americanized church and its inescapable vocation to play a pivotal role for justice within international Catholicism. Those who are urging that American Catholic scholarship and pastoral strategies address themselves to the persisting phenomenon of ethnicity argue, persuasively it seems to me, that it is highly unlikely that the dominant American culture will be open to challenge and enrichment by other cultures across the globe if it is unable to respect cultural diversity in its own midst. If one wants to state it in the strongest possible terms, the ethnic groups may be the primary provokers for us to heed what John C. Bennett has called "the radical imperative" of the gospel toward justice and peace. Placing a strategic priority upon understanding and fostering ethnicity and Catholic pluralism would commit the American church to a strategy that might not only challenge and complement the dominant American ethos but promise to nudge the American church toward becoming as thoroughly Catholic as it is American. For, as James Joyce seemed to sense in *Finnegans Wake,* "Catholicism means, here comes everybody."

Finally, a serious confrontation with ethnicity bids fair to be for Catholicism a resource for dealing with its new sensibility to its denominational particularity and historical-contextual relativism. With the effective collapse of neo-Scholasticism, Catholicism has lost all pretensions to have a secure, universal and static language. It is beginning to face squarely the particularity and limits of the Catholic tradition, generally, and that of the American Catholic experience. It knows that it is but one, finite symbol system, one language, one tradition among the many.

If the sectarian Catholic theology is dead, so is the Enlightenment. Truth, once again, only comes riding a donkey. For, particularity, like history, is the human fate. In a sense, the recent puncturing of inflated Catholic pretensions to speak *the* universal language should make Catholics especially sensitive to the complaints of the various liberation movements among women and blacks that attack the imperial claims of male or upper-class white language or presumptive attempts to speak *for* those who have been robbed of active and passive voice.

If this sense of one's finite particularity requires extensive and multidirectional dialogue with a variety of other traditions, religious and secular, it no less demands a careful nurturing of one's own collective symbols. For if a people's collective symbols are allowed to wither and die, the people will die. Without a distinctive language and collective story, there simply is no vigorous sense of peoplehood. Just as the great collective symbols are ever so much more powerful than individual symbols, so the history and tradition of a people is of a richer texture than any individual life can fully absorb, embody or creatively shape. In dialogue, there is, of course, a place for a careful selective absorption of alien symbols from other traditions.

It is probably the case that only in dialogue with alien traditions can one even discover and retrieve lost echoes within one's own tradition. Selective absorption and transformation of alien symbols may be in order, although it is not always so easy a task as it sounds. In a pluralistic society, one resists, to be sure, inordinate claims that one's own symbolic is necessarily more universal or the exact counterpart to the other. One contents oneself with the satisfaction that the Catholic symbol, in all its particularity and finiteness, is one's own and offers the symbol to others who may find it useful or illuminative to help them understand the reality of their tradition, as Catholics, in turn, find alien symbols illuminative of theirs. One avoids sheer relativism, in turn, by adopting a twofold strategy of, on the one hand, epistemological humility and, on the other, the careful nurturing of one's own tradition, not simply because it is one's own but because one assumes it is in some sense a special vehicle of truth. It is only with the stance of epistemological humility that Catholic truth claims can ever be publicly tested. If this strategy of *resourcement* is a call for the American church to become more deeply Catholic than it has perhaps ever been, it should be clear that it is a call to become a very different kind of Catholic than prevailed in the pre-Vatican II church. For what I am proposing as the most creative intellectual strategy for dealing with the crisis in American Catholicism is the kind of *resourcement* that Michael Novak has referred to as an "openness with roots": "To attempt to be open to all other cultures, without having roots of one's own, is almost certainly to misperceive the otherness of such culture. It is, perhaps, even to be incapable of culture. For culture is a kind of rootedness. The word itself suggests the patient cultivation of a living, growing plant. To have culture is to be shaped by a social tradition, shaped willingly and joyously, so that the shaping is appropriated as one's own, and so that the culture, as it were, becomes alive in oneself under one's own direction. One does not choose the culture into which one is born; but one may choose to go as deeply into it as one can, to realize every human potential it affords. Paradoxically, it is through the route of becoming particular that one finds, at the depths, genuine universality."

64.

Immigrants in the Labor Market

The Industrial Revolution in the United States was built from the labor of millions of immigrants who came to the country between 1820 and 1925. Cheap non-union labor enabled the "captains of industry" to operate the mines, factories, and railroads and to make the United States the leading economic power in the modern world. But the labor scene has changed dramatically since the end of the Great Migration, fifty years ago. Labor is no longer cheap; there are many industrial and trade unions; and the labor market, especially in times of economic stress, can become very tight. Yet immigrants still flock to America hoping to make their fortune. In this selection Colin Greer and Marvin Surkin examine the impact of recent immigrants upon an economy in recession.

Source: *New York Times,* November 6, 1976. "Paving Streets With His Life."

THIS IS STILL A NATION of immigrants. Immigration, now as in the past, is a permanent fixture. But the situation today requires a fresh look and critical analysis, since immigration has been on the rise precisely at a time of high unemployment.

Immigration has been increasingly associated with unemployment so simplistically as to imply that closing the doors on foreign labor will solve the unemployment problem. On the contrary, both immigration and unemployment are established pillars of American socioeconomic life and are not merely the products of current economic trends.

Altogether, 3.5 million legal immigrants entered the United States between 1964 and 1974. If illegal immigrants are included at the rates estimated by the Immigration and Naturalization Service and the Labor Department, the number would reach a staggering 8 to 12 million.

More than 10 percent of the labor force is made up of recent immigrant workers. In New York City, there are more than 1.5 million recent immigrants; 10 percent of needles-trade labor consists of immigrants. In Detroit, there are 15,-000 Arab workers in the auto industry. In Mahwah, N.J., at the Ford plant, Puerto Rican, Dominican, Honduran, Haitian and other Caribbean and Latin-American peoples have been hired in recent years in increasingly large numbers.

National unemployment is still at its highest since the 1930's. Unemployment in such cities as New York and Detroit underscores the extent of the new joblessness. More and more, people are being thrown out of work it has taken generations of aspirations to achieve. Indeed, current unemployment is dominated by the children of earlier immigrants. And if, as seems the case, the Ford Administration is ready to accept 6 percent unemployment as the definition of full employment, it is ensuring limited, even downward mobility for more and more Americans.

It is important to recognize that the new hard-core unemployed are, in fact,

These Vietnamese immigrants at Fenton, Michigan, are purchasing the house they pose in front of.

the immigrants and in-migrants who had supposedly "made it" through protective labor contracts, white collar status, and the security of public employment.

Yet, new immigrants are still coming to find work. They are prepared to work for pay that is below the minimum wage, and find themselves in pre-Depression labor conditions. The unwritten agreement is that their hard work, which generates business profits, will also generate personal success. Consequently, they expect precisely the security and mobility that earlier immigrants are losing.

Meanwhile, the heavy concentration of illegals among those who arrive from Asia, Africa, the Middle East, Latin America, the Caribbean and Southern Europe are the latest manifestation of the way American society—and that of other Western nations—continually reproduce the bottom of the social structure.

Illegals are not legitimate workers and so function outside the law and outside the protections that labor has won over the years. Apparently, this is the only way that American business enterprise can turn a "reasonable" profit.

Illegals work under conditions that all immigrants were subject to in earlier periods; immigrant labor has historically provided the basis for business flexibility in the face of the economic cycle.

Illegal immigration underscores the costs paid for this flexibility, reminding us of the continuing need for foreign workers and proving that the profit/labor equation it represents can only exist on a sufficiently large scale by operating outside the law.

Furthermore, illegal immigration in the face of high unemployment means that the opportunity and mobility that immigrants historically came here for has been exceedingly fragile. Making room for new people at the bottom of the social ladder has frequently given the impression that the push upward for those who preceded them is widespread and durable. But it isn't!

As in the past, cheap labor is imported. But on an unprecedented scale, these workers are now illegal immigrants whose labor and living conditions go virtually unprotected by the norms of law. The new unemployed and the new immigrants, especially illegals, show how the priorities of profit in American economic life continue to demand impoverished workers. Nowadays, however, the dream that attracts them and the profit their labor produces have to operate outside the law to work at all.

65.

ELI GINZBERG: The Pluralistic Economy of the U.S.

The economy of the United States is so huge and diversified that no one, not even the best informed economist, can hope to comprehend all of its complexities. Most Americans are satisfied to accept a few conventional ideas about "free enterprise," a market economy, laws of supply and demand, and so forth. We reject, at least theoretically, all forms of "collectivism," the planned economy, and any obvious moves toward "socialism." But the commonly accepted theories hardly match the prevailing practice, as this selection demonstrates. Eli Ginzberg is chairman of the National Commission for Manpower Policy. He and his associates have studied the whole of the American economy and have come up with conclusions about it that are at variance with many of the standard views.

Source: *Scientific American*, December 1976.

THE NATION HAS been through another quadrennial election campaign in which voters were exhorted to preserve (or strengthen or revitalize or more equally distribute the fruits of) our private-enterprise system. Few truisms are so firmly implanted in the American consciousness as the notion that our economy is a private-enterprise one. The fact is that it is not. It is private and public, profit-making and not-for-profit: a pluralistic economy of private enterprise, nonprofit institutions and government. Persistent failure to recognize this pluralism and to perceive the interrelations of the economy's various elements clouds understanding of important economic issues and makes it harder to deal with some current problems.

More than 10 years ago Dale L. Hiestand, Beatrice G. Reubens and I became convinced that the dominant picture of the U.S. economy as a private-enterprise system was in need of revision. Even before we looked closely at the figures we surmised that the cumulative growth of government—national, state and local—had permanently altered the structure and functioning of the economy, and that the economy could no longer be encapsulated within a private-enterprise, profit-maximizing model. The main effort of our inquiry was to find the answer to one critical question: What proportion of the U.S. economy's output and employment was accounted for by activities outside the private, profit-oriented sector? Our considered answer was that about a fourth of the gross national product and no less than a third (and possibly as much as two-fifths) of the country's employment was generated by nonprofit institutions and government, which is to say by the not-for-profit sector.

One might have expected such a finding, published in 1965 in our book *The Pluralistic Economy*, to attract attention. It did, but primarily abroad; it was largely ignored by economists and journalists at home. Foreign observers in both developed and developing countries had no difficulty absorbing the evidence of the rapid growth of the not-for-profit sector in the U.S. economy. They knew that their own governments played a dominant role in shaping their economies, and they had no reason to question the finding that government had come to play a critical role in this country too. Our colleagues at home preferred to ignore our findings rather than confronting them. Conservatives and liberals alike were comfortable with the old view that the private sector continued to dominate the American economy, the one group applauding and the other group criticizing that basic state of affairs. It was less disturbing intellectually and less threatening ideologically (regardless of the particular ideology) to reaffirm the conventional wisdom that the economy operates under market forces, with government's role limited to adjustments of the rules of the game and the distribution of rewards.

Little has changed in the decade since our book was published. Presidents Johnson, Nixon and Ford—and many other people—have continued to emphasize that "five out of six jobs" are based in the private sector, as if repetition and emphasis could alter arithmetic. What are the facts? Hiestand recently brought our 1963 data up to 1973. With total national employment in that year at 84.7 million, "general government" employees came to 13.4 million (full-time-equivalent workers). That is the basis for the five-out-of-six reference. It makes no sense, however, to isolate direct government employment and call everything else private. The important distinction is between the private, profit-seeking sector and the total not-for-profit sector.

To begin with, the private sector is not all that private. When the Federal Government buys missiles from Lockheed or naval vessels from Litton, workers employed in those companies' West Coast plants or Gulf Coast shipyards are classified as employees of the private-enterprise sector, but no economist should be comfortable with such a designation. The wages those workers earn are paid for out of Federal Government funds, and their output is absorbed exclusively by the Government. For years the Army has manufactured some of its ammunition in its own arsenals whose workers have always been counted as Government employees. It is hard to see the logic of classifying those who work for defense contractors as belonging in the private sector any more than the arsenal workers belong in it, since their output is absorbed by government.

This principle of classification extends far beyond defense. In seeking to draw realistic boundaries between the private and the not-for-profit sectors we believe all employment generated by government purchases of all kinds in the private sector must be counted as part of the not-for-profit sector. This can be done by converting the dollars government spends on such purchases into an equivalent employment figure. Hiestand's calculations for 1973 show government purchases from the private sector as amounting to 9.9 percent of the gross national product. He calculates that this represents 8.4 percent of the total employment of 84.7 million, or 7.1 million workers. The combined direct and indirect employment of all government in 1973, then, was 13.4 million plus 7.1 million, or 20.5 million. About one American worker in four depends for his job on the activities of government, directly or indirectly.

Although government is the largest component of the not-for-profit sector, it is not the only one. The other significant segment comprises the nonprofit institutions: churches, colleges, voluntary hospitals, labor unions, social organizations, special-interest associations and many more. Hiestand's calculations for 1973 show a total direct employment of five million in these nonprofit institutions, or 5.9 percent of total employment. Here as in the case of government, however, one must take into account the purchases by nonprofit institutions from the private sector in order to obtain a total view of the economic impact of those institutions. Converting the purchases into employment adds another 1.8 percent, giving the nonprofit institutions a total of 7.7 percent of U.S. employment.

We are now in a position to derive a more realistic estimate of the role played by the entire not-for-profit sector in terms of employment. Government is responsible for 24.2 percent of U.S. employment and nonprofit institutions for 7.7: the two add up to 31.9 percent. It would be desirable to add to that a small increment reflecting government or quasi-governmental employees in, for example, the Postal Service, municipal hospital systems and state liquor stores. Those figures are obscured, however, because we are converting dollars of purchases into employment, and the Department of Commerce includes such enterprises not in the government sector but in the business sector of its national-income accounts! Even if they represent only a percent or two of total employment, it is clear that the not-for-profit sector as a whole is responsible for one out of three, rather than one out of six, American workers. A complementary picture in terms of dollars can be developed by calculating the total output of goods and services accounted for by government and nonprofit institutions as a proportion of the gross national product. The larger role of the not-for-profit sector in employment than in gross national product reflects two factors: a larger proportion of that sector's total ex-

penditures goes to payrolls and below-average wages are paid by nonprofit institutions.

The weight of this evidence is unequivocal. The American economy is much less private than either its defenders or its critics have assumed. Moreover, one should note that government transfer payments to or on behalf of individuals, such as food stamps or Medicaid payments to private nursing homes, are not included in national-income accounts. Such transfers would add another 3 to 5 percent to the not-for-profit sector's share of output and of equivalent employment.

A second critical question relates to the trend. Conservatives call for action to halt the rapid rise in government spending, which they consider to be the road to inflation and ruin. Through recourse to linear extrapolation they insist that unless the trend is broken it will not be long until government controls most of the country's resources and output. (In the countries of Western Europe, on the other hand, there has been much less concern about the growth of the government sector, at least until recently.) Hiestand has looked at the U.S. trend since 1929. In that year the not-for-profit sector accounted for about 15 percent of total employment and 12.5 percent of output. In terms of either measure, employment or share of the gross national product, the increase through the Depression years and World War II was gradual; the most striking advance for the not-for-profit sector came in the 1950's. There was some additional growth in the 1960's but it was much slower. And in the early years of this decade there was a slight decline.

The analysis up to this point has assumed that there is a clear-cut differentiation between the private profit-seeking sector and the not-for-profit one. A more sensitive delineation of the boundaries of the profit-seeking arena would have to take note of the fact that several of the nation's largest industries operate under government controls that constrict their freedom with respect to both prices and profits. At a minimum one would have to consider as something less than completely private those enterprises engaged in transportation, communications and the production of power. In 1974 they accounted for approximately 4.7 million employees, or about 5 percent of the total employment, and they contributed 11 percent of the total gross national product. There is no point in exploiting the data further to expand the "controlled" sector, except perhaps to note that three additional industries—agriculture, banking and insurance—operate at least in part under price and profit controls.

The heated political debate on the relative sizes of the private sector and the public one is frequently conducted with such slogans as "the market" v. "economic planning" or, in their more extreme form, "capitalism" v. "socialism." Less emotionally charged terms are more appropriate. Potent factors have been operating to enlarge the not-for-profit sector. Among the most important has been the much enlarged role of the Federal Government since World War II in defense and in defense-related areas such as space, atomic energy and a broad range of research-and-development activities. More recently the expanding Federal commitment in education, manpower and health has also been a potent factor.

Yet the fastest-growing sector of government, particularly in terms of employment, has not been the Federal Government at all but state and local government. These jurisdictions were forced to respond to the demands of an expanding population for improved services in such fields as education, health and welfare and for such conventional services as police and fire protection and sanitation. In terms of personnel, state and local governments have been the most rapidly expanding sector of the American economy. In 1950 their total employment was 4.3 million; in 1974 it came to 11.8 million, an increase of 174 percent. Total employment in the same period increased by only 46 percent. Many of the same forces that stimulated the growth of government were also responsible for the relatively rapid growth of nonprofit institutions, particularly in higher education and hospitals.

Those who see the growth of the not-for-profit sector primarily as an ideological issue fail to appreciate the extent to which it reflects the inability of the private sector to respond to priority needs and desires of the American people. One can argue about whether or not the U.S. overreacted to the threat of Russian expansion, but once the threat was defined as being serious it was inevitable that the nation's defense and defense-related expenditures would increase. Similarly, ideology has had very little to do with the desire of the public for improved access to higher education and health services. It took many years for the health reformers to overcome the opposition of the American Medical Association, but the eventual passage of Medicare in 1965 was effected by broad-based political support.

Once the American people had made choices for strong defense, more access to higher education and improved medical care, the die was cast in favor of an enlarged role for the not-for-profit sector. Moreover, there was no way for the nation to accommodate its rapidly rising population and the irrepressible demand for a suburban way of life unless all levels of government expanded. The growth of the not-for-profit sector was inevitable because the goods and services that a more affluent America wanted could not be provided by private-sector entrepreneurs operating through the market. Important as the private sector has been in stimulating the growth of the economy, there is no way to read our recent history without recognizing the strategic part government and nonprofit institutions have played in providing new entrepreneurial structures for meeting new needs and desires of the public.

The focus on defense, education and health provides a background to one of the most important economic transformations now under way: the growth of the service economy. The full details and implications of this transformation have still not been adequately examined or assessed. One simple way to gauge its scale is to compare the four goods-producing industries—agriculture, mining, manufacturing and construction—with all other activities, which are conventionally grouped under the heading of services.

Almost the entire growth in post-World War II employment has been in the service sector. Among the goods-producing industries only construction shows any sizable increase. Agriculture declined by more than half, from some 7.6 to 3.5 million: mining declined by approximately a third, from 955,000 to 672,000; manufacturing—the backbone of the economy—showed only a small absolute increase: approximately a third, from 15.6 to 20 million, which meant that its share of total employment dropped from about 27 percent to 21 percent. In terms of contribution to the gross national product the relative decline of the goods-producing sector was less steep. Between 1950 and 1974 manufacturing actually registered a small increase in its share of output: in 1950 that share was 29.7 percent and in 1974 it was 30.8 percent.

The rapid growth of services and their newly acquired dominance in the expansion of employment, along with the bias toward commodity transactions that is inherent in economic analysis, guarantee that many efforts to diagnose economic ills and to devise new programs are doomed to error and frustration. A few illustrations will make this clear.

There has recently been much comment in Washington and among captains of industry about a disastrous decline in the productivity of the American economy and the danger such a decline presents to our international competitive position and our long-run economic well-being. People have also sought to explain the fact that our rate of growth is slower than, say, Japan's by arguing that we devote too much of our income to consumption and too little to saving and investment. That we save and invest proportionately less than Japan is true, but the productivity-growth argument has a further dimension that is related to the size of the government sector in the two countries. By convention the output of the larger U.S. government sector is measured in terms of the inputs: the dollars spent for payrolls and other purposes, which are assumed to equal the value of the services provided. Hence there is no way for this large sector to contribute to an increase in total productivity. National-income accounting practices force the much-reduced private sector to carry the entire burden of registering productivity gains.

The difficulties run deeper than that, however. The key to service output is quality, not quantity. For example, before there were antibiotics people with severe infections often died and others required weeks or months of care before they recovered. Today such patients are often cured within a few days by one injection or a series of them. The national-income accounts do not reflect the improved quality of medical care or of other services. We measure the gains in productivity in the manufacture of television sets but assume that the quality of programming remains the same.

The burden of these few illustrations is to argue the case that the shift from goods production to services, a cause and a concomitant of the growth of the not-for-profit sector, has fundamentally distorted our system of national accounts, has complicated our ability to locate points of weakness in our economic system and has compounded the difficulties of designing effective solutions.

We are still at an early stage in our ability to differentiate among the component parts of the service sector, which in 1974 accounted for two-thirds of total employment and $534 billion of output. People tend to think in terms of consumer services, from medical care to hairdressing. There has also been large growth in the producer services: the services, such as trucking, advertising, the law, management consulting and computing and all the rest, that support the profit-making activities of the business sector. It is surprising that Harry I. Greenfield's 1967 book *Manpower and the Growth of Producer Services* was the first serious consideration of the role of those important services in economic development. My colleagues and I in our ongoing studies of New York City (which is overwhelmingly a service economy, with more than 80 percent of total employment in the service sector) stress that the city's future depends less on attracting back some of the manufacturing firms that have left it than it does on retaining and strengthening its complex of corporate headquarters and the advanced services—banking, legal, accounting, communications, public relations—that are linked together and mutually support one another and the corporate headquarters.

It is no sign of disrespect to point out in this bicentennial year of the publication of Adam Smith's *The Wealth of Nations* that economists, politicians and journalists are caught up in a Smithian fallacy. Smith argued that the test of productive labor was whether the work resulted in material output: a physical representation of the time and effort expended. In short, the craftsman who builds a violin is productive but Heifetz and Menuhin are not; the manufacturer of a scalpel is productive, but not the surgeon who excises a tumor and thereby saves a life.

Smith wanted to emphasize an important point. He was concerned by the fact that, as he saw it, a great many people were being "kept." He included the extraordinarily large number of household retainers, bureaucrats whose sole activity was to get in the way of ambitious businessmen, members of the court and other supernumeraries. In Smith's view such people contributed nothing to the growth of the economy. Today only a dyed-in-the-wool Keynesian (who would prefer to have government pay men to dig holes than to have them idle) would challenge him. In striving after the distinction between productive and unproductive labor, however, Smith pressed too hard and went too far. And many who came after him absorbed his prejudice without appreciating the particular distinction he was trying to make.

There have been several important manpower concomitants to the rapid growth of the not-for-profit and service sectors of the economy. The services have facilitated the rapid growth of female employment. Between 1950 and 1974 the civilian employment of males 16 years

On the floor of the New York Stock Exchange.

and over increased from 41.6 to 52.5 million, or by approximately 26 percent. During the same period the number of female workers employed increased from 17.3 to 33.4 million, or by 93 percent: three and a half times as much.

Not only did the number of new job openings available to women increase but also the services were more able to offer less-than-full-time employment, a schedule of work that both the employers and many women preferred. This accommodation was not all gain, to be sure: it meant that many women workers were not able to obtain desirable full-time jobs with fringe benefits, security and opportunity for career development. Whereas many women found what they wanted—work that was not too demanding and gave them an opportunity to supplement their family income and to get out of the home—many others who were the head of a family or who had strong career drives were hard-pressed to find suitable job and career openings.

The rapid expansion of service employment also opened up many opportunities for part-time or intermittent work for young people whose main activity was pursuing their education. The period after World War II witnessed a rapid expansion in postsecondary education supported in no small measure by the enlarged earning opportunities that were opened up for students in a broad array of service industries.

One of the striking consequences of the increase in the proportion of women and of students employed and in the labor force was the extent to which the prototype of a worker as a person employed full time for the full year from young adulthood until retirement no longer fits the American scene. As Dean Morse pointed out some years ago in *The Peripheral Worker*, of all people who work during the course of a year almost 45 percent are employed less than full time for the full year: only 55 percent fit the stereotype of the conventional worker. Even if the calculation is shifted from the number of workers to the total work performed, one finds that about 30 percent of all work is performed by those who are not full-time workers.

Another important manpower concomitant of the recent expansion of services has been the substantial growth of professionals, in education, health, management, science, engineering and many other fields. For two and a half decades, from 1945 to 1970, the economy was able to absorb the increasing output of the colleges, graduate schools and professional schools with no serious evidence of any weakening in demand. In part this balance reflected the relatively long time required to expand the structure of higher education and to fill the pipeline. In part it reflected the enlarged expenditures by government for research and development, which created a new market that absorbed many of the newly trained specialists. By 1970, however, the supply had overtaken the demand, and since then the outlook for educated manpower has appreciably worsened, particularly for people with degrees in the humanities.

In my view there is a strong linkage among the following: the growth of the not-for-profit sector, the substantial increase in educated manpower, the rapid growth of the advanced services and the generally good record of performance of the American economy. To the extent that these developments are interrelated — and it is difficult to see how they could not be — we find confirmation for the basic thesis on which the pluralistic economy of the U.S. is based. It is not simply the growth of the not-for-profit sector that is critical. It is rather the new articulations between the not-for-profit sector and the private sector based on the principle of complementarity. The prosperity of the automotive industry has long depended on an expanding national highway system. Similarly, the argument can be made, the research-based and science-based industries and advanced services that continue to provide the frontiers of the economy — from more powerful computers to strengthened capital markets — depend on the trained manpower produced in the colleges and universities based in the not-for-profit sector. To discuss the not-for-profit sector as a profligate spender of scarce resources without reference to its critical contribution to enlarging the wealth and welfare of the American economy and society may arouse enthusiasm among certain components of the body politic, but it is not likely to win much favor or have much influence on public policy, even among a people that considers its tax burden onerous.

A society can act more intelligently if it has a clearer perception of the nature and functioning of its basic institutions. This article has sought to provide a few modest clarifications, which I shall summarize.

The U.S. economy, while still dependent on a large and vigorous private sector, is in fact a pluralistic economy in which the not-for-profit sector accounts for one in every three jobs.

With the goods-producing industries accounting for an ever smaller part of the nation's output and employment, it is critically important that we abandon simplistic reliance on a manufacturing model and deepen our understanding of the role of services in the production of wealth and welfare. For example, concern about the slow growth of productivity may or may not be justified, but nobody really knows whether it is because we have not learned how to measure productivity in the services.

The foundation for an advanced service economy is trained manpower. This manpower is educated in the not-for-profit sector, thereby establishing the principle of complementarity between it and the private sector and illustrating the interdependence of the various elements of our pluralistic economy.

President Ford delivers a Bicentennial address in front of Independence Hall in Philadelphia.

LOOKING BACKWARD, LOOKING FORWARD

The year of the Bicentennial was a time that portended change. Americans remembered and re-enacted their Revolutionary past, but they did so in the shadow of a tragic and lost war abroad and a devastating political scandal at home. The United States of America, on its two-hundredth anniversary, seemed poised for renewal of faith in itself, ready to set about solving the many domestic problems that had gone so long unattended.

Bicentennial celebration at Lexington-Concord, Massachusetts. Vice President Nelson Rockefeller at the Republican National Convention in Kansas City, Missouri.

Another view of the Bicentennial celebration at Lexington-Concord. Jimmy Carter and President Ford meet in the first of three televised campaign debates.

The Bicentennial celebration had hardly ended when the 1976 presidential campaign got under way. In convention at Madison Square Garden in New York, the Democrats nominated former Georgia governor Jimmy Carter and Senator Walter Mondale to be their standard bearers. And at Kansas City, Missouri, a hotly contested Republican race ended when President Ford defeated a serious challenge by former California governor Ronald Reagan. Senator Robert Dole was Ford's running mate. Carter began the campaign with a strong lead in the public opinion polls, but by election day this lead had been whittled away to almost nothing; and Carter won the election by a slim majority. Otherwise the election was a Democratic sweep; the party maintained a sure control in Congress and held most of the state governorships.

Jimmy Carter and Senator Walter Mondale on the platform at the Democratic National Convention, July 1976. July 4, 1976, in Detroit, Michigan.

66.

ANTHONY SAMPSON: The Lockheed Connection

In August 1975, Lockheed Corporation, the nations's largest defense contractor, admitted having paid out more than $24 million in bribes to officials of foreign countries in order to promote the sales of its airplanes. In the wake of this announcement it was learned that dozens of other corporations had made similar overseas payments. This news about corporate bribery had serious repercussions in several countries. The Japanese government was severely shaken by the scandal, and former Prime Minister Kakuei Tanaka was indicted for accepting $1.7 million from Lockheed. In The Netherlands, Prince Bernhard, husband of Queen Juliana, was accused of accepting more than one million dollars. In February 1976 the two top officials of Lockheed resigned. This article by Anthony Sampson provides a detailed account of Lockheed's overseas activities. It originally appeared in the London Observer.

Source: *Atlas World Press Review*, May 1976.

THE LOCKHEED CORP of California has, according to the latest evidence, been paying bribes in at least fourteen countries. In at least six it has caused a major government crisis. "Not since Lenin," one member of the multinationals committee in Washington remarked, "have so many governments been threatened at once."

The Lockheed testimony and the vivid memoranda that have been subpoenaed furnish a narrative of how a dynamic but heavy-handed corporation built up an aggressive network of salesmen through Europe over the past twenty years: and the story raises many questions wider than bribes.

To see the Lockheed story in perspective it is necessary to flash back briefly to the late Fifties when this thrusting California company was first pushing itself into Europe. Its planes were crucial weapons of the Cold War and its links with the Pentagon and the CIA were necessarily close. Lockheed had built the spectacular U-2 spy plane which could photograph Soviet installations from a height of 50,000 feet (and whose discovery by the Russians brought the collapse of the 1960 summit).

In the Cold War atmosphere of the time the selling of aircraft and the security of the West were specially close. For anyone inside the military-industrial complex the business was a crusade. The California companies had a special confidence and romance, and the great Lockheed headquarters at Burbank, just north of Hollywood, was one of the wonders of the West.

In this dedicated atmosphere Lockheed in the late Fifties produced a brand new fighter which was uniquely versatile, called the Starfighter, or F-104. It climbed steeply, accelerated easily: it could attack, reconnoiter, support, and bomb. Pilots regarded it as a wonder plane; but it was, as one aviation expert described it, an unforgiving aircraft. The Starfighter was the spearhead of the Lockheed invasion of Europe, and the executives went abroad with a well-based confidence in their plane and with a driving zeal. Behind all their enthusiasm—as so often in aircraft companies—lay the personality of one man.

He is Daniel Jeremiah Haughton, one of the last charismatic names in American business. A country boy from Alabama with a wide grin and boyish style, he began in Lockheed as a cost accountant but came to breathe the very spirit of aeronautic adventure: even in London, addressing hardboiled civil servants, he has been observed to bring tears to their eyes. "I had an alarming feeling," said one Rolls-Royce executive, "that if he told us to march out of the window we would follow him." Haughton became president in 1961 and inspired the Lockheed men to go out and sell their planes; and it was his enthusiasm, filtering its way down, which became transmuted into subterranean methods.

The Americans' concern with bribery was partly promoted by their conviction that the Europeans—and particularly the French—were the master bribers: and the documents reveal a positive obsession with Gallic corruption. No doubt there was some evidence that Dassault, their chief French rivals, were passing bribes (a Dassault employee is currently charged with bribing a Dutch official). But what the Americans were also up against, as one memo lamented, was French "tact and diplomacy"—together with the effective coordination between French diplomats and businessmen. And into this subtle territory the gung-ho Lockheed agents moved with heavy tread, and with an obsessive insistence on writing everything down—to impress the boss.

The Lockheed executives, spurred on by Haughton, set about selling the Starfighter to the countries of NATO. They were not only making money but helping

to unify the Western world by standardizing its aircraft; and this notion was to be officially endorsed in 1961 when U.S. Defense Secretary MacNamara decided to set up a Government sales organization to stimulate exports and reduce the growing deficit.

Lockheed already had its own organization in Europe. At the head of it was a dynamic Dutchman called Fred Meuser who had worked in KLM and served in the Royal Air Force during the war, after which he became a naturalized American citizen working for Lockheed. In 1954 Meuser was transferred to Switzerland to be Lockheed's director for Europe, Africa, and the Near East. Meuser had a nexus of "top-of-the-top" contacts (as he called them) through Europe to advise him; and to help him he chose an old Swiss college friend, Hubert Weisbrod, an expert skier and amateur pilot who had practiced international law in Zurich.

Much of the success in selling the Starfighter (Meuser recalled later in a characteristically candid Lockheed letter) "was in no small measure due to his expert counseling and behind-the-scenes pulling of strings. Hardly ever did Hubert appear in the open for the support of Lockheed's interests; practically all his constructive work was done discreetly, indirectly." Weisbrod, as a lawyer, had a special advantage: under Swiss law he was protected (like a banker) from investigation. Meuser and Weisbrod, with their discreet Swiss bank accounts, were at the center of the Lockheed web, from Geneva to Jakarta.

Fred Meuser also recruited an influential Dutch friend, an old colleague from KLM, to help in Lockheed's sales effort: a Resistance hero called Hans Gerritsen. As a young man Gerritsen had been a famous sportsman, an Olympic skier who also played soccer for Holland; in the war he was an underground leader, was captured, tortured, and nearly killed; his body was used in medical experiments which affected his health. After the war he was very active in a club of ex-Resistance members that included important Dutch leaders.

But there is little doubt that the chief attraction of Gerritsen for Lockheed was his friendship with Prince Bernhard. He had first met the Prince before the war at an ice hockey match; and after the war Bernhard (who had been flying with the RAF) made a point of meeting Dutch Resistance heroes. The two formed a close friendship which ripened over the next thirty years. On Fred Meuser's advice Lockheed hired Gerritsen as a consultant at $18,000 a year.

Lockheed was not disappointed with its new agent: Gerritsen reckoned that his help in selling their planes, including the Starfighters, to the Dutch was worth ten times what he earned. Through the Resistance club he developed excellent contacts, particularly at the Ministry of Economics.

But certainly Lockheed paid very special attention to Prince Bernhard at the time when the Starfighters were being promoted. The Prince had better contacts than anyone: he was a director of many companies, including KLM, and he was Inspector General of the Armed Forces. And it was between 1961 and 1963 according to Lockheed's sworn testimony that Prince Bernhard was paid a million dollars. Fred Meuser has claimed that he kept the money. The staff of the senate multinationals committee in Washington still insist, despite the Prince's denials, that the money reached Bernhard. It was a gift, they explained, "to establish a climate of goodwill to foster our sales."

The Lockheed agents in Holland, Belgium, and elsewhere (though notably not in Japan) were men with fine war records and postwar links with intelligence who doubtless saw their employment as part of the great cause of maintaining the Atlantic alliance. In each country Lockheed tried to fly high; in Britain it employed for a time Prince Philip's friend and former private secretary Michael Parker.

In the late Fifties Lockheed was also energetically selling the Starfighter in the most important market of all, West Germany, against strong competition from the Dassault Mirage III and the Grumman Super Tiger. The German Minister of Defense, Franz-Josef Strauss, the combative Bavarian with close American ties, was persuaded by the Luftwaffe of the advantages of the Starfighter and was naturally attracted to the sophisticated Lockheed plane, which he saw as part of Germany's catching up with advanced military technology to become part of the nuclear deterrent. But Lockheed was taking no chances, and it launched a lobbying offensive in Bonn which became notorious for its relentlessness, even by German standards.

The campaign was triumphant: Strauss first ordered 250 Starfighters in 1959, then 700 more next year. But the results were politically catastrophic. The Luftwaffe insisted on equipping the plane with extra devices which Lockheed was glad to supply. These increased the weight and the problems of the plane, and it required highly skilled pilots and careful maintenance. In the following seven years ninety-one Starfighters crashed, the plane became known as the "Flying Coffin," and the Starfighter widows became—as they still are—a formidable lobby. The resulting scandal reverberated for years.

Among the Lockheed salesmen in Germany from 1961 to 1964 was a fast-talking American ex-Army intelligence officer called Ernest Hauser, who had become friendly with Strauss in the Army and whom Strauss had later recommended to Lockheed. His evidence in Washington has not been found wholly reliable but it is certain that he kept a diary—his handwriting has been authenticated—which contained incriminating references: some mentioned Prince Bernhard receiving money through Fred Meuser's bank account: others referred to Lockheed payments made to the Christian Social Union, the party headed by Strauss. One entry even described Strauss' anger because a commission had not been passed on to his party as promised. Strauss denies everything.

The Strauss question remains possibly the most explosive of all the questions raised by Lockheed. But what is clear is that Lockheed continued to be involved with bribery in Germany—in rather blundering fashion. A comic example has emerged in a memo in which a Lockheed executive describes in 1971 how he had just dined with the new agent in Dusseldorf, Christian Steinrücke. He had been very impressed: it was a magnificent mansion, Mrs. Steinrücke was a "lovely lady," and the dinner party for sixteen was "as splendidly presented as any I have attended in Europe."

Steinrücke asked them for $16,000 to bribe political parties in order to persuade the West German Bundesbank to buy some Lockheed Jetstar executive planes. But Steinrücke (according to an official statement from the Bonn Government) kept the money for himself and the Bundesbank never bought the planes. Like other episodes in the Lockheed dossier, it raises the question: who was corrupting whom?

Lockheed's dealings in Italy reveal the company still deeper in a confused bog of corruption. In Rome in the mid-Sixties it was trying to sell its first Orion turbo-jets, then Hercules transports, and to this end its legal counsel, Roger Bixby Smith, was employing a demanding lawyer in Rome called Lefebvre D'Ovidio, who acted as intermediary with the Italian Minister of Defense. With his help the customary delays inside the Ministry were miraculously circumvented: but Smith found himself facing increasing demands from Lefebvre.

By March, 1969, he was writing anxiously to his Lockheed bosses ("please hold on to your seat") to explain that his agent might now need $120,000 for each Hercules aircraft sold—because, he explained, he was having to outbid the French and German bribes. His bosses acceded and the money was duly paid through a discreet company in Panama with the innocent-sounding name of the Temperate Zone Research Foundation. The order for the aircraft went through.

It is often difficult from the memos to decide who is behaving worst. The Americans were relentless, naive, and impatient; but their European agents were wily and grasping: they extorted huge sums while the Americans, in some cases it seems, sold them planes they did not really need.

Certainly the Lockheed bribes were sometimes able to achieve remarkable outcomes. Probably the most remarkable was in Japan. In November, 1972, Japan Air Lines in Tokyo ordered six Lockheed Tri-Star airliners powered with Rolls-Royce engines, against heavy competition from Boeing and McDonnell Douglas. The choice seemed very odd at the time. It has now emerged that Lockheed had paid $7 million to a right-wing ex-war criminal, Yoshio Kodama to persuade Japan Air Lines.

Undoubtedly the Pentagon was doing little to discourage bribery: as recently as

July, 1974, a Pentagon official, Joe Hoenig, gave a pep talk to electronics salesmen about the Middle East, stressing the importance of buying "influence." Yet in all the published papers there is a striking lack of reference to serious defense requirements or anything that the Russians or Chinese might be doing: the enemy is not Moscow but rival plane manufacturers.

The Pentagon virtually unleashed the arms salesmen, and exports became increasingly important as a means to earn foreign currency and maintain employment and production lines at home — par ticularly after the oil price increases in 1973. But today the Pentagon is in a tricky relationship with Lockheed; it is the biggest American defense contractor and yet is in a perilous financial position. Dan Haughton has resigned with his deputy Carl Kotchian.

Both American and European governments will now have to take up the task of cleaning up business methods — particularly in the arms business. For corruption in the defense companies raises the question: what kind of society are they supposed to be defending?

67.

Coping With Terrorism

The wave of international terrorism that has been on the increase since the late 1960s consists largely of political crimes such as hijacking, assassination, kidnaping, and bombings. The success of such incidents has been abetted by sophisticated technology and weaponry; and the failure to arrest terrorism can be blamed in great measure on the inadequacies of international law enforcement, coupled with the willingness of some nations to provide sanctuary for the terrorists. Most of the sensational and well publicized terrorist activities have taken place outside the United States, although Americans in foreign lands have frequently been the victims of kidnap and assassination plots. The spectacular July 3/4, 1976 rescue of airline passengers from Entebbe Airport in Uganda by Israeli troops caught the imagination of the world and sparked new debate on how to deal with terrorists. Subsequent to the Entebbe affair, Atlas magazine conducted a panel discussion in New York City on the topic, "Coping with Terrorism." Panelists were Gitta Bauer of Springer Foreign News Service; Brian Saxton, United Nations correspondent for the British Broadcasting Corporation; and George Wolff, UN correspondent for Agence France-Presse. Atlas editors Alfred Balk and Marion K. Sanders posed the questions.

Source: *Atlas World Press Review*, September 1976.

Historically there have always been individuals and groups who used acts of terror to make political statements. Is there something different about the terrorism of our time?

Bauer: Yes, there is a new terrorism today. It's not just a matter of Palestinians against Israel or German anarchists against the German government. There is a coalition of terrorists who threaten all of us who are free. This is one new phenomenon. Another is the fact that terrorists today enjoy the active or tacit cooperation of legitimate governments, as we so well saw this summer in the hijacking of the Air France plane which found a haven in Uganda. This puts the matter on a totally different level.

Saxton: There's no doubt that this is a new form of terrorism. Historically of course, there have always been anarchists and others who've used violence to achieve political ends, to overthrow governments. But advances in science and technology and intensified political hostilities between nations and groups have increased the level and style of violence. There is much more freedom to act, for example, and groups that might once have worked for change through orthodox political machinery now find terrorism an easier way. It seems to have become somewhat simple to hijack a plane or burst into a bank or stage a violent demonstration in an airport.

Wolff: I don't see today's terrorism as something really new. Terrorism is warfare. It is a weapon used in war. In World War II terror took all sorts of forms. I remember when convoys were hijacked and ships with civilian passengers were torpedoed and cities filled with civilians were bombed to the ground. Nowadays determined political factions use terrorism—like the hijacking of the French plane that went to Uganda, like the massacre in the Tel Aviv airport in 1972, like the gunning down of athletes at the Munich Olympics. This is just an adaptation of a weapon that has existed through centuries, to modern circumstances. But we have only had mass air transport since the end of World War II. So now you can have an airport massacre. This is warfare and it must be dealt with by the methods of war.

In the struggle against terrorists—whether they are the anarchists in Germany or Palestinian extremists who hijack planes or the fanatics who bomb the car of the British ambassador in Dublin—all of them must be dealt with very coolly, realistically, and pragmatically.

Resolutions at the UN, speeches in parliaments—these are not the way. Of course there has to be a political component, but essentially this is a military staff job and it requires the kind of cooperation that we have among various national police forces in the framework of Interpol. It is war. And we need people specializing in this particular kind of warfare, just as we have specialists in artillery, an air force, infantry, and intelligence. We have in France a special section of the police who are trained to cope with terrorist situations, with the taking of hostages.

Saxton: The trouble is, if you start setting up armies of shock troops—call them what you will—creating armies of highly trained people, you are recognizing terrorism as being part of the establishment and I think that might prolong it, escalate it. These additional agencies, which have this special label, in a sense legitimize terrorism.

There is also the problem of preserving a society's basic freedoms and the rule of law. How do you avoid shooting up innocent people and exacerbating the situation if you depend on the military approach?

Wolff: I admit this is a problem. The military approach is neither my philosophy nor my way of life. But if the people engaged in the form of warfare you call terrorism don't face the very acute danger of being killed while they do their job you will never get rid of them. The special section of the French police, which is nationwide, which is in charge of coping with terrorism—political and criminal—is trained to shoot to kill.

That's the only way, sad to say.

About a year and a half ago some gangsters held up a bank on the Champs Elysées in the middle of Paris and took as hostages innocent people, business people, employees, passersby. These gangsters were killed on the spot by sharpshooters of the special . . . police.

But if there is a jumbo jet full of passengers, with the hijackers and explosives on board, what does one do then?

Saxton: It seems to me that various situations require different approaches. The sharpshooter approach, for example, is acceptable in special circumstances, where you can pick off the terrorist, get rid of him, and save the hostages. But then there's a situation in which a large group of innocent people are involved, as on a jetliner; there you have to employ other methods. If you're too drastic you risk losing those people. Ideally, of course, the question of terrorism shouldn't be a problem at all in this day and age of so-called sophistication. Personally I feel the time has come for world action to stop it once and for all.

What preventative measures might be effective?

Saxton: One problem is the apparently easy access to weapons, which has to be tightened up. It's much easier today to obtain weapons.

Bauer: I don't see any way that we can prevent the flow of weapons into terrorist hands. I don't even know that we can control the armament business anywhere. It's one of the most thriving businesses in the world with a lot of muscle behind it. The problem is that governments like the Soviets or the Libyans are arming terrorists and training them to use newfangled weapons. The Libyans buy the arms with their oil money and the Soviets deliver the goods. So I don't see how we could persuade these governments to stop doing

this. The right forum would be the UN, which we know is totally blocked, totally ineffective.

If we can't reduce the availability of weapons is there some way to reduce the access by people who have the weapons to situations in which they can blackmail?

Bauer: You could prevent what happened in Athens, where the hijackers boarded the Air France plane that finally went to Uganda. These terrorists came from Kuwait, I believe, and were sitting in the transit lounge and boarded the plane without any security check. You cannot go from Seattle to Cincinnati without two or three security checks. So why can't that be done everywhere? There should be an international agreement among aviation authorities everywhere at least on the point of security measures.

Wolff: The situation at the Athens airport, where those people could board the plane with their bags full of grenades and pistols, is simply intolerable. There has not been for the last several years any hijacking attempt on an El Al plane. I am told this is simply because you can't board an Israeli plane without being completely searched. This is the thing to do. It's not a remedy. It's prevention.

The "Toronto Star" recently suggested a way in which the industrialized nations might eliminate safe havens for hijacked planes. If any country did not cooperate then air service to it would be suspended and its airlines would be refused landing rights everywhere. Is that a possible solution?

Bauer: Boycotts have been tried in the free world every so often and have failed because you simply cannot get private enterprise to back up the government at the cost of profits. I don't want to be impolite but I am thinking of the way the French handled the Entebbe situation because they wanted their airliner back. Even the French deputy representative at the UN was very, very cautious because he was thinking of the $50 million airliner sitting in Entebbe. This is the way profit-oriented organizations act. So you can't get an international boycott to work. Of course, we do have an agreement between the European nine to extradite terrorists who have taken hostages or to punish them in the country where they are captured. That is encouraging, and probably we could get the U.S. and Japan involved. But do we get the Third World to cooperate?

Wolff: You would never get the nations that wanted to condemn Israel for rescuing its own people to take any action against terrorist groups. For them the terrorists are Palestinians and should be helped and abetted.

Saxton: There's no doubt international cooperation is the only solution. And of course, as George was saying, it's fraught with political difficulties and calls for a great deal of political preparation before it could ever be successful. The UN Secretary General back in 1972 on his initiative was trying to get some action on this in the General Assembly.

Wolff: And was almost forced to resign.

Saxton: It was relegated to the Legal Committee, the Sixth Committee of the UN General Assembly, but no positive action has ever been taken on it. Now this month I understand some of the Western European countries are expected to press for a new debate in the UN. They are aiming for a new convention, an international agreement to cope with terrorism. I don't think they will succeed because I don't think the will is there right now, so we'll probably end up by getting action by a splinter group. The U.S. and other Western countries will probably go off on their own and perhaps adopt their own agreement. As things stand at the moment

it's impossible for the UN to do anything about it. And since the UN is a reflection of the political realities of today's world you won't get international action even if there were some international body other than the UN.

Are you being perhaps too pessimistic? Cuba is no friend of the U.S. but after Cuba agreed not to give asylum to hijackers American planes were no longer hijacked to Latin America.

Bauer: That was a totally different situation. Those were not political terrorists. Those were largely criminals who just wanted a safe haven, and Cuba was not very happy with the influx of ordinary robbers or criminals. They were put in the sugarcane harvest and were not happy with that. They were relieved by the Cuban government of the money they had blackmailed from the airlines, which in some cases I think delivered it back to those who had paid. This was a craze. And every unstable person who could not go on with his life anymore or who had just robbed a bank or killed his wife thought, "It's easy to go to Cuba." It was in the interest of the Cubans as well as our interest to stop this. There you had a coincidence of interests.

Before the Security Council debate about Entebbe there was widespread expectation of a resolution condemning the Israelis. This didn't happen. Isn't this significant?

Wolff: The fact that no veto was necessary to kill the resolution condemning Israel depended on one thing . . . the vote of the Republic of Panama. It might sound laughable but that's a fact. Panama currently represents Latin America on the Security Council; had Latin America been represented by, let us say, Cuba, there would have been enough votes to condemn Israel. But Panama is a civilized country, a country with a great tradition of legal training which has produced great jurists. Panama simply said, "We are all for the liberation of Palestine but we cannot accept the fact that not one word in this text mentions that innocent people, legal passengers of an airplane, were taken in an act of banditry and threatened. This we cannot accept and we cannot vote for the resolution."

How about other aspects of the problem, like Northern Ireland? The U.S. is somewhat involved because it has been alleged that some arms for Northern Irish terrorists come from the U.S. and are financed by individual Americans.

Saxton: I don't think there's any easy answer to the question of Northern Ireland. Any process to resolve the problem is going to be slow and painful, and I can't see any immediate end to the dispute. It will take very patient negotiations and very patient strategy to settle a question which is almost as agonizing as Lebanon. . . .

In London, must strategy against terrorism be reactive?

Saxton: Security has been tightened considerably in many places. Fortunately the number of incidents of violence seems to have dropped lately. But not long ago restaurants were being blown up, there were attacks in public places, and bombs in stores. Now this sort of thing was unthinkable in London at one time. The reason why London was suddenly plagued with the problem was perhaps a reflection of what I mentioned earlier. Terrorism has become fashionable. If certain groups want to prove a point they resort to violence.

Germany has the famous Baader-Meinhof terrorist gang. What has the Government learned about dealing with them?

Bauer: Fortunately we have been able to capture most of them, at least the hard core. But we have been less lucky in bringing them to trial and keeping them

in captivity. On the very weekend of Entebbe four women escaped from a Berlin prison. Among them was one of those whose freedom had been demanded by the Entebbe hijackers. One thing we have learned is that this is not just a German problem, that the Baader-Meinhof group has working relations with the Carlos people in France, who were part and parcel of the group at Entebbe. So we have an international terrorist community. I agree that this calls for international military action.

But strangely we in Germany are not very competent in warfare anymore. There's a new generation of soldiers coming up and they are not very good at it, as we saw in Munich to our deepest regret in 1972. Five terrorists were killed, but we were not able to rescue the Israelis. So I do think that what we need is perhaps a trained, international police force, shock troops like the Israeli group that went to Entebbe, in every country, working on an international level — at least with the countries that cooperate.

Do you think that the threat of terrorism has been exaggerated or perhaps exacerbated by the media?

Bauer: A spectacular event like a terrorist attack is bound to have a lot of media coverage. Actually the communication between terrorists and the people they are blackmailing is often done through TV and other media. Formerly terrorists were often after personal glory but today they are out for very drastic political objectives.

Saxton: Terrorism in itself tends to take a spectacular and dramatic form. The recent hijacking of the French plane — and of course the Israeli rescue operation at Entebbe, for example — produced a spectacular story. The media didn't exaggerate it. Most acts of terrorism *are* dramatic, involving murder, bloodshed, hostages, sometimes dramas which go halfway around the world and back.

What could be done about terrorist acts against diplomats?

Bauer: Again these incidents show the limitations of the UN. We have some sort of convention on the protection of diplomats. It says that at all costs they must be saved in time of war. But then it goes on to say that in the course of a war of liberation which has "just and legitimate causes" the whole situation is different. The diplomat may be dead but if he dies in a war of liberation that's too bad, and he may be a hero.

Wolff: The U.S. and the Belgian ambassadors in Khartoum were both murdered. When war is raging all international conventions are suspended.

Is the American policy of never negotiating with terrorists even when a diplomat's life is at stake a wise one?

Saxton: It's hard to generalize. Personally, while I have always attached great importance to the work of a diplomat I'm not sure his life is any more important than that of a housewife from Illinois who happens to be caught up, innocently, on a hijacked plane. I think diplomats simply have to take their chances along with everybody else. What I'm saying is that *everybody* should be protected from terrorism, Diplomats should not be singled out for special preference.

Bauer: The most frightening thing is the prospect of a terrorist with an atomic device in his hands. What are we going to do then? There are some safeguards that the International Atomic Energy Agency places on nuclear installations all over the world and to which all the signators adhere. I don't think there is any real and ultimate safeguard which will prevent terrorists—people who have decided to declare war on the world—from getting a nuclear device if they want to. We can

guard our nuclear breeders and all the installations very closely, put them under police control, but I've been told that a schoolboy with the scientific education of a high school senior could develop a device.

Saxton: If a major power were supporting a minor power—let's say a liberation movement or group of extremists in a conventional orthodox way—I don't think it's beyond the realm of possibility that in some secret place nuclear material could be handed over on a small scale.

Wolff: Especially a tactical nuclear device.

Saxton: Let's not forget, too, that a lot of countries these days are being supplied with missiles and that they could be given a nuclear capability.

Wolff: Again this is a problem of international cooperation to fight terrorism in its many forms.

Saxton: The nub of the problem in this new situation is that we actually have some governments supporting and condoning what are regarded as being acts of terrorism. Now, the question is: who or what is a terrorist? It took the UN many years to define aggression, and it's taking a lot of people a great deal of time now to persuade the UN even to discuss terrorism. Today's so-called terrorist might be tomorrow's foreign minister and today's freedom fighters could become tomorrow's politicians. Because certain governments realize this and because they want to see certain countries or groups realize various political aspirations, they are prepared to support the means to achieve them.

Do you think there's a sufficient sense of urgency about this?

Bauer: There is a sense of urgency and I think the Entebbe incident really dramatized it, and so did the Security Council debate. It put the problem in focus even though certain countries tried their hardest to evade the issue by talking about the rescue operation and not about the preceding hijacking and hostage-taking. The sense of urgency is there but with the world being what it is I don't see much prospect of a global approach.

Saxton: I agree. I don't think there is the necessary political will in the majority of nations. So even though the Western group at this month's General Assembly will probably press for it I don't think they will get the necessary support. But I do think the West is taking terrorism seriously. One gets the impression that their attitude now is, "Well, if the rest of the world doesn't join with us then we'll go alone. We'll get our own convention, get our own systems organized, and improve our protective agencies and the safeguarding of our people." I think we'll see that this month.

68.

CARL SAGAN: The Viking Landing on Mars

A significant part of the Bicentennial celebration took place millions of miles from Earth. On July 20, 1976, spacecraft Viking I touched down on Mars to begin exploration of the planet's surface. Early in September a second spacecraft, Viking II, landed on the Martian surface. This selection from a much longer article explains the operation of the Viking mission. Mr. Sagan is director of the Laboratory for Planetary Studies at Cornell University and is also affiliated with the National Aeronautics and Space Administration.

Source: NASA News Release 76-74, as reprinted in *Space World*, October 1976.

THIS IS THE SUMMER of the Viking landings on Mars. If all goes well, two landers and two orbiters will arrive at the planet during mid-1976 in an event unique in human history—the first extended and closeup reconnaissance of the surface of another planet.

The Viking spacecraft includes orbital experiments for imaging, infrared thermal mapping, infrared water vapor detection, and radio science; atmospheric entry experiments for analysis of the neutral and ionized components of the Martian upper atmosphere; and lander experiments for imaging of the surface, atmosphere and other astronomical objects, for inorganic chemistry, meteorology, seismometry, magnetic properties of sand grains, organic chemistry of surface samples and analysis of lower atmosphere, plus three compact biological experiments designed to search for any Martian microorganisms.

Viking is an expensive mission, costing almost a billion dollars; it has occupied hundreds of scientists and engineers for many years, some of us for more than a decade; and if it works, it promises to revolutionize the planetary sciences in general and the study of Mars in particular.

While the orbit television system will obtain photographs of Mars with a resolution of two to three times better than the best images from Mariner 9, the prime function of the orbiter is lander support: to act as a radio link to Earth for the lander and to help certify preselected landing sites. The orbiters do not have, for example, the infrared and ultraviolet spectrometers that were so successful on Mariner 9. The primary objective of the mission is to search for life on Mars, and this is not something easily performed remotely.

The key elements in both orbiter and lander are their onboard computers. The lander possesses—like a human being with his corpus callosum cut—two identical brains. Each has an 18,000-word memory, with 24 bits per word, stored on two coupled magnetic wires. A memory of 18,000 words is quite large. Basic English, which is alleged to be serviceable in many layers of American society, consists of fewer than 1,000 words.

A scientific and engineering protocol is already in the Viking memory banks. Each lander's computers will be checked by a data dump to see how well they remember and understand their program. In each case, the computer that has forgotten the least will be put in charge. A third computer on Earth selects the winner. The loser will be put to sleep, but will wait in readiness; in case of an accident or senility in the winner it may be called upon later.

While it is certainly large, an 18,000-word vocabulary is inadequate for everything the Viking lander may be asked to do. (The sample arm motions alone require several hundred words.) Only 5,000 of its words are for functions to be performed exclusively after landing. The remainder are for executive matters, involving the structure of the entire computer program; checkout of engineering functions; and functions performed during descent to the Martian surface.

For this reason, the mission controllers have devised a "primary design," according to which every six days a set of new commands, comprising hundreds to thousands of words, will be radioed uplink from Earth to Mars.

But this corresponds to a very sluggish response to what may be astounding discoveries made on the planet's surface, and an "adaptive design" (update every three days) seems to be the first mission design in which it will be possible to perform appropriately responsive experiments on the surface.

One clear lesson from past spacecraft is that enormous scientific payoffs follow from the ability to do new experiments on the basis of what we have just learned. Many of the most famous discoveries made by Mariner 9—the great volcanoes, the surfaces of Phobos and Deimos, variable features, great sand-dune fields and details of the large sinuous channels—required the space probe's adaptive mode. An entirely preprogrammed Viking mission would be relatively feeble scientifically. It could not even select with the lander cameras the place where the sample arm is to dig. But a Viking mission in which we can perform an experiment tomorrow on the basis of what we learned the day before yesterday—that is a scientific capability of stunning potentialities.

Both Viking launches took place in August and September 1975 from Pad 41 at the Kennedy Space Center, Cape Canaveral, Fla.

Any launch later than about September 20 would have seriously degraded the mission, and might have required a 23-month "hold" until the next opportunity in 1977. NASA has a very good launch record, but there has never been as complex a scientific mission as Viking. The launch vehicle is the Titan 3E, a Titan booster with a Centaur second stage, a configuration that had been tried only twice before.

In the nominal mission, the A orbiter-lander combination is injected into orbit around Mars on June 19, 1976, giving it 15 days for landing site certification before the July 4 landing. After certification, several propulsion maneuvers are required to make the orbit Mars-synchronous, with a 24.6-hour period and a low point in the orbit of about 1,500 kilometers (900 miles) over the landing site. The orbit is highly elliptical. The Viking 2 mission arrives in the vicinity of Mars on August 7, 45 days after the Viking 1 configuration. It has about 30 days to orbit for Viking 2 lander site certification and scientific investigations before its lander deboosts.

Lander 1 has a nominal working lifetime on Mars' surface of 58 days; Lander 2, 62 days (although the spacecraft are likely to work for a full year). The resources available to the Viking mission will apparently permit almost no simultaneous operation of major scientific experiments on the two landers.

This is a great pity, since synoptic observations are the key to a variety of fundamental problems. The difficulty is not spacecraft capability, but rather money to pay for ground personnel and mission control computers. Despite its high cost, Viking is severely hampered by lack of funds.

The descent maneuver begins when a mechanical spring separates the orbiter and the lander, giving a relative velocity of a meter (slightly more than a yard) or two per second. The two follow essentially the same orbit for two hours, during which the lander orients itself for entry and examines the thin upper atmosphere of the Red Planet. It radios its findings to the nearby orbiter, which relays them directly to Earth as well as recording them on tape recorders for future playback. The entire descent sequence is under control of the active lander computer; the ground "controllers" will be able only to bite their fingernails.

After an initial rocket burn, the lander enters the denser atmosphere, ablation shield first. After this burns off, the parachute is deployed and then, under control of the accelerometers with backup timing devices, is jettisoned. Finally, the terminal-descent rockets burn, to be burned off only about 3 meters (10 feet) above the Martian surface.

The entire delicate landing maneuver is actively controlled by the lander, relying on its descent radar and other instruments and maintaining a careful attitude control. It is an intricate servomechanism, making decisions on the basis of its sensory information, as we do. The lander free falls the final few feet and—many of us sincerely hope—safely lands on its three spring-loaded footpads on the surface of distant Mars.

Immediately upon setting down, at about 4:30 in the afternoon Chryse standard time, the spacecraft initiates a range of engineering and housekeeping functions. It asks itself if it is feeling well. The lander will relay data to Earth via the orbiter (when that is above the lander's horizon) at 16,000 bits per second; and at other times directly to Earth, but at the much slower rate of 500 bits per second. During the next three days, it principally takes seismometric and meteorological data, as well as the first closeup pictures of the Martian terrain.

The meteorology package, on a small boom, will examine other atmospheric properties including wind velocity and direction. Evening weather reports on American television in the summer of 1976 may include reports on meteorological conditions at the two locales on Mars. We know that, despite the thinness of the Martian atmosphere, winds are occasionally strong enough to raise enormous clouds of sand and dust and it would be very interesting to correlate wind speeds as measured by the meteorology experiments with the amount of atmospheric dust as measured from above by the orbiter, and from below by the two Viking television cameras. The cameras will be able to see dust clouds in the vicinity of the spacecraft and at the horizon, and will also determine the mobility of samples of dust and sand dumped by the sample arm on a specially prepared grid on the horizontal surface of the spacecraft.

The lander cameras will be able to see detail about as well as a human being standing on Mars. In some respects it will be superior. It will be able to image as far as 1.2 microns into the infrared and it will be able to perform much better stereo imaging than human eyes can because the two cameras will be placed much farther apart than our characteristic few inches. There will be color stereoscopic panoramic photographs of two landing sites on Mars, horizon to horizon, perhaps even stretched out over a period of many months.

The Mariner 9 experience is that quite new sets of features appear on Mars as we are able to see smaller and smaller detail. No one is able to predict what we will see within a few yards of the Viking landers. For all we know there may be amazing discoveries as we take the first closeup images of Mars.

On the third day after landing, the first set of uplink commands arrives. By the sixth day, a decision will have been made on where to obtain the first soil sample with the sample arm. On the eighth day, after the onboard computer has demonstrated that it truly understands its newly arrived instructions on where to dig a hole, the sample arm gingerly extends itself towards the surface. It can reach a soil sample (or a more interesting object) as much as 3 meters (10 feet) away. With a

nervous jittery backhoe motion it lifts its sample into the air and gradually retracts, telescoping itself until it is only a few inches from the lander's main body. Photographs are taken before, during and after the sampling operation. The arm then positions itself over one or more of the three entry bays. One is for the X-ray fluorescence experiment, to examine the inorganic chemistry of molecules with atoms heavier than about mass number 20; another is for the gas chromatograph-mass spectrometer (GCMS) to examine the organic chemistry of the samples; and the last is for the three different microbiology experiments.

The arm opens its little claw, shakes itself and deposits the sample into a funnel which is covered by a wire mesh screen. Experimenters back on Earth will have decided whether they want the same sample for each experiment.

The experiments then do their stuff, which may take some days. The biology experiments, for example, require an incubation period before the results can be radioed downlink to Earth. In all, three samples will be examined by each of the three biology experiments, four by the GCMS, and five by X-ray fluorescence, all during the nominal mission of each lander.

We will be examining the properties of the Martian surface near the lander fairly thoroughly. The sample arm will be able to dig trenches and with Viking's eye-hand combination, we will perform simple experiments on surface properties. The Viking 1 mission is scheduled to land near the banks of old sinuous valleys thought to have once been mighty rivers. If we are very lucky we might get some information on the ages and mechanisms of the channel cutting process. The deeper interior of the planet will be investigated by an elegant seismometer which will listen for marsquakes if there are any. Since from our Mariner 9 experience we know that Mars has recently been tectonically active, we expect much higher levels of seismic activity than were detected by seismometers on the Moon.

An X-ray fluorescence spectrometer should provide insights into the mineralogy and geochemistry of the Martian surface, and an indication of what sorts of geological processes have been operating. For example, it is possible that this experiment might be able, from an examination of salt content, to check whether liquid water once flowed on Mars.

If there is life on Mars we may see characteristic chemical signatures of its presence from the GCMS experiment. Alternatively there may be organic compounds there from carbonaceous chondrites, organic-rich meteorites originating in the asteroid belt and falling now and then on Mars. Finally there may be non-biological synthesis of organic matter by ultraviolet light in the present oxygen-poor Martian atmosphere. It is hoped that the GCMS experiment will be able to distinguish among these possibilities. It will also search for time variations in the chemistry of the Martian atmosphere. The microbiology experiments range from one which makes very specific assumptions about Martian microbial metabolism but which has very high sensitivity to one which makes only very general assumptions but which has a much lower detectivity.

The GCMS and biology experiments are by far the most expensive scientific instruments ever flown in the unmanned planetary program. But the questions being asked are very fundamental. We do not know beforehand the nature of Martian life, if any, and there has been no previous experience in designing, testing and flying space vehicle experiments oriented towards organic chemistry and microbiology. We get what we pay for, by and large. With these instruments developed, the incremental cost of future investigations of the organic chemistry and biology on Mars will be much less.

The Viking lander cameras may also be used for biological investigations if there are organisms large enough to see. No one knows if this is the case. If it is, Martian organisms may be detectable independent of any assumptions we make on their biochemistry. The range of Viking investigations directed towards the search for life on Mars is of course not perfect. But it seems to be an excellent mix for the first preliminary biological reconnaissance of another planet. If all works well, Viking is almost sure to find a great deal that is of meteorological and geological interest. And if we are lucky, we may hit the cosmic jackpot and find something of biological interest.

After the Viking 2 lands, high-data-rate transmission from the Viking 1 lander is turned off for the economy reasons mentioned above. Only low-data-rate experiments on the direct link to Earth can be performed, chiefly seismometry, meteorology and single-line video scans. The Viking 1 orbiter, freed of its relay responsibility for its lander, now exuberantly explores Mars from orbit. Many questions posed by Mariner 9 may be answered at this stage.

This is also the first time in the mission when radio occultation experiments will be performed, as the atmosphere and the planet intercept the transmission from orbiter to Earth. Eventually, the Orbiter 1 may be called back to service the Lander 2 (a function possible only if the longitudes of the nominal 1 and 2 landing sites are very nearly the same). If this occurs, the inclination of 2's orbital plane to the equatorial plane of Mars can be increased to 75 degrees, converting the Viking 2 orbiter into a Martian polar observatory. Many other comparably elegant combined mission strategies are possible.

Mars will be in solar conjunction on Nov. 25, 1976, when the Sun will be between the planet and the Earth. Communication with the Viking spacecraft will be interrupted from November 8 until about Christmas Day.

The generosity of nature is evident here: Viking scientists will finally be able to take time out from data gathering to ponder what the data mean. Many space missions never provide such an opportunity until they are over.

If all is still working well, the Viking Extended Mission may begin early in 1977. While the nominal lifetime of a Viking spacecraft is only about 90 days, Mariner 9, with a similar life expectancy, performed for a full year. . . . Viking's power source is independent of sunlight; it runs on the decay of radioactive plutonium. If it is as well engineered as Mariner 9 was, the really interesting part of the Viking mission may begin in January, 1977. In any case, if Viking works even moderately well, planetary astronomy will never be the same again.

If after a long series of post-Viking investigations of Mars we find no sign of life on the planet, we will then have discovered something of considerable importance about the unlikelihood of life originating and surviving on another planet not very dissimilar to our own, a finding which will underscore the preciousness and rarity of what has happened here on our small Earth. And if we are lucky enough to find life on Mars, that event will clearly open a new epoch in the history of biology, our view of ourselves and our place in the cosmos.

69.

THOMAS A. VANDERSLICE: Technology as Problem Solver

Half a century ago, a European traveler in the United States noted: "The average American sets an absolute and positive value on technique. . . . The clatter of machinery . . . is music to the true American ear." Know-how is, in fact, an American term: and it has been a way of life since the nation's inception. Yet in the last quarter of the 20th century there has been expressed much concern that the United States is forfeiting its lead in technology, that other industrialized nations have become the innovators. Environmentalists have focused on the problems that technology causes, and many citizens have called for a slowdown, or even a halt, to manufacturing growth. With a recession in the 1970s, many companies have seemed to heed the environmentalists by cutting back on expenditures for expansion and new products. In an address to the Executives' Club of Chicago, Dr. Thomas A. Vanderslice reviewed recent trends in technology and gave a prognosis for the coming decade. Mr. Vanderslice is a vice president of the General Electric Company and works at the company's Research and Development Center in Schenectady, New York.

Source: *Executives' Club News*, November 5, 1976.

OUR PREDECESSORS were very strong on infrastructure. They built a transcontinental system of roads, railroads, and canals; of basic industries and abundant energy resources; the most productive agriculture the world has ever known—all of which has served this nation well for more than a hundred years. We don't realize how fortunate we are, until we spend some time in a country where this basic infrastructure is lacking.

Now, essential parts of that infrastructure are badly in need of upgrading and modernization.

I shall confine myself today to one aspect of this infrastructure that is of particular concern to me, to many of my associates at General Electric, and to the scientific and technical community: the state of U.S. research and engineering and its implication for the future of our society.

Insofar as General Electric is concerned, the question "Whither technology?" is almost equivalent to the question, "Whither General Electric?"

Are we becoming so self-conscious about technology, "the problem-creator," that we tend to forget the long role of technology as the problem-solver?

Thus, today, we are properly concerned about oil supplies, but back in 1900, a single South American country had the same "lock" on nitrate fertilizers that the Arabs now have on oil. Then a German scientist named Haber learned how to pull nitrogen out of the air, and pulled the rug out from under the Chilean monopoly.

Likewise, at the beginning of WW-II, Japan took over Southeast Asia and achieved a stranglehold on the world's natural rubber supply. At first the idea of conservation got most of the attention. Some of you may remember the scrap rubber drives during the war. But in spite of all the patriotism and all the efforts the results were far from meeting essential wartime needs—where each airplane required half a ton of rubber, and each tank required a ton.

Fortunately, an accelerated program to develop synthetic rubber for tires was also being mounted—from a technological viewpoint perhaps the most successful "project Independence" this nation has ever carried out. In 1940, not a single pound of general purpose synthetic rubber was produced in the U.S. By 1944, an annual production of over 670,000 tons was achieved, and the product was so superior for most purposes that we never went back to dependence on natural rubber again.

There is a moral to these stories. The events would not have taken place, or at least not at the same rate, if the technological infrastructure had not already been in place; with a reservoir of scientific and engineering talent to apply to the problem; and a chemical industry with the managerial talent and productive know-how to perfect and mass produce the product in very short order. Another lesson to be learned is that it is sometimes easier to provide a technological "fix" than to get people to make a major change in their lifestyle.

I hope we are all as concerned today about being as fortunate with regard to our present and future resource problems.

The 25 years following WW-II saw some of the most dramatic commercial innovations in history—stemming at least in part from the R&D of the 1940's: television; computers; the transistor and integrated circuits; gas turbines and nuclear reactors; jet air transport; Xerox copiers; synthetic diamonds (which relieved yet another monopoly); structural "engineered" plastics; radar; communication, weather and navigational satellites.

For the most of this period the U.S. had a comparative advantage in new and improved products and processes, an advantage that has continued to the present in agricultural and so-called high-technology products.

For example, one study shows that of some 500 major technological innovations introduced into the commercial market between 1953 and 1973 by the major industrial countries the U.S. led by a wide margin. However, the U.S. lead declined from the late 1950's to mid 1960's, falling from 82% to 55% of innovations. The slight upward bleep at the end of the line does not represent a gain for us, but further decline for the United Kingdom, vis-a-vis the rest of the industrial world. The largest actual gains, as might be expected, were recorded by Japan and West Germany.

Patents show the same kind of trend, with U.S. patents granted to foreign inventors more than doubling from the '60's to the '70's. The favorable balance with Japan has declined steadily since 1962, as its patenting of inventions in the U.S. increased some three-fold.

With the rich heritage of technical competence resident in our labor and managerial forces, it may seem strange to say that U.S. technology is in trouble today. Yet, I believe, there are trends that, unless corrected, could lead to a rapidly maturing crisis, such as the United Kingdom is now undergoing in translating her technology into economic growth. This is a road we dare not go down.

Research and development has been well nourished in the U.S. But in recent years, R&D has been suffering from malnutrition—and it may be suffering not just from a lack of federal and corporate calories, but also from an imbalanced diet.

Let's look at some of the trends, bearing in mind Lewis Mumford's admonition that "trend is not destiny."

In the U.S., the percent of GNP devoted to R&D has dropped steadily for more than nine years. Meanwhile other countries have registered substantial gains. Underlying the gains of Japan and West Germany were continuous large increases in funding from both industry and government.

R&D is a comparatively small part of the total Federal budget. It is also apparent that while total Federal outlays approximately doubled between 1965 and 1975, approaching $400 billion, R&D remained relatively constant. The share of the Federal budget represented by R&D and by R&D plant programs has declined continuously from 1965, not even keeping pace with inflation.

Corporate spending for R&D, on the other hand, has just about managed to keep pace with inflation, remaining nearly constant for most of the period at around 1% of the GNP, while Federal R&D spending has dropped from almost 2% of the GNP in 1966 to an estimated 1.2% in 1976. The record suggests that American industry more fully recognized the value of maintaining constant, continuing levels of support for R&D than has the Federal government.

The impact of this reduced Federal spending for R&D has fallen most heavily on the universities. Not only have programs been drastically cut back or curtailed, but the shift in emphasis from basic to applied research has compounded the problems of university research staffs.

Basic research—in high-energy physics, materials, plasma physics, nuclear chemistry—provides much of the fundamental knowledge upon which modern scientifically-based industry is built. This also includes a safer, more attractive environment; effective treatment, or better still, the prevention of such diseases as cancer, mental illness; the development of new energy sources and more energy-economical homes, transportation, and industry; new sources of raw materials and a more effective agriculture. Much of what we expect science and technology to provide in the future will, in the opinion of many in the scientific community, be slower in coming unless present trends are reversed.

Perhaps the most drastic cutbacks made by the Federal government have been in the graduate fellowship and traineeship programs—which provide the trained scientists and engineers we will need in the years ahead. These are the people who, traditionally, by their works create not only jobs for themselves but also employment for hundreds and thousands of others.

The free and exuberant atmosphere of technical innovation that sustained research and engineering in the '50's and '60's has disappeared as we seem to be heading toward a nation in which the number of people able to articulate the problems will be greater than the number of people capable of solving them. The number of scientists and engineers engaged in R&D per 10,000 population has declined from the late '60's to the present. The U.S. is the only one of these major industrial nations which shows a decline over this period.

Another indicator is the occupational preference shown by college freshmen between 1968 and 1974. Interest decreased in careers in education, business, engineering, and science—with only the life and social sciences holding, or registering a healthy increase.

The basic anachronism in these trends is that the polls tell us that most Americans still believe that the best way to achieve the complicated and sometimes competing goals we now seek remains the same: through economic growth.

And the economists tell us that the best route to economic growth is through technical innovation.

For example, Robert Solow states that considerably more than half of the increase in American productivity has been due to scientific and engineering advances, to industrial improvements and to know-how of management methods, and the education of labor.

The economist E.F. Denison estimates that advances in knowledge—including technology, education, and managerial know-how—are the most fundamental route to long-term growth of output per unit of input.

Other economists—Thurow and Kendrick among them—divide the pie into slightly different categories, but come to the same basic conclusion: technological advances account for from one-third to two-thirds of our improvement in productivity.

Simon Kuznets goes so far as to state that the major capital stock of an industrially advanced nation is not its physical equipment; it is the body of knowledge amassed from testing findings of empirical science and the capacity and training of its population to use this knowledge effectively.

A good example of Kuznets' thesis was the rapid recovery of German industry after WW-II, when its capital equipment lay in ruins. It is conventionally held that capital from the U.S. under the Marshall Plan played a leading part in this, and it did, but it was above all the technical competence and knowledge that resided in the German people, that enabled them to rebound so quickly.

The remarkable agreement of these economists on technology as one of the most important factors affecting productivity takes on added significance at a time when U.S. productivity is in trouble. Using the United States as 100, overall output per employed person is still higher in the U.S. than any other nation. Although this is also true of manufacturing, the rate of increase in U.S. productivity has been among the lowest in the Western World and Japan.

A high-wage economy such as the U.S. —in a world where new knowledge and technological innovations rapidly diffuse to lower-wage economies—must be able to innovate and adopt new technologies with equal rapidity. In fact, we must run faster and faster, just to stand still.

What is the relationship of technology to jobs? This can be seen most clearly in the international arena, where the growth in U.S. jobs has been greatest where the technology was most advanced, and where we enjoyed the greatest comparative advantage.

U.S. total exports in 1975 came to $147 billion, which created about 8½ million jobs in this country—some 10% of the nation's total jobs.

This shows what has been happening to the U.S. trade balance in products with "low" technical content—down from breakeven in 1960 to a $16 billion deficit.

And here is the positive contribution of high-technology products—now up to a plus of over $25 billion per year. . . .

And what applies in the international arena is also reflected in our domestic economy. Low-technology companies, in a period of generally rapid growth for the U.S. economy, have had a job formation rate of about 2% per year; while high-technology companies have created jobs five times as fast. They have also had a growth in sales approximately double that of low-technology companies.

We have seen that technological advances lead to:

Improvements in productivity—which in a mature industrial nation such as the U.S. play a crucial role in the maintenance of a sound domestic economy. It is the only route to improvement in national income really available to us—we cannot trade our natural resources for increased wealth as say, a small oil- or mineral-rich nation can.

Advanced technology leads to *the ability to compete* in the world marketplace—with exports of "high-technology" products and services, and a favorable balance of payments to offset the increasing cost of imported energy and the declining supply of domestic natural resources.

Technology creates new jobs—both in the domestic economy, making products and performing services that did not exist before, and from exports of these products and services overseas.

As we listened to the election campaign in the last few weeks, and months, both parties and all candidates seemed to agree that solving the unemployment problem, solving the economic problem, has to take priority in the nation's goals.

Yet as we have seen from the charts presented this morning, expenditures for R&D, the "seed corn" of our technology, have been declining for nine straight years, and are continuing to decline relative to our GNP.

If we project the present *trends* ten years out here's what the Federal budget would look like in 1986. Breaking out some of the components: human resources, including Health Education and Manpower, Income Security and Veterans Benefits, are projected to more than double; expenditures for physical resources, including Agriculture, Environmental and Natural Resources, Commerce and Transportation, and Community Development and Housing, will also double. General Government is fore-

The Concorde supersonic jet lands at Charles De Gaulle Airport near Paris.

cast to expand by 184% and national security by 104%.

During the same period, when the total federal budget is projected to triple, federal expenditures for R&D, according to the authoritative National Science Foundation, are expected to increase only 2.5% per year; with industrial R&D spending growing about 3.5% per year; and universities and other non-profit institutions showing a 1% growth rate.

The gradual decline in the ratio of R&D expenditures to the gross national product experienced since 1966 is expected to continue through 1985.

In the face of a great need for economic growth and the solution of social problems we have to ask ourselves: is this the right balance, and the right track for America?

This shows the number of new jobs we will need by 1986. This is not an estimate, but is based on the number of people already born and growing up in America who will need jobs if we are to attain only a 5% unemployment rate. By 1986 we will need to have created 18 million new jobs in this country or more than 2 million new jobs a year between now and then.

I was reminded of this by reading in the New York Times of October 15, of the problems in Great Britain. According to the article, "successive British Governments took much of the money that might have gone into industry to build an ambitious welfare State to the point where borrowed money now supports it."

Meanwhile, other countries, including West Germany and Japan, copied with notable success the original American model of innovation and technological development, built up their economies and now support their welfare service from taxes on the profits of their expanded industries and the wages of their highly paid workers.

To sum up, I would say that U.S. Science and Technology remains strong— but as Casey Stengel once said about the Mets, "in many areas we have too damned strong a weakness."

Our resources are not unlimited. A Federal, or a corporate, budget represents a lot of political and economic decisions and should be backed up by sound strategic planning.

But at this stage, on the trend lines we have been examining today, there are many—economists, scientists, representatives of government, industry and the academic community—who believe the facts show that technological innovation in this country is approaching a critical point.

There are many factors—domestic and worldwide—influencing this. But we, I think, have to ask ourselves if we can afford to allow these trends to continue—for instance, the growing imbalance between our support for R&D and the funding to meet our other needs.

In the long run, I can think of nothing that can give us more leverage on all of the problems that confront us now and in the future, than to protect the "seed corn" of scientific and technological competence that resides in our universities, industry, government in-house, and privately funded research organizations—our vital technological infrastructure.

This is a "relatively" modest proposal—the amounts of money involved are "relatively" moderate compared to other items in the Federal budget.

There are many other things that could be done by government, industry, and the universities to improve the climate for U.S. technological innovation, and to restore the incentives to invest in improved technology. But that is another discussion.

This, at least, is a place to begin to get back to the fundamentals that built this country, and it would create "new" jobs, not only for the scientists and engineers, who in the larger sense create their own jobs, but also jobs for hundreds and thousands of others.

70.

R. EMMETT TYRRELL: The American Novel in Decline

The great age of the novel was the 19th century. The works of Dickens, Hugo, Dostoevsky, Tolstoi, Austen, Eliot, Melville, and Twain comprise a peak of literary excellence that has not been surpassed. In the United States, apart from Twain and Melville, the novel matured later, in the early decades of the 20th century, with the works of such authors as Lewis, Faulkner, Hemingway, Dreiser, and Steinbeck, to name a few. That the style of the novel has changed in the meantime is certain. Some critics, such as the author of this selection, would argue that it has changed so much that the novel as a literary form no longer exists. R. Emmett Tyrrell of Bloomington, Indiana, is editor of The Alternative: An American Spectator.

Source: *New York Times*, March 5, 1976. "Kiss Me, She Cried."

IT STRIKES ME as a calamity that when the novel died the American novelist did not die too. It would have saved us time, money, perhaps even a few redwoods.

Norman Mailer would have been spared the mortification he feels about having written but one good novel, and we would have been spared Truman Capote, who has yet to match even Mr. Mailer's scrawny accomplishment.

Further, the great publishing houses could continue to disgorge their trash without any spasms of conscience; that is, they could continue to publish those dreadful nonce editions that always hover about the best-seller list: books of popular luridity, of bogus revelation about the system and the self, of socio-political tosh, and that book about an admirable sea gull so steeped in the wisdom of Bertrand

Russell that he broke away and became truly his own bird. It is hard to say who is more responsible for the rubbish publishing houses extrude, the Philistines who publish it or who read it. Generally I would blame the consumer, for as with so many other free-market transactions the consumer's vote elects what is produced. Unfortunately, readers, and for that matter most members of the culturati, are rarely so demanding or so independent as, say, automobile consumers. Rather, readers are generally the most abject slaves of fashion known to man.

The gentle and pliable nature of the reader has been noted forever and anon, and lately he appears even more gullible than in the past. With increasing frequency, readers are the shabby products of our industrial-mill university system. Some graduates are so embittered by the experience that they become lifelong foes of the written word, but, though they are the avowed enemies of writers and readers alike, their influence is practically benign compared to that of graduates whose minds have been bedaubed with intellectual pretense and a vague yearning for whiffs of "culture."

Today charlatans are doing a brisk business. Publishers realize that publishing junk is much easier and more lucrative than publishing quality. There are no apparent Faulkners or Hemingways—notwithstanding the thousands of our creative-writing greenhouses—and it is costly and difficult to ferret out talented writers. So publishers turn out poorly edited books written for enthusiasms of the moment. They make them long beyond belief, because it is more profitable.

Television is our dominant pastime, and if a book is to sell it must be written in the form of TV drama or news. It has to be simple, pretentious, nerve-racking. It has to soar ostentatiously on the winds of the *Zeitgeist*. Hence, the popularity of general-interest books like those of Theodore H. White and all the potboilers about Patty Hearst, etc. Hardly one of these books ever informs readers of anything that the press has not reported. Nonetheless they become publishing events of great moment, and for weeks they sell famously and their authors gab incontinently on talk shows. The same can be said for our works of fiction—all either gimmicky tales like "Ragtime" and that repulsive story of the seagull, or ventures into romantic turpitude.

There is hardly a novelist in America worth reading, and none is capable of sustained quality. I doubt that very many of the books published are ever read. Few are actually read in their entirety. They are carried by secretaries who hope to trap culturally inclined lawyers, or they are purchased by readers for whom the very financial transaction is a kind of cultural fix.

Anyone must tire of reading about the bold, candid, teleological orgasms of Smith-educated princesses or of *belles lettres'* he-man types. Endless recastings of the adventures of Raskolnikov, Madam Bovary and Huckleberry Finn have eventually got to weary even the Book-of-the-Month Club clientele.

What the novel needs is real people sweating it out in credible or interesting conditions. People, not clinical statistics, make novels informative, amusing, engaging, beautiful.

Which suggests another desideratum: Novels can impart a sense of the beautiful. What is beautiful is a complicated question, but I do not think that there is any question that beauty has a great deal to do with art. And here we come to just what contemporary writing lacks most: art. It is too limited. It is pseudo-journalism, sophisticated gossip. But it is *not* art. Until art returns to writing, books will be hard to take seriously.

71.

HENRY FAIRLIE: Eating in America

The American diet has long been characterized by sheer abundance and a predilection for sweets. To these two features have been added in the past two or three decades an availability of "fast foods," and fad, or junk, foods. British author-journalist Fairlie used the Bicentennial visit of Queen Elizabeth II to the United States as an occasion to comment on the way Americans eat.

Source: *Manchester Guardian Weekly*, August 1, 1976. "An American Ordeal—The Barbecue."

DURING THE VISIT of my Queen, I was interested in the observation of Julia Child that, if one is going to give a banquet in the White House, one cannot give it with American food; that a menu of clam chowder, turkey or ham and strawberry cheesecake would simply not do.

But before I advance my own theory of American food, let me acknowledge that I am aware of the weakness of my ground. The reputation of English cooking is not high. In fact, against the conspiracy theory of the Bonapartists—that Napoleon was poisoned on St. Helena by his English jailers—I incline to the view that, if food had anything to do with his death, it was that he could not, as a Frenchman, stand the English cooking; and so gave up the ghost.

But to business. With the coming of every summer which I spend in America, I find I am afflicted by one fear: that I will be invited to a barbecue. "Why, they're still savages over there," Freud once said of America. "They cook their food on heated stones in the woods." I know exactly what he meant.

The Americans provide themselves with the best-equipped kitchens in the world, but when the weather permits—or as often as not, when it does not permit—they abandon them, to cook and eat in conditions of unspeakable discomfort, by a method of which the masters could be counted on a single hand.

On one occasion, I had to play three prolonged games of chess with my hostess, while my host concealed his head in the cloud of smoke where the pathetic corpses of six Cornish hens were supposed to be being cooked. At 11:30 p.m., he announced that they were ready, and a moment later each of our knives tore vainly at the still-raw flesh. In his humiliation, he took the corpses and stuffed them down the disposal, with a ferocity which had to be seen to be believed.

This story has its own relevance, of course, because one of the truths about the barbecue is that American men, who would not dream of lifting a finger in their kitchens, suddenly persuade themselves that out of doors they are translated into chefs as great as the Marquis de Bechamel.

But not only do the Americans leave their kitchens, they also leave the screens which they have with such intelligence fixed to their windows and their doors. Out one must go, into their yards or onto their patios, where myriads of tropical and sub-tropical insects of all sizes gather in formation, and dive to the attack with the malign determination of kamikaze pilots.

One arrives at an American home for

dinner in summer to overhear the whisper of the host to the hostess, "I think we can eat outside," and he then turns to one and says, with a mixture of bravado and gloating: "Well, let's go outside; we'll barbecue some steaks." The sky is overcast and heavy, the temperature is 89, the humidity is 86, one can hear the insects revving their engines; but out one must go.

I have various theories of the barbecue, of which macho is only one. (It is the son who is allowed to help the husband cook; the daughter is allowed only to carry out the plates.) I simply think that Americans do not like meals as social occasions or mannered behavior.

For example, my English colleague, Mervyn Jones, has constructed his own theory of the American sandwich, a fabrication which of course bears no relation to the slender slices of bread, with a little cucumber between them, which one gets in Britain.

His theory runs something like this: At first there was something like a sandwich —two pieces of bread or toast, or bun, with something else between them. But then the Americans began putting more and more things in between. On top of the slice of meat went lettuce and onion and pickle and tomato and cheese and bacon and mayonnaise and ketchup, until the structure would not hold together as a sandwich. So it had to be served open; there was no sandwich, but it was still called one.

At this point, he says, the idea of a sandwich had already become "largely metaphysical." But once the sandwich was open, then one could put other things on the plate. The sandwich had vanished; one was eating a full course.

Mervyn Jones' theory of all this is that, by continuing to call it a sandwich, the Americans persuade themselves that they are eating lightly. The American sandwich is thus an elaborate disguise for gluttonous eating, and he extends his theory with a description of the bountiful hospitality one receives if one spends a weekend with an American family.

Quite early in the day, one is set down in a chair, in the living room or on the deck, round a small table which is immediately filled with plates and bowls of all kinds of snacks. They are never allowed to be empty. The day drifts by. Neighbors drop in and, as they talk, automatically put out their hands to the bowls, which are as automatically refilled. They go; other neighbors come to visit. Again the bowls are emptied, again they are filled, and so it goes on until the sun has long set.

In this way, he argues, one is under the impression that one has not eaten very much, whereas in fact one has steadily consumed, throughout the day, as much as in the most elaborate five-course meal.

I see Mervyn Jones's point. The Americans are phenomenal eaters of what appears to be nothing. The filled refrigerator, to which each member of the family goes when he or she feels like it, is really just a larder of snacks. In fact, all the prepared and packaged food with which the shelves of the supermarkets are stocked is only another addition to the ever-abundant, ever-ready snacks by which the American manages to be a glutton while pretending that he or she does not each much.

But I think there is more to it than that. When the Englishman first came to peer at the Americans "through an opera lorgnette," as one American complained, he was appalled at the haste with which the Americans ate. "No intervals of repose in mastication," said Thomas Hamilton in 1833; "No loitering nor longing . . . Each individual seemed to pitchfork his food down his gullet, without the smallest attention to the needs of his neighbor."

More than a hundred years later, when he was ambassador to the United States, the Earl of Halifax commented on "the tendency of Americans to regard mealtimes not as a period of relaxation but as an extension of office hours"; and a little later still, it is as true as ever.

Unless an occasion is intended to be formal, the ordinary meal in an American family is hurried and disjointed, and often an extension not only of office hours but of the school hours of the children. Luncheon in particular is not an occasion for leisure in America, whereas in Europe it is a time often of dalliance.

And here I come to my own theory of American food.

The true mark of American society is an informality which itself forms its own patterns and codes. Although the outsider at first cannot detect it, there is a rhythm to American life. This rhythm is a constant improvisation, a flexibility that will accommodate the wishes and whims of every member of a group. No voice in an American family takes precedence over the rest.

Someone is always leaving or coming back; someone is always asking if she or he can have the car; someone is always going to the refrigerator for a snack instead of a meal; someone is always arriving late at a meal or leaving it early. The word "visit"—or "visit with"—is used in America as it is not in England, and even the family seems to be a series of "visits."

The rhythm of the American family is to be found in a system of communication by which the improvised activities of each of its members is made known to all of them, so that they can be taken into account. What holds the home together is a pattern of wires and castings, hidden from view as in a transistor, along which a ceaseless flow of messages is carried from each to all, and an accommodation is made to them.

The American aversion to meals, therefore, is not really an aversion to food. As every statistic shows, Americans consume vast quantities of food. They merely parcel their food into things that can be eaten with the hand.

The American habit of using only the fork, instead of a knife and fork, is in fact carried further by having neither, and having the sandwich—the hamburger— or the snack instead. One cannot imagine the phrase, "Come dressed properly to table," in America; hence, one of the appeals of the barbecue, the ultimate excuse for eating at home as if one is on a picnic.

In Washington this summer, I have been watching whole American families in ordinary restaurants, when they are for once having a meal together. One by one, each grows restless to get away, and the meal degenerates into a pitiless—voice added to voice—nagging of the person who is actually enjoying the occasion.

But in their homes this does not happen. There the transistor works, and every member of the family passes through the kitchen, grabbing on the way what is always plentiful to hand.

It is this informality—these manners— which have spread to the rest of the world; and although something has been lost—"Come dressed properly to table" was the promise of security, as well as the imposition of discipline—I have no doubt that much also has been gained.

But I wish merely that, in the process, the Americans did not pretend that they do not eat a lot. They eat even with their drinks. They put onions in them, or olives, or lemons, or limes; and it is almost impossible to get a Bloody Mary without a tree of celery in it.

Order the "chef's salad" in almost any American restaurant. The day is hot; it is lunchtime; one wants to have something light; one orders the "chef's salad." At which there is brought to one's table a bowl which could hold the rations for an entire Roman legion after a hard day's march. One puts in one's fork, and at once strikes what one is certain can only be a piece of linoleum. One takes out one's fork, and looks at what is on the end.

A tablet of hard cheese. A slab of meat, hewn from the breast of a turkey. A chunk of ham. A congealed flake of tuna. And beneath their weight sinks the salad.

Gone is the light toss of lettuce, gone the slither of tomato, gone the barely perceptible scoop of avocado, gone the spring onion.

One has been given a meal, not a salad, without the attractions of a meal. But what is really at the heart of it all is that the American, thus stuffed, says with assurance, "I only had a salad for lunch"— and reaches out for the next light snack.

72.

JIMMY CARTER: Acceptance Speech

The 1976 presidential race was a marked contrast to most of the other political campaigns of this century. On the Republican side, President Gerald R. Ford was seriously challenged for the nomination by former California governor Ronald Reagan, representing the most conservative wing of the party. This was the strongest threat to deny an incumbent the nomination since Chester A. Arthur lost to James G. Blaine in 1884. By early 1976 the Democrats had not occupied the White House for nearly two terms, and they provided an abundance of presidential aspirants to try to regain it. Because there were so many candidates, it was generally believed that none of them would emerge with enough delegate strength at the July convention to win the nomination on the first ballot. Many politicians even thought that former Vice President Hubert Humphrey might win the nomination by default, even though he refused to enter any primaries. But before the "primary season" was very far along, former governor Jimmy Carter of Georgia appeared as a far stronger contestant than most political pundits had deemed likely. His emergence as a strong candidate by late spring surprised most Americans. He seemed to come out of nowhere to capture the party's nomination. Running for the presidency while holding no political office, Carter was not a member of the Washington "establishment," and he was from the Deep South. Yet he was really not so unknown a quantity as his opponents made him out to be. He had campaigned for nearly two years, traveling the country relentlessly, getting acquainted with local Democrats, and telling them— and all who would listen—his views on the problems facing the nation. Carter entered every primary, garnering enough delegates to win the nomination on the first ballot. On November 2, by winning the general election, he capped one of the most extraordinary political feats in American history. This selection reprints most of Carter's acceptance speech, delivered on Thursday, July 15, 1976, in Madison Square Garden, New York City.

Source: *Vital Speeches*, August 15, 1976.

I ACCEPT your nomination. I accept it in the words of John F. Kennedy: "With a full and grateful heart—and with only one obligation—to devote every effort of body, mind and spirit to lead our party back to victory and our nation back to greatness."

1976 will not be a year of politics as usual. It is a year of concern, and of quiet and sober reassessment of our nation's character and purpose—a year when voters have already confounded the political experts.

It can be a year of inspiration and hope.

And I guarantee you, it will be the year when we give the government of this country back to the people of this country.

There is a new mood in America.

We have been shaken by a tragic war abroad and by scandals and broken promises at home.

Our people are seeking new voices, new ideas and new leaders.

Although government has its limits and cannot solve all our problems, we Americans reject the view that we must be reconciled to failures and mediocrity, or to an inferior quality of life.

For I believe that we can come through this time of trouble stronger than ever before. Like troops who have seen combat, we have been tempered in the fire— we have been disciplined and educated. Guided by lasting and simple moral values, we have emerged idealists without illusions, realists who still know the old dreams of justice and liberty—of country and community. . . .

But in recent years, our nation has seen a failure of leadership. We have been hurt and disillusioned. We have seen a wall go up that separates us from our own government.

We have lost some precious things that historically have bound our people and our government together.

We feel that moral decay has weakened our country, that it is crippled by a lack of goals and values, and that our public officials have lost faith in us.

We have been a nation adrift too long. We have been without leadership too long. We have had divided, deadlocked government too long. We have been governed by veto too long. We have suffered enough at the hands of a tired, worn out administration without new ideas, without youth or vitality, without vision, and without the confidence of the American people.

There is a fear that our best years are behind us, but I say to you that our nation's best is still ahead.

Our country has lived through a time of torment. It is now a time for healing.

We want to have faith again!

We want to be proud again!

We *just* want the truth again!

It is time for the people to run the government, and not the other way around.

It is time to honor and strengthen our families, our neighborhoods, and our diverse cultures and customs.

We need a Democratic President and a Congress to work in harmony for a change, with mutual respect for a change, in the open for a change. Next year we will have that new leadership.

It is time for America to move and to speak, not with boasting and belligerence, but with a quiet strength—to depend in world affairs not merely on the size of an arsenal but on the nobility of ideas—and to govern at home not by confusion and crisis, but with grace and imagination and common sense.

Too many have had to suffer at the hands of a political and economic elite who have shaped decisions and never had to account for mistakes nor to suffer from injustice. When unemployment prevails, they never stand in line looking for a job. When deprivation results from a confused welfare system, they never do without food or clothing or a place to sleep. When the public schools are inferior or torn by strife their children go to exclusive private schools. And when the bureaucracy is bloated and confused, the powerful always manage to discover and to occupy niches of special influence and privilege. An unfair tax structure is designed to serve their needs. And tight secrecy always seems to prevent reform.

All of us must be careful not to cheat each other.

Too often, unholy, self-perpetuating alliances have been formed between money and politics, and the average American citizen has been held at arms length.

Recently, each time our nation has made a serious mistake, our people have been excluded from the process. The tragedy of Vietnam and Cambodia, the disgrace of Watergate, and the embarrassment of the CIA revelations could have been avoided if our government had reflected the sound judgment, good common sense and high moral character of the American people.

It is time for us to take a new look at our own government, to strip away the secrecy, to expose the pressure of lobbyists, to eliminate waste, to release our civil servants from bureaucratic chaos, to provide tough management, and always to remember that in any city or town, the mayor, the governor and the president all represent exactly the same constituents.

As governor I had to deal each day with the complicated, confused, overlapping and wasteful federal government bureaucracy. As president, I want you to help me evolve an efficient, economical, purposeful and manageable government for our nation. I recognize the difficulty, but if I'm elected, it's going to be done!

We must strengthen the government closest to the people.

Business, labor, agriculture, education, science and government should not struggle in isolation from one another, but should be able to strive toward mutual goals and shared opportunities.

We should make our major investments in people, not in buildings and weapons. The poor, the weak, the aged, the afflicted must be treated with respect and compassion and with love.

I have spoken many times about love, but love must be aggressively translated into simple justice.

The test of any government is not how popular it is with the powerful, but how honestly and fairly it deals with the many who must depend on it.

It is time for a complete overhaul of our tax system. It is a disgrace to the human race. All my life I have heard promises of tax reform, but it never quite happens. With your help, we are finally going to make it happen!

It is time for universal voter registration.

It is time for a nationwide, comprehensive health program for all our people.

It is a time to guarantee an end to discrimination because of race or sex by full involvement in the decision making processes of our government by those who know what it is to suffer from that discrimination.

It is time for the law to be enforced. We cannot educate children, create harmony among our people, or preserve basic human freedom unless we have an orderly society. Crime and lack of justice are especially cruel to those who are least able to protect themselves. Swift arrest and trial, and fair and uniform punishment should be expected by those who would break our laws.

It is time for our government leaders to respect the law no less than the humblest citizen, so that we can end the double standard of justice in America. I see no reason why big shot crooks should go free while the poor ones go to jail.

A proper function of government is to make it easy for us to do good and difficult for us to do wrong.

As an engineer, a planner and a businessman, I see clearly the value of a strong system of free enterprise based on increased productivity and adequate wages. We Democrats believe that competition is preferable to regulation, and we intend to combine strong safeguards for consumers with minimal intrusion of government in our free economic system.

I believe that anyone who is able to work ought to work — and have a chance to work. We will never end the inflationary spiral, nor have a balanced budget, which I am determined to see, as long as we have eight or nine million Americans who cannot find a job.

Any system of economics is bankrupt if it sees value or virtue in unemployment. We simply cannot check inflation by keeping people out of work.

The foremost responsibility of any president is to guarantee the security of our nation — a guarantee of freedom from the threat of successful attack or blackmail and the ability with our allies to maintain peace.

But peace is not the mere absence of war. Peace is action to stamp out international terrorism. Peace is the unceasing effort to preserve human rights. Peace is a combined demonstration of strength and good will. We will pray for peace and we will work for peace, until we have removed from all nations the threat of nuclear destruction.

America's birth opened a new chapter in mankind's history. Ours was the first nation to dedicate itself so clearly to basic moral and philosophical principles:

That all people are created equal and endowed with inalienable rights to life, liberty, and the pursuit of happiness; and that the power of government is derived from the consent of the governed.

This national commitment was a singular act of wisdom and courage, and it brought the best and the bravest to our shores.

It was a revolutionary development that captured the imagination of mankind.

It created the basis for a unique world role for America — that of pioneer in shaping more decent and just relations among people and societies.

Today, 200 years later, we must address ourselves to that role, both in what we do at home and in how we act abroad — among people everywhere who have become politically more alert, socially more congested, increasingly impatient with global inequities, and who are now organized into some 150 different nations.

This calls for nothing less than a sustained architectural effort to shape an international framework of peace within which our own ideals gradually can become a global reality.

Our nation should always derive its character directly from our people and let this be the strength and the image to be presented to the world.

To our friends and allies I say that what unites us through our common dedication to democracy is more important than that which occasionally divides us on economics or politics.

To the nations that seek to lift themselves from poverty I say that America shares your aspiration and extends its hand to you.

To those nation-states that wish to compete with us I say that we neither fear competition nor see it as an obstacle to wider cooperation.

To all I say that after 200 years America remains confident and youthful in its commitment to freedom and equality.

During this election year we candidates will ask for votes, and from us will be demanded our vision.

My vision of this nation and its future has deepened and matured during the nineteen months that I have campaigned for president.

I have never had more faith in America than I do today.

We have an America that, in Bob Dylan's phrase, is busy being born, not busy dying.

We *can* have an American government that has turned away from scandal and corruption and official cynicism and is once again as decent and as competent as our people.

We *can* have an America that has reconciled its economic needs with its desire for an environment we can pass on with pride to the next generation.

We *can* have an America that provides excellence in the education of my child and your child and every child.

We *can* have an America that encourages and takes pride in our ethnic diversity, our religious diversity, and our cultural diversity, knowing that out of our pluralistic heritage has come the strength and vitality and creativity that made us great and will keep us great.

We *can* have an American government that does not oppress or spy on its own people, but respects our dignity and privacy and our right to be let alone.

We *can* have an America where freedom and equality are mutually supportive and not in conflict, and where the dreams of our nation's first leaders are fully realized in our own day and age.

We *can* have an America which harnesses the idealism of the student, the compassion of the nurse or social worker, the determination of the farmer, the wisdom of the teacher, the practicality of the business leader, the experience of the senior citizen, and the hope of the laborer to build a better life for us all.

As I have said before, we can have an American President who does not govern with negativism and fear of the future, but with vigor and vision and aggressive leadership—a president who is not isolated from our people, but who feels your pain and shares your dreams, and takes his strength and wisdom and courage from you.

I see an America on the move again, united, a diverse and vital and tolerant nation, entering our third century with pride and confidence—an America that lives up to the majesty of our constitution and the simple decency of our people.

This is the America we want.

This is the America we will have.

We go forward from this convention with some differences of opinion, perhaps, but nonetheless united in our calm determination to make our country large and driving and generous in spirit once again, ready to embark on great national deeds. And once again, as brothers and sisters, our hearts will swell with pride to call ourselves Americans.

73.

The American Bicentennial: A Special Report

The two hundredth anniversary of the Declaration of Independence was celebrated during a period beginning in March 1975 and ending with nationwide festivities on July 4, 1976. This special section is a three-part evocation of the Bicentennial. 1. An account of some of the many ways July 4, 1976, was celebrated in communities throughout the land. 2. An address, "Bicentennial of What?" by Archibald MacLeish, celebrated poet and former Librarian of Congress. 3. A compilation of statements by foreign journalists on the United States at 200. Since America began, some of the most perceptive and significant assessments of the United States have been made by outsiders such as these. Commentators such as de Tocqueville, James Bryce, Frances Trollope, Charles Dickens, Francis Lieber, and Peter Kalm have frequently been able to see what America is about with more clarity, or at least a different perspective, than those of us who live here. We do not always agree with their views, but we can use their ideas to gain a better understanding of our country.

The Bicentennial Celebration, July 4, 1976

Source: *Time* Magazine, July 5, 1976.

FROM NEW YORK harbor, the tall ships will move up the Hudson River under a cumulus of sail, like a stately apparition from another century. Some days later, if all goes well, over 200 million miles away, America's Viking lander will glide through the thin Martian atmosphere and settle on the Red Planet like a gray metal mantis.

Within such brackets of past and future, the United States will celebrate its 200th anniversary this weekend—a culminating moment of raucous blowout compounded of Disneyland pageantry and kitsch, perfervid oratory, sentiment and sentimentality, dissent, 10,000 miles of bunting, phalanxes of politicians and majorettes in a din of John Philip Sousa brass, and tons of fireworks splashing in the dazzled night air.

The Queen of the mother country will appear in Washington, Philadelphia and elsewhere—though not until a couple of days after the main event. The elfin pop singer Elton John will come to a Boston Bicentennial concert tricked out as the Statue of Liberty in silver-sequined robe. Italian Americans in Rome, N.Y., will celebrate with one of history's biggest spaghetti dinners—600 lbs. of pasta and 600 lbs. of sausage for a crowd of up to 3,000. For 76 consecutive hours, the Declaration of Independence, the Constitution and the Bill of Rights will be on display at the National Archives to the hundreds of thousands of visitors converging on the capital.

Abraham Lincoln once said of Fourth of July celebrations that "we go from these meetings in better humor with ourselves, we feel more attached, the one to the other, and more firmly bound to the country we inhabit." It would have been difficult even a year ago, as the Bicentennial began, to credit the thought. But much has changed.

The nation may be in better shape this July 4 than it has been since at least Nov. 22, 1963. The economy's recuperation is progressing. An odd and fascinating primary season seems to have demonstrated the health of the political system—and produced a new face or two to engage voters' imaginations for the future. Watergate is finally interred. Above all, after 13 consecutive years of assassinations, race riots, youth rebellion, Viet Nam, political scandal, presidential collapse, energy crisis and recession, the nation's mood seems optimistic again. Today's leading scandal—sex on Capitol Hill—seems comparatively harmless. Louis Tucker, executive director of the New York State Bicentennial Commission, believes that "the Bicentennial is acting as a kind of catharsis. It's become a way of clearing the American soul in a very positive way."

The dawn's early light will first strike the continental U.S. at 4:31 on July 4 at Mars Hill, Me. (pop. 1,875).

The northeastern Maine potato-growing town will celebrate, sedately enough, with a flag-raising ceremony, nationally televised. Farther down the New England coast, perhaps the nation's longest and oldest July 4 birthday party (every year for 190 years) will take place in Bristol, R.I. During its 13-day celebration, Bristol will have, among other things, a beard-judging contest, a Portuguese song fest and a four-mile-long parade. Newport, R.I., will place a buttonwood Liberty Tree beside one that was planted at the 1876 Centennial in symbolic reply to the retreating British army that cut down every tree on Aquidneck Island during the Revolution.

New England's most grandiose event will occur on Boston's mile-long Esplanade facing the Charles River, where Arthur Fiedler will conduct the Boston Pops Orchestra before an expected crowd of 200,000. The climax of the program will be Tchaikovsky's *1812 Overture.* As the piece reaches its resounding finale, five 105-mm. howitzers will bark out about 40 blasts; eight bells in the belfry of the nearby Church of the Advent will peal, and for 23 minutes fireworks will detonate in the sky. The Boston show (cost: $25,000) is the private contribution of the Armenian immigrant family of Stephen Mugar, a millionaire businessman. Says his son David Mugar: "We are doing this to show our appreciation to this land of freedom for what it has given us."

Perhaps none of the Bicentennial spectacles will match the gathering of 225 sailing ships from 30 nations that will collect July 3 in New York harbor. From there, they will see, hanging from the Verrazano-Narrows Bridge, the largest national flag ever lofted.

On the morning of the Fourth, the ships will proceed in a majestic parade up the Hudson River as far as the George Washington Bridge, then head back down the river past Manhattan's imperious towers. Among them are scheduled to be 16 of the world's largest windjammers, or tall ships (a phrase John Masefield used in his line "All I ask is a tall ship, and a star to steer her by"). . . .

The flotilla promises to be one of the great spectator events of the century. As many as 5 million visitors are expected to jam the riverbanks on the New York and New Jersey sides. More than 16,000 bleacher seats set up at a landfill off southern Manhattan are selling for $25 apiece. In lower Manhattan, Wall Street brokerage firms with offices in the upper stories are staying open to give employees, friends and customers a look. The Coast Guard worries that thousands of small boats will jam the river and harbor. "We expect all kinds of incidents—collisions, capsizings, drownings," said the local Coast Guard commandant. "It's got to happen, with that many boats in the water."

Philadelphia, birthplace of the Declaration of Independence, plans its longest July 4 parade yet—five hours. Queen Elizabeth and Prince Philip will present a six-ton Bicentennial Bell as a gift from the British. Yet there has been a certain ironic sourness in Philadelphia's celebration. The expected hordes of visitors have not appeared, possibly because they feared, incorrectly, that all the hotels would be full. Moreover, dissident groups have promised July 4 demonstrations. Mayor Frank Rizzo has tried to get Washington to dispatch 15,000 federal troops to keep order against, as he says, "a bunch of radicals, leftists [who] intend to come here in the thousands from all over the country to disrupt." The Justice Department, after studying the threat, refused Rizzo's request. One major group planning protests is the July 4th Coalition, made up of disparate organizations, including Puerto Rican nationalists, gay activists, American Indians, feminists and black radicals.

Washington's celebrations will go on for a week. On July 1, President Ford will speak at dedication ceremonies of the Smithsonian Institution's new National Air and Space Museum, where planes and spaceships are suspended from the ceiling like toys. The Fourth of July fireworks will be the most dazzling ever. Instead of the customary two tons set off on the Washington Monument grounds, 33½ tons will be detonated at four places around the Washington Monument, Tidal Basin and Lincoln Memorial. The display costs $200,000 and is being put together by Etablissements Ruggieri, the same French firm that concocted a display seen by Thomas Jefferson in Paris in 1786.

In Bartow, Fla., as is the custom, the townspeople will hold a birthday party for Charlie Smith, who on the Fourth will celebrate what he believes will be his 134th birthday. Smith, who arrived in New Orleans on a slave ship in 1854, is acknowledged by the Social Security Administration to be the oldest living American. The only man in town who remembers the Centennial, Smith will serve as honorary grand marshal for Bartow's Bicentennial parade.

In Atlanta, more than half a million people are expected to watch the Fourth of July parade. In New Orleans' Superdome the night of July 3, performers like Jazzman Al Hirt and Country Fiddler Doug Kershaw will provide five hours of entertainment.

So it will go across the nation. In St. Louis, the celebration under, around and through the city's Gateway Arch will last four hours and include an air show with a wing walker and a five-man free-fall parachute jump. At Chicago Stadium, the Immigration and Naturalization Service will swear in 1,776 new citizens. In the Miami Beach Convention Hall, 7,000 new citizens will be naturalized.

For months, Southern California has been advertising its July 4 "All Nations, All Peoples" Los Angeles County Bicentennial parade as the longest in the nation. When the parade leaves Los Angeles en route to the Pacific Ocean, it will stretch for 10.8 miles. But the sidewalk excitement will be absent in Beverly Hills and Santa Monica, which will not provide police escorts. Once it reaches the Beverly Hills city limits, the parade must disband. On the other side of town new marching units will form and hike to the edge of Santa Monica. There the parade will fizzle, two miles short of its goal at the ocean.

Fireworks, bands and picnics are predictable. The Bicentennial has also aroused inventive imaginations. Some time ago, Chicago Attorney Marvin Rosenblum dreamed up "hands across America," a grand scheme to link the nation from coast to coast with a human chain to symbolize American unity. The plan would require at least 5 million people grasping hands, so Rosenblum has lowered his expectations. Now there will be only bits and pieces of the human chain —about ten miles' worth on Chicago's South Side, for example.

Time capsules are as popular now as they were on July 4, 1876. In Seward, Neb., a discount hardware store owner named Harold Davisson last year interred a 1975 Chevrolet in a crypt of concrete and steel. This year he is adding a blue Kawasaki motorcycle. Also in the vault are a Teflon frying pan, a bolt of polyester fabric, a zipper, a pair of bikini panties and a man's aquamarine leisure suit.

Another Bicentennial enterprise: the horse-drawn wagon trains that have embarked from various sections of the country and will rendezvous July 3 at Valley Forge.

Up in Alaska, at least ten different parties of mountain climbers are trying to reach the summit of Mount McKinley, the tallest peak in North America, by July 4. These Bicentennial climbs will put 800 to 1,000 people near the top at one time. One of the parties plans to try to raise President Ford by radio once it has reached the crest.

Many Americans, of course, find it difficult to summon up such energetic enthusiasm for the grand, excessive project. Blacks, for example, have remained on the margins of Bicentennial celebrations. But they have launched some notable projects. The National Urban League has distributed a series of booklets called *Black Perspectives on the Bicentennial* — covering black economic progress, the black press, education and politics. Two weeks ago, the Afro-American Historical and Cultural Museum opened in Philadelphia, 1½ blocks away from Independence Hall. It houses the most extensive collection of black American documents and artifacts yet assembled in the U.S.

In the South, blacks have been involved in other ways. In Evergreen, Ala. (pop. 5,700), the Rev. H.K. Matthews, pastor of three small A.M.E. Zion churches in the piney backwoods, will observe the Fourth by leading a parade and gospel show to protest surviving rural Alabama bigotry. In Wilmington, N.C., over the weekend, there will be a four-day "Black Freedom Festival" of picnics, "gospelramas," sports events, concerts and workshops.

Charles Rangel, a black Congressman from New York, remarked last week: "If the Bicentennial is some kind of self-congratulatory celebration, it is frivolous and meaningless to the black community. It should be a cause to blacks to bring to light just how far America needs to go to achieve equality under the Constitution. If the Bicentennial can be seen as a rededication to full equality, then it would be relevant to blacks."

It may be that by next week the dominant emotion about the Bicentennial will be one of immense relief that it is finally over — most of it, anyway. Still, for all the blare and schlock — the "Collector's Item" Bicentennial beer cans one brewery put out, the Frisbee tourneys, the air of Styrofoam patriotism — the birthday party promises to include much genuine excitement, significance and dedication. It may be a sign of renewed national health. From all the advance signs, and despite ample predictions of boredom, it should also be fun.

74.

Archibald MacLeish: Bicentennial of What?

An address at the Bicentennial commemoration of the American Philosophical Society in Philadelphia.

Source: *Aspects of American Liberty; Memoirs of the American Philosophical Society,* vol. 118.

It is a common human practice to answer questions without truly asking them and the American Bicentennial is merely the latest instance. Everyone knows what the Bicentennial celebrates: the 200th anniversary of the adoption, by the Continental Congress, of the Declaration of Independence. But no one asks what the Bicentennial *is* because no one asks what the Declaration *was.* The instrument of announcing American independence from Great Britain? Clearly that: but is that all it was? Is it only American independence from Great Britain we are celebrating on July 4, 1976? — only the instrument which declared our independence? There have been other declarations of unilateral independence from Great Britain (Rhodesia's comes most recently to mind) which no one is likely to remember for 200 years, much less to celebrate. Just as there are words, including the best-remembered words, in the American Declaration which seem to have more in mind than an American independence from the British crown.

"All men" are said in that document to be created equal and to have been endowed with certain unalienable rights. All governments are alleged to have been instituted among men to secure those rights — to protect them. Are these, then, American rights? Doubtless — but only American? Is it the British Government which is declared to have violated them?

Unquestionably — but the British Government alone? And the revolution against tyranny and arrogance which is here implied — is it a revolution which American independence from the mediocre majesty of George III will win or is there something more intended? — something for all mankind? — for all the world?

In the old days when college undergraduates still read history, any undergraduate could have told you that these are not rhetorical questions: that there were, from the beginning, two opinions about the Declaration and that they were held by (among others) the two great men who had most to do with its composition and its adoption by the Congress.

John Adams, who supported the Declaration with all his formidable powers, inclined to the view that it was just what it called itself: a declaration of *American* independence. Thomas Jefferson, who wrote it, held the opposite opinion: it was a revolutionary proclamation applicable to all mankind.

"May it be to the world," he wrote to the citizens of Washington a few days before he died, "what I believe it will be: to some parts sooner, to others later, but finally to all, the signal of arousing men to burst the chains. . . ."

And he went on in reverberating words which later and less-honorable revolutionaries have aborted to a different end: "The mass of mankind has not been born with saddles on their backs for a favored few, booted and spurred, ready to ride them by the grace of God."

Moreover, these two great and famous men were not the only Presidents of the Republic to choose between the alternatives: A third, as great as either, speaking in Philadelphia at the darkest moment in our history—bearing indeed the whole weight of that history on his shoulders as he spoke—turned to the Declaration for guidance for himself and for his country and made his choice between the meanings.

Mr. Lincoln had been making his way slowly eastward in February 1861 from Springfield to Washington to take the oath of office as President of a divided people on the verge of Civil War. He had been making little speeches in city after city as he went, saying nothing, marking time, attempting to quiet apprehensions which his irrelevancies only aggravated. He had reached Philadelphia on the 21st of February where he had been told by the detective Pinkerton and by Secretary Seward's son of the conspiracy to murder him in Baltimore as he passed through that city. He had gone to Independence Hall before daylight on the 22d. He had found a crowd waiting. He had spoken to them.

He had often asked himself, Mr. Lincoln said, what great principle or idea it was which had held the Union so long together. "It was not," he said, as though replying directly to John Adams, "the mere matter of the separation from the mother country."

It was something more. "Something in the Declaration," they heard him say. "Something giving liberty not alone to the people of this country but hope to the world." "It was that which gave promise that in due time the weights should be lifted from the shoulders of all men."

His hearers seem to have remembered his words in different ways and it is understandable that they should, for these were private words spoken as much to himself as to them—a speech as moving as a great soliloquy in a tragic play. Anyone else, any modern President certainly, would have said, as most of them regularly do, that his hope for the country was fixed in huge expenditures for arms, in the possession of overwhelming power. Not Mr. Lincoln. Not Mr. Lincoln even at that desperate moment. *His* hope was fixed in a great affirmation of belief made almost a century before. It was fixed in the commitment of the American people, at the beginning of their history as a people, to "a great principle or idea": the principle or idea of human liberty—of human liberty not for themselves alone but for mankind.

It was a daring gamble of Mr. Lincoln's —but so too was Mr. Jefferson's Declaration—so was the cause which Mr. Jefferson's Declaration had defined. Could a nation be founded on the belief in liberty? Could belief in liberty preserve it? Two American generations argued that issue but not ours—not the generation of the celebrants of the 200th anniversary of that great event. We assume, I suppose, that Mr. Jefferson's policy was right for him and right for Mr. Lincoln, because it was successful. The Civil War was won when it became openly and explicitly a war for human liberty—a war to lift the weights from the shoulders of all men. But whatever we think about Mr. Lincoln's view of the Declaration, whatever we believe about the Declaration in the past, in other men's lives, in other men's wars, we do not ask ourselves, as we celebrate its Bicentennial, what it is today, what it is to us.

Our present President has never intimated by so much as a word that such a question might be relevant—that it even exists. The Congress has not debated it.

The state and Federal commissions charged with Bicentennial responsibility express no opinions. Only the generation of the young, so far as I am informed, has even mentioned it, and the present generation of the young has certain understandable prejudices, inherited from the disillusionments of recent years, which color their comments.

Tell your children—or, if you prefer, tell my grandchildren—what Thomas Jefferson thought of his Declaration and you will get a blank look with overtones of embarrassment—embarrassment *for you*. Inform them that in your opinion Mr. Jefferson's Declaration remains the most profoundly revolutionary document ever published by a responsible people—the only revolutionary declaration ever made on behalf, not of a class or a creed or a special interest of one kind or another but of all mankind, all men, of every man—and you will be told, with courteous amusement, that you have to be kidding.

Express your view that the nation brought into being by that great document was, and had no choice but be, a revolutionary nation, and you will be reminded that, but for the accidental discovery of a piece of tape on a door latch, the President of the United States in the Bicentennial year would have been Richard Nixon. And so it will go until you are told at last that the American Revolution is a figure of obsolescent speech; that the Declaration has become a museum exhibit in the National Archives; and that, as for the Bicentennial, it is a year-long commercial which ought to be turned off.

Well, the indignation of the young is always admirable regardless of its verbal excesses—far more admirable, certainly, than the indifference of the elders. But, unfortunately, it is the indifference of the elders we have to consider. And not only because it is a puzzling, a paradoxical, indifference but because it is as disturbing as it is paradoxical.

Does our indifference to the explicitly revolutionary purpose of the Declaration—our silence about Mr. Jefferson's interpretation of that purpose—mean that we no longer believe in that purpose—no longer believe in human liberty? Hardly.

Two years ago we forced the resignation of a President we had just elected by an overwhelming majority because we discovered that he had been engaged in a conspiracy to conceal the truth from us—which means, a conspiracy to obstruct the processes of self-government—which means a conspiracy to suppress our liberties. Rarely has the country been united as it was, and still is, in the sense of outrage which forced that resignation. There can be no doubt, I think, that we in our generation believe in our liberties, in human liberty, in Mr. Jefferson's cause.

But if this is so, if we still believe in the cause of human liberty, why do we celebrate the anniversary of the document which defined it for us without a thought for the meaning of the definition, then or now? Why have we not heard from our representatives and our officials on this great theme?

Is it because, although the Republic continues to believe in human liberty for itself, it no longer hopes for it in the world? Because it no longer thinks such a hope "realistic"? Because, aware of the apparently inexorable conquest of the earth by the most monstrous of all forms of despotism, the modern police state, the country has concluded that the Declaration of Independence is an instrument of purely historical interest and that the American Revolution is a fable for infants like *The Ride of Paul Revere*?

If we think that, we had better give up thinking. It is true, of course, that the police states, whatever their ideologies (the ideologies no longer matter, only the police), have succeeded in subjugating more than half humanity. They are the new "establishment," the new "existing order."

But it is also true that there is not a single police state of any ideology which does not confess by its Berlin Walls, its nets of concentration camps, its prison hospitals for the "insane," its censorship of books, its silencing of mouths, its suppression of minds, that it is afraid. And what it is most afraid of is precisely the ghost of Thomas Jefferson. Opposition from within, the police state can put down. Wars it can win for a time as Hitler won wars — for a time. But the free man, the free mind, it cannot conquer, it can only imprison, only torture, only kill.

So far, indeed, is Mr. Jefferson's revolution from being obsolete that it is now the only truly revolutionary force in the age we live in. And not despite the police states but because of them. When the K.G.B. is king the only possible revolution is the revolution of mankind. The revolution of Sakharov, of Solzhenitsyn.

This, then, is the second puzzle, the second paradox, of the Bicentennial. If we still believe in the cause of human liberty for ourselves, as the events of the last three years prove we do, and if the cause of human liberty is now the one great revolutionary cause in this inhuman world, as the police states know it is, whether we know or not, then why is this greatest of our anniversaries celebrated without a word to start that music in the heart again?

Because we are afraid to affirm our purpose as a people for fear of angering those who have a different purpose? I don't think so. Because we have fixed our minds so long on the menace of the Russian purpose that we have forgotten what our own great purpose was? That is ar-

guable. And the words which would make the argument are three: containment, McCarthyism and Vietnam — containment abroad, McCarthyism at home and Vietnam as the inevitable consequence of both.

In 1945, when we had driven the Nazis out of Europe and the Japanese out of the Pacific in the name of human freedom and human decency, we stood at the peak, not only of our power as a nation but of our greatness as a people. We were more nearly ourselves, our true selves as the inheritors of Thomas Jefferson and Abraham Lincoln, than we had ever been before. And yet within a few years of that tremendous triumph, of the unexampled generosity of our nuclear offer to the world, of the magnificence of the Marshall Plan, we were lost in the hysterical fears and ignoble deceits of Joe McCarthy and his followers and had adopted, as our foreign policy, the notion that if we "contained" the Russian initiative, we would somehow or other be better off ourselves than if we pursued our historic purpose as Jefferson conceived it.

The result, as we now know, was disaster. And not only in Southeast Asia and Portugal and Africa but throughout the world. Containment put us in bed with every anti-Communist we could find including some of the most offensive despots then in business — despots almost as offensive as the Commissars themselves. It produced flagrantly subversive and shameful plots by American agencies against the duly elected governments of other countries. And it ended by persuading the new countries of the postwar world, the emerging nations, that the United States was to them and to their hopes what the Holy Alliance had been to us and ours 200 years before.

But bad as all this was, the worst and most destructive effect of this breach of faith, this treason to our own past, was what it did, precisely, to ourselves. It aged us. When I was a young man, 60 years ago, Americans thought of their country as young—thought of the Republic as a nation still at the beginning of its history. A generation later, after the hysteria of McCarthyism and the corrosion of containment, we had become an elderly society huddled over an old man's dream— the dream of "security."

Mr. Jefferson knew, as those who honor him know still, that there is no such thing in human life, no such thing in human history, as what we call "security." He knew that what makes a people great, a nation powerful, is purpose. And what our nation celebrates this year—what it should be celebrating—is precisely the purpose Mr. Jefferson bequeathed to us, the purpose Mr. Lincoln took for answer in his agony.

We are as great as our belief in human liberty—no greater. And our belief in human liberty is only ours when it is larger than ourselves: liberty, as Mr. Lincoln put it, "not alone to the people of this country but hope to the world." We must become again his "last, best hope of earth" if we wish to be the great Republic which his love once saved. We know that. We must say so even now, even toward dark, without a voice to lead us, without a leader standing to come forth. We must say it for ourselves. No one else will say it for us.

75.

Ourselves As Others See Us: Foreign Press Commentary On the United States In the Bicentennial Year

Source: *Atlas World Press Review,* July and September 1976

Klaus Liedtke, in Stern *magazine, Hamburg, West Germany. April 8, 1976.*

America on its 200th birthday is perplexed. Abroad it suffers one foreign policy defeat after another, at home it stumbles into scandal after scandal. The god who supposedly watches after drunks, little children, and the United States of America seems to have departed. According to George Gallup, inventor of the public opinion poll, Americans have never been so pessimistic. For the first time a majority of those polled believe their standard of living has declined.

Two-thirds are dissatisfied with the whole system—economic and political.

Political campaigns are no longer run *from* Washington but *against* Washington. The country that brought us blue jeans, computers, *Bonanza,* jazz, and drive-in churches now seems to export only bad news—a murder rate doubling every few years, cities on the edge of bankruptcy, a secret agency conspiring to murder heads of state, and companies that in pursuit of profits would have bribed the Pope.

The leader of this unhappy scene is a

likable president who stumbles over his words and whose predecessor uttered the famous line: "I am not a crook." Small wonder that Uncle Sam is in a funk, far removed from his onetime belief in a happy ending—that tomorrow will inevitably be a little better than today. The future no longer appears exclusively American. For example, almost half the Germans questioned in a recent poll believe that in fifty years the U.S.S.R. will be stronger than the U.S.

In sum the American Century is over. It lasted only thirty years—born in 1945; died April 29, 1975, at 7:52 a.m. when a helicopter lifted the last GI from the rooftop of the U.S. embassy in Saigon. This defeat demonstrated to the world the limits of U.S. power. The humiliation was completed a few days later with the recapture from the Cambodians of the U.S. freighter *Mayaguez.* Touted as a "victory," this was merely a phony compensation for a war that had been lost.

Is America still in a position to win the next war? Many Americans fear it is not. Nor does its standard of living any longer set the U.S. apart from the rest of the world. In 1960 Americans were twice as well off as northern Europeans. Today this lead has shrunk and several nations may soon be better off.

For most of their history Americans have believed they were exceptional, enjoying more sense, civilization, and freedom than anyone else on earth. The Pilgrim fathers sailed to America convinced of their holy mandate to build a model society that would show the Old World the path to the future. By 1776 this sense of mission had become dogma. For the first time the concept of human rights was incorporated in a legally binding constitution. The Stars and Stripes became the banner of human progress. America, wrote Alexis de Tocqueville in 1835, was

to become a beacon for the rest of the world. To Walt Whitman the expansion of American territory was an "expansion of human happiness and freedom."

When and where did this sense of mission degenerate into naked imperialism? Was it in 1898 when the Americans wrested the Philippines from Spain and in succeeding years killed millions of Filipino guerrillas? Or was it in the rice paddies of Vietnam? Certainly in recent years whenever the U.S. could choose between supporting a liberation movement or a dictatorship it chose the latter—the side that was pro-Western, pro-ITT, pro-Coca-Cola. The new freedom the superpower cherished was freedom for trade and maximum profits.

Actually there never was an equal division of the pie in this land of biblical piety. Whites enslaved blacks, the North crushed the South, the U.S. cavalry the Indians, and the Rockefellers the little companies that balked at joining the trust. Money had replaced the people as the fundamental source of power. By rough estimates $100,000 would buy a House seat and a million, one in the Senate. Less than 1 per cent of the population contributed 90 per cent of these campaign funds.

America likes its heroes to be rich. A poor Kennedy would have been only half as interesting. And Eisenhower was the only World War II leader whose people devised a special tax law to enable him to become a millionaire. This is a land where generations of dishwashers have worked hard and dreamed of becoming millionaires.

America has never developed a class consciousness or supported a socialist movement worthy of the name. The reason can be perceived in the classic Western which embodies the basic American urge to move, settle on a piece of land, each man for himself, and against all comers. Those who failed blamed themselves and not their surroundings or society.

The European visitor is shocked to find that in the land of abundance some 25 million persons live below the official poverty line of $5,000 annual income; that the nation which reached the moon also includes 21 million illiterates; that almost every other marriage leads to divorce; and that a third of the twenty-to thirty-year-olds indulge in some form of drugs. Here in God's own country more laws are passed and then broken than anywhere else on earth. The violent past has spawned a pistol culture that proliferates crime, to the point where there is no way of protecting the Kennedys or a Martin Luther King.

So far this has been a litany of failures, defeats, problems. But has the American experiment really failed? In this nation of stark contrasts one could draw just the opposite conclusion. On the one hand, the Watergate, Lockheed, and other scandals exposed the dark side of the American system. Yet the Americans' capacity for self-cleansing that spared no politicians or secrets could scarcely be equaled in Europe. Was this not, as the *Times* of London wrote, almost "democratic excess"? The American war machine has caused widespread suffering. But did it not free the world from fascism? Americans may have oppressed their minorities. But they have also provided refuge for millions of oppressed, displaced, and hopeless people from all over the world.

Europeans make fun of American vulgarity and tastelessness—of their senior citizens, for example, vegetating in plastic gardens. Yet is this not a sort of tolerance, a freedom to do as one wants? So many cultures have collided in this "nation of nations" that the composite they have created is a miracle of sorts. And America is the home of movements—environmental and consumer protection; civil and women's rights. It has exported the Jesus cult, hippie culture, student revolution, and wheat to the Russians. Yet the U.S. is not loved.

European intellectuals' enthusiasm for America has turned, especially since Vietnam, into a blind anti-Americanism which is as mindless as dogmatic anti-Communism. But it is in West Germany that an anti-radical law has been passed that borders on thought control and a sedition act that intrudes on press freedom. Meanwhile in Washington a new "Freedom of Information Law" gives every citizen a right to peer into public documents. The U.S., too, is a rare country that does not issue identity cards to its citizens and then issues a driver's license to a blind person so that he, too might have some sort of identification.

The last fifteen years in this wonderland have been turbulent. Blacks have fired the cities because they no longer wanted to shine white shoes. Youth fought the police and governmental authority to develop alternative lifestyles. Protesters who mounted the barricades forced the removal of U.S. troops from Vietnam. The press, now the Fourth Estate in fact as well as theory, drove a vice president and president from office. America now knows that it, too, can have a "crook" at the helm and that barbarians who commit massacres are not always "Japs," "Ivans," "Krauts."

America has shed the arrogance of power and lost its delusion of moral superiority. Severe conflicts still lie ahead. Somehow the disparity of incomes between its white and black citizens must be bridged. A strong neoconservative tide threatens to wash away social welfare programs. A battle is looming between economic boosters and anti-growth activists who would curb industrial growth in order to save the environment and quality of life. And the dream of good life — of a $25,000 annual income, a seven-room house in the suburbs with two cars in the garage — will remain just that for nine out of ten Americans.

Now, at the beginning of its third century, the U.S. is licking its wounds. But the convalescence will be temporary. The world is too small for isolationism and America too big. Besides, who would fill the vacuum? America's comeback is simply a question of when, not whether. There is no doubt that Uncle Sam wants again to stand tall.

And if we have one wish for our big brother across the ocean for the Bicentennial it should be that in future he should reflect more on his revolutionary heritage and line up with the oppressed, the disadvantaged, and those in the world who are without hope.

And with that thought: Happy Birthday, U.S.A.!

Alain Clément, in Le Monde, *Paris, France. May 11, 1976.*
Ever since the late 19th century Americanization has been synonymous with modernization. There were, to be sure, some in old Europe — chiefly of the political Right — who deplored the dominance of the machines and of money — a cause that would later be taken up by the Left. Even Tocqueville, whose dream for France was of an "American style" blend of freedoms and beliefs, could not altogether conceal his repugnance for the pursuit of the dollar.

Yet America's vitality and daring compelled admiration. After all, with an army of a mere 3,000 men Washington's successor John Adams proposed to wage war on France, whose pirates were preying on U.S. shipping. Yesterday, as to-day, the outside world was captivated by such audacity.

The same magnetism persists. The slaughter of Indians, for example, instead of exciting horror provides the inexhaustible component of successful "Westerns." America's perpetual motion, its social jumble, the garish vulgarity of its civilization, the eccentricities of its politics, the whole "pop" lifestyle exercise a powerful fascination. Would John Kennedy, for instance, in so short a time and on such slim achievements, have captivated five continents without the charm of his cowboy dandyism?

But today — after Johnson, Nixon, and now Gerald Ford — the White House is no longer exuberant. Americans are, in fact, merely witnesses to a political system which narrowly rations their participation in government. The electorate, sovereign in theory, is consulted only on fixed dates (every two years for Congress, every four years for the presidency). Congress cannot be dissolved before the end of the term, and even the resignation of the president does not shorten an incumbency, which is a kind of regency. Thus institutions originally conceived to obliterate hereditary power came to codify succession, preventing recourse to the polls until a time fixed by an inflexible calendar.

What is called the power of public opinion in America is merely an accumulation of emotions and tensions between electoral dates unchanged by the most acute crises. Yet this malaise does not breed extralegal opposition or a drive to overturn the established order. The years of demonstrations against the Vietnam War proved this. For the first time in decades millions of Americans took to the streets. To raise barricades? Not at all. Their marches were liturgical processions led by ministers of the cult, never by politicians or labor union leaders. Even in those stormy days "subversion" was not afoot anywhere except in the minds of FBI agents, who increased their provocations in the hope of driving it into the open.

Herein lies a paradox: in this supposedly violent country nothing is happening. Events unfold according to a fixed seasonal calendar. It can be disturbed by the gun of a deranged person but not by a mass movement, a general strike, or a military uprising which is totally improbable. Even moderate revisionism has little chance to penetrate either of the two big political parties, which are merely agglomerations of individuals with sectional interests.

Yet beneath this surface dullness 215 million inhabitants are deeply worried, though these anxieties do not take the form of an "event." So there is something disturbing in the current American calm. It is sometimes explained as a "need for rest" after the excesses of Vietnam and Watergate, as a "backswing of the pendulum" toward a timid conservatism after fifteen years of vertiginous adventurism. Actually it seems other phenomena are at work.

In the first place I believe the Americans have completed their Americanization, despite the talk of "ethnic awakenings" and demands. The annual figure of legal and illegal immigrants is climbing back to the levels of the years before the restrictions of the 1920s. However, more than 95 per cent of actively employed Americans (as against 85 per cent in 1930) were born in the U.S. and received an entirely American education.

The result is a relaxed conformity which has replaced the strident conformism of the McCarthy era. The American mode of government has succeeded in making people forget that there are competing models. The U.S. easily puts up with its "counter culture" since there is no "counter-constitution" that can make it genuinely disruptive.

The timid proposals for reorganization of powers put forth from 1960 to 1970 and the initial verve of the Democratic congressmen elected in the wake of the 1974 Nixonian debacle vanished in the sands of routine indifference. The only durable innovations of those years were signed by a solitary outsider: Henry Kissinger, the incarnation of the triumph of Americanization, the champion abroad of what he had called a policy of "repose," of settling-down.

All generations it seems are happily joined in condemning constraints, taxes, and interdependence. All are harking back to the country's primordial dream that American society is mature enough to control itself, the state is a necessary evil that must be kept in rein, for, in the words of Thomas Paine, it is "the badge of lost innocence."

But instead the State is proliferating. In fifty years the federal administration has almost sextupled in personnel. Since 1960 it has grown by 215 new bureaus and agencies which consume four times as many dollars. How much better everything would be if the gardener was master of his own house!

Against this ideological background various Congressional committees for more than a year have been investigating the monstrous Pentagon, CIA, and FBI. Their cardinal sin is not in the abuses revealed; it is in their exposure as the apparatus of a secular power which betrays the spiritual basis of American democracy by imitating the vile intrigues and sordid despotisms of Europe.

This discovery was made when weapons had fallen silent. From Pearl Harbor to the fall of Saigon, from 1941 to 1975 virtually all Americans except for a handful of rebels felt they were engaged in world missions that absolved in advance the means used to carry them out: the "European crusade," the Korean War, the Cold War, the Vietnam War. During all this time they gave their leaders carte blanche. Now they are awakening at peace but not pacified: the external enemy they had fought, totalitarianism, the police-state, spying on private citizens, tyranny in all its forms, had invaded the sanctuary of freedom. America feeling itself surrounded by darkness is trying to repurify the temple.

Statements by five U. S. correspondents of the weekly Shukan Asahi, *Tokyo, Japan, January 16, 1976. The unattributed remarks are by Yukio Matsuyama, Jutaro Tsuchida, Yoshio Murakami, Hisashi Ujiie, and Tsugio Kato.*

I feel the U.S. has lost the dynamism it had during the Nixon-Kissinger era. Disarmanent talks are at a standstill, the U.S. role in the international economy is stagnant, there is still the East-West confrontation, and détente has not measured up to American expectations. The U.S. seems now to be drifting. But the country will soon have the first elected president in several years and I think we can look for a break in the stagnation that followed Vietnam and Watergate, a renewed dynamism.

The U.S. has been confronted with one crisis after another for more than ten years—the Berlin crisis, Cuban crisis, the Kennedy and King assassinations, racial violence, Vietnam, and Watergate. Now that the latest crises are over the country has a sense of relief, and also of emptiness. There is no crisis to face but neither is there anything to feel especially happy

about. And there are no clearcut issues in this election like how to cope with the Soviet Union or what to do about Cuba. Democrats, Republicans, it really doesn't make that much difference.

The Bicentennial certainly offers Americans an opportunity for self-examination. But afterward will they turn inward or look outward? It is hard to say. There are strong indications that the U.S. will turn inward in the years ahead. But this is not the same kind of isolationism which once characterized U.S. foreign policy. Even among conservatives few believe the U.S. should drastically curtail its world relationships.

I think the U.S. was disgusted with itself after Vietnam. It will not make the same kind of commitment again. And it has also lost the traditional missionary zeal, which was recently manifested in the Peace Corps. On the other hand it is naive to expect the U.S. to halt aid to non-Communist countries. I think the State Department has not changed its view that Communism would advance at the first sign of relaxation in Western defenses.

I'd call U.S. foreign policy after Vietnam selective isolationism or selective internationalism, depending on how you look at it. The U.S. will still regard as crucial its ties with Western Europe and Northeast Asia, including Japan and Korea. But it will not play an active role in Southeast Asia or on the Asian continent. I think this will be the national consensus in the near future.

I think the U.S. will be forced into isolationism because of money. For instance Kissinger tries to work out a peace agreement in the Middle East by hinting at military aid. But when he comes home he has to ask Congress for money and it can say no. The U.S. can no longer police the world.

I think the Bicentennial celebration is giving Americans a sense of history. They will be less inclined to feel they can settle any problem in the world and there will be a decline in their provincialism, which is based on their worship of industrial technology.

Everyone is talking about the presidential election. But I doubt the present political system is really suitable for today's America. A noted U.S. scholar wrote me the other day that he believes the parliamentary system in Japan and Britain may work better than the presidential system in this age. I followed Goldwater, Rockefeller, and Johnson on their campaigns and six months or a year of campaigning is enough to exhaust anyone. After the election year turmoil it's difficult for the man who gets to the White House to think straight. Nixon's personality may have been responsible for Watergate but I suspect the scandal also resulted from America's political system.

An outstanding difference between the U.S. today and 200 years ago is that at the time of independence first-rate people were involved in politics—Washington, Adams, Franklin, and Jefferson. Today politics has lost respect—and not only in the U.S. So bright young people don't go into politics anymore and the status of politicians in the eyes of the public has dropped. The U.S. election system should be changed so that really able people can easily run for office. Today they can be brought into the top of bureaucracy but the Cabinet often lacks first-rate talent.

Judging from the people I see, money and taxes are the greatest concerns of Americans. Yet at the same time there is a sentiment that "we are going to build the country once again," in the spirit of those who came on the *Mayflower*. They are still proud of being Americans despite the huge problems that confront them.

There was an interesting survey recently. Two questions were asked: Do you think your life will be better five or ten years from now? And do you think American society will become correspondingly better? Many answered that their lives would improve but not the society. This is a kind of doomsday view—that the world is coming to an end. I think this attitude will make Americans more hesitant and self-centered in the future.

Carlos Alberto Montaner, in El Nacional *of Caracas, Venezuela. April 3, 1976.*
The Bicentennial affords us a good opportunity to dissect the big country up north. The contractions, the rhythm, and the nature of the birth at Philadelphia left a permanent mark on the infant. Let me explain: to throw the monarchy overboard and to embrace the arithmetic of democracy was an amazing and unprecedented deed. Washington, Jefferson, and their crowd innovated. They inaugurated a system—in fact they invented the time in which they lived. They didn't look back. They didn't copy. They didn't modify. They created. And in creating, at the exact instant of birth they introduced into the genetic pool of the country an irrepressible need for originality.

In 200 years the U.S. has done nothing but create. The initial push has not stopped. The first big bang has kept that universe expanding in the same direction.

The gringos don't look back. They create incessantly. And on this frightening peculiarity hangs the fate of the rest of the planet. For the Americans are the leaders. They decide the speed at which we travel, the illnesses of which we're cured, and even the conversations we have.

For many years now every important thought in the world has been thought in English. I say this with sorrow, with shame, and frustration. Spanish is a language of *boleros* and bad novels. A system of communication that either translates or mimics. Our people sing rock music in English.

When we speak of the U.S. as the leading nation we invariably think of its airplanes and bombs. What nonsense! Leadership doesn't derive from a country's military arsenal but from the research done in its laboratories, from the creativity of its people, and their maddening ability to change. For two centuries these people have been inventing the world. What simpleton thinks we could ever catch them? When we arrive out of breath at Point X they'll already be gone. They'll have taken off with their protean society, always on the move chasing more comfortable and complex destinies as if they were Indians.

And we can't go back, as Gandhi wished, to the vegetable garden and the spinning wheel, forgetting about electronic gadgets. We're hooked in. It's almost an act of cultural obscenity to project the image of a moon-landing on a home television set in Nicaragua. Mere possession of a television set borders on black humor. But it's inevitable. The magic flute of gringo leadership sends its music through our pores. We're condemned to sing in the chorus.

Can we seriously talk of Yankee decadence? Yes, if we talk of the subordinate little world of politics. But the Yankees have not been important to humanity—from the perspective of centuries—for having won two world wars or lost in Angola, Vietnam, or Cuba. They are important for having raised their values to a universal level and impregnated all earthlings with the American way of life. And for having put all of humanity to work copying their ingenuity, translating their texts, and imitating their manners.

In the role of big daddy there's no hint of decadence. Quite the contrary. As Americans abandon their police functions abroad their domestic vitality will grow. When the Linus Paulings and Noam Chomskys have nothing better to do they'll devote themselves to research. That is, to changing the world. (Ironically, these efforts will increase the chasm between the developed and underdeveloped countries.)

I, for one, won't participate in the stupid current anti-American craze. The parrots of journalism and literature may accuse me of selling myself for Yankee gold, but at least I won't be an idiot. It pains me enough to belong to a subsidiary world. But I admire creativity, whatever its source. And I regret that our little world—which speaks in Spanish and prays to Jesus Christ, won't take up the scepter.

Stephen Barber, in the Australian, *Canberra, Australia. February 20, 1976.*

America's friends and allies have been dismayed—and her adversaries bewildered, if not dangerously misled—by Washington's current seeming obsession with self-denigration. To the year-long torrent of leaks about the alleged past misdeeds of the CIA, the FBI, and other security services have been added embarrassing disclosures of diplomatic cables and revelations of corruption on an international scale in the aircraft industry. Committees of both the Senate and the House of Representatives keep dredging up one scandal after another in an orgy of denunciations of past errors, real or imaginary, as if thereby to purge the entire nation of its supposed wickedness.

Outsiders looking on may well have wondered whether America has gone mad. What is even more alarming—for those of us who rely, in the final analysis, on the ability of this, the most powerful of nations economically and (so far) militarily, to act as a counterweight to Russia—is the thought that it had lost its will and sense of national purpose.

Having said this, however, I am glad to be able to report that once one gets out of Washington, and into the heartland of the real America one is swiftly reassured that things are nothing like as bad as they look. Mr. Ford, on the campaign trail for the Republican Presidential nomination, has been cheered most lustily whenever he called for an end to the self-destructive tendencies displayed in recent Congressional witchhunts. Ordinary Americans are increasingly angry with Congress about this.

A thoughtful Wisconsin farmer whom I met on a recent trip to California expressed genuine surprise when I told him that many of America's friends were worried about the seemingly endless self-abasement indulged in by Washington's legislators in recent months. It had not occurred to him, he said, that it could lead others to doubt America's commitment to its ideals or even to its allies. "This is such a big country," he said, recalling that his father had come from Norway in the Depression years, "that we can be careless. You see, it just doesn't occur to us that we might look weak to others because we know we are not.

"Have you ever seen a hen sitting on her eggs and then got her to hatch a goose egg at the same time?" he asked. "Well, in due course all the eggs hatch. The gosling is there with the chicks. He grows up quickly but he does not know he is different from them and never thinks of it. But one day he starts to flop around with those great big web-feet and he stomps on a few chicks without meaning to harm them. I think maybe we are like that."

A university dean from Colorado, a Johnson Democrat, made another comment, after agreeing with the farmer. "In a way the fact that we have to go through all this trauma—and most of us are getting very tired of it—shows not that we are weak but that we are really strong. It comes as a shock to us that others are afraid for us. If you leave aside the self-conscious Liberal Establishment intelligentsia, you will find us really rather optimistic that we can surmount the problems that confront mankind. That may sound smug but it is so."

He also told me, as did many others from various walks of life I talked with at random in a cross-country week outside the capital, that there has been a strong reaction in the universities recently against the pot-smoking, hippie, peacenik "counterculture" that burgeoned in the late Sixties and early Seventies. Student radicalism is decidedly on the wane. Conservativism is coming back into vogue among the young, and so is old-fashioned patriotism. This is the message I got on the West Coast . . . and the Middle West.

Americans remain basically self-reliant and optimistic over the long term even though they love to grumble and pick at old sores over the short term. All the opinion polls confirm that many trendy commentators tend to dwell too much on the nitpicking mood of their own kind.

Bruce Hutchinson, in the Globe and Mail, Toronto, Ontario. November 28, 1975.

The room where the Declaration of Independence was signed on July 4, 1776, by a group of obscure colonists with the mutual pledge of their Lives, Fortunes, and Sacred Honor, seems quite small, austere, and chilly—an improbable birthplace for the most powerful nation of the contemporary world, a repository of old certainties and new doubts.

Amid the swarm of hushed and nostalgic pilgrims who crowd Independence Hall in honor of the nation's Bicentennial year one asks whether two centuries of human events have measured up to the hopes of the signers and the subsequent framers of the Constitution in this room. This is a time of reassessment and bittersweet memories.

What has gone wrong with the original dream and what right? Where does the nation really stand today in its own judgment and the respectful opinion of mankind? Of course there is no agreed answer. But clearly events have not flowed as the constitutional architects planned, even though history judges them the most brilliant company of political genius ever assembled, an elite unrivaled in modern times.

Instead the U.S. has become what we call a democracy (often without understanding either the system or the citizen's responsibility to it). And democracy as we know it now was not in the minds of the founders, who would not even trust the people to elect their president and asserted merely their vague right to Life, Liberty, and the Pursuit of Happiness.

"Democracy," said John Adams, the second president and, next to Thomas Jefferson, perhaps the ablest of the founders, "never lasts long. It soon wastes, exhausts, and murders itself. There never was a democracy yet that did not commit suicide." After two centuries that warning, long ignored and forgotten, is as relevant today as when Adams uttered it. More relevant, indeed, and haunting, not only in the U.S. but in all democratic nations.

Is democracy won in bloodshed and then taken for granted still a viable form of government in the unforeseen age of galloping technology, a brittle interlocking worldwide economy, increasing State control of men's lives, and overhanging them the shadow of nuclear lunacy? Was Jefferson realistic or deluded in assuming that free men are capable of governing themselves and Adams mistaken when he denied that bold heresy?

Nowadays such a question is submerged or dismissed as absurd in the debate of so-called practical politics when a dozen ambitious candidates scheme and struggle for the next presidency. But compared to the health and survival of democracy itself, here and elsewhere, the fate of any man or government is of small import, a trivial episode, a brief whistle stop. What matters is the basic Jeffersonian postulate, and to a good many thinkers, American and foreign, it begins to look pretty dubious. Dubious or not, the postulate raises the supreme question of the Bicentennial.

The ocean tide of rhetoric, the parades, bands, and clumsy tableaux, the thriving industry of cheap souvenirs, flags, and gaudy ribbons, George Washington's face on every lapel button, the blatant commercialization of the Self-Evident Truths—these things are human enough, and harmless, but they only disguise and postpone the real question.

After all, the Pursuit of Happiness does not end in confetti and fireworks. Life and Liberty cannot be reckoned in a Gross National Product nor ensured by an inflated deficit budget. Such measurements and devices have their place but they are only economic and men and women are not wholly economic animals. For if they were no more than that the glaring paradox of our times would not have appeared—the paradox of government always expanding its legal power, institutions, and machinery while steadily losing its moral power, the faith of the citizen. A paradox so deep and so little understood, the core of the democratic dilemma everywhere, will not be much affected by this year's celebrations nor by the accompanying flood of historic scholarship.

As I was leaving a famous university its greatest scholar gave me a copy of a rather shaking document which sums up the question posed in the first and unanswered at the end of the second American century. In a letter to John Quincy, his son and the sixth president, on Aug. 26, 1816, John Adams wrote:

"The people of U.S. are the most conceited People that ever existed on this Globe. The most proud, vain, ambitious, suspicious, jealous, umbrageous, and envious (and I am as guilty as any of them). Have a care of them! . . . If ever a People had the Proof of Happiness it is the people of U.S. We cannot bear prosperity. Calamity alone and extreme distress will ever bring forth the real character of this Nation. . . . Nothing short of foreign War, and civil War once, will ever effect it. And then you may depend upon it they will follow a Bonaparte or several Bonapartes rather than Jeffersons, Madisons, John or Quincy Adams's. Hamiltons and Burrs will be preferred to Hancocks and Washingtons."

So far Adams has been proved wrong. The two centuries produced no Bonaparte. At worst they produced only a Nixon of futile Napoleonic instincts (who is now in his own luxurious St. Helena) and then an honest, well-meaning Ford.

But the adventure that began in Philadelphia is a moment's twinkling in history's eye and Adams' verdict has yet to be finally proved or disproved. The question of questions—seldom asked today, inescapable tomorrow—is whether any free people can bear prosperity without debauching their economic system and corrupting their democracy. That has still to be decided.

From The Observer, *London, England. July 4, 1976.*

It must look odd to most of the world that this year we, the British, celebrate the greatest act of treason ever committed against us. The unilateral Declaration of Independence in part was a factious and niggling document, almost any point of which should have been settled by negotiation. But the break had to come as certainly as a great growing tree must break into leaf.

We should have won the fighting. We commanded the sea. We had a professional British and German Army. We were beaten by the equivalent of territorials and mercenaries. By right we should greet July 4 in sullen silence. But in fact we were uncommonly fortunate to have lost that particular war.

Had we won the fight there would have had to be scaffolds to rival Tower Hill and Tyburn in the nobility of their burdens. We would have had something far worse than Ireland on our hands. And bigger. The bitterness would have grown like a fever, as it did after the suppression of the Dublin Easter Rising. Instead we have got on uncommonly well.

Some people used to think that countries born marvelously and bravely into independence and their own version of freedom, countries like India and Israel, would be morally different from us, who were old and ill and evil.

The U.S. has never been innocent since the time it began cruelly to persecute those who had remained loyal to the Crown. It has indulged in a classical imperialism that compares morally with our own. And it did less physical good in the process. It has indulged in the social perversion of slavery and its aftermath. It has worshipped great wealth as we worshipped hereditary or royal honor. It has had its own hereditary aristocracy and cities run by oligarchies. In all this the U.S. hardly differs in anything but scale from the nation of which it is a majestic offspring.

But there is more to it than this human weakness. Its revolution was the most rational in history. Its intentions — even when they were perverted by self-deception — were the highest any State ever dared to set for itself. Its vast generosity has been frequently selfless. Its politics are enchanting and involuted, though messier than ours. It chooses, like other States, great leaders only by accident (Abraham Lincoln was laughed into office).

The Fourth of July cannot be our feast. But we can be a little proud that no other nation, not even Imperial Rome, produced so great and nobly independent an offspring.

From The Guardian, *Manchester, England. May 17, 1976.*

America has always been, and continues, a great debate. A 200th birthday — a wholesale slaughtering of turkeys and prime beef cattle amid an ocean of Coca-Cola — will end no debates and produce no fresh conclusions. There is, however, one old conclusion it seems right to reiterate now. That America, for all its doubts and frailties, has been for 200 years a triumph for humanity. Do we doubt the possibility of a U.S. of Europe? The British and the Irish and the Poles and the Swedes and the Italians and countless more have made that a reality in the U.S.

Do we doubt that democracy still works? Six months of insanely gruelling primary elections may have strained credibility; but at the end there is a peanut farmer grinning. Do we doubt that a handful of men, barely knowing what they intend, can take a continent and make something beyond imagining of it, the weary old earth built again and built differently? That is America. There will be more words, but for the moment a simpler, quieter reaction suffices. A moment of awe. Men made America and perhaps other men might make it differently. Nonetheless the achievement itself is awesome.

From The Sunday Times, *London, England. July 4, 1976.*

We salute the U.S. and the American people. Of course if the thirteen colonies had not rebelled the world might have escaped a number of infelicities, the tea bag, the Ku Klux Klan, formula television, chewing gum, funerary habits, confected salad dressing, the phrase "have a nice day," bread like cotton wool, and second-hand auto salesmen. Anyone can make up his own list, but not even the most productive of us can produce one that weighs more than a feather in the scale. The political, economic, and philosophical consequences of the U.S. are profound and beneficial and an inspiration for a Western civilization sustained by faith in the individual and his capacity for virtue.

The past and the individualist philosophy bequeath a harsh side to American life: the violence of the cities, the racial antagonism, the tolerance for gun-carrying, the insistence on individual effort which at its extremes produces glaring neglect of minorities and a fierce urge for material success that corrupts men and destroys landscapes. But against these stark enough problems and the glaring existence of poverty, and especially black poverty, must be set the testified capacity of the society for candor, for self-criticism, for idealism, and for climbing the unscaleable peaks. On this American birthday, the British people should have no difficulty in recognizing, like Churchill, that "Westward, look, the land is bright."

From L'Express, *Paris, France. May 17, 1976.*

The U.S. is celebrating the 200th anniversary of its independence this year. How far has it come? And how far have we come? America. the most criticized country in the world, is also the most imitated, and nothing that goes on in America is wholly alien to Europe or the rest of the world, including China and the Soviet Union.

The Russians depend on American agriculture in order to feed themselves, and without American technology Siberia would remain barren. The European leftists who demonstrated against the Vietnam War were dressed in jeans and listened to Bob Dylan every night. The America that was plunged deep into political despair by the Watergate scandal is listening to the biblical tones of the Founding Fathers in the voice of Jimmy Carter. This continent, on which the shadows of the Great Depression fell during the economic crisis, is now the first to achieve new growth records, and without inflation.

America includes the Mafia, the CIA, and multinational companies' bribes; there may be awesome doubts about the political and military balance between East and West. But as Francoise Giroud [Secretary of State for Women] told students at Ann Arbor recently: "Two hundred years after your birth it is your rebirth, your Renaissance, that we hope soon to celebrate."

Nicola Matteucci, in II Giornale, *Milan, Italy. July 4, 1976.*

It is not reckless to predict that Italy will celebrate America's Bicentennial in a listless fashion. The American revolution scarcely figures in European historical discourse and a tendentious anti-Americanism pervades our mass media.

The American revolution does not, in fact, fit neatly into European categories. Other revolutions aimed at installing a new order, a new society. In contrast the goal of the American revolution was to reinstall a constitutional order violated by the British Parliament. Paradoxically this was a revolt without a revolution. Nor was it an expression of nationalism. The Americans never considered the British foreigners: they rebelled against a Parliamentary decision they considered illegal, and based their action on English judicial political tradition.

The revolt of the thirteen colonies was also the first chapter of the history of decolonialization, of rebellion against the dominance of a Europe whose sun had set. The battle against the well-equipped and disciplined British army was won by modern guerrilla tactics.

Throughout American colonial history there is a constant moral rejection of Europe in favor of a mythical America as a land of refuge from European corruption and misery. However, Americans rejected Europe in the name of typically European values, from Locke to Calvin, while Africa and Asia today seek to reinforce their own traditions, espouse values and ideals extraneous to our civilization. The modern wars of liberation are also social revolutions which seek to create new elites.

Above all the American revolution was a Constitutional revolution. Alexis de Tocqueville in *Democracy in America* tried to understand through the U.S. the new world emerging in Europe. As bulwarks against the danger of tyranny of the majority and paternal despotism, he pointed to pluralism and participation, words which today are too often misunderstood.

The American revolution is an obligatory crossroad both for our historical and political cultures. It is the path to the great traditions of democratic nations which Third World populism and its new left intellectuals want us to abandon.

Ugo Stille, in Corriere della Sera, *Milan, Italy. July 4, 1976.*

The movie *Nashville* begins with a song: "We must be doing something right to last 200 years." In director Robert Altman's mind the refrain has a bitter and ironic flavor. But when we emerge from the penumbra of the movie theater to the light of real life we are surprised to find the song stripped of satiric intent, in everyday talk. Behind the picturesque and commercial facade of the Bicentennial ceremonies the Americans are celebrating the validity of a political system which in two centuries has withstood the most severe trials and has brought the U.S. to the pinnacle of wealth and power while preserving the original principles of liberty and democracy.

A hundred and fifty years ago Ralph Waldo Emerson said: "Americans search for the future without carrying on their shoulders the weight of the past." But there is another aspect which emerges in moments of crisis: the desire to return to the past, a past conceived mythically rather than historically, the will to redis-

cover "fundamental principles." This singular mix of empirical pragmatism and tradition is incomprehensible to Europeans.

The Bicentennial has come at the end of a decade of traumatic shocks—Vietnam, Watergate, the black revolt in the ghettos, the student revolution—which created a climate of moral and psychological crisis and doubts about the course of American society. But in the past months the tensions of the past have eased. The dramatic phase of polarization and internal conflicts seems ended: the nation's prevalent tendency is to return to moderate positions which avoid excesses.

Because he understood this state of mind earlier and better than his rivals Jimmy Carter won the Democratic nomination and probably will become the next president of the U.S. The Carter phenomenon also highlights the most positive aspect of the American system, its mobility and decentralized structure which facilitate change at the summit and prevent the leadership class from becoming rigid.

In its second century the effort of American democracy—from the progressive reforms of the 19th century to the New Deal—was directed towards limiting and controlling the excessive power of financial and industrial capitalism. In the third century this objective is joined by the desire to control the excessive power of the new technocratic, bureaucratic, and intellectual elites. This is one of the most important themes in the American debate today.

Eric Mettler, in Neue Zürcher Zeitung, *Zurich, Switzerland. July 4–5, 1976.*

The American Bicentennial celebrates the greatest success story in modern history. The 1776 beacon, rekindled and invigorated in various ways—not least by puritan self-criticism—has endured.

Marx conceded that the American democracy was future-oriented but believed erroneously that sooner or later it would fall into the pattern of his class-struggle scheme. His followers, the Great Power Leninist leaders of the 20th century, used the vocabulary of freedom and democracy, yet without exception they preside over tyranny, over new forms of the old despotisms. Indeed the "absolute tyranny" with which the rebellious colonists of 1776 charged George III was first brought to full perfection by Stalin.

It is hard to conceive of the shape of things in our century if—say—the Chinese or the Russians had come to America via the Bering Strait and had settled the land or if the Red Man still held sway over the Mississippi.

Radomar Bogdanov, Novosti, Moscow, U.S.S.R.

The historic significance of the American War of Independence was, according to Marx, that it advanced the idea of a great democratic republic which proclaimed the first declaration of human rights and gave the first impetus to the European revolution of the 18th century. Marx also stressed the historically limited character of this revolution, which proved incapable of steadily implementing the democratic principles it proclaimed.

After the October Revolution of 1917 Lenin, founder of the Soviet State, called the American Revolution one of those "great, really liberating, really revolutionary wars" against colonialism and feudal oppression.

The list of sociopolitical literature published by central Moscow publishing houses in 1974–1976 to mark the U.S. Bicentennial includes more than 100 titles of large monographs and research papers, apart from many other articles and publications. Soviet researchers consider this revolution to have laid the groundwork of the American State and initiated the national self-consciousness of Americans. It also produced outstanding public leaders, scientists, and writers.

However, America of today has forgotten many democratic principles of the revolution. An intensification of conservative and neo-conservative trends has occurred. Acting upon Cold War premises, they try to galvanize the ideas of chauvinism and American exclusiveness, among others. Yet the ideological discussion now in progress in the U.S. demonstrates that a sector represented by those who support the policy of the relaxation of tension and act in the democratic traditions of American history actually does exist.

Ideas formulated in the Declaration of Independence were invested with a new, deeper meaning under different social conditions and in other countries. This specifically refers to the idea of the genuine equality of people, which is why we do not share the nihilistic attitude of some rightists, ultra-leftist, and extremist groups in the U.S. today.

The proclamation of the ideal of equality and happiness for everybody was a major achievement of the American revolution. The Soviet Union highly values these principles and has created social conditions under which everyone can practice them in full. The idea of equality and the right to happiness which forms the core of the spiritual legacy of the American Revolution also contains international significance of great import today. We appreciate the democratic traditions of American history promoted by the advanced and progressive forces of American society.

Anders Mellbourne, in Dagens Nyheter, *Stockholm, Sweden. July 4, 1976.*

America celebrates as its 200th birthday the Declaration of Independence from England. But actually the U.S. did not start to become what it really is until the mass migrations of the 1800s when millions of poor Europeans fled from poverty and oppression to a new continent.

The U.S. differs from all other large nations in being a land of immigrants. The Americans are united not by social and cultural ties. They don't live in a country where for generations their ancestors have spoken the same language and tilled the earth. Instead they are bound together by the American dream itself. The Constitution, the political institutions, and the flag take on a particular symbolic value and are sacred in a way that to an outsider often appears ridiculous. Every crisis of the nation's political institutions is potentially more serious in the U.S. than anywhere else. When the political and social system is challenged the foundation of the entire nation is shaken.

It is because of its great variety that the U.S. has become the home of the greater part of what Western cultural circles can offer in the way of free and spontaneous innovation. This is not an unmixed blessing. Freedom of the airwaves brings with it an abundance of vulgar advertising but also permits existence of an occasional radio station with good music and controversial talk.

The U.S. has always been an attempt by Europeans to realize European ideas and to solve European problems in a place outside Europe. The debt of the U.S. over 200 years—to the Indians and the blacks or in our own day to the Vietnamese and other Third World peoples—is a debt shared by the entire Western world. And if the time comes, centuries from now, when the U.S. is forced to seek new economic and political solutions and to find its national identity in something other than the traditional American dream, it will mean a painful end to a European dream.

Babatunde Jose, Jr., in Sunday Tide, *Port Harcourt, Nigeria. July 3, 1976.*

Since July 4, 1776, the U.S. has grown to become the most powerful nation in the world, the richest, and most affluent. She has become a colossus, feared by small and big nations alike. She's made many friends and a lot of enemies.

Though the U.S. has not been a major participant in the African scene, she has nonetheless demonstrated her desire to help in the building up of the continent. American technological, scientific, educational, and cultural aid is what Africans want from America. We want the cooperation of the U.S. in the development of our friendships.

What we Africans do not want, however, is American imperialism and domination, the American CIA, and the undermining of our national efforts. We strongly resent any attempt by America to dictate to us the terms of our friendship or who should be our friends.

In the liberation of the remaining parts of our continent we do not want the interference of America. She should either help in the liberation or remain silent forever. We also do not want false promises from America. On this historic occasion, of America's 200th birthday, America must think of the role she wants to play in Africa. To the people of America, I say, HAPPY BIRTHDAY.

Ahmad Baha El-Din, in al-Arabi, *Kuwait. July 1976*

America has always presented an image of greatness, power, and progress. . . .

Yet America remains a bewildering riddle, a land of contradictions. In America one finds the most prestigious centers of learning, research, and specialization. One is also aware of an elaborate network for spying and collecting data. Yet this nation, which ostensibly weighs every move carefully, can commit the most obvious and rash mistakes, sometimes drowning a country in blood or tearing its very fabric apart, as in Vietnam.

What is the enigma behind this giant land, where one finds the finest centers for scientific and humanistic studies and where the most powerful organized crime syndicates hold sway? . . .

In no other equally civilized country is the possession of firearms on such a wide scale so easy. . . . Every new invention in America brought about revolutionary changes in lifestyle. . . . Instead of the traditional attachment to the land the norm has become movement to wherever opportunity beckons.

The lightning success achieved by Democratic presidential candidate Carter is attributed to his appeal to the latent hostility which Americans now harbor toward Washington with all that it stands for: bureaucracy, influence-peddling, corruption, Vietnam-type involvement and encroachment on the right to privacy. This expression of hostility . . . would seem to be the American individual's protest against what he perceives to be the end of his forefathers' "dream" to build a world totally different from the Old World.

Girilal Jain, in the Times of India, *Bombay and New Delhi. July 7, 1976.*

The U.S. has entered the third century of its existence as an independent nation full of doubts regarding its own future. And yet no other country is as vigorous, innovative, productive, and well placed to influence the course of events in coming years and decades. Indeed, it will not be much of an exaggeration to say that peace and stability in our era and the well-being of the rest of mankind are to no small extent dependent on the strength and prosperity of the U.S.

The U.S., of course, no longer dominates the international economic scene as it did in the Fifties and Sixties. But America is still the world's largest and most dynamic economy. Many countries have seen the U.S. as a disturber rather than as a promoter of stability and peace — a point of view which cannot be dismissed out of hand in view of the American performance in Vietnam, its role in the overthrow of President Allende, and its extraordinarily inept attitude toward China till the late Sixties. But peace in the larger sense of the absence of a worldwide conflagration has in our era been the product broadly of something like an overall power balance between the U.S. and the U.S.S.R.

Right now the voice of the pessimists is dominant in the U.S. This will doubtless change if the process of recovery, economic and psychological, continues. America's may not be institutions toward which, to quote Lord Bryce, "as if by law of fate, the rest of civilized mankind are forced to move." But they will continue to inspire and influence man in his endless journey towards freedom.

From Excelsior, *Mexico City, Mexico. July 3, 1976.*

The 200th year since the beginning of the American war of independence is an occasion to ask whether the true manifest destiny of the U.S. will continue to be fulfilled. Has this bicentennial society created the seeds of its own destruction or has it produced enough healthy cells to restore itself?

The birth of the U.S. was the fruit of a libertarian zeal which spread throughout the world and provided a model for the rise of the Latin American countries. Later, devotion to the fundamental liberties led to war against Fascist barbarity.

It is a strange paradox, however, that the U.S. has sustained its own freedom through the subjection of other countries. There is no substantive difference between the purchase of Manhattan Island for $24 and the domination of the Panama Canal, or between the theft of Mexican land and the finally frustrated siege of Vietnam. It is as if the principles of good and evil were permanently at war in the breast of America.

Rich and multiform, fed by human currents from all over the world, American society epitomizes humanity's highest achievements and its most degrading depths. The stereotype of the American soul is concerned only with material gain, technical knowledge, and the subduing of nature to the service of man. But the American spirit is also capable of the highest cultural and artistic creation.

Many of the builders of the Mexican nation of today found refuge on American soil. But that same soil also nurtured the seeds of vices—economic dependence, cultural subjection—which grew in Mexico with the help of our own inadequacies and aberrations. Today, on the celebration of this Bicentennial, without forgetting—how could we?—its imperial nature, we salute the nation that founded democracy.

From O Estado de São Paulo, *Brazil. July 4, 1976.*

In the two centuries since the Founding Fathers created a form of government *sui generis* the U.S. has overcome the most profound internal crisis and participated in the international power game without abandoning the democratic principles of the great Virginia liberal [Jefferson]. It is these same principles, despite the permissiveness of the affluent society and the strategic retreat of the U.S. in international affairs, that are forcing all sectors of the American nation to make a painful examination of conscience and are leading men of good faith to believe in the restoration of national unity after the ravages of the racial problem, the Vietnam War, and the Watergate scandal.

Thanks to the balance of power among the government, the great private corporations, the labor unions, and free community organizations—the U.S. today constitutes the true example of the social democracy of which humanity dreams. Balance and real prudence are the heritage of the American nation and they are rooted in the moral force which Jefferson invoked in proclaiming the right to life, liberty, and the pursuit of happiness. These are the eternal aspirations of man.

INDEX

Note: An asterisk (*) following a proper name indicates that the person is the author of one or more selections in this volume. In the case of multiple references, the more important ones are listed first.